THE NUREMBERG TRIALS

THE COMPLETE PROCEEDINGS

Vol 1. The Indictment and Opening Statements

Edited and introduced by Bob Carruthers

CODA
BOOKS LTD

This edition published in Great Britain in 2011 by
Coda Books Ltd, The Barn, Cutlers Farm Business Centre, Edstone,
Wootton Wawen, Henley in Arden, Warwickshire, B95 6DJ
www.codahistory.com

A CIP catalogue record for this book is available from the British Library

ISBN 978 1 908538 75 8

Originally published as
"The Trial of German Major War Criminals
Proceedings of the International Military Tribunal Sitting at Nuremberg,
Germany"
under the authority of
H.M. Attorney-General by His Majesty's Stationery Office
London : 1946

CONTENTS

INTRODUCTION

The trial of the German major war criminals is better known to posterity as the Nuremberg Trials. This was a revolutionary new form of justice which was without parallel in the history of warfare.

In the wake of six years of savagery, inhumanity and turmoil it was sensed that a series of summary executions would not bring closure to the years of violence which had seen unheralded scenes of brutality as civilian populations were targeted for bombardment on a scale never before witnessed.

In 1945, faced with the stark evidence of the appalling crimes against humanity committed by the Nazi regime, there was an understandable clamour, particularly from the Soviet camp, for a series of quick summary executions to draw the line under the past and allow the world to get back to civilised behaviour. Given the scale of the crimes and the gruesome evidence emerging from Dachau, Auschwitz and Bergen-Belsen, it was certainly difficult to argue against making a rapid example of men like Hermann Göring, the father of the Gestapo.

Fortunately clearer heads prevailed and it was felt necessary to create some form of judicial process which would mark the transition back from barbarism to the rule of law. However there was then no such thing as an international court and there was no precedent for the legal trial of defeated belligerents. The plan for the "Trial of European War Criminals" was therefore drafted by Secretary of War Henry L. Stimson and the War Department. Following Roosevelt's death in April 1945, the new president, Harry S. Truman, gave strong approval for a judicial process. After a series of negotiations between Britain, the US, the Soviet Union and France, details of the trial were finally agreed. The trials were to commence on 20th November 1945, in the Bavarian city of Nuremberg.

At the meetings in Potsdam (1945), the three major wartime powers, the United Kingdom, the United States, and the Union of Soviet Socialist Republics finally agreed on the principles of punishment for those responsible for war crimes during World War II. France was also awarded a place on the tribunal.

The legal basis for the trial was established by the London Charter, issued on August 8th, 1945, which restricted the trial to "punishment of the major war criminals of the European Axis countries". Some 200 German war crimes defendants were ultimately tried at Nuremberg, and 1,600 others were tried under the traditional channels of military justice. The legal basis for the jurisdiction of the court was that defined by the Instrument of Surrender of Germany. Political authority for Germany had been transferred to the Allied Control Council which, having sovereign power over Germany, could choose to punish violations of international law and the laws of war. Because the court was limited to violations of the laws of war, it did not have jurisdiction over crimes that took place before the outbreak of war on September 3rd, 1939.

Leipzig, Munich and Luxembourg were briefly considered as the location for the trial. The Soviet Union had wanted the trials to take place in Berlin, as the capital city of the 'fascist conspirators', but Nuremberg was chosen as the site for the trials for two specific reasons: firstly because the Palace of Justice was spacious and largely undamaged (one of the few civic buildings that had remained largely intact through extensive Allied bombing), and secondly that a large prison was also part of the complex.

Nuremberg was also considered the ceremonial birthplace of the Nazi Party, and hosted annual rallies. It was thus considered a fitting place to mark the Party's symbolic demise.

As a compromise with the Soviet Union, it was agreed that while the location of the trial would be Nuremberg, Berlin would be the official home of the Tribunal authorities. It was also agreed that France would become the permanent seat of the IMT and that the first trial (several were planned) would take place in Nuremberg.

Each of the four countries provided one judge and an alternate, as well as a prosecutor.
- Major General Iona Nikitchenko (Soviet main)
- Lieutenant Colonel Alexander Volchkov (Soviet alternate)
- Colonel Sir Geoffrey Lawrence (British main and president)
- Sir Norman Birkett (British alternate)
- Francis Biddle (American main)
- John J. Parker (American alternate)
- Professor Henri Donnedieu de Vabres (French main)
- Robert Falco (French alternate)

The chief prosecutors were as follows:
- Attorney General Sir Hartley Shawcross (United Kingdom)
- Supreme Court Justice Robert H. Jackson (United States)
- Lieutenant-General Roman Andreyevich Rudenko (Soviet Union)
- François de Menthon (France)

Assisting Jackson was the lawyer Telford Taylor, Thomas J. Dodd and a young US Army interpreter named Richard Sonnenfeldt. Assisting Shawcross were Major Sir David Maxwell-Fyfe and Sir John Wheeler-Bennett. Mervyn Griffith-Jones, later to become famous as the chief prosecutor in the Lady Chatterley's Lover obscenity trial, was also on Shawcross's team. Shawcross also recruited a young barrister, Anthony Marreco, who was the son of a friend of his, to help the British team with the heavy workload. Assisting de Menthon was Auguste Champetier de Ribes.

The International Military Tribunal was opened on October 18th, 1945, in the Palace of Justice in Nuremberg. The first session was presided over by the Soviet judge, Nikitchenko. The prosecution entered indictments against 24 major war criminals and six criminal organizations – the leadership of the Nazi party, the Schutzstaffel (SS) and Sicherheitsdienst (SD), the Gestapo, the Sturmabteilung (SA) and the "General Staff and High Command," comprising several categories of senior military officers.

The indictments were for:
- Participation in a common plan or conspiracy for the accomplishment of a crime

against peace

• Planning, initiating and waging wars of aggression and other crimes against peace

• War crimes

• Crimes against humanity

Under the circumstances the Proceedings of the International Military Tribunal just about passes muster as an exercise in establishing a platform from which to dispense a reasonably balanced form of justice. There was, of course, the questionable involvement of Stalin's legal team and it was ironic that his crimes against peace and humanity matched, if not surpassed those of Adolf Hitler. Ribbentrop and Molotov between them had secretly carved up Poland and in so doing had certainly been guilty of crimes against peace, planning war. Stalin had also waged an aggressive was against Finland and had annexed the Baltic States. Had Stalin been on trial his own actions would have condemned him to a guilty verdict on all four counts, but history is always written by the victors, and Stalin's crimes were airbrushed out of history in order that his team could sit in judgement as if nothing untoward had ever happened.

It has been asked many times were the trials fair. In strict legal terms they certainly were not. Declaring the instruments of the Nazi state to be illegal was illogical and unreasonable, but this was certainly no Stalinist show trial with a guilty verdict and a hangman's noose already awaiting the defendants. Under the circumstances the court was incredibly well balanced as was evidenced by the fact that three of the Defendants were acquitted and others received comparatively light sentences. Of the twenty-four accused only twelve received death sentences.

Ultimately the process had its flaws but it did provide a civilised alternative to Stalin's suggestion that 50,000 to 100,000 German officers should be executed without trial, and it was to serve as a forerunner for the International Court now located at the Hague.

This is the first volume in the complete proceedings of the Nuremberg trial of the German major war criminals before the International Military Tribunal sitting at Nuremberg, Germany.

Taken from the original court transcript this volume covers the proceedings from 20th November 1945 to 1st December 1945 and represents an essential primary source for scholars and general readers alike. The transcripts are complete and contain the whole of the proceedings as taken from the original court documents.

This key volume contains the charges brought against the Defendants and the opening statements by the Prosecution as originally published under the authority of H.M. Attorney-General by His Majesty's Stationery Office London in 1946.

Bob Carruthers

FOREWORD

This is the first of a series of publications which will, in due course, cover the whole trial of Major War Criminals now in progress at Nuremberg. The publication will be issued in fortnightly parts.

A copy of the official text of the transcript has been made available to the Attorney-General for this purpose by the International Military Tribunal, who, however, accept no responsibility for this publication.

The names of the respective speakers are set out in the general heading together with the capacities in which they are appearing. When the speakers used a language in Court other than English, the text is a translation of that language. The American and British Judges and Prosecutors spoke throughout in English, The French in French, and those for the U.S.S.R. in Russian. The Defendants pleaded, and Defence Counsel addressed the Tribunal, in German.

THE INTERNATIONAL MILITARY TRIBUNAL IN SESSION AT NUREMBERG, GERMANY

BEFORE:

THE RT. HON. SIR GEOFFREY LAWRENCE, (member for the United Kingdom of Great Britain and Northern Ireland) President

The Hon. Sir William BIRKETT, (alternate member for the United Kingdom of Great Britain and Northern Ireland)

MR. FRANCIS BIDDLE (member for the United States of America)

JUDGE JOHN J. PARKER (alternate member for the United States of America)

M. LE PROFESSEUR DONNEDIEU DE VABRES (member for the French Republic)

M. LE CONSEILLER R. FALCO (alternate member for the French Republic)

MAJOR GENERAL I.T. NIKITCHENKO (member for the Union of Soviet Socialist Republics)

LIEUTENANT COLONEL A.F. VOLCHKOV (alternate member for the Union of Soviet Socialist Republics)

The United States of America, The French Republic, The United Kingdom of Great Britain and Northern Ireland, and the Union of Soviet Socialist Republics

AGAINST:

Hermann Wilhelm Göring, Rudolf Hess, Joachim von Ribbentrop, Robert Ley, Wilhelm Keitel, Ernst Kaltenbrunner, Alfred Rosenberg, Hans Frank, Wilhelm Frick, Julius Streicher, Walter Funk, Hjalmar Schacht, Gustav Krupp von Bohlen und Halbach, Karl Dönitz, Erich Raeder, Baldur von Schirach, Fritz Sauckel, Alfred Jodl, Martin Bormann, Franz von Papen, Artur Seyss-Inquart, Albert Speer, Constantin von Neurath and Hans Fritzsche, individually and as members of any of the following groups or organisations to which they respectively belonged, namely: Die Reichsregierung (Reich Cabinet); Das Korps der Politischen Leiter der Nationalsozialistischen Deutschen Arbeiterpartei (Leadership Corps of the Nazi Party); Die Schutzstaffeln der Nationalsozialistischen Deutschen Arbeiterpartei (commonly known as the "SS") and including Der Sicherheitsdienst (commonly known as the "SD"); Die Geheime Staatspolizei (Secret State Police, commonly known as the "GESTAPO"); Die Sturmabteilungen der N.S.D.A.P. (commonly known as the "SA") and the General Staff and High Command of the German Armed Forces.

COUNSEL FOR THE PROSECUTION

For the United States of America
CHIEF OF COUNSEL:
Mr. Justice Robert H. Jackson
EXECUTIVE TRIAL COUNSEL:
Colonel Robert G, Storey
Mr. Thomas J. Dodd
ASSOCIATE TRIAL COUNSEL:
Mr. Sidney S. Alderman
Brigadier General Telford Taylor
Colonel John Harlan Amen
Mr. Ralph G. Albrecht
ASSISTANT TRIAL COUNSEL:
Colonel Leonard Wheeler, Jr.
Lieutenant Colonel William H. Baldwin
Lieutenant Colonel Smith W. Brockhart, Jr.
Commander James Britt Donovan (U.S.N.R.)
Major Frank B. Wallis
Mnjor William F. Walsh
Major Warren F. Farr
Captain Samuel Harris
Captain Drexel A. Sprecher
Lieutenant Commander Whitney R. Harris (U.S.N.R.)
Liewlenant Thomas F. Lambert, Jr., (U.S.N.R.)
Lieutenant Henry K. Atherton
Lieutenant Brady O Bryson (U.S.N.R.)
Lieutenant Bernard D. Meltzer (U.S.N.R.)
Dr. Robert M. Kempner
Mr. Walter W. Brudno

For the French Republic
CHIEF PROSECUTOR:
M. Francois de Menthon
DEPUTY CHIEF PROSECUTORS:
M. Charles Dubost
M. Edgar Faure
ASSISTANT PROSECUTORS (Chiefs of Sections) :
M. Pierre Mounier
M. Charles Gerthoffer
ASSISTANT PROSECUTORS:
M. Henry Delpech
M. Jacques B. Herzog

M. Conslant Quatre
M. Serge Fuster

For the United Kingdom of Great Britain and Northern Ireland
CHIEF PROSECUTOR:
H.M. Attorney General, Sir Harley Shawcross, K.C., M.P.
DEPUTY CHIEF PROSECUTOR:
The Rt. Hon. Sir David Maxwell-Fyfe, P.C., K.C., M.P.
LEADING COUNSEL:
Mr. G. D. Roberts, K.C., O.B.E.
JUNIOR COUNSEL:
Lieutenant Colonel J. M. G. Griffith-Jones, M.C, Barrisler-at-Law
Colonel H. J. Phillimore, O.B.E., Barrister-at-Law
Major F. Elwyn Jones, M.P., Barrister-at-Law
Major J. Harcourt Barrington, Barrister-at-Law

For the Union of Soviet Socialist Republics
CHIEF PROSECUTOR:
General R. A. Rudenko
DEPUTY CHIEF PROSECUTOR:
Colunel Y. V. Pokrovsky
ASSISTANT PROSECUTORS:
State Counsellor of Justice of the 2nd Class, L. R. Shenin
State Counsellor of Justice of the 2nd Class, M. Y Raginsky
State Counsellor of Justice of the 3rd Class, N. D. Zorya
Chief Counsellor of Justice, L. N. Smirnov
Colonel D. S, Karev
Lieutenant Colonel J. A. Ozol
Captain V. V. Kuchin

COUNSEL FOR THE DEFENDANTS

GOERING : Dr. Otto Stahmer
HESS : Dr. Gunther von Rohrscheidt
VON RIBBENTROP : Dr. Fritz Sauter (to 6 January 1946)
KIETEL : Dr. Otto Nelte
KALTENBRUNNER : Dr. Kurt Kauffmann
ROSENBERG : Dr. Alfred Thoma
FRANK : Dr. Alfred Seidl
FRICK : Dr. Otto Pannenbeeker
STREICHER : Dr. Hanns Marx
FUNK : Dr. Fritz Sauter

SCHACHT : Dr. Rudolf Dix
DOENITZ : Flottenrichte Otto Kranzbuchler
RAEDER : Dr. Walter Siemers
VON SCHIRACH : Dr. Fritz Sauter
SAUCKEL : Dr. Robert Servatius
JODL : Professor Dr. Franz Exner
BORMANN : Dr. Friedrich Bergold
VON PAPEN : Dr. Egon Kubuschok
SEYSS-INQUART : Dr. Gustav Steinbauer
SPEER : Dr. Hans Flachsner
VON NEURATH : Dr. Otto Frelherr von Ludinghausen
FRITZSCHE : Dr. Heinz Fritz

For the Groups and Organisations Counsel:
Reich Cabinet : Dr. Egon Kubuschok
Leadership Corps of Nazi Party : Dr. Robert Servatius
S.S. and S.D. : Ludwig Babel
SA : Georg Boehm
Gestapo : Dr. Rudolf Merkel
General Staff And High Command : Professor Dr. Franz Exner

Notes:
All individual defendants named in the indictment were present in Court throughout
the period covered by this Part except the following:
  (i) Robert Ley, who committed suicide on the 25th October 1945,
  (ii) Ernst Kaltenbrunner, absent through illness on each day,
  (iii) Gustav Krupp von Bohlen und Halbach whose trial had been postponed by
      order of the Tribunal, and
  (iv) Martin Bormann, who was not in custody and whom the Tribunal decided to
      try in his absence.

PROCEEDINGS OF THE INTERNATIONAL MILITARY TRIBUNAL SITTING AT NUREMBERG, GERMANY

FIRST DAY:
Tuesday, 20th November, 1945

THE PRESIDENT: Before the defendants in this case are called upon to make their pleas to the indictment which has been lodged against them, and in which they are charged with Crimes against Peace, War Crimes, and Crimes against Humanity, and with a Common Plan or Conspiracy to commit those Crimes, it is the wish of the Tribunal that I should make a very brief statement on behalf of the Tribunal.

This International Military Tribunal has been established pursuant to the Agreement of London, dated the 8th of August, 1945, and the Charter of the Tribunal annexed thereto. The purpose for which the Tribunal has been established is stated in Article I of the Charter to be the just and prompt trial and punishment of the Major War Criminals of the European Axis.

The signatories to the Agreement and Charter are the Government of the United Kingdom of Great Britain and Northern Ireland, the Government of the United States of America, the Provisional Government of the French Republic and the Government of the Union of Soviet Socialist Republics.

The Committee of the Chief Prosecutors, appointed by the four signatories, have settled the final designation of the War Criminals to be tried by the Tribunal, and have approved the indictment on which the present defendants stand charged here today.

On Thursday, the 18th of October, 1945, in Berlin, the indictment was lodged with the Tribunal and a copy of that indictment in German has been furnished to each defendant, and has been in his possession for more than thirty days.

All the defendants are represented by counsel. In almost all cases the counsel appearing for the defendants have been chosen by the defendants themselves, but in cases where counsel could not be obtained the Tribunal has itself selected suitable counsel agreeable to the defendant.

The Tribunal has heard with great satisfaction of the steps which have been taken by the Chief Prosecutors to make available to defending counsel the numerous documents upon which the prosecution rely, with the aim of giving to the defendants every possibility for a just defence.

The trial which is now about to begin is unique in the history of the jurisprudence of the world and it is of supreme importance to millions of people all over the globe. For these reasons, there is laid upon everybody who takes any part in this trial a solemn responsibility to discharge his duties without fear or favour, in accordance with the sacred principles of law and justice.

The four signatories having invoked the judicial process, it is the duty of all concerned to see that the trial in no way departs from those principles and traditions which alone give justice its authority and the place it ought to occupy in the affairs of all civilised states.

This trial is a public trial in the fullest sense of those words, and I must, therefore, remind the public that the Tribunal will insist upon the complete maintenance of order and decorum, and will take the strictest measures to enforce it. It only remains for me to direct, in accordance with the provisions of the Charter, that the indictment shall now be read.

MR. SIDNEY ALDERMAN: May it please the Tribunal:

INDICTMENT

I. The United States of America, the French Republic, the United Kingdom of Great Britain and Northern Ireland and the Union of Soviet Socialist Republics by the undersigned, Robert H. Jackson, Francois de Menthon, Hartley Shawcross and R. A. Rudenko, duly appointed to represent their respective Governments in the investigation of the charges against and the prosecution of the major War Criminals, pursuant to the Agreement of London, dated 8th August, 1945, and the Charter of this Tribunal annexed thereto, hereby accuse as guilty, in the respects hereinafter set forth, of Crimes against Peace, War Crimes, and Crimes against Humanity, and of a Common Plan or Conspiracy to commit those Crimes, all as defined in the Charter of the Tribunal, and accordingly name as defendants in this cause and as indicted on the counts hereinafter set out: HERMANN WILHELM GOERING, RUDOLF HESS, JOACHIM VON RIBBENTROP, ROBERT LEY, WILHELM KEITEL, ERNST KALTENBRUNNER, ALFRED ROSENBERG, HANS FRANK, WILHELM FRICK, JULIUS STREICHER, WALTER FUNK, HJALMAR SCHACHT, GUSTAV KRUPP VON BOHLEN UND HALBACH, KARL DOENITZ, ERICH RAEDER, BALDUR VON SCHIRACH, FRITZ SAUCKEL, ALFRED JODL, MARTIN BORMANN, FRANZ VON PAPEN, ARTUR SEYSS-INQUART, ALBERT SPEER, CONSTANTIN VON NEURATH and HANS FRITZSCHE, individually and as members of any of the Groups or Organisations next hereinafter named.

II. The following are named as Groups or Organisations (since dissolved) which should be declared criminal by reason of their aims and the means used for the accomplishment thereof, and in connection with the conviction of such of the named defendants as were members thereof: DIE REICHSREGIERUNG (REICH CABINET); DAS KORPS DER POLITISCHEN LEITER DER NATIONALSOZIALISTISCHEN DEUTSCFIEN ARBEITERPARTEI (LEADERSHIP CORPS OF THE NAZI PARTY); DIE SCHUTZSTAFFELN DER NATIONALSOZIALISTISCHEN DEUTSCHEN ARBEITERPARTEI (commonly known as the "SS") and including the SICHERHEITSDIENST (commonly known as the "SD"); DIE GEHEIME STAATSPOLIZEI (SECRET

STATE POLICE), (commonly known as the "GESTAPO"); DIE STURMABTEILUNGEN DER N.S.D.A.P. (commonly known as the "SA"); and the GENERAL STAFF and the HIGH COMMAND of the GERMAN ARMED FORCES. The identity and membership of the Groups or Organisations referred to in the foregoing titles are hereinafter in Appendix B more particularly defined.

COUNT ONE - THE COMMON PLAN OR CONSPIRACY
(Charter, Article 6, especially 6 (a))
III. Statement of the Offence

All the defendants, with divers other persons, during a period of years preceding 8th May, 1945, participated as leaders', organisers, instigators or accomplices in the formulation or execution of a common plan or conspiracy to commit, or which involved the commission of, Crimes against Peace, War Crimes, and Crimes against Humanity, as defined in the Charter of this Tribunal, and, in accordance with the provisions of the Charter, are individually responsible for their own acts and for all acts committed by any persons in the execution of such plan or conspiracy. The common plan or conspiracy embraced the commission of Crimes against Peace, in that the defendants planned, prepared, initiated and waged wars of aggression, which were also wars in violation of international treaties, agreements or assurances. In the development and course of the common plan or conspiracy it came to embrace the commission of War Crimes, in that it contemplated, and the defendants determined upon and carried out, ruthless wars against countries and populations, in violation of the rules and customs of war, including as typical and systematic means by which the wars were prosecuted, murder, ill-treatment, deportation for slave labour and for other purposes of civilian populations of occupied territories, murder and ill-treatment of prisoners of war and of persons on the high seas, the taking and killing of hostages, the plunder of public and private property, the wanton destruction of cities, towns, and villages, and devastation not justified by military necessity. The common plan or conspiracy contemplated and came to embrace as typical and systematic, and the defendants determined upon and committed, Crimes against Humanity, both within Germany and within occupied territories, including murder, extermination, enslavement, deportation and other inhumane acts committed against civilian populations before and during the war, and persecutions on political, racial, or religious grounds, in execution of the plan for preparing and prosecuting aggressive or illegal wars, many of such acts and persecutions being violations of the domestic laws of the countries where perpetrated.

IV. Particulars of the nature and development of the common plan or conspiracy

(A) NAZI PARTY AS THE CENTRAL CORE OF THE COMMON PLAN OR CONSPIRACY

In 1921 Adolf Hitler became the supreme leader or Fuehrer of the Nationalsozialistische Deutsche Arbeiterpartei (National Socialist German Workers Party) also known as the Nazi Party, which had been founded in Germany in 1920. He continued as such throughout the period covered by this Indictment. The Nazi Party, together with certain of its subsidiary organisations, became the instrument of cohesion among the defendants and their co-conspirators and an instrument for the carrying out of the aims and purposes of their conspiracy. Each defendant became a member of the Nazi Party and of the conspiracy, with knowledge of their aims and purposes, or, with such knowledge, became an accessory to their aims and purposes at some stage of the development of the conspiracy.

(B) COMMON OBJECTIVES AND METHODS OF CONSPIRACY

The aims and purposes of the Nazi Party and of the defendants and divers other persons from time to time associated as leaders, members, supporters or adherents of the Nazi Party (hereinafter called collectively the "Nazi conspirators") were, or came to be, to accomplish the following by any means deemed opportune, including unlawful means, and contemplating ultimate resort to threat of force, force and aggressive war:

(i) to abrogate and overthrow the Treaty of Versailles and its restrictions upon the military armament and activity of Germany;

(ii) to acquire the territories lost by Germany as the result of the World War of 1914-1918 and other territories in Europe asserted by the Nazi conspirators to be occupied principally by so-called "racial Germans";

(iii) to acquire still further territories in continental Europe and elsewhere claimed by the Nazi conspirators to be required by the "racial Germans" as "Lebensraum," or living space, all at the expense of neighbouring and other countries.

The aims and purposes of the Nazi conspirators were not fixed or static, but evolved and expanded as they acquired progressively greater power and became able to make more effective application of threats of force and threats of aggressive war. When their expanding aims and purposes became finally so great as to provoke such strength of resistance as could be overthrown only by armed force and aggressive war, and not simply by the opportunistic methods theretofore used, such as fraud, deceit, threats, intimidation, fifth column activities and propaganda, the Nazi conspirators deliberately planned, determined upon and launched their aggressive wars and wars in violation of international treaties, agreements and assurances by the phases and steps hereinafter more particularly described.

(C) DOCTRINAL TECHNIQUES OF THE COMMON PLAN OR CONSPIRACY

To incite others to join in the common plan or conspiracy, and as a means of securing for the Nazi conspirators the highest degree of control over the German community, they put forth, disseminated, and exploited certain doctrines, among others, as follows :-

1. That persons of so-called "German blood" (as specified by the Nazi conspirators) were a "master race" and were accordingly entitled to subjugate,

dominate or exterminate other "races" and peoples

2. That the German people should be ruled under the Fuehrerprinzip (leadership principle) according to which power was to reside in a Fuehrer from whom sub-leader were to derive authority in a hierarchical order, each sub-leader to owe unconditional obedience to his immediate superior but to be absolute in his own sphere of jurisdiction; and the power of the leadership was to be unlimited, extending to all phases of public and private life

3. That war was a noble and necessary activity of Germans

4. That the leadership of the Nazi Party, as the sole bearer of the foregoing and other doctrines of the Nazi Party, was entitled to shape the structure, policies and practices of the German State and all related institutions, to direct and supervise activities of all individuals within the State, and to destroy all opponents.

(D) THE ACQUIRING OF TOTALITARIAN CONTROL OF GERMANY: POLITICAL

1. First steps in acquisition of control of State machinery

In order to accomplish their aims and purposes, the Nazi conspirators prepared to seize totalitarian control over Germany to secure that no effective resistance against them could arise within Germany itself. After the failure of the Munich Putsch of 1923 aimed at the overthrow of the Weimar Republic by direct action, the Nazi conspirators set out through the Nazi Party to undermine and capture the German Government by "legal" forms supported by terrorism. They created and utilised, as a Party formation, Die Sturmabteilungen (SA), a semimilitary, voluntary Organisation of young men trained for and committed to the use of violence, whose mission was to make the Party the master of the streets.

2. Control acquired

On 30th January, 1933, Hitler became Chancellor of the German Republic. After the Reichstag fire of 28th February, 1933, clauses of the Weimar constitution guaranteeing personal liberty, freedom of speech, of the Press, of association and assembly were suspended. The Nazi conspirators secured the passage by the Reichstag of a "law for the Protection of the People and the Reich" giving Hitler and the members of his then cabinet plenary powers of legislation. The Nazi conspirators retained such powers after having changed the members of the cabinet. The conspirators caused all political parties except the Nazi Party to be prohibited. They caused the Nazi Party to be established as a para-governmental Organisation with extensive and extraordinary privileges.

3. Consolidation of control

Thus possessed of the machinery of the German State, the Nazi conspirators set about the consolidation of their position of power within Germany, the extermination of potential internal resistance and the placing of the German nation on a military footing.

(a) The Nazi conspirators reduced the Reichstag to a body of their own nominees and curtailed the freedom of popular elections throughout the country. They transformed the several states, provinces and municipalities, which had formerly exercised semiautonomous powers, into hardly more than administrative organs of the Central Government. They united the offices of the President and the Chancellor in the person Of Hitler, instituted a widespread purge of civil servants, and severely restricted the independence of the judiciary and rendered it subservient to Nazi ends. The conspirators greatly enlarged existing State and Party organisations, established a network of new State and Party organisations, and "coordinated" State agencies with the Nazi Party and its branches and affiliates, with the result that German life was dominated by Nazi doctrine and practice and progressively mobilised for the accomplishment of their aims.

(b) in order to make their rule secure from attack and to instil fear in the hearts of the German people, the Nazi conspirators established and extended a system of terror against opponents and supposed or suspected opponents of the regime. They imprisoned such persons without judicial process, holding them in "protective custody" and concentration camps, and subjected them to persecution, degradation, despoilment, enslavement, torture and murder. These concentration camps were established early in 1933 under the direction of the defendant Goering and expanded as a fixed part of the terroristic policy and method of the conspirators and used by them for the commission of the Crimes against Humanity hereinafter alleged. Among the principal agencies utilised in the perpetration of these crimes were the SS and the Gestapo, which, together with other favoured branches or agencies of the State and Party, were permitted to operate without restraint of law.

(c) The Nazi conspirators conceived that, in addition to the suppression of distinctively political opposition, it was necessary to suppress or exterminate certain other movements or groups which they regarded as obstacles to their retention of total control in Germany, and to the aggressive aims of the conspiracy abroad.

Accordingly :

(1) The Nazi conspirators destroyed the free trade unions in Germany by confiscating their funds and properties, persecuting their leaders, prohibiting their activities, and supplanting them by an affiliated Party Organisation. The leadership principle was introduced into industrial relations, the entrepreneur becoming the leader and the workers becoming his followers. Thus any potential resistance of the workers was frustrated and the productive labour capacity of the German nation was brought under the effective control of the conspirators.

(2) The Nazi conspirators, by promoting beliefs and practices incompatible with Christian teaching, sought to subvert the influence of the Churches over the people and, in particular over the youth of Germany. They avowed their aim to eliminate the Christian Churches in Germany and sought to substitute therefor Nazi institutions and Nazi beliefs, and pursued a programme of persecution of priests, clergy and members of monastic orders whom they deemed opposed to their purposes, and confiscated

church property.

(3) The persecution by the Nazi conspirators of pacifist groups, including religious movements dedicated to pacifism, was particularly relentless and cruel.

(d) Implementing their "master race" policy, the conspirators joined in a programme of relentless persecution of the Jews, designed to exterminate them. Annihilation of the Jews became an official State policy, carried out both by official action and by incitements to mob, and individual violence. The conspirators openly avowed their purpose. For example, the defendant Rosenberg stated: " Anti-Semitism is the unifying element of the reconstruction of Germany." On another occasion he also stated: "Germany will regard the Jewish question as solved only after the very last Jew has left the greater German living space...Europe will have its Jewish question solved only after the very last Jew has left the continent." The defendant Ley declared: "We swear we are not going to abandon the struggle until the last Jew in Europe has been exterminated and is actually dead. It is not enough to isolate the Jewish enemy of mankind - the Jew has got to be exterminated." On another occasion he also declared: "The second German secret weapon is anti-Semitism, because if it is consistently pursued by Germany, it will become a universal problem which all nations will be forced to consider." The defendant Streicher declared: "The sun will not shine on the nations of the earth until the last Jew is dead." These avowals and incitements were typical of the declarations of the Nazi conspirators throughout the course of their conspiracy. The programme of action against the Jews included disfranchisement, stigmatisation, denial of civil rights,subjecting their persons and property to violence, deportation, enslavement, enforced labour, starvation, murder and mass extermination. The extent to which the conspirators succeeded in their purpose can only be estimated, but the annihilation was substantiallycomplete in many localities of Europe. Of the 9,6000,00 Jews who lived in the parts of Europe under Nazi domination, it is conservatively estimated that 5,700,000 have disappeared, most of them deliberately put to death by the Nazi conspirators. Only remnants of the Jewish population of Europe remain.

(e) In order to make the German people amenable to their. will, and to prepare them psychologically for war, the Nazi conspirators reshaped the educational system and particularly the education and training of the German youth. The leadership principle was introduced into the schools and the Party and affiliated organisations were given wide supervisory powers over education. The Nazi conspirators imposed a supervision of all cultural activities, controlled the dissemination of information and the expression of opinion within Germany as well as the movement of intelligence of all kinds from and into Germany, and created vast propaganda machines.

(f) The Nazi conspirators placed a considerable number of their dominated organisations on a progressively militarised footing with a view to the rapid transformation and use of such organisations whenever necessary as instruments of war.

(E) THE ACQUIRING OF TOTALITARIAN CONTROL IN GERMANY: ECONOMIC; AND THE ECONOMIC PLANNING AND MOBILISATION FOR AGGRESSIVE WAR

Having gained political power, the conspirators organised Germany's economy to give effect to their political aims.

In order to eliminate the possibility of resistance in the economic sphere, they deprived labour of its rights of free industrial and political association as particularised in paragraph (D) 3 (c) (1) herein.

They used organisations of German business as instruments of economic mobilisation for war.

They directed Germany's economy towards preparation and equipment of the military machine. To this end they directed finance, capital investment, and foreign trade.

The Nazi conspirators, and in particular the industrialists among them embarked upon a huge rearmament programme and set out to produce and develop huge quantities of materials of war and to create a powerful military potential.

With the object of carrying through the preparation for war the Nazi conspirators set up a series of administrative agencies and authorities. For example, in 1936 they established for this purpose the office of the Four Year Plan with the defendant Goering as Plenipotentiary, vesting it with overriding control over Germany's economy. Furthermore, on 28th August, 1939, immediately before launching their aggression against Poland, they appointed the defendant Funk Plenipotentiary for Economics; and on 30th August, 1939, they set up the Ministerial Council for the Defence of the Reich to act as a War Cabinet.

(F) UTILISATION OF NAZI CONTROL FOR FOREIGN AGGRESSION

1. Status of the conspiracy by the middle of 1933 and projected plans

By the middle of the year 1933 the Nazi conspirators, having acquired governmental control over Germany, were in a position to enter upon further and more detailed planning with particular relationship to foreign policy. Their plan was to re-arm and to re-occupy and fortify the Rhineland, in violation of the Treaty of Versailles and other treaties, in order to acquire military strength and political bargaining power to be used against other nations.

2. The Nazi conspirators decided that for their purpose the Treaty of Versailles must definitely be abrogated, and specific plans were made by them and put into operation by 7th March, 1936, all of which opened the way for the major aggressive steps to follow, as hereinafter set forth. In the execution of this phase of the conspiracy the Nazi conspirators did the following acts :-

    (a) They led Germany to enter upon a course of secret re- armament from 1933 to March, 1935, including the training of military personnel and the production of munitions of war, and the building of an Air Force.

    (b) On 4th October, 1933, they led Germany to leave the International Disarmament Conference and the League of Nations.

    (c) On 10th March, 1935, the defendant Goering announced that Germany was building a Military Air Force.

(d) On 16th March, 1935, the Nazi conspirators promulgated a law for universal military service, in which they stated the peace-time strength of the German Army would be fixed at 500,000 men.

(e) On 21St May, 1935, they falsely announced to the world, with intent to deceive and allay fears of aggressive intentions, that they would respect the territorial limitations of the Versailles Treaty and comply with the Locarno Pacts.

(f) On 7th March, 1936, they re-occupied and fortified the Rhineland, in violation of the Treaty of Versailles and the Rhine Pact of Locarno of 16th October, 1925, and falsely announced to the world that "we have no territorial demands to make in Europe."

3. Aggressive Action against Austria and Czechoslovakia

(a) The 1936-1938 phase of the plan: planning for the assault on Austria and Czechoslovakia.

The Nazi conspirators next entered upon the specific planning for the acquisition of Austria and Czechoslovakia, realising it would be necessary, for military reasons, first to seize Austria before assaulting Czechoslovakia. On 21St May, 1935, in a speech to the Reichstag, Hitler stated that: "Germany neither intends nor wishes to interfere in the internal affairs of Austria, to annex Austria or to conclude an Anschluss." On 1st May, 1936, within two months after the re-occupation of the Rhineland, Hitler stated: "The lie goes forth again that Germany tomorrow or the day after will fall upon Austria or Czechoslovakia." Thereafter, the Nazi conspirators caused a treaty to be entered into between Austria and Germany on 11th July, 1936, Article I of which stated that "The German Government recognises the full sovereignty of the Federal State of Austria in the spirit of the pronouncements of the German Fuehrer and Chancellor of 21st May, 1935." Meanwhile, plans for aggression in violation of that treaty were being made. By the autumn of 1937, all noteworthy opposition within the Reich had been crushed. Military preparation for the Austrian action was virtually concluded. An influential group of the Nazi conspirators met with Hitler on 5th November, 1937, to review the situation. It was reaffirmed that Nazi Germany must have "Lebensraum" in Central Europe. It was recognised that such conquest would probably meet resistance which would have to be crushed by force and that their decision might lead to a general war, but this prospect was discounted as a risk worth taking. There emerged from this meeting three possible plans for the conquest of Austria and Czechoslovakia. Which of the three was to be used was to depend upon the developments in the political and military situation in Europe. It was contemplated that the conquest of Austria and Czechoslovakia would, through compulsory emigration of 2,000,000 persons from Czechoslovakia and 1,000,000 persons from Austria, provide additional food to the Reich for 5,000,000 to 6,000,000 people, strengthen it militarily by providing shorter and better frontiers, and make possible the constituting of new armies up to about twelve divisions. Thus, the aim of the plan against Austria and

Czechoslovakia was conceived of not as an end in itself but as a preparatory measure toward the next aggressive steps in the Nazi conspiracy.

(b) The execution of the plan to invade Austria : November, 1937, to March, 1938 Hitler on 8th February, 1938, called Chancellor Schuschnigg to a conference at Berchtesgaden. At the meeting of 12th February, 1938, under threat of invasion, Schuschnigg yielded a promise of amnesty to imprisoned Nazis and appointment of Nazis to ministerial posts. He agreed to remain silent until Hitler's next speech in which Austria's independence was to be reaffirmed, but Hitler in that speech, instead of affirming Austrian independence, declared himself protector of all. Germans. Meanwhile, subversive activities of Nazis in Austria increased. Schuschnigg on 9th March, 1938, announced a plebiscite for the following Sunday on the question of Austrian independence. On 11th March Hitler sent an ultimatum, demanding that the plebiscite be called off or Germany would invade Austria. Later the same day a second ultimatum threatened invasion unless Schuschnigg should resign in three hours. Schuschnigg resigned. The defendant Seyss-Inquart, who was appointed Chancellor, immediately invited Hitler to send German troops into Austria to "preserve order." The invasion began on 12th March, 1938 On 13th March, Hitler by proclamation assumed office as Chief of State of Austria and took command of her armed forces. By a law of the same date Austria was annexed to Germany.

(c) The execution of the plan to invade Czechoslovakia: April, 1938, to March, 1939

   1. Simultaneously with their annexation of Austria, the Nazi conspirators gave false assurances to the Czechoslovak Government that they would not attack that country. But within a month they met to plan specific ways and means of attacking Czechoslovakia, and to revise, in the light of the acquisition of Austria, the previous plans for aggression against Czechoslovakia.

   2. On 21st April, 1938, the Nazi conspirators met and prepared to launch an attack on Czechoslovakia not later than 1st October, 1938. They planned to create an "incident" to "justify" the attack. They decided to launch a military attack only after a period of diplomatic squabbling which, growing more serious, would lead to the excuse for war, or, in the alternative, to unleash a lightning attack as a result of an " incident" of their own creation. Consideration was given to assassinating the German Ambassador at Prague to create the requisite incident. From and after 21st April, 1938, the Nazi conspirators caused to be prepared detailed and precise military plans designed to carry out such an attack at any opportune moment and calculated to overthrow all Czechoslovak resistance within four days, this presenting the world with a fait accompli, and so forestalling outside resistance. Throughout the months of May, June, July, August and September, these plans were made more specific and detailed, and by 3rd September, it was decided that all troops were to be ready for action on

28th September, 1983.

3. Throughout this same period, the Nazi conspirators were agitating the minorities' question in Czechoslovakia, and particularly in the Sudetenland, leading to a diplomatic crisis in August and September, 1938. After the Nazi conspirators threatened war, the United Kingdom and France concluded a pact with Germany and Italy at Munich on 29th September, 1938, involving the cession of the Sudetenland by Czechoslovakia to Germany. Czechoslovakia was required to acquiesce. On 1st October, 1938, German troops occupied the Sudetenland.

4. On 5th March, 1939, contrary to the provisions of the Munich Pact itself, the Nazi conspirators completed their plan by seizing and occupying the major part of Czechoslovakia, i.e., Bohemia and Moravia, not ceded to German by the Munich Pact.

4. Formulation of the plan to attack Poland : preparation and initiation of aggressive war : March, 1939, to September, 1939

(a) With these aggressions successfully consummated, the conspirators had obtained much desired resources and bases and were ready to undertake further aggressions by means of war. Following the assurances to the world of peaceful intentions, an influential group of the conspirators met on 23rd May, 1939, to consider the further implementation of their plan. The situation was reviewed and it was observed that "the past six years have been put to good use and all measures have been taken in correct sequence and in accordance with our aims," that the national- political unity of the Germans had been substantially achieved, and that further successes could not be achieved without war and bloodshed. It was decided nevertheless next to attack Poland at the first suitable opportunity. It was admitted that the questions concerning Danzig which they had agitated with Poland were not true questions, but rather that the question was one of aggressive expansion for food and "Lebensraum." It was recognised that Poland would fight if attacked and that a repetition of the Nazi success against Czechoslovakia without war could not be expected. Accordingly, it was determined that the problem was to isolate Poland and, if possible, prevent a simultaneous conflict with the Western Powers. Nevertheless, it was agreed that England was an enemy to their aspirations, and that war with England and her ally France must eventually result, and therefore that in that war every attempt must be made to overwhelm England with a "Blitzkrieg" or lightning war. It was thereupon determined immediately to prepare detailed plans for an attack on Poland at the first suitable opportunity and thereafter for an attack on England and France, together with plans for the simultaneous occupation by armed force of air bases in the Netherlands and Belgium.

(b) Accordingly, after having denounced the German-Polish Pact Of 1934, on false grounds, the Nazi conspirators proceeded to stir up the Danzig issue, to prepare frontier "incidents" to "justify" the attack, and to make demands for the cession of Polish territory. Upon refusal by Poland to yield, they caused German armed forces to invade Poland on 1st September, 1939, thus precipitating war also

22

with the United Kingdom and France.

5. Expansion of the war into a general war of aggression: planning and execution of attacks on Denmark, Norway, Belgium, The Netherlands, Luxembourg, Yugoslavia, and Greece: 1939 to April, 1941

Thus the aggressive war prepared for by the Nazi conspirators through their attacks on Austria and Czechoslovakia was actively launched by their attack on Poland, in violation of the terms of the Briand-Kellogg Pact, 1928. After the total defeat of Poland, in order to facilitate the carrying out of their military operations against France and the United Kingdom, the Nazi conspirators made active preparations for an extension of the war in Europe. In accordance with these plans, they caused the German armed forces to invade Denmark and Norway on 9th April, 1940; Belgium, the Netherlands and Luxembourg on 10th May, 1940; Yugoslavia and Greece on 6th April, 1941. All these invasions had been specifically planned in advance.

6. German invasion on 22nd June, 1941, of the U.S.S.R. territory in violation of the Non-Aggression Pact Of 23rd August, 1939

On 22nd June, 1941, the Nazi conspirators deceitfully denounced the Non-Aggression Pact between Germany and the U.S.S.R. and without any declaration of war invaded Soviet territory, thereby beginning a war of aggression against the U.S.S.R. Schuschnigg yielded a promise of amnesty to imprisoned Nazis and appointment of Nazis to ministerial posts. He agreed to remain silent until Hitler's next speech in which Austria's independence was to be reaffirmed, but Hitler in that speech, instead of affirming Austrian independence, declared himself protector of all. Germans. Meanwhile, subversive activities of Nazis in Austria increased. Schuschnigg on 9th March, 1938, announced a plebiscite for the following Sunday on the question of Austrian independence. On 11th March Hitler sent an ultimatum, demanding that the plebiscite be called off or Germany would invade Austria. Later the same day a second ultimatum threatened invasion unless Schuschnigg should resign in three hours. Schuschnigg resigned. The defendant Seyss-Inquart, who was appointed Chancellor, immediately invited Hitler to send German troops into Austria to "preserve order." The invasion began on 12th March, I938 On 13th March, Hitler by proclamation assumed office as Chief of State of Austria and took command of her armed forces. By a law of the same date Austria was annexed to Germany.

From the first day of launching their attack on Soviet territory the Nazi conspirators, in accordance with their detailed plans, began to carry out the destruction of cities, towns and villages, the demolition of factories, collective farms, electric stations and railroads, the robbery and barbaric devastation of the natural cultural institutions of the peoples of the U.S.S.R., the devastation of museums, churches, historic monuments, and mass deportation of the Soviet citizens for slave labour to Germany, as well as the annihilation of old people, women and children, especially Byelo-Russians and Ukrainians. The extermination of Jews was committed throughout the territory of the Soviet Union.

The above-mentioned criminal offences were perpetrated by the German troops in accordance with the orders of the Nazi Government and the General Staff and

High Command of the German Armed Forces.

7. Collaboration with Italy and Japan and aggressive war against the United States
: November, 1936, to December, 1941

After the initiation of the Nazi wars of aggression the Nazi conspirators brought about a German-Italian-Japanese ten- year military-economic alliance signed at Berlin on 27th September, 1940. This agreement, representing a strengthening of the bonds among those nations, established by the earlier but more limited pact of 25th November, 1936, stated: " The Governments of Germany, Italy and Japan, considering it as a condition precedent of any lasting peace that all nations of the world be given each its own proper place, have decided to stand by and co-operate with one another in regard of their efforts in Greater East Asia and regions of Europe respectively wherein it is their prime purpose to establish and maintain a new order of things calculated to promote the mutual prosperity and welfare of the peoples concerned." The Nazi conspirators conceived that Japanese aggression would weaken and handicap those nations with which they were at war, and those with whom they contemplated war. Accordingly, the Nazi conspirators exhorted Japan to seek "a new order of things." Taking advantage of the wars of aggression then being waged by the Nazi conspirators, Japan commenced an attack on 7th December, 1941, against the United States of America at Pearl Harbour and the Philippines, and against the British Commonwealth of Nations, French Indo-China and the Netherlands in the South-west Pacific. Germany declared war against the United States on 11th December, 1941.

(G) WAR CRIMES AND CRIMES AGAINST HUMANITY COMMITTED IN THE COURSE OF EXECUTING THE CONSPIRACY FOR WHICH THE CONSPIRATORS ARE RESPONSIBLE:

1. Beginning with the initiation of the aggressive war on 1st September, 1939, and throughout its extension into wars involving almost the entire world, the Nazi conspirators carried out their Common Plan or Conspiracy to wage war in ruthless and complete disregard and violation of the laws and customs of war. In the course of executing the Common Plan or Conspiracy, there were committed the War Crimes detailed hereinafter in Count Three of this Indictment.

2. Beginning with the initiation of their plan to seize and retain total control of the German State, and thereafter throughout their utilisation of that control for foreign aggression, the Nazi conspirators carried out their Common Plan or Conspiracy in ruthless and complete disregard and violation of the laws of Humanity. In the course of executing the Common Plan or Conspiracy there were committed the Crimes against Humanity detailed hereinafter in Count Four of this Indictment.

3. By reason of all the foregoing, the defendants with divers other persons are guilty of a Common Plan or Conspiracy for the accomplishment of Crimes against Peace; of a conspiracy to commit Crimes against Humanity in the course of preparation for war and in the course of prosecution of war; and of a conspiracy to commit War Crimes not only against the armed forces of their enemies but also against non-belligerent civilian populations.

(H) INDIVIDUAL, GROUP AND ORGANISATION RESPONSIBILITY

FOR THE OFFENCE STATED IN COUNT ONE:

Reference is hereby made to Appendix A of this Indictment for a statement of the responsibility of the individual defendants for the offence set forth in this Count One of the Indictment. Reference is hereby made to Appendix B of this Indictment for a statement of the responsibility of the groups and organisation named herein as criminal groups and organisations for the offences set forth in this Count One of the Indictment.

MR. SIDNEY ALDERMAN: If the Tribunal please, that ends Count One, which is America's responsibility. Great Britain will present Count Two.

SIR DAVID MAXWELL FYFE: If your Lordship pleases.

COUNT TWO - CRIMES AGAINST PEACE (Charter, Article 6 (a))

V. Statement of the Offence

All the defendants with divers other persons, during a period of years preceding 8th May, 1945, participated in the planning, preparation, initiation and waging of wars of aggression, which were also wars in violation of international treaties, agreements and assurances.

VI. Particulars of the wars planned, prepared, initiated and waged

(A) The wars referred to in the Statement of Offence in this Count Two of the Indictment and the dates of their initiation were the following: against Poland, 1st September, 1939; against the United Kingdom and France, 3rd September, 1939; against Denmark and Norway, 9th April, 1940; against Belgium, the Netherlands and Luxembourg, 10th May, 1940; against Yugoslavia and Greece, 6th April, 1941; against the U.S.S.R., 22nd June, 1941; and against the United States of America, 11th December, 1941.

(B) Reference is hereby made to Count One of the Indictment for the allegations charging that these wars were wars of aggression on the part of the defendants.

(C) Reference is hereby made to Appendix C annexed to this Indictment for a statement of particulars of the charges of violations of international treaties, agreements and assurances caused by the defendants in the course of planning, preparing and initiating these wars.

VII. Individual, group and Organisation responsibility for the offence stated in Count Two

Reference is hereby made to Appendix A of this Indictment for a statement of the responsibility of the individual defendants for the offence set forth in this Count Two of the Indictment. Reference is hereby made to Appendix B of this Indictment for a statement of the responsibility of the groups and organisations named herein as criminal groups and organisations for the offence set forth in this Count Two of the Indictment.

That finishes, Mr. President, Count Two of the Indictment.

THE PRESIDENT: Sir David.

SIR DAVID MAXWELL FYFE: If your Lordship pleases.

THE PRESIDENT: The Tribunal will now adjourn for 15 minutes.

SIR DAVID MAXWELL FYFE: If your Lordship pleases. The reading will be resumed by a representative of the French Republic.

(A recess was taken.)

THE PRESIDENT: The Tribunal understands that the defendant Ernst Kaltenbrunner is temporarily ill. The trial will continue in his absence. I call upon the Chief Prosecutor for the Provisional Republic of France.

M. MOUNIER:

COUNT THREE - WAR CRIMES
(Charter, Article 6, especially 6 (b))

VIII. Statement of the Offence

All the defendants committed War Crimes between 1st September, 1939, and 8th May, 1945, in Germany and in all those countries and territories occupied by the German armed forces since 1st September, 1939, and in Austria, Czechoslovakia and Italy, and on the High Seas.

All the defendants, acting in concert with others, formulated and executed a Common Plan or Conspiracy to commit War Crimes as defined in Article 6 (b) of the Charter. This plan involved, among other things, the practice of "total war" including methods of combat and of military occupation in direct conflict with the laws and customs of war, and the perpetration of crimes committed on the field of battle during encounters with enemy armies, against prisoners of war, and in occupied territories against the civilian population of such territories.

The said War Crimes were committed by the defendants and by other persons for whose acts the defendants are responsible (under Article 6 of the Charter) as such other persons when committing the said War Crimes performed their acts in execution of a Common Plan or Conspiracy to commit the said War Crimes, in the formulation and execution of which plan and conspiracy all the defendants participated as leaders, organisers, instigators and accomplices.

These methods and crimes constituted violations of international conventions, of internal penal laws and of the general principles of criminal law as derived from the criminal law of all civilised nations, and were involved in and part of a systematic course of conduct.

(A) MURDER AND ILL-TREATMENT OF CIVILIAN POPULATIONS OF OR IN OCCUPIED TERRITORY AND ON THE HIGH SEAS

Throughout the period of their occupation of territories overrun by their armed forces, the defendants, for the purpose of systematically terrorising the inhabitants, ill- treated civilians, imprisoned them without legal process, tortured and murdered them.

The murders and ill-treatment were carried out by divers means, such as shooting, hanging, gassing, starvation, gross overcrowding, systematic under-nutrition, systematic imposition of labour tasks beyond the strength of those ordered to carry them out, inadequate provision of surgical and medical services, kickings, beatings. brutality and torture of all kinds, including the use of hot irons and pulling out of finger nails and the performance of experiments by means of operations and otherwise on living human subjects. In some occupied territories the defendants interfered with religious services, persecuted members of the clergy and monastic orders, and expropriated church property. They conducted deliberate and systematic genocide, viz. the extermination of racial and national groups, against the civilian population of certain occupied territories in order to destroy particular races and classes of people, and national, racial or religious groups, particularly Jews, Poles and Gypsies, and others.

Civilians were systematically subjected to tortures of all kinds, with the object of obtaining information.

Civilians of occupied countries were subjected systematically to "protective arrests," that is to say they were arrested and imprisoned without any trial and any of the ordinary protections of the law, and they were imprisoned under the most unhealthy and inhumane conditions.

In the concentration camps were many prisoners who were classified " Nacht und Nebel." These were entirely cut off from the world and were allowed neither to receive nor to send letters. They disappeared without trace and no announcement of their fate was ever made by the German authorities.

Such crimes and ill-treatment are contrary to International Conventions, in particular to Article 46 of The Hague Regulations, 1907, the laws and customs of war, the general principles of criminal law as derived from the criminal laws of all civilised nations, the internal penal laws of the countries in which such crimes were committed, and to Article 6 (b) of the Charter.

The following particulars and all the particulars appearing later in this count are set out herein by way of example only, are not exclusive of other particular cases, and are stated without prejudice to the right of the prosecution to adduce evidence of other cases of murder and ill-treatment of civilians.

I. In France, Belgium, Holland, Denmark, Norway, Luxembourg, Italy and the Channel Islands (hereinafter called the "Western Countries") and in that part of Germany which lies West of a line draw due North and South through the centre of Berlin (hereinafter called "Western *Germany").*

Such murder and ill-treatment took place in concentration camps and similar establishments set up by the defendants, and particularly in the concentration camps set up at Belsen, Buchenwald, Dachau, Breendonck, Grini, Natzweiler, Ravensbrueck, Vught and Amersfoort, and in numerous cities, towns and villages, including Oradour sur Glane, Trondheim and Oslo.

Crimes committed in France or against French citizens took the following Forms:

Arbitrary arrests were carried out under political or racial pretexts; they were either individual or collective; notably in Paris (round-up of the 18th Arrondissement by the Field Gendarmerie, round-up of the Jewish population of the 11th Arrondissement in August, 1941, round-up of Jewish intellectuals in December, 1941, round-up in July, 1942); at Clermont-Ferrand (round-up of professors and students of the University of Strasbourg, which had been evacuated to Clermont-Ferrand, on 25th November, 1943); at Lyons, at Marseilles (round-up of 40,000 persons in January, 1943); at Cluny (round-up on 24th December, 1944); at Figeac (round-tip in May, 1944); at Saint-Pol-de-Leon (round-up in July, 1944); at Locmine (round-up on 3rd July, 1944); at Eyzieux (round-up in May, 1944) and at Moussey (round-up in September, 1944). These arrests were followed by brutal treatment and tortures carried out by the most diverse methods, such as immersion in icy water, asphyxiation, torture of the limbs, and the use of instruments of torture, such as the iron helmet and electric current, and practised in all the prisons of France, notably in Paris, Lyons, Marseilles, Rennes, Metz, Clermont-Ferrand, Toulouse, Nice, Grenoble, Annecy, Arras, Bethune, Lille, Loos, Valenciennes, Nancy, Troyes and Caen, and in the torture chambers fitted up at the Gestapo centres.

In the concentration camps, the health regime and the labour regime were such that the rate of mortality (alleged to be from natural causes) attained enormous proportions, for instance

1. Out of a convoy of 250 French women deported from Compeigne to Auschwitz in January, 1943, 180 had died of exhaustion at the end of four months.
2. 143 Frenchmen died of exhaustion between 23rd March and 6th May 1943, in Block 8 at Dachau.
3. 1,797 Frenchmen died of exhaustion between 21st November, 1943, and 15th March, 1945, in the Block at Dora.
4. 465 Frenchmen died of general debility in November, I944, at Dora.
5. 22,761 deportees died of exhaustion at Buchenwald between 1st January, 1943, and 15th April, 1945.
6. 11,560 detainees died of exhaustion at Dachau Camp (most of them in Block 30 reserved for the sick and the infirm) between 1st January and 15th April, I945.
7. 780 priests died of exhaustion at Mauthausen.
8. Out of 2,200 Frenchmen registered at Flossenburg Camp, 1,600 died from supposedly natural causes.

Methods used for the work of extermination in concentration camps were: bad treatment, pseudo-scientific experiments (sterilisation of women at Auschwitz and at Ravensbrueck, study of the evolution of cancer of the womb at Auschwitz, of typhus at Buchenwald, anatomical research at Natzweiler, heart injections at Buchenwald, bone grafting and muscular excisions at Ravensbrueck, etc.), gas chambers, gas wagons and crematory ovens. Of 228,000 French political and racial deportees in concentration camps, only 28,000 survived.

In France also systematic extermination was practised, notably at Asq on 1st April, 1944, at Colpe on 22nd July, 1944, at Buzet-sur- Tarn on 6th July, 1944, and on 17th August, 1944, at Pluvignier on 8th July, 1944, at Rennes on 8th June, 1944, at Grenoble on 8th July, 1944, at Saint Flour on 10th June, 1944, at Ruisnes on 10th June, 1944, at Nimes, at Tulle, and at Nice, where, in July, 1944, the victims of torture were exposed to the population, and at Oradour-sur-Glane where the entire village population was shot or burned alive in the church.

The many charnel pits give proof of anonymous massacres. Most notable of these are the charnel pits of Paris (Cascade du Bois de Boulogne), Lyons, Saint-Genies-Laval, Besancon, Petit Saint-Bernard, Anlnat, Caen, Port-Louis, Charleval, Fontainebleau, Bouconne, Cabaudet, L'hermitage-Lorges, Morlas, Bordelongue, Signe.

In the course of a premeditated campaign of terrorism, initiated in Denmark by the Germans in the latter part of 1943, 600 Danish subjects were murdered and, in addition, throughout the German occupation of Denmark, large numbers of Danish subjects were subjected to torture and ill- treatment of all sorts. In addition, approximately 500 Danish subjects were murdered, by torture and other-wise, in German prisons and concentration camps.

In Belgium between 1940 and 1944 torture by various means, but identical in each place, was carried out at Brussels, Liege, Mons, Ghent, Namur, Antwerp, Tournai, Arlon, Charleroi and Dinant.

At Vught, in Holland, when the camp was evacuated, about 400 persons were shot.

In Luxembourg, during the German occupation, 500 persons were murdered and, in addition, another 521 were illegally executed, by order of such special tribunals as the so- called "Sondergericht." Many more persons in Luxembourg were subjected to torture and ill-treatment by the Gestapo. At least 4,000 Luxembourg nationals were imprisoned during the period of German occupation, and of these at least 400 were murdered.

Between March, 1944, and April, 1945, in Italy, at least 7,500 men, women and children, ranging in years from infancy to extreme old age, were murdered by the German soldiery at Civitella, in the Ardestine Caves in Rome, and at other places.

(B) DEPORTATION, FOR SLAVE LABOUR AND FOR OTHER PURPOSES, OF THE CIVILIAN POPULATIONS OF AND IN OCCUPIED TERRITORIES

During the whole period of the occupation by Germany of both the Western and the Eastern Countries, it was the policy of the German Government and of the German High Command to deport able-bodied citizens from such occupied countries to Germany and to other occupied countries to force them to work on fortifications, in factories, and in other tasks connected with the German War effort.

In pursuance of such policy there were mass deportations from all the Western and Eastern Countries for such purposes during the whole period of the occupation.

These deportations were contrary to the international conventions, in particular to Article 46 of the Hague Regulations, 1907, the laws and customs of war, the general principles of criminal law as derived from the criminal laws of all civilised nations, the internal penal laws of the countries in which such crimes were committed, and to Article 6 (b) of the Charter.

Particulars of deportations, by way of example only and without prejudice to the production of evidence of other cases, are as follows:-

1. From the Western Countries:-

From France the following "deportations" of persons for political and racial reasons took place-each of which consisted of from 1,500-2,500 deportees:-

    1940 ---   3 Transports.

    194I ---   14 Transports.

    1942 --- 104 Transports.

    1943 --- 257 Transports.

    1944 --- 326 Transports.

Such deportees were subjected to the most barbarous conditions of overcrowding; they were provided with wholly insufficient clothing and were given little or no food for several days.

The conditions of transport were such that many deportees died in the course of the voyage, for example:

In one of the wagons of the train which left Compiegne for Buchenwald, on the 17th of September, 1943, 80 men died out of 130.

On 4th June, 1944, 484 bodies were taken out of a train at Sarrebourg.

In a train which left Compiegne on the 2nd July, 1944, for Dachau, more than 600 dead were found on arrival, i.e., one- third of the total number.

In a train which left Compiegne on the 16th January, 1944, for Buchenwald, more than 100 persons were confined in each wagon, the dead and the wounded being heaped in the last wagon during the voyage.

In April, I945, of I2,000 internees evacuated from Buchenwald, 4,000 only were still alive when the marching column arrived near Regensburg.

During the German occupation of Denmark, 5,200 Danish subjects were deported to Germany and there imprisoned in concentration camps and other places.

In 1942 and thereafter, 6,000 nationals of Luxembourg were deported from their country under deplorable conditions and many of them perished.

From Belgium between 194o and 1944, at least 190,000 civilians were deported to Germany and used as slave labour. Such deportees were subjected to ill-treatment and many of them were compelled to work in armament factories.

From Holland, between 1940 and 1944 nearly half a million civilians were deported to Germany and to other occupied countries.

(C) MURDER AND ILL-TREATMENT OF PRISONERS OF WAR, AND OF OTHER MEMBERS OF THE ARMED FORCES OF THE COUNTRIES WITH WHOM GERMANY WAS AT WAR, AND OF PERSONS ON THE HIGH SEAS

The defendants ill-treated and murdered prisoners of war by denying them suitable food, shelter, clothing and medical care and other attention; by forcing them to labour in inhumane conditions; by humiliating them, torturing them and by killing them. The German Government and the German High Command imprisoned prisoners of war in various concentration camps, where they were killed or subjected to inhuman treatment by the various methods set forth in paragraph VIII (A).

Members of the armed forces of the countries with whom Germany was at war were frequently murdered while in the act of surrendering. These murders and ill-treatment were contrary to International Conventions, particularly Articles 4, 5, 6 and 7 of the Hague Regulations, 1907, and to Articles 2,3, 4 and 6 of the Prisoners of War Convention (Geneva, 1929), the laws and customs of war, the general principles of criminal law as derived from the criminal laws of all civilised nations, the internal penal laws of the countries in which such crimes were committed and to Article 6 (b) of the Charter.

Particulars by way of example and without prejudice to the production of evidence of other cases, are as follows:-

In the Western Countries :-

French officers who escaped from Oflag XC were handed over to the Gestapo and disappeared; others were murdered by their guards; others sent to concentration camps and exterminated. Among others, the men of Stalag VI C were sent to Buchenwald.

Frequently prisoners captured on the Western Front were obliged to march to camps until they completely collapsed. Some of them walked more than 600 kilometres with hardly any food; they marched on for 48 hours running, without being fed; among them a certain number died of exhaustion or of hunger; stragglers were systematically murdered.

The same crimes were committed in 1943, 1944 and 1945, when the occupants of the camps were withdrawn before the Allied advance, particularly during the withdrawal of the prisoner from Sagan on February 8th, 1945.

Bodily punishments were inflicted upon non-commissioned officers and cadets who refused to work. On December 24th, 1943, three French N.C.0's. were murdered for that motive in Stalag IV A. Much ill-treatment was inflicted without motive on other ranks; stabbing with bayonets, striking with rifle- butts and whipping; in Stalag XX B the sick themselves were beaten many times by sentries; in Stalag III B and Stalag III C, worn-out prisoners were murdered or grievously wounded. In military gaols, in Graudenz for instance, in reprisal camps as in Rava-Ruska, the food was so insufficient that the men lost more than 15 kilograms in a few weeks. In May, one loaf of bread only was distributed in Rava-Ruska to each group of 35 men.

Orders were given to transfer French officers in chains to the camp of Mauthausen after they had tried to escape. At their arrival in camp they were murdered, either by shooting or by gas and their bodies destroyed in the crematorium.

American prisoners, officers and men, were murdered in Normandy during the summer of 1944 and in the Ardennes in December, 1944. American prisoners were starved, beaten and mutilated in various ways in numerous Stalags in Germany or in the occupied countries, particularly in 1943, 1944 and 1945.

(D) KILLING OF HOSTAGES

Throughout the territories occupied by the German armed forces in the course of waging their aggressive wars, the defendants adopted and put into effect on a wide scale the practice of taking and killing hostages from the civilian population. These acts were contrary to International Conventions, particularly Article 50 of the Hague Regulations, 1907, the laws and customs of war, the general principles of criminal law, as derived from the criminal laws of all civilised nations, the internal penal laws of the countries in which such crimes were committed and to Article 6(b) of the Charter.

Particulars by way of example and without prejudice to the production of evidence of other cases, are as follows:-

In the Western Countries :-

In France hostages were executed either individually or collectively; these executions took place in all the big cities of France, among others in Paris, Bordeaux and Nantes, as well as at Chateaubriant.

In Holland many hundreds of hostages were shot at the following among other places - Rotterdam, Apeldoorn, Amsterdam, Benschop and Haarlem.

In Belgium many hundreds of hostages were shot during the period 1940 to 1944.

M. GERTHOFFER (continuing the reading of the Indictment)

(E) PLUNDER OF PUBLIC AND PRIVATE PROPERTY

The defendants ruthlessly exploited the people and the material resources of the countries they occupied, in order to strengthen the Nazi war machine, to depopulate and impoverish the rest of Europe, to enrich themselves and their adherents, and to promote German economic supremacy over Europe.

The defendants engaged in the following acts and practices, among others:

1. They degraded the standard of life of the people of occupied countries and caused starvation, by stripping occupied countries of foodstuffs for removal to Germany.

2. They seized raw materials and industrial machinery in all of the occupied countries, removed them to Germany and used them in the interest of the German war effort, and the German economy.

In all the occupied countries, in varying degrees, they confiscated businesses, plants and other property.

4. In an attempt to give colour of legality to illegal acquisitions of property, the forced owners of property to go through the forms of "voluntary" and "legal" transfers.

5. They established comprehensive controls over the economies of all of the occupied countries and directed their resources, their production and their labour in the interests of the German war economy, depriving the local populations of the, products of essential industries.

6. By a variety of financial mechanisms, they despoiled all of the occupied countries of essential commodities and accumulated wealth, debased the local currency systems and disrupted the local economics. They financed extensive purchases in occupied countries through clearing arrangements by which they exacted loans from the occupied countries. They imposed occupation levies, exacted financial contributions, and issued occupation currency, far in excess of occupation costs. They used these excess funds to finance the purchase of business properties and supplies in the occupied countries.

7. They abrogated the rights of the local populations in the occupied portions of the U.S.S.R. and in Poland and in other countries to develop or manage agricultural and industrial properties, and reserved this area for exclusive settlement, development, and ownership by Germans and their so-called racial brethren.

8. In further development of their plan of criminal exploitation, they destroyed industrial cities, cultural. monuments, scientific institutions, and property of all types in the occupied territories to eliminate the possibility of competition with Germany.

9. From their programme of terror, slavery, spoliation and organised outrage, the Nazi conspirators created an instrument for the personal profit and aggrandisement of themselves and their adherents. They secured for themselves and their adherents:

   (a) Positions in administration of business involving power, influence, and lucrative prerequisites.

   (b) The use of cheap forced labour.

   (c) The acquisition on advantageous terms of foreign properties, raw materials, and business interests.

   (d) The basis for the industrial supremacy of Germany.

These acts were contrary to International Conventions, particularly Articles 46 to 56 inclusive of the Hague Regulations, 1907, the laws and customs of war, the general principles of criminal law as derived from the criminal laws of all civilised nations, the internal penal laws of the countries in which such crimes were committed and to Article 6 (b) of the Charter.

Particulars by way of example and without prejudice to the production of evidence of other cases are as follows:-

1. Western Countries :

There was plundered from the Western Countries from 1940 to 1944, works of art, artistic objects, pictures, plastics, furniture, textiles, antique pieces and similar articles of enormous value to the number of 21,903.

In France statistics show the following:

REMOVAL OF RAW MATERIALS

Coal	63,000,000 tons
Electric energy	20,976 kw
Petrol and fuel	1,943,750 tons
Iron ore	74,848,000 tons
Siderurgical products	3,822,000 tons
Bauxite	1,211,800 tons
Cement	5,984,000 tons
Lime	1,888,000 tons
Quarry products	25,872,000 tons

and various other by-products to a total value of 79,961,423,000 francs.

REMOVAL OF INDUSTRIAL EQUIPMENT

Total 9,759,861,000 francs, of which 2,626,479,000 francs of machine tools.

REMOVAL OF AGRICULTURAL PRODUCE

Total ....126,655,852,000 francs.

i.e., for the principal products-

Wheat ....2,947,337 tons

Oats ....2,354,080 tons

Milk ....790,000 hectolitres

Milk (concentrated and in powder) ....460,000 hectolitres

Butter...76,000 tons

Cheese ....49,000 tons

Potatoes ....725,975 tons

Various vegetables.. 575,000 tons

Wine ....7,647,000 hectolitres

Champagne ....87,000,000 bottles

Beer . ...3,821,520 hectolitres

Various kinds of alcohol ....1,830,000 hectolitres

REMOVAL OF MANUFACTURED PRODUCTS

to a total of 184,640,000,000 francs.

PLUNDERING

Francs 257,020,024,000 from private enterprise.

Francs 55,000,100,000 from the state.

FINANCIAL EXPLOITATION

From June, 1940, to September, 1944, the French Treasury was compelled to pay to Germany 631,966,000,000 francs.

LOOTING AND DESTRUCTION OF WORKS OF ART

The museums of Nantes, Nancy, Old-Marseilles were looted. Private collections of great value were stolen. In this way, Raphaels, Vermeers, Van Dycks and works of Rubens, Holbein, Rembrandt, Watteau, Boucher disappeared. Germany compelled France to deliver up "The Mystic Lamb" by Van Eyck, which Belgium had entrusted to her.

In Norway and other occupied countries decrees were made by which the property of many civilians, societies, etc., was confiscated. An immense amount of property of every kind was plundered from France, Belgium, Norway, Holland and Luxembourg.

As a result of the economic plundering of Belgium between 1940 and 1944 the damage suffered amounted to 175 billions of Belgian francs.

(F) THE EXACTION OF COLLECTIVE PENALTIES

The Germans pursued a systematic policy of inflicting, in all the occupied countries, collective penalties, pecuniary and otherwise, upon the population for acts of individuals for which it could not be regarded as collectively responsible; this was done at many places, including Oslo, Stavanger, Trondheim and Rogaland.

Similar instances occurred in France, among others in Dijon, Nantes and as regards the Jewish population in the occupied territories. The total amount of fines imposed on French communities add up to 1,157,179,484 francs made up as follows:

A fine on the Jewish population...........................1,000,000,000

Various fines..157,179,484

These acts violated Article 50, Hague Regulations, 1907, the laws and customs of war, the general principles of criminal law as derived from the criminal laws of all civilised nations, the internal penal laws of the countries in which such crimes were committed and Article 6 (b) of the Charter.

(G) WANTON DESTRUCTION OF CITIES, TOWNS AND VILLAGES AND DEVASTATION NOT JUSTIFIED BY MILITARY NECESSITY

The defendants wantonly destroyed cities, towns, and villages and committed other acts of devastation without military justification or necessity. These acts violated Articles 46 and So of the Hague Regulations, 1907, the laws and customs of war, the general principles of criminal law as derived from the criminal laws of all civilised nations, the internal penal laws of the countries in which such crimes were committed and Article 6 (b) of the Charter.

Particulars by way of example only and without prejudice to the production of evidence of other cases, are as follows:

1. Western Countries:

In March, 1941, part of Lofoten in Norway was destroyed.

In April, 1942, the town of Telerag in Norway was destroyed.

Entire villages were destroyed in France, among others, Oradour-sur-Glane, Saint-Nizier in Gascogne, La Mure, Vassieu, La Chappelle en Vercors. The town of Saint Die was burnt down and destroyed. The Old Port District of Marseilles was dynamited in the beginning of 1943 and resorts along the Atlantic and the Mediterranean coasts, particularly the town of Sanary, were demolished.

In Holland there was most widespread and extensive destruction, not justified by military necessity, including the destruction of harbours, locks, dykes and bridges; immense devastation was also caused by inundations which equally were not justified by military necessity.

(H) CONSCRIPTION OF CIVILIAN LABOUR

Throughout the occupied territories the defendants conscripted and forced the inhabitants to labour and requisitioned their services for purposes other than meeting the needs of the armies of occupation and to an extent far out of proportion to the resources of the countries involved. All the civilians so conscripted, were forced to work for the German war effort. Civilians were required to register and many of those who registered were forced to join the Todt Organisation and the Speer Legion, both of which were semi-military organisations involving some military training. These acts violated Articles 46 and 52 of the Hague Regulations, 1907, the laws and customs of war, the general principles of criminal law as derived from the criminal laws of all civilised nations, the internal penal laws of the countries in which such crimes were committed and Article 6 (b) of the Charter.

Particulars, by way of example only and without prejudice to the production of evidence of other cases, are as follows

1. Western Countries:

In France, from 1942 to 1944, 963,813 persons were compelled to work in Germany and 737,000 to work in France for the German Army.

In Luxembourg in 1944 alone, 2,500 men and 500 girls were conscripted for forced labour.

(I) FORCING CIVILIANS OF OCCUPIED TERRITORIES TO SWEAR ALLEGIANCE TO A HOSTILE POWER

Civilians who joined the Speer Legion, as set forth in paragraph (H) were required, under threat of depriving them of food, money and identity papers, to swear a solemn oath acknowledging unconditional obedience to Adolf Hitler, the Fuehrer of Germany, which was to them a hostile power.

THE PRESIDENT: The Tribunal will now adjourn until 2 o'clock.

(A recess was taken until 14.00 hours.)

THE PRESIDENT: Will the Chief Prosecutor for the French Republic continue the reading of the indictment.

M. MOUNIER:

(I) FORCING CIVILIANS OF OCCUPIED TERRITORIES TO SWEAR ALLEGIANCE TO A HOSTILE POWER

Civilians who joined the Speer Legion, as set forth in paragraph (H) were required, under threat of depriving them of food, money and identity papers, to swear a solemn oath acknowledging unconditional obedience to Adolf Hitler, the Fuehrer of Germany, which was to them a hostile power.

In Lorraine, civil servants were obliged, in order to retain their positions, to sign a declaration by which they acknowledged the "return of their country to the Reich," pledged themselves to obey - without reservation the orders of their chiefs and put themselves "at the active service of the Fuehrer and the Great National Socialist Germany."

A similar pledge was imposed on Alsatian civil servants by threat of deportation or internment.

These acts violated Article 45 of the Hague Regulations, 1907, the laws and customs of war, the general principles of International Law and Article 6 (b) of the Charter.

(J) GERMANISATION OF OCCUPIED TERRITORIES

In certain occupied territories purportedly annexed to Germany the defendants methodically and pursuant to plan endeavoured to assimilate those territories politically, culturally, socially and economically into the German Reich. The defendants endeavoured to obliterate the former national character of these territories. In pursuance of these plans and endeavours, the defendants forcibly deported inhabitants who were predominantly non-German and introduced thousands of German colonists.

This plan included economic domination, physical conquest, installation of puppet Governments, purported de jure annexation and enforced conscription into the German Armed Forces.

This was carried out in most of the Occupied Countries including: Norway, France (particularly in the departments of Upper Rhine, Lower Rhine, Moselle,

Ardennes, Aisne, Nord, and Meurthe), Luxembourg, the Soviet Union, Denmark, Belgium, Holland.

In France in the Departments of the Aisne, the Nord, the Meurthe and Moselle, and especially in that of the Ardennes, rural properties were seized by a German State Organisation which tried to have them exploited under German direction; the landowners of these exploitations were dispossessed and turned into agricultural labourers.

In the Department of the Upper Rhine, the Lower Rhine and the Moselle, the methods of Germanisation were those of annexation followed by conscription.

1. From the month of August, 1940, officials who refused to take the oath of allegiance to the Reich were expelled. On 21st September expulsions and deportation of populations began and on 22nd November, 1940, more than 70,000 Lorrainers or Alsatians were driven into the South zone of France. From 31st July, 1941, onwards, more than 100,000 persons were deported into the Eastern regions of the Reich or to Poland. All the property of the deportees or expelled persons was confiscated. At the same time, 80,000 Germans coming from the Saar or from Westphalia were installed in Lorraine and 2,000 farms belonging to French people were transferred to Germans.

2. From 2nd January, 1942, all the young people of the Departments of the Upper Rhine and the Lower Rhine, aged from 10 to 18 years, were incorporated in the Hitler Youth. The same thing was done in the Moselle from 4th August, 1942. From 1940 all the French schools were closed, their staffs expelled, and the German school system was introduced in the three departments.

3. On 28th September, 1940, an order applicable to the Department of the Moselle ordained the Germanisation of all the surnames and Christian names which were French in form. The same thing was done from 15th January, 1943, in the Departments of the Upper Rhine and the Lower Rhine.

4. Two orders from 23rd to 24th August, 1942, imposed by force German nationality on French citizens.

5. On 8th May, 1941, for the Upper Rhine and the Lower Rhine, 23rd April, 1941, for the Moselle, orders were promulgated enforcing compulsory labour service on all French citizens of either sex aged from 17 to 25 years. From 1st January, 1942, for young men and from 26th January, 1942, for young girls, national labour service was effectively organised in the Moselle. It was from 27th August, 1942, in the Upper Rhine and in the Lower Rhine for young men only. The classes 1940, 1941, 1942 were called up.

6. These classes were retained in the Wehrmacht on the expiration of their time and labour service. On 19th August, 1942, an order instituted compulsory military service in the Moselle. On 25th August, 1942, the classes 1940-1944 were called up in three departments. Conscription was enforced by the German authorities in conformity with the provisions of German legislation. The first revision boards took place from 3rd September, 1942. Later in the Upper Rhine and the Lower Rhine new levies were effected everywhere on classes 1928 to 1939 inclusive. The French people who refused to obey these laws were considered as deserters

and their families were deported, while their property was confiscated.

These acts violated Articles 43, 46, 55 and 56 of the Hague Regulations, 1907, the laws and customs of war, the general principles of criminal law as derived from the criminal laws of all civilised nations, the internal penal laws of the countries in which such crimes were committed and Article 6 (b) of the Charter.

IX. Individual, Group and Organisation Responsibility for the Offence stated in Count Three

Reference is hereby made to Appendix A of this Indictment for a statement of the responsibility of the individual defendants for the offence set forth in this Count Three of the Indictment. Reference is hereby made to Appendix B of this Indictment for a statement of the responsibility of the groups and organisations named herein as criminal groups and organisations for the offence set forth in this Count Three of the Indictment.

THE PRESIDENT: I will now call upon the Chief Prosecutor for the Soviet Union.
CAPTAIN V. V. KUCHIN:

COUNT THREE - WAR CRIMES

All the defendants committed War Crimes between 1st September, 1939 and 8th May, 1945, in Germany and in all those countries and territories occupied by the German armed forces since 1st September, 1939, and in Austria, Czechoslovakia, Italy, and on the High Seas.

All the defendants, acting in concert with others, formulated and executed a common plan or conspiracy to commit War Crimes as (refined in Article 6 (b) of the Charter.. This plan involved, among other things, the practice of "total war" including methods of combat and of military occupation in direct conflict with the laws and customs of war, and the commission of crimes perpetrated on the field of battle during encounters with enemy armies, and against prisoners of war, and in occupied territories against the civilian population of such territories.

The said War Crimes were committed by the defendants and by other persons for whose acts the defendants are responsible (under Article 6 of the Charter) as such other persons when committing the said War Crimes performed their acts in execution of a common plan and conspiracy to commit the said War Crimes, in the formulation and execution of which plan and conspiracy all the defendants participated as leaders, organisers, instigators and accomplices.

These methods and crimes constituted violations of international conventions, of internal penal laws and of the general principles of criminal law as derived from the criminal law of all civilised nations, and were involved in and part of a systematic course of conduct.

(A) MURDER AND ILL-TREATMENT OF CIVILIAN POPULATIONS OF OR IN OCCUPIED TERRITORY AND ON THE HIGH SEAS.

Throughout the period of their occupation of territories overrun by their armed forces the defendants, for the purpose of systematically terrorising the inhabitants, murdered and tortured civilians, and ill-treated them, and imprisoned them without legal process.

The murders and ill-treatment were carried out by divers means, including shooting, hanging, gassing, starvation, gross overcrowding, systematic under-nutrition, systematic imposition of labour tasks beyond the strength of those ordered to carry them out, inadequate provision of surgical and medical services, kickings, beatings, brutality and torture of all kinds, including the use of hot irons and pulling out of fingernails and the performance of experiments by means of operations and otherwise on living human subjects. In some occupied territories the defendants interfered with religious services, persecuted members of the clergy and monastic orders, and expropriated church property. They conducted deliberate and systematic genocide, viz., the extermination of racial and national groups, against the civilian populations of certain occupied territories in order to destroy particular races and classes of people and national, racial or religious groups, particularly Jews, Poles and Gypsies and others.

Civilians were systematically subjected to tortures of all kinds, with the object of obtaining information.

Civilians of occupied countries were subjected systematically to "protective arrests" whereby they were arrested and imprisoned without any trial and any of the ordinary protections of the law, and they were imprisoned under the most unhealthy and inhumane conditions.

In the concentration camps were many prisoners who were classified "Nacht und Nebel." These were entirely cut off from the world and were allowed neither to receive nor to send letters. They disappeared without trace and no announcement of their fate was ever made by the German authorities.

Such murders and ill-treatment were contrary to International Conventions, in particular to Article 46 of the Hague Regulations, 1907, the laws and customs of war, the general principles of criminal law as derived from the criminal laws of all civilised nations, the internal penal laws of the countries in which such crimes were committed, and to Article 6 (b) of the Charter.

The following particulars and all the particulars appearing later in this count are set out herein by way of example only, are not exclusive of other particular cases, and are stated without prejudice to the right of the prosecution to adduce evidence of other cases of murder and ill-treatment of civilians.

2. In the U.S.S.R., i.e., in the Byelo-Russian, Ukrainian, Esthonia, Latvian, Lithuanian, Karelo-Finnish and Moldavian Soviet Socialist Republics, in nineteen regions of the Russian Soviet Federated Socialist Republic, and in Poland, Czechoslovakia, Yugoslavia, Greece, and the Balkans (hereinafter called "the Eastern Countries").

From 1st September, 1939, when the German armed forces invaded Poland, and from 22nd June, 1941, when they invaded the U.S.S.R., the German Government and the German High Command adopted a systematic policy of murder and ill-treatment of the civilian populations of and in the Eastern Countries as they were successively occupied by the German armed forces. These murders and ill-treatments were carried on continuously until the German armed forces were driven out of the said countries.

Such murders and ill-treatments included:

(a) Murders and ill-treatments at concentration camps and similar establishments set up by the Germans in the Eastern Countries and in Eastern Germany including those set up at Maidanek and Auschwitz.

The said murders and ill-treatments were carried out by divers means including all those set out above, as follows :

About 1,500,000 persons were exterminated in Maidanek and about 4,000,000 persons were exterminated in Auschwitz, among whom were citizens of Poland, the U.S.S.R., the United States of America, Great Britain, Czechoslovakia, France and other countries.

In the Lwow region and in the city of Lwow the Germans exterminated about 700,000 Soviet people, including seventy persons in the field of the arts, science and technology, and also citizens of the U.S.A., Great Britain, Czechoslovakia, Yugoslavia and Holland, brought to this region from other concentration camps.

In the Jewish ghetto from 7th September, 1941, to 6th July, 1943, over 133,000 persons were tortured and shot.

Mass shooting of the population occurred in the suburbs of the city and in the Livenitz forest.

In the Ganov camp 200,000 citizens were exterminated. The most refined methods of cruelty were employed in this extermination, such as disembowelling and the freezing of human beings in tubs of water. Mass shooting took place to the accompaniment of the music of an orchestra recruited from the persons interned.

Beginning with June, 1943, the Germans carried out measures to hide the evidence of their crimes. They exhumed and burned corpses, and they crushed the bones with machines and used them for fertiliser.

At the beginning of 1944, in the Ozarichi region of the Bielorussian S.S.R., before liberation by the Red Army, the Germans established three concentration camps without shelters, to which they committed tens of thousands of persons from the neighbouring territories. They intentionally brought many people to these camps from typhus hospitals, for the purpose of infecting the other persons interned and for spreading the disease in territories from which the Germans were driven by the Red Army. In these camps there were many murders and crimes.

In the Esthonian S.S.R. they shot tens of thousands of persons and in one day alone, 19th September, 1944, in Camp Kloga, the Germans shot 2,000 peaceful citizens. They burned the bodies on bonfires.

In the Lithuanian S.S.R. there were mass killings of Soviet citizens, namely in Panerai at least 1,000,000; in Kaunas more than 70,000; in Alitus about 60,000, at Prenai more than 3,000; in Villiampol about 8,000; in Mariampol about 7,000; in Trakai and neighbouring towns 37,640.

In the Latvian S.S.R. 577,000 persons were murdered.

As a result of the whole system of internal order maintained in all camps, the interned persons were doomed to die.

In a secret instruction entitled "the internal regime in concentration camps," signed personally by Himmler in 1941, severe measures or punishment were set forth for the internees. Masses of prisoners of war were shot, or died from the cold and torture.

(b) Murders and ill-treatments at places in the Eastern Countries and in the Soviet Union, other than in the camps referred to in (a) above, included, on various dates during the occupation by the German armed forces:

The destruction in the Smolensk region of over 135,000 Soviet citizens.

Among these, near the village of Kholmetz of the Sychev region, when the military authorities were required to remove the mines from an area, on the order of the Commander of the 101st German Infantry Division, Major-General Fizler, the German soldiers gathered the inhabitants of the village of Kholmetz and forced them to remove mines from the road. All of these people lost their lives as a result of exploding mines.

In the Leningrad region there were shot and tortured over 172,000 persons, including over 20,000 persons who were killed in the city of Leningrad by the barbarous artillery barrage and the bombings.

In the Stavropol region in an anti-tank trench close to the station of Mineralny Vody, and in other cities, tens of thousands of persons were exterminated.

In Pyatigorsk many were subjected to torture and criminal treatment, including suspension from the ceiling and other methods. Many of the victims of these tortures were then shot.

In Krasnodar some 6,000 civilians were murdered by poison gas in gas vans, or were shot and tortured.

In the Stalingrad region more than 40,000 persons were killed and tortured. After the Germans were expelled from Stalingrad, more than a thousand mutilated bodies of local inhabitants were found with marks of torture. One hundred and thirty-nine women had their arms painfully bent backward and held by wires. From some their breasts had been cut off, and their ears, fingers and toes had been amputated, The bodies bore the marks of burns. On the bodies of the men the five-pointed star was burned with an iron or cut with a knife. Some were disembowelled.

In Orel over 5,000 persons were murdered.

In Novgorod and in the Novgorod region many thousands of Soviet citizens were killed by shooting, starvation and torture. In Minsk tens of thousands of citizens were similarly killed.

In the Crimea peaceful citizens were gathered on barges, taken out to sea and drowned, over 144,000 persons being exterminated in this manner.

In the Soviet Ukraine there were monstrous criminal acts of the Nazi conspirators. In Babi Yar, near Kiev, they shot over 100,00 men, women, children and old people. In this city in January, 1941, after the explosion in German headquarters on Dzerzhinsky Street the Germans arrested as hostages 1,250 - persons old men, minors, women with nursing infants. In Kiev they killed over 195,000 persons.

In Rovno and the Rovno region they killed and tortured over 100,000 peaceful citizens.

In Dnepropetrovsk, near the Transport Institute, they shot or threw alive into a great ravine 11,000 women, old men and children.

In the Kamenetz-Podolsk region 31,000 Jews were shot and exterminated, including 13,000 persons brought there from Hungary.

In the Odessa region at least 200,000 Soviet citizens were killed.

In Kharkov about 195,000 persons were either tortured to death, shot or gassed in gas vans.

In Gomel the Germans rounded up the population in prison, and tortured and tormented them, and then took them to the centre of the city and shot them in public.

In the city of Lyda in the Grodnen region on 8th May, 1942, 5,670 persons were completely undressed, driven into pens in groups of 100 and then shot by machine guns. Many were thrown in the graves while they were still alive.

Along with adults the Nazi conspirators mercilessly destroyed even children. They killed them with their parents, in groups and alone. They killed them in children's homes and hospitals, burying the living in the graves, throwing them into flames, stabbing them with bayonets, poisoning them, conducting experiments upon them, extracting their blood for the use of the German Army, throwing them into prison and Gestapo torture chambers and concentration camps, where the children died from hunger, torture, and epidemic diseases.

From 6th September to 24th November, 1942, in the region of Brest, Pinsk, Kobryn, Dyvina, Maloryta and Bereza-Kartuzka about 400 children were shot by German punitive units.

In the Yanov camp in the city of Lwow the Germans killed 8,000 children in two months.

In the resort of Tiberda the Germans annihilated 500 children suffering fromtuberculosis of the bone, who were in the sanatorium for the cure.

On the territory of the Latvian S.S.R. the German usurpers killed thousands of children, whom they had brought there with their parents from the Byelo-Russian S.S.R., and from the Kalinin, Kaluga and other regions of the R.S.F.S.R.

In Czechoslovakia, as a result of torture, beating, hanging, and shooting, there were annihilated in Gestapo prisons in Brno, Seim and other places over 20,000 persons. Moreover many thousands of internees were subjected to criminal treatment, beatings and torture.

Both before the war, as well as during the war, thousands of Czech patriots, in particular Catholics and Protestants, lawyers, doctors, teachers, etc., were arrested as hostages and imprisoned. A large number of these hostages were killed by the Germans.

In Greece in October, 1941, the male populations between 16 and 60 years of age of the Greek villages Amelofito, Kliston, Kizonia Mesevunos, Selli, Ano-Kerzillon and Kato- Kerzilion were shot-in all 416 persons.

In Yugoslavia many thousands of civilians were murdered. Other examples are given under paragraph (D), "Killing of Hostages," below.

THE PRESIDENT: Paragraph (B) on page 16 was read by the Chief Prosecutor for the French Republic. Paragraph 2 on page 17 was omitted by him. So had you better not go on at paragraph 2 at page 17?

CAPTAIN KUCHIN:

2. From the Eastern Countries

The German occupying authorities deported from the Soviet Union to slavery about 4,978,000 Soviet citizens.

750,000 Czechoslovakian citizens were taken away for forced labour outside the Czechoslovak frontiers in the interior of the German war machine.

On 4th June, 1941, in the city of Zagreb (Yugoslavia) a meeting of German representatives was called with the Councillor Von Troll presiding. The purpose was to set up the means of deporting the Yugoslav population from Slovenia. Tens of thousands of persons were deported in carrying out this plan.

(C) MURDER AND ILL-TREATMENT OF PRISONERS OF WAR

THE PRESIDENT: Will you read paragraph 2 at page 18?

CAPTAIN KUCHIN:

2. In. the Eastern Countries: At Orel prisoners of war were exterminated by starvation, shooting, exposure, and poisoning.

Soviet prisoners of war were murdered en masse on orders from the High Command and the Headquarters of the SIPO and SD. Tens of thousands of Soviet prisoners of war were tortured and murdered at the "Cross Lazaret" at Slavuta.

In addition, many thousands of the persons referred to in paragraph VIII (A)2, above, were Soviet prisoners of war.

Prisoners of war who escaped and were recaptured were handed over to SIPO and SD for shooting.

Frenchmen fighting with the Soviet Army who were captured were handed over to the Vichy Government for "proceedings."

In March, 1944, fifty R.A.F. officers who escaped from Stalag Luft III at Sagan, were murdered when captured.

In September, 1941, 11,000 Polish officers, who were prisoners of war were killed in the Katyn Forest near Smolensk.

In Yugoslavia the German Command and the occupying authorities in the person of the chief officials of the Police, the SS troops (Police Lieutenant General Rosener) and the Divisional Group Command (General Kubler and others) in the period 1941-43 ordered the shooting of prisoners of war.

THE PRESIDENT: Now paragraph 2 of (D).

LIEUTENANT-COLONEL J. A. OZOL (continuing the reading of the indictment):

2. In the Eastern Countries:

At Kragnevatz in Yugoslavia 2,300 hostages were shot in October, 1941.

At Kraljevo in Yugoslavia 5,000 hostages were shot.

THE PRESIDENT: Will you turn now to (E), paragraph 2, page 21?

LIEUTENANT-COLONEL OZOL:

2. Eastern Countries: During the occupation of the Eastern Countries the German Government and the German High Command carried out, as a systematic policy, a continuous course of plunder and destruction including:

On the territory of the Soviet Union the Nazi conspirators destroyed or severely damaged 1,710 cities and more than 70,000 villages and hamlets, more than 6,000,000 buildings and rendered homeless about 25,000,000 persons.

Among the cities which suffered most destruction are Stalingrad, Sevastopol, Kiev, Minsk, Odessa, Smolensk, Novgorod, Pskov, Orel, Kharkov, Voronezh, Rostov-on-Don, Stalino and Leningrad.

As is evident from an official memorandum of the German Command, the Nazi conspirators planned the complete annihilation of entire Soviet cities. In a completely secret order of the Chief of the Naval Staff (Staff 1A No. 1601/41, dated 29.IX.1941) addressed only to staff officers, it was said:

"The Fuehrer has decided to erase St. Petersburg from the face of the earth. The existence of this large city will have no further interest after Soviet Russia is destroyed. Finland has also said that the existence of this city on her new border is not desirable from her point of view. The original request of the Navy that docks, harbour, etc., necessary for the fleet be preserved - is known to the Supreme Commander of the Military Forces but the basic principles of carrying out operations against St. Petersburg do not make it possible to satisfy this request.

It is proposed to approach near to the city and to destroy it with the aid of an artillery barrage from weapons of different calibres and with long air attacks ...

The problem of the lives of the population and of their provisioning is a problem which cannot and must not be decided by us.

In this war ... we are not interested in preserving even a part of the population of this large city."

The Germans destroyed 427 museums, among them the wealthy museums of Leningrad, Smolensk, Stalingrad, Novgorod, Poltava and others.

In Pyatigorsk the art objects brought there from the Rostov museum were seized.

The losses suffered by the coal mining industry alone in the Stalin region amount to 2,000,000,000 roubles. There was colossal destruction of industrial establishments in Malerevka, Carlovka, Yeliakievo, Monstantinovka, Kariupol, from which most of the machinery and factories were removed.

Stealing of huge dimensions and the destruction of industrial, cultural and other property was typified in Kiev. More than 4,000,000 books, magazines and manuscripts (many of which were very valuable and even unique) and a large number of artistic productions and divers valuables were stolen and carried away.

Many valuable art productions were taken away from Riga.

The extent of the plunder of cultural valuables is evidenced by the fact that 100,000 valuable volumes and seventy cases of ancient periodicals and precious monographs were carried away by Rosenberg's staff alone.

Among further examples of these crimes are:

Wanton devastation of the city of Novgorod and of many historical and artistic monuments there. Wanton devastation and plunder of the city of Rovno and of its province. The destruction of the industrial, cultural and other property in Odessa. The destruction of cities and villages in Soviet Karelia. The destruction in Esthonia of cultural, industrial and other buildings.

The destruction of medical and prophylactic institutes, the destruction of agriculture and industry in Lithuania, the destruction of cities in Latvia.

The Germans approached monuments of culture, dear to the Soviet people, with special hatred. They broke up the estate of the poet Pushkin in Mikhailova-koye, desecrated his grave, and destroyed the neighbouring villages and the Svyatogor monastery.

They destroyed the estate and museum of Leo Tolstoi, "Yasnaya Polyana" and desecrated the grave of the great writer. They destroyed, in Klin, the museum of Tchaikovsky and, in Penaty, the museum of the painter Repin and many others.

The Nazi conspirators destroyed 1,670 Greek Orthodox Churches, 237 Roman Catholic Churches, 67 Chapels, 532 Synagogues, etc.

They also broke up, desecrated and senselessly destroyed the most valuable monuments of the Christian Church, such as the Kievo-Pecherskaya Lavra, Novy Jerusalem in the Istrin region, and the most ancient monasteries and churches.

Destruction in Esthonia of cultural, industrial and other premises; burning down of many thousands of residential buildings; removal of 10,000 works of art; destruction of medical and prophylactic institutions. Plunder and removal to Germany of immense quantities of agricultural stock including horses, cows, pigs, poultry, beehives and agricultural machines of all kinds.

Destruction of agriculture, enslavement of peasants and looting of stock and produce in Lithuania.

In the Latvian Republic destruction of the agriculture by the looting of all stock, machinery and produce.

Carrying away by Rosenberg's Headquarters of 100,000 valuable volumes and seventy cases of ancient periodicals and precious monographs; wanton destruction of libraries and other cultural buildings; destruction of the agriculture of the Latvian Republic by the looting of all stock, machinery and produce.

The result of this policy of plunder and destruction was to lay waste the land and cause utter desolation.

The overall value of the material loss which the U.S.S.R. has borne, is computed to be 679,000,000,000 roubles, in State prices of 1941.

Following the German occupation of Czechoslovakia on 15th March, 1939, the defendants seized and stole large stocks of raw materials, copper, tin, iron, cotton, and food; caused to be taken to Germany large amounts of railway rolling stock, and many engines, carriages, steam vessels and trolley buses; robbed libraries, laboratories, and art museums of books, pictures, objects of art, scientific apparatus and furniture; stole all gold reserves and foreign exchange of Czechoslovakia, including 23,000 kilograms of gold, of a nominal value of 5,265,000 pounds; fraudulently acquired control and thereafter looted the Czech banks and many Czech industrial enterprises; and otherwise stole, looted and misappropriated Czechoslovak public and private property. The total sum of defendants' economic spoliation of Czechoslovakia from 1938 to 1945 is estimated at 200,000,000,000 Czechoslovak crowns.

(G) WANTON DESTRUCTION OF CITIES, TOWNS AND VILLAGES, AND DEVASTATION NOT JUSTIFIED BY MILITARY NECESSITY

The defendants wantonly destroyed cities...

THE PRESIDENT: Will you go to paragraph 2 of (G) ? The French read the first paragraph. Do you want to go to paragraph 2 of (G)?

LIEUTENANT-COLONEL OZOL: I have begun

THE PRESIDENT: I thought we had read paragraph 1. We might take up at paragraph 2, beginning "In the Eastern Countries the defendants pursued...

LIEUTENANT-COLONEL OZOL:

2. Eastern Countries:

In the Eastern Countries the defendants pursued a policy of wanton destruction and devastation: some particulars of this (without prejudice to the production of evidence of other cases) are set out above under the heading "Plunder of Public and Private Property."

In Greece in 1941, the villages of Amelofito, Kliston, Kizonia, Messovunos, Selli, Ano-Kerzilion and Kato-Kerzilion were utterly destroyed.

In Yugoslavia on 15th August, 1941, the German military command officially announced that the village of Skela was burned to the ground and the inhabitants killed on the order of the command.

On the order of the Field Commander Hoersterberg a punitive expedition from the SS troops and the field police destroyed the villages of Machkovats, and Kriva Reka in Serbia and all the inhabitants were killed.

General Fritz Neidbold (369 Infantry Division) on 11th September, 1944, gave an order to destroy the villages of Zagnlezde and Udora, hanging all the men and driving away all the women and children.

In Czechoslovakia the Nazi conspirators also practised the senseless destruction of populated places. Lezaky and Lidice were burned to the ground and the inhabitants killed.

(H) CONSCRIPTION OF CIVILIAN LABOUR

Throughout the occupied territories the defendants conscripted and forced the inhabitants to labour and requisitioned their services -

THE PRESIDENT: I think paragraph (H) has been read, the first paragraph of it. There only remains for you to read paragraph 2 of (H).

LIEUTENANT-COLONEL OZOL:

2. Eastern Countries :

Of the large number of citizens of the Soviet Union and of Czechoslovakia referred to under Count Three Vlll (B) 2 above many were so conscripted for forced labour.

IX. Individual, Group and Organisation Responsibility for the Offence stated in Count Three

Reference is hereby made to Appendix A of this Indictment for a statement of the responsibility of the individual defendants for the offence set forth in this Count Three of the Indictment. Reference is hereby made to Appendix B of this Indictment for a statement of the responsibility of the groups and organisations named herein as criminal groups and organisations for the offence set forth in this Count Three of the Indictment.

COUNT FOUR - CRIMES AGAINST HUMANITY
(Charter, Article 6, especially 6 (c))

X. Statement of the Offence

All the defendants committed Crimes against Humanity during a period of years preceding 8th May, 1945, in Germany and in all those countries and territories occupied by the German armed forces since 1st September, 1939, and in Austria and Czechoslovakia and in Italy and on the High Seas.

All the defendants, acting in concert with others, formulated and executed a Common Plan or Conspiracy to commit Crimes against Humanity as defined in Article 6 (c) of the Charter. This plan involved, among other things, the murder and persecution of all who were, or who were suspected of being, hostile to the Nazi Party and all who were, or who were suspected of being, opposed to the common plan alleged in Count One.

The said Crimes against humanity were committed by the defendants, and by other persons for whose acts the defendants are responsible (under Article 6 of the Charter) as such other persons, when committing the said War Crimes, performed their acts in execution of a Common Plan or Conspiracy to commit the said War Crimes, in the formulation and execution of which plan and conspiracy all the defendants participated as leaders, organisers, instigators and accomplices.

These methods and crimes constituted violations of international conventions, of internal penal laws, of the general principles of criminal law as derived from the criminal law of all civilised nations and were involved in and part of a systematic course of conduct. The said acts were contrary to Article 6 of the Charter.

The prosecution will rely upon the facts pleaded under Count Three as also constituting Crimes against Humanity.

(A) MURDER, EXTERMINATION, ENSLAVEMENT, DEPORTATION AND OTHER INHUMANE ACTS COMMITTED AGAINST CIVILIAN POPULATIONS BEFORE AND DURING THE WAR

For the purposes set out above, the defendants adopted a policy of persecution, repression, and extermination of all civilians in Germany who were, or who were believed to be, or who were believed likely to become, hostile to the Nazi Government and the Common Plan or Conspiracy described in Count One. They imprisoned such persons without judicial process, holding them in "protective custody" and concentration camps, and subjected them to persecution, degradation, despoilment, enslavement, torture and murder.

Special courts were established to carry out the will of the conspirators; favoured branches or agencies of the State and Party were permitted to operate outside the range even of Nazified law and to crush all tendencies and elements which were considered "undesirable." The various concentration camps included Buchenwald, which was established in 1933 and Dachau, which was established in 1934. At these and other camps the civilians were put to slave labour and murdered and ill-treated by divers means, including those set out in Count Three above, and these acts and policies were continued and extended to the occupied countries after the 1st September, 1939, and until 8th May, 1945.

(B) PERSECUTION ON POLITICAL, RACIAL AND RELIGIOUS GROUNDS IN EXECUTION OF AND IN CONNECTION WITH THE COMMON PLAN MENTIONED IN COUNT ONE

As above stated, in execution of and in connection with the common plan mentioned in Count One, opponents of the German Government were exterminated and persecuted. These persecutions were directed against Jews. They were also directed against persons whose political belief or spiritual aspirations were deemed to be in conflict with the aims of the Nazis.

Jews were systematically persecuted since 1933; they were deprived of liberty, thrown into concentration camps where they were murdered and ill-treated. Their property was confiscated. Hundreds of thousands of Jews were so treated before the 1st September, 1939.

Since the 1st September, 1939, the persecution of the Jews was redoubled; millions of Jews from Germany and from the occupied Western Countries were sent to the Eastern Countries for extermination.

Particulars by way of example and without prejudice to the production of evidence of other cases are as follows:

The Nazis murdered amongst others Chancellor Dollfuss, the Social Democrat Breitscheid and the Communist Thaelmann. They imprisoned in concentration camps numerous political and religious personages, for example, Chancellor Schuschnigg and Pastor Nieimoller.

In November, 1938, by orders of the Chief of the Gestapo, anti-Jewish demonstrations all over Germany took place. Jewish property was destroyed, 30,000 Jews were arrested and sent to concentration camps and their property confiscated.

Under paragraph VIII (A), above, millions of the persons there mentioned as having been murdered and ill-treated were Jews.

Among other mass murders of Jews were the following:

At Kislovdosk all Jews were made to give up their property; 2,000 were shot in an anti-tank ditch at Mineralniye Vodi; 4,300 other Jews were shot in the same ditch.

60,000 Jews were shot on an island on the Dvina near Riga.

20,000 Jews were shot at Lutsk.

32,000 Jews were shot at Sarny.

60,000 Jews were shot at Kiev and Dniepropetrovsk.

Thousands of Jews were gassed weekly by means of gas-wagons which broke down from overwork.

As the Germans retreated before the Soviet Army they exterminated Jews rather than allow them to be liberated. Many concentration camps and ghettos were set up in which Jews were incarcerated and tortured, starved, subjected to merciless atrocities and finally exterminated.

About 70 000 Jews were exterminated in Yugoslavia.

XI. Individual, Group and Organisation Responsibility for the Offence stated in Count Four

Reference is hereby made to Appendix A of this Indictment for a statement of the responsibility of the individual defendants for the offence set forth in this Count Four of the Indictment. Reference is hereby made to Appendix B of this Indictment for a statement of the responsibility of the groups and organisations named herein as criminal groups and organisations for the offence set forth in the Count Four of the Indictment.

Wherefore, this Indictment is lodged with the Tribunal in English, French and Russian, each text having equal authenticity, and the charges herein made against the above-named defendants are hereby presented to the Tribunal.

HARTLEY SHAWCROSS Acting on Behalf of the United Kingdom of Great Britain and Northern Ireland.

ROBERT H. JACKSON Acting on Behalf of the United States of America.

FRANCOIS DE MENTHON. Acting on Behalf of the French Republic.

R. RUDENKO. Acting on Behalf of the Union of Soviet Socialist Republics.

Berlin, 6th October, 1945

THE PRESIDENT: Has anybody been designated to read the appendices?

MR. ALDERMAN: May it please the Tribunal, I shall read Appendix A and Appendix B, and the British delegation will read Appendix C. One word of explanation as to Appendix A. The Court will have observed that the defendants are seated in the dock in the same order in which they are named in the Indictment. By a mechanical slip-up they are not named in Appendix A in exactly the same order. I think it would be too much difficulty for the interpreters or for me to arrange them in the same order, and if the Court will permit I will read Appendix A as it is printed-

APPENDIX A

STATEMENT OF INDIVIDUAL RESPONSIBILITY FOR CRIMES SET OUT IN COUNTS ONE, TWO, THREE AND FOUR

The statements hereinafter set forth following the name of each individual defendant constitute matters upon which the prosecution will rely inter alia as establishing the individual responsibility of the defendant

Goering:

The defendant Goering between 1932-1945 was: a member of the Nazi Party, Supreme Leader of the S.A., General in the S.S., a member and President of the Reichstag, Minister of the Interior of Prussia, Chief of the Prussian Police and Prussian Secret State Police, Chief of the Prussian State Council, Trustee of the Four-Year Plan, Reich Minister for Air, Commander in Chief of the Air Force, President of the Council of Ministers for the Defence of the Reich, member of the Secret

Cabinet Council, head of the Hermann Goering Industrial Combine, and Successor Designate to Hitler. The defendant Goering used the foregoing positions, his personal influence, and his intimate connection with the Fuehrer in such a manner that: he promoted the accession to power of the Nazi conspirators and the consolidation of their control over Germany set forth in Count One of the Indictment; he promoted the military and economic preparation for war set forth in Count One of the Indictment; he participated in the planning and preparation of the Nazi conspirators for Wars of Aggression and Wars in Violation of International Treaties, Agreements and Assurances set forth in Counts One and Two of the Indictment; and he authorised, directed and participated in the War Crimes set forth in Count Three of the Indictment, and the Crimes against Humanity set forth in Count Four of the Indictment, including a wide variety of crimes against persons and property.

Ribbentrop:

The defendant Ribbentrop between 1932-1945 was: a member of the Nazi Party, a member of the Nazi Reichstag, Adviser to the Fuehrer on matters of foreign policy, representative of the Nazi Party for matters of foreign policy, special German delegate for disarmament questions, Ambassador Extraordinary, Ambassador in London, organiser and director of Dienststelle Ribbentrop, Reich Minister for Foreign Affairs, member of the Secret Cabinet Council, member of the Fuehrer's political staff at general headquarters, and General in the S.S. The defendant Ribbentrop used the foregoing positions, his personal influence, and his intimate connection with the Fuehrer in such a manner that: he promoted the accession to power of the Nazi conspirators as set forth in Count One of the Indictment he promoted the preparations for war set forth in Count One of the Indictment he participated in the political planning and preparation of the Nazi conspirators for Wars of Aggression and Wars in Violation of International Treaties, Agreements and Assurances as set forth in Counts One and Two of the Indictment in accordance with the Fuehrer Principle he executed and assumed responsibility for the execution of the foreign policy plans of the Nazi conspirators set forth in Count One of the Indictment; and he authorised, directed and participated in the War Crimes set forth in Count Three of the indictment and the Crimes against Humanity set forth in Count Four of the Indictment, including more particularly the crimes against persons and property in occupied territories.

Hess:

The defendant Hess between 1921 and 1941 was: a member of the Nazi Party, Deputy to the Fuehrer, Reich Minister without Portfolio, member of the Reichstag, member of the Council of Ministers for the Defence of the Reich, member of the Secret Cabinet Council, Successor Designate to the Fuehrer after the defendant Goering, a General in the S.S. and a General in the S.A. The defendant Hess used the foregoing positions, his personal influence and his intimate connection with the Fuehrer in such a manner that: he promoted the accession to power of the Nazi conspirators and the consolidation of their control over Germany set forth in Count One of the Indictment; he promoted the military, economic and psychological preparations for war set forth in Count One of the Indictment; he participated in the political planning and preparation for Wars of Aggression and Wars in Violation of International Treaties, Agreements and Assurances set forth in Counts One and Two of the Indictment; he participated in the preparation and planning of foreign policy plans of the Nazi conspirators set forth in Count One of the Indictment; he authorised, directed. and participated in the War Crimes set forth in Count Three of the Indictment and the Crimes against Humanity set forth in Count Four of the Indictment, including a wide variety of crimes against persons and property.

Kaltenbrunner:

The defendant Kaltenbrunner between 1932-1945 was: a member of the Nazi Party, a General in the S.S., a member of the Reichstag, a General of the Police, State Secretary for Security in Austria in charge of the Austrian Police, Police Leader of Vienna, Lower and Upper Austria, Head of the Reich Main Security Office and Chief of the Security Police and Security Service. The defendant Kaltenbrunner used the foregoing positions and his personal influence in such a manner that: he promoted the consolidation of control over Austria seized by the Nazi conspirators as set forth in Count One of the Indictment; and he authorised, directed and participated in the War Crimes set forth in Count Three of the Indictment and the Crimes against Humanity set forth in Court Four of the Indictment including particularly the Crimes against Humanity involved in the system of concentration camps.

Rosenberg:

The defendant Rosenberg between 1920 and 1945 was: a member of the Nazi Party, Nazi member of the Reichstag, Reichsteiter in the Nazi Party for Ideology and Foreign Policy, the Editor of the Nazi newspaper Volkischer Beobachter, and the NS Monatshefte, head of the Foreign Political Office of the Nazi Party, Special Delegate for the entire Spiritual and Ideological Training of the Nazi Party, Reich Minister for the Eastern Occupied Territories, organiser of the "Einsatzstab Rosenberg," a General in the S.S. and a General in the S.A. The defendant Rosenberg used the foregoing positions, his personal influence and his intimate connection with the Fuehrer in such a manner that: he developed, disseminated and exploited the doctrinal techniques of the Nazi conspirators set forth in Count One of the Indictment; lie promoted the accession to power of the Nazi conspirators and the consolidation of their control over Germany set forth in Count One of the Indictment; he promoted the psychological preparations for war set forth in Count One of the Indictment; he participated in the political planning and preparation for Wars of Aggression and Wars in Violation of International Treaties, Agreements and Assurances set forth in Counts One and Two of the Indictment; and he authorised, directed and participated in the War Crimes set forth in Count Three of the Indictment and the Crimes against Humanity set forth in Count Four of the Indictment, including a wide variety of crimes against persons and property.

Frank:

The defendant Frank between 1932-1945 was: a member of the Nazi Party, a

General in the S.S., a member of the Reichstag, Reich Minister without Portfolio, Reich Commissar for the Co-ordination of Justice, President of the International Chamber of Law and Academy of German Law, Chief of the Civil Administration of Lodz, Supreme Administrative Chief of the military district of West Prussia, Poznan, Odz and Krakow, and Governor General of the Occupied Polish territories. The defendant Frank used the foregoing positions, his personal influence, and his intimate connection with the Fuehrer in such a manner that: he promoted the accession to power of the Nazi conspirators and the consolidation of their control over Germany set forth in Count One of the Indictment; he authorised, directed and participated in the War Crimes set forth in Count Three of the Indictment and the Crimes against Humanity set forth in Count Four of the Indictment, including particularly the War Crimes and Crimes against Humanity involved in the administration of occupied territories.

Bormann:

The defendant Bormann between 1925-1945 was: a member of the Nazi Party, member of the Reichstag, a member of the Staff of the Supreme Command of the S.A., founder and head of "Hilfskasse der NSDAP", Reichsleiter, Chief of Staff Office of the Fuehrer's Deputy, head of the Party Chancery, Secretary of the Fuehrer, member of the Council of Ministers for the Defence of the Reich, organiser and head of the Volkssturm, a General in the S.S. and a General in the S.A. The defendant Bormann used the foregoing positions, his personal influence and his intimate connection with the Fuehrer in such a manner that: he promoted the accession to power of the Nazi conspirators and the consolidation of their control over Germany set forth in Count One of the indictment he promoted the preparations for war set forth in Count One of the Indictment and he authorised, directed and participated in the War Crimes set forth in Count Three of the Indictment and the Crimes against Humanity set forth in Count Four of the Indictment, including a wide variety of crimes against persons and property.

Frick:

The defendant Frick between 1932-1945 was: a member of the Nazi Party, Reichsleiter, General in the S.S., member of the Reichstag, Reich Minister of the Interior, Prussian Minister of the Interior, Reich Director of Elections, General Plenipotentiary for the Administration of the Reich, head of the Central Office for the Reunification of Austria and the Reich, Director of the Central Office for the Incorporation of Sudetenland, Memel, Danzig, the Eastern incorporated territories, Eupen, Malmedy, and Moresnet, Director of the Central Office for the Protectorate of Bohemia, Moravia, the Government General, Lower Styria, Upper Carinthia, Norway, Alsace, Lorraine and all other occupied territories and Reich Protector for Bohemia and Moravia. The defendant Frick used the foregoing positions, his personal influence, and his intimate connection with the Fuehrer in such a manner that: he promoted the accession to power of the Nazi conspirators and the consolidation of their control over Germany set forth in Count One of the Indictment; he participated in the planning and preparation of the Nazi conspirators for Wars of

Aggression and Wars in Violation of International Treaties, Agreements and Assurances set forth in Counts One and Two of the Indictment; and he authorised, directed and participated in the War Crimes set forth in Count Three of the Indictment and the Crimes against Humanity set forth in Count Four of the Indictment, including more particularly the crimes against persons and property in occupied territories.

Ley:

The defendant Ley between 1932-1945 was: a member of the Nazi Party, Reichsleiter, Nazi Party Organisation Manager, member of the Reichstag, leader of the German Labour Front, a General in the S.A., and Joint Organiser of the Central Inspection for the Care of Foreign Workers. The defendant Ley used the foregoing positions, his personal influence and his intimate connection with the Fuehrer in such a manner that: he promoted the accession to power of the Nazi conspirators and the consolidation of their control over Germany as set forth in Count One of the Indictment; he promoted the preparation for war set forth in Count One of the Indictment; he authorised, directed and participated in the War Crimes set forth in Count Three of the Indictment, and in the Crimes against Humanity set forth in Count Four of the Indictment, including particularly the War Crimes and Crimes against Humanity relating to the abuse of human beings for labour in the conduct of the aggressive wars.

Sauckel:

The defendant Sauckel between 1921-1945 was: a member of the Nazi Party, Gauleiter and Reichsstatthalter of Thuringia, a member of the Reichstag, General Plenipotentiary for the Employment of Labour under the Four Year Plan, Joint Organiser with the defendant Ley of the Central Inspection for the Care of Foreign Workers, a General in the S.S. and a General in the S.A. The defendant Sauckel used the foregoing positions and his personal influence in such manner that: he promoted the accession to power of the Nazi conspirators set forth in Count One of the Indictment; he participated in the economic preparations for Wars of Aggression and Wars in Violation of Treaties, Agreements and Assurances set forth in Counts One and Two of the Indictment; he authorised, directed and participated in the War Crimes set forth in Count Three of the Indictment and the Crimes against Humanity set forth in Count Four of the Indictment, including particularly the War Crimes and Crimes against Humanity involved in forcing the inhabitants of occupied countries to work as slave labourers in occupied countries and in Germany.

Speer:

The defendant Speer between 1932-1945 was a member of the Nazi Party, Reichsleiter, member of the Reichstag, Reich Minister for Armament and Munitions, Chief of the Organisation Todt, General Plenipotentiary for Armaments in the Office of the Four Year Plan, and Chairman of the Armaments Council. The defendant Speer used the foregoing positions and his personal influence in such a manner that: he participated in the military and economic planning and preparation of the Nazi conspirators for Wars of Aggression and Wars in Violation of International Treaties,

Agreements and Assurances set forth in Counts One and Two of the Indictment; and he authorised, directed and participated in the War Crimes set forth in Count Three of the Indictment and the Crimes against Humanity set forth in Count Four of the Indictment, including more particularly the abuse and exploitation of human beings for forced labour in the conduct of aggressive war.

Funk:

The defendant Funk between 1932-1945 was : a member of the Nazi Party, Economic Adviser of Hitler, National Socialist Deputy to the Reichstag, Press Chief of the Reich Government, State Secretary of the Reich Ministry of Public Enlightenment and Propaganda, Reich Minister of Economics, Prussian Minister of Economics, President of the German Reichsbank, Plenipotentiary for Economy, and member of the Ministerial Council for the Defence of the Reich. The defendant Funk used the foregoing positions, his personal influence, and his close connection with the Fuehrer in such a manner that: he promoted the accession to power of the Nazi conspirators and the consolidation of their control over Germany set forth in Count One of the Indictment; he promoted the preparations for war set forth in Count One of the Indictment; he participated in the military and economic planning and preparation of the Nazi conspirators for Wars of Aggression and Wars in Violation of International Treaties, Agreements and Assurances set forth in Counts One and Two of the Indictment; and he authorised, directed and participated in the War Crimes set forth in Count Three of the Indictment and the Crimes against Humanity set forth in Count Four of the Indictment, including more particularly crimes against persons and property in connection with the economic exploitation of occupied territories.

Schacht:

The defendant Schacht between 1932-1945 was: a member of the Nazi Party, a member of the Reichstag, Reich Minister of Economics, Reich Minister without Portfolio and President of the German Reichsbank. The defendant Schacht used the foregoing positions, his personal influence, and his connection with the Fuehrer in such a manner that: he promoted the accession to power of the Nazi Conspirators and the Consolidation of their control over Germany set forth in Count One of the Indictment; he promoted the preparations for war ,set forth in Count One of the Indictment; and he participated in the military and economic plans and preparation of the Nazi conspirators for Wars of Aggression, and Wars in Violation of International Treaties, Agreements and Assurances set forth in Counts One and Two of the Indictment.

Papen:

The defendant Papen between 1932-1945 was: a member of the Nazi Party, a member of the Reichstag, Reich Chancellor, Vice Chancellor under Hitler, special Plenipotentiary for the Saar, negotiator of the Concordat with the Vatican, Ambassador in Vienna and Ambassador in Turkey. The defendant Papen used the foregoing positions, his personal influence, and his close connection with the Fuehrer in such a manner that: he promoted the accession to power of the Nazi conspirators and participated in the consolidation of their control over Germany set forth in Count One of the Indictment; he promoted the preparations for war set forth in Count One of the Indictment; and he participated in the political planning and preparation of the Nazi Conspirators for Wars of Aggression and Wars in Violation of International Treaties, Agreements and Assurances set forth in Counts One and Two of the indictment.

Krupp:

The defendant Krupp between 1932-1945 was: head of Friedrich Krupp A.G., a member of the General Economic Council, President of the Reich Union of German Industry, and head of the Group for mining and Production of Iron and metals under the Reich Ministry of Economics. The defendant Krupp used the foregoing positions, his personal influence, and his connection with the Fuehrer in such a manner that: he promoted the accession to power of the Nazi conspirators and the consolidation of their control over Germany set forth in Count One of the Indictment, he promoted the preparation for war set forth in Count One of the Indictment, he participated in the military and economic planning and preparation of the Nazi conspirators for Wars of Aggression and Wars in Violation of International Treaties, Agreements and Assurances set forth in Counts One and Two of the Indictment; and he authorised, directed and participated in the War Crimes set forth in Count Three of the Indictment and the Crimes against Humanity set forth in Count Four of the Indictment, including more particularly the exploitation and abuse of human beings for labour in the conduct of aggressive wars.

Neurath:

The defendant Neurath between 1932-1945 was: a member of the Nazi Party, a General in the S.S., a member of the Reichstag, Reich Minister, Reich Minister of Foreign Affairs, President of the Secret Cabinet Council, and Reich Protector for Bohemia and Moravia. The defendant Neurath used the foregoing positions, his personal influence, and his close connection with the Fuehrer in such a manner that: he promoted the accession to power of the Nazi conspirators set forth in Count One of the Indictment; he promoted the preparations for war set forth in Count One of the Indictment; he participated in the political planning and preparation of the Nazi conspirators for Wars of Aggression and Wars in Violation of International Treaties, Agreements and Assurances set forth in Counts One and Two of the Indictment; in accordance with the Fuehrer Principle he executed, and assumed responsibility for the execution of the foreign policy plans of the Nazi conspirators set forth in Count One of the Indictment; and he authorised, directed and participated in the War Crimes set forth in Count Three of the Indictment and the Crimes against Humanity set forth in Count Four of the Indictment, including particularly the crimes against persons and property in the occupied territories.

Schirach:

The defendant Schirach between 1924-1945 was: a member of the Nazi Party, a member of the Reichstag, Reich Youth Leader on the Staff of the S.A. Supreme Command, Reichsleiter in the Nazi Party for Youth Education, Leader of Youth of the German Reich, head of the Hitler Jugend, Reich Defence Commissioner and Reichstatthalter and Gauleiter of Vienna. The defendant Schirach used the foregoing positions, his personal influence and his intimate connection with the Fuehrer in such a manner that: he promoted the accession to power of the Nazi conspirators and the consolidation of their control over Germany set forth in Count One of the Indictment; he promoted the psychological and educational preparations for war and the militarisation of Nazi-dominated organisations set forth in Count One of the Indictment; and he authorised, directed and participated in the Crimes against Humanity set forth in Count Four of the Indictment, including, particularly, anti-Jewish measures.

Seyss-Inquart:

The defendant Seyss-Inquart between 1932 1945 was: a member of the Nazi Party, a General in the S.S., State Councillor of Austria, Minister of the Interior and Security of Austria, Chancellor of Austria, a member of the Reichstag, a member of the Reich Cabinet, Reich Minister without Portfolio, Chief of the Civil Administration in South Poland, Deputy Governor-General of the Polish Occupied Territory, and Reich Commissar for the Occupied Netherlands. The defendant Seyss-Inquart used the foregoing positions and his personal influence in such a manner that: he promoted the seizure and the consolidation of control over Austria by the Nazi conspirators set forth in Count One of the Indictment; he participated in the political planning, and preparation of the Nazi conspirators for Wars of Aggression and Wars in Violation of International Treaties, Agreements and Assurances set forth in Counts One and Two of the Indictment; and he authorised, directed and participated in the War Crimes set forth in Count Three of the Indictment and the Crimes against Humanity set forth in Count Four of the Indictment, including a wide variety of crimes against persons and property.

Streicher:

The defendant Streicher between 1932-1945 was: a member of the Nazi Party, a member of the Reichstag, a General in the S.A., Gauleiter of Franconia, Editor-in-Chief of the anti- Semitic newspaper " Der Sturmer " The defendant Streicher used the foregoing positions, his personal influence, and his close connection with the Fuehrer in such a manner that: he promoted the accession to power of the Nazi conspirators and the consolidation of their control over Germany set forth in Count One of the Indictment; he authorised, directed and participated in the Crimes against Humanity set forth in Count Four of the Indictment, including particularly the incitement of the persecution of the Jews set forth in Count One and Count Four of the Indictment.

Keitel:

The defendant Keitel between 1938-I945 was: Chief of the High Command of the German Armed Forces, member of the Secret Cabinet Council, member of the

Council of Ministers for the Defence of the Reich, and Field Marshal. The defendant Keitel used the foregoing positions, his personal influence and his intimate connection with the Fuehrer in such a manner that: he promoted the military preparations for war set forth in Count One of the Indictment; he participated in the political planning and preparation of the Nazi conspirators for Wars of Aggression and Wars in Violation of International Treaties, Agreements and Assurances set forth in Counts One and Two of the Indictment; he executed and assumed responsibility for the execution of the plans of the Nazi conspirators for Wars of Aggression and Wars in Violation of International Treaties, Agreements and Assurances set forth in Counts One and Two of the Indictment; he authorised, directed and participated in the War Crimes set forth in Count Three of the indictment, and the Crimes against Humanity set forth in Count Four of the Indictment, including particularly the War Crimes and Crimes against Humanity involved in the ill- treatment of prisoners of war and of the civilian population of occupied territories.

Jodl:

The defendant Jodl between 1932-1945 was: Lieut.-Colonel, Army Operations Department of the Wehrmacht, Colonel, Chief of OKW Operations Department, Major-General and Chief of Staff OKW and Colonel-General. The defendant Jodl used the foregoing positions, his personal influence, and his close connection with the Fuehrer in such a manner that: he promoted the accession to power of the Nazi conspirators and the consolidation of their control over Germany set forth in Count One of the Indictment; he promoted the preparations for war set forth in Count One of the Indictment; he participated in the military planning and preparation of the Nazi conspirators for Wars of Aggression and Wars in Violation of International Treaties, Agreements and Assurances set forth in Counts One and Two of the Indictment; and he authorised, directed and participated in the War Crimes set forth in Count Three of the Indictment and the Crimes against Humanity set forth in Count Four of the Indictment, including a wide variety of crimes against persons and property.

Raeder:

The defendant Raeder between 1928-1945 was: Commander-in- Chief of the German Navy, Generaladmiral. Grossadmiral, Admiralspektor of the German navy, and a member of the Secret Cabinet Council. The defendant Raeder used the foregoing positions and his personal influence in such a manner that: he promoted the preparations for war set forth in Count One of the Indictment; he participated in the political planning and preparation of the Nazi conspirators for Wars of Aggression and Wars in Violation of International Treaties, Agreements and Assurances set forth in Counts One and Two of the Indictment; he executed, and assumed responsibility for the execution of the plans of the Nazi conspirators for Wars of Aggression and Wars in Violation of International Treaties, Agreements and Assurances set forth in Counts One and Two of the Indictment; and he authorised, directed and participated in the War Crimes set forth in Count Three of the Indictment, including particularly War Crimes arising out of sea warfare.

Donitz:

The defendant Donitz between 1932-1945 was: Commanding Officer of the Weddigen U-boat Flotilla, Commander-in-Chief of the U-boar arm, Vice-Admiral, Admiral, Grossadmiral and Commander-in-Chief of the German Navy, Adviser to Hitler, and Successor to Hitler as head of the German Government. The defendant Donitz used the foregoing positions, his personal influence, and his intimate connection with the Fuehrer in such a manner that he promoted the preparations for war set forth in Count One of the Indictment; he participated in the military planning and preparation of the Nazi conspirators for Wars of Aggression and Wars in Violation of International Treaties, Agreements and Assurances set forth in Counts One and Two of the Indictment; and he authorised, directed and participated in the War Crimes set forth in Count Three of the Indictment, including particularly the crimes against persons and property on the High Seas.

Fritzsche:

The defendant Fritzsche between 1933-1945 was: a member of the Nazi Party, Editor-in-Chief of the official German news agency, "Deutsche Nachrichten Buro", Head of the Wireless News Service and of the Home Press Division of the Reich Ministry of Propaganda, Ministerialdirektor of the Reich Ministry of Propaganda, Head of the Radio Division of the Propaganda Department of the Nazi Party, and Plenipotentiary for the Political Organisation of the Greater German Radio. The defendant Fritzsche used the foregoing positions and his personal influence to disseminate and exploit the principal doctrines of the Nazi conspirators set forth in Count One of the Indictment, and to advocate, encourage and incite the commission of the War Crimes set forth in Count Three of the Indictment and the Crimes against Humanity set forth in Count Four of the Indictment including, particularly, anti-Jewish measures and the ruthless exploitation of occupied territories.

APPENDIX B
Statement Of Criminality Of Groups And Organisations

The statements hereinafter set forth, following the name of each Group or Organisation named in the Indictment as one which should be declared criminal, constitute matters upon which the prosecution will rely inter alia as establishing the criminality of the Group or Organisation :

Die Reichsregierung (Reich Cabinet)

"Die Reichsregierung (Reich Cabinet)" referred to in the Indictment consists of persons who were:

(i) Members of the ordinary cabinet after 30th January, 1933, the date on which Hitler became Chancellor of the German Republic. The term "ordinary cabinet " as used herein means the Reich Ministers, i.e., heads of departments of the central government; Reich-Ministers without portfolio; State ministers acting as Reich Ministers; and other officials entitled to take part in meetings of this cabinet.

(ii) Members of der Ministerrat fur die Reichsverteldigung (Council of Ministers for the Defence of the Reich).

(iii) Members of der Gebeimer Kabinettsrat (Secret Cabinet Council).

Under the Fuehrer, these persons functioning in the foregoing capacities and in association as a group, possessed and exercised legislative, executive, administrative and political powers and functions of a very high order in the system of German government. Accordingly, they are charged with responsibility for the policies adopted and put into effect by the Government including those which comprehended and involved the commission of the crimes referred to in Counts One, Two, Three and Four of the Indictment.

Das Korps der Politischen Leiter der Nationalsozialistischen Deutschen Arbeiterpartei (Leadership Corps of the Nazi Party)

"Das Korps der Politischeii Leiter der Nationalsozialistischen Deutschen Arbeiterpartei (Leadership Corps of the Nazi Party)" referred to in the Indictment consists of persons who were at any time, according to common Nazi terminology, Politische Leiter " (Political Leaders) of any grade or rank.

The Politischen Leiter comprised the leaders of the various functional offices of the Party (for example, the Reichsleitung or Party Reich Directorate, and the Gauleitung, or Party Gau Directorate), as well as the territorial leaders of the Party (for example, the Gauleiter).

The Politischen Leiter were a distinctive and elite group within the Nazi Party proper, and as such were vested with special prerogatives. They were organised according to the leadership principle and were charged with planning, developing and imposing upon their followers the policies of the Nazi Party. Thus the territorial leaders among them were called Hoheitstrager, or bearers of sovereignty, and were entitled to call upon and utilise the various Party formations when necessary for the execution of Party policies.

Reference is hereby made to the allegations in Count One of the Indictment showing that the Nazi Party was the central core of the Common Plan or Conspiracy therein set forth. The Politischen Leiter, as a major power within the Nazi party proper, and functioning in the capacities above described and in association as a group, joined in the Common Plan or Conspiracy, and accordingly share responsibility for the crimes set forth in Counts One, Two, Three and Four of the Indictment.

The prosecution expressly reserves the right to request, at any time before sentence is pronounced, that Politische Leiter of subordinate grades or ranks or of other types or classes, to be specified by the prosecution, be excepted from further proceedings in this Case No. 1, but without prejudice to other proceedings or actions against them.

Die Schutzstaffeln der Nationalsozialistischen Deutschen

Arbeiterpartei (commonly known as the SS) including Der Sicherheitsdienst (commonly known as the SD)

Die Schutzstaffeln der Nationalsozialistischen Deutschen Arbeiterpartei (commonly known as the SS) including Der Sicherheitsdienst (commonly known as the SD) and all offices, departments, services, agencies, branches, formations, organisations and groups of which it was at any time comprised or which were at any time integrated in it, including but not limited to, the Allgemeine SS, the Waffen SS, the SS Totenkopf Verbande, SS Polizei Regimente and Der Sicherheitsdienst des Reichsfuehrers-SS (commonly known as the SD).

The SS, originally established by Hitler in 1925 as an elite section of the SA to furnish a protective guard for the Fuehrer and Nazi Party leaders, became an independent formation of the Nazi Party in 1934 under the leadership of the Reichsfuehrer-SS, Heinrich Himmler. It was composed of voluntary members, selected in accordance with Nazi biological, racial and political theories, completely indoctrinated in Nazi ideology and pledged to uncompromising obedience to the Fuehrer. After the accession of the Nazi conspirators to power, it developed many departments, agencies, formations and branches and extended its influence and control over numerous fields of governmental and Party activity. Through Heinrich Himmler, as Reichsfuehrer-SS and Chief of the German Police, agencies and units of the SS and of the Reich were joined in operation to form a unified repressive police force. Der Sicherheitsdienst des Reichsfuehrers-SS '(commonly known as the SD), a department of the SS, was developed into a vast espionage and counter-intelligence system which operated in conjunction with the Gestapo and criminal police in detecting, suppressing and eliminating tendencies, groups and individuals deemed hostile or potentially hostile to the Nazi Party, its leaders, principles and objectives, and eventually was combined with the Gestapo and criminal police in a single security police department, the Reich Main Security Office.

Other branches of the SS developed into an armed force and served in the wars of aggression referred to in Counts One and Two of the Indictment. Through other departments and branches the SS controlled the administration of concentration camps and the execution of Nazi racial, biological and resettlement policies. Through its numerous functions and activities it served as the instrument for ensuring the domination of Nazi ideology and protecting and extending the Nazi regime over Germany and occupied territories. It thus participated in and is responsible for the crimes referred to in Counts One, Two, Three and Four of the Indictment.

Die Geheime Staatspolizei (Secret State Police, commonly known as the Gestapo)

"Die Geheime Staatspolizei (Secret State Police, commonly known as the Gestapo) " referred to in the Indictment consists of the headquarters, departments, offices, branches and all the forces and personnel of the Geheime Staatspolizei organised or existing it any time after 30th January, 1933, including the Geheime Staatspolizei of Prussia and equivalent secret or political police forces of the Reich and the components thereof.

The Gestapo was created by the Nazi conspirators immediately after their accession to power, first in Prussia by the defendant Goering and shortly thereafter in all other States in the Reich. These separate secret and political police forces were developed into a centralised, uniform organisation operating through a central headquarters and through a network of regional offices in Germany and in occupied territories. Its officials and operatives were selected on the basis of unconditional acceptance of Nazi ideology, were largely drawn from members of the SS, and were trained in SS and SD schools. It acted to suppress and eliminate tendencies, groups and individuals deemed hostile or potentially hostile to the Nazi Party, its leaders, principles and objectives, and to repress resistance and potential resistance to German control in occupied territories. In performing these functions it operated free from legal control, taking any measures it deemed necessary for the accomplishment of its missions.

Through its purposes activities and the means it used, it participated in and is responsible for the commission of the crimes set forth in Counts One, Two, Three and Four of the Indictment.

Die Sturmabteilungen der Nationalsozialistischen Deutschen Arbeiterpartei (commonly known as the SA)

"Die Sturmabteilungen der Nationalsozialistischen Deutschen Arbeiterpartei (commonly known as the SA)" referred to in the Indictment was a formation of the Nazi Party under the immediate jurisdiction of the Fuehrer, organised on military lines, whose membership was composed of volunteers serving as political soldiers of the Party. It was one of the earliest formations of the Nazi Party and the original guardian of the National Socialist movement. Founded in 1921 on a voluntary militant formation, it was developed by the Nazi conspirators before their accession to power into a vast private army and utilised for the purpose of creating disorder, and terrorising and eliminating political opponents. It continued to serve as an instrument for the physical, ideological and military training of Party members and as a reserve for the German Armed Forces. After the launching of the wars of aggression, referred to in Counts One and Two of the Indictment, the SA not only operated as an organisation for military training but provided auxiliary police and security forces in occupied territories, guarded prisoner-of-war camps and concentration camps and supervised and controlled persons forced to labour in Germany and occupied territories.

Through its purposes and activities and the means it used, it participated in and is responsible for the commission of the crimes set forth in Counts One, Two, Three and Four of the Indictment.

General Staff and High Command of the German Armed Forces

The "General Staff and High Command of the German Armed Forces' referred to in the Indictment consist of those individuals who, between February 1938, and May, 1945, were the highest commanders of the Wehrmacht, the Army, the Navy, and the Air Forces. The individuals comprising this group are the persons who held the following appointments :

Oberbefehlshaber der Kriegsniarine (Commander-in-Chief of the Navy).

Chef (and, formerly, Chef des Stabes) der Seckriegsleitung (Chief of Naval War Staff).

Oberbefehlsheber des Heeres (Commander-in-Chief of the Army).

Chef des Generalstabes des Heeres (Chief of the General Staff of the Army).

Oberbefehlshaber der Luftwaffe (Commander-in-Chief of the Air Force).

Chef des Generalstabes der Luftwaffe (Chief of the General Staff of the Air Force).

Chef des Oberkommandos der Wehrmacht (Chief of the High Command of the Armed Forces).

Chef des Fuhrungstabes des Oberkommandos der Wehrmacht (Chief of the Operations Staff of the High Command of the Armed Forces).

Stellvertretender Chef des Fuhrungstabes des Oberkommandos der Wehrmacht (Deputy Chief of the Operations Staff of the High Command of the Armed Forces).

Commanders-in-Chief in the field, with the status of Oberbefehlshaber, of the Wehrmacht, Navy, Army, Air Force.

SIR DAVID MAXWELL FYFE (continuing the reading of the Indictment):

APPENDIX C
Charges And Particulars Of Violations Of International Treaties, Agreements And Assurances Caused By The Defendants In The Course Of Planning, Preparing And Initiating The Wars

I

Charge: Violation of the Convention for the Pacific Settlement of International Disputes signed at The Hague, 29th July, 1899.

Particulars: In that Germany did, by force and arms, on the dates specified in Column I, invade the territory of the sovereigns specified in Column 2, respectively, without first having attempted to settle its disputes with said sovereigns by pacific means.

Column 1	Column 2
6th April, 1941	Kingdom of Greece
6th April,1941	Kingdom of Yugoslavia

II

Charge: Violation of the Convention for the Pacific Settlement of International Disputes signed at The Hague, 18th October, 1907.

Particulars : In that Germany did, on or about the dates specified in Column 1, by force of arms invade the territory of the sovereigns specified in Column 2, respectively, without having first attempted to settle its disputes with said sovereigns by pacific means.

Column 1	Column 2
1st September, 1939	Republic of Poland
9th April, 1940	Kingdom of Norway
9th April, 1940	Kingdom of Denmark
10th May, 1940	Grand-Duchy of Luxembourg
10th May, 1940	Kingdom of Belgium
10th May, 1940	Kingdom of the Netherlands
22nd June, 1941	Union of Soviet Socialist Republics

III

Charge: Violation of Hague Convention III Relative to the Opening of Hostilities, signed 18th October, 1907.

Particulars: In that Germany did, on or about the dates specified in Column 1, commence hostilities against the countries specified in Column 2, respectively, without previous warning in the form of a reasoned declaration of war or an ultimatum with conditional declaration of war.

Column 1	Column 2
1st September, 1939	Republic of Poland
9th April, 1940	Kingdom of Norway
9th April, 1940	Kingdom of Denmark
10th May, 1940	Kingdom of Belgium
10th May, 1940	Kingdom of the Netherlands
10th May, 1940	Grand-Duchy of Luxembourg
22nd June, 1941	Union of Soviet Socialist Republics

IV

Charge: Violation of Hague Convention V Respecting the Rights and Duties of Neutral Powers and Persons in Case of War on Land, signed 18th October, 1907.

Particulars: In that Germany did, on or about the dates specified in Column 1, by force and arms of its military forces, cross into, invade, and occupy the territories of the sovereigns specified in Column 2, respectively, then and thereby violating the neutrality of said sovereigns.

Column 1	Column 2
9th April, 1940	Kingdom of Norway
9th April, 1940	Kingdom of Denmark
10th May, 1940	Grand-Duchy of Luxembourg
10th May, 1940	Kingdom of Belgium
10th May, 1940	Kingdom of the Netherlands
22nd June, 1941	Union of Soviet Socialist Republics

V

Charge: Violation of the Treaty of Peace between the Allied and Associated Powers and Germany, signed at Versailles, 28th June, 1919, known as the Versailles Treaty.

Particulars:

(1) In that Germany did, on and after 7th March, 1936, maintain and assemble armed forces and maintain and construct military fortifications in the demilitarised zone of the Rhineland in violation of the provisions of Articles 42 to 44 of the Treaty of Versailles.

(2) In that Germany did, on or about 13th March, 1938, annex Austria into the German Reich in violation of the provisions of Article 80 of the Treaty of Versailles.

(3) In that Germany did, on or about 22nd March, 1939, incorporate the district of Memel into the German Reich in violation of the provisions of Article 99 of the Treaty of Versailles.

(4) In that Germany did, on or about 1st September, 1939, incorporate the Free City of Danzig into the German Reich in violation of the provisions of Article 100 of the Treaty of Versailles.

(5) In that Germany did, on or about 16th March, 1939, incorporate the provinces of Bohemia and Moravia, formerly part of Czechoslovakia, into the German Reich in violation of the provisions of Article 81 of the Treaty of Versailles.

(6) In that Germany did, at various times in March, 1935, and thereafter, repudiate various parts of Part V, Military, Naval and Air Clauses of the Treaty of Versailles, by creating an air force, by use of compulsory military service, by increasing the size of the army beyond treaty limits, and by increasing the size of the navy beyond treaty limits.

VI

Charge: Violation of the Treaty between the United States and Germany Restoring Friendly Relations, signed at Berlin, 25th August, 1921.

Particulars: In that Germany did, at various times in March, 1935, and thereafter, repudiate various parts of Part V, Military, Naval and Air Clauses of the Treaty between the United States and Germany Restoring Friendly Relations by creating an air force, by use of compulsory military service, by increasing the size of the army beyond treaty limits, and by increasing the size of the navy beyond treaty limits.

VII

Charge: Violation of the Treaty of Mutual Guarantee between Germany, Belgium, France, Great Britain and Italy, done at Locarno, 16th October, 1925.

Particulars :

(1) In that Germany did, on or about 7th March, 1936, unlawfully send armed forces into the Rhineland demilitarised zone of Germany, in violation of Article 1 of the Treaty of Mutual Guarantee.

(2) In that Germany did, in or about March, 1936, and thereafter, unlawfully maintain armed forces in the Rhineland demilitarised zone of Germany, in violation of Article 1 of the Treaty of Mutual Guarantee.

(3) In that Germany did, on or about 7th March, 1936, and thereafter, unlawfully construct and maintain fortifications in the Rhineland demilitarised zone of

Germany, in violation of Article I of the Treaty of Mutual Guarantee.

(4) In that Germany did, on or about 10th May, unlawfully attack and invade Belgium, in violation of Article 2 of the Treaty of Mutual Guarantee.

(5) In that Germany did, on or about 10th May, I940, unlawfully attack and invade Belgium, without first having attempted to settle its dispute with Belgium by peaceful means, in violation of Article 3 of the Treaty of Mutual Guarantee.

VIII

Charge: Violation of the Arbitration Treaty between Germany and Czechoslovakia, done at Locarno, 16th October, I925-

Particulars: In that Germany did, on or about 15th March, 1939, unlawfully by duress and threats of military might force Czechoslovakia to deliver the destiny of Czechoslovakia and its inhabitants into the hands of the Fuehrer and Reichschancellor of Germany without having attempted to settle its dispute with Czechoslovakia by peaceful means.

IX

Charge: Violation of the Arbitration Convention between Germany and Belgium, done at Locarno, 16th October, l955

Particulars: In that Germany did, on or about 10th May, 1940, unlawfully attack and invade Belgium without first having attempted to settle its dispute with Belgium by peaceful means.

X

Charge: Violation of the Arbitration Treaty between Germany and Poland, done at Locarno, 16th October, l925.

Particulars: In that Germany did, on or about 1st September, 1939, unlawfully attack and invade Poland without first having attempted to settle its dispute with Poland by peaceful means.

XI

Charge: Violation of Convention of Arbitration and Conciliation entered into between Germany and the Netherlands on 20th May, 1926.

Particulars: In that Germany, without warning, and notwithstanding its solemn covenant to settle by peaceful means all disputes of any nature whatever which might arise between it and the Netherlands which were not capable of settlement by diplomacy and which had not been referred by mutual agreement to the Permanent Court of International Justice, did, on or about 10th May, 1940, with a military force, attack, invade, and occupy the Netherlands, thereby violating its neutrality and territorial integrity and destroying its sovereign independence.

XII

Charge: Violation of Convention of Arbitration and Conciliation entered into between Germany and Denmark on 2nd June, 1926.

Particulars: In that Germany, without warning, and notwithstanding its solemn covenant to settle by peaceful means all disputes of any nature whatever which might arise between it and Denmark which were not capable of settlement by diplomacy and which had not been referred by mutual agreement to the Permanent Court of International Justice, did, on or about 9th April, 1940, with a military force, attack, invade, and occupy Denmark, thereby violating its neutrality and territorial integrity and destroying its sovereign independence.

XIII

Charge: Violation of Treaty between Germany and other Powers providing for Renunciation of War as an Instrument of National Policy, signed at Paris 27th August, 1928, known as the Kellogg-Briand Pact.

Particulars: In that Germany did, on or about the dates specified in Column 1, with a military force, attack the sovereigns specified in Column 2, respectively, and resort to war against such sovereigns, in violation of its solemn declaration condemning recourse to war for the solution of international controversies, its solemn renunciation of war as an instrument of national policy in its relations with such sovereigns, and its solemn covenant that settlement or solution of all disputes or conflicts of whatever nature or origin arising between it and such sovereigns should never be sought except by pacific means.

Column 1	Column 2
1st September, 1939	Republic of Poland
9th April, 1940	Kingdom of Norway
9th April, 1940	Kingdom of Denmark
10th May, 1940	Kingdom of Belgium
10th May, 1940	Grand-Duchy of Luxembourg
10th May, 1940	Kingdom of the Netherlands
6th April, 1941	Kingdom of Greece
6th April, 1941	Kingdom of Yugoslavia
22nd June, 1941	Union of Soviet Socialist Republics
11th December, 1941	United States of America

XIV

Charge: Violation of Treaty of Arbitration and Conciliation entered into between Germany and Luxembourg on 11th September, 1929.

Particulars: In that Germany, without warning, and notwithstanding its solemn covenant to settle by peaceful means all disputes which might arise between it and Luxembourg which were not capable of settlement by diplomacy, did, on or about 10th May, 1940, with a military force, attack, invade, and occupy Luxembourg, thereby violating its neutrality and territorial integrity and destroying its sovereign independence.

XV

Charge: Violation of the Declaration of Non-Aggression entered into between Germany and Poland on 26th January, 1934.

Particulars: In that Germany proceeding to the application of force for the purpose of reaching a decision did, on or about 13th September, 1939, at various places along the German-Polish frontier, employ military forces to attack, invade and commit other acts of aggression against Poland.

XVI

Charge: Violation of German Assurance given on 21st May, 1935, that the Inviolability and Integrity of the Federal State of Austria would be Recognised.

Particulars: In that Germany did, on or about 12th March, 1938, at various points, and places along the German- Austrian frontier, with a military force and in violation of its solemn declaration and assurance, invade and annex to Germany the territory of the Federal State of Austria.

XVII

Charge: Violation of Austro-German Agreement of 11th July, 1936.

Particulars: In that Germany during the period from 11th February, 1938 to 13th March, 1938, did by duress and various aggressive acts, including the use of military force, cause the Federal State of Austria to yield up its sovereignty to the German State in violation of Germany's agreement to recognise the full sovereignty of the Federal State of Austria.

XVIII

Charge: Violation of German Assurances given on 30th January, 1937, 28th April, 1939, 26th August, 1939 and 6th October, 1939, to Respect the Neutrality and Territorial Inviolability of the Netherlands.

Particulars: In that Germany, without warning, and without recourse to peaceful means of settling any considered differences did, on or about 10th May, 1940, with a military force and in violation of its solemn assurances, invade, occupy, and attempt to subjugate the sovereign territory of the Netherlands.

XIX

Charge: Violation of German Assurances given on 30th January, 1937, 13th October, 1937, 28th April, 1939, 26th August, 1939, and 6th October, 1939, to Respect the Neutrality and Territorial Integrity and Inviolability of Belgium.

Particulars: In that Germany, without warning, did on or about 10th May, 1940, with a military force and in violation of its solemn assurances and declarations, attack, invade, and occupy the sovereign territory of Belgium.

XX

Charge: Violation of Assurances given on 11th March, 1938, and 26th September, 1938, to Czechoslovakia.

Particulars: In that Germany, on or about 15th March, 1939, did, by establishing a Protectorate of Bohemia and Moravia under duress and by the threat of force, violate the assurance given on 11th March, 1938, to respect the territorial integrity of the Czechoslovak Republic and the assurance given on 26th September, 1938, that, if the so- called Sudeten territories were ceded to Germany, no further German territorial claims on Czechoslovakia would be made.

XXI

Charge: Violation of the Munich Agreement and Annexes of 29th September, 1938.
Particulars :

(1) In that Germany on or about 15th March, 1939, did by duress and the threat of military intervention force the Republic of Czechoslovakia to deliver the destiny of the Czech people and country into the hands of the Fuehrer of the German Reich.

(2) In that Germany refused and failed to join in an international guarantee of the new boundaries of the Czechoslovakian State as provided for in Annex No. I to the Munich Agreement.

XXII

Charge: Violation of the Solemn Assurances of Germany given On 3rd September, 1939, 28th April, 1939, and 6th October, 1939, that they would not Violate the Independence or Sovereignty of the Kingdom of Norway.

Particulars: In that Germany, without warning did, on or about 9th April, 1940, with its military and naval forces attack, invade and commit other acts of aggression against the Kingdom of Norway.

XXIII

Charge: Violation of German Assurances given on 28th April, 1939, and 26th August, 1939, to Respect the Neutrality and Territorial Inviolability of Luxembourg.

Particulars : In that Germany, without warning, and without recourse to peaceful means of settling any considered differences, did, on or about 10th May, 1940, with a military force and in violation of the solemn assurances, invade, occupy, and absorb into Germany the sovereign territory of Luxembourg.

XXIV

Charge: Violation of the Treaty of Non-Aggression between Germany and Denmark signed at Berlin, 31st May, 1939.

Particulars: In that Germany without prior warning, did, on or about 9th April, 1940, with its military forces, attack, invade and commit other acts of aggression against the Kingdom of Denmark.

XXV

Charge: Violation of Treaty of Non-Aggression entered into between Germany and U.S.S.R. on 23rd August, 1939.
Particulars:

(1) In that Germany did, on or about 22nd June, 1941, employ military forces to attack and commit acts of aggression against the U.S.S.R.

(2) In that Germany without warning or recourse to a friendly exchange of views or arbitration did, on or about 22nd June, 1941, employ military forces to attack and commit acts of aggression against the U.S.S.R.

XXVI

Charge: Violation of German Assurance given on 6th October, 1939, to Respect the Neutrality and Territorial Integrity of Yugoslavia.

Particulars: In that Germany without prior warning did, on or about 6th April, 1941, with its military forces attack, invade and commit other acts of aggression against the Kingdom of Yugoslavia.

THE PRESIDENT: The Tribunal will now adjourn until 10 o'clock to-morrow morning.

(The Tribunal adjourned to 21st November, 1945, at 10.00 hours.)

SECOND DAY:
Wednesday, 21st November, 1945

THE PRESIDENT: A motion has been filed with the Tribunal and the Tribunal has given it consideration. In so far as it may be a plea to the jurisdiction the Tribunal, it conflicts with Article 3 of the Charter and will not be entertained. In so far as it may contain other arguments which may be open to the defendants they may be heard at a later stage.

Now, in accordance with Article 24 of the Charter, which provides that, the indictment has been read in Court, the defendants shall be called upon plead guilty or not guilty, I direct the defendants to plead either guilty or not guilty.

DR. RUDOLF DIX (Counsel for defendant Schacht): May I speak to Your Lordship for just a moment?

THE PRESIDENT: You may not speak to me in support of the motion with I have just dealt on behalf of the Tribunal. I have told you so far as that motion is a plea to the jurisdiction of the Tribunal, it conflicts with Article 2 of the Charter and will not be entertained. In so far as it contains or may contain arguments which may be open to the defendants, those arguments may be heard hereafter.

DR. DIX: I do not wish to speak on the subject of a motion. As speaker for the defence I should like to broach a technical question and voice a request to this effect on behalf of the defence. May I do so? The defence counsel were forbidden to talk to the defendants this morning. It is absolutely necessary that the defence counsel should be able to speak to the defendants before the session. It often happens that after the session one cannot reach one's client at night. In all probability it might prove necessary to prepare matters overnight for the next morning which one wants to talk over with him. According to our experience it is always permissible for the defence counsel to speak to the defendant the session. The question of conferring between defence counsel and clients during sessions could be dealt with at a later date. At present I request, on behalf of the entire defence, that we be allowed to confer with our clients in the courtroom itself, into which they usually are brought at a very early hour. Otherwise we shall not be in a position to conduct the defence in an efficient and appropriate manner.

THE PRESIDENT: I am afraid that you cannot consult with your clients in the courtroom except by written communication. When you are out of the courtroom, security regulations can be carried out and you have, so far as those security regulations go, full opportunity to consult with your clients. In the courtroom we must confine you to written communications to your clients. At the end of each day's sitting, you will have full opportunity to consult with them in private.

DR. DIX: I shall discuss this with my colleagues of the defence and we should like if possible to return to this question.

DR. RALPH THOMA (Counsel for defendant Rosenberg): May I have the floor?

THE PRESIDENT: Will you state your name please.

DR. THOMA: Dr. Ralph Thoma. I represent the defendant Rosenberg. Yesterday my client gave me a statement as regards the question of guilt or innocence. I took this statement and promised him to talk with him about it. Neither last night nor this morning have I had an opportunity to talk with him; and, consequently, neither I nor my client are in a position to make a statement to-day as to whether he is guilty or not guilty. I therefore request an interruption of the trial so that I may speak with my client.

THE PRESIDENT: Dr. Thoma, the Tribunal will be prepared to adjourn for fifteen minutes in order that you may have an opportunity of consulting with your clients.

DR. THOMA: Thank you. I should like to make another statement. Some of my colleagues have just told me that they are in the same position as I, particularly ...

THE PRESIDENT: I meant that all defence counsel should have an opportunity of consulting with their clients; but I would point out to the defence counsel that they have had several weeks preparation for this trial, and that they must have anticipated that the provisions of Article 24 would be followed. Now we will adjourn for fifteen minutes in which all of you may consult with your clients.

DR. THOMA: May I say something further in that respect, your Honour ?

THE PRESIDENT: Yes.

DR. THOMA: The defence asked whether the question of guilty or not guilty could only be answered with "yes" or "no" or whether a more extensive and longer statement could be made. We have obtained information on this point only the day before yesterday. I therefore had no opportunity to confer at length with my client on this matter.

THE PRESIDENT: One moment. The question will have to be answered in the words of Article 24 of the Charter, and those words are printed in italics:

"The tribunal shall ask each defendant whether he pleads guilty or not guilty."

That is what they have to do at that stage. Of course, the defendants will have a full opportunity themselves, if they are called as witnesses, and by their counsel, to make their defence fully at a later stage.

(A recess was taken.)

THE PRESIDENT: I will now call upon the defendants to plead guilty or not guilty to the charges against them. They will proceed in turn to a point in the dock opposite to the microphone.

THE PRESIDENT: Hermann Goering.

HERMANN GOERING: Before I answer the question of the high court whether or not I am guilty -

THE PRESIDENT: I announced that defendants were not entitled to make a statement. You must plead guilty or not guilty.

HERRMANN GOERING: I declare myself in the sense of the indictment not guilty.

THE PRESIDENT: Rudolf Hess.

71

RUDOLF HESS: No.

THE PRESIDENT: That will be entered as a plea of not guilty. (Laughter.)

THE PRESIDENT: If there is any disturbance in Court, those who make it will have to leave the Court.

THE PRESIDENT: Joachim von Ribbentrop.

JOACHIM VON RIBBENTROP: I declare myself in the sense of the indictment not guilty.

THE PRESIDENT: Wilhelm Keitel.

WILHELM KEITEL: I declare myself not guilty.

THE PRESIDENT: In the absence of Ernst Kaltenbrunner, the trial will proceed against him, but he will have an opportunity of pleading when he is sufficiently well to be brought back into court.

THE PRESIDENT: Alfred Rosenberg.

ALFRED ROSENBERG: I declare myself in the sense of the indictment not guilty.

THE PRESIDENT: Hans Frank.

HANS FRANK: I declare myself not guilty.

THE PRESIDENT: Wilhelm Frick.

WILHELM FRICK: Not guilty.

THE PRESIDENT: Julius Streicher.

JULIUS STREICHER: Not guilty.

THE PRESIDENT: Walter Funk.

WALTER FUNK: I declare myself not guilty.

THE PRESIDENT: Hjalmar Schacht.

HJALMAR SCHACHT: I am not guilty in any respect.

THE PRESIDENT: Karl Donitz.

KARL DONITZ: Not guilty.

THE PRESIDENT: Erich Raeder.

ERICH RAEDER: I declare myself not guilty.

THE PRESIDENT: Baldur von Schirach.

BALDUR VON SCHIRACH: I declare myself in the sense of the indictment not guilty.

THE PRESIDENT: Fritz Sauckel.

FRITZ SAUCKEL: I declare myself in the sense of the indictment, before God and the world and particularly before my people, not guilty.

THE PRESIDENT: Alfred Jodl.

ALFRED JODL: Not guilty. What I have done or had to do, I have a pure conscience form before God, before history and my people.

THE PRESIDENT: Franz von Papen.

FRANZ VON PAPEN: I declare myself in no way guilty.

THE PRESIDENT: Artur Seyss-Inquart.

ARTUR SEYSS-INQUART: I declare myself not guilty.

THE PRESIDENT: Albert Speer.

ALBERT SPEER: Not guilty.

THE PRESIDENT: Constantin von Neurath.

CONSTANTIN VON NEURATH: I answer the question in the negative.

THE PRESIDENT: Hans Fritzsche.

HANS FRITZSCHE: As regard this indictment, not guilty.

(At this point Hermann Goering arose in the prisoners' box.)

THE PRESIDENT: You are not entitled to address the Tribunal, except through your counsel, at the present time. I will now call upon the Chief Prosecutor for the United States of America.

(At this point defendant Goering stood up in the prisoners' dock and attempted to address the Tribunal.)

MR. JUSTICE JACKSON: May it please Your Honour, the privilege of opening the first trial in history for crimes against the peace of the world imposes a grave responsibility. The wrongs which we seek to condemn and punish have been so calculated, so malignant and so devastating, that civilisation cannot tolerate their being ignored, because it cannot survive their being repeated. That four great nations, flushed with victory and stung with injury, stay the hands of vengeance and voluntarily submit their captive enemies to the judgement of the law, is one of the most significant tributes that Power ever has paid to Reason.

This Tribunal, while it is novel and experimental, is not the product of abstract speculations nor is it created to vindicate legalistic theories. This inquest represents the practical effort of four of the most mighty of nations, with the support of seventeen more, to utilise International Law to meet the greatest menace of our times - aggressive war. The common sense of mankind demands that law shall not stop with the punishment of petty crimes by little people. It must also reach men who possess themselves of great power and make deliberate and concerted use of it to set in motion evils which leave no home in the world untouched. It is a cause of that magnitude that the United Nations will lay before Your Honour.

In the prisoners' dock sit twenty-odd broken men. Reproached by the humiliation of those they have led, almost as bitterly as by the desolation of those they have attacked, their personal capacity for evil is forever past. It is hard now to perceive in these miserable men as captives the power by which as Nazi leaders they once dominated much of the world and terrified most of it. Merely as individuals their fate is of little consequence to the world.

What makes this inquest significant is that these prisoners represent sinister influences that will lurk in the world long after their bodies have returned to dust. We will show them to be living symbols of racial hatreds, of terrorism and violence, and of the arrogance and cruelty of power. They are symbols of fierce nationalism and of militarism, of intrigue and war-making which embroiled Europe, generation after generation, crushing its manhood, destroying its homes, and impoverishing its life. They have so identified themselves with the philosophies they conceived, and with the forces they have directed, that tenderness to them is a victory and an encouragement to all the evils which attached to their names. Civilisation can afford no compromise with the forces which would gain renewed strength if we deal ambiguously or with the men in whom those forces now precariously survive.

What these men stand for we will patiently and temperately disclose. We will give you undeniable proofs of incredible events. The catalogue of crimes will omit nothing that could be conceived by a pathological pride, cruelty, and lust for power. These men created in Germany, under the "Fuehrerprinzip," a National Socialist despotism equalled only by the dynasties of the ancient East. They took from the German people all those dignities and freedoms that we hold natural and inalienable rights in every human being, The people were compensated by inflaming and gratifying hatreds towards those who were marked as "scapegoats." Against their opponents, including Jews, Catholics, and free labour the Nazis directed such a campaign of arrogance, brutality, and annihilation as the world has not witnessed since the pre-Christian ages. They excited the German ambition to be a "master race," which of course implies serfdom others. They led their people on a mad gamble for domination. They diverted social energies and resources to the creation of what they thought to be an invincible war machine. They overran their neighbours. To sustain the "master race" in its war-making, they enslaved millions of human beings and brought them into Germany, where these hapless creatures now wander as "displaced persons." At length, bestiality and bad faith reached such excess that they aroused the sleeping strength of imperilled Civilisation. Its united efforts have ground the German war machine to fragments. But the struggle has left Europe a liberated yet prostrate land where a demoralised society struggles to survive. These are the fruits of the sinister forces that sit with these defendants in the prisoners' dock.

In justice to the nations and the men associated in this prosecution, I must remind you of certain difficulties which may leave their mark on this case. Never before in legal history has an effort been made to bring within the scope of a single litigation the developments of a decade covering a whole continent, and involving a score of nations, countless individuals, and innumerable events. Despite the magnitude of the task, the world has demanded immediate action. This demand has had to be met, though perhaps at the cost of finished craftsmanship. In my country, established courts, following familiar procedures, applying well-thumbed precedents, and dealing with the legal consequences of local and limited events, seldom commence a trial within a year of the event in litigation. Yet less than eight months ago to- day the courtroom in which you sit was an enemy fortress in the hands of German S.S. troops. Less than eight months ago nearly all our witnesses and documents were in enemy hands. The law had not been codified, no procedures had been established, no tribunal was in existence, no usable courthouse stood here, none of the hundreds of tons of official German documents had been examined, no prosecuting staff had been assembled, nearly all of the present defendants were at large, and the four prosecuting powers had not yet joined in common cause to try them. I should be the last to deny that the case may well suffer from incomplete researches, and quite likely will not be the example of professional work which any of the prosecuting nations would normally wish to sponsor. It is, however, a completely adequate case to the judgement we shall ask you to render, and its full development we shall be obliged to leave to historians.

Before I discuss particulars of evidence, some general considerations which may affect the credit of this trial in the eyes of the world should be candidly faced. There is a dramatic disparity between the circumstances of the accusers and of the accused that might discredit our work if we should falter, in even minor matters, in being fair and temperate.

Unfortunately, the nature of these crimes is such that both prosecution and judgement must be by victor nations over vanquished foes. The world-wide scope of the aggressions carried out by these men has left but few real neutrals. Either the victors must judge the vanquished or we must leave the defeated to judge themselves. After the First World War we learned the futility of the latter course. The former high station of these defendants, the notoriety of their acts, and the adaptability of their conduct to provoke retaliation make it hard to distinguish between the demand for a just and measured retribution, and the unthinking cry for vengeance which arises from the anguish of war. It is our task, so far as is humanly possible, to draw the line between the two. We must never forget that the record on which we judge these defendants today is the record on which history will judge us tomorrow. To pass these defendants a poisoned chalice is to put it to our lips as well. We must summon such detachment and intellectual integrity to our task that this trial will commend itself to posterity as fulfilling humanity's aspirations to do justice.

At the very outset, let us dispose of the contention that to put these men to trial is to do them an injustice entitling them to some special consideration. These defendants may be hard pressed but they are not ill used. Let us see what alternative they would have to being tried.

More than a majority of these prisoners surrendered to or were tracked down by the forces of the United States. Could they expect us to make American custody a shelter for our enemies against the just wrath of our Allies? Did we spend American lives to capture them only to save them from punishment? Under the principles of the Moscow Declaration, those suspected war criminals who are not to be tried internationally must be turned over to individual governments for trial at the scene of their outrages. Many less responsible and less culpable American-held prisoners have been and will continue to be turned over to other United Nations for local trial. If these defendants should succeed, for any reason, in escaping the condemnation of this Tribunal, or if they obstruct or abort this trial, those who are American-held prisoners will be delivered up to our continental Allies. For these defendants, however, we have set up an International Tribunal, and have undertaken the burden of participating in a complicated effort to give them fair and dispassionate hearings. That is the best known protection to any man with a defence worthy of being heard.

If these men are the first war leaders of a defeated nation to be prosecuted in the name of the law, they are also the first to be given a chance to plead for their lives in the name of the law. Realistically, the Charter of this Tribunal, which gives them a hearing, is also the source of their only hope. It may be that these men of troubled conscience, whose only wish is that the world forget them, do not regard a trial as a favour. But they do have a fair opportunity to defend themselves - a favour which, when in power, they rarely extended even to their fellow countrymen. Despite the fact that public opinion already condemns their acts, we agree that here they must be given a presumption of innocence, and we accept the burden of proving criminal acts and the responsibility of these defendants for their commission.

When I say that we do not ask for convictions unless we prove crime, I do not mean mere technical or incidental transgression of international conventions. We charge guilt on planned and intended conduct that involves moral as well as legal wrong. And we do not mean conduct that is a natural and human, even if illegal, cutting of corners, such as many of us might well have committed had we been in the defendants' positions. It is not because they yielded to the normal frailties of human beings that we accuse them. It is their abnormal and inhuman conduct which brings them to this bar.

We will not ask you to convict these men on the testimony of their foes. There is no count in the Indictment that cannot be proved by books and records. The Germans were always meticulous record keepers, and these defendants had their share of the Teutonic passion for thoroughness in putting things on paper. Nor were they without vanity. They arranged frequently to be photographed in action. We will show you their own films. You will see their own conduct and hear their own voices as these defendants re-enact for you, from the screen, some of the events in the course of the conspiracy.

We would also make clear that we have no purpose to incriminate the whole German people. We know that the Nazi Party was not put in power by a majority of the German vote. We know it came to power by an evil alliance between the most extreme of the Nazi revolutionists, the most unrestrained of the German reactionaries, and the most aggressive of the German militarists. If the German populace had willingly accepted the Nazi programme, no Storm-troopers would have been needed in the early days of the Party, and there would have been no need for concentration camps or the Gestapo, both of which institutions were inaugurated as soon as the Nazis gained control of the German state. Only after these lawless innovations proved successful at home were they taken abroad.

The German people should know by now that the people of the United States hold them in no fear, and in no hate. It is true that the Germans have taught us the horrors of modern warfare, but the ruin that lies from the Rhine to the Danube shows that we, like our Allies, have not been dull pupils. If we are not awed German fortitude and proficiency in war, and if we are not persuaded of their political maturity, we do respect their skill in the arts of peace, their technical competence, and the sober, industrious and self-disciplined character of the masses of the German people. In 1933, we saw the German people recovering prestige in the commercial, industrial and artistic world after the set-back of the last war. We beheld their progress neither with envy nor malice. The Nazi regime interrupted this advance. The recoil of the Nazi aggression has left Germany in ruins. The Nazi readiness to pledge the German word without hesitation and to break it without shame has fastened upon German diplomacy a reputation for duplicity that will handicap it for years. Nazi arrogance has made the boast of the "master race" a taunt that will be thrown at Germans the world over for generations. The Nazi nightmare has given the German name a new and sinister significance throughout the world, which will retard Germany a century. The German, no less than the non-German world, has accounts to settle with these defendants.

The fact of the war and the course of the war, which is the central theme of our case, is history. From September 1st, 1939, when the German armies crossed the Polish frontier, until September, 1942, when they met epic resistance at Stalingrad, German arms seemed invincible. Denmark and Norway, the Netherlands and France, Belgium and Luxembourg, the Balkans and Africa, Poland and the Baltic States, and parts of Russia, all had, been overrun and conquered by swift, powerful, well-aimed blows. That attack on the peace of the world is the crime against international society which brings into international cognizance crimes in its aid and preparation which otherwise might be only internal concerns. It was aggressive war, which the nations of the world had renounced. It was war in violation of treaties, by which the peace of the world was sought to be safeguarded.

This war did not just happen - it was planned and prepared for over a long period of time and with no small skill and cunning. The world has perhaps never seen such a concentration and stimulation of the energies of any people as that which enabled Germany, twenty years after it was defeated, disarmed and dismembered, to come so near carrying out its plan to dominate Europe. Whatever else we may say of those who were the authors of this war, they did achieve a stupendous work in organisation, and our first task is to examine the means by which these defendants and their fellow conspirators prepared and incited Germany to go to war.

In general, our case will disclose these defendants all uniting at some time with the Nazi Party in a plan which they well knew could be accomplished only by an outbreak of war in Europe. Their seizure of the German State, their subjugation of the German people, their terrorism and extermination of dissident elements, their planning and waging of war, their calculated and planned ruthlessness in the conduct of warfare, their deliberate and planned criminality toward conquered peoples - all these are ends for which they acted in concert; and all these are phases of the conspiracy, a conspiracy which reached one goal only to set out for another and more ambitious one. We shall also trace for you the intricate web of organisations which these men formed and utilised to accomplish these ends. We will show how the entire structure of offices and officials was dedicated to the criminal purposes and committed to the use of the criminal methods planned by these defendants and their co-conspirators, many of whom war and suicide have put beyond reach.

It is my purpose to open the case, particularly under Count One of the Indictment, and to deal with the Common plan or Conspiracy to achieve ends possible only by resort to Crimes against Peace, War Crimes, and Crimes against Humanity. My emphasis will not be on individual perversions which may have occurred independently of any central plan. One of the dangers ever present in this trial is that it may be protracted by details of particular wrongs and that we will become lost in a "wilderness of single instances." Nor will I now dwell on the activity of individual defendants except as it may contribute to exposition of the Common Plan.

The case as presented by the United States will be concerned with the brains and authority behind all the crimes. These defendants were men of a station and rank which does not soil its own hands with blood. They were men who knew how to use lesser folk as tools. We want to reach the planners and designers, the inciters and leaders without whose evil architecture, the world would not have been for so long scourged with the violence and lawlessness, and racked with the agonies and convulsions, of this terrible war.

I shall first take up the lawless road by which these men came to possess the power which they have so used. The chief instrumentality of cohesion in plan and action was the National Socialist German Workers Party, known as the Nazi Party. Some of the defendants were with it from the beginning. Others joined only after success seemed to have validated its lawlessness or power had invested it with immunity from the processes of the law. Adolf Hitler became its supreme leader or "Fuehrer" in 1921.

On the 24th February, 1920, at Munich, it publicly had proclaimed its programme (1708-PS). Some of its purposes would commend themselves to many good citizens, such as the demands for "profit-sharing in the great industries," "generous development of provision for old age," "a land reform suitable to our national requirements," and "raising the standard of health." It also made a strong appeal to that sort of nationalism which in ourselves we call patriotism and in our rivals chauvinism. It demanded "equality of rights for the German people in its dealing with other nations and the evolution of the peace treaties of Versailles and St. Germain." It demanded the "union of all Germans on the basis of the right of self-determination of peoples to form a Great Germany." It demanded "land and territory (colonies) for the enrichment of our people and the settlement of our surplus population." All of these, of course, were legitimate objectives if they were to be attained without resort to aggressive warfare.

The Nazi Party from its inception, however, contemplated war. It demanded the "abolition of mercenary troops and the formation of a national army." It proclaimed that "in view of the enormous sacrifice of life and property demanded of a nation by every war, personal enrichment through war must be regarded as a crime against the nation. We demand, therefore, ruthless confiscation of all war profits." I do not criticise this policy. Indeed, I wish it were universal. I merely wish to point out that in a time of peace, war was a preoccupation of the Party, and it started the work of making war less offensive to the masses of the people. With this it combined a programme of physical training and sports for youth that became, as we shall see, the cloak for a secret programme of military training.

The Nazi Party declaration also committed its members to an anti-Semitic programme. It declared that no Jew or any person of non-German blood could be a member of the nation. Such persons were to be disfranchised, disqualified for office, subject to the alien laws, and entitled to nourishment only after the German population had first been provided for. All who had entered Germany after 2nd August, 1914, were to be required forthwith to depart, and all non- German immigration was to be prohibited.

The Party also avowed, even in those early days, an authoritarian and totalitarian programme for Germany. It demanded creation of a strong central power with unconditional authority, nationalisation of all businesses which had been "amalgamated," and a "reconstruction" of the national system of education, which "must aim at teaching the pupil to understand the idea of the State (state sociology)." Its hostility to civil liberties and freedom of the Press was distinctly announced in these words: "It must be forbidden to publish newspapers which do not conduce to the national welfare. We demand the legal prosecution of all tendencies in art or literature of a kind likely to disintegrate our life as a nation, and the suppression of institutions which might militate against the above requirements."

The forecast of religious persecution was clothed in the language of religious liberty, for the Nazi programme stated "We demand liberty for all religious denominations in the State." But it continued with the limitation, "so far as they are not a danger to it and do not militate against the morality and moral sense of the German race."

The Party programme foreshadowed the campaign of terrorism. It announced, "we demand ruthless war upon those whose activities are injurious to the common interests," and it demanded that such offences be punished with death.

It is significant that the leaders of this Party interpreted this programme as a belligerent one, certain to precipitate conflict. The Party platform concluded:

"The leaders of the Party swear to proceed regardless of consequences - if necessary, at the sacrifice of their lives - toward the fulfilment of the foregoing points."

It is this Leadership Corps of the Party, not its entire membership, that stands accused before you as a criminal Organisation.

We have not sought to include every person who may, at some time, have supported the Nazi Party, but only the leadership core which pledged itself to achieve its ends at the risk of their lives.

Let us now see how the leaders of the Party fulfilled their pledge to proceed regardless of consequences. Obviously, their foreign objectives, which were nothing less than to undo international treaties and to wrest territory from foreign control, as well as most of their internal programme, could be accomplished only by possession of the machinery of the German State. The first effort, accordingly, was to subvert the Weimar Republic by violent revolution. An abortive "putsch" at Munich in 1921 landed many of them in jail. A period of meditation which followed produced "Mein Kampf," henceforth the source of law for the Party workers and a source of considerable revenue to its supreme leader. The Nazi plans for the violent overthrow of the feeble Republic then turned to plans for its capture.

No greater mistake could be made than to think of the Nazi Party in terms of the loose organisations which we of the Western world call "political parties." In discipline, structure, and method the Nazi Party was not adapted to the democratic process of persuasion. It was an instrument of conspiracy and of coercion. The Party was not organised to take over power in the German State by winning the support of a majority of the German people; it was organised to seize power in defiance of the will of the people.

The Nazi Party, under the "Fuehrerprinzip," was bound by an iron discipline into a pyramid, with the Fuehrer, Adolf Hitler, at the top and broadening into a numerous Leadership Corps, composed of overlords of a very extensive Party membership at the base. By no means all of those who may have supported the movement in one way or another were actual Party members. The membership took the Party oath which in effect amounted to an abdication of personal intelligence and moral responsibility. This was the oath: "I vow inviolable fidelity to Adolf Hitler; I vow absolute obedience to him and to the leaders he designates for me." The membership in daily practise followed its leaders with an idolatry and self-surrender more Oriental than Western. We will not be obliged to guess as to the motives or goal of the Nazi Party. The immediate aim was to undermine the Weimar Republic. The order to all Party members to work to that end was given in a letter from Hitler of 24th August, 1931, to Rosenberg, of which we will produce the original. Hitler wrote:-

"I am just reading in the Volkischer Beobachter, edition 235/236 page 1, an article entitled 'Does Wirth intend to come over?' The tendency of the article is to prevent on our part a crumbling away from the present form of government. I myself am travelling all over Germany to achieve exactly the opposite. May I therefore ask that my own paper will not stab me in the back with tactically unwise articles ..." (047-PS)

Captured film enables us to present the defendant, Alfred Rosenberg, who from the screen will himself tell you the story. The S.A. practised violent interference with the elections. We have here the reports of the S.D., describing in detail how its members later violated the secrecy of elections in order to identify those who opposed them. One of the reports makes this explanation:-

"The control was effected in the following way: some members of the election-committee marked all the ballot- papers with numbers. During the ballot itself, a voters list was made up. The ballot-papers were handed out in numerical order, therefore it was possible afterwards with the aid of this list to find out the persons who cast no-votes or invalid votes. One sample of these marked ballot-papers is enclosed. The marking was done on the back of the ballot-papers with skimmed-milk." (R- 142)

The Party activity, in addition to all the familiar forms of political contest, took on the aspect of a rehearsal for warfare. It utilised a Party formation, "Die Sturmabteilungen," commonly known as the S.A. This was a voluntary organisation of youthful and fanatical Nazis trained for the use of violence under semi-military discipline. Its members began by acting as bodyguards for the Nazi leaders and rapidly expanded from defensive to offensive tactics. They became disciplined ruffians for breaking up opposition meetings and the terrorisation of adversaries. They boasted that their task was to make the Nazi Party "master of the streets." The S.A. was the parent organisation of a number of others. Its offspring included "Die Schutzstaffeln" commonly known as the S.S., formed in 1925, and distinguished for the fanaticism and cruelty of its members; "Der Sicherheitsdienst," known as the S.D.; and "Die Geheime Staatspolizei," the Secret State Police, the infamous Gestapo formed in 1934 immediately after Nazi accession to power.

A glance at a chart of the Party Organisation is enough to show how completely it differed from the political parties we know. It had its own source of law in the Fuehrer and it had its own courts and its own police. The conspirators set up a government within the Party to exercise outside the law every sanction that any legitimate State could exercise and many that it could not. Its chain of command was military, and its formations were martial in name as well as in function. They were composed of battalions set up to bear arms under military discipline, motorised corps, flying corps, and the infamous "Death Head Corps," which was not misnamed. The Party had its own secret police, its security units, its intelligence and espionage division, its raiding forces, and its youth forces. It established elaborate administrative mechanisms to identify and liquidate spies and informers, to manage concentration camps, to operate death vans, and to finance the whole movement. Through concentric circles of authority, the Nazi Party, as its leadership later boasted, eventually organised and dominated every phase of German life - but not until they had waged a bitter internal struggle characterised by brutal criminality. In preparation for this phase of their struggle they created a party police system. This became the pattern and the instrument of the police State, which was the first goal in their plan.

The Party formation, including the Leadership Corps of the Party, the S.D., the S.S. the S.A. and the infamous Secret State Police, or Gestapo - all these stand accused before you as criminal organisations; organisations which, as we will prove from their own documents, were recruited only from the recklessly devoted Nazis, ready in conviction and temperament to do the most violent of deeds to advance the common programme. They terrorised and silenced democratic opposition and were able at length to combine with political opportunists, militarists, industrialists, monarchists, and political reactionaries.

On January 30,1933 Adolf Hitler became Chancellor of the German Republic. An evil combination, represented in the prisoner's dock by its most eminent survivors, had succeeded in possessing itself of the machinery of the German Government, a facade behind which they thenceforth would operate to make reality of the war of conquest they so long had plotted. The conspiracy had passed into its second phase.

We shall now consider the steps, which embraced the most hideous of crimes against humanity, to which the conspirators resorted In perfecting control of the German State and in preparing Germany for the aggressive war indispensable to their ends.

The Germans of the 1920's were a frustrated and baffled people as a result of defeat and the disintegration of their traditional government. The democratic elements, which were trying to govern Germany through the new and feeble machinery of the Weimar Republic, got inadequate support from the democratic forces of the rest of the world. It is not to be denied that Germany, when world-wide depression added to her other problems, was faced with urgent intricate pressures in her economic and political life, which necessitated bold measures.

The internal measures by which a nation attempts to solve its problems are ordinarily of no concern to other nations. But the Nazi programme from the first was recognised as a desperate programme for a people still suffering the effects of an unsuccessful war. The Nazi policy ends recognised as attainable only by a renewal and more successful outcome of war. The conspirators' answer to Germany's problems was nothing less than to plot the regaining of territories lost in the First World War and the acquisition of other fertile lands of Central Europe by dispossessing or exterminating those who inhabited them. They also contemplated destroying or permanently weakening all other neighbouring peoples so as to win virtual domination over Europe and probably over the world. The precise limits of their ambition we need not define, for it was and is as illegal to wage aggressive war for small stakes as for large ones.

We find at this period two governments in Germany-the real and the ostensible. The form of the German Republic was maintained for a time, and it was the outward and visible government. But the real authority in the State was outside of and above the law and rested in the Leadership Corps of the Nazi Party.

On February 27, 1933, less than a month after Hitler became Chancellor, the Reichstag building was set on fire. The burning of this symbol of free parliamentary government was so providential for the Nazis that it was believed they staged the fire themselves. Certainly when we contemplate their known crimes, we cannot believe they would shrink from mere arson. It is not necessary, however, to resolve the controversy as to who set the fire. The significant point is in the use that was made of the fire and of the state of public mind it produced. The Nazis immediately accused the Communist Party of instigating and committing the crime, and turned every effort to portray this single act of arson as the beginning of a Communist revolution. Then, taking advantage of the hysteria, the Nazis met this phantom revolution with a real one. In the following December, the German Supreme Court, with commendable courage and independence, acquitted the accused Communists, but it was too late to influence the tragic course of events which the Nazi conspirators had set rushing forward.

Hitler, on the morning after the fire, obtained from the aged and ailing President von Hindenburg a Presidential decree suspending the extensive guarantees of individual liberty contained in the constitution of the Weimar Republic. The decree provided that "Sections 114, 115, 117, 118, 123, 124, and 153 of the constitution of the German Reich are suspended until further notice. Thus, restrictions on personal liberty, on the right of free expression of opinion, including freedom of the Press, on the right of assembly and the right of association, and violations of the privacy of postal, telegraphic, and telephonic communications and warrants for house searches, orders for confiscation as well as restrictions on property, are also permissible beyond the legal limits otherwise prescribed." (1390-PS)

The extent of the restriction on personal liberty under the decree of 28th February, 1933, may be understood by reference to the rights under the Weimar Constitution which were suspended:-

Article 114. The freedom of the person is inviolable. Curtailment or deprivation of personal freedom by a public authority is only permissible on a legal basis. Persons who have been deprived of their personal freedom must be informed at the latest on the following day by whose authority and for what reasons the deprivation of freedom was ordered. Opportunity shall be afforded them without delay of submitting objection to their deprivation of freedom.

Article 115. Every German's home is his sanctuary and is inviolable. Exceptions may only be made as provided by law.

Article 117. The secrecy of letters and all postal, telegraphic and telephone communications is inviolable. Exceptions are inadmissible except by Reich law.

Article 118. Every German has the right, within the limits of the general laws, to express his opinions freely in speech, in writing, in print, in picture form or in any other way. No condition of work or employment may detract from this right and no disadvantage may accrue to him from any person making use of this right.

Article 123. All Germans have the right to assemble peacefully and unarmed without giving notice and without special permission. A Reich law may make previous notification obligatory for assemblies in the open air, and may prohibit them in the case of immediate danger to the public safety.

Article 124. All Germans have the right to form associations or societies for purposes not contrary to criminal law. This right may not be curtailed by preventive measures. The same provisions apply to religious associations and societies. Every association may become incorporated (Erwerb der Rechtsfaehigkeit) according to the provisions of the civil law. The right may not be refused to any association on the grounds that its aims are political, social-political or religious.

Article 153. Property is guaranteed by the Constitution. Its content and limits are defined by the laws. Expropriation can only take place for the public benefitand on a legal basis. Adequate compensation shall be granted, unless a Reich law orders otherwise. In the case of dispute concerning the matter to the ordinary civil courts, unless Reich laws determine otherwise. Compensation must be paid if the Reich expropriates property belonging to the Lands, Communes, or public utility associations. Property carries obligations. Its use shall also serve the common good." (2050-PS)

It must be said, in fairness to von Hindenburg, that the Constitution itself authorised him temporarily to suspend these fundamental rights "if the public safety and order in the German Reich are considerably disturbed or endangered." It must also be acknowledged that President Ebert previously had invoked this power.

But the National Socialist coup was made possible because the terms of the Hitler-Hindenburg decree departed from all previous ones in which the power of suspension had been invoked. Whenever President Ebert had suspended constitutional guarantees of individual rights, his decree had expressly revived the Protective Custody Act adopted by the Reichstag in igi6 during the previous war. This Act guaranteed a judicial hearing within twenty-four hours of arrest, gave a right to have counsel and to inspect all relevant records, provided for appeal, and authorised compensation from Treasury funds for erroneous arrests.

The Hitler-Hindenburg decree of 28th February, 1933, contained no such safeguards. The omission may not have been noted by von Hindenburg. Certainly he did not appreciate its effect. It left the Nazi police and party formations, already existing and functioning under Hitler, completely unrestrained and irresponsible. Secret arrest and indefinite detention without charges, without evidence, without hearing, without counsel, became the method of inflicting inhuman punishment on any whom the Nazi police suspected or disliked. No court could issue an injunction, or writ of habeas corpus, or certiorari. The German people were in the hands of the police, the police were in the hands of the Nazi Party, and the Party was in the hands of a ring of evil men, of whom the defendants here before you are surviving and representative leaders.

The Nazi conspiracy, as we shall show, always contemplated not merely overcoming current opposition, but exterminating elements which could not be reconciled with its philosophy of the State. It not only sought to establish the Nazi "new order" but to secure its way, as Hitler predicted, "for a thousand years." Nazis were never in doubt or disagreement as to what those dissident elements were. They were concisely described by one of them, Col. General von Fritzsche, on 11th December, 1938, in these words:

"Shortly after the first war I came to the conclusion that we should have to be victorious in three battles if Germany were to become powerful again: (1)The battle against the working class - Hitler has won this; (2)Against the Catholic Church, perhaps better expressed against Ultramontanism (3) Against the Jews." (1947-PS)

The warfare against these elements was continuous. The battle in Germany was but a practice skirmish for the world- wide drive against them. We have here in point of geography and of time two groups of crimes against humanity - one within Germany before and during the war, the other in occupied territory during the war. But the two are not separated in Nazi planning. They are a continuous unfolding of the Nazi plan to exterminate peoples and institutions which might serve as a focus or instrument for overturning their "new world order" at any time. We consider these Crimes against Humanity in this address as manifestations of the one Nazi Plan and discuss them according to General von Fritsche's classification.

1. THE BATTLE AGAINST THE WORKING CLASS

When Hitler came to power there were in Germany three groups of trade unions. The General German Trade Union Confederation (A.D.G.B.) with twenty-eight affiliated unions, and the General Independent Employees Confederation (A.F.A.) with thirteen federated unions together numbered more than 4,500,000 members. The Christian Trade Union had over 1,250,000 members.

The working people of Germany, like the working people of other nations, had little to gain personally by war. While labour is usually brought around to the support of the nation at war, labour by and large is a pacific, though by no means a pacifist force in the world. The working people of Germany had not forgotten in 1933 how heavy the yoke of the war lord can be. It was the working men who had joined with the sailors and soldiers in the revolt of 1918 to the First World War. The Nazis had neither forgiven nor forgotten. The Nazi programme required that this part of the German population not only be stripped of power to resist diversion of its scanty comforts to armament, but also be wheedled or whipped into new and unheard-of sacrifices as a part of the Nazi war preparation. Labour must be cowed, and that meant its organisations and means of cohesion and defence must be destroyed.

The purpose to regiment labour for the Nazi Party was avowed by Ley in a speech to workers on 2nd May, 1933, as follows:-

"You may say what else do you want, you have the absolute power. True we have the power, but we do not have the whole people, we do not have you workers 100 per cent, and it is you whom we want; we will not let you be until you stand with us in complete, genuine acknowledgement." (614-PS)

The first Nazi attack was upon the two larger unions. On 21st April, 1933, an order, not even in the name of the Government, but of the Nazi Party, was issued by the conspirator Robert Ley as "Chief of Staff of the political Organisation of the N.S.D.A.P" applicable to the Trade Union Confederation and the Independent Employees Confederation. It directed seizure of their properties and arrest of their principal leaders. The Party order directed Party organs which we here denounce as criminal associations, the S.A. and S.S., "to be employed for the occupation of the trade union properties, and for the taking into custody of personalities who come into question." And it directed the taking into "protective custody" of all chairmen and district secretaries and union and branch directors of the labour bank. (392-PS)

These orders were carried out on 2nd May, 1933. All funds of the labour unions, including pension and benefit funds, were seized. Union leaders were sent to concentration camps. A few days later, on 10th May, 1933, Hitler appointed Ley leader of the German Labour Front (Deutsche Arbeitsfront), which succeeded to the confiscated union funds. The German Labour Front, a Nazi controlled labour bureau, was set up under Ley to teach the Nazi philosophy to German workers and to weed out from industrial employment all who were backward in their lessons. (940-PS) "Factory Troops" were organised as an "ideological shock squad within the factory" (1817- PS). The Party order provided that "outside of the German Labour Front, no other Organisation (whether of workers or of employees) is to exist." On 24th June, 1933, the remaining Christian Trade Unions were seized, pursuant to an order of the Nazi Party, signed by Ley.

On 19th May, 1933, this time by a Government decree, it was provided that "trustees" of labour, appointed by Hitler, should regulate the conditions of all labour contracts, replacing the former process of collective bargaining (405- PS). On 30th November, 1934, a decree "regulating national labour" introduced the Fuehrer principle into industrial relations. It provided that the owners of enterprises should be the "Fuehrers" and the workers should be the followers. The enterprise-fuehrers should "make decisions for employees and labourers in all matters concerning the enterprise" (1861-PS). It was by such bait that the great German industrialists were induced to support the Nazi cause, to their own ultimate ruin.

85

Not only did the Nazis dominate and regiment German labour, but they forced the youth into the ranks of the labouring people they had thus led into chains. Under a compulsory labour service decree on 26th June, 1935, young men and women between the ages of 18 and 25 were conscripted for labour (1654-PS). Thus was the purpose to subjugate German labour accomplished.

In the words of Ley, the accomplishment consisted "in eliminating the association character of the trade union and employees' associations, and in its place we have substituted the conception 'soldiers of work'." The productive manpower of the German nation was in Nazi control. By these steps the defendants won the battle to liquidate labour unions as potential opposition and were enabled to impose upon the working class the burdens of preparing for aggressive warfare.

Robert Ley, the field marshal of this battle against labour, answered our indictment with suicide. Apparently he knew no better answer.

2. THE BATTLE AGAINST THE CHURCHES

The Nazi Party was always predominantly anti-Christian by ideology. But we who believe in freedom of conscience and of religion base no charge of criminality on anybody's ideology. It is not because the Nazis themselves were irreligious or pagan, but because they persecuted others of the Christian faith that they became guilty of crime, and it is because the persecution was a step in the preparation for aggressive warfare that the offence becomes one of international consequence. To remove every moderating influence among the German people and to put its population on a total war footing, the conspirators devised and carried out a systematic and relentless repression of all Christian sects and churches.

We will ask you to convict the Nazis on their own evidence, Martin Bormann in June 1941 issued a secret decree on the relation of Christianity and National Socialism. The decree provided:

"For the first time in German history the Fuehrer consciously and completely has the leadership of the people in his own hand. With the Party, its components, and attached units, the Fuehrer has created for himself, and thereby for the German Reich leadership, an instrument which makes him independent of the church. All influences which might impair or damage the leadership of the people exercised by the Fuehrer with the help of the N.S.D.A.P. must be eliminated. More and more the people must be separated from the churches and their organs, the pastors. Of course, the churches must and will, seen from their viewpoint, defend themselves against this loss of power. But never again must an influence on leadership of the people be yielded to the churches. This influence must be broken completely and finally. Only the Reich government, and by its direction the Party, its components, and attached units, have a right to leadership of the people. Just as the deleterious influence of astrologers, seers, and other fakers are eliminated and suppressed by the State, so must the possibility of church influence also be totally removed. Not until this has happened does the State leadership have influence on the individual citizens. Not until then are the people and Reich secure in their existence for all the future" (D-75).

And how the Party had been securing the Reich from Christian influence will be proved by such items as this teletype from the Gestapo, Berlin, to the Gestapo Nuremburg, on 24th July, 1938. Let us hear from their own account of events in Rottenburg:-

"The Party, on 23rd July, 1939, from 2100 carried out the third demonstration against Bishop Sproll. Participants, about 2,500-3,000, were brought in from outside by bus, etc. The Rottenburg populace again did not participate in the demonstration. This town took rather a hostile attitude to the demonstrations. The action got completely out of hand of the Party Member responsible for it. The demonstrators stormed the palace, beat in the gates and doors. About 150 to 200 people forced their way into the palace, searched the rooms, threw files out of the windows, and rummaged through the beds in the rooms of the palace. One bed was ignited. Before the fire got to the other objects or equipment in the rooms and the palace, the flaming bed was throw from the window and the fire extinguished. The Bishop was with Archbishop Groeber of Freiburg, and the ladies and gentlemen of his menage in the chapel at prayer. About 25 to 30 pressed into this chapel and molested those present. Bishop Groeber was taken for Bishop Sproll. He was grabbed by the robe and dragged back and forth, Finally the intruders realised that Bishop Groeber was not the one they were seeking. They could then be persuaded to leave the building. After the evacuation of the palace by the demonstrators I had an interview with Archbishop Groeber, who left Rottenburg in the night. Groeber wants to turn to the Fuehrer and Reich Minister of the Interior Dr. Frick anew. On the course of the action, the damage done, as well as the homage of the Rottenburg populace beginning today for the Bishop, I shall immediately hand in a full report, after I begin suppressing counter mass meetings. In case the Fuehrer has instructions to give in this matter, I request that these be transmitted most quickly." (848-PS).

Later, defendant Rosenberg wrote to Bormann reviewing the proposal of Herrl as Church minister to place the Protestant Church under State tutelage and proclaim Hitler its supreme head. Rosenberg was opposed, hinting that Naziism was to suppress the Christian Church completely after the war.

The persecution of all pacifist and dissenting sects, such as Jehovah's Witnesses and the Pentecostal Association, was peculiarly relentless and cruel. The policy toward the Evangelical Churches, however, was to use their influence for the Nazi's own purposes. In September, 1933, Muller was appointed the Fuehrer's representative with power to deal with the "affairs of the Evangelical Church" in its relations to the State. Eventually, steps were taken to create a Reich Bishop vested with power to control this Church. A long conflict followed, Pastor Niemoller was sent to a concentration camp, and extended interference with the internal discipline and administration of the Churches occurred.

A most intense drive was directed against the Roman Catholic Church. After a strategic Concordat with the Holy See, signed in July, 1933, in Rome, which never was observed by the Nazi Party, a long and persistent persecution of the Catholic Church, its priesthood and its members, was carried out. Church Schools and educational institutions were suppressed or subjected to requirements of Nazi teaching inconsistent with the Christian faith. The property of the Church was confiscated and inspired vandalism directed against the Church property was left unpunished. Religious instruction was impeded and the exercise of religion made difficult. Priests and bishops were laid upon, riots were stimulated to harass them, and many were sent to concentration camps.

After occupation of foreign soil, these persecutions went on with greater vigour than ever. We will present to you from the files of the Vatican the earnest protests made by the Vatican to Ribbentrop summarising the persecutions to which the priesthood and the Church had been subjected in this Twentieth Century under the Nazi regime. Ribbentrop never answered them. He could not deny. He dared not justify.

I now come to "Crimes against the Jews."

THE PRESIDENT: We shall now take our noon recess.

(A recess was taken until 1400 hours.)

THE PRESIDENT: The Tribunal will adjourn for fifteen minutes at half past three and then continue until half past four.

MR. JUSTICE JACKSON: I was about to take up the "Crimes Committed Against the Jews."

3. CRIMES COMMITTED AGAINST THE JEWS

The most savage and numerous crimes committed by the Nazis were those against the Jews. Those in Germany, in 1933, numbered about 500,000. In the aggregate, they had made for themselves positions which excited envy, and had accumulated properties which excited the avarice of the Nazis. They were few enough to be helpless and numerous enough to be held up as a menace.

Let there be no misunderstanding about the charge of persecuting Jews. What we charge against these defendants is not those arrogances and pretensions which frequently accompany the intermingling of different peoples and which are likely, despite the honest efforts of Government, to produce regrettable crimes and convulsions. It is my purpose to show a plan and design to which all Nazis were fanatically committed to annihilate all Jewish people. These crimes were organised and promoted by the Party Leadership, executed and protected by the Nazi officials, as we shall convince you by written orders of the Secret State Police itself.

The persecution of the Jews was a continuous and deliberate policy. It was a policy directed against other nations as well as against the Jews themselves. Anti-Semitism was promoted to divide and embitter the democratic peoples and to soften their resistance to the Nazi aggression. As Robert Ley declared in Der Angriff on 14 May, 1944, "the second German secret weapon is Anti-Semitism because, if it is constantly pursued by Germany, it will become a universal problem which all nations will be forced to consider."

Anti-Semitism also has been aptly credited with being a "spearhead of terror."

The ghetto was the laboratory for testing repressive measures. Jewish property was the first to be expropriated, but the custom grew and included similar measures against Anti-Nazi Germans, Poles, Czechs, Frenchmen, and Belgians. Extermination of the Jews enabled the Nazis to bring a practised hand to similar measures against Poles, Serbs, and Greeks. The plight of the Jew was a constant threat to opposition or discontent among other elements of Europe's population - Pacifists, Conservatives, Communists, Catholics, Protestants, Socialists. It was in fact, a threat to every dissenting opinion and to every non- Nazi's life.

The persecution policy against the Jews commenced with non- violent measures, such as disfranchisement and discriminations against their religion, and the placing of impediments in the way of success in economic life. It moved rapidly to organised mass violence against them, physical isolation in ghettos, deportation, forced labour, mass starvation, and extermination. The Government, the Party formations indicted before you as criminal organisations, the Secret State Police, the Army, private and semi-public associations, and "spontaneous" mobs that were carefully inspired from official sources, were all agencies that were concerned in this persecution. Nor was it directed against individual Jews for personal bad citizenship or unpopularity. The avowed purpose was the destruction of the Jewish people as a whole, as an end in itself, as a measure of preparation for war, and as a discipline for conquered peoples.

The conspiracy or common plan to exterminate the Jew was so methodically and thoroughly pursued, that despite the German defeat and Nazi prostration this Nazi aim largely has succeeded. Only remnants of the European Jewish population remain in Germany, in the countries which Germany occupied, and in those which were her satellites or collaborators. Of the 9,600,000 Jews who lived in Nazi-dominated Europe, 6o per cent. are authoritatively estimated to have perished- 5,700,000 Jews are missing from the countries in which they formerly lived, and over 4,500,000 cannot be accounted for by the normal death rate nor by immigration; nor are they included among displaced persons. History does not record a crime ever perpetrated against so many victims or one ever carried out with such calculated cruelty.

You will have difficulty, as I have, to look into the faces of these defendants and believe that in this Twentieth Century human beings could inflict such sufferings as will be proved here, on their own countrymen as well as upon their so-called "inferior" enemies. Particular crimes, and the responsibility defendants for them, are to be dealt with by the Soviet Government's Counsel, when committed in the East, and by Counsel for the Republic of France committed in the West. I advert to them only to show their magnitude as evidence of a purpose and a knowledge common to all defendants, of an official plan rather than of a capricious policy of some individual commander, and to show such a continuity of Jewish persecution, from the rise of the Nazi conspiracy to its collapse, as forbids us to believe that any person could be identified with any part of Nazi action without approving this most conspicuous item in their programme.

The Indictment itself recites many evidences of the anti- Semitic persecutions. The defendant Streicher led the Nazis in anti-Semitic bitterness and extremism. In an article appearing in Der Sturmer on 19th March, he complained that Christian teachings have stood in the way of "racial solution of the Jewish question in Europe," and quoted enthusiastically as the Twentieth Century solution the Fuehrer's proclamation Of 24th February, 194z, that "the Jew will be exterminated." And on 4th November, 1943, Streicher declared in Der Sturmer that the Jews "have disappeared from Europe and that the Jewish 'Reservoir of the East' from which the Jewish plague has for centuries beset the people of Europe, has ceased to exist." Streicher now has the effrontery to tell us he is "only a Zionist"; he says he only wants to return the Jews to Palestine. But on 7th May, 1942, his newspaper Der Sturmer had this to say:

"It is also not only a European problem! The Jewish question is a world question! Not only is Germany not safe in the face of the Jews as long as one Jew lives in Europe, but also the Jewish question is hardly solved in Europe so long as Jews live in the rest of the world."

And the defendant Hans Frank, a lawyer by profession I say with shame, summarised in his diary in 1944 the Nazi policy thus:

"The Jews are a race which has to be eliminated; whenever we catch one, it is his end." (Document No. 2233-PS, Vol. 1944, p. 26.)

And earlier, speaking of his function as Governor-General of Poland, he confided to his diary this sentiment:

"Of course I cannot eliminate all lice and Jews in only a year's time." (2233-PS, Vol. IV, 1940, p. 1159)

I could multiply endlessly this kind of Nazi ranting, but I will leave it to the evidence and turn to the fruit of this perverted thinking.

The most serious of the actions against Jews were outside of any law, but the law itself was employed to some extent. There were the infamous Nuremberg decrees of 15th September, 1935. ("Reichsgesetzblatt," 1935, Part 1, p. 1146.) The Jews were segregated into ghettos and put into forced labour; they were expelled from their professions; their property was expropriated; all cultural life, the Press, the theatre, and schools were prohibited them; and the S.D. was made responsible for them. (212-PS, 069-PS.) This was an ominous guardianship as the following order for "The Handling of the Jewish Question" shows:-

"The competency of the Chief of the Security Police and Security Service, who is charged with the mission of solving the European Jewish question, extends even to the occupied eastern provinces. . . .

An eventual act by the civilian population against the Jews is not to be prevented as long as this is compatible with the maintenance of order and security in the rear of the fighting troops. . . .

The first main goal of the German measures must be the strict segregation of Jewry from the rest of the population. In the execution of this, first of all, is the seizing of the Jewish populace by the introduction of a registration order and similar appropriate measures..

Then immediately, the wearing of the recognition sign, consisting of a yellow Jewish star, is to be brought about and all rights of freedom for Jews are to be withdrawn. They are to be placed in ghettos, and at the same time, are to be separated according to sex. The presence of many more or less closed Jewish settlements in White Ruthenia and in the Ukraine makes this mission easier. Moreover, places are to be chosen which make possible the full use of the Jewish manpower in case labour needs are present. The entire Jewish property is to be seized and confiscated, with the exception of that which is necessary for a bare existence. As far as the economical situation permits, the power of disposal of their property is to be taken from the Jews as soon as possible through orders and other measures given by the commissariat, so that the moving of property will quickly cease."

"Any cultural activity will be completely forbidden to the Jew. This includes the outlawing of the Jewish Press, the Jewish theatres and schools.

"The slaughtering of animals according to Jewish rites is also to be prohibited." (212-PS).

The anti-Jewish campaign became furious following the assassination in Paris of the German Legation Councillor von Rath. Heydrich, Gestapo head, sent a telegram to all Gestapo and S.D. offices with directions for handling "spontaneous" uprisings anticipated for the nights of 9th and 10th November, 1938, so as to aid in destruction of Jewish-owned property and protect that of Germans. No more cynical document ever came into evidence. Then there is a report by an S.S. Brigade Leader, Dr. Stahlecher to Himmler, which recites that:-

"Similarly, native anti-Semitic forces were induced to start pogroms against Jews after capture, though this inducement proved to be very difficult.

Following out orders, the Security Police was determined to solve the Jewish question with all possible means and most decisively. But it was desirable that the Security Police should not put in an immediate appearance, at least at the beginning, since the extraordinarily harsh measures were apt to stir even German circles. It had to be shown to the world that the native population itself took the first action by way of natural reaction against the suppression by Jews during several decades and against the terror exercised by the Communists during the preceding period."

In view of the extension of the area of operations and the great number of duties which had to be performed by the Security Police, it was intended from the very beginning to obtain the co-operation of the reliable population for the fight against vermin - that is mainly the Jews and Communists. Beyond our directing of the first spontaneous actions of self-cleansing, which will be reported elsewhere, care had to be taken that reliable people should be put to the cleansing job, and that they were appointed auxiliary members of the Security Police."

Kowno. To our surprise it was not easy at first to set in motion an extensive pogrom against Jews. Klimatis, the leader of the partisan unit, mentioned above, who was used for this purpose primarily, succeeded in starting a pogrom on the basis of advice given to him by a small advanced detachment acting in Kowno, and in such a way that no German order or German instigation was noticed from the outside. During the first pogrom in the night from 25 to 26.6 the Lithuanian partisans did away with more than 1,500 Jews, set fire to several Synagogues or destroyed them by other means and burned down a Jewish dwelling district consisting of about 60 houses. During the following nights about 2,300 Jews were made harmless in a similar way. In other parts of Lithuania similar actions followed the example of Kowno, though smaller and extending to the Communists who had been left behind.

These self-cleansing actions went smoothly because the Army authorities who had been informed showed understanding for this procedure. From the beginning it was obvious that only the first days after the occupation would offer the opportunity for carrying out pogroms. After the disarmament of the partisans the self-cleansing actions ceased necessarily.

It proved much more difficult to set in motion similar cleaning actions in Latvia."

From the beginning it was to be expected that the Jewish problem in the East could not be solved by pogroms alone. In accordance with basic orders received, however, the cleansing activities of the Security Police had to aim at a complete annihilation of the Jews. . . .

"The sum total of Jews liquidated in Lithuania amounts to 71,105. . . ." (L-180)

Of course, it is self-evident that these "uprisings" were managed by the government and the Nazi Party. If we were in doubt, we could resort to Streicher's memorandum of 14th April, 1939, which says, "The anti-Jewish action of November, 1938, did not arise spontaneously from the people.. Part of the party formation has been charged with the execution of the anti-Jewish action." (406-PS) Jews as a whole were fined a billion Reichsmarks. They were excluded from all businesses, and claims against insurance companies for their burned properties were confiscated, all by the decree of the defendant Goering. (Reichsgesetzblatt, 1938, Part 1, pp. 1579-1582.)

Synagogues were the objects of a special vengeance. On 10th November, 1938, the following order was given:

"By order of the Group Commander, all Jewish Synagogues in the area of Brigade 50 have to be blown up or set afire. .The operation will be carried out in civilian clothing.... Execution of the order will be reported....(1721- PS.) Some 40 teletype messages, from police headquarters, which will be introduced to you, will tell the fury with which all Jews were pursued in Germany on those awful November nights. The S.S. troops were turned loose and the Gestapo supervised. Jewish-owned property was destroyed. The Gestapo ordered twenty to thirty thousand "well-to-do Jews" to be arrested. Concentration camps were to receive them and the order provided healthy Jews, fit for labour, were to be taken (3051-PS).

As the German frontiers were expanded by war, so the campaign against the Jews expanded. The Nazi plan never was limited to in Germany; always it contemplated extinguishing the Jew in Europe and often in the world. In the West, the Jews were killed and their property, taken over. But the campaign achieved its zenith of savagery in the East. The Eastern Jew has suffered as no people ever suffered. Their sufferings were carefully reported to the Nazi authorities to show faithful adherence to the Nazi design. I shall refer only to enough of the evidence of these to show the extent of the Nazi design for killing Jews.

If I should recite these horrors in words of my own, you would think me intemperate and unreliable. Fortunately, we need not take the word of any witness but the Germans themselves. I invite you now to look at a few of the vast number of captured German orders and reports that will be offered in evidence, to see what a Nazi invasion meant. We will present such evidence as the report of "Einsatzgruppe (Action Group) A" of 15th October, 1941, which boasts that in overrunning the Baltic States, "Native Anti-Semitic forces were induced to start pogroms against the Jews during the first hours after occupation." The report continues:-

"From the beginning it was to be expected that the Jewish problem in the East could not be solved by pogroms alone. In accordance with the basic orders received, however, the cleansing activities of the Security Police had to aim at a complete annihilation of the Jews. Special detachments reinforced by selected units - in Lithuania partisan detachments, in Latvia units of the Latvian auxiliary police - therefore performed extensive executions both in the towns and in rural areas. The actions of the execution detachments were performed smoothly."

"The sum total of the Jews liquidated in Lithuania, according to the report, amounts to 71,105. During the pogroms in Kowno 3,800 Jews were eliminated, in the smaller towns about 1,200 Jews."

"In Latvia, up to now a total of 30,000 Jews was executed. Five hundred were eliminated by pogroms in Riga." (L-180.)

This is a captured report from the Commissioner of Sluzk on 20th October, 1941, which describes the scene in more detail. It says:-

"...The first lieutenant explained that the police battalion had received the assignment to effect the liquidation of all Jews here in the town of Sluzk, within two days ... Then I requested him to postpone the action one day. However, he rejected this with the remark that he had to carry out this action everywhere and in all towns and that only two days were allotted for Sluzk. Within these two days the town of Sluzk had to be cleared of Jews by all means ... All Jews without exception were taken out of the factories and shops and deported in spite of our agreement. It is true that part of the Jews was moved by way of the ghetto, where many of them were processed and still segregated by me, but a large part was loaded directly on trucks and liquidated without further delay outside of the town.. For the rest, as regards the execution of the action, I must point out to my deepest regret that the latter bordered already on sadism. The town itself offered a picture of horror during the action. With indescribable brutality on the part of the German police officers and particularly the Lithuanian partisans, the Jewish people, but also among them White Ruthenians, were taken out of their dwellings and herded together. Everywhere in the town shots were to be heard and in different streets the corpses of shot Jews accumulated. The White Ruthenians were in greatest distress to free themselves from the encirclement. Regardless of the fact that the Jewish people, among whom were also tradesmen, were mistreated in a terribly barbarous way in the face of the White Ruthenian people, the White Ruthenians themselves were also worked over with rubber clubs and rifle butts. There was no question of an action against the Jews anymore. It rather looked like a revolution..."(1104-PS.)

There are reports which merely tabulate the numbers slaughtered. Another example is an account of the work of Einsatzgruppen of Sipo and S.D. in the East which relates that "in Estonia, all Jews were arrested immediately upon the arrival of the Wehrmacht."

Jewish men and women above the age of sixteen and capable of work were drafted for forced labour. Jews were subjected to all sorts of restrictions and all Jewish property was confiscated.

All Jewish males above the age of sixteen were executed, with the exception of doctors and elders. Only 500 of an original 4,500 Jews remained.

37,180 persons have been liquidated by the Sipo and S.D. in White Ruthenia during October.

In one town, 337 Jewish women were executed for demonstrating a "provocative attitude." In another, 380 Jews were shot for spreading vicious propaganda.

And so the report continues, listing town after town, where hundreds upon hundreds of Jews were murdered.

In Vitebsk 3,000 Jews were liquidated because of the danger of epidemics.

In Kiev, 33,771 Jews were executed On 29th/30th September in retaliation for some fires which were set off there.

In Zhitomir, 3,145 Jews "had to be shot" because, judging from experience they had to be considered as the carriers of Bolshevik propaganda.

In Kherson, 410 Jews were executed in reprisal against acts of sabotage. In the territory east of the Djnepr, the Jewish problem was "solved" by the liquidation Of 4,891 Jews and by putting the remainder into labour battalions of up to 1,000 persons. (R- 102.)

Other accounts tell not of the slaughter so much as of the depths of degradation to which the tormentors stooped. For example, we will show the report made to defendant Rosenberg about the Army and the S.S. in the area under Rosenberg's jurisdiction, which recited the following:-

" Details in the presence of S.S. man, a Jewish dentist has to break all gold teeth and fillings out of mouth of German and Russian Jews before they are executed." Men, women and children are locked into barns and burned alive.

Peasants, women and children, are shot on the pretext that they are suspected of belonging to bands. (R-135.)

We of the Western world heard of gas wagons in which Jews and political opponents were asphyxiated. We could not believe it. But here we have the report of 16th May, I942, from the German S.S. Officer Becker, to his supervisor in Berlin, which tells this story;-

"Gas vans in C group can be driven to execution spot, which is generally stationed ten to fifteen kilometres from main road, only in dry weather. Since those to be executed become frantic if conducted to this place, such vans become immobilised in wet weather.

Gas vans in D group were camouflaged as cabin trailers, but vehicles well known to authorities and civilian population which calls them 'Death Vans.'

The writer of the letter, Becker, ordered all men to keep as far away as possible during gassing. Unloading van after the gassing has 'atrocious spiritual and physical effect' on men and they should be ordered not to participate in such work." (501-PS.)

I shall not dwell on this subject longer than to quote one more sickening document which evidences the planned and systematic character of these Jewish persecutions. I hold a report written with Teutonic thoroughness as to detail, illustrated with photographs to authenticate its almost incredible text, and beautifully bound in leather with the loving care bestowed to a proud work. It is the original report of the S.S. Brigade General Stroop in charge of the destruction of the Warsaw Ghetto, and its title page carries the inscription, "The Jewish Ghetto in Warsaw no longer exists." It is characteristic that one of the captions explains that the photograph concerned shows the driving out of Jewish "bandits"; those whom the photograph shows being driven out are almost entirely women and little children. It contains a day-by-day account of the killings mainly carried out by the S.S. Organisation, too long to relate, but let me quote General Stroop's summary:

"The resistance put up by the Jews and bandits could only be suppressed by energetic actions of our troops day and night. The Reichsfuehrer S.S. ordered therefore on 23rd April, 1943, the cleaning out of the ghetto with utter ruthlessness and merciless tenacity. I, therefore, decided to destroy and burn down the entire ghetto without regard to the armament factories. These factories were systematically dismantled and then burned. Jews usually left their hideouts, but frequently remained in the burning buildings and jumped out of the windows only when the heat became unbearable. They then tried to crawl with broken bones across the street into buildings which were not afire. Sometimes they changed their hideouts during the night into the ruins of burned buildings. Life in the sewers was not pleasant after the first week. Many times we could hear loud voices in them. S.S. men or policemen climbed bravely through the manholes to capture these Jews. Sometimes they stumbled over Jewish corpses; sometimes they were shot at. Tear gas bombs were thrown into the manholes and the Jews driven out of the sewers and captured. Countless numbers of Jews were liquidated in sewers and bunkers through blasting. The longer the resistance continued the tougher became the members of the Waffen S.S., Police and Wehrmacht, who always discharged their duties in an exemplary manner. Frequently Jews who tried to replenish. their food supplies during the night or to communicate with neighbouring groups were exterminated." (1061-PS)

"This action eliminated," says the S.S. commander, "a proved total of 56,065. To that we have to add the number killed through blasting, fire, etc., which cannot be counted."

We charge that all atrocities against Jews were the manifestation and culmination of the Nazi plan to which every defendant here was a party. I know very well that some of these men did take steps to spare some particular Jew for some personal reason from the horrors that awaited the unrescued Jew. Some protested that particular atrocities were excessive, and discredited the general policy. While a few defendants may show efforts to make specific exceptions to the policy of Jewish extermination, I have found no instance in which any defendant opposed the policy itself or sought to revoke or even modify it.

Determination to destroy the Jews was a binding force which at all times cemented the elements of this conspiracy. On many internal policies there were differences among the defendants. But there is not one of them who has not echoed the rallying cry of Naziism: DEUTSCIILAND ERWACHE-JUDA VERRECKE (Germany Awake-Jewry Perish!)

I come to the discussion of terrorism and to preparation for the war.

How a Government treats its own inhabitants generally is thought to be no concern of other Governments or of international society. Certainly few oppressions or cruelties would warrant the intervention of foreign powers. But the German mistreatment of Germans is now known to pass in magnitude and savagery any limits of what is tolerated by modern civilisation. Other nations, by silence, would take a consenting part in such crimes. These Nazi persecutions, moreover, take character as international crimes because of the purpose for which they were undertaken.

The purpose, as we have seen, of getting rid of the influence of free labour, the churches and the Jews was to clear their obstruction to the precipitation of aggressive war. If aggressive warfare in violation of treaty obligation is a matter of international cognisance, the preparations for it must also be of concern to the international community. Terrorism was the chief instrument for securing the cohesion of the German people in war purposes. Moreover, these cruelties in Germany served as atrocity practice to discipline the membership of the criminal organisation to follow the pattern later in occupied countries.

Through the police formations that are before you accused as criminal organisations, the Nazi Party leaders, aided at some point in their basic and notorious purpose by each of the individual defendants, instituted a reign of terror. These espionage and police organisations were utilised to hunt down every form of opposition and to penalise every nonconformity. These organisations early founded and administered concentration camps - Buchenwald in 1933, Dachau in 1934. But these notorious names were not alone. Concentration camps came to dot the German map and to number scores. At first they met with resistance from some Germans. We have a captured letter from Minister of Justice Gurtner to Hitler which is revealing. A Gestapo official had been prosecuted for crimes committed in a camp at Hohenstein, and the Nazi Governor of Saxony had promptly asked that the proceeding be quashed. The Minister of Justice in June of 1935 protested because, as he said, "In this camp unusually grave mistreatments of prisoners has occurred at least since Summer 1939. The prisoners not only were beaten with whips, without cause, similarly as in the Concentration Camp Bredow near Stettin until they lost consciousness, but they were also tortured in other manners, e.g., with the help of a dripping apparatus constructed exclusively for this purpose, under which prisoners had to stand until they were suffering from serious purulent wounds of the scalp."

(787-PS)

I shall not take time to detail the ghastly proceedings in these concentration camps. Beatings, starvings, tortures, and killings were routine - so routine that the tormentors became blase and careless. We have a report of discovery that in Plotzensee one night, 186 persons were executed while there were orders for only 150. Another report describes how the family of one victim received two urns of ashes by mistake. Inmates were compelled to execute each other. In 1942, they were paid five Reichsmarks per execution, but on 27th June, 1942, S.S. General Glucke ordered commandants of all concentration camps to reduce this honorarium to three cigarettes. In 1943, the Reichs leader of the S.S. and Chief of German Police ordered the corporal punishment on Russian women to be applied by Polish women and vice versa, but the price was not frozen. "As a reward, a few cigarettes" was authorised. Under the Nazis, human life had been progressively devalued, until it finally became worth less than a handful of tobacco - Ersatz tobacco. There were, however, some traces of the milk of human kindness. On 11th August,1942, an order went from Himmler to the commandants of fourteen concentration camps that "only German prisoners are allowed to beat other German prisoners." (2189-PS).

Mystery and suspense was added to cruelty in order to spread torture from the inmate to his family and friends. Men and women disappeared from their homes or business or from the streets, and no word came of them. The omission of notice was not due to overworked staff; it was due to policy. The Chief of the S.D. and Sipo reported that, in accordance with orders from the Fuehrer, anxiety should be created in the minds of the family of the arrested person. (668-PS.) Deportations and secret arrests were labelled, with a Nazi wit which seems a little ghoulish, "Nacht und Nebel" (Night and Fog). (L,90, 833-PS.)

One of the many orders for these actions, gave this explanation:-

"The decree carries a basic innovation. The Fuehrer and Commander-in-Chief of the Armed Forces commands that crimes of the specified sort by civilians of the occupied territories are to be punished by the pertinent courts martial in the occupied territories only when (a) the sentence calls for the death penalty; and (b) the sentence is pronounced within eight days of arrest. Only when both conditions are met does the Fuehrer and Commander-in Chief of the Armed Forces hope for the desired deterrent effect from the conduct of punitive proceedings in the occupied territories. In other cases in the future, the accused are to be secretly brought to Germany, and the further conduct of the trial carried on here. The deterrent effect of these measures lies (a) in allowing the disappearance of the accused without a trace; (b) therein that no information whatsoever may be given about their whereabouts and their fate." (833-PS.)

To clumsy cruelty, scientific skill was added. "Undesirables" were exterminated by injection of drugs into the bloodstream, by asphyxiation in gas chambers. They were shot with poison bullets, to study the effects (L-103);

Then, to cruel experiments the Nazi added obscene ones. These were not the work of underling-degenerates, but of master-minds high in the Nazi conspiracy. On 20th May, 1942, General Field Marshal Milch authorised S.S. General Wolff to go ahead at Dachau Camp with so-called "cold experiments"; and four female gypsies were selected for the purpose. Himmler gave permission to carry on these "experiments" also in other camps (1617-PS). At Dachau, the reports of the "doctor" in charge show that victims were immersed in cold water until their body temperature was reduced to 26 degrees centigrade (8.24 degrees Fahrenheit) when they all died immediately. (1618-PS.) This was in August, 1942. But the "doctor's" technique improved. By February, 1943, he was able to report that thirty persons were chilled to 27 to 29 degrees, their hands and feet frozen white, and their bodies "rewarmed" by a hot bath. But the Nazi scientific triumph was "rewarming with animal heat." The victim, all but frozen to death, was surrounded with the bodies of living women until he revived and responded to his environment by having sexual intercourse. (1616-PS.) Here Nazi degeneracy reached its nadir.

I dislike to encumber the record with such morbid tales, but we are in the grim business of trying men as criminals, and these are the things that their own agents say happened. We will show you these concentration camps in motion pictures. just as the Allied armies found them when they arrived, and the measures General Eisenhower had to take to clean them up. Our proof will be disgusting and you will say I have robbed you of your sleep. But these are the things which have turned the stomach of the world and set every civilised hand against Nazi Germany.

Germany became one vast torture chamber. Cries of its victims were heard round the world and brought shudders to civilised people everywhere. I am one who received during this war most atrocity tales with suspicion and scepticism. But the proof here will be so overwhelming that I venture to predict not one word I have spoken will be denied. These defendants will only deny personal responsibility or knowledge.

Under the clutch of the most intricate web of espionage and intrigue that any modern State has endured, and persecution and torture of a kind that has not been visited upon the world in many centuries, the elements of the German population which were both decent and courageous were annihilated. Those which were decent but weak were intimidated. Open resistance, which had never been more than feeble and irresolute, disappeared. But resistance, I am happy to say, always remained, although it was manifest in only such events as the abortive effort to assassinate Hitler on 20th July, 1944. With resistance driven underground, the Nazi had the German State in his own hands.

But the Nazis not only silenced discordant voices. They created positive controls as effective as their negative case. Propaganda organs, on a scale never before known, stimulated the party and party formations with a permanent enthusiasm and abandon such as we, democratic people, can work up only for a few days before a general election. They inculcated and practised the Fuehrer-prinzip which centralised control of the Party and of the Party-controlled State over the lives and thought of the German people, who are accustomed to look upon the German State, by whomever controlled, with a mysticism that is incomprehensible to my people.

All these controls, from their inception were exerted with unparalleled energy and single-mindedness to put Germany on a war footing. We will show from the

Nazis' own documents their secret training of military personnel, their secret creation of a military air force. Finally, a conscript army was brought into being. Financiers, economists, industrialists, joined in the plan and promoted elaborate alterations in industry and finance to support an unprecedented concentration of resources and energies upon preparations for war. Germany's rearmament so outstripped the strength of her neighbours that in about a year she was able to crush the whole military force of Continental Europe, exclusive of that of Soviet Russia, and then to push the Russian armies back to the Volga. These preparations were of a magnitude which surpassed all need of defence, and every defendant, and every intelligent German, well understood them to be for aggressive purposes.

Before resorting to open aggressive warfare, the Nazis undertook some rather cautious experiments to test the spirit of resistance of those who lay across their path. They advanced, but only as others yielded, and kept in a position to draw back if they found a temperament that made persistence dangerous.

On 7th March, 1936, the Nazis reoccupied the Rhineland and then proceeded to fortify it in violation of the Treaty of Versailles and the Pact of Locarno. They encountered no substantial resistance and were emboldened to take the next step, which was the acquisition of Austria. Despite repeated assurances that Germany had no designs on Austria, invasion was perfected. Threat of attack forced Schuschnigg to resign as Chancellor of Austria and put the Nazi defendant Seyss- Inquart in his place. The latter immediately opened the frontier and invited Hitler to invade Austria "to preserve order". On 12th March the invasion began. The next day, Hitler proclaimed himself Chief of the Austrian State, took command of its armed forces, and a law was enacted annexing Austria to Germany.

Threats of aggression had succeeded without arousing resistance. Fears nevertheless had been stirred. They were lulled by an assurance to the Czechoslovak Government that there would be no attack on that country. We will show that the Nazi Government already had detailed plans for the attack. We will lay before you the documents in which those conspirators planned to create an incident to justify their attack. They even gave consideration to assassinating their own Ambassador at Prague in order to create a sufficiently dramatic incident. They did precipitate a diplomatic crisis which endured throughout the summer. Hitler set 30th September as the day when troops should be ready for action. Under the threat of immediate war, the United Kingdom and France concluded a pact with Germany and Italy at Munich on 29th September, 1938, which required Czechoslovakia to acquiesce in the cession of the Sudetenland to Germany. It was consummated by German occupation on 1st October, 1938.

The Munich Pact pledged no further aggression against Czechoslovakia, but the Nazi pledge was lightly given and quickly broken. On 15th March, 1939, in defiance of the Treaty of Munich itself, the Nazis seized and occupied Bohemia and Moravia, which constituted the major part of Czechoslovakia not already ceded to Germany. Once again the West stood aghast, but it dreaded war, it saw no remedy except war, and it hoped against hope that the Nazi fever for expansion had run its course. But the Nazi world was intoxicated by these unresisted successes in open alliance with

Mussolini and in covert alliance with Franco. Then, having made a deceitful, delaying peace with Russia, the conspirators entered upon the final phase of the plan to renew war.

I will not prolong this address by detailing the steps leading to the war of aggression which began with the invasion of Poland on 1st September, 1939. The further story will be unfolded to you by the British Delegation from documents including those of the German High Command itself. The plans had been laid long in advance. As early as 1935 Hitler appointed the defendant Schacht to the position of "General Deputy for the War Economy." (2261-PS) We have the diary of General Jodl (1780-PS); the "Plan Otto," Hitler's own order for attack on Austria in case trickery failed (C- 102); the "Plan Green" which was the blueprint for attack on Czechoslovakia (338-PS); the plan for the War in the West (376-PS, 375-PS); Funk's letter to Hitler dated 25th August, 1939, detailing the long course of economic preparation for war (699-PS); Keitel's top-secret mobilisation order for 1939-40 prescribing steps to be taken during a "period of tension," as it was described, during which no "'state of war' will be publicly declared even if open war measures against the enemy will be taken." This latter order (1699- PS) is in our possession despite a secret order issued on 16th March, 1945, when Allied troops were advancing into the heart of Germany, to burn these plans. We have also Hitler's directive, dated 18th December, 1940, for the "Barbarossa Contingency," which was a code name, outlining the strategy of the attack on Russia. That plan, in the original, bears the initials of the defendants Keitel and Jodl. They were planning the attack and planning it long in advance of the declaration of war. We have detailed information concerning the "Case White," the plan for attack on Poland (2327-PS). That attack began the war. The plan was issued by Keitel on 3rd April, 1939. The attack did not come until September. Steps in preparation for the attack were taken by subordinate commanders, one of whom issued an order on 14th June providing that:-

"The Commander-in-Chief of the Armies has ordered the working out of a plan of deployment against Poland which takes in account the demands of political leadership for the opening of the war by surprise and for quick successes.. I declare it the duty of the Commanding Generals, the Divisional Commanders, and the Commandants to limit as much as possible the number of persons who will be informed, and to limit the extent of the information, and ask that all suitable measures be taken to prevent persons not concerned from getting information..

The operation, in order to forestall an orderly Polish mobilisation and concentration, is to be opened by surprise with forces which are for the most part armoured and motorised, placed on alert in the neighbourhood of the border. The initial superiority over the Polish frontier-guards and surprise that can be expected with certainty are to be maintained by quickly bringing up other parts of the army as well to counteract the marching up of the Polish Army..

If the development of the political situation should show that a surprise at the beginning of the war is out of question, because of well-advanced defence preparations on the part of the Polish Army, the Commander-in-Chief of the

Army will order the opening of the hostilities only after the assembling of sufficient additional forces The basis of all preparations will be to surprise the enemy.."(2327-PS)

We also have the order for the attack on England, initialled again by Keitel and Jodl. It is interesting that it commences with a recognition that although the British military position is "hopeless," they show not the slightest sign of giving in. (442-PS)

Not the least incriminating are the minutes of Hitler's meeting with his high advisers.

As early as 5th November, 1937, Hitler told defendants Goering, Raeder, and Neurath, among others, that German rearmament was practically accomplished and that he had decided to secure by force, starting with a lightening attack on Czechoslovakia and Austria, greater living space for Germans in Europe no later that 1943-5 and perhaps as early as 1938. (368-PS) On the 23rd May, 1939, the Fuehrer advised his staff that:

"It is a question of expanding our living space in the East and of securing our food supplies over and above the natural fertility, thoroughgoing German exploitation will enormously increase the surplus.

There is therefore no question of sparing Poland, and we are left with the decision:

To attack Poland at the first suitable opportunity.

We cannot expect a repetition of the Czech affair. There will be war." (L-79)

On 22nd August, 1939, Hitler again addressed members of the High Command, telling them when the start of military operations would be ordered. He disclosed that for propaganda purposes, he would provocate a good reason. "It will make no difference," he announced, "whether this reason will sound convincing or not. After all, the victor will not be asked whether he talked the truth or not. We have to proceed brutally. The stronger is always right." (1014-PS) On 23rd November, 1939, after the Germans had invaded Poland, Hitler made this explanation: "For the first time in history we have to fight on only one front. The other front is at present free, but no one can know how long that will remain so. I have doubted for a long time whether I would strike in the East and then in the West. Basically, I did not organise the armed forces in order not to strike. The decision to strike was always in me. Earlier or later I wanted to solve the problem. Under pressure it was decided that the East was to be attacked first." (789-PS)

We know the bloody sequel. Frontier incidents were staged. Demands were made for cession of territory. When Poland refused, the German forces invaded on 1st September, 1939. Warsaw was destroyed; Poland fell. The Nazis, in accordance with plans, moved swiftly to extend their aggression throughout Europe and to gain the advantage of surprise over their unprepared neighbours, Despite repeated and solemn assurances of peaceful intentions, they invaded Denmark and Norway on 9th April, 1940; Belgium, the Netherlands and Luxembourg on 10th May, 1940, Yugoslavia and Greece on 6th April 1941.

As part of the Nazi preparation for aggression against Poland and her allies,

Germany, on 23rd April, 1939 had entered into a non-aggression pact with Soviet Russia. It uses only a delaying treaty intended to be kept no longer than necessary to prepare for its violation. On 22nd June, 1941, pursuant to long matured plans, the Nazis hurled troops into Soviet territory without any declaration of war. The entire European world was aflame.

The Nazi plans of aggression called for use of Asiatic allies, and they found among the Japanese men of kindred mind and purpose. They were brothers, under the skin.

Himmler records a conversation that he had on 31st January, 1939, with General Oshima, Japanese Ambassador at Berlin. He wrote

Furthermore, he (Oshima) had succeeded up to now in sending 10 Russians with bombs across the Caucasian frontier. These Russians had the mission to kill Stalin. A number of additional Russians, whom he had also sent across, had been shot at the frontier." (2195-PS.)

On 27th September, 1940, the Nazis concluded a German- Italian-Japanese ten-year military and economic alliance by which those powers agreed "to stand by and co-operate with one another in regard to their efforts in Greater East Asia and regions of Europe respectively, wherein it is their prime purpose to establish and maintain a new order of things."

On 5th March, 1941, a top secret directive was issued by defendant Keitel. It stated that "The Fuehrer had ordered instigation of Japan's active participation in the war" and directed that "Japan's military power has to be strengthened by the disclosure of German war experiences and support of a military, economic and technical nature has to be given." The aim was stated to be to crush England quickly, thereby keeping the United States out of the war. (C-75)

On 29th March, 1941, Ribbentrop told Matsuoka, the Japanese Foreign Minister, that the German Army was ready to strike against Russia. Matsuoka in turn reassured Ribbentrop about the Far East. Japan, he reported, was acting at the moment as though she had no interest whatever in Singapore, but "intends to strike when the right moment comes." (1877-PS) On April, 1941, Ribbentrop urged Matsuoka that entry of Japan into the war would "hasten the victory" and would be more in the interest of Japan than of Germany, since it would Japan a unique chance to fulfil her national aims and to play a leading part in Eastern Asia. (1882-PS.)

The proofs in this case will also show that the leaders of Germany were planning war against the United States from its Atlantic as well as instigating it from its Pacific approaches. A captured memorandum from the Fuehrer's headquarters, dated 29th October, 1940, asks certain information as to air bases and reports further that:-

The Fuehrer is at present occupied with the question of the occupation of the Atlantic islands with a view to the prosecution of war against America at a later date. Deliberations on this subject are being embarked upon here." (376-PS.)

On 7th December, 1941, a day which the late President Roosevelt declared "will live in infamy," victory for German aggression seemed certain. The Wehrmacht was at the gates of Moscow. Taking advantage of the situation, and while her plenipotentiaries were creating a diplomatic diversion in Washington, Japan without declaration of war treacherously attacked the United States at Pearl Harbour and the Philippines. Attacks followed swiftly on the British Commonwealth and The Netherlands in the South-west Pacific. These aggressions met in the only way that they could be met, with instant declarations of war and with armed resistance which mounted slowly through many long months of reverse until finally the Axis was crushed to earth and deliverance for its victims was won.

Your Honour, I am about to take up "Crimes in the Conduct of War," which is quite a separate subject. We are within five minutes of the recessing time. It will be very convenient for me it if will be agreeable to you.

THE PRESIDENT: We will sit again in 15 minutes' time.

(A recess was taken.)

THE PRESIDENT: The Tribunal must request that if it adjourns for I5 minutes, that members of the bar and others are back in their seats after an interval of 15 minutes. Mr. Justice Jackson, I understand that you wish to continue to 5.15, when you may be able to conclude your speech?

MR. JUSTICE JACKSON: I think that would be the most orderly way.

THE PRESIDENT: Yes, the Tribunal will be glad to do so.

MR. JUSTICE JACKSON: May it please your Honour, I will now take up the subject of "Crimes in the Conduct of War."

4. CRIMES IN THE CONDUCT OF WAR

Even the most warlike of peoples have recognised in the name of humanity some limitations on the savagery of warfare. Rules to that end have been embodied in international conventions to which Germany became a party. This code had prescribed certain restraints as to the treatment of belligerents. The enemy was entitled to surrender and to receive quarter and good treatment as a prisoner of war. We will show by German documents that these rights were denied, that prisoners of war were given brutal treatment and often murdered. This was particularly true in the case of captured airmen, often my countrymen.

It was ordered that captured English and American airmen should no longer be granted the status of prisoners of war. They were to be treated as criminals and the Army was ordered to refrain from protecting them against lynching by the populace (R-118). The Nazi Government, through its police and propaganda agencies, took pains to incite the civilian population to attack and kill airmen who crash- landed. The order, given by the Reichsfuehrer S.S., Himmler, on 10th August, 1943, directed that:

"It is not the task of the police to interfere in clashes between German and English and American fliers who have bailed out."

This order was transmitted on the same day by S.S. Obersturmbannfuehrer Brandof, Himmler's Personal Staff to all Senior Executive S.S. and Police Officers, with these directions:

"I am sending you the enclosed order with the request that the Chief of the Regular Police and of the Security Police be informed. They are to make this instruction known to their subordinate officers verbally." (R-110)

Similarly, we will show Hitler's top secret order, dated 18th October, 1942, that Commandos, regardless of condition, were "to be slaughtered to the last man" after capture. (498- PS) We will show the circulation of secret orders, one of which was signed by Hess, to be passed orally to civilians, that enemy fliers or parachutists were to be arrested or liquidated. (062-PS). By such means were murders incited and directed.

This Nazi campaign of ruthless treatment of enemy forces assumed its greatest proportions in the fight against Russia. Eventually all prisoners of war were taken out of control of the Army and put in the hands of Himmler and the S.S. (058-PS.) In the East, the German fury spent itself. Russian prisoners of war were ordered to be branded. They were starved. I shall quote passages from a letter written 28th February, 1942, by defendant Rosenberg to defendant Keitel:

"The fate of the Soviet prisoners of war in Germany is, on the contrary, a tragedy of the greatest extent. Of 3,600,000 prisoners of war, only several hundred thousand are still able to work fully. A large part of them has starved, or died, because of the hazards of the weather. Thousands also died from spotted fever.

The camp commanders have forbidden the civilian population to put food at the disposal of the prisoners, and they have rather let them starve to death.

In many cases, when prisoners of war could no longer keep up on the march because of hunger and exhaustion, they were shot before the eyes of the horrified population, and the corpses were left.

In numerous camps, no shelter for the prisoners of war was provided at all.

They lay under the open sky during rain or snow. Even tools were not made available to dig holes or caves.

Finally, the shooting of prisoners of war must be mentioned; for instance, in various camps, all the 'Asiatics' were shot." (081-PS.)

Civilised usage and conventions, to which Germany was a party, had prescribed certain immunities for civilian populations unfortunate enough to dwell in lands overrun by hostile armies. The German occupation forces, controlled or commanded by men on trial before you, committed a long series of outrages against the inhabitants of occupied territory that would be incredible except for captured orders and captured reports which show the fidelity with which those orders were executed.

We deal here with a phase of common criminality designed by the conspirators as part of the Common Plan. We can appreciate why these crimes against their European enemies were not of a casual character but were planned and disciplined crimes when we get at the reason for them. Hitler told his officers on 22nd August, 1939, that "The main objective in Poland is the destruction of the enemy and not the reaching of a certain geographical line." (1014-PS.) Those words were quoted. The project of deporting promising youth from occupied territories was approved by Rosenberg on the theory that "a desired weakening of the biological force of the conquered people is being achieved." (03I-PS) To Germanise or to destroy was the programme. Himmler announced, "Either we win over any good blood that we can use for ourselves and give it a place in our people, or, gentlemen - you may call this cruel, but nature is cruel - we destroy this blood." As to "racially good types" Himmler further advised, "Therefore, I think that it is our duty to take their children with us, to remove them from their environment, if necessary, by robbing or stealing them." (L- 90.) He urged deportation of Slavic children to deprive potential enemies of future soldiers.

The Nazi purpose was to leave Germany's neighbours so weakened that even if she should eventually lose the war, she would still be the most powerful nation in Europe. Against this background, we must view the plan for ruthless warfare, which means a plan for the commission of War Crimes and Crimes against Humanity.

Hostages in large numbers were demanded and killed. Mass punishments were inflicted, so savage that whole communities were extinguished. Rosenberg was advised of the annihilation of three unidentified villages in Slovakia. In May of 1943, another village of about 40 farms and 220 inhabitants was ordered to be wiped out. The entire population was ordered to be shot, the cattle and property impounded, and the order required that "the village will be destroyed totally by fire." A secret report from Rosenberg's Reich Ministry of Eastern territory, where he was responsible reveals that:

"Food rations allowed to the Russian population are so low that they fail to secure their existence and provide only for minimum subsistence of limited duration. The population does not know if they will still live. They are faced with death by starvation.

The roads are clogged by hundreds of thousands of people, sometimes as many as one million according to the estimate of experts, who wander around in search of nourishment.

Sauckel's action has caused great unrest among the civilians. Russian girls were deloused by men, nude photos in forced positions were taken, women doctors were locked into freight cars for the pleasure of the transport commanders, women in night shirts were fettered and forced through the Russian towns to the railroad station, etc. All this material has been sent to the OKH."

Perhaps the deportation to slave-labour was the most horrible and extensive slaving operation in history. On few other subjects is our evidence so abundant and so damaging. In a speech made on 25th January, 1944, the defendant Frank, Governor-General of Poland, boasted: "I have sent 1,200,000 Polish workers into the Reich." The defendant Sauckel reported that "out of the five million foreign workers who arrived in Germany, not even 200,000 came voluntarily." This fact was reported to the Fuehrer and to the defendants Speer, Goering, and Keitel. (R-124) Children of 10 to 14 years were impressed into service by telegraphic order of Rosenberg's Ministry for the Occupied Eastern Territories:

"The Command is further charged with the transferring of worthwhile Russian youth between 10-14 years of age, to the Reich. The authority is not affected by the changes connected with the evacuation and transportation to the reception camps of Bialystok, Krajewo, and Olitei, The Fuehrer wishes that this activity be increased even more. (200-PS.)

When enough labour was not forthcoming, prisoners of war were forced into war work in flagrant violation of international conventions. (016-PS.) Slave labour came from France, Belgium, Holland, Italy, and the East. Methods of recruitment were violent. (R-124, 018-PS, 204-PS,) The treatment of these slave labourers was stated in general terms, not difficult to translate into concrete deprivations, in a letter to the defendant Rosenberg from the defendant Sauckel, which stated:

"All prisoners of war, from the territories of the West as well as of the East, actually in Germany, must be completely incorporated into the German armament and munition industries. Their production must be brought to the highest possible level."

The complete employment of prisoners of war as well as the use of a gigantic number of new civilian workers, men and women, has become an undisputable necessity for the solution of the mobilisation of labour programme in this war.

All the men must be fed, sheltered and treated in such a way as to exploit them to the highest possible extent at the lowest conceivable degrees of expenditure.."(016-PS.)

In pursuance of the Nazi plan permanently to reduce the living standards of their neighbours and to weaken them physically and economically, a long series of crimes were committed. There was extensive destruction, serving no military purpose, of the property of civilians. Dikes were thrown open in Holland almost at the close of the war, not to achieve military ends but to destroy the resources, and retard the economy, of the thrifty Netherlanders.

There was carefully planned economic siphoning off of the assets of occupied countries. An example of the planning is shown by a report on France dated 7th December, 1942, made by the Economic Research Department of the Reichsbank. The question arose whether French occupation costs should be increased from 15 million Reichsmarks per day to 25 million Reichsmarks per day. The Reichsbank analysed French economy to determine whether it could bear the burden. It pointed out that the armistice had burdened France to that date to the extent of 18 1/4 billion Reichsmarks, equalling 370 billion Francs. It pointed out that the burden of these payments within two and a half years equalled the aggregate French national income in the year 1940, and that the amount of payments handed over to Germany in the first six months of 1942 corresponded to the estimate for the total French revenue for that whole year. The report concluded, "In any case, the conclusion is inescapable that relatively heavier tributes have been imposed on France since the armistice in June, 1940, than upon Germany after the First World War. In this connection, it must be noted that the economic powers of France never equalled those of the German Reich, and that the vanquished France could not draw on foreign economic and financial resources in the same degree as Germany after the First World War."

The defendant Funk was the Reich Minister of Economics and President of the Reichsbank; the defendant Ribbentrop was Foreign Minister; the defendant Goering was Plenipotentiary of the Four-Year Plan; all of them participated in the exchange of views of which this captured document is a part (2149-PS) Notwithstanding this analysis by the Reichsbank, they proceeded to increase the imposition on France from 15 million Reichsmarks to daily to 25 million per day.

It is small wonder that the bottom had been knocked out of French economy. The plan and purpose of the thing appears in a letter from General Stupnagel, head of the German Armistice Commission, to the defendant Jodl as early as 14th September, 1940, when he wrote: "The slogan 'Systematic weakening of France' has already been surpassed by far in reality."

Not only was there a purpose to debilitate and demoralise the economy of Germany's neighbours for the purpose of destroying their competitive position, but there was looting and pilfering on an unprecedented scale. We need not be hypocritical about this business Of looting. I recognise that no army moves through occupied territory without some pilfering as it goes. Usually the amount of pilfering increases as discipline wanes. If the evidence in this case showed no looting except of that sort, I certainly would ask no conviction of these defendants for it.

But we will show you that looting was not due to the lack of discipline or to the ordinary weaknesses of human nature. The German organised plundering, planned it, disciplined it, and made it official just as he organised everything else, and then he compiled the most meticulous records to show that he had done the best job of looting that was possible under the circumstances. And we have those records.

The defendant Rosenberg was put in charge of a systematic plundering of the objet d'art of Europe by direct order of Hitler dated 29th January 1940. (136-PS) On the 16th April, 1943, Rosenberg reported that up to the 7th April, ninety- two railway cars with 2,775 cases containing objets d'art had been sent to Germany; and that fifty-three pieces of art had been shipped to Hitler direct and 594 to the defendant Goering. (015-PS) The report mentioned something like 20,000 pieces of seized art and the main locations where they were stored.

Moreover, this looting was glorified by Rosenberg. Here we have thirty-nine leather-bound tabulated volumes of his inventory, which in due time we will offer in evidence. One cannot but admire the artistry of this Rosenberg report. The Nazi taste was cosmopolitan. Of the 9,455 articles inventories, there were included 5,255 paintings, 297 sculptures, 1,372 pieces of antique furniture, 307 textiles, and 2,224 small objects of art. Rosenberg observed that there were approximately 10,000 more objects still to be inventoried. (015-PS.) Rosenberg himself estimated that the values involved would come close to a billion dollars. (090- PS.)

I shall not go into further details of the War Crimes and Crimes against Humanity committed by the Nazi gangster ring whose leaders are before you. It is not the purpose in my part of this case to deal with the individual crimes. I am dealing with the Common Plan or design for crime and will not dwell on individual offences. My task is to show the scale on which those crimes occurred, and to show that these are the men who were in the responsible positions and who conceived the plan and design which renders them answerable, regardless of the fact that the plan was actually executed by others.

At length, this reckless and lawless course outraged the world. It recovered from the demoralisation of surprise attack, assembled its forces and stopped these men in their tracks. Once success deserted their banners, one by one the Nazi satellites fell away. Sawdust Caesar collapsed. Resistance forces in every occupied country arose to harry the invader. Even at home, Germans saw that Germany was being led to ruin by those mad men, and the attempt on 20th July, 1944, to assassinate Hitler, an attempt fostered by men of highest station, was a desperate effort by internal forces in Germany to stop short of ruin. Quarrels broke out among the failing conspirators, and the decline of the Nazi power was more swift than its ascendancy. German armed forces surrendered, its government disintegrated, its leaders committed suicide by the dozen, and by the fortunes of war these defendants fell into our hands. Although they are not, by any means, all the guilty ones, they are survivors among the most responsible. Their names appear over and over again in the documents and their faces grace the photographic evidence. We have here the surviving top politicians, militarists, financiers, diplomats, administrators, and propagandists, of the Nazi movement. Who was responsible for these crimes if they were not?

The end of the war and capture of these prisoners presented the victorious Allies with the question whether there is any legal responsibility on high-ranking men for acts which I have described. Must such wrongs either be ignored or redressed in hot blood? Is there no standard in the law for a deliberate and reasoned judgement on such conduct?

The Charter of this Tribunal evidences a faith that the law is not only to govern the conduct of little men, but that even rulers are, as Lord Chief Justice Coke it to King James, "under God and the law." The United States believed that the law has long afforded standards by which a juridical hearing could be conducted to make sure that we punish only the right men and for the right reasons. Following the instructions of the late President Roosevelt and the decision of the Yalta Conference, President Truman directed representatives of the United States to formulate a proposed International Agreement, which was submitted during the San Francisco Conference to the Foreign Ministers of the United Kingdom, the Soviet Union, and the Provisional Government of France. With many modifications, that proposal has become the Charter of this Tribunal.

But the Agreement which sets up the standards by which these prisoners are to be judged does not express the views of the signatory nations alone. Other nations with diverse but highly respected systems of jurisprudence also have signified adherence to it. These are Belgium, The Netherlands, Denmark, Norway, Czechoslovakia, Luxembourg, Poland, Greece, Yugoslavia, Ethiopia, Australia, Haiti, Honduras, Panama, New Zealand, Venezuela and India. You judge, therefore, under an organic act which represents the wisdom, the sense of justice, and the will of twenty-one governments, representing an overwhelming majority of all civilised people.

The Charter by which this Tribunal has its being, embodies certain legal concepts which are inseparable from its jurisdiction and which must govern its decision. These, as I have said, also are conditions attached to the grant of any hearing to defendants. The validity of the provisions of the Charter is conclusive upon us all, whether we have accepted the duty of judging or of prosecuting under it, as well as upon the defendants, who can point to no other law which gives them a right to be heard at all. My able and experienced colleagues believe, as do I, that it will contribute to the expedition and clarity of this trial if I expound briefly the application of the legal philosophy of the Charter to the facts I have recited.

While this declaration of the law by the Charter is final, it may be contended that the prisoners on trial are entitled to have it applied to their conduct only most charitably if at all. It may be said that this is new law, not authoritatively declared at the time they did the acts it condemns, and that this declaration of the law has taken them by surprise.

I cannot, of course, deny that these men are surprised that this is the law; they really are surprised that there is any such thing as law. These defendants did not rely on any law at all. Their programme ignored and defied all law. That this is so will appear from many acts and statements, of which I cite but a few. In the Fuehrer's speech to all military commanders on 23rd November, 1939, he reminded them that at the moment Germany had a pact with Russia, but declared "Agreements are to be kept only as long as they serve a certain purpose." Later in the same speech he announced "A violation of the neutrality of Holland and Belgium will be of no importance." (789-PS.) A Top Secret document, entitled " Warfare as a Problem of Organisation," dispatched by the Chief of the High Command to all Commanders on 19th April, 1938, declared that "the normal rules of war toward neutrals must be considered to apply on the basis whether operation of these rules will create greater advantages or disadvantages for the belligerents. (L- 211.) And from the files of the German Navy Staff, we have a "Memorandum on Intensified Naval War," dated 15th October, 1939, which begins by stating a desire to comply with International Law. "However," it continues, "if decisive successes are expected from any measure considered as a war necessity, it must be carried through even if it is not in agreement with International Law." (L-184) International Law, Natural Law, German Law, any law at all was to these men simply a propaganda device to be invoked when it helped and to be ignored when it would condemn what they wanted to do. That men may be protected in relying upon the law at the time they act is the reason we find laws of retrospective operation unjust. But these men cannot bring themselves within the reason of the rule which in some systems of jurisprudence prohibits ex post facto laws. They cannot show that they ever relied upon International Law in any state or paid it the slightest regard.

The Third Count of the Indictment is based on the definition of War Crimes contained in the Charter. I have outlined to you the systematic course of conduct toward civilian populations and combat forces which violates international conventions to which Germany was a party. Of the criminal nature of these acts at least, the defendants had, as we shall show, knowledge. Accordingly, they took pains to conceal their violations. It will appear that the defendants Keitel and Jodl were informed by official legal advisers that the orders to brand Russian prisoners of war, to shackle British prisoners of war, and to execute Commando prisoners were clear violations of International Law. Nevertheless, these orders were put into effect. The same is true of orders issued for the assassination of General Giraud and General Weygand, which failed to be executed only because of a ruse on the part of Admiral Canaris, who was himself later executed for his part in the plot to take Hitler's life on 20th July, 1944.

The Fourth Count of the Indictment is based on Crimes against Humanity. Chief among these are mass killings of countless human beings in cold blood. Does it take these men by surprise that murder is treated as a crime ?

The First and Second Counts of the Indictment add to these crimes the crime of plotting and waging wars of aggression and wars in violation of nine treaties to which Germany was a party. There was a time, in fact, I think, the time of the first World War, when it could not have been said that war inciting or war making was a crime in law, however reprehensible in morals.

Of course, it was, under the law of all civilised peoples, a crime for one man with his bare knuckles to assault another. How did it come about that multiplying this crime by a million, and adding fire-arms to bare knuckles, made it a legally innocent act ? The doctrine was that one could not be regarded as criminal for committing the usual violent acts in the conduct of legitimate warfare. The age of imperialistic expansion during the eighteenth and nineteenth centuries added the foul doctrine, contrary to the teachings of early Christian and International Law scholars such as Grotius, that all wars are to be regarded as legitimate wars. The sum of these two doctrines was to give war-making a complete immunity from accountability to law.

This was intolerable for an age that called itself civilised. Plain people, with their earthy common sense, revolted at such fictions and legalisms so contrary to ethical principles and demanded checks on war immunities. Statesmen and international lawyers at first cautiously responded by adopting rules of warfare designed to make the conduct of war more civilised. The effort was to set legal limits to the violence that could be done to civilian populations and to combatants as well.

The common sense of men after the First World War demanded, however, that the law's condemnation of war reach deeper, and that the law condemn not merely uncivilised ways of waging war, but also the waging in any way of uncivilised wars - wars of aggression. The world's statesmen again, went only as far as they were forced to go. Their efforts were timid and cautious and often less explicit than we might have hoped. But the 1920's did outlaw aggressive war.

The re-establishment of the principle that there are unjust wars and that unjust wars are illegal is traceable in many steps. One of the most significant is the Briand-Kellogg Pact of 1928, by which Germany, Italy and Japan, in common with practically all nations of the world, renounced war as an instrument national policy, bound themselves to seek the settlement of disputes only by pacific means, and condemned recourse to war for the solution of international controversies. This pact altered the legal status of a war of aggression. As Mr. Stimson, the United States Secretary of State put it in 1932, such a war "is no longer to be the source and subject of rights. It is no longer to be the principle around which the duties, the conduct, and the rights of nations revolve. It is an illegal thing.. By that very act, we have made obsolete many legal precedents and have given the legal profession the task of re-examining many of its codes and treaties."

The Geneva Protocol of 1924 for the Pacific Settlement of International Disputes, signed by the representatives of forty-eight governments, declared that "a war of aggression constitutes . an international crime." The Eighth Assembly of the League of Nations in 1927, on unanimous resolution of the representatives forty-eight member nations, including Germany, declared that a war of aggression constitutes an international crime. At the Sixth Pan-American Conference of 1928, the twenty-one American Republics unanimously adopted a resolution stating that "war of aggression constitutes an international crime against the human species."

A failure of these Nazis to heed, or to understand the force and meaning of this evolution in the legal thought of the world, is not a defence or a mitigation. If anything, it aggravates their offence and makes it the more mandatory that the law they have flouted be vindicated by juridical application to their lawless conduct. Indeed, by their own law - had they heeded any law - these principle were binding on these defendants. Article 4 of the Weimar Constitution provided that " The generally accepted rules of International Law are to be considered as binding integral parts of the law of the German Reich." (2050-PS.) Can there be any that the outlawry of aggressive war was one of the "generally accepted rules of International Law" in 1939?

Any resort to war - to any kind of a war - is a resort to means that are inherently criminal. War inevitably is a course of killings, assaults, deprivations of liberty, and destruction of property. An honestly defensive war is, of course, legal and saves those lawfully conducting it from criminality. But inherently criminal acts cannot be defended by showing that those who committed them were engaged of in a war, when war itself is illegal. The very minimum legal consequence of the treaties making aggressive wars illegal is to strip those who incite or wage them of every defence the law ever gave, and to leave war-makers subject to judgement by the usually accepted principles of the law of crimes.

But if it be thought that the Charter, whose declarations concededly bind us all, does contain new Law I still do not shrink from demanding its strict application by this Tribunal. The rule of law in the world, flouted by the lawlessness incited by these defendants, had to be restored at the cost to my country of over a million casualties, not to mention those of other nations. I cannot subscribe to the perverted reasoning that society may advance and strengthen the rule of law by the expenditure of morally innocent lives, but that progress in the law may never be made at the price of morally guilty lives.

It is true, of course, that we have no judicial precedent for the Charter. But International Law is more than a scholarly collection of abstract and immutable principles. It is an outgrowth of treaties and agreements between nations and of accepted customs. Yet every custom has its origin in some single act, and every agreement has to be initiated by the action of some State. Unless we are prepared to abandon every principle of growth for International Law, we cannot deny that our own day has the right to institute customs and to conclude agreements that will themselves become sources of a newer and strengthened International Law. International Law is not capable of development by the normal processes of legislation, for there is no continuing international legislative authority. Innovations and revisions in International Law are brought about by the action of governments such as those I have cited, designed to meet a change in circumstances, It grows, as did the Common Law, through decisions reached from time to time in adapting settled principles new situations. The fact is that when the law evolves by the case method, as did the Common Law and as International Law must do if they are to advance at all, it advances at the expense of those who wrongly guessed the law and learned too late their error. The law, as far as International Law can be decreed, had been clearly pronounced when these acts took place. Hence we are not disturbed by the lack of judicial precedent for the inquiry it is proposed to conduct.

The events I have earlier recited clearly fall within the standards of crimes, set out in the Charter, whose perpetrators this Tribunal is convened to judge and to punish fittingly. The standards for War Crimes and Crimes against Humanity are too familiar to need comment. There are, however, certain novel problems in applying other precepts of the Charter which I should call to your attention.

A basic provision of the Charter is that to plan, prepare, initiate, or wage a war of aggression, or a war in violation of international treaties, agreements, and assurances, or to conspire or participate in a common plan to do so, is a crime.

It is perhaps a weakness in this Charter that it fails itself to define a war of aggression. Abstractly, the subject is full of difficult and all kinds of troublesome hypothetical cases can be conjured up. It is a subject which, if the defence should be permitted to go afield beyond the very narrow charge ion the Indictment, would prolong the trial and involve the Tribunal in insoluble political issues. But so far as the question can property be involved in this case, the issue is one of no novelty and is one on which legal opinion has well crystallised.

One of the most authoritative sources of International Law on this subject is the Convention for the Definition of Aggression signed at London on 3rd July, 1933, by Roumania, Estonia, Latvia, Poland, Turkey, the Soviet Union, Persia and Afghanistan. The subject has also been considered by international committees and by commentators whose views are entitled to the greatest respect. It had been little discussed prior to the First World War but has received much attention as International Law has evolved its outlawry of aggressive war. In the light of these materials of International Law, and so far as relevant to the evidence in this case, I suggest that an "aggressor " is generally held to be that state which is the first to commit any of the following actions:

(1) Declaration of war upon another State;
(2) Invasion by its armed forces, with or without a declaration of war, of the territory of another State;
(3) Attack by its land, naval, or air forces, with or without a declaration of war, on the territory, vessels or aircraft of another State; and
(4) Provision of support to armed bands formed in the territory of another State, or refusal, notwithstanding the request of the invaded State, to take in its own territory, all the measures in its power to deprive those bands of all assistance or protection.

And I further suggest that it is the general view that no political, military, economic or other considerations shall serve as an excuse or justification for such actions but exercise of the right of legitimate self-defence - that is to say, resistance to an act of aggression, or action to assist a State which has been subjected to aggression, shall not constitute a war of aggression.

It is upon such an understanding of the law that our evidence of a conspiracy to provoke and wage an aggressive war is prepared and presented. By this test each of the series of wars begun by these Nazi leaders was unambiguously aggressive.

It is important to the duration and scope of this trial that we bear in mind the difference between our charge that this war was one of aggression and a position that Germany had no grievances. We are not inquiring into the conditions which contributed to causing this war. They are for history to unravel. It is no part of our task to vindicate the European status quo as of 1933, or as of any other date. The United States does not desire to enter into discussion of the complicated pre-war currents of European politics, and it hopes this trial will not be protracted by their consideration. The remote causations avowed are too insincere and inconsistent, too complicated and doctrinaire to be the subject of profitable inquiry in this trial. A familiar example is to be found in the "Lebensraum" slogan, which summarised the contention that Germany needed more living space as a justification for expansion. At the same time that the Nazis were demanding more space for the German people, they were demanding more German people to occupy space. Every known means to increase the birth rate, legitimate and illegitimate, was utilised. "Lebensraum" represented a vicious circle of demand-from neighbours more space, and from Germans more progeny. We need not investigate the verity of doctrines which led to constantly expanding circles of aggression. It is the plot and the act of aggression which we charge to be crimes.

Our position is that whatever grievances a nation may have, however objectionable it finds the status quo, aggressive warfare is not a legal means for settling those grievances or for altering those conditions. It may be that the Germany of the 1920's and 1930's faced desperate problems, problems that would have warranted the boldest measures short of war. All other methods - persuasion, propaganda, economic competition, diplomacy-were open to an aggrieved country, but aggressive warfare was outlawed. These defendants did make aggressive war, a war in violation of treaties. They did attack and invade their neighbours in order to effectuate a foreign policy which they knew could not be accomplished by measures short of war. And that is as far as we accuse or propose to inquire.

The Charter also recognises individual responsibility on the part of those who commit acts defined as crimes, or who incite others to do so, or who join a common plan with other persons, groups or organisations to bring about their commission.

The principle of individual responsibility for piracy and brigandage, which have long been recognised as crimes punishable under International Law, is old and well established. That is what illegal warfare is. This principle of personal liability is a necessary as well as a logical one if International Law is to render real help to the maintenance of peace. An International Law which operates only on States can be enforced only by war because the most practicable method of coercing a State is warfare. Those familiar with American history know that one of the compelling reasons for adoption of our Constitution was that the laws of the Confederation, which operated only on constituent States, were found in-effective to maintain order among them. The only answer to recalcitrance was impotence or war. Only sanctions which reach individuals can peacefully and effectively be enforced. Hence, the principle of the criminality of aggressive is implemented by the Charter with the principle of personal responsibility.

Of course, the idea that a State, any more than a corporation, commits crimes, is a fiction. Crimes always are committed only by persons. While it is quite proper to employ the fiction of responsibility of a State or corporation for the purpose of imposing a collective liability, it is quite intolerable to let such a legalism become the basis of personal immunity.

The Charter recognises that one who has committed criminal acts may not take refuge in superior orders nor in the doctrine that his crimes were acts of States. These twin principles, working together, have heretofore resulted in immunity for practically everyone concerned in the really great crimes against peace and mankind. Those in lower ranks were protected against liability by the orders of their superiors. The superiors were protected because their orders were called acts of State. Under the Charter, no defence based on either of these doctrines can be entertained. Modern civilisation puts unlimited weapons of destruction in the hands of men. It cannot tolerate so vast an area of legal irresponsibility.

Even the German Military Code provides that:-

"If the execution of a military order in the course of duty violates the criminal law, then the superior officer giving the order will bear the sole responsibility therefor. However, the obeying subordinate will share the punishment of the participant: (1) if he has exceeded the order given to him, or (2) if it was within his knowledge that the order of his superior officer concerned an act by which it was intended to commit a civil or military crime or transgression." (Reichsgesetzblatt, 1926, No. 37, P. 278, Art. 47)

Of course, we do not argue that the circumstances under which one commits an act should be disregarded in judging its legal effect. A conscripted private on a firing squad cannot expect to hold an inquest on the validity of the execution. The Charter implies common sense limits to liability, just as it places common sense limits upon immunity. But none of these men before you acted in minor parts. Each of them was entrusted with broad discretion and exercised great power. Their responsibility is correspondingly great and may not be shifted to that fictional being, "the State," which cannot be produced for trial, cannot testify, and cannot be sentenced.

The Charter also recognises a vicarious liability, which responsibility is recognised by most modern systems of law, for acts committed by others in carrying out a common plan or conspiracy to which the defendant has become a party. I need not discuss the familiar principles of such liability. Every day in the courts of countries associated in this prosecution, men are convicted for acts that they did not personally commit, but for which they were held responsible of membership in illegal combinations or plans or conspiracies.

Accused before this Tribunal as criminal organisations, are certain political police organisations which the evidence will show to have been instruments of cohesion in planning and executing the crimes I have detailed. Perhaps the worst of the movement were the Leadership Corps of the N.S.D.A.P., the Schutz-stappeln or "S.S.," and the Sturmabteilung or "S.A.," and the subsidiary formations which these include. These were the Nazi Party leadership, espionage, and policing groups. They were the real government, above and outside of any law. Also accused as organisations are the Reich Cabinet and the Secret Police, or Gestapo, which were fixtures of the Government but animated solely by the Party.

Except for a late period when some compulsory recruiting was done in the S.S. membership in all these militarised organisations was voluntary. The police organisations were recruited from ardent partisans who enlisted blindly to do the dirty work the leaders planned. The Reich Cabinet was the governmental facade for Nazi Party Government and in its members legal as well as actual responsibility was vested for the programme. Collectively they were responsible for the programme in general, individually they were especially reponsible for segments of it. The finding which we will ask you to make, that these are criminal organisations, will subject members to punishment to be hereafter determined by appropriate tribunals, unless some personal defence - such as becoming a member under threat to person or to family, or inducement by false respresentation, or the like be established. Every member will have a chance to be heard in the subsequent forum on his personal relation to the organisation, but your finding in this trial will conclusively establuish the criminal character of the organisation as a whole.

We have also accused as criminal organisations the High Command and the General Staff of the German Armed Forces. We recognise that to plan warfare is the business of professional soldiers in all countries. But it is one thing to plan strategic moves in the event of war coming, and it is another thing to plot and intrigue to bring on that war. We will prove the leaders of the German General Staff and of the High Command to have been guilty of just that. Military men are not before you because they served their country. They are here because they mastered it, and along with others, drove it to war. They are not here because they lost the war, but because they started it. Politicians may have thought of them as soldiers, but soldiers know they were politicians. We ask that the General Staff and the High Command, as defined in the Indictment, be condemned as a criminal group whose existence and tradition constitute a standing menace to the peace of the world.

These individual defendants did not stand alone in crime and will not stand alone in punishment. Your verdict of "guilty" against these organisations will render prima facie, as nearly as we can learn, thousands upon thousands of members now in custody of the United States and of other Armies.

To apply the sanctions of the law to those whose conduct is found criminal by the standards I have outlined, is the responsibility committed to this Tribunal. It is the first court ever to undertake the difficult task of overcoming the confusion of many tongues the conflicting concepts of just procedure among divers systems of law, so as to reach a common judgement. The tasks of all of us are such as to make heavy demands on patience and good will. Although the need for prompt action has admittedly resulted in imperfect work on the part of the prosecution, our great nations bring you their hurriedly assembled contributions of evidence. What remains undiscovered we can only guess. We could, with testimony, prolong the recitals of crime for years - but to what avail? We shall rest the case when we have offered what seems convincing and adequate proof of the crimes charged without unnecessary cumulation of evidence. We doubt very much whether it will be seriously denied that the crimes I have outlined took place. The effort will undoubtedly be to mitigate or escape personal responsibility.

Among the nations which unite in accusing these defendants, the United States is perhaps in a position to be the most dispassionate, for having sustained the least injury, it is perhaps the least animated by vengeance. Our American cities have not been bombed by day and by night, by humans, and by robots. It is not our temples that have been laid in ruins. Our countrymen have not had their homes destroyed over their heads. The menace of Nazi aggression, except to those in actual service, has seemed less personal and immediate to us than to European peoples. But while the United States is not first in rancour, it is not second in determination that the forces of law and order be made equal to the task of dealing with such international lawlessness as I have recited here.

Twice in my lifetime, the United States has sent its Young manhood across the Atlantic, drained its resources, and burdened itself with debt to help defeat Germany. But the real hope and faith that has sustained the American people in these great efforts was that victory for ourselves and our Allies would lay the basis for an ordered international relationship in Europe and would end the centuries of strife on this embattled continent.

Twice we have held back in the early stages of European conflict in the belief that it might be confined to a purely European affair. In the United States, we have tried to build an economy without armament, a system of government without militarism, and a society where men are not regimented for war. This purpose, we know, now, can never be realised if the world periodically is to be embroiled in war. The United States cannot, generation after generation, throw its youth or its resources on to the battlefields of Europe to redress the lack of balance between Germany's strength and that of her enemies, and to keep the battles from our shores.

The American dream of a peace and plenty economy, as well as the hopes of other nations, can never be fulfilled if these nations are involved in a war every generation, so vast and devastating as to crush the generation that fights and but burden the generation that follows. Experience has shown that wars are no longer local. All modem wars become world wars eventually. And none of the big nations at least can stay out. If we cannot stay out of wars, our only hope is to prevent wars.

I am too well aware of the weaknesses of juridical action alone to contend that in itself your decision under this Charter can prevent future wars. Judicial action always comes after the event. Wars are started only on the theory and in the confidence that they can be won. Personal punishment, to be suffered only in the event the war is lost, will probably not be a sufficient deterrent to prevent a war where the warmers feel the chances of defeat to be negligible.

But the ultimate step in avoiding periodic wars, which are inevitable in a system of international lawlessness, is to make statesmen responsible to law. And let me make clear that while this law is first applied against German aggressors, the law includes, and if it is to serve a useful purpose it must condemn, aggression by any other nations, including those which sit here now in judgement. We are able to do away with domestic tyranny and violence and aggression by those in power against the rights of their own people only when we make all men answerable to the law. This trial represents mankind's desperate effort to apply the discipline of the law to statesmen who have used, their powers of state to attack the foundations of the world's peace, and to commit aggressions against the rights of their neighbours.

The usefulness of this effort to do justice is not to be measured by considering the law or your judgement in isolation. This trial is part of the great effort to make the peace more secure. One step in this direction is the United Nations Organisation, which may take joint political action to prevent war if possible, and joint military action to insure that any nation which starts a war will lose it. This Charter and this trial, implementing the Kellogg-Briand Pact, constitute another step in the same direction- juridical action of a kind to ensure that those who start a war will pay for it personally.

While the defendants and the prosecutors stand before you as individuals, it is not the triumph of either group alone that is committed to your judgement. Above all personalities there are anonymous and impersonal forces whose conflict makes up much of human history. It is yours to throw the strength of the law behind either the one or the other of these forces for at least another generation. What are the forces that are contending before you?

No charity can disguise the fact that the forces which these defendants represent, the forces that would advantage and delight in their acquittal, are the darkest and most sinister forces in society-dictatorship and oppression, malevolence and passion, militarism and lawlessness. By their fruits we best know them. Their acts have bathed the world in blood and set civilisation back a century. They have subjected their European neighbours to every outrage and torture, every spoliation and deprivation that insolence, cruelty, and greed could inflict. They have brought the German people to the lowest pitch of wretchedness, from which they can entertain no hope of early deliverance. They have stirred hatreds and incited domestic violence on every continent. There are the things that stand in the dock shoulder to shoulder with these prisoners.

The real complaining party at your bar is Civilisation. In all our countries it is still a struggling and imperfect thing. It does not plead that the United States, or any other country, has been blameless of the conditions which made the German people easy victims to the blandishments and intimidations of the Nazi conspirators.

But it points to the dreadful sequence of aggression and crimes I have recited, it points to the weariness of flesh, the exhaustion of resources, and the destruction of all that was beautiful or useful in so much of the world, and to greater potentialities for destruction in the days to come. It is not necessary among the ruins of this ancient and beautiful city with untold members of its civilian inhabitants still buried in its rubble, to argue the proposition that to start or wage an aggressive war has the moral qualities of the worst of crimes. The refuge of the defendants can be only their hope that International Law will lag so far behind the moral sense of mankind that conduct which is crime in the moral sense must be regarded as innocent in law.

Civilisation asks whether law is so laggard as to be utterly helpless to deal with crimes of this magnitude by criminals of this order of importance. It does not expect that you can make war impossible. It does expect that your juridical action will put the forces of International Law, its prospects, its prohibitions and, most of all, its sanctions, on the side of peace, so that men and women of good will, in all countries, may have "leave to live by no man's leave, underneath the law."

THE PRESIDENT: The Tribunal will now adjourn until 10 o'clock tomorrow morning.

(The Tribunal adjourned to 22nd November, 1945, at 10.00 hours.)

THIRD DAY:
Thursday, 22st November, 1945

THE PRESIDENT: Before the Chief Prosecutor for the United States proceeds to present the evidence on Count 1, the Tribunal wishes me to announce the decision on the application made on behalf of the defendant Julius Streicher by his counsel that his condition be examined. It has been examined by three medical experts on behalf of the Tribunal and their report has been submitted to and considered by the Tribunal; and it is as follows:

1. The defendant Julius Streicher is sane.
2. The defendant Julius Streicher is fit to appear before the Tribunal, and to present his defence.
3. It being the unanimous conclusion of the examiners that Julius Streicher is sane, he is for that reason capable of understanding the nature and policy of his acts during the period of time covered by the indictment."

The Tribunal accepts the report of the medical experts and the trial against Julius Streicher will, therefore, proceed.

The other matter to which I have to refer is a motion on behalf of counsel for Bormann, whom the Tribunal have decided to try in his absence in pursuance of Article 12 of the Charter. Counsel for Bormann has made a motion that the trial against him should be postponed, but, in view of the fact that the provisions of the Charter and the Tribunal's rules of procedure have been strictly carried out in the notices which have been given, and the fact that counsel for Bormann will have ample time before he is called upon to present defence on his behalf, the motion is denied.

I will now call upon counsel for the United States to present the evidence on Count 1.

COLONEL STOREY: May it please the Tribunal: As the first order of business concerning the evidence, it shall be my purpose to outline the method of assembling, processing and authenticating documents to be presented in evidence by the United States. I shall also describe and illustrate the plan of presenting documents and briefs relating to the United States Case in Chief.

As the United States Army advanced into German territory, there were attached to each Army and subordinate Organisation specialised military personnel, whose duties were to capture and preserve enemy information in the form of documents, records, reports and other files. The Germans kept accurate and voluminous records. They were found in Army headquarters, government buildings and elsewhere. During the later stages of the war, particularly, such documents were found in salt mines, buried in the ground, behind false walls and many other places believed secure by the Germans. For example, the personal correspondence and diaries of defendant Rosenberg, including his Nazi Party correspondence, were found behind a false wall in an old castle in Eastern Bavaria. The records of the OKL, or Luftwaffe, of which the defendant Goering was Commander-in- Chief - equivalent to the records of the Headquarters of the Air Staff of our Army Air Forces of the United States, were found in various places in the Bavarian Alps. Most of such Luftwaffe records were assembled and processed by the Army at Berchtesgaden.

When the Army first captured documents and records, they immediately placed the materials under guard and later assembled them in temporary document centres. Many times the records were so voluminous that they were hauled by fleets of Army trucks to document centres. Finally, as the territory seized was [Page 88] made secure, Army zones were established and each Army established a fixed document centre to which were transported the assembled documents and records. Later this material was indexed and catalogued, which was a slow process.

Beginning last June, Mr. Justice Jackson requested me to direct the assembling of documentary evidence on the continent for the U.S. Case. Field teams from our office were organised under the direction of Major William H. Coogan, who established U.S. liaison officers at the main Army document centres. Such officers were directed to screen and analyse the mass of captured documents, and select those having evidentiary value for our case. Literally hundreds of tons of enemy documents and records were screened and examined, and those selected were forwarded to Nuremberg for processing. I now offer in evidence an affidavit by Major Coogan, dated 19th November, 1945, attached hereto, describing the method of procedure, capture, screening and delivery of such documents to Nuremberg.

At this time, if your Honour pleases, and in order to present this matter to the Tribunal, I believe it wise to read at least substantial portions of this affidavit. It is dated 19th November, 1945.

I, MAJOR WILLIAM H. COOGAN, 0-455814, Q.M.C., a commissioned officer of the Army of the United States of America, do hereby certify as follows

(1) The United States Chief of Counsel in July, 1945, charged the Field Branch of the Documentation Division with the responsibility of collecting, evaluating and assembling documentary evidence in the European Theatre for use in the prosecution of the major Axis War Criminals before the International Military Tribunal. I was appointed Chief of the Field Branch on 20th July, 1945. I am now the Chief of the Documentation Division, Office of United States Chief of Counsel.

(2) I have served in the United States Army for more than four years and am a practising attorney by profession. Based upon my experience as an attorney and as a United States Army officer, I am familiar with the operation of the United States Army in connection with seizing and processing captured enemy documents. In my capacity as Chief of the Documentation Division, Office of the United States Chief of Counsel, I am familiar with and have supervised the processing, filing, translating and photostating of all documentary evidence for the United States Chief of Counsel."

I skip to paragraph 4.

"(4) The Field Branch of the Documentation Division was staffed by personnel thoroughly conversant with the German language. Their task was to search for and select captured enemy documents in the European theatre which disclosed information relating to the prosecution of the major Axis War Criminals. Officers under my command were placed on duty at various document centres and also dispatched on individual missions to obtain original documents. When the documents were located, my representatives made a record of the circumstances under which they were found, and all information available concerning their authenticity was recorded. Such documents were further identified by Field Branch pre-trial serial numbers, assigned by my representatives who would then periodically dispatch the original documents by courier to the Office of the United States Chief of Counsel.

(5) Upon receipt of these documents they were duly recorded and indexed. After this operation, they were delivered to the Screening and Analysis Branch of the Documentation Division of the Office of United States Chief of Counsel, which Branch re-examined the documents in order to finally determine whether or not they should be retained as evidence for the prosecutors. This final screening was done by German- speaking analysts on the staff of the United States Chief of Counsel. When the document passed the screeners, it was then transmitted to the document room of the Office of United States Chief of Counsel, with a covering sheet prepared by the screeners showing the title or nature of the document, the personalities involved, and its importance. In the document room, a trial identification number was given to each document or to each group of documents in cases where it was desirable for the sake of clarity to file several documents together.

(6) United States documents were given trial identification numbers in one of five series designated by the letters: "PS", "L", "R", "C", and "EC," indicating the means of acquisition of the documents. Within each series documents were listed numerically.

(7) After a document was so numbered, it was then sent to a German-speaking analyst, who prepared a summary of it with appropriate references to personalities involved, index headings, information as to the source of the document as indicated by the Field Branch, and the importance of the document to a particular phase of the case. Next, the original document was returned to the document room and then checked out to the photostating department, where photostatic copies were made. Upon return from photostating, it was placed in an envelope in one of the several fireproof safes in the rear of the document room. One of the photostatic copies of the document was sent to the translators, thereafter leaving the original itself in the safe. A commissioned officer has been, and is, responsible for the documents in the safe. At all times when he is not present the safe is locked and a military guard is on duty outside the only door. If the officers preparing the certified translation, or one of the officers working on the briefs, found it necessary to examine the original document, this was done within the document room in the section set aside for that purpose. The only exception to this strict rule has been where it has been occasionally necessary to present the

original document to the defence counsel for examination. In this case, the document as entrusted to a responsible officer of the prosecution staff.

(8) All original documents are now located in safes in the document room, where they will be secured until they are presented by the prosecution to the court during the process of this trial.

(9) Some of the documents which will be offered in evidence by the United States were seized and processed by the British Army. Also, personnel from the Office of the United States Chief of Counsel and the British War Crimes Executive have acted jointly in locating, seizing and processing such documents.

(10) Substantially the same system of acquiring documentary evidence was utilised by the British Army and the British War Crimes Executive as that hereinabove set forth with respect to the United States Army and the Office of the United States Chief of Counsel.

(11) Therefore, I certify in my official capacity as hereinabove stated, to the best of my knowledge and belief, that the documents captured in the British Zone of Operations and Occupation, which will be offered in evidence by the United States Chief of Counsel, have been authenticated, translated, and processed in substantially the same manner as hereinabove set forth with respect to the operations of the United States Chief of Counsel.

(12) Finally, I certify that all documentary evidence offered by the United States Chief of Counsel, including those documents from British Army sources, are in the same condition as captured by the United States and British Armies; that they have been translated by competent and qualified translators; that all photostatic copies are true and correct copies of the originals and that they have been correctly filed, numbered and processed as above outlined."

Signed by

WILLIAM H. COOGAN, Major QMC 0-455814

After the documents selected by the screening process outlined reached our office they were again examined, re-screened, and translated by expert U.S. Army personnel, as outlined by Major Coogan.

Finally, more than 2,500 documents were selected and filed here in the Court House. At least several hundred will be offered in evidence. They have been photographed, translated into English, filed, indexed, and processed. The same general procedure was followed by the British War Crimes Executive with regard to documents captured by the British Army, and there has been complete integration and co- operation of activities with the British in that regard.

In order to present our case and to assist the Tribunal, we have prepared written briefs on each phase of our case, which cite the documents by appropriate numbers. Legal propositions of the United States will also be presented in such briefs. The briefs and documents will cover each allegation of the Indictment which is the United States' responsibility. I hold in my hand one of the trial briefs entitled "Reshaping of Education, Training of Youth," which will be offered later on this day. Accompanying each brief is a document book containing true copies in English of all documents referred to in the brief. I hold in my hand the document book that will be submitted to this Tribunal in support of the brief which I have just exhibited to your Honour. Likewise, copies in German have been or will be, furnished to defence counsel at the time such documents are offered in evidence. Upon conclusion of the presentation of each phase or section of our case by counsel, the entire book of documents will be offered in evidence such as this book. At the same time, Lt. Barrett, who will sit here during the whole trial and who is on our staff, will hand to the clerk of this Tribunal the original documents that may be offered in evidence in this form. It will have the seal of the Tribunal, will be exhibit USA --, 2836-PS, and in turn Lt. Barrett will hand the original document to the Tribunal. In the same manner, the document book will be passed by Lt. Barrett to the clerk of the Court, and these trial briefs for the assistance of the Tribunal will be made available to the Court and to the defence counsel. Likewise, copies of documents actually introduced in evidence will be made available to the Press. Thus, may your Honour please, it is hoped that by this procedure the usual laborious and tedious method of introducing documentary evidence may be expedited.

May I, therefore, respectfully inquire of the Tribunal and of defence counsel if there is any objection to the procedure outlined? If not, the United States will proceed with the presentation of the documentary evidence and trial briefs as outlined herein.

THE PRESIDENT: Will you wait one moment?

COLONEL STOREY: Yes, Sir.

THE PRESIDENT: The Tribunal has no objection to the course that you propose.

COLONEL STOREY: If your Honour pleases, may I now announce what will be presented immediately following by the United States?

THE PRESIDENT: I think perhaps that I ought to say to counsel for the defendants that their silence will be taken as their assent to the course proposed. In the absence of any objection by them to the course proposed by Col. Storey on behalf of the Chief Prosecutor for the United States, the Tribunal will take it, that they agree that the course is convenient.

Thank you, gentlemen.

COLONEL STOREY: If your Honour pleases, the next presentation will be the briefs and documents on the Common Plan or Conspiracy up to 1939. We will open by presentation of charts of the Nazi Party and Reich Government with exhibits and explanation by Mr. Albrecht. That will be followed by a presentation of the trial briefs and documents on the other phases of the Common Plan or Conspiracy up to 1939.

Mr. Albrecht.

MR. ALBRECHT: May it please the Tribunal, the prosecution will now allude briefly to certain facts, which may well be considered to be within judicial purview, the consideration of which the prosecution has found useful in understanding and evaluating the evidence that will be presented to the Tribunal during the trial, in support of the allegations of the Indictment.

In the opinion of the prosecution, some preliminary references must be made to the National Socialist German Labour Party, the NSDAP, which in itself is one of the defendant organisations in this proceeding, but which is represented among the defendant organisations by its most important formations, namely the Leadership Corps of the NSDAP, which you will hear referred to as "Das Korps der Politischen Leiter der NSDAP," the "SS" (Die Schutzstaffeln der NSDAP), and the "SA" (Die Sturmabteilungen der NSDAP).

With the permission of the Tribunal the prosecution will offer at this point, as its first exhibit, a chart showing, the structure and Organisation of the NSDAP substantially as it existed at the peak of its development in March, 1945. This chart has been prepared by the prosecution on the basis of information contained in important and well-known official publications of the National Socialist Party with which the defendants must be presumed to have been well acquainted. We refer particularly to the Organisation Book of the Party, "Das Organisationsbuch der NSDAP", and to the National Socialist Year Book," Nationalsozialistisches Jahrbuch", of both of which, be it noted, the late defendant, Robert Ley was the chief editor or publisher. Both books appeared, in the course of time, in many editions and appeared in hundreds of thousands of copies, throughout the period when the National Socialist Party was in control of the German Reich and of the German people. The chart, furthermore, which we are offering, has been certified on its face as correct by a high official of the Nazi Party, namely Franz Xaver Schwarz, its Treasurer (Reichsschatzmeister der NSDAP), and official in charge of Party administration. This affidavit is being submitted with the chart, and I now wish to offer this chart in evidence.

We have been able to have this chart duplicated, and, with the permission of the Tribunal, are making it available to all concerned.

Before I offer some remarks of explanation concerning the Organisation of the National Socialist German Labour Party, which, we believe, will be found useful in connection with the prosecution's case, I would just like to call the attention of the Tribunal to the fact, that the larger chart which now appears is a simplification of the duplicated chart with which your Honour has been furnished. For if it had been reproduced in the same detail, I am afraid many of the boxes would not have appeared intelligible from this point.

I would like to call your attention first of all to an Organisation with which we will have to become very familiar: the Leadership Corps of the NSDAP, the "Reichsleiter," which has been named as a defendant Organisation and which comprises the sum of the officials and leaders of the Nazi Party. If your Honour will be good enough to follow me down the centre line of the chart, we come to the main horizontal line of division where the word "Reichsleiter" appears. That is the first category of the Leadership Corps, I should say, the main category, perhaps, of the Leadership Corps.

The Fuehrer, of course, stands above it. As we follow the vertical line of division to the lower part of the chart, we reach five additional boxes, which may be referred to collectively as the "Hoheitstraeger," the bearers of the sovereignty of the Party, and those are the "Gauleiter," the "Kreisleiter," the "Ortsgruppenleiter," the "Zellenleiter," and the "Blockleiter."

The Fuehrer at the top of our chart is the supreme and the only leader in the Nazi hierarchy. His successor-designate was first, the defendant Hess, and subsequently the defendant Goering.

The "Reichsleiter," of whom sixteen are shown on this chart, comprise collectively the Party Directorate (Reichsleitung). Through them, co-ordination of the Party and State machinery was achieved. A number of these "Reichsleiter," each of whom, at some time, was in charge of at least one office within the Party Directorate, were also the heads of other Party formations and affiliated or supervised organisations of the Party and also of agencies of the State, or even held ministerial positions. The "Reichsleitung " may be said to represent the horizontal organisation of the Party according to functions, within which all threads controlling the varied life of the German people met. Each office within the "Reichsleitung" of the NSDAP executed definite tasks assigned to it by the Fuehrer, or by the leader of the Party Chancellery (Chef der Parteikanzlei), who on the chart before you appears directly under the Fuehrer. In 1945 the chief of the Party Chancellery was Martin Bormann, the defendant in this proceeding, and before him, and until his flight to England in 1941, the defendant Rudolf Hess. It was the duty of the Reichsleitung to make certain that these tasks assigned to it by the Fuehrer were carried out with expedition and without interruption, so that the will of the Fuehrer was quickly and accurately communicated to the lowest Party echelon, the lowliest Zelle or Block. The individual offices of the Reichsleitung had the mission to remain in constant and closest contact with the life of the people through the agency of the subdivisions of the component Party organisations in the "Gau," within the "Kreis," or the "Ort" or the lower group. These leaders had been taught that the right to organise human beings accrued through the appreciation of the fact that a people must be educated ideologically; "weltanschaulich," the Germans call it, that is to say, according to the philosophy of National Socialism.

Among the former Reichsleiter, on trial in this cause, may be included the following defendants:-

If your Honour will follow me to this broad, horizontal line, we started at the extreme left at the box marked with the defendant Frank's name. At one time, although not in March, 1945, he was the Head of the Legal Office of the Party. He was the "Reichsleiter des Reichsrechtsamtes."

In the third square appears the defendant Rosenberg, the delegate of the Fuehrer for Ideological Training and Education of the Party. He was called "Der Beauftragte des Fuehrers fur die Uberwachung der gesammten geistigen und weltanschaulichen Schulung und Erziehung der NSDAP." Next to him, to the right, is the defendant von Schirach, Leader of Youth Education (Leiter fur die Jugenderziehung). Next to him, appears the late defendant Robert Ley, at one time Head of the Party Organisation (Reichsorganisationsleiter der NSDAP) and also the Leader of the German Labour Front (Leiter der Deutschen Arbeitsfront).

Then, if we cross the vertical line, and proceed to the right, in passing I might allude to the box marked with the name of Schwarz. He was the Party Official and Reichsleiter, who certified to the chart before the Tribunal. As we proceed further to the right, next to the last box, we find the name of Frick, who was the leader of the

Reichstag fraction (Leiter des NS Reichstags-fraktion).

The next categories to be considered are the "Hoheitstraeger," at the bottom of the vertical line, in the centre of the chart. The National Socialists called them the bearers of sovereignty. To them was assigned the political sovereignty over specially designated subdivisions of the State, of which they were the appointed leaders. The "Hoheitstraeger " may be said to represent the vertical Organisation of the Party.

These leaders, these "Hoheitstraeger" included all Gauleiters, of whom there were 42 within the Reich in 1945. A "Gauleiter" was a political leader of the largest subdivision of the State. He was charged by the Fuehrer with the political, cultural and economic control over all forms and manifestations of the life of the people and the co- ordination of the same with National Socialist philosophy and ideology.

A number of the defendants, before the bar of this Tribunal, were former "Gauleiter" of the NSDAP. I mention, in this connection, the defendant Streicher, Gauleiter of Franconia, "Franken-Fuehrer" they called him, whose seat was in the city of Nuremburg. Von Schirach was Gauleiter of Vienna and the defendant Sauckel was Gauleiter of Thuringia.

The next lower category on the chart, were the "Kreisleiter," the political leaders of the largest subdivision within a Gau. Then follow the "Ortsgruppen- leiter," the political leaders of the largest subdivision within the Kreis. And a Kreis consisted perhaps of several towns or villages or, in the case of a larger city, anywhere from 1,500 to 3,000 households.

The next "Hoheitstraeger" were the Zellenleiter, the political leaders of a group from four to eight city blocks, or of a corresponding group within country districts, and then follow the Blockleiter, the political leaders of from 40 to 60 households.

Now, each of these political leaders, of these "Hoheitstraeger," or bearers of sovereignty, was directly responsible to the next highest leader in the Nazi hierarchy. The Gauleiter was directly responsible to the Fuehrer himself; the Kreisleiter was directly responsible to the Gauleiter; the Ortsgruppenleiter to the Kreisleiter, and so on.

The Fuehrer himself, reserved to himself, in accordance with the philosophy that runs through the Party, the right to name all fuehrers. It was he, personally, that named the Reichsleiter, all members of the Party Directorate. It was he that appointed all Gauleiter and Kreisleiter and all political leaders, down to the grade of "Gauamtsleiter," which was a lower classification of political leader within the Party Organisation of the Gau.

These "Hoheitstraeger," together with the Reichsleitung, constituted the all-powerful group of leaders by means of which the Nazi Party reached right down into the lives of the people, consolidated its control of them and compelled them to conform to the National Socialist pattern. For this purpose broad powers were given to them, including the right to call upon all Party formations to effectuate their plans. They could requisition the services of the SA and of the SS, as well as of the HJ and of the NSKK. If I may direct your attention, for the moment, to the Party organisations that appear at the extreme left of the chart, I would just like to say that structurally these were organised regionally to with the offices and regions controlled by the "Hoheitstraeger." If I might be more explicit, let us take the SA. The subsidiary formations of the SA came down and corresponded, in its lower organisations, to the Gau, so that we have "Gauleitung" in the SA, and further down, to the Kreis, so that we have a Kreisleitung within the Kreis. Thus, we have a Kreisleitung in the SA so that the Gauleiter and the Kreisleiter, to cite two examples, charged with a particular duty by the Fuehrer, could call on these organisations for assistance in carrying out their tasks.

These sinister implications of the use of this power will become more apparent as the prosecution's case develops, and as the wealth of evidentiary material is introduced into evidence to prove the criminality of the defendant organisations.

The component Party-organisations, called "Gliederungen" within the Party, are shown at the extreme left of the chart, and are the organisations to which I directed the attention of your Honour a moment ago. These organisations actually constitute the Party itself, and substantially the entire Party-membership is contained within them. The four principal organisations are sometimes referred to as "paramilitary" organisations. They were uniformed organisations and they were armed. These were the notorious SA and SS, who are named as party-defendants in this case, the HJ (Hitler Youth) and the NSKK (the Motor Corps of the Party'). Then there were also the National Socialist Women's Organisation, the National Socialist German Students Bund (Deutscher Studentenbund), and the National Socialist University Teachers' Bund.

There are additional organisations that were officially designated within the Party, as affiliated organisations, not "Gliederungen" nor controlled organisations, but affiliated organisations (Angeschlossene Verbaende der NSDAP). Among those organisations we have the German Labour Front (Deutsche Arbeiterfront) the DAF; we have an organisation that controlled the Civil Service (Reichsbund der Deutschen Beamten). There were the physicians in the Deutscher Aerztebund; there were the teachers in the "Lehrerbund;" there were the lawyers within the National Socialist "Rechtswahrerbund," of which, at one time, the defendant Frank was the head.

There is another group of organisations, which was officially known as supervised organisations (Betreute Organisationen der NSDAP), organisations that included certain specialised women's organisations (Deutsches Frauenwerk), certain student societies (Deutsche Studentenschaft) and former university students (Altherrenbund der Deutschen Studenten). There was a group that had reference to the German communes (National- Sozialistischer Deutscher Gemeindetag) and there was a "Reichsbund fur Leibesuebungen," that interested itself in controlling all those interested in physical exercise.

According to the official Party designations applicable to the various organisations and associations that controlled German life, there was a fourth classification, which is the last organisation that appears to the right on the chart before your Honour, which is sometimes simply called "Weitere Nationalsozialistische Organisationen," and here, in some respects, we are in "No Man's Land," because the party was not static, it was dynamic and our latest information is now to the effect that the organisations that ordinarily came within this category, well known organisations like the RAD (Reich Labour Service) and the NSFK (National Sozialistisches Fliegerkorps), may no longer be included there. At least that was the opinion of the Party Treasurer, who certified to this chart.

I think with these few remarks, I have given some general impression of the structure of the Party with which we are dealing, in this Proceeding before your Honours.

Before leaving the Chart perhaps I would just like to point out several other instances where some of the defendants appear in this set-up.

At the very top, to the left of the Fuehrer, as marked on the chart before your Honour, are the successors-designate of the Fuehrer. First is defendant Hess, until 1941, and followed by the defendant Goering. Under the Fuehrer appears the Chief of the Party Chancellery, the defendant Martin Bormann, and then, if we come to the left of the Reichsleiter, and go to the left, opposite Rosenberg's name, we find somewhat below that his name is repeated as the Head of an office on a lower level, namely, the Foreign Relations Office of the Party, which played such a sinister influence in the early work of the Party, as will later appear in the documentary evidence to be presented to your Honour.

We then come to the late defendant Ley's name, on the main horizontal division, and follow the dotted line to a lower level, and we will find he was the Chief of the German Labour Service, and if we come closer to the vertical line, to a lower level, below the "Reichsleiter," we find the defendant Speer, in the "Hauptamt Fur Technik," the Office of Technical Affairs, and below that, as the Chief of the "Bund Deutscher Technik " (German Technological League).

With the permission of the Tribunal, the prosecution will now pass to the consideration of the governmental machinery of the German State, which, like the Organisation of the Nazi Party, requires some brief observations before the prosecution proceeds with the submission of proof on the Common Plan or Conspiracy, with which the defendants have been charged.

If the Tribunal will allow, the prosecution will offer as its second exhibit, another chart, delineating substantially the governmental structure of the Third Reich, as it existed in March, 1945, and also "The chief leadership corps of the Reich Government and the Reich Administration during those years."

This chart has been prepared by the prosecution on the basis of information contained in two official publications, "Das Taschenbuch fur Verwaltungsbeamte," the Manual for Administrative Officers, and the National Socialist Year Book, to which I have already alluded, edited by the defendant Ley.

This chart has been examined, corrected and certified by the defendant Wilhelm Frick, whose affidavit is submitted with it. In fact, it is reproduced directly on the copies of the charts before your Honour.

It seems plain that the defendant Frick, a former Minister of Interior of the Reich from January, 1933, to August, 1943, was well qualified, by reason of his position and long service in public office during the National Socialist regime, to certify to the substantial accuracy of the facts disclosed in this chart.

Now, with the permission of the Tribunal, I would like to make some brief comments on this chart.

First of all, we refer to the "Reichsregierung," which is the big box in the centre of the chart on the vertical line, directly below Hitler. The " Reichsregierung" is a word that may not be translated literally as "government of the Reich." The word "Reichsregierung" is a word of art and is applied collectively to the ministers who composed the German Cabinet.

The "Reichsregierung" has been named as a defendant in this proceeding, and as used in the Indictment, the expression is used to identify a group which, we will urge, should be declared to have been a criminal organisation.

This group includes all the men named in that centre box, who were members of the Cabinet after 30th January, 1933, that is Reich Ministers with and without Portfolio, and all other officials entitled to participate in the deliberations of the Cabinet.

Secondly, it includes members of the Council of Ministers for the Defence of the Reich. It is called "Ministerrat Fur die Reichsverteidigung," which is the large box to the right of the vertical line.

Then, it includes the members of the Secret Cabinet Council, which is the small box to the left of the vertical line, the "Geheimer Kabinettarat," of which the defendant von Neurath was the President.

Unlike the Cabinets and Ministerial Councils in countries that were not within the orbit of the Axis, the "Reichsregierung," after 30th January, 1933, when Adolf Hitler became Chancellor of the German Reich, did not remain merely the executive branch of the Government. In short order it also came to possess, and it exercised, legislative and other functions as well, in the governmental system into which the German Government developed while under the domination of the National Socialist Party.

It is proper to observe here that, unlike such Party organisations as the S.A. and S.S., the " Reichsregierung," before 1933, certainly, was not a body created exclusively or even predominantly for the purpose of committing illegal acts. The "Reichsregierung' was an instrument of government provided for by the Weimar Constitution. Under the Nazi regime, however, the "Reichsregierung" gradually became a primary agent of the Party, with functions formulated in accordance with the objectives and methods of the Party itself. The Party, to all intents and purposes, was intended to be a "Fuehrerorden," an order of fuehrers, a pool of political leaders. And while the Party was, in the words of a German law, "the bearer of the concept of the German State," it was not identical with the State.

Thus, in order to realise its ideological and political objectives and to reach the German people, the Party had to avail itself of official State channels.

The Reichsregierung, and such agencies and offices established by it, were the chosen instruments by means of which Party politics were converted into legislative and administrative acts, binding upon the German people as a whole.

In order to accomplish this result, the "Reichsregierung" was thoroughly remodelled by the Party. Some of the steps may be here recorded, by which the co-ordination of Party and State machinery was assured in order to impose the will of the Fuehrer on the German people.

On 30th January, 1933, the date that the Fuehrer became Reich Chancellor, there were few National Socialists that were Cabinet members. But, as the power of the Party in the Reich grew, the Cabinet came to include an ever-increasing number of Nazis, until by January, 1937, no non-Party member remained in the "Reichsregierung." Now cabinet posts were created and Nazis appointed to them. Many of these cabinet members were also in the "Reichsleitung" of the Party.

To give but a few examples:-

The defendant Rosenberg, whose name your Honours will find in that central box on the vertical line, the delegate of the Fuehrer for Ideological Training and Education of the Party, was a member of the "Reichsregierung," in its capacity as Minister for the Occupied Eastern Areas, the "Reichsminister fur die besetsten Ostgebiete."

And if your Honours will follow me on the vertical line to the main horizontal line and proceed to the very end, you will find a box marked "Ministry for the Occupied Eastern Territories," of which the head was the defendant Rosenberg.

The defendant Frick, the leader of the National Socialist faction in the " Reichstag," was also Minister of the Interior.

If your Honours will follow me down to the main horizontal line and two boxes over you will find the Ministry presided over by the defendant Frick. Goebbels, the " Reichsleiter fur Propaganda," also sat in the Cabinet as Minister for Public Enlightenment and Propaganda, "Reichsminister fur Volksaufklaerung und Propaganda." He is in Propaganda, the next box to the right from the Ministry of the Interior.

After the 25th of July, 1934, participation in the work of the cabinet was at all times achieved through the person of the defendant Rudolf Hess, the Deputy Fuehrer. By a decree of Hitler the defendant Hess was invested with the power to take part in the editing of legislative bills with all the departments of the Reich. Later this power of the Fuehrer's deputy was expanded to include all executive decisions and orders that were published in the "Reichsgesetzblatt," the official volume in which are contained the decrees of the State. After Hess's flight to England in 1941, the defendant Martin Bormann, as his successor, took over the same functions, and in addition he was given the authority of a "Reichsminister " so that he could sit in the Cabinet.

Now, another item of importance:-

On 30th January, 1937, four years after Hitler became Chancellor, the Fuehrer executed the acceptances into the Party of those last few Cabinet members who still remained out of the Party. Only one Cabinet member had the strength of character to reject membership in the Party. That was the Minister of Transportation and Minister of Posts, Mr. Eltz- Ruebenau. His example was not followed by the defendant von Neurath. His example was not followed by the defendant Raeder. And if the defendant Schacht was not yet at that time a member of the Party, I might say that his example was not followed by the defendant Schacht.

The chart shows many other instances where Party members on the highest, as well as subordinate levels, occupied corresponding or other positions in the organisation of the State. Take Hitler himself as the Fuehrer of the N.S.D.A.P. He was also the Chancellor of the Reich with which office, furthermore, the office of President of the Reich was joined and merged after the death of President von Hindenburg in 1934.

Take the defendant Goering, the successor-designate of Hitler. As Fuehrer of the S.A. he sat in the Cabinet as Air Minister, "Luftfahrtminister," and he also held many other important positions, including that of Commander-in-Chief of the "Luftwaffe," the German Air Force, and that of Delegate for the Four Year Plan.

Himmler, the notorious head of the S.S., the Reichsfuehrer S.S., was also the Chief of the German Police, reporting to the defendant Frick. He himself later became Minister of the Interior after the attempted assassination of Hitler on 20th June, 1944, which event also catapulted him into the position of Commander-in-Chief of the German Reserve Army.

Now, at the extreme upper left of the chart is a box that is labelled "Reichstag," the former German parliament.

(A short recess was taken.)

In that box is the label "Reichstag," the former German parliament.

The " Reichstag " presents an anomaly in this picture. Under the Republic it had been the supreme law-making body of the Reich, subject only to a limited check by the "Reichsrat" - the Council of the Reich, by the President and by the people themselves by way of Initiative and Referendum.

Putting their opposition to all forms of Parliamentarianism into effect at once, the Nazis proceeded to curtail the powers of the " Reichstag," to eliminate the "Reichsrat," and to merge the Presidency with the Office of Chancellor occupied by the Fuehrer. By the Act of 24th March, 1933, the Cabinet was given unlimited legislative powers, including the right to deviate from the Constitution. Subsequently, as I stated, the Reichsrat was abolished, and with that act the residuum of the power to legislate in the Reichstag was reduced to a minimum. I say the power was reduced to a minimum, because the actual power to legislate was never taken away from the Reichstag, but certainly after the advent of the Party to power it was never permitted to exercise as a legislature.

The "Reichsregierung" retained its legislative powers throughout, even though from time to time other agencies of the "Reichsregierung," such as the Plenipotentiary for Administration, in the upper right of the chart, the "Generalbevollmaechtigter fur die Reichsverwaltung," the Plenipotentiary for Economy, also in the right-hand corner of the chart, the "Generalbevollmaectitigter fur die Wirtschaft" and the Council of Ministers for the Defence of the Reich, were created. That is the big box to the right of the vertical line. And these agencies of the Reichsregierung received certain concurrent legislative powers.

The development of the Reichstag into an emasculated legislative body was, however, only an intermediate step on the road to rule by Fuehrer decrees. That was the ultimate goal of the Party, and a goal which they achieved.

The Nazis then proceeded to delegate some of the powers of the Reich Cabinet to all sorts of newly created agencies, some of which I have already mentioned. Cabinet functions were delegated first of all to the Reich Defence Council, the "Reichsverteidigungsrat," possibly as early as 4th April, 1933, but we believe certainly not later than 1935. I might say in this connection that with respect to a number of these agencies of the Reichsregierung which received delegated powers, we are moving in a somewhat shadowy land, because in developing this organisation we are dealing - to some extent, at least - with decrees and actions that were secret, or secretive, in character.

A number of these decrees were never definitely fixed in time. A number of them were never published, and the German people themselves never became acquainted with them. And that is why I say that the Reich Defence Council may possibly have been created as early as two and one-half months after the advent of Hitler to power, but we believe that we will be able to show to the satisfaction of the Tribunal that that important body in the government of the Reich was created certainly not later than May, 1935.

I say it was an important body. This was the war-planning group, of which Hitler himself was chairman and the defendant Goering the alternate. It was a large war-planning body, as your Honour will note, that included many cabinet members, and there was also a working committee - the true numerical size of which does not appear from the chart - which was presided over by the defendant

Keitel. That also was composed of Cabinet members and of Reich defence officials, the majority of whom were appointed by Cabinet officers and subject to their control. Other powers were delegated to the Plenipotentiary, whom I have named before, for Administration, appearing at the extreme right of the chart. That was the defendant Frick, and later the notorious Himmler.

Subordinate to Frick in his capacity as Plenipotentiary for Administration were complete ministries, the Ministry of the Interior, Frick's old ministry, Ministry of Justice, Education, Church Affairs, and " Raumordnung," the Ministry for Special Planning.

Other powers went to the delegate for the Four Year Plan, again the defendant Goering, whose box appears to the left of the median line, half way to the edge.

There were certain other powers that went to an organisation within the shadow-land I mentioned, and which, unfortunately, does not have it, name on this chart, the "Dreierkollegium," the College of Three, which title should really be imposed over the last three boxes in the upper right-band corner; because the "Dreierkollegium " consisted not alone of the Plenipotentiary for Administration, but also the Plenipotentiary for War Economy. And the Chairman of that group, I believe, was the defendant Keitel, as the head of the O.K.W., the Wehrmacht, all the armed forces. The duties of the "Dreierkollegium " would seem to have included the drafting of decrees in preparation of and for use during war. To the Secret Cabinet Council, the "Geheimer Kabinettsrat," of which the defendant von Neurath was Chairman, or President I believe was his title, went other powers. That secret Cabinet Council was created by a decree of the Fuehrer in 1938.

Certain other delegation of power took place to the "Ministerrat fur die Reichsverteidigung," the Ministerial Council for the Defence of the Realm, which is the smallest box appearing under the large box of the Reich Defence Council, to the right of the vertical line.

The Council of Ministers for the Defence of the Reich was responsible to the Fuehrer alone. Its membership, as would seem to be indicated on the chart, was taken from the Reich Council. It had broad powers to issue decrees with the force of law in so far as the Reichsregierung itself had not legislated on the subject. It should be stressed that this delegation of Cabinet functions to various groups, composed largely of its own members, helped to conceal some of the important policies of the " Reichsregierung," namely, those relating to the preparation of war, which delegated the necessary authority to secret and semi-secret agencies. Thus in a general way, as I have outlined, did the National Socialist Party succeed in putting Nazi policies into effect through its dummy, through the machinery of the State, the Reichsregierung, in its revised form.

I think it might be helpful if your Honour will permit me to point out on this chart the large number of instances in which the defendants' names reappear in connection with the functions of the Government of the Reich.

Now, first of all, the Reichsregierung itself - I am sorry to say in that connection that there is one omission, a very important omission. It is the name of the Vice Chancellor under Hitler, von Papen, who was Vice Chancellor from the seizure of power until some time around the purge in June, 1934.

Your Honours will see a grouping of Reich Ministers with portfolio, and under it of Ministers without portfolio, in which mostly the names of the defendants in court are listed. There are State Ministers acting as Reich Ministers listed, and you will note the name of the defendant Frank. There are other participants in cabinet meetings, among which you will notice the name of the defendant von Schirach.

Now, this whole line on which the cabinet hangs is the level of the Reich Cabinet, and as I have stated, organisations that grew out of this maternal organism, the "Reichsregierung."

To the left the Secret Cabinet Council includes the names of the defendants. Still further to the left is the delegate for the Four Year Plan. And over to the very end is the Reichstag, of which the president was the defendant Goering, and the leader of the "Reichstagsfraktion," the defendant Frick.

If we proceed to the right of the median line, we have the Reich Defence Council, with Hitler himself as Chairman, the Reich Defence Committee under it, and the Ministerial Council for the Defence of the Realm, which grew out of the Reich Defence Council. And we see mostly the names of cabinet ministers, including, if I may refer to that fact, particularly the names of purely military leaders, such as the defendant Raeder and the defendant Keitel.

And farther to the right, all names mentioned as defendants in these proceedings, Schacht, the first Plenipotentiary for War Economy, later succeeded by Funk Field Marshal Keitel as the Chief of the O.K.W., and the defendant Funk again as

Plenipotentiary for Administration, in the triangle which became known as the "Dreierkollegium."

If we descend the vertical line to the horizontal line in the middle, we have the various ministries over which these cabinet ministers, this "Reichsregierung," presided. We have also at the extreme left and the extreme right, very important and special offices that were set up at the instigation of the Party, and those offices reported directly to the Fuehrer himself.

If I may start at the extreme left, I will point out that as the civil government moved after the military machine into the Lowlands, the defendant Seyss-Inquart became the Reichskommissar for the Netherlands.

A few names below that of Seyss-Inquart is the name of the defendant von Neurath, the "Reichsprotektor" for Bohemia and Moravia, who was later succeeded by the defendant Frick; and under those names, the name of the defendant Frank, the "General-gouvenieur" of Poland.

Adjoining the box of these administrators who reported directly to the Reich Chancellor and President was the Foreign Office, presided over first by the defendant von Neurath, and subsequently by the defendant von Ribbentrop.

If we proceed down below the elongation under the smaller box dealing with German legations, there should, of course, in any itemised, detailed treatment of that box appear the name of the defendant von Papen, the representative of the Reich in Austria for a time, and later in Turkey.

The next box on the horizontal line is the Ministry of Economics, the "Reichs-wirtschaftsministerium." First is the name of the defendant Schacht, followed by the name of the defendant Goering, and by the name of the defendant Funk.

The next box, the Ministry for Armament and War Production, the "Reichs-ministerium fur Ruestung und Kriegsproduktion," was presided over by the defendant Speer. And out of this organisation, and subordinate to it, in the box devoted to the Organisation Todt, again the name of the defendant Speer, who succeeded Todt in the Leadership of that organisation upon the death of the latter.

Two boxes over, the Ministry of Justice, if your Honour will follow me, down close to the bottom of the page to the last left-hand box, appearing under the Ministry of Justice, is the "Reichsrechtsanwaltskammer" - I am sorry, the box next to the bottom at the left which is devoted to the Academy for German Law, "Die Akademie fur deutsches Recht," over which the defendant Frank presided for a time.

Almost at the vertical line, the Air Ministry, of which the defendant Goering was Oberkommandant; and next to it again the Ministry of the Interior, presided over by the defendant Frick.

If your Honour will follow me again to the bottom of all the squares to the small horizontal line at the bottom of the Ministry of the Interior, we come to certain state officials, called Reich Governors, " Reichstatthalter." And if those boxes were sufficiently detailed there would appear thereon the name, among others, of the defendant Sauckel, who besides being the Gauleiter of Thuringia, was also the Reichstatthalter or Governor there. There would also appear the name of the defendant von Schirach, who was not only the Gauleiter of Vienna, but also the State representative there, the Governor, the "Reichstatthalter," of Vienna.

And springing out of the Ministry of the Interior is the box or boxes devoted to the German police, and in the first sub-division appearing to the right, the Chief of the Security Police and SD, is the name of the defendant Kaltenbrunner.

In the Ministry of Propaganda, about midway down in this box, appears the name of the defendant Fritzsche, who, as the chart is drawn, although he would not appear in the position of one of the chief directing heads of the Ministry, actually was very much more important than his position there will indicate; and proof will be submitted to your Honour in support of that contention.

At the end of the horizontal line is the Ministry for the Occupied Eastern Territories, the " Reichsministerium fur die Besetzten Ostgebiete," of which the defendant Rosenberg was the head.

And to the right of that box, among the agencies immediately subordinate to Hitler as Reichskanzler and President, there is the office of General Inspector for Highways, with the name of the defendant Speer associated with it; the General Inspector for Water and Energy, again with the name of the defendant Speer associated with it.

There follows the Reich Office for Forestry, the "Reichsforstamt," under the defendant Goering; the "Reichsjugendfuehrer," the leader of the Reich Youth, the defendant von Schirach, the Reich Housing Commissioner, "Reichswohnungs-kommissar," the late defendant Robert Ley; and among the subsequent agencies, that of the important "Reichsbank," over which the defendant Schacht presided, to be succeeded subsequently by the defendant Funk; the General Inspector for the Reich Capital, "Generalbauinspekt fur die Reichshauptstadt," the defendant Speer.

I think I have named all of the defendants as they appear on this chart, and of those now before your Honour in this cause I think they all appear on this chart in one capacity or another; in one or more capacities, all, I might add, except the defendant Jodl. Jodl was the Chief of Staff of all the Armed Forces. He was the head of the "Wehrmacht Fuehrungsstab," and in the chart as evidential material which will be subsequently brought before your Honour, the name Jodl will figure prominently in connection with the Organisation of the Armed Forces.

If I may make one correction at this point, a slip of the tongue that was called to my attention, in discussing the chart of the Party, in the small box to the left containing the designates of the Fuehrer to succeed him to the Party leadership, I made the statement that Goering succeeded Hess as Fuehrer designate. Actually, when the designations were announced by the Fuehrer, Goering was always the first designate, and the defendant Hess the second.

In Annex A of the Indictment, the various offices, Party functions and State offices which these defendants held in the course of the period under discussion, these various offices are mentioned. And we would like to submit at this time and offer into evidence as exhibits, proof of the offices that were occupied by these defendants. This proof consists of 17 statements, more or less, signed by the defendants themselves and/or their counsel, certifying to the Party and State offices that they have held from time to time. Some of these statements were not as complete as we desired to have them, and we have appended thereto a statement showing such additional offices or proof of Party membership as was available to us. I would like to offer those into evidence.

(Several documents were distributed to defence counsel)

MR. ALBRECHT: And now, if your Honour pleases, I offer into evidence the two charts to which my remarks have been addressed in the course of the morning.

THE PRESIDENT: Will Counsel for the United States continue the evidence until 1230 hours ?

COLONEL STOREY: If your Honour pleases, it lacks two minutes until 11230 hours. Mr. Albrecht has finished, and will it be convenient for your Honour for Major Wallis to start at 1400 hours ?

THE PRESIDENT: Very well.

(The court is adjourned)

COLONEL STOREY: If the Tribunal please, Major Frank Wallis will now present the briefs, and documents supporting the briefs, on behalf of the phase of the case known as the Common Plan or Conspiracy, from 1939.

MAJOR WALLIS: Mr. President, members of the Tribunal:

It will be my purpose to establish most of the material allegations of the Indictment running from Paragraph IV on page 3, to sub-paragraph E on page 6. The subjects involved are:

The aims of the Nazi Party.

Their doctrinal techniques.

Their rise to power, and

The consolidation of control over Germany between 1933 and 1939 in preparation for aggressive war.

This story has already been sketched by the American Chief Prosecutor. Moreover, it is history, beyond challenge by the defendants. For the most part, we rely upon the Tribunal to take judicial notice of it. What we offer is merely illustrative material - including statements by the defendants and other Nazi leaders - laws, decrees, and the like. We do not need to rest upon captured documents or other special sources, although some have been used.

For the convenience of the Court and defence counsel, the illustrative material has been put together in document books, and the arguments derived from them have been set out in trial briefs.

I intend only to comment briefly on some of the materials and to summarise the main lines of the briefs.

What is the charge in Count One?

The Charge in Count One is that the defendants, with divers other persons, participated in the formulation or execution of a Common Plan or Conspiracy to commit, or which involved the commission of Crimes against Humanity (both within and without Germany), War Crimes, and Crimes against Peace.

The charge is, further, that the instrument of cohesion among the defendants, as well as an instrument for the execution of the purposes of the conspiracy, was the Nazi Party, of which each defendant was a member or to which he became an adherent.

The scope of the proof which I shall offer is:

First, that the Nazi Party set for itself certain aims and objectives, involving basically the acquisition of "Lebensraum," or living space, for all "racial Germans.

Second, that it was committed to the use of any methods, whether or not legal, in attaining these objectives, and that it did in fact use illegal methods.

Third, that it put forward and disseminated various lines of propaganda, and used various propaganda techniques to assist it in its unprincipled rise to power.

Fourth, that it ultimately did seize all governmental power in Germany.

Fifth, that it used this power to complete the political conquest of the State, to crush all opposition, and to prepare the nation psychologically and otherwise for the foreign aggression upon which it was bent from the outset.

In general, we undertake to outline, so far as relevant to the charge, what happened in Germany during the pre-war period, leaving it to others to carry the story and proof through the war years.

The aims of this conspiracy were open and notorious. It was far different from any other conspiracy ever unfolded before a court of justice, not only because of the gigantic number of people involved, the period of time covered, the magnitude and audacity of it, but because, unlike other criminal conspirators, these conspirators often boastfully proclaimed to the world what they planned to do, before they did it.

As an illustration, Hitler, in his speech of 30th January, 1941, said:

"My programme was to abolish the Versailles Treaty. It is futile nonsense for the rest of the world to pretend today that I did not reveal this programme until 1933 or 1935 or 1937. . . .Instead of listening to the foolish chatter of emigres, these gentlemen would have been wiser to read what I have written thousands of times. No human being has declared or recorded what he wanted more than I. Again and again I wrote these words, 'the abolition of the Treaty of Versailles'."

First, a brief reference to the history of the Nazi Party.

The Court will no doubt recollect that the National Socialist Part had its origin in the German Labor Party, which was founded on 5 January 1919 in Munich. It was this organization which Hitler joined as seventh member on 12 September 1919. At a meeting of the German Labor Party held on 24 February 1920, Hitler announced to the world the "25 Thesis" that subsequently became known as the "unalterable" program of the National Socialist German Workers Party.

A few days later, on 4 March 1920, the name of the German Labor Party was changed to the "National Socialist German Workers Party," frequently referred to as the NSDAP, or Nazi Party. It is under that name that the Nazi Party continued to exist until its dissolution after the collapse and unconditional surrender of Germany in 1945.

The disagreements and intrigues within the Party between Hitler's followers and those who opposed him were finally resolved on 29 July 1921, when Hitler became "First Chairman" and was invested with extraordinary powers. Hitler immediately reorganized the Party and imposed upon it the Führerprinzip--the leadership principle--of which you will hear more later. Thereafter Hitler, the Führer, determined all questions and made all decisions for the Party.

The main objectives of the Party, which are fastened upon the defendants and their co-conspirators by reason of their membership in, or knowing adherence to the Party, were openly and notoriously avowed. They were set out in the Party program of 1920, were publicized in Mein Kampf and in Nazi literature generally, and were obvious from the continuous pattern of public action of the Party from the date of its founding.

Now two consequences, of importance in the Trial of this case, derive from the fact that the major objectives of the Party were publicly and repeatedly proclaimed:

First, the Court may take judicial notice of them.

Second, the defendants and their co-conspirators cannot be heard to deny them or to assert that they were ignorant of them.

The Prosecution offers proof of the major objectives of the Party-and hence of the objectives of the conspiracy--only to refresh or implement judicial recollection. The main objectives were:

First, to overthrow the Treaty of Versailles and its restrictions on military armament and activity in Germany;

Second, to acquire territories lost by Germany in World War I;

Third, to acquire other territories inhabited by so-called "racial Germans"; and

Fourth, to acquire still further territories said to be needed as living space by the racial Germans so incorporated--all at the expense of neighboring and other countries.

In speaking of the first aim, Hitler made an admission which applied equally to the other aims, namely, that he had stated and written a thousand times or more that he demanded the abolition of the Versailles Treaty.

These aims are fully documented in the evidence offered by the prosecution on this phase of the case, and it is not my purpose at this time to recite to the Court numerous declarations made by the defendants and others with respect to these aims.

Moreover, these conspirators again and again publicly announced to the still unbelieving world that they proposed to accomplish these objectives by any means found opportune, including illegal means and resort to threat of force, force, and aggressive war. The use of force was distinctly sanctioned, in fact guaranteed, by official statements and directives of the conspirators which made activism and aggressiveness a political quality obligatory for Party members.

As Hitler stated in "Mein Kampf":

"What we needed and still need are not a hundred or two hundred reckless conspirators, but a hundred thousand and a second hundred thousand fighters for our philosophy of life."

In 1929 Hitler stated:

"We confess further that we will tear anyone to pieces who would dare hinder us in this undertaking. Our rights will be protected only when the German Reich is again supported by the point of the German dagger."

Hitler, in 1934, in addressing the Party Congress at Nuremburg, stated the duties of Party members in the following terms:

"Only a part of the people will consist of really active fighters. It is they who were fighters of the National Socialist revolution. Of them, more is demanded than of the millions among the rest of the population. For them it is not sufficient to confess, 'I believe,' but to swear, 'I fight.'"

In proof of the fact that the Party was committed to the use of any means, whether or not legal or honourable, it is only necessary to remind the Court that the Party virtually opened its public career by staging a revolution-the Munich Putsch of 1923.

Now let us consider for a moment the doctrinal techniques of the Common Plan or Conspiracy which are alleged in the Indictment.

To incite others to join in the Common Plan or Conspiracy and as a means of securing for the Nazi conspirators the highest degree of control over the German community, they disseminated and exploited certain doctrines.

The first of these was the "master race" doctrine - that persons of so-called German blood were a master race. This doctrine of racial supremacy was incorporated as Point 4 in the Party Programme, which provided:

"Only a member of the race can be a citizen. A member of the race can only be one who is of German blood without consideration of confession. Consequently, no Jew can be a member of the race."

They outlined this master race doctrine as a new religion- the faith of the blood - superseding in individual allegiance all other religions and institutions. The defendant Rosenberg and the defendant Streicher were particularly prominent in disseminating this doctrine. Much of the evidence to be offered in this case will illustrate the Nazi conspirators' continued espousal and exploitation of this master race doctrine.

This doctrine had an eliminatory purpose; call anything "non- German" or Jewish, and you have a clear right, indeed a duty, to cast it out. In fact purges did not stop at so- called racial lines, but went far beyond.

The second important doctrine, which permeates the entire conspiracy and is one of the important links in establishing the guilt of each of these defendants, is the doctrine or concept of the "Fuehrerprinzip" or leadership principle.

This doctrine permeated the Nazi Party and all its formations and allied organisations and eventually permeated the Nazi State and all institutions, and is of such importance that I would like to dwell upon it for a few moments and attempt to explain the concepts which it embraces.

The "Fuehrerprinzip" embodies two major political concepts:

1. Authoritarianism.

2. Totalitarianism.

Authoritarianism implies the following: All authority is concentrated at the top and is vested in one person only, the Fuehrer. It further implies that the Fuehrer is infallible as well as omnipotent. The Party Manual states:

"Under the Commandments of the National Socialists:- The Fuehrer is always right."

Also, there are no legal or political limits to the authority of the Fuehrer. Whatever authority is wielded by others is derived from the authority of the Fuehrer. Moreover, within the sphere of jurisdiction allotted to him, each appointee of the Fuehrer manipulates his power in equally unrestricted fashion, subordinate only to the command of those above him. Each appointee owes unconditional obedience to the Fuehrer and to the superior Party leaders in the hierarchy.

Each political leader was sworn in yearly. According to the Party Manual, which will be introduced in evidence, the wording of the oath was as follows:

"I pledge eternal allegiance to Adolf Hitler. I pledge unconditional obedience to him and the fuehrers appointed by him."

The Party Manual also provides that:

"The political leader is inseparably tied to the ideology and the Organisation of the N.S.D.A.P. His oath only ends with his death or with his expulsion from the National Socialist Community."

As the defendant Hans Frank stated in one of his publications:

"Leadership principle in the administration means: always to replace decision by majority, by decision on the part of a specific person with clear jurisdiction and with sole responsibility to those above, and to entrust to his authority the realisation of the decision to those below."

And finally the concept of Authoritarianism contained in the "Fuehrerprinzip" implies: The authority-of the Fuehrer extends into all spheres of public and private life.

The second main concept of the "Fuehrerprinzip" is Totalitarianism which implies the following: The authority of the Fuehrer, his appointees and, through them, of the Party as a whole, extends into all spheres of public and private life.

The Party dominates the State.

The Party dominates the Armed Forces.

The Party dominates all individuals within the State.

The Party eliminates all institutions, groups and individuals unwilling to accept the leadership of the Fuehrer.

As the Party manual states:

"Only those organisations can lay claim to the institution of the leadership principle and to the National Socialist meaning of the State and people in the National Socialist meaning of the term, which . . . have been integrated into, supervised and formed by the Party and which, in the future, will continue to do so."

The Manual goes on to state:

"All others which conduct an organisational life of their own are to be rejected as outsiders and will either have to adjust themselves or disappear from public life."

Illustrations of the Fuehrerprinzip and its application to the Party, the State and allied organisations are fully set forth in the brief and accompanying documents, which will be offered in evidence.

The third doctrine or technique employed by the Nazi conspirators to make the German people amenable to their will and aims was the doctrine that war was a noble and necessary activity of Germans. The purpose of this doctrine was well expressed by Hitler in "Mein Kampf" when he said:-

"The question of restoration of German power is not a question of how to fabricate arms, but a question of how to create the spirit which makes a people capable of bearing arms. If this spirit dominates a people, the will finds a thousand ways to secure weapons."

Hitler's writings and public utterances are replete with declarations rationalising the use of force and glorifying war. The following is typical, when he said:-

"Always before God and the world, the stronger has the right to carry through his will. History proves it! He who has no might has no use for right."

As will be shown in subsequent proof, this doctrine of the glorification of war played a major part in the education of the German youth of the pre-war era.

I now offer the documents which establish the aims of the Nazi Party and their doctrinal techniques. I also have for the assistance of the Court and defence counsel, briefs which make the argument part of these documents.

I now direct your attention to the rise to power of the Nazi Party.

The first attempt to acquire political control was by force. In fact at no time during this period did the Party participate in any electoral campaigns, nor did it see fit to collaborate with other political groups and parties.

THE PRESIDENT: Major Wallis, have you got copies of these for defendants' counsel ?

MAJOR WALLIS: In Room 54-

THE PRESIDENT: Well, they will be wanting to follow them now.

MAJOR WALLIS: Mr. President, my remarks, with which I am proceeding, will cover an entirely different subject than in the briefs before you. The briefs cover what I have already said, Sir.

THE PRESIDENT: Are you depositing a copy of these briefs for each of the defendants' counsel ?

MAJOR WALLIS: I am informed, if your Honour pleases, that the same procedure has been followed with respect to these briefs as has been followed with respect to the documents, namely, a total of six has been made available to the defendants in Room 54.

THE PRESIDENT: What do you say?

MAJOR WALLIS: A total of six copies has been made available to the defendants in Room 54. If your Honour does not deem that number sufficient, I feel sure that I can give assurance, on behalf of the Chief Prosecutor of the United States, that before the close of the day an ample supply of copies will be there for use.

THE PRESIDENT: The Tribunal thinks that the defence counsel should each have a copy of these briefs.

MAJOR WALLIS: That will be done, sir.

THE PRESIDENT: Members of the defence counsel, you will understand that I have directed on behalf of the Tribunal that you should each have a copy of this brief.

DR. RUDOLF DIX: (Counsel for defendant Schacht): We are very grateful for this directive, but none of us has seen any of these documents so far. I assume and hope that these documents will be given to the defence in the German translation.

THE PRESIDENT: Yes. (Pause) Yes, Major Wallis.

MAJOR WALLIS: I now direct your attention to the rise to power of the Nazi Party.

The 9th November, 1923, warranted the end as well as the beginning of an era. On the 9th November occurred the historical fact popularly known as the Hitler Putsch. During the night of the 8th to 9th November, Hitler, supported by the S.A. under the defendant Goering, at a meeting in Munich, proclaimed the National Revolution and his dictatorship of Germany, and announced himself as the Chancellor of the Reich. On the following morning the duly constituted authorities of the State, after some bloodshed in Munich, put an end to this illegal attempt to seize the government. Hitler and some of his followers were arrested and tried, and sentenced to imprisonment.

The new era in the National Socialist movement commences with Hitler's parole from prison in December 1924. With the return of its leader, the Party took up its fight for power once again. The prohibitions invoked by the government against the Nazi Party at the time of the Munich Putsch gradually were removed, and Hitler the Fuehrer of the Party, formally announced that in seeking to achieve its aims to overthrow the Weimar Government, the Party would resort only to "legal" means. A valid inference from these facts may well be suggested, namely that the Party's resort to "legality" was in reality only a condition on which it was permitted to carry on its activities in a democratically organised State. But, consistent with its professed resort to "legality," the Party now participated in the popular elections of the German people and generally took part in political activity. At the same time it engaged in feverish activity to expand the party membership, its organisational structure and activities. The S.A. and the S.S. recruited numerous new members. Hitler's "Mein Kampf" appeared in 1925. The Hitler Youth was founded. Newspapers were published, among them the Volkischer Beobachter of which the defendant Rosenberg was editor, and Der Angriff published by Goebbels, later the notorious Minister of Propaganda and Public Enlightenment. Meetings of other political parties were interfered with and broken up, and there was much street brawling.

The results of the Party's attempt to gain political power made little headway for a number of years, despite the strenuous efforts exerted to that end. In 30 elections in which the National Socialists participated from 1925 to 1930 for seats in the "Reichstag" and in the "Landtage" or Provincial Diets of the various German states, the Nazis received mandates in but 16 and gained no seats at all in 14 elections. The National Socialist vote in the 1927 elections did not exceed 4 per cent of the total number of votes cast. The year 1929 marks the first modest success at the polls in the State of Thuringia. The Nazi received over 11 per cent of the popular vote, elected six representatives out of the total of fifty-three to the Diet, and the defendant Frick became Minister of Interior of Thuringia, the first National Socialist chosen to ministerial rank.

With such encouragement and proof of the success of its methods to win support, the Nazi Party redoubled its traditional efforts (by means of terror and coercion). These met with some rebuff on the part of the Reich and various German States. Prussia required its civil servants to terminate their membership in the Party and forbade the wearing of brown shirts, which were worn by the S.A. of the Party. Baden likewise ruled against the wearing of brown shirts, and Bavaria prohibited the wearing of uniforms by political organisations. New National Socialist writings appeared in Germany. The new "National Socialist Monthly" appeared under the editorship of the defendant Rosenberg, and shortly thereafter, in June, 1930, Rosenberg's "Myth of the 20th century" was published.

Against this background - President von Hindenburg having meanwhile dissolved the Reichstag when Chancellor Bruning failed to obtain a vote of confidence - Germany moved to the polls once more on the 14th September, 1930. By this election their representation in the Reichstag was increased from 12 seats to 107 seats out of a total of 577.

The new Reichstag met and 107 Nazis marched into the session dressed in brown shirts. Rowdy opposition at once developed, intent on causing the fall of the Bruning Cabinet. Taking advantage of the issues caused by the then prevailing general economic distress, the Nazis sought a vote of non- confidence and dissolution of the Reichstag. Failing in these obstructionary tactics, the Nazis walked out of the Reichstag.

With 107 members in the Reichstag, the Nazi propaganda increased in violence. The obstruction by the Nazi deputies of the Reichstag continued with the same pattern of conduct. Repeatedly motions of non-confidence in Bruning and for dissolution of the Reichstag were offered and were lost. And after every failure the Nazi members stalked out of the chamber anew.

By spring of 1932, Brunings' position became untenable and the defendant von Papen was appointed Chancellor. The Reichstag was dissolved and new elections held in which the Nazis increased the number of their seats to 230 out of a total of 608. The Nazi Party was becoming a strong party in Germany, but it had failed to become the Majority Party. The obstructive tactics of the Nazi deputies in the Reichstag continued, and by the fall of 1932 von Papen's government was no longer able to continue. President von Hindenburg again dissolved the Reichstag, and in the new elections of November the Nazi representation in the Reichstag actually decreased to 196 seats. The short-lived von Schleicher government then came into being - it was the 3rd December, 1932 - and by the end of January, 1933, it went out of existence. With the support of the Nationalist Party under Hugenberg and other political assistance, Hitler became Chancellor of Germany by designation of von Hindenburg.

That is the end of the prologue, as it were, to the dramatic and sinister story that will be developed by the prosecution in the course of this trial. Let it be noted here, however, and remembered, as the story of the misdeeds and crimes of these defendants and their fellow conspirators are exposed, that at no time in the course of their alleged "legal" efforts to gain possession of the State, did the conspirators represent a majority of the people.

Now it is commonly said that the Nazi conspirators "seized control" when Hitler became Chancellor of the German Republic on 3oth January, 1933. It may be more truly said that they seized control upon securing the passage of the law for the Protection of the People and the State on 24th March, 1933. The steps leading to this actual seizure of power are worthy of recital. The Nazi conspirators were fully cognisant of their lack of control over the legislative powers of the republic. They needed, if they were to carry out the first steps of their grand conspiracy under the cloak of law, an enabling act which would vest supreme legislative power in Hitler's Cabinet, free from all restraints of the Weimar Constitution. Such an enabling act, however, required a change in the Constitution which, in turn, required two-thirds of the regular members of the Reichstag to be present, and at least two-thirds of the votes of those present.

The time-table of events leading up to the passage of this enabling act, known as the law for the Protection of the People and the State, is as follows:-

1. On 30th January, 1933, Hitler held his first Cabinet meeting, and we have the original minutes of that meeting, which will be offered in evidence. The defendants von Papen, von Neurath, Frick, Goering, and Funk were present. According to the minutes of this meeting, Hitler pointed out that the adjournment of the Reichstag would be impossible without the collaboration of the Centre Party. He went on to say:

"We might, however, consider suppressing the Communist Party to eliminate its votes in the Reichstag and by this measure achieve a majority in the Reichstag."

He expressed the fear, however, that this might result in a general strike. The Reich Minister of Economy, according to their official minutes, stated that in his opinion, it was impossible to avoid the suppression of the Communist Party of Germany, for, if that were not done they could not achieve a majority in the Reichstag, certainly not a majority of two-thirds but that, after the suppression of the Communist Party, the passage of an enabling act through the Reichstag would be possible. The defendant Frick suggested that it would be best initially to request an enabling law from the Reichstag. At this meeting Hitler agreed to contact representatives of the Centre Party the next morning to see what could be done by way of making a deal with them.

2. The next event on this time-table was the Reichstag fire on the 28th of February, 1933.

3. Taking advantage ot the uncertainty and unrest created by the Reichstag fire, and the disturbances being created by the S.A., the provisions of the Weimar Constitution guaranteeing personal freedom, and other personal liberties were suspended by a decree of the Reich President on February 28th, 1933.

Then on 5th March, 1933, elections to the Reichstag were held. The Nazis acquired 288 seats out of a total of 647.

On the 15th March, 1933, another meeting of the Reich Cabinet was held, and we also have the original official minutes of that meeting which bears the initials, opposite their names, of the defendants who were present at that meeting, signifying that they have read - I contend that it is a reasonable inference to state that it signifies that they read these minutes and approved them. The following defendants were present at this meeting: von Papen, von Neurath, Frick, Goering, and Funk. At this meeting, according to these official minutes, Hitler stated that the putting over of the enabling act in the Reichstag by a two- thirds majority would, in his opinion, meet with no opposition. The defendant Frick pointed out that the Reichstag had to ratify the enabling act with a constitutional majority within three days, and that the Centre Party had not expressed itself negatively. He went on to say the enabling act would have to be broadly conceived in a manner to allow for deviation from the provisions of the Constitution of the Reich. He further stated that as far as the constitutional requirements of a two-thirds majority was concerned, a total of 432 delegates would have to be present for the ratification of the enabling act. The defendant Goering expressed his conviction at this meeting that the enabling act would be ratified with the required two-thirds vote for, if necessary, the majority could be obtained by refusing admittance to the Reichstag of some Social Democrats. Now on the 20th March another Cabinet meeting was held, and we also have the official, original records of this meeting which will be offered in evidence. The defendants Frick, von Papen, von Neurath, Goering and Funk were present. The proposed enabling act was again the subject of a discussion. Hitler reported on the conference he had completed with the representatives of the Centre Party, The defendant Neurath proposed a note concerning the arrangement to be agreed to by the representatives of the Centre Party. The defendant Frick expounded to the meeting the contents of the draft of the proposed law, and further stated that changes in the standing orders or rules of the Reichstag were also necessary, that an explicit rule must be made that unexcused absent delegates be considered present, and if that was done it would probably be possible to ratify the enabling act on the following Thursday in all three readings.

It is interesting to note that, among the things recorded in the official minutes of this Cabinet meeting, was the defendant Goering's announcement that he had ordered SA troops on the Polish border to be cautious and not to show themselves in uniform, and that the defendant Neurath recommended also that the SA be cautious, especially in Danzig. In addition, the defendant Neurath pointed out that Communists in SA uniforms were being caught continuously. These stool pigeons had to be banned. justice had to find means and ways to make possible such punishment for Communist stool pigeons, according to the defendant Neurath. On 14th March, 1933, the defendant Frick announced: "When the Reichstag meets on the 21st March the Communists will be prevented by urgent labour elsewhere from participation in the session. In concentration camps they will be re-educated for productive work. We will know how to render harmless permanently, sub- humans who don't want to be re-educated."

During this period, taking advantage of the decree suspending constitutional guarantees of freedom, a large number of Communists, including party officials and Reichstag deputies, and a smaller number of Social Democrat officials and deputies, were placed in protective custody. On 23rd March, 1933, in urging the passage of the enabling act, Hitler stated before the Reichstag:

"It is up to you, Gentlemen, to make the decision now. It will be for peace or war."

On 24th March, 1933, only 535 out of the regular 747 deputies of the Reichstag were present. The absence of some was unexcused; they were in protective custody in concentration camps. Subject to the full weight of the Nazi pressure and terror, the Reichstag passed an enabling act known as the "Law for the Protection of the People and State", with a vote of 441 in favour. This law marks the real seizure of political control by the conspirators. Article 1 provided: that the Reich laws can be enacted by the Reich Cabinet. Article 2: provided the National laws enacted by the Reich Cabinet may deviate from the Constitution. Article 3: provided: National Laws enacted by the Reich Cabinet are prepared by the Chancellor and published in the Reichsgesetzblatt. Article 4 provided: Treaties of the Reich with foreign states, which concern matters of national legislation, do not require the consent of the parties participating in legislation. The Reich Cabinet is empowered to issue the necessary provisions for the execution of these treaties.

Thus the Nazis acquired full political control, completely unrestrained by any provision of the Weimar Constitution.

I now offer the documents which establish the facts which I have just stated, and I also present, for the assistance of the Court and the defence counsel, the briefs covering this portion of the case.

THE PRESIDENT: I wish to speak to Major Wallis. Would it be possible for the prosecution to let defendants' counsel have at least one copy between each two of them here in court ? If not to-day, then to-morrow ?

COL. STOREY: If the Tribunal please, there has been some misunderstanding and the briefs were delivered to the defendants' document room. We have sent for some of them and they should be here shortly. However, Sir, in all fairness the briefs themselves are not in the German language, because we had intended to take the trial brief and let the lawyers follow it over the translating system and thus, when it was finished, it would be translated into all languages.

However, in order to shorten the proceeding, Major Wallis has made a summary, and he is giving the summary and will offer the documents in evidence and later the briefs, as needed, to the Tribunal, and to defence counsel, and, unfortunately, in the rush of time, they have been put down in the defendants' document room and we have sent for some of them. We understand, also, if the Tribunal please, that Dr. Kempner approached some of the distinguished counsel for the defence, and learned that a great many of them not only speak English, but understand it when they read it, and to save the tremendous physical burden on facilities, the briefs have not, as yet, been translated into German. If there is objection, the only thing we can do is to withhold them at this time, but we understood it would be agreeable to pass them to them in English, and that is what we propose to do at the present moment, and have German-speaking officers in the document room who will translate for any of them who may not be able to read German. Pardon me, to read English.

THE PRESIDENT: Did you hear what Col. Storey said, Dr. Dix ?

DR. DIX: I have one request. We are here, as German defence counsel, and in face of great difficulties. These proceedings are conducted according to Anglo-American customs. We are doing our best to make our way through these principles, and would be very grateful if the President would take into consideration our difficult situation.

I have heard - I am not quite sure if it was right-that according to these Anglo-American principles, it is necessary to prepare objections immediately, if one has any objections to the contents of a document, and that this is not possible unless one does it at once. This is a point on which I would like to make my request. I am convinced that both the trial brief and the documents will be made available to us, and we will see if we can have a German translation of one or the other. If this trouble can be spared, if the defence counsel needs a translation, we shall have it, but I should like-I have one request-that we have leisure to raise an objection later when we have had a chance of discussing it.

I think in that way we shall easily overcome the difficulties raised by the present situation, and we are trying to cooperate in order to overcome any difficulties.

THE PRESIDENT: The Tribunal is glad that defendants' counsel are making efforts to co-operate in the trial. After the adjournment, the Tribunal will consider the best method of providing defendants' counsel with as many translations as possible, and you are right in thinking that you will be able to make objections to any document after you have had time to consider it.

DR. DIX: Thank you, Sir.

PRESIDENT: Yes, Major Wallis ?

MAJOR WALLIS: Having acquired full political control, the Nazi conspirators now proceeded to consolidate their power, and at this point I would like to impress upon the Tribunal once again that with the exception of a very few documents, the subject matter of my remarks is within the purview of Judicial notice of the court, a matter of history well known to these defendants and their counsel. Their first step was ruthlessly to purge their political opponents by confining them to concentration camps or by murder. Concentration camps made their first appearance in 1933, and were first used as means of putting political opponents out of circulation by confining them to a so-called "protective custody." This system of concentration camps grew and expanded within Germany. At a subsequent stage in these proceedings full and complete evidence of the concentration camp system and the atrocities committed therein will be presented to the Court, both by documents and films.

Illustrative documentary evidence of the arrest, mistreatment and murder by the Nazi conspirators of their political opponents is contained in the documentary evidence offered by the United States.

As an illustration, affidavit of Raymond H. Geist, former American Consul and First Secretary of the Embassy in Berlin from 1929 to 1938, states (which will be offered):

"Immediately in 1933, the concentration camps were established and put under charge of the Gestapo. Only political prisoners were held in concentration camps.

The first wave of terroristic acts began in March, 1933, more particularly from March 6th to 13th, 1933, accompanied by unusual mob violence. When the Nazi Party won the elections in March, 1933, the accumulated passion blew off in wholesale attacks on the Communists, Jews and others suspected of being either. Mobs of SA men roamed the streets, beating up, looting and even killing persons. For Germans taken into custody by the Gestapo there was a regular pattern of brutality and terror. All over Germany victims were numbered by the hundred thousand."

On the 30th of June and 1st and 2nd July, 1934, the conspirators proceeded to destroy opposition within their own ranks by wholesale murder. In discussing this purge, the defendant Frick stated, in an affidavit under oath, signed on the i19th day of November, 1945, in the presence of his defence counsel, as follows: This is document 2950-PS, It has not yet been introduced in evidence, Sir:

"Himmler, in June of 1934, was able to convince Hitler that Roehm wanted to start a putsch. The Fuehrer ordered Himmler to suppress the putsch, which was supposed to take place at the Tegernsee, where all the SA leaders were coming together. For Northern Germany, the Fuehrer gave the order to suppress the putsch to Goering."

Frick goes on to say:

" Pursuant to this order, a great many people - something like a hundred, and possibly more-accused of high treason, were arrested and even put to death. They were just killed on the spot. Many people were killed - I don't know how many -w ho actually did not have anything to do with the putsch. People who just weren't liked very well as, for instance, Schleicher, the former Reich Chancellor, were killed. Schleicher's wife was also killed. Also Gregor Strasser, who had been the Reich Organisation Leader and second man in the Party after Hitler. Strasser, at the time he was murdered, was not active in political affairs any more; he had however separated himself from the Fuehrer in November or December of 1932."

Frick goes on to say: "The S.S. was used by Himmler for the execution of these orders to suppress the putsch."

During this period the conspirators created, by a series of decrees of the Reich Cabinet, a number of new political crimes. Any act or statement contrary to the Nazi Party was deemed to be treason and punished accordingly. The formations of the Party, the S.A., S.S., as well as the S.D. and the Gestapo, were the vicious tools used in the extermination of all opposition, real or potential. As the defendant Goering said on 24th July, 1933 (I refer to document 2494-PS, which will be introduced in evidence):

"Whoever in the future raises a hand against a representative of the National Socialist movement or of the State, must know that he will lose his life in a very short while. Furthermore, it will be entirely sufficient, if he is proven to have intended the act, or, if the act results not in a death, but only in an injury."

The defendant Frick stated, in a magazine of the Academy for German Law, 1936, which will be introduced as document 2533- PS, as follows:

"By the world we are blamed again and again because of the concentration camps. We are asked, 'Why do you arrest without a warrant of arrest?' I say, 'Put yourself into the position of our nation'. Don't forget that the very great and still untouched world of Bolshevism cannot forget that we have made final victory for them impossible in Europe, right here on German soil."

And Raymond Geist, whose affidavit I previously referred to, being document 1759-PS, states:

"The German people were well acquainted with what was happening in concentration camps, and it was well known that the fate of anyone too actively opposed to any part of the Nazi programme was liable to be one of great suffering. Indeed, before the Hitler regime was many months old, almost every family in Germany had received first-hand accounts of the brutalities inflicted in the concentration camps from someone, either in the family circle or in the circle of friends who had served a sentence, and consequently the fear of such camps was a very effective brake on any possible opposition."

And as the defendant Goering said in 1934 (and I refer to document 2344-PS, which will be offered in evidence)

"Against the enemies of the State we must proceed ruthlessly ... therefore the concentration camps have been created, where we have first confined thousands of Communist and Socialist Democrat functionaries.

In addition to ruthlessly purging all political opponents, the Nazi conspirators further consolidated their position by promptly proceeding to eliminate all other political parties. On 21st March, 1933, the defendant Frick announced that the Communists would be prevented from taking part in the Reichstag proceedings. This was accomplished, as has been pointed out, by placing them in "protective custody in 21 concentration camps." On 26th May, 1933, a Reich Cabinet decree, signed by Hitler and the defendant Frick, provided for the confiscation of the Communist property. On 22nd June, 1933, the Social Democratic Party was suppressed in Prussia, it previously having been seriously weakened by placing a number of its members in concentration camps. On 7th July, 1933, a Reich decree eliminated Social Democrats from the Reichstag and from the governing bodies of the provinces and municipalities. On 14th July, 1933, by a decree of the Reich Cabinet, the property of the Social Democrats was confiscated, and the Nazi Party was constituted as the sole political party in Germany, and thereupon it became illegal to maintain or to form another political party. Thus, Hitler was able to say within hardly more than five months after becoming Chancellor, I quote,

"The Party has become the State."

The Nazi conspirators immediately proceeded to make that statement a recorded fact, for on 1st December, 1933, the Reich Cabinet issued a law for "Securing the Unity of Party and State". This law was signed by Hitler and the defendant Frick.

Article 1 provided that the Nazi Party "is the bearer of the concept of the State and is inseparably the State. It will be a part of the public law. Its organisation will be determined by the Fuehrer."

Article 2 provided: "The Deputy of the Fuehrer and the Chief of Staff of the S.A.

will become members of the Reich Cabinet in order to insure close co-operation of the offices of the Party and S.A. with public authorities."

Article 3 provided: "The members of the National Socialist German Workers Party and the S.A. (including their subordinate organisations) as the leading and driving force of the National Socialist State will bear greater responsibility toward Fuehrer, People and State."

(A recess was taken.)

COLONEL STORY: During the recess defendants' counsel and the prosecution arrived at an agreement for the furnishing of briefs to the defendants, which I understand to be this:

Copies of the documents offered in evidence in German will be delivered in the defendants' information centre, with the understanding that if any defence counsel needs to show the German photostatic copy to his client he may do so in the defendants' counsel room adjacent thereto; that the briefs which we are passing to the Tribunal as an aid will likewise be passed to defendants' counsel in English, and that if any of them have trouble in the translation of any portion of the briefs we have German-speaking officers in defendants' information centre who will assist counsel. I understand that all of these defendants' counsel have so agreed.

THE PRESIDENT: Thank you. Now, Major Wallis.

MAJOR WALLIS: May it please the Court, at the moment of recess I was referring to the law which was passed on 1st December, 1933, for securing the unity of Party and State.

Article 6 of that law provided: "The public authorities have to grant legal and administrative assistance to the officers of the Party and the S.A. which are entrusted with the execution of the jurisdiction of the Party and S.A."

Article 8 provided: "The Reich Chancellor as Fuehrer of the National Socialistic German Workers Party and, as the supreme commander of the S.A., will issue the regulations necessary for the execution and augmentation of this law, particularly with respect to the organisation and procedure of the jurisdiction of the Party and S.A." Thus by this law the Nazi Party became a paragovernmental Organisation in Germany.

The further merger of the Party and State occurred on the death of Hindenburg. Instead of holding an election to fill the office of President, the merger of the offices of President and Chancellor, in the person of Hitler, was accomplished by the law of ist August, 1934, signed by the entire Reich Cabinet. One of the significant consequences of this law was to give to Hitler the supreme command of the German Armed Forces, always a prerequisite of the presidency, and every soldier was immediately required to take an oath of loyalty and unconditional obedience to Hitler. On 4th February, 1938, Hitler issued a decree which stated in part (and I quote from document 1915-P2), which will be offered in the document book at the close of my remarks) as follows: "From now on, I take over directly the command of the whole Armed Forces."

150

As a further step in the consolidation of their political control, the Nazi conspirators reduced national elections to mere formalities devoid of the element of freedom of choice. Elections, properly speaking, could not take place under the Nazi system. In the first place, the basic doctrine of the Fuehrerprinzip dictated that all subordinates must be appointed by their superiors in the government hierarchy. Although it had already become the practice, in 1938 it was specifically provided by law that only one list of candidates was to be submitted to the people. By the end of this pre-war period little of substance remained in the election law. The majority of the substantive provisions had become obsolete.

By a series of laws and decrees the Nazi conspirators reduced the powers of regional and local governments and substantially transformed them into territorial subdivisions of the Reich Government. With the abolition of representative assemblies and elective officials in the Lander, and the municipalities, regional and local elections ceased to exist. On 31st January, 1934, the last vestiges of Land independence was destroyed by the Law for the Reconstruction of the Reich. The defendant Frick, Minister of the Interior throughout this period, has written of this Law for the Reconstruction of the Reich as follows:

"The reconstruction law abolished the sovereign rights and executive powers of the Lander and made the Reich the sole bearer of the rights of sovereignty. The supreme powers of the Lander do not exist any longer. The natural result of this was the subordination of the Land government to the Reich Government and the Land ministers to the corresponding Reich ministers. On 30th January, 1934, the German Reich becomes one State."

Another step taken by the Nazi conspirators in consolidating their political power was the purge of civil servants on racial and political grounds and their replacement by Party members and supporters. This purge was accomplished through a series of Nazi laws and decrees. The first was on 7th April, 1933, entitled " Law for the Restoration of the Professional Civil Service." Article 3 of the law applied the Nazi blood and master race theories in providing that officials who were not of Aryan descent were to be retired. The political purge provision of the law is contained in Article 4 and I quote:

"Officials who, because of their previous political activities, do not offer security that they will assert themselves for the National State without reservations may be dismissed."

The effect of this law and the decrees and regulations issued thereunder was to fill every responsible position in the government with a Nazi and to prevent the appointment of any applicant opposed, or suspected of being opposed, to the Nazi programme and policy.

Even the judiciary did not escape the purge of the Nazi conspirators.

All judges who failed to fulfil the racial and political requirements of the conspirators were quickly removed. In addition, the Nazis set up a new system of special criminal courts independent of the regular judiciary and directly subservient to the Party programme.

Moreover, the Nazis controlled all judges through special directives and orders from the central government, their aim being, as expressed by one Garland, one of the leading Nazi lawyers of that time, "to make the word 'terrorisation' in the penal law respectable again."

As their control was consolidated, the conspirators greatly enlarged existing State and Party organisations and established an elaborate network of new formations and agencies. The Party spread octopus-like throughout all of Germany. This process of growth was summed up late in 1937 in an official statement of the Party Chancellery, as follows:-

"In order to control the whole German nation in all spheres of life - and I repeat, 'in order to control the whole German nation in all spheres of life'- the N.S.D.A.P., after assuming power, set up under its leadership the new Party formations and affiliated organisations."

At this point I would like to offer to the court the document book which contains the laws and conditions which I have referred to in this part of my presentation together with the briefs covering this part of it.

I would like to direct the Tribunal's attention to some case histories in the consolidation of control by the conspirators.

The first case history in the consolidation of the Nazi conspirators' control of Germany is the destruction of the free trade unions and the obtaining of control over the productive labour capacity of the German nation.

The position of organised labour in Germany, at the time of the Nazi seizure of power, the obstacles they afforded to the Nazi plans, the speed with which they were destroyed, the terror and maltreatment ranging from assault to murder of union leaders, were fully outlined in the opening address of the Chief Prosecutor of the United States, and are fully set forth in the document book - which I will present to the Court on this phase of the case.

The result achieved by the Nazi conspirators is best expressed in the words of Robert Ley. Ley's confidence in the Nazis' effective control over the productive labour capacity of Germany in peace or in war was declared as early as 1936 to the Nuremberg Party Congress. I refer to document 2283-PS which is included in the document book which will be presented on this phase of the case. He stated:-

"The idea of the factory troops is making good progress in the plants, and I am able to report to you, my Fuehrer, that security and peace in the factories has been guaranteed, not only in normal times, but also in times of the most serious crisis. Disturbances, such as the munitions strikes of the traitor Ebert and confederates, are out of the question. National Socialism has conquered the factories. Factory troops are the National Socialist shock troops within the factory, and their motto is "The Fuehrer is always right."

At this time I would like to offer to the Court the document on this phase of the case, namely, "The destruction of Labour unions and the gaining of control of all productive labour in Germany" together with the brief on that subject. At the same time, if it pleases the Court, I would like to offer the document book concerning the consolidation of control with respect to the utilisation and moulding of political machinery, which is, in law, a decree which I referred to just prior to my discussion of the destruction of labour unions.

I would now direct your attention to the second case history in the consolidation of control.

The Nazi conspirators early realised that the influence of the Christian churches in Germany was an obstacle to their complete domination of the German people and contra to their master race dogma. As the defendant Martin Bormann stated in a secret decree of the Party Chancellery, signed by him and distributed to all Gauleiters on 7th June, 1941 - it is identified as document D-75 and will be included in the document book which will be presented to the Court - he stated as follows:-

"More and more must the people be separated from the churches and their organisations and pastors.. Not until this has happened does the State leadership have influence on the individual citizens."

Accordingly, the Nazi conspirators, seeking to subvert the influence of the churches over the people of Germany proceeded to attempt to eliminate these churches.

1. By promoting beliefs and practices incompatible with Christian teachings.
2. By persecuting priests, clergy and members of monastic orders. This persecution, as the documentary evidence will show, ran the gauntlet of insults and indignities, physical assault, confinement and concentration camps and murder.
3. By the confiscation of church properties.
4. By suppressing religious publications.
5. By the suppression of religious organisations.

Moreover, they also suppressed religious education. This is illustrated by the secret decree of the Party Chancellery which I just referred to in document D-75, when the defendant Bormann stated:-

"No human being would know anything of Christianity if it had not been drilled into him in his childhood by his pastors. The so-called 'dear God' in no wise gives knowledge of his existence to young people in advance, but in an astonishing manner, in spite of His omnipotence, leaves this to the efforts of the pastors. If, therefore, in the future our youth learns nothing more of this Christianity, whose doctrines are far below ours, Christianity will disappear by itself."

At a subsequent stage in these proceedings, additional documentary evidence of the acts of the conspirators in their attempt to subvert the influence of the Christian churches will be offered. At this time I offer the document book in support of this phase of the case together with the accompanying brief.

We now come to what might be called the third case history, the persecution of the Jews. The Nazi conspirators adopted and publicised a programme of ruthless persecution of Jews.

It is not our purpose at this time to present to the Court a full and complete story, in all its sickening details, of the Nazi conspirators' plans and acts for the elimination and liquidation of the Jewish population of Europe. This will be done in due course, at a subsequent stage of these proceedings, but it is our purpose at this time to bring before you, as one of the elements in the Nazi scheme for the consolidation of their control of Germany, the action which was planned and taken with respect to the Jews within Germany during the pre-war period.

As a means of implementing their master race policy and as a means of rallying otherwise discordant elements behind the Nazi banner, the conspirators adopted and publicised a programme of relentless persecution of Jews. This programme was contained in the official, unalterable twenty-five points of the Nazi Party, of which six were devoted to the master race doctrine. The defendants Goering, Hess, Rosenberg, Frank, Frick, Streicher, Funk, Schirach, Bormann and others, all took prominent parts in publicising this programme. Upon the Nazis' coming into power, this Party programme became the official State programme. The first organised act was the boycott of Jewish enterprises on the 1st April, 1933. The defendant Streicher, in a signed statement, admits that he was in charge of this programme only for one day. We, of course, reserve the right to show additional evidence with respect to that fact. The Nazi conspirators then embarked upon a legislative programme which was gradual and which dates from 7th April, 1933 until September, 1935. During this period a series of laws was passed removing the Jews from civil service, from the professions and from the schools and military service. It was clear, however, that the Nazi conspirators had a far more ambitious programme for the Jewish problem and only put off its realisation for reasons of expediency. After the usual propaganda barrage, in which the speeches and writings of the defendant Streicher were most prominent, the Nazi conspirators initiated the second period of anti-Jewish legislation, namely, from 15th September, 1935 to September,1938. In this period the famous Nuremberg laws were passed, depriving the Jews of their rights as citizens, forbidding them to marry Aryans and eliminating them from additional professions. In the autumn of 1938, the Nazi conspirators began to put into effect a programme of complete elimination of the Jews from German life. The measures taken were partly presented as a retaliation against world Jewry in connection with the killing of a German embassy official in Paris. Unlike the boycott action in April, 1933, when care was taken to avoid extensive violence, an allegedly spontaneous pogrom was staged and carried out all over Germany (see 374- PS). The legislative measures which followed were discussed and approved in their final form at a meeting on 12th November, 1938, under the chairmanship of the defendant Goering, with the participation of the defendants Frick and Funk and others. I refer to document 516-PS, which will appear in the document book. The meeting was called following Hitler's orders "requesting that the Jewish question be now, once and for all, co-ordinated and solved one way or the other." The participants agreed on measures to be taken for the elimination of the Jew from German economy. The laws issued in this period were signed mostly by the defendant Goering in his capacity as Deputy of the Four-Year Plan, and were thus strictly connected with the consolidation of control of the German economy and preparation for aggressive war. These laws obliged all German Jews to pay a collective fine of one billion Reichsmarks; barred the Jews from trades and crafts; limited movement of Jews to certain localities and hours; limited the time for the sale or liquidation of Jewish enterprises; forced Jews to deposit shares and securities held by them; forbade the sale or acquisition of gold or precious stones by a Jew; granted landlords the right to give notice to Jewish tenants before legal expiration of the leases, and forced all Jews over six years of age to wear the Star of David. In the final period of the anti-Jewish crusade of the Nazi conspirators within Germany, very few legislative measures were passed. The Jews were just delivered to the S.S., Gestapo and the various extermination staffs. The last law dealing with Jews in Germany put them entirely outside the law and ordered the confiscation by the State of the property of dead Jews. This law was a weak reflection of a factual situation already in existence. As Dr. Stuckart, assistant to the defendant Frick, stated at the time:-

"The aim of the racial legislation may be regarded as already achieved and consequently the racial legislation as essentially closed. It led to the temporary solution of the Jewish problem and at the same time essentially prepared for the final solution. Many regulations will lose their practical importance as Germany approaches the achievement of the final goal on the Jewish problem."

Hitler, on 30th January, 1939, in a speech before the Reichstag, made the following prophecy:-

"The result (of a war) will be the annihilation of the Jewish race in Europe."

I will leave to others in this case the task of presenting to the Court the evidence as to how well that prophecy was fulfilled.

I would now offer to the Court the document book, which contains the laws referred to, with respect to the persecution of the Jews, and the brief outlining that subject.

THE PRESIDENT: The Tribunal will now adjourn until 10 o'clock to-morrow morning.

(The Tribunal adjourned until 23rd November at 1000 hours.)

FOURTH DAY:
Friday, 23rd November, 1945

DR. OTTO NELTE (Counsel for the defendant Keitel): Mr. President, you advised the defence in yesterday's session that they should at once, at this stage of the trial, raise objections if they believe they have any against the documentary evidence introduced by the Prosecution.

The Chief Prosecutor introduced in Court yesterday a graphic presentation concerning the Reich Ministries and other bureaux and offices at the highest level of the German government. My client is of the opinion that this presentation is erroneous in the following respects which concern his own person:

(1) A Reich Defence Council has never existed. The Reich Defence Law, which foresaw a Reich Defence Council in the event of war, has never been published; a session of a Reich Defence Council has never taken place. For this reason, the defendant Keitel was never a member of a Reich Defence Council.

(2) The Secret Cabinet Council which was to be created in accordance with the law of 4th February, 1938, never came into existence. It was never constituted; it never held a session.

(3) The defendant Keitel never was Reich Minister. Like the commanders in chief of the Army and the Navy, he merely had the rank of a Reich Minister. Consequently, he never was a Minister without portfolio either. He did not participate in any advisory Cabinet session.

I should like to ask the Court for its opinion as to whether these objections may be made the object of an examination at this stage of the trial or whether they are to be reserved for a later stage?

THE PRESIDENT: The Tribunal rules that the documents are admissible, but the defendants can prove at a later stage any matters, which are relevant to the documents. It is not necessary for the defendants to make objections at this stage. At a later stage they can prove any matters which are relevant to the weight of the documents.

DR. RUDOLF DIX (defence Counsel): May I ask the Tribunal a question:

We have now been able to see, in part, the briefs and documents which were introduced in Court yesterday. In that connection we have established that these documents comprise some with which the representative of the prosecution did not acquaint the Court either in their entire contents or as regards their nature. My question now is: Shall the contents, the entire contents of all the documents which were presented to Court form part of the basis for the Court's decision, even in cases where the prosecutor who presented the documents did not refer to their contents?

In other words, must we consider all of the documents presented in Court - including those the contents of which were not verbally referred to - as a basis for the judgement and, consequently, should they be examined with a view to determining whether the defendants wish to raise any objections?

In conclusion, I ask the Tribunal whether we are to understand that the entire contents of all the documents which were introduced in Court yesterday, or which still may be introduced at a future date, will form the basis for formulation of the judgement, even in cases concerning documents which the prosecutor has not presented verbatim, whose contents he has not given and to which he has not referred otherwise?

THE PRESIDENT: Every document, when it is put in, becomes part of the record and is in evidence before the Tribunal, but it is open to the defendants to criticise and comment upon any part of the document when their case is presented.

DR. DIX: Thank you. The question is clarified herewith.

THE PRESIDENT: There are three announcements which I have to make on behalf of the Tribunal; and the first is this: That we propose that the Tribunal shall not sit on Saturday morning in this week, in order that defendants' counsel may have more time for the consideration of the documents and arguments, which have been made up to that time. That is the first matter.

The second matter is that the Tribunal desires that all motions and applications shall, so far as practicable, be made in writing, both by the prosecution and by the defence. There are occasions, of course, such as this morning when motions and applications for the purpose of explanation, are more conveniently made orally, but as far as practicable, it is the desire of the Tribunal that they shall be made in writing, both by the prosecution and by the defence.

The other matter is an observation, which the Tribunal desires me to make to the prosecution, and to suggest to them that it would be more convenient to the Tribunal and possibly also to the defence that their briefs and volumes of documents should be presented to the Tribunal before counsel-speaking begins that branch of the case, so that the brief and volume of documents should be before the Tribunal while counsel is addressing the Tribunal upon that branch of the case; and also that it would be convenient to the Tribunal - if it is convenient to counsel for the prosecution-that he should give a short explanation - not a prolonged explanation - of the documents which he is presenting to the Court, drawing their attention to any passages in the documents to which be particularly wishes to draw attention.

I will now call upon the Chief Prosecutor for the United States to continue his address.

COLONEL STOREY: May it please the Tribunal: Yesterday afternoon it appeared that there was some question about the identification of documents formally offered in evidence yesterday. Therefore, with the Tribunal's permission I should like to offer them by number, formally, so that the Clerk can get them on his record and they may be identified, with your Honour's permission.

The United States - and may I say, Sir, that we offer each one of these exhibits in evidence - requests that they be received and filed as evidence for the United States of America, with the understanding that defence counsel may later interpose objections. If that is agreeable, Sir, the first is exhibit U.S.A. 1, the affidavit of Major William H. Coogan, concerning the capture, processing and authentication of documents, together with Robert C. Storey's accompanying statement:

Exhibit USA 2 being document 2903-PS, being the Nazi Party Chart, together with authentication certificates.

Exhibit USA 3, being document 2905-PS, the Nazi State Chart, together with authenticating certificates;

Exhibit USA 4, document 2836-PS, the original statement of defendant Goering as to positions held;

Exhibit USA 5, document 2829-PS, the same, concerning defendant Ribbentrop;

Exhibit USA 6, document 2851-PS, being the same with reference to defendant Rosenberg;

Exhibit USA 7, being document 2979-PS, the same concerning defendant Frank;

Exhibit USA 8, being document 2978-PS, the same relating to defendant Frick;

Exhibit USA 9, being document 2975-PS, regarding defendant Streicher

Exhibit USA 10, being document 2977-PS, relating to defendant Funk

Exhibit USA 11, being document 3021-PS, relating to defendant Schacht;Exhibit USA 12, being document 2887-PS, relating to defendant Donitz;

Exhibit USA 13, being document 2688-PS, relating to defendant Raeder;

Exhibit USA 14--

THE PRESIDENT: Colonel Storey, might not the numbering of those documents be done by the General Secretary?

COLONEL STOREY: Yes, Sir, that is correct. That is agreeable with us, Sir, but the General Secretary raised the question that it was not in the record. We have the complete tabulation describing each document by number, and if it is agreeable to your Honour I will offer the description of this page, correctly describing, by exhibit number, each one that was offered in evidence yesterday.

THE PRESIDENT: We will authorise the General Secretary to accept the documents so numbered.

COLONEL STOREY: Thank you, Sir. The tabulation referred to is set forth in the following words and figures:

USA 1 Major Coogan's affidavit with Col. Storey's statement.

USA 2 (2903-PS) Nazi Party Chart and authenticating papers.

USA 3 (2905-PS) Nazi State Chart and authenticating papers.

USA 4 (2695-PS) Original statement of Goering's positions.

USA 5 (2829-PS) Original statement of Ribbentrop's positions.

USA 6 (2851-PS) Original statement of Rosenberg's positions.

USA 7 (2979-PS) Original statement of Frank's positions.

USA 8 (2978-PS) Original statement of Frick's positions.

USA 9 (2975-PS) Original statement of Streicher's positions.

USA 10 (2977-PS) Original statement of Funk's positions.

USA 11 (3021-PS) Original statement of Schacht's positions.

USA 12 (2887-PS) Original statement of Donitz' positions.

USA 13 (2888-PS) Original statement of Raeder's positions.

USA 14 (2973-PS) Original statement of von Schirach's positions.

USA 15 (2974-PS) Original statement of Sauckel's positions.

USA 16 (2865-PS) Original statement of Jodl's positions.

USA 17 (2910-PS) statement of Seyss-Inquart's positions.

USA 18 (2980-PS) Original statement of Speer's positions.

USA 19 (2972-PS) Original statement of von Neurath's positions.

USA 20 (2976-PS) Original statement of Fritzsche's positions.

DOCUMENT BOOKS

USA A Common Objectives, Methods, and Doctrines of Conspiracy.

USA B The Acquiring of Totalitarian Control over Germany; Political First Steps; Control Acquired.

USA C Consolidation of Control (Utilisation and Moulding of Political Machinery.

USA F Purge of Political Opponents; Terrorisation.

USA G Destruction of Trade Unions and Acquisition of Control over Productive Labour Capacity in Germany.

USA H Suppression of the Christian Churches in Germany.

USA I Adoption and Publication of the Programme for Persecution of the Jews.

May it please the Tribunal, Mr. Justice Jackson called my attention while we were offering all of these exhibits on behalf of the United States; naturally they are for the benefit of and on behalf of all the other nations who are co- operating in this case.

THE PRESIDENT: That is understood.

MAJOR WALLIS: May it please the Court, when we adjourned yesterday afternoon, I was in the process of developing the various means by which these conspirators acquired a totalitarian control of Germany. I wish to continue on that subject this morning, and I will first discuss the reshaping of education and the training of youth; and in accordance with your Honour's suggestion, I offer the document book, United States Exhibit D, and would call to the Court's attention that this book contains translations of the documents which we rely upon with respect to this portion of the case. These documents consist of German writings, German speeches of the defendants, and other Nazi leaders, and are matters that we suggest are clearly within the purview of judicial notice of the Court. In the brief which is offered for the assistance of the Court in connection with this subject, the exact portions of the documents which are desired to be brought to the attention of the Tribunal are set forth either by quotation from the documents, or by reference to the specific page number of the documents.

Meanwhile, during this entire pre-war period, the nation was being psychologically prepared for war. One of the most important steps was the re-shaping of the educational system so as to educate the German youth to be amenable to their will. Hitler publicly announced this purpose in November, 1933, and I am quoting from document 2455-PS, when he said:

"When an opponent declares, 'I will not come over to your side, and you will not get me on your side,' I calmly say, 'Your child belongs to me already. A people lives forever. What are you? You will pass on. Your descendants, however, now stand in the new camps. In a short time they will know nothing else but this new community.'"

159

He further said in May, 1937, and I refer to document 2454- PS:

"This new Reich will give its youth to no one, but will itself take youth and give to youth its education and its own upbringing."

The first steps taken in making the German schools the tools of the Nazi education system were two decrees in May 1934, whereby the Reich Ministry of Education was established and the control of education by local authorities was replaced by the absolute authority of the Reich in all educational matters. These decrees are set out in documents 2078-PS, 2088-PS, 2992-PS. Thereafter, the curricula and organisation of the German schools and universities were modified by a series of decrees in order to make these schools effective instruments for the teaching of Nazi doctrines.

The Civil Service Law of 1933, which was presented in evidence yesterday, made it possible for the Nazi conspirators to re-examine thoroughly all German teachers and to remove all "harmful and unworthy elements", harmful and unworthy in the Nazi opinion. Many teachers and professors, mostly of them Jews, were dismissed and were replaced with State-spirited teachers. All teachers were required to belong to the National Socialist Teachers' League, which Organisation was charged with the training of all teachers in the theories and doctrines of the N.S.D.A.P. This is set forth in document 2452-PS. The Fuehrerprinzip was introduced into the schools and universities. I refer to document 2393-PS.

In addition, the Nazi conspirators supplemented the school system by training the youth through the "Hitler Jugend." The law of the Hitler Jugend, which is set forth in document 1392-PS, states:

"The German youth, besides being reared within the family and school, shall be educated physically, intellectually and morally in the spirit of National Socialism to serve the people and community through the Hitler Youth."

In 1925 the Hitler Youth was officially recognised by the Nazi Party and became a junior branch of the S.A. In 1931 the defendant Schirach was appointed Reich Youth Leader of the N.S.D.A.P. with the rank of S.A. Gruppenfuehrer. I refer to document 1458-PS. In June, 1933, the defendant Schirach was appointed Youth Leader of the German Reich. I refer to the same document, 1458-PS. In that same month, on orders of the defendant Schirach, the Nazi conspirators destroyed or took over all other youth organisations. This was accomplished by force in the first instance. The defendant Schirach, by decree dated 22nd June, 1933, dissolved the Reich Committee of the German Youth Associations and took over their property. I refer to document 2229-PS. By similar decrees, all of which are set forth in the document book, all the youth organisations of Germany were destroyed. Then the Nazi conspirators made membership in the Hitler Jugend compulsory. I refer to document 1392-PS.

The Hitler Jugend from its inception had been a formation of the Nazi Party. By virtue of the 1936 Youth-Law, making membership compulsory, it became an agency of the Reich Government while still retaining its position as a formation of the Nazi Party. This is set forth in document 1392-PS. By 1940 membership in the Hitler Jugend was over 7,000,000. I refer you to document 2435-PS. Through the Hitler

Jugend the Nazi conspirators imbued the youth with Nazi ideology. The master race doctrine and anti-Semitism, including physical attack on the Jews, were systematically taught in the training programme. I refer you to document 2436-PS. The Hitler Jugend indoctrinated the youth with the idea that war is a noble activity. I refer to document 1458-PS. One of the most important functions of the Hitler Jugend was to prepare the youth for membership in the Party and its formations. The Hitler Jugend was the agency used for extensive pre- military and military training of youth. I refer to document 1850-PS. In addition to general military training, special training was given in special formations. These included flying units, naval units, motorised units, signal units, etc.

The full details, with the accompanying documents of the methods used by the Nazi conspirators in re-shaping the educational system and supplementing it with the Hitler Jugend so as to educate the German youth to be amenable to the Nazi will, and prepare youth for war, are set forth in the document book which has been offered, and in the accompanying briefs.

Now I would like to direct your attention to the weapon of propaganda that was used during this period, and for this purpose I offer exhibit USA E with the accompanying brief. This document book and the briefs which accompany it.

THE PRESIDENT: Have any copies of these documents been provided for the defence counsel?

COLONEL STOREY: I understand they have been sent to the Defendants' Information Centre. I may say, Sir, that by to- morrow we will have then in advance for everybody, including the Court and the defence counsel.

THE PRESIDENT: Very well.

MAJOR WALLIS: This document book and the accompanying brief entitled "Propaganda Censorship and Supervision of Cultural Activities."

During this period one of the strongest weapons of the conspirators was propaganda. From the outset they appreciated the urgency of the task of inculcating the German masses with the National Socialist principles and ideology. The early utterances of Hitler and his fellow conspirators evidenced full recognition of the fact that their power could endure only if it rested on general acceptance of their political and social views.

Immediately following their accession to power, the Nazi conspirators instituted a determined programme for wholesale Organisation of the masses by seizing control of all vehicles of public expression. The widespread use of propaganda by the political machine thus created became a key device in establishing control over all phases of the German economy, public and private. They conceived that the proper function of propaganda was:-

"To prepare the ground psychologically for political action and military aggression, and to guarantee popular support of a system which was based on a permanent and steadily intensified application of terror and aggression, both in the sphere of domestic politics and foreign relations."

To attain these objectives, propaganda was used to create a specific thought pattern designed to make the people amenable to the aims and programme of the Nazis and to foster their active participation therein to the greatest extent possible. The nature of this propaganda is within the judicial purview of the Court. As Goebbels put it, it was aimed at "the conquest of the masses." Its intended effect was the elimination of all serious resistance in the masses. To achieve this result, as will be shown later in the evidence, the Nazi conspirators were utterly unscrupulous in their choice of means, a total disregard of veracity that presented their case purely from the standpoint of political expediency and their conception of national self-interest. Inasmuch as propaganda was the means to an end, "the conquest of the masses," it required different strategy at different times, depending on the objectives issued and pursued by the Nazi conspirators at any given moment. According to Hitler: "the first task of propaganda is gaining of people for the future organisation."

The recruiting of people for enlistment in the Party and supervised organisations was the primary objective in the years preceding and immediately following the seizure of power. After the rise to power, this task was broadened to include the enlistment of the people as a whole for the active support of the regime and its policies. As the Reich Propaganda Leader of the Party and Reich Minister for Propaganda, Goebbels stated:-

"Propaganda, the strongest weapon in the conquest of the State, remains the strongest weapon in the consolidation and building up of the State."

The methods which they used to control this strongest weapon in the power of the State are set forth in a chart which I would like to call to the Court's attention at this time, and would like to introduce in evidence as exhibit USA 21.

As you will note from the charts, there were three separate levels of control within the German Reich. The first level was the Party Controls, which are represented on the chart by the top block. And you will see that the Party through its Examining Commission controlled the books and magazines, and issues of books and magazines setting forth the ideology of the Party.

The second block, the Press Leader Division, supervised all publishers, and headed the Party newspapers and book publishers.

The third block, Press Chief - this office controlled the Press Political Office, the Press Personnel Office, and supervised the Party treatment of the Press and treatment of Party affairs in the Press.

The centre block, the Office of Propaganda Leader, had under its control not only the Press, but Exhibits, Affairs, Speaker's Bureau, Films, Radio, Culture, and other means of expression, and dissemination of the ideology of the Party and its purposes.

The next block, Ideology, was devoted exclusively to the ideology of the Party headed by the defendant Rosenberg. It supplied all the training periodicals, prepared for the schools, and the indoctrination of the people into the ideology of the Party. On that same level is Youth Education, presided over by the defendant Schirach, who had under his control the Hitler Jugend; and then there were the University Students and Teachers Division of the Party Control.

On the next level you have the controls that were exercised by the State, and reading from left to right you have the Propaganda Co-ordination, Foreign Co-ordination, and Co- operation.

Radio, which was under the control of the defendant Fritzsche, Film, Literature, the German Press, Periodicals, Theatre, Arts, Other Cultural Things, and the Ministry for Education.

Then, in the last, there is what is known as the Corporate Controls. These were under a semi-official control of both the Party and the State. These are the so-called Cultural Chambers. Their purpose was to have full control over the personnel engaged in the various arts and cultures, and engaged in the preparation and dissemination of news. First the Press. All reporters and writers belonged to that section. The next section was Fine Arts, Music, Theatre, Film, Literature, Radio, and then going over into the Educational Branch the organisation which the University Teachers, the Students, the former Corps Members of the University had to belong to.

By means of this vast network of propaganda machinery, the Nazi conspirators had full control over the expression and dissemination of all thought, cultural activities, and dissemination of news within the Reich. Nothing was or could be published in Germany that did not have the approval, express or implied of the Party and State. The defendant Schacht in his personal notes explains the effect of the killing of a piece of news in a totalitarian dictatorship. As he states it, it has never become publicly known that there have been thousands of martyrs in the Hitler regime. They have all disappeared in the cells or graves of the concentration camps, without ever having been heard of again; and he goes on to say, "what is the use of martyrdom in the fight against terror if it has no chance of becoming known and thus serving as an example for others."

I would . . .

THE PRESIDENT: What were you reading from then? From what document were you reading when you quoted Schacht?

MAJOR WALLIS: I am afraid . . .

THE PRESIDENT: You can tell us later on.

MAJOR WALLIS: I will tell you later on, Sir. I would now like to turn your attention . . .

THE PRESIDENT: Before you pass from this subject, there is a note on the documents which shows that certain documents are missing. What does that mean?

MAJOR WALLIS: Those documents are in the process of being reproduced and will be furnished to the Court, I hope, before the close of the day, Sir. They have been added to that book and, as yet, have not been completed in their process of reproduction.

THE PRESIDENT: Thank you. Have they been translated ?

MAJOR WALLIS: Yes, Sir, they have been translated, and the translations are in the process of being reproduced.

THE PRESIDENT: Are the documents in their original form in German?

MAJOR WALLIS: Yes, I believe they are, Sir.

THE PRESIDENT: Very well.

MAJOR WALLIS: I would now like to direct the Court's attention to the militarisation of Nazi-dominated organisations during this pre-war period, and for that purpose I offer Exhibit USA J, which consists of a document book with English translations, and I present to the Court also a brief which accompanies this portion of the case.

Throughout this pre-war period, and while the Nazi conspirators were achieving and consolidating their totalitarian control of Germany, they did not lose sight of their main objective-aggressive war. Accordingly, they placed a considerable number of their dominated organisations on a progressively militarised footing, with a view to the rapid transformation of these organisations whenever necessary, as instruments of war. These organisations were the SS, the SA, the Hitler Jugend, the NSKK or National Socialist Motor Corps, the NSFK (the National Socialist Aviation Corps), the RAD (Reich Labour Service), and the OT, the Todt Organisation.

The manner in which the militarisation was accomplished is detailed in part in the documents, which have been presented to us, and will be detailed further when the particular organisations are taken up and discussed and their criminality established at subsequent stages in the case. At this time, I would like to call the Court's attention to a chart, and while the chart is physically being placed on the board, I would offer exhibits USA 22 and 23, I beg your pardon--exhibit 22, which is document 2899-PS, and is a reproduction of Page 15 of the book entitled, "History of the Nazi Party". You will note that on the left lower corner of the chart placed oil the board, there are some papers attached. The top paper is an affidavit which reads as follows: "I certify that the above enlargement is a true and correct copy prepared under my direct supervision, of document Number 2833-PS, Page 15 of the book entitled "History of the Nazi Part," and you will note underneath is a second paper and this affidavit states it is a correct photographic copy, and which appears in the left-hand corner of the panel. This affidavit is signed by David Zablodowsky, sworn to and subscribed 23rd November, 1945, at Nuremburg, Germany, before James H. Johnston, 1st Lt., Office of U.S. Chief of Counsel.

This chart visualises, as vividly as possible, just how this militarisation took place in Germany. The chart is entitled, "The Organic Incorporation of German Nationals into the National Socialist System, and the Way to Political Leadership".

Starting at the bottom of the chart, you see the young folk, between the ages of 10 and 14. The arrows point both right and left. The arrow to the right is the Adolf Hitler School, for youth between the ages of 12 and 18. Both from the School and from the young folk, they proceed to the Hitler Jugend. At 18 years of age, they graduate from the Hitler Jugend into the various party formations, the SA, SS, the NSKK, and the NSFK. At the age of 20 they continue from these party formations into the Labour Service, and from the Labour Service, after they have served their period of time there, back again to the party formations, of the SA, the SS, NSKK, and NSFK, until they reach the age of 21. Then they proceed into the Army, serve in the Army from the ages of 21 to 23, and then back again into the party formations of SA, SS, etc.

And from that group, the select move to be Political Leaders (Leiter) of the Nazi Party, and from that group are selected the cream of the crop who go to the Nazi Party Special Schools and from these schools, as is represented on the top of the chart, graduate the political Fuehrers of the People.

I would emphasise again to the Court that this chart is not anything that was prepared by counsel in this case. It was prepared by the Nazi Party people and it comes from their own history.

Thus, by the end of the pre-war period, the Nazi conspirators had achieved one of the first major steps in their grand conspiracy. All phases of German life were dominated by Nazi doctrine and practice and mobilised for the accomplishment of their militant aims. The extent to which this was accomplished can be no better expressed than by the words of Hitler when he spoke to the Reichstag on 20th February, 1938. I refer to document 2715-PS. He said:

"Only now have we succeeded in setting before us the great tasks and in possessing the material things which are the prerequisites for the realisation of great creative plans in all fields of our national existence. Thus, National Socialism has made up with a few years for what centuries before it had omitted. . . . National Socialism has given the German people that leadership which as Party not only mobilises the nation but also organises it, so that on the basis of the natural principle of selection, the continuance of a stable political leadership is safeguarded forever . . . National Socialism . . .possesses Germany entirely and completely since the day when, five years ago, I left the house in Wilhelmsplatz as Reich Chancellor. There is no institution in this State which is not National Socialist. Above all, however, the National Socialist Party in these five years not only has made the nation National Socialist, but has given itself the perfect organisational structure which guarantees its permanence for all future. The greatest guarantee of the National Socialist revolution lies in the complete domination of the Reich and all its institutions and organisations, internally and externally, by the National Socialist Party. Its protection against the world abroad, however, lies in its New National Socialist armed forces. . . .

In this Reich, anybody who has a responsible position is a National Socialist. . . . Every institution of this Reich is under the orders of the supreme political leadership. . . . The Party leads the Reich politically, the armed forces defend it militarily. . . . There is nobody in any responsible position in this State who doubts that I am the authorised leader of this Reich." Thus spoke Adolf Hitler at the end of this period on the 2oth February, 1938.

COLONEL STOREY: If the Tribunal please ...

DR. SEIDL (Counsel for defendant Frank): Mr. President, may I make a few short remarks in this connection? The defendants were given, along with the Indictment, a list of the documents, which is introduced as follows:

"Every one of the defendants is hereby being informed that the prosecution will use several or all the documents listed in the enclosure..."

THE PRESIDENT:(interposing): You must speak more slowly.

DR. SEIDL (continuing):

"...in order to implement the points enumerated in the Indictment."

Now, the Chief Prosecutor introduced in Court this morning about twelve documents and a check of that list revealed that not a single one of the documents is mentioned.

Thus, already now, at the very beginning of the trial, we are confronted with the fact that documents are presented to the Court with the contents of which the defendant is unacquainted and, further, that documents which are not even listed are being used as documentary evidence. Not a single one of these documents is mentioned in the list, and I must confess that an adequate defence is altogether impossible under these circumstances. I therefore move:

(1) That the Tribunal supply the prosecution with a list of all documents available, which are to be placed before the Court as evidence.

(2) To instruct the prosecution to make available to the defence and their counsel - at the latest on the day when documents are being presented to the Court - a copy of the German text; and

(3) That the main proceedings be suspended until the prosecution will be in a position to comply with these requests. Otherwise I, at least, will not be able to proceed with the defence.

THE PRESIDENT: Colonel Storey, or counsel for the prosecution, will you say what answer you have to make to this objection?

COLONEL STOREY: If the Tribunal please, in the first place practically every document referred to by Major Wallis is a document of which the Court would take judicial knowledge. Secondly, a list of documents was filed in the Defendants' Information Centre on 1st November. I am not sure as to whether all of these or a part of them were included. Each attorney presenting each segment of the case sends down to the Defendants' Information Centre a list of the documents which he proposes to offer in evidence Upon his presentation. Thirdly, I wonder if the Tribunal and defence counsel realise the physical problems that are imposed? I am informed that copies of these documents in English as well as copies of the briefs, were delivered either last night or this morning in Defendants' Information Centre. Lastly, other presentations that follow, we will abide by the Tribunal's request, namely, that, prior to the presentation the Court will be furnished with these documents books, with these briefs, and defence counsel will also be furnished with them in advance. The week-end will permit us to do that.

THE PRESIDENT: The Tribunal thinks that the trial must now continue without any adjournment, but that in future as soon as possible the defendants' counsel will be furnished with copies of the documents which are to be put in evidence.

DR. SERVATIUS (Counsel for defendant Sauckel): I should like to present the following: The documents are presented to the Court also in an English translation. An examination of these translations should be made available to the defence. I point out particularly that the translation of technical terms could possibly lead to misunderstandings. Moreover, the documents are provided with an introductory remark and a table of contents. The defence should also have opportunity to read through this table of contents and examine it.

I make the motion that these English translations and their preliminary remarks be made available to the defence.

THE PRESIDENT: Colonel Storey, I understood from you that you proposed to make available to the defendants the trial briefs which contain certain observations upon the documents put in.

COLONEL STOREY: That is right, sir. They have been, are now, and will be completed during the week-end, and, as I understand defence counsel were willing for the briefs to be furnished in English, and if they want a translation, there will be German speaking officers in Defendants' Information Centre at their service. I understood that was agreeable yesterday.

Sir, while I am on my feet, and in order to obviate some misapprehension, for the benefit of defence counsel, when we refer to document numbers as, say, 1850-PS, in many instances that is a document which is a copy of a citation or a decree in the Reichsgesetzblatt, and, therefore, is not a separate document of ours. We have placed In the Defendants' Information Centre ample copies and sets of the Reichsgesetzblatt, and I dare say that one-half of the documents referred to in Major Walllis's presentation will be found in the Reichsgesetzblatt. I assure your Honour that over the week-end we will do the utmost to explain to defence counsel and to make available to them all information that we have and will do so in the future in advance.

THE PRESIDENT: Thank you. The Tribunal will now adjourn for ten minutes.

(The Tribunal then took a ten-minute recess, after which proceedings continued as follows:)

COLONEL STOREY: If your Honour pleases, the next subject to be presented is the economic preparation for aggressive war, by Mr. Dodd.

MR. THOMAS J. DODD: May it please the Tribunal, Mr. President, and Members of the Tribunal: In view of the discussions which took place just before the recess period, I believe it proper for me to inform the Tribunal that a list of the documents to which I shall make reference, has been lodged in the Defendants' Information Centre, and photostatic copies of the originals have also been placed there this morning.

It is my responsibility on behalf of the Chief Prosecutor for the United States of America to present the proof with reference to the allegations of the indictment under Section XV E, on page 6 of the English version of the Indictment, and particularly beginning with the second paragraph under E, which is entitled, "The Acquiring of Totalitarian Control in Germany, Economic, and the Economic Planning and Mobilisation for Aggressive War." The second paragraph:-

" 2. They used organisations of German business as instruments of economic mobilisation for war.

3. They directed Germany's economy towards preparation and equipment of the military machine. To this end they directed finance, capital investment, and foreign trade.

4. The Nazi conspirators, and in particular the industrialists among them, embarked upon a huge rearmament programme, and set out to produce and develop huge quantities of materials of war and to create a powerful military potential."

The fifth paragraph under that same heading A, and the final one in so far as my responsibility goes this morning, is that which reads

"With the object of carrying through the preparation for war the Nazi conspirators

167

set up a series of administrative agencies and authorities. For example, in 1936 they established for this purpose the office of the Four-Year Plan with the defendant Goering as plenipotentiary, vesting it with overriding control over Germany's economy. Furthermore, on 26th August, 1939, immediately before launching their aggression against Poland, they appointed the defendant Funk Plenipotentiary for Economics; and on 30th August, 1939, they set up the Ministerial Council for the Defence of the Reich to act as a War Cabinet."

I will not take the time of this Tribunal to prove what the world already knows that the Nazi conspirators rearmed Germany on a vast scale. I propose to place in evidence the secret records of the plans and deliberations of the inner councils of the Nazis, which prove that the reorganisation of the German government, the financial wizardry of the defendant Schacht, and the total mobilisation of the German economy largely under the defendants Schacht, Goering and Funk, were directed at a single goal - aggressive war.

I should like to hand to the Court at this point the so- called document book which contains the English translation of the original German document. I do not make an offer at this time of these documents in evidence, but hand them to the Court for the purpose of easing the task of the Court in following the discussion concerning these documents. I might say at this point also that I should like to submit at a little later date a brief for the assistance of the Court after I have concluded my remarks before it this morning.

The significance of the economic measures adopted and applied by the conspirators can, of course, be properly appraised only if they are placed in the larger social and political context of Nazi Germany. The economic measures were adopted while the conspirators were, as has already been shown, directing their vast propaganda to the glorification of war. They were adopted while the conspirators were perverting physical training into training for war. They were adopted while, as my colleagues will show, these conspirators were threatening to use force and were planning to use force to achieve their material and political objects. In short, if your Honour pleases, these measures constitute in the field of economics and government administration the same preparation for aggressive war which dominated every aspect of the Nazi State.

In 1939 and 1940 after the Nazi aggression upon Poland, Holland, Belgium, and France, it became perfectly clear to the world that the Nazi conspirators had created probably the greatest instrument of aggression in history. That machine was built up in its entirety in a period of less than one decade. In May of 1939, Major-General George Thomas, former Chief of the Military-Economic Staff in the Reich War Ministry, reported that the German Army had grown from seven infantry divisions in 1933 to thirty-nine infantry divisions, among them four fully motorised and three mountain divisions; eighteen corps headquarters; five panzer divisions; twenty-two machine-gun battalions. Moreover, General Thomas stated that the German Navy had greatly expanded by the launching, among other vessels, of two battleships Of 35,000 tons, four heavy cruisers of 10,000 tons, and other warships; further, that the Luftwaffe had grown to a point where it had a strength of 260,000 men, twenty-one squadrons, consisting Of 240 echelons, and thirty- three anti-aircraft batteries.

He likewise reported that out of the few factories permitted by the Versailles Treaty there had arisen - and I now quote him from the document EC 28, which consists of a lecture which he delivered on the 24th May, 1939 - in the Nazi Foreign Office: "The mightiest armament industry"; or rather he reported that out of the few factories permitted by the Treaty of Versailles there had arisen "the mightiest armament industry now existing in the world. It has attained the performances which in part equal the German wartime performances and in part even surpasses them. Germany's crude steel production is to-day the largest in the world after the Americans. The aluminium production exceeds that of America and of other countries of the world very considerably. The output of our rifle, machine gun, and artillery factories is at present larger than that of any other State."

That quotation, I repeat, was from a document hearing the lettering "EC" and the number after the dash "28."

These results - the results which General Thomas spoke about in his lecture in May of 1939--were achieved only by making preparation for war the dominating objective of German economy. And, to quote General Thomas from that same speech, he stated: "History will know only a few examples of cases where a country has directed, even in peace time, all its economic forces so deliberately and systematically towards the requirements of war, as Germany was compelled to do in the period between the two World Wars."*

*[*NB. This quotation is not taken from the lecture given by General Thomas in may 1939, but from his manuscript entitled "Basic Facts for a History of German War Armaments Economy" (1944).]*

That quotation from General Thomas will be found in the document 2353-PS.

THE PRESIDENT:(interposing): Mr. Dodd, it would help me personally if I knew where, in the document, you were reading from.

MR. DODD: Very well, Sir. Would you like me to refer back to number EC-28.

THE PRESIDENT: I have it before me, but I haven't the particular passage in the document which you were reading.

MR. DODD: That document - the one which I have just been reading, your Honour - is document 2353-PS.

THE PRESIDENT: It is not in EC-28?

MR. DODD: No. It is another quotation from General Thomas, but from another writing of his.

THE PRESIDENT: 2353?

MR. DODD: The document is 2353-PS. The passage will be found on the third page of that document.

THE PRESIDENT: I seem to have only two pages of that document 2353-PS.

MR. DODD: I am sorry; there should be a third page.

THE PRESIDENT: There is a page in between?

MR. DODD: There should be a third page. There may be one page missing.

THE PRESIDENT: Oh, yes; I have it now.

MR. DODD: The task of mobilising the German economy for aggressive war began promptly after the Nazi conspirators' seizure of power. It was entrusted principally to the defendants, Goering and Funk.

The defendant Schacht, as is well known, was appointed President of the Reichsbank in March of 1933 and Minister of Economics in August of 1934. The world did not know, however, that the responsibility for the execution of this programme was entrusted to the office of the Four Year Plan under the defendant Goering.

I should now like to call to your Honour's attention document EC-408, and I should also like to refer at this time to another document for your Honour's attention while I discuss the material, which is number 2261-PS. To continue.

Nor did the world know that the defendant Schacht was designated Plenipotentiary for the War Economy on 21St May, 1935, with complete control over the German civilian economy for war production in the Reich Defence Council, established by a top secret Hitler decree.

I invite your Honour's attention to document 2261-PS, which I referred to a few minutes ago.

The defendant Schacht recognised that the preparation for war came before all else for, in a memorandum concerning the problem of financing rearmament written on 3rd May, 1935, he stated that his comments were based on the assumption that the accomplishment of the armament programme--

THE PRESIDENT:(interposing): Pardon me, but you referred us to document 2261.

MR. DODD: Yes, your Honour.

THE PRESIDENT: But you haven't read anything from it.

MR. DODD: I did not; I merely referred the Court to it since it -

THE PRESIDENT: (interposing): It would help us, I think, if, when you refer to a document, you refer to some particular passage in it.

MR. DODD: Very well.

THE PRESIDENT: I think it must be the middle paragraph in the document: "The Fuehrer has nominated the President of the Directorate of the Reichsbank, Dr. Schacht."

MR. DODD: Yes, that is the paragraph to which I wish to make reference. If your Honour pleases, I refer to the second paragraph, or the middle paragraph, which states, in a letter dated 24th June, 1935, at Berlin:

"The Fuehrer and Reichs Chancellor has nominated the President of the Directorate, Dr. Schacht, to be Plenipotentiary General for the War Economy."

I might point out, in addition to the second paragraph, the last paragraph or the last sentence of that letter, which reads: "I point out the necessity of strictest secrecy once more"; the letter being signed, "von Blomberg."

Through Schacht's financial genius monetary measures were devised to restore German industry to full production; and through the control of imports and exports, which he devised under his plan of 1934, German production was channelled in accordance with the requirements of the German war machine.

I shall, with the Court's permission, later discuss the details of documentary proof of this assertion.

In 1936, with an eye to the experience in the First World War, the Nazi conspirators embarked on an ambitious plan to make Germany completely self-sufficient in strategic war materials such as rubber, gasoline, and steel, in a period of four years, so that the Nazi conspirators would be fully prepared for aggressive war. The responsibility for the execution of this programme was entrusted to the office of the Four-Year Plan under the defendant Goering - and at this point I should like to refer to the document bearing the number and the lettering EC-408. It is dated the 30th day of December, 1936, marked "Secret Command Matter", and entitled, "Report, Memorandum on the Four-Year Plan and Preparation of the War Economy."

This document sets out that the Fuehrer and Reich Chancellor has conferred powers in regard to mobilisation preparations in the economic field that need further definition. In the third paragraph it refers specifically to Minister President, Generaloberst Goering, as Commissioner of the Four-Year Plan, by authority of the Fuehrer and Reich Chancellor granted the 18th day of October, 1936. The existence of this programme involved the reorganisation and control of the whole German economy for war.

Again referring to Major General Thomas - and specifically to our document EC-27 - General Thomas, in a lecture on the 28th of January, 1939, made at the Staff Instructor's Course, stated:

"The National Socialist State, soon after taking over power, reorganised the German economy in all sections and directed it towards a military view-point, which had been requested by the Army for years. Due to the reorganisation, agriculture, commerce and professions become those powerful instruments the Fuehrer needs for his extensive plans, and we can say to-day that Hitler's mobile politics, as well as the powerful efforts of the Army and economy, would not have been possible without the necessary reorganisation by the National Socialist Government. We can now say that the economic organisation as a whole corresponds with the needs, although slight adjustments will have to be made yet. These reorganisations made a new system of economics possible which was necessary in view of our internal and foreign political situation as well as our financial problems. The directed economy, as we have it to-day concerning agriculture, commerce and Industry, is not only the expression of the present State principles, but at the same time also the economy of the country's defence."

If your Honour pleases, this programme was not undertaken in a vacuum it was deliberately designed and executed to provide the necessary instrument of the Nazi conspirators' plans for aggressive war.

In September of 1934 the defendant Schacht frankly acknowledged to the American Ambassador in Berlin that the Hitler Party was absolutely committed to war, and the people too ready and willing. That quotation is found in the Ambassador's diary and is document 2832-PS, particularly on page 176 of that diary.

At the same time, the defendant Schacht promulgated his new plan for the control of imports and exports in the interest of rearmament. A year later he was appointed Plenipotentiary for the War Economy by the top secret decree referred to a few minutes ago.

In September, 1936, the defendant Goering announced - at a meeting attended by the defendant Schacht and others - that Hitler had issued instructions to the Reich Minister on the basis that the show-down with Russia is inevitable, and added that "all measures have to be taken just as if we were actually in the stage of imminent danger of war."

I refer the Court to document EC-416. Before I discuss the quotation I might indicate that this document is also marked a secret Reich matter in the minutes of the Cabinet meeting of 4th September, 1936, at 12 o'clock noon. It tells who was present: the defendant Goering, von Blomberg, the defendant Schacht, and others.

On the second page of that document, in the second paragraph, is found the quotation by Goering. It starts from the basic thought that: "The show-down with Russia is inevitable. What Russia has done in the field of reconstruction we too can do."

On the third page of that document, in the second paragraph, Goering stated: "All measures have to be taken just as if we were actually in the stage of imminent danger of war."

In the same month the office of the Four-Year Plan was created with the mission of making Germany self-sufficient for war in four years. I refer back, at this point, to document EC-408, and I particularly refer your Honour to the third paragraph, again, of that document, where the statement is made as regards the war economy: Minister President Generaloberst Goering sees it as his task, within four years, to put the entire economy in a state of readiness for war.

The Nazi Government officials provided the leadership in preparing Germany for war. They received, however, the enthusiastic co-operation of the German industrialists. The role played by industrialists in converting Germany to a war economy is an important one, and I turn briefly to that aspect of the economic picture.

On the invitation of the defendant Goering, approximately twenty-five of the leading industrialists of Germany, and the defendant Schacht, attended a meeting in Berlin on the 20th day of February, 1933. This was shortly before the election of 5th March, 1933, in Germany. At this meeting Hitler announced the conspirators' aim to seize totalitarian control over Germany, to destroy the parliamentary system, to crush all opposition by force, and to restore the power of the Wehrmacht.

Among those present on that day, in February of 1933 in Berlin, were Gustav Krupp, head of the huge munitions firm, Alfred Krupp, A.G.; four leading officials of I.G. Farben, one of the world's largest chemical concerns; and, I repeat, also present was the defendant Schacht. Albert Vogler, the head of the huge steel trusts, the United Steel Works of Germany, was there too, as were other leading industrialists.

In support of the assertion with respect to that meeting at that time and in that place, I refer your Honour to the document EC-439, it being an affidavit of George von Schnitzler, which reads as follows:-

"I, George von Schnitzler, a member of the Vorstand of I.G. Farben, make the following deposition under oath:

At the end of February, 1933, four members of the Vorstand of I.G. Farben, including Dr. Boech, the head of the Vorstand, and myself were asked by the office of the President of the Reichstag to attend a meeting in his house, the purpose of which was not given. I do not remember the two other colleagues of mine who were also invited. I believe the invitation reached me during one of my business trips to Berlin. I went to the meeting which was attended by about twenty persons, who I believe were mostly leading industrialists from the Ruhr.

Among those present, I remember: Dr. Schacht, who at that time was not yet head of the Reichsbank again and not yet Minister of Economics.

Krupp von Bohlen, who in the beginning of 1933 presided over the Reichsverband der Deutschen Industrie, which later on was changed in the semi-official Organisation 'Reichsgruppe Industrie.'

Dr. Albert Vogler, head of the Vereinigte Stahlwerke.

Von Loewenfeld, from an industrial works in Essen.

Dr. Stein who was head of the I.G. Farben owned mine - Gewerkschaft Auguste Victoria - and also an active member of the Deutsche Volkspartei.

I remember that Dr. Schacht acted as a kind of host.

While I had expected the appearance of Goering, Hitler entered the room, shook hands with everybody and took a seat at the table. In a long speech he talked mainly about the danger of Communism over which he pretended that he had just won a decisive victory.

He then talked about the Bundnis - alliance - into which his party and the Deutschnationale Volkspartei had entered. This latter party, in the mean-time, had been reorganised by Herr von Papen. At the end he came to the point which seemed to me the purpose of the meeting. Hitler stressed the importance that the two aforementioned parties should gain the majority in the coming Reichstag election. Krupp von Bohlen thanked Hitler for his speech. After Hitler had left the room, Dr. Schacht proposed to the meeting the raising of an election fund of, as far as I remember, RM3,000,000. The fund should be distributed between the two ' allies' according to their relative strength at the time being. Dr. Stein suggested that the Deutsche Volkspartei should be included- "

THE PRESIDENT: (interposing): Mr. Dodd, it seems to me that really all that that document shows is that there was a meeting at which Schacht was present, and at which it was determined to subscribe an election fund in 1933.

MR. DODD: That is quite so, your Honour. I will not trouble to read it all. There were some other references, but not of major importance, in the last paragraph, to a division of the election fund. I just call your Honour's attention to it in passing.

I should like, at this point, to call your Honour's attention to the document D-203, which is a three-page document.

THE PRESIDENT: What is the number?

MR. DODD: D-203. I wish to read only excerpts from it very briefly. It is the speech delivered to the industrialists by Hitler, and I refer particularly to the second paragraph of that document:-

"Private enterprise cannot be maintained in the age of democracy;" .

THE PRESIDENT:(interposing): What is the date of that?

MR. DODD: It is the speech made at the meeting on the 20th February, 1933, at Berlin.

THE PRESIDENT: Yes.

MR. DODD:

"Private enterprise cannot be maintained in the age of democracy; it is conceivable only if the people have a sound idea of authority and personality."

I refer now to page 2 of the document, and I should like to read an excerpt from the first paragraph on page 9, about thirteen sentences down, beginning with the words: "I recognised even while in the hospital that one had to search for new ideas conducive to reconstruction. I found them in Nationalism, in the value of strength and power of individual personality."

Then, a little further down, the next to the last and the last sentence of that same paragraph, Hitler said:-

"If one rejects pacifism, one must put a new idea in its place immediately. Everything must be pushed aside, must be replaced by something better."

Then, in the third paragraph, the last sentence beginning: "We must not forget that all the benefits of culture must be introduced more or less with an iron fist, just as once upon a time the farmers were forced to plant potatoes."

Then finally, on that page, in the fourth paragraph - nearly at the end of it: "With the very same courage with which we go to work to make up for what had been sinned during the last fourteen years, we have withstood all attempts to move us from the right way."

Then, at the top of the next page, in the second paragraph, these words: "Now we stand before the last election. Regardless of the outcome there will be no retreat, even if the coming election does not bring about a decision."

THE PRESIDENT: Why did you not read the last line on page 2: " While still gaining power, one should not start the struggle against the opponent"?

MR. DODD: Beginning with the words "while still gaining power"?

THE PRESIDENT: The sentence before, "We must first gain complete power if we want to crush the other side completely. While still gaining power, one should not start the struggle against the opponent. Only when one knows that one has reached the pinnacle of power, that there is no further possible development, shall one strike."

MR. DODD: I was going to refer to that, if your Honour pleases, in a minute.

However, I think it is quite proper to have it inserted here.

Before starting to read this last paragraph, I suggest that as it is now the accustomed time, as I understand it, and it is a rather lengthy paragraph -

THE PRESIDENT:(interposing): Yes, we will adjourn until two o'clock.

(Whereupon at 12.30 hours the Tribunal adjourned, to reconvene at 14.00 hours of the same date.)

MR. DODD: If your Honour pleases, if I may go back for just a very little bit to take up the train of thought where I left off at the noon recess.

We were discussing document D-203, and I had referred particularly to the third page of that document, and even more particularly to the second paragraph on that page; and I wish to read from a sentence approximately eight or ten lines down in that second paragraph, which reads as follows:

"The question of restoration of the Wehrmacht will not be decided at Geneva but in Germany, when we have gained internal strength through internal peace."

I wish to refer again to the same page of the same document, and to the last paragraph and the last sentence, which refers to the defendant Goering, who was present at that same meeting to which this document refers, the meeting of 20th February, 1933, in Berlin. Goering said:

"That the sacrifices asked for surely would be so much easier for industry to bear if it realised that the election of 5th March will surely be the last one for the next ten years, probably even for the next hundred years."

In a memorandum, dated the 22nd day of February, 1933, and, for the information of the Court, in the document book, bearing the number D-204, Gustav Krupp described this meeting briefly, and in the memorandum wrote that he had expressed to Hitler the gratitude of the twenty-five industrialists present at the meeting on 20th February, 1933.

There were other expressions in that memorandum, which we do not deem to be particularly pertinent to the allegations of the Indictment with which we are now concerned.

I might point out to the Court that this memorandum, together with the report of the speech of Hitler, were found by the British and the United States Armies in the personal files of the defendant Krupp.

I am aware, if your Honours please, that the method I am pursuing here is a little tedious, because I am trying to refer specifically to the documents, and particularly to the excerpts referred to in my remarks, and therefore this presentation differs very considerably from that which has gone before. I trust, however, that you will bear with me, because this part of the case requires some rather careful and detailed explanations.

In April of 1933, after Hitler had entrenched himself in power, Gustav Krupp, as Chairman of the Reich Association of German Industry, which was the largest association of German industrialists, submitted to Hitler the plan of that association for the reorganisation of German industry, and in connection therewith, undertook to bring the Association into line with the aims of the conspirators, and to make it an effective instrument for the execution of their policies.

In a letter of transmittal, Krupp stated that the plan of reorganisation which he submitted on behalf of the Association of Industrialists, was characterised by the desire to co-ordinate economic measures and political necessity, adopting the Fuehrer conception of the new German State. A copy of that letter of transmittal is set out in the document book under the number D-157.

In the plan of reorganisation itself, Krupp stated:

"The turn of political events is in line with the wishes which I myself and the

Board of Directors have cherished for a long time. In reorganising the Reich Association of German Industry, I shall be guided by the idea of bringing the new organisation into agreement with the political aims of the Reich Government."

The ideas expressed by Krupp on behalf of the members of the Reich Association of German Industry for introducing the leadership principle into industry, were subsequently adopted.

I respectfully refer the Court to the Reichsgesetzblatt of 1934, Part I, 1194, Sections 11, 12 and 16.

Under the decrees introducing the leadership principle into industry, each group of industry was required to have a leader who was to serve without compensation. The leaders were to be appointed and could be removed at the discretion of the Minister of Economics. The charter of each group was to be created by the leader, who was bound to lead his group in accordance with the principles of the National Socialist State.

I think it is fair to argue that the introduction of the leadership principle into the organisations of business permitted the centralisation of authority, and guaranteed the efficient execution of orders, which the government issued to business, in the interest of a promotion of a war economy. And the overwhelming support given by the German industrialists to the Nazi war programme is very vividly described in a speech prepared by Gustav Krupp in January of 1944, for delivery at the University of Berlin; and I must again respectfully refer your Honour to the document in your book bearing the identification number D-317.

I shall not, of course, bore this court with a reading of the whole document, but I should like to quote from it without wrenching any of the material from its true context.

And this statement is found beginning in the third and fourth paragraphs, being the first large paragraph on the first page:

"War material is life-saving for one's own people, and whoever works and performs in these spheres can be proud of it. Here, enterprise, as a whole, finds its highest justification of existence. This justification, I may inject this here, crystallised especially during the time of interregnum between 1919 and 1933, when Germany was lying down disarmed."

And further on:

"It is the one great merit of the entire German war economy that it did not remain idle during those bad years, even though its activity could not be brought to light for obvious reasons. Through years of secret work, scientific and basic groundwork was laid in order to be ready again to work for the German Armed Forces at the appointed hour without loss of time or experience."

And further quoting from that same speech, and the last paragraph, particularly on the first page:

"Only through the secret activity of German enterprise, together with the experience gained meanwhile through production of peacetime goods, was it possible, after 1933, to fall into step with the new tasks arrived at, restoring

Germany's military power. Only through all that could the entirely new and various problems, brought up by the Fuehrer's Four-Year Plan for German enterprise, be mastered. It was necessary to supply the new raw materials, to explore and experiment, to invest capital in order to make German economy independent and strong - in short, to make it war-worthy."

Quoting even further from the same speech:-

"I think I may state here that the German enterprises followed the new ways enthusiastically, that they made the greatest intentions of the Fuehrer their own, by fair competition and conscious gratitude, and became his faithful followers. How else could the tasks between 1933 and 1939, and especially those after 1939, have been overcome?"

It must be emphasised that the secret rearmament programme was launched immediately upon the seizure of power by the Nazi conspirators. On 4th April, 1933, the Reich Cabinet passed a resolution establishing a Reich Defence Council. The function of this council was secretly to mobilise for war; and at the second meeting of the Working Committee of the Councillors for Reich Defence, which was, by the way, the predecessor of the Reich Defence Council, at that second meeting which was held on 22nd May, 1933, the Chairman was the defendant Keitel, then Colonel Keitel; and he stated that the Reich Defence Council would immediately undertake to prepare for war emergency. He stressed the urgency of the task of organisms a war economy, and announced that the Council stood ready to brush aside all @f their obstacles. Fully aware of the fact that their action was in flagrant violation of the Treaty of Versailles, the defendant Keitel emphasised the extreme importance of absolute secrecy - I quote from page 5, document EC-177 - when he said:-

"No document ought to be lost, since otherwise it may fall into the hands of the enemies' Intelligence Service. Orally transmitted matters are not provable; they can be denied by us in Geneva."

The singleness of purpose with which the Nazi conspirators geared the German economy to the forging of a war machine is even further shown by the secret minutes of the second meeting of the Working Committee of the so-called Reich Defence Council, held on the 7th of February, 1934, as shown in the document EC-404, marked "Secret Command Matter," and dated the 7th of February, 1934. At this meeting, Lieutenant- General Beck pointed out that " The actual state of preparation is the purpose of this session."

Parenthetically, I may say that on the first page of that document it appears that besides Lieutenant-General Beck, the defendant Jodl was present, then Lieutenant-Colonel Jodl. There were also present a Captain Schmundt, a Colonel Guderian, a Major-General von Reichenau and a Major Warlimont. All these are names that your Honour will hear more of in the course of the presentation of this case.

Detailed measures of financing a future war were discussed and it was pointed out that the financial aspects of the war economy would be regulated by the Reich Finance Ministry and the Reichsbank, which was headed by the defendant Schacht.

On May 31st, 1935, as stated earlier -

THE PRESIDENT: Are you passing from EC-404?

MR. DODD: I am, your Honour.

THE PRESIDENT: Very well, go on.

MR. DODD: As was stated earlier in this morning's discussion, the defendant
Schacht was secretly appointed Plenipotentiary-General of the War Economy, and
he had the express function of placing all economic forces of the nation in the
services of the Nazi war machine.

By the secret defence law of 21st May, 1935, under which Schacht received this
secret appointment, he was in effect, given charge of the entire war economy. In case
of war, he was to be virtual economic dictator of Germany. His task was to place all
economic forces into the service for the conduct of the war and to secure
economically the life of the German people. The Ministers of Economy, of Food,
Agriculture, Labour, Forestry, as well as all Reich agencies directly under the
Fuehrer, were subordinated to him. He was to be responsible for the financing as
well as for the conduct of the war; and he was even authorised to issue ordinances
within his sphere of responsibility, even if these deviated from the existing laws.

The rearmament of Germany proceeded at an amazingly rapid pace. By the
summer of 1935, the Nazi conspirators were emboldened to make plans for the
reoccupation of the Rhineland, and at the tenth meeting of this same Working
Committee of the Council, the question of measures to be taken in connection with
the proposed reoccupation of the Rhineland were discussed.

I refer to the document EC-40S:

At that meeting, held on the 26th day of June, 1935, it was said that the Rhineland
required special treatment, because of the assurances given by Hitler to the French
that no military action was being undertaken in the de-militarised zone. Among the
matters requiring special treatment was the preparation of economic mobilisation, a
task specifically entrusted to the defendant Schacht, as secret Plenipotentiary for the
War Economy.

THE PRESIDENT: Are you reading from this document?

MR. DODD: I am quoting in part from it, your Honour, and it is upon pages 4 and
5 of this document that I base my statements. I dislike annoying the Court with
constant references to these documents, but I thought it would be the best way to
proceed.

THE PRESIDENT: If you tell us exactly where it is in the document we can find
it there.

MR. DODD: It is on page 4, if your Honour pleases.

THE PRESIDENT: Yes, go on.

MR. DODD: On page 4, the middle of the page, the fifth paragraph, the first
sentence, "the de-militarised zone requires special treatment."

THE PRESIDENT: Yes.

MR. DODD: And on page 5, " J," under "The Preparations," "preparation of
economic mobilisation." On page 4, the last paragraph just before the setting-out
of the " A," "B," "C," and "D," it said -

THE PRESIDENT: I think you ought to read on page 4, the last paragraph 1 -"since
political entanglements."

MR. DODD: That was the one I had proceeded to read.

THE PRESIDENT: I thought you had gone on to page 5.

MR. DODD:

"Since political entanglements abroad must be avoided at present under all conditions, only those preparatory measures that are urgently necessary may be carried out. The existence of such preparations, or the intention of them must be kept in strictest secrecy in the zone itself as well as in the rest of the Reich."

Preparations are then set out, and they include, as I have indicated a few minutes ago, as the last one in the list, the preparations for economic mobilisation.

There are many others, of course, for preliminary restoring of measures, and for the financial preparation for evacuation measured, and so forth. We shall pass now from that document to the rapid success of the German re- armament, primarily attributable to the work of the defendant Schacht. In the Fall of 1934, the Nazi conspirators announced the so-called "New Plan," aiming at the control of imports and exports in order to obtain the raw materials, which were needed for armaments and the foreign currency which was required to sustain the armament programme. The new plan was the creation of the defendant Schacht, and under the plan, the defendant Schacht controlled imports by extending the system of Supervisory Boards for import control, which was previously limited to the main groups of raw materials, and all goods imported into Germany, whether those raw materials were semi-manufactured goods or finished products. The requirement of licences for imports enabled the Nazi conspirators to restrict imports to those commodities which served their war aims.

Subsequently, in February, 1935, the "Devisen" Law was passed which can be found by referring to the Reichsgesetzblatt 1935, 1, 105. Under it, all transactions involving foreign exchange were subject to the approval of Devisenstellen (Foreign Exchange Control Offices). By thus controlling the disposition of foreign exchange, the conspirators were able to manipulate foreign trade so as to serve their needs and desires.

Thus every aspect of German economy was being geared to war under the guidance of the Nazi conspirators, particularly of the defendant Schacht. In a study of the economic mobilisation for war as of 30th September, 1934, it was stated that steps had already been taken to build up stock piles, to construct new facilities for the production of scarce goods, to re-deploy industry, to secure areas and to control fiscal and trade policies. References were made to the fact that the task of stock piling had been hampered by the requirement of secrecy and camouflage. Reserves of automobile fuels and stocks of coal were accumulated and the production of synthetic oil was accelerated. Civilian supply was purposely organised so that most plants would be working for the German Armed Forces. Studies were made of the possibility of barter trade with "supposedly" neutral countries in case of war.

The matter of financing the armament programme presented a difficult problem for the conspirators. In 1934 and 1935 the German economy could by no possibility have raised funds for their extensive rearmament programme through taxes and public loans. From the outset, the armament programme involved "the engagement of the last reserves."

Apart from the problem of raising the huge sums required to sustain this programme, the Nazi conspirators were exceedingly anxious, in the early stages to conceal the extent of their feverish armament activities.

After considering various techniques of financing the armament programme, the defendant Schacht proposed the use of "mefo" bills. One of the primary advantages of this method was the fact that figures indicating the extent of rearmament, that would have become public through the use of other methods, could be kept secret through the use of mefo bills. These mefo bills were used exclusively for armament financing.

Transactions in mefo bills worked as follows:

Mefo bills were drawn by armament contractors and accepted by a limited liability company, the Metallurgische Forscbungsgesellschaft m.b.H., whose initials spell the word "mefo" from which the transaction takes its name. This company had a nominal capital of one million Reichsmarks and was therefore merely a dummy Organisation. The bills were received by all German banks for possible rediscounting with the Reichsbank, and the bills were guaranteed by the Reich. Their secrecy was assured by the fact that they appeared neither in the published statements of the Reichsbank nor in the budget figures.

The mefo bill system continued to be used until 1st April, 1938. To that date, twelve billion Reichsmarks of mefo bills for the financing of rearmament had been issued. Since it was no longer deemed necessary to conceal the vast progress of German rearmament, mefo financing was discontinued at that time.

A further source of funds which defendant Schacht drew upon to finance the secret armament programme was the funds of political opponents of the Nazi regime, and marks of foreigners on deposit in the Reichsbank. As Schacht stated, "Our armaments are also financed partly with the credits of our political opponents."

That statement was made in the memorandum from the defendant Schacht to Hitler, dated 3rd May, 1935, and is in document 1168-PS, and the specific sentence I found in the second paragraph is:

"The outstanding mefo bills at all times represented a threat to the stability of the currency because they could be tendered to the Reichsbank for discount, in which case the currency circulation would automatically have to be increased."

Thus, there was an ever-present threat of inflation. But Schacht continued on his course, because "he stands with unswerving loyalty to the Fuehrer, because he fully recognises the basic idea of National Socialism and because at the end, the disturbances, as compared to the great task, can be considered irrelevant."

High ranking military officers paid tribute to the defendant Schacht's contrivances on behalf of the Nazi war machine. In an article written for the "Military Weekly Gazette" in January, 1937, it is said:

"The German Defence Force commemorates Dr. Schacht to- day as one of the men who have done imperishable things for it and its development in accordance with directions from the Fuehrer and Reich Chancellor. The Defence Force owes it to Schacht's skill and great ability that, in defiance of all currency difficulties, it has, according to plan, been able to grow up to its present strength from an army of 100,000 men."

After the reoccupation of the Rhineland, the Nazi conspirators redoubled their efforts to prepare Germany for a major war. The Four-Year Plan was proclaimed by Hitler in his address at the Nuremberg Party Convention on 9th September, 1936, and it was given a statutory foundation by the decree concerning the execution of the Four-Year Plan dated 18th October, 1936, which I found in Reichsgesetzblatt 1936, 1, 887. By this decree the defendant Goering was put in charge of the plan. He was authorised to enact any legal and administrative measures deemed necessary by him for the accomplishment of his task, and to issue orders and instructions to all government agencies, including the highest Reich authorities.

The purpose of the plan was to enable Nazi Germany to attain complete self-sufficiency in essential raw materials, notably motor fuel, rubber, textile fibre, and non-ferrous metals, and to intensify preparations for war. The development of synthetic products was greatly accelerated despite their high costs.

Apart from the self-sufficiency programme, however, the Nazi conspirators required foreign exchange to finance propaganda and espionage activities abroad. Thus, in a speech on 1st November, 1937, before the Wehrmachtakademie, General Thomas stated:

"If you consider that one will need during the war considerable means in order to organise the necessary propaganda, to pay for the espionage services and similar purposes, then it will be clear that our internal Mark can therefore be of no use, and that foreign exchange will be needed."

This particular need for foreign exchange was reduced in part by the virtue of the espionage and propaganda services rendered free of charge to the Nazi State by some leading German industrial concerns.

I hold in my hand document D-206, dated at Essen 12th October, 1935. It was found in the files of the Krupp Company by representatives of United States and the British Isles. I shall not read all of it unless your Honour requires it, but I will start at the beginning by way of establishing its purpose and the information contained therein. It is entitled "Memorandum". There is the subheading: "Concerns-distribution official propaganda literature abroad with help of our foreign connections". It goes on and says that on the morning of 11th October the district representative of Ribbentrop's Private Foreign Office, Dienststelle Ribbentrop, made an appointment by telephone for a Mr. Lachman to arrive at an appointed time. " In answer to my question as to with whom I was dealing, and which official bureau he represented, he informed me that he was not himself the district representative of Ribbentrop's Private Foreign Office, but that a Mr. Landrat Bollman was such, and that he himself had come at Mr. Bollman's orders."

The next paragraph states that "there exists a very great mix-up in the field of foreign propaganda, and Ribbentrop's Foreign Office wants to create a tighter organisation for foreign propaganda. For this purpose the support of our firm and above all an index of addresses were needed." The next sentence, in the third paragraph, I would like to read. "I informed Mr. Lachman that our firm had put itself years ago at the disposal of official bureaux for purposes of foreign propaganda, and that we had supported all requests addressed to us to the utmost."

I now hold in my hand document P-167. This is also a copy of a document found in the files of the Krupp Company by representatives of the Americans and of the British Isles. It is dated 12th October-14th October, 1937, and states it is a memorandum of Herr Sonnenberg of the meeting at Essen on 12th October, 1937. It indicates that only in the "Maze" representing the Intelligence with the combined service of the ministry is the department coming under the Defence Office, as for the Intelligence in the foreign department, but not including matters published in newspapers. The intelligence received by Koch was from agents, and threading through other channels to be passed on by the services of the Intelligence.

Finally, the third paragraph states: On our part we undertook to supply cases to combine the service of ministry as required.

I have concluded reading from that document, and I pass on now to discuss the conspirators' programme, carried out, as I have said so many times here to-day, with amazing-really amazing speed; the production of steel, for example, as shown in the official German publications, rose as follows:

In the year of 1933---   74,000 tons
.......................1934 ---108,000 tons
.......................1935 --- 145,000 tons
.......................1936 --- 186,000 tons
.......................1937 ---217,000 tons
and in the year 1938 -- 477,000 tons

The production of gasoline increased at an even greater tempo: from 370,000 tons in 1934 to 1,494,000 tons in 1938.

The Nazi conspirators pressed the completion of the armament programme with a sense of urgency which clearly betrayed their awareness of the imminence of war. At a 4th September, 1938, meeting, Goering pointed out that "all measures have to be taken just as if we were actually in the state of imminent danger of war." He pointed out that "if war should break out tomorrow we would be forced to take measures from which we might possibly shy away at the present moment. They are therefore to be taken." The extreme urgency was manifested by Goering's remark that "existent reserves will have to be touched for the purpose of carrying us over this difficulty until the goal ordered by the Fuehrer has been reached; in case of war, he added, they are not a reliable backing in any case."

By a letter marked "top secret" and "an important secret, top secret," on 21st August, 1936, the defendant Schacht was informed of Hitler's order that all formations of the Air Force be ready by 1st April, 1937. This served to accentuate the urgent sense of immediacy that had pervaded the Nazi economy from the outside, thus laying the groundwork for further aggressive action.

Reading from other sections in Hitler Nazi-

THE PRESIDENT: I am going to interrupt you. In so far as I understand, you have not referred us to any document since document 167.

MR. DODD: No, your Honour, the figures there on the production of steel, and of oil, are from the statistical year book of the German Reich, 1939 and 1940, and the statistical year book of the German Reich 1941 and 1942 inclusive. That is, with respect to the steel figures; and the figures which I quoted with respect to the production of gasoline are from the statistical year book of the German Reich, 1941 and 1942. The statements of the defendant Goering are based upon the document marked EC-416, in document book.

I quoted a remark about the-

THE PRESIDENT: That is the document you already referred to?

MR. DODD: Yes, it has been referred to heretofore, I believe. Some of these documents contain references to more than one part of the presentation, and I have to refer to them at different times in the presentation I make.

THE PRESIDENT: All right. Go on, if you want to refer to it.

MR. DODD: The sixth paragraph on the first page: "Existing reserves will have to be touched for the purpose of carrying through over this difficulty until the goal ordered by the Fuehrer has been reached, and then in the case of war, they are not a reliable backing in any case." And on the second page, the eighth paragraph down: "If war should break out to-morrow, we would be forced to take measures from which we might possibly still find a way at the present moment. They are therefore to be taken." With reference to the assertion that the defendant Schacht was advised that Hitler ordered that all formations of the Air Force be ready by 1st April, 1937, I respectfully refer to document 1301-PS, dated 31st August, 1936. 1 am advised that the document should bear an additional number. It should read 1301-PS-7. On the first page, if your Honour pleases, the third paragraph, or the paragraph marked 3 and after the words "air force"--

THE PRESIDENT: The third page?

MR. DODD: No, on the first page, 1301-PS-7. In your folio, it is page 19 of the group of documents bearing the serial number 1301-PS.

THE PRESIDENT: Our documents are not paged.

MR. DODD: I think you will find the number on the upper left-hand corner, very near to the top and at the extreme left.

THE PRESIDENT: Yes, I've got this document now.

MR. DODD: Paragraph No. 3 after the words "air force."

THE PRESIDENT: Yes.

MR. DODD: It states that according to an order of the Fuehrer, the setting up if all air force units had to be completed on 1st April, 1937; and if your Honour will turn the page, page 20, about midway in the page, you will observe that a copy of this document was sent to the President of the Reichsbank, Dr. Schacht.

THE PRESIDENT: Yes, what are you passing to now?

MR. DODD: I am passing to another document immediately, your Honour. After their successes in Austria and in the Sudetenland, the Nazi conspirators redoubled their efforts to equip themselves for the war of aggression, and in a conference on 14th October, 1938, shortly before the Nazi conspirators made their first demands on Poland, the defendant Goering stated that, "The Fuehrer had instructed him to carry out a gigantic programme, by comparison with which the performances thus far were insignificant. These difficulties must be overcome with the greatest energy and ruthlessness." And that statement may be found in the document 1301-PS, on page 25 of that document, and particularly the second sentence of the opening paragraph: "Everybody knows from the Press what the world situation looks like, and therefore the Fuehrer has issued an order to him-"

THE PRESIDENT: That's not on page 25, is it? Is that on page 25 of 1301 ?

MR. DODD: Yes, your Honour.

THE PRESIDENT: Yes.

MR. DODD:

"Everybody knows from the Press what the world situation looks like, and therefore the Fuehrer has issued an order to him to carry out a gigantic programme compared to which previous achievements are insignificant. There are difficulties in the way which he will overcome with the utmost energy and ruthlessness."

The supply of foreign currency had shrunk because of preparations for the invasion of Czechoslovakia, and it was considered necessary to replenish it. These - and I am now referring to the third paragraph of that same page 25 of document 1301-PS - "these gains made through export are to be used for an increased armament. The armament should not be curtailed by the export activities." He received the order from the Fuehrer to increase the armament to an abnormal extent, the Air Force having first priority. " Within the shortest time, the Air Force should be increased five-fold; also the Navy should create war weapons more rapidly, and the Army should procure large amounts of war weapons at a faster rate, particularly heavy artillery and heavy tanks. Along with this manufacture of armaments a larger production of armament, especially fuel, rubber, powders and explosives must be moved to the foreground. This should be coupled with an accelerated expansion of highways, canals, and particularly of the railroads."

In the course of these preparations for war, a clash of wills ensued between two men, the defendant Goering and the defendant Schacht, as a result of which the defendant Schacht resigned his position as head of the Ministry of Economics and Plenipotentiary for the War Economy in November of 1937 and was removed from the presidency of the Reichsbank in January of 1939, I do not propose, at this moment, to go into the details of this controversy. There will be more said on that subject at a later stage in these proceedings, but for the present, I should like to have it noted that it is our contention that Schacht's departure in no way implied any disagreement with the major war aims of the Nazis. The defendant Schacht took particular pride in his vast attainments in the financial and economic fields in aid of the Nazi war machine. And in the document EC-257, which is a copy of a letter from the defendant Schacht to General Thomas, in the first paragraph of the letter, he wrote, "I think back with much satisfaction to the work in the rearmament of the German people as 'conditio sine qua non' of the establishment of a new German nation." The second paragraph is of a more personal nature. It has no real bearing on the issues before us at this time.

In the document EC-252, a letter written to General von Blomberg, dated 8th

July, 1937, the defendant Schacht wrote,

"The direction of the war economy by the plenipotentiary would in that event never take place entirely independent of the rest of the war mechanism, but would be aimed at an accomplishment of the political war purpose with the assistance of all economic forces. I am entirely willing, therefore, to participate in this way in the preparation of the forthcoming order giving effect to the Defence Act."

In the spring of 1937, the defendant Schacht participated with representatives of the three branches of the Armed Forces in war games in war economy which is probably something new by way - or was something new by way of military exercises. The war games in war economy were held at Godesberg, Germany.

And I refer to the document EC-174. It has as a heading, or subheading, under the summary, "War economy tasks in Godesberg undertaken by General Staff between 25th May and 2nd June," and it goes on to outline, in some slight detail, that there was a welcome to the General Staff war economy trip. It tells something in a rather vague and not altogether clear way of just how a war game in war economy was conducted, but it leaves no doubt in the mind that such a war game in war economy had been conducted at Godesberg at that time. And on the second page of this document, the last paragraph, is the translation of Part 1 of the speech welcoming Dr. Schacht. It says: "Before I start with the discussion of the war game in war economy, I have to express how grateful we all are that you, President Dr. Schacht, have gone to the trouble to personally participate in our final discussion to-day despite all your other activities. This proves to us your deep interest in war economy tasks shown at all times, and your presence is renewed proof that you are willing to facilitate for us the difficult war economic preparations and to strengthen the harmonious co- operation with your offices."

I should also like to call the Court's attention to the next, to the last paragraph, on the first page. It is a one- sentence paragraph, and it simply says, "I want to point out, however, that all material and all information received has to be kept in strict secrecy," and it refers to the preceding paragraph concerning the war games in war economy.

It appears that the annexation of Austria was a goal which the defendant Schacht had long sought, for in a speech to the employees of the former Austrian National Bank, as set out in the document bearing the label EC-297, and particularly the second paragraph of the first page of that document, nearly at the end, four or five lines from the end of that paragraph, we find these words, immediately after "large applause":

"Austria has certainly a great mission, namely, to be the bearer of German culture, to ensure respect and regard for the German name, especially in the direction of the South-east. Such a mission can only be performed within the Great German Reich and based on the power of a nation of 75,000,000, which, regardless of the wish of the opponents, forms the heart and the soul of Europe." Dr. Schacht goes on to say, "We have read a lot in the foreign Press during the last few days that this aim, the union of both countries, was to a certain degree justified, but that the method of effecting this union was terrible. This method, which certainly did not suit one or the other power, was nothing but the consequence of countless perfidies and brutal acts and violence which foreign countries have practised against us." And I refer now to page 3 of this same document and to the fourth paragraph, about the centre of the page, and reading from it: "I am known for sometimes expressing thoughts which give offence and there I would not like to depart from this consideration. I know that there are even here, in this country, a few people - I believe they arc not too numerous- who find fault with the events of the last few days; but nobody, I believe, doubts the goal, and it should be said to all grumblers that you can't satisfy everybody. One person says he would have done it maybe one way, but the remarkable thing is that they did not do it, and that it was only done by our Adolf Hitler; and if there is still something left to be improved, then those grumblers should try to bring about these improvements from the German Reich, and within the German community, but not to disturb us from without."

In the memorandum of 7th January, 1939, written by the defendant Schacht and other directors of the Reichsbank to Hitler, urging a balancing of the budget in view of the threatening danger of inflation, it was stated, and I now refer to the document bearing the label EC-369 and particularly to the paragraph at the bottom of the first page of that document: "From the beginning the Reichsbank has been aware of the fact that a successful foreign policy can be attained only by the reconstruction of the German Armed Forces. It (the Reichsbank) therefore assumed to a very great extent the responsibility of financing the rearmament in spite of the inherent dangers to the currency. The justification therefore was the necessity, which pushed all other considerations into the background, to carry through the armament at once, out of nothing, and furthermore under camouflage, which made a respect-commanding foreign policy possible."

The Reichsbank directors, as experts on money, believed that a point had been reached where greater production of armaments was no longer possible. That was merely a judgement on the situation and not a moral principle, for there was no opposition to Hitler's policy of aggression. Doubts were entertained as to whether he could finance that policy. Hitler's letter to Schacht on the occasion of Schacht's departure from the Reichsbank, as contained in document EC-397, paid high tribute to Schacht's great efforts in furthering the programme of the Nazi conspirators. The armed forces by now had enabled Hitler to take Austria and the Sudetenland. We say Schacht's task up to that point had been well done. And to quote from document EC-397, in the words of Hitler, in a letter which he wrote to the defendant Schacht, "Your name, above all, will always be connected with the first epoch of the national rearmament."

Even though dismissed from the presidency of the Reichsbank, Schacht was retained as a minister without portfolio and special confidential adviser to Hitler. The defendant Funk stepped into Schacht's position as president of the Reichsbank. And I ask at this point that the Court might take judicial notice of the Volkischer Beobachter Of 21St January, 1939. The defendant Funk was completely uninhibited by fears of inflation, for like Goering, under whom he had served in the Four-Year Plan, he recognised no obstacles to the plan to attack Poland.

In document 699-PS, a letter from the defendant Funk to Hitler, written on 25th August, 1939, only a few days before the attack on Poland, the defendant Funk reported to Hitler that the Reichsbank was prepared to withstand any disturbances of the international currency and credit system occasioned by a large-scale war. He said that he had secretly transferred all available funds of the Reichsbank abroad into gold, and that Germany stood ready to meet the financial and economic tasks which lay ahead.

And it seems plain and clear from the writings, from the acts, from the speeches of the Nazi conspirators themselves, that they did in fact direct the whole of the German economy toward preparation for aggressive war. To paraphrase the words the defendant Goering once used, the conspirators gave the German people "guns instead of butter " and they also gave - we say, they also gave history its most striking example of a nation gearing itself in time of peace to the single purpose of aggressive war. Their economic preparations, formulated and applied with the ruthless energy of Goering, the cynical financial wizardry of the defendant Schacht, and the willing complicity of Funk, among others, were the indispensable first act in the heart-breaking tragedy which their aggression inflicted upon the world.

I should like to offer, if I may at this time, your Honour, those documents which I have referred to in the course of this discussion. We have here the original documents in the folders, and they compare with the translations which have been submitted to the court.

THE PRESIDENT: Have the defendants had the opportunity of inspecting these documents?

MR. DODD: I doubt that they have had full opportunity to inspect them, your Honour. The documents are there, but I don't think they have had the opportunity to inspect them because they haven't been there long enough for that.

THE PRESIDENT: Well, the Tribunal - I think that they should be given full opportunity of inspecting them and comparing them with the copies which have been submitted to us before the originals are put in.

MR. DODD: Very well, your Honour. We may offer these later, as I understand?

THE PRESIDENT: Certainly. The Tribunal will adjourn for ten minutes.

(Whereupon the Court, at 15.25 o'clock, recessed for ten minutes.)

COLONEL STOREY: May it please the Tribunal:

The United States Prosecution now passes into the aggressive war phase of the case and it will be presented by Mr. Alderman.

MR. SIDNEY S. ALDERMAN: May it please the Tribunal:

I rise to present on behalf of the United States Chief of Counsel, evidence to support the allegation of Count 1 of the Indictment relating to the planning, preparation, initiation, and waging of illegal and aggressive war, and relating to the conspiracy to commit that crime.

The aggressive war phase of the case, the aggressive war phase of the conspiracy case under Count 1, and the aggressive war phase of the entire case is really, we think, the heart of the case. If we did not reach it in our presentation we would not reach the heart of the case. If we did not present it to the Tribunal in the necessary detail, we would fail to present what is necessary to the heart of the case.

After all, everything else in this case, however dramatic, however sordid, however shocking and revolting to the common instinct of civilised peoples, is incidental to, or subordinate to, the aggressive war aspect of the case.

All the dramatic story of what went on in Germany in the early phases of the conspiracy, the ideologies used, the technics of terror used, the suppressions of human freedom employed in the seizure of power, and even the concentration camps and the Crimes against Humanity, the persecutions, tortures and murders committed, all of these things would have had little juridical international significance except for the fact that they were the preparation for the commission of aggressions against peaceful neighbouring peoples.

Even the aspects of the case involving War Crimes in the strict sense are aspects which are merely the inevitable, proximate result of the wars of aggression launched and waged by these conspirators, and of the kind of warfare they waged, that is total war, the natural result of the totalitarian party-dominated State that waged it, and atrocious war, the natural result of the atrocious doctrines, designs and purposes of these war-makers.

For these reasons, I repeat, that in our view the phases of the case dealing with territorial gains acquired by threats of force and with actual aggressions and aggressive wars, constitute the real heart of the case. Accordingly, we ask the indulgence of the Tribunal if for these reasons we may make the presentation of this part of the case as detailed as seems to us necessary in view of the outstanding importance of the subject matter.

The general scope of the case to be presented by the American prosecution has been stated in the opening address of Mr. Justice Jackson. That address indicated to the Tribunal the general nature and character of the evidence to be offered by the American prosecution in support of the allegations with which I shall deal. However, before approaching the actual presentation of that evidence, it seems to us it would be helpful to an orderly presentation of the case, to address the Tribunal in an introductory way concerning this specific segment of the prosecution's case. In doing so, I shall not attempt to retrace the ground so ably covered by Mr. Justice Jackson. On the contrary, I shall confine my introductory remarks to matters specifically and peculiarly applicable to that part of the American case relating to the crime of illegal warfare, and the Common Plan or Conspiracy to commit that crime.

The substantive rule of law which must guide the considerations of the Tribunal on this aspect of the case, and the rule of law which must be controlling in the final judgement of the Tribunal on this part of the case, is stated in Article 6 of the Charter of the International Military Tribunal. Article 6, so far as is pertinent here, reads as follows:-

"Article 6. The Tribunal established by the Agreement referred to in Article 1 hereof for the trial and punishment of the Major War Criminals of the European Axis countries shall have the power to try and punish persons who, acting in the interests of the European Axis countries, either as individuals or as members of organisations, committed any of the following crimes.

The following acts, or any of them, are crimes coming within the jurisdiction of the Tribunal for which there shall be individual responsibility.

(a) Crimes Against Peace: namely, planning, preparation, initiation or waging of a war of aggression, or a war in violation of international treaties, agreements or assurances, or participation in a Common Plan or Conspiracy for the accomplishment of any of the foregoing; "

Sub-paragraph's (b) and (c) of Article 6 are not pertinent to this aspect of the case. However, the unnumbered final paragraph of Article 6 is of controlling importance on this aspect of the case. That paragraph reads:-

"Leaders, organisers, instigators and accomplices participating in the formulation or execution of a Common Plan or Conspiracy to commit any of the foregoing crimes are responsible for all acts performed by any persons in execution of such plan."

In receiving evidence on this aspect of the case I would request the Tribunal to have in mind five principles derived from the portions of the Charter I have just read:

(1) The Charter imposes "individual responsibility" for acts constituting "Crimes against Peace;"

(2) The term "Crimes against Peace" embraces planning, preparation, initiation, or waging of illegal war;

(3) The term "Crimes against Peace" also embraces participation in a Common Plan or Conspiracy to commit illegal war;

(4) an illegal war consists of either a war of aggression, or a war in violation of international treaties, agreements or assurances.

These two kinds of illegal war might not necessarily be the same. It will be sufficient for the prosecution to show that the war was aggressive, irrespective of breach of international treaties, agreements or assurances. On the other hand it would be sufficient for the prosecution to show that the war was in violation of international treaties, agreements or assurances irrespective of whether or not it was a war of aggression. We think the evidence in this case will establish conclusively that the wars planned, prepared, initiated, and waged by these defendants, and the wars which were the object of their Common Plan and Conspiracy, were illegal for both reasons. The fifth principle which I ask you to bear in mind, is that individual criminal responsibility of a defendant is imposed by the Charter not merely by reasons of direct, immediate participation in the crime. It is sufficient for the prosecution to show that a defendant was a leader, an organiser, instigator, or accomplice who participated either in the formulation or in the execution of a Common Plan or Conspiracy to commit Crimes against Peace. In the case of many of the defendants the evidence will show direct and immediate personal participation in the substantive crime itself. In the case of some of the defendants the evidence goes to their participation in the formulation and execution of a Common Plan or Conspiracy. In the case of each defendant we think the evidence will establish full individual responsibility for Crimes against Peace, as defined in the Charter of this Tribunal.

In this connection I wish to emphasise that the Charter declares that the responsibility of conspirators extends not only to their own acts, but also to all acts performed by any persons in execution of the Conspiracy.

It is familiar law in my country that if two or more persons set out to rob a bank, in accordance with a criminal scheme to that end, and in the course of carrying out their scheme one of the conspirators commits the crime of murder, all the participants in the planning and execution of the bank robbery are guilty of murder, whether or not they had any personal participation in the killing. This is a simple rule of law declared in the Charter. All the parties to a Common Plan or Conspiracy are the agents of each other and each is responsible as principal for the acts of all the others as his agents.

So much for the terms of the Charter having a bearing on this aspect of the case.

I invite the attention of the Tribunal to the portions of the Indictment lodged against the defendants on trial which relate to the crimes of illegal war or war of aggression. Particularly I ask the Tribunal to advert to the statements of offences under Count 1 and Count 2 of the Indictment in this case.

The statement of offences under Count 1 of the Indictment is contained in paragraph III. The offences there stated, so far as pertinent to the present discussion, are:-

"All the defendants, with divers other persons, during a period of years preceding 8th May, 1945, participated as leaders, organisers, instigators, or accomplices in the formulation or execution of a Common Plan or Conspiracy to commit, or which involved the commission of, Crimes against Peace, as defined in the Charter of this Tribunal. . . . The Common Plan or Conspiracy embraced the commission of Crimes against Peace, in that the defendants planned, prepared, initiated and waged wars of aggression, which were also wars in violation of international treaties, agreements or assurances." . . .

The statement of offences under Count 2 of the Indictment is also relevant at this point. It must be obvious that essentially Counts 1 and 2 interlock in this Indictment. The substance of the offence stated under Count 2, paragraph V of the Indictment is this:-

"The emphasis in the statement of offences under Count 1 of the Indictment is on the Common Plan or Conspiracy. The emphasis under Count 2 of the Indictment is on the substantive crimes to which the Conspiracy related and which were committed in the course of and pursuant to that conspiracy."

I should hasten to add at this point that in the division of the case as between the Chief Prosecutors of the four Prosecuting Governments, primary responsibility for the presentation of the evidence supporting Count 1 has been placed on the American prosecutor, and primary responsibility for the presentation of the evidence supporting Count 2 of the Indictment has been placed on the British prosecutor.

But as we shall show somewhat later, there will, to some extent, be a co-operative effort as between the prosecutors to present both counts together. In addition to the statement of offence relating to illegal warfare in paragraph III under Count 1 of the Indictment, Count 1 also contains what amounts to a bill of particulars of that offence. In so far as those particulars relate to illegal warfare, they are contained in paragraph IV (F) of the Indictment which sets out in the English text on page 7 through to the top of page 10 under the general heading "Utilisation of Nazi Control for Foreign Aggression." The allegations of this bill of particulars have been read in open Court, in the presence of the defendants; and the Tribunal, as well as the defendants, are certainly familiar with the contents of those allegations. I call attention to them, however, in order to focus attention on the parts of the Indictment which are relevant in consideration of the evidence which I intend to bring before the Tribunal.

My introduction to the presentation of evidence in this matter would be faulty if I did not invite the Tribunal to consider with me the relationship between history and the evidence in this case. Neither Counsel nor Tribunal can orient themselves to the problem at hand-neither counsel nor Tribunal can present or consider the evidence in this case in its proper context- neither can argue nor evaluate the staggering implications of the evidence at hand to be presented without reading that history, reading that evidence against the background of recorded history, and by recorded history, I mean the history merely of the last twelve years.

Justice Oliver Wendell Holmes, of the U.S. Supreme Court, found in his judicial experience that "a page of history is worth a volume of logic." My recollection is that he stated it perhaps better, perhaps earlier in the preface to his book on the common law where he said, I think, " The life of the law has been not logic but experience." I submit, that in the present case, a page of history is worth a hundred tons of evidence. As lawyers and judges we cannot blind ourselves to what we know as men. The history of the past twelve years is a burning, living thing in our immediate memory. The facts of history crowd themselves upon us and demand our attention.

It is common ground among all systems of jurisprudence that matters of common knowledge need not be proved, but may receive the judicial notice of courts without other evidence. The Charter of this Tribunal, drawing on this uniformly recognised principle, declares in Article 21:-

"The Tribunal shall not require proof of facts of common knowledge but it shall take judicial notice thereof."

The facts of recorded history are the prime example of facts of common knowledge which require no proof. No court would require evidence to prove that the Battle of Hastings occurred in the year 1066, or that the Bastille fell on the 14th of July, 1789, or that Czar Alexander II freed the serfs in i863, or that George Washington was the first President of the United States, or that George III was the reigning King of England at that time.

If I may be allowed to interpolate, an old lawyer-professor of mine used to present a curiosity of the law - that a judge is held to responsibility for no knowledge of the law whatsoever, that a lawyer is held to a reasonable knowledge of the law, and a layman is held to an absolute knowledge of all the laws. It works inversely as to facts, or facts of common knowledge. There, the judge is imputed to know all of those facts, however many of them he may have forgotten as an individual man. So one of the purposes of this presentation will be to implement the judicial knowledge, if a hypothesis actually exists.

It is not our purpose however, to convert the record of these proceedings into a history book. The evidence which we offer in this case is evidence which for the moment has been concealed from historians. It will fill in recorded history, but it must be read against the background which common knowledge provides. The evidence in this case consists primarily of captured documents - these captured documents fill in the inside story underlying the historical record which we all already knew. The evidence which we will offer constitutes an illustrative spot-check on the history of recent times as the world knows it. The evidence to be offered is not a substitute for history. We hope the Tribunal will find it to be an authentication of history. The evidence which we have drawn from captured documents establishes the validity of the recent history of the past twelve years - a history of many aggressions by the Nazi conspirators accused in this case.

As I offer to the Tribunal document after document, I ask the Court to see in those documents definite additions to history, the addition of new elements long suspected and now proved. The elements which the captured documents on this particular aspect of the case will add to recorded history are the following:-

(1) the conspiratorial nature of the planning and preparation which underlay the Nazi aggressions already known to history;
(2) the deliberate premeditation which preceded those acts of aggression;
(3) the evil motives which led to the crimes;
(4) the individual participation of named persons in the Nazi conspiracy for aggression;
(5) the deliberate falsification of the pretexts claimed by the Nazi aggressors as their reason for their criminal activities.

These elements the captured documents will demonstrate beyond possible doubt, and these elements, in the context of historical facts, we think are all that need be shown.

The critical period between the Nazi seizure of power and the initiation of the first war of aggression was a very short period. This critical period of lawless preparation and illegal scheming which ultimately set the whole world aflame was unbelievably short. It covered six years, 1933 to 1939. The speed with which all this was accomplished evidences at once the fanatical intensity of the conspirators and their diabolical efficiency. Crowded into these six short years is the making of the greatest tragedy that has ever befallen mankind.

A full understanding of these six years, and the vibrant six years of war that followed, demands that we see this period of time divided into rather definite phases, phases that reflect the development and execution of the Nazi master plan. I suggest that the Tribunal as it receives evidence, fit it into five phases. The first was primarily preparatory, although it did involve overt acts. That phase covers roughly the period from 1933 to 1936. In that period the Nazi conspirators, having acquired government control of Germany by the middle of 1933, turned their attention toward utilisation of that control for foreign aggression. Their plan at this stage was to acquire military strength and political bargaining power to be used against other nations. In this they succeeded. The second phase of their aggression was short. It is rather interesting to see that as the conspiracy gained strength, it gained speed. During each phase the conspirators succeeded in accomplishing more and more in less and less time until toward the end of the period, the rate of acceleration of their conspiratorial movement was enormous. The second phase of their utilisation of control for foreign aggression involved the actual seizure and absorption of Austria and Czechoslovakia in that order. By March, the third month of 1939, they had succeeded in that phase. The third phase may be measured in months rather than years, from March 1939 to September 1939. The previous aggression being successful, having been consummated without the necessity of resorting to actual war, the conspirators had obtained much desired resources and bases and were ready to undertake further aggressions by means of war, if necessary. By September 1939 war was upon the world. The fourth phase of the aggression consisted of expanding the war into a general European war of aggression. By April 1941, the war which had heretofore involved Poland, the United Kingdom and France, had been expanded by invasions into Scandinavia and into the Low Countries and into the Balkans. In the next phase the Nazi conspirators carried the war Eastward by invasion of the territory of the Union of Soviet Socialist Republics, and finally, through their Pacific ally, Japan, precipitated the attack on the United States at Pearl Harbour.

The final result of these aggressions is fresh in the mind of all of us.

I turn now to certain outstanding evidence at hand. While on this phase of the case we shall not rest exclusively on them alone, the essential elements of the crime which I have already pointed out can be made out by a mere handful of captured documents. My order of presentation of these will be first to present one by one this handful of documents, documents which prove the essential elements of the case on aggressive war up to the hilt. These documents will leave no reasonable doubt concerning the aggressive character of the Nazi war or concerning the conspiratorial premeditation of that war. Some of this group of documents are the specific basis for particular allegations in the Indictment. As I reach those documents, I shall invite the attention of the Tribunal to the allegations of the Indictment which are specifically supported by them. Having proved the corpus of the crime in this way, I will follow the presentation of this evidence with a more or less chronological presentation of the details of the aggressive war, producing more detailed evidence of the relevant activities of the conspirators from 1933 to 1941.

The documents which we have selected for single presentation at this point, before developing the case in detail, are ten in number. The documents have been selected to establish the basic facts concerning each phase of the development of the Nazi conspiracy for aggression. Each document is conspiratorial in nature. Each document is one, I believe, heretofore unknown to history and each document is self- contained and tells its own story. Those are the three standards of selection which we have sought to apply.

I turn to the period of 1933 to l936, a period characterised by an orderly, planned sequence of preparations for war. This is the period covered by paragraphs 1 and 2 of section IV (F) of the Indictment, to be found at page 7 of the printed English text. The essential character of this period was the formulation and execution of the plan to re-arm and to re-occupy the Rhineland, in violation of the treaty of Versailles and other treaties, in order to acquire military strength and political bargaining power to be used against other nations.

If the Tribunal please, we have what have been referred to as document books. They are English translations of German documents, in some cases German versions. I shall ask that they be handed up and we will hand one copy at the moment to counsel for the defendants. It has been physically impossible to prepare twenty-one sets of them. If possible, we shall try to furnish further copies to the defendants.

DR. DIX (Counsel for defendant Schacht): I would be very much obliged. In order that there should be no misunderstanding, we have arranged that tomorrow-

THE PRESIDENT: Speak a little bit slower.

DR. DIX: We have arranged that tomorrow we will discuss with the authorities in what way in the future the whole of the evidence may be made available to all the defence counsel. It is, of course, necessary that no one has the advantage over the other. For this reason, I should like to acknowledge the goodwill on the part of the prosecution in this difficult situation.

I should like to take one copy, but if I were to do so this would be an unfair advantage over the others. I am not in a position during this procedure to give my colleagues the evidence. For this reason, I hope you will understand if I do not accept this document. I am convinced that tomorrow we shall be able to agree on a perfect method of obtaining the evidence, and we shall try to continue to-day as we have done so far.

THE PRESIDENT: Mr. Alderman, can you inform the Tribunal how many copies of these documents you will be able to furnish to defence counsel by Monday?

MR. ALDERMAN: I cannot at the moment. If your Honour pleases, may I make this suggestion in connection with it, which I think may be of help to all concerned? I think many of us have underestimated the contribution of this interpreting system to this trial. We all see how it has speeded the proceeding, but in so far as my presentation of German documents is concerned, I shall let the documents speak. I expect to read the pertinent parts of the documents into the system so that they will go into the transcript of the record. Counsel for the German defendants will get their transcript in German; our French and Russian Allies will get their transcript in their language, and it seems to me that that is the most helpful way to overcome this language barrier. I can recognise that for Dr. Dix to receive a volume of documents which are English translations of German documents might not seem very helpful to him. Further, as an aid, we will have an original German document in Court, one copy, and if the Court will allow, I would ask that the original German document, from which I shall read, be passed to the German interpreter under Colonel Dostert, so that instead of undertaking to translate an English translation back into perhaps a bad German, he will have the original document before him and in that way, the exact German text will be delivered in the daily transcript to all of the counsel for the defendants. I hope that may be a helpful suggestion.

THE PRESIDENT: That, to some extent depends, does it not, upon how much of the document you omit?

MR. ALDERMAN: That is quite true, Sir, as to these ten documents with which I propose to deal immediately. I expect to read into the transcript practically the whole of the documents, because the whole of them is significant, much more significant than anything I could say. Also all of these ten documents were listed in the list of documents which we furnished counsel for the defendants on, I believe, the 1st of November.

THE PRESIDENT: You say that they were in the list. Are the documents very long?

MR. ALDERMAN: Some of them are very long and some of them are very short; you can't generalise. Whenever it is a speech of Adolf Hitler you can count it is fairly long.

THE PRESIDENT: Can you not by Monday have in the hands of every member of the defence counsel copies of these ten documents? It is suggested to me that the photostating could be done quite easily.

MR. ALDERMAN: I understand our photostatic facilities and our mimeographing facilities are right up to the hilt with work. It is a very difficult mechanical problem.

COLONEL STOREY: If the Tribunal please, in further explanation, the documents which Mr. Alderman intends to offer were on the defendants' list filed in the document centre on 1st November, 1945. Lt. Barrett had twenty-three of each one photostated as far as he could on that list. Six copies went into the Defendants' Information Centre. Now, we can't say at this time whether six copies, that is photostatic copies of each one, have been furnished to the defendants, but, whenever they wanted copies of any particular one, either the original was exhibited to them or photostatic copies were made.

Again, Sir, I call attention to the physical problems that are almost insurmountable to make twenty-three photostatic copies which are required of every document.

THE PRESIDENT: If I may interrupt you, I imagine the list which was deposited on 1st November didn't contain only these ten documents but contained a great number of other documents.

COLONEL STOREY: That is correct, Sir.

THE PRESIDENT: So that the defendants' counsel wouldn't know which out of that list of documents were going to be relied upon.

COLONEL STOREY: Except, Sir, they were notified that the Prosecution would use all or some of those documents if necessary and if the copies were not furnished upon request, they have since been made and delivered to them.

May I say, Sir, that working twenty-four hours a day, we are trying to furnish ten sets of all of these to defendants' counsel and there will be one complete set. One complete set was delivered to defendants' counsel here now as a convenience to follow. The other sets, I feel certain, will be in their hands sometime Sunday, but one complete list we now turn over to them - not a list, complete copies.

DR. SIEMERS (Counsel for defendant Raeder): I beg the pardon of the Court for being rather hoarse. I should like to point out one fact. The prosecution had declared this morning that those documents that will be put before us today are contained in the list which on the 1st of November was made available to us, or were in the list which was made available to us this morning. This morning a list was made available to us in room fifty-five. I have it in my hand. This morning nine documents were named. Of these documents only one, contrary to what the prosecution said, was present; the other eight or nine documents were neither in the old list, nor in the new list. The eight other documents are as I ascertained at lunch-time today, not in the document room, not available in photostatic copies, so they could not be made available to me. I think, Sirs, that it will not be possible for us to work on this basis. I therefore request that, first of all, we may wait until we have had our discussion tomorrow with the prosecution, which they have kindly offered to us and see how this -

THE PRESIDENT: The Tribunal proposes to adjourn now and to give defence counsel the opportunity of meeting counsel for the prosecution tomorrow morning. Both counsel for the prosecution and defence counsel appear to be perfectly ready to make every possible effort to deal with the case in a most reasonable way, and at that meeting you will be able to discuss these documents which you say have been omitted and the counsel for the prosecution will try to satisfy you with reference to the other documents.

DR. SIEMERS: Yes, I have one more request. It has just been said by the prosecution that it will hardly be possible to make twenty-three photostatic copies. I believe, Sirs, if this is a case of such very important documents, as the prosecution said today, it is a conditio sine qua non that every defence counsel and every accused should have a photostatic copy of these documents.

As we all know it is easy to produce a photostat in a few hours' time. With the excellent apparatus here available to the prosecution it should, in my opinion, be easy to produce twenty or forty photostats of these ten documents in forty- eight hours.

THE PRESIDENT: Well, you will meet the counsel for the prosecution tomorrow and attempt to come to some satisfactory arrangement with them then; and now the Tribunal will adjourn.

(The Tribunal adjourned until 26th November, 1945, at 10.00 hours.)

FIFTH DAY:
Monday, 26th November, 1945

DR. SAUTER: May it please the Court, I should like to make an application. I am Dr. Sauter and defend the defendant von Ribbentrop. On the 30th October the defendant von Ribbentrop requested that his former secretary, Margarete Blank, at that time in the Remand Prison in Nuremberg, be made available to him in order that he might make his reply to the Indictment, as well as a survey of the manner in which he performed his official duties in the last seven or eight years. He wished to dictate the facts.

On the 11th November, 1945, the Tribunal allowed this plea. The defendant von Ribbentrop thereupon was able to dictate for a few hours, but this was stopped for reasons unknown to him. The defendant von Ribbentrop has not yet had returned to him either the shorthand notes or the type script dictated to Fraulein Blank. He therefore makes application to the Court that the President be good enough to decree that his former secretary, Margarete Blank, be made available to him for the transcription of the requisite data. Such permission would appear to be essential for the proper preparation of his testimony and for the preparation of the testimony of the defence witnesses.

Particularly in the case of the defendant von Ribbentrop, the material to be treated is so voluminous, that no other way of treating it appears feasible to us. Von Ribbentrop has a further request to put forward. He has repeatedly asked that some of his former colleagues, in particular Ambassador Gauss, Ambassador von Rintelen, Minister von Sonnleitner, Professor Fritz Berber and Under-Secretary of State Henke, be brought to Nuremberg as witnesses, and that he be permitted to speak to these witnesses in the presence of his counsel. This request has, in part, been refused by the Court on the 10th November. The remaining part has not yet been decided.

It is quite impossible for the defendant von Ribbentrop, considering the question of the entire foreign policy for the last seven or eight years, to give a clear and exhaustive account, if nothing is placed at his disposal except a pencil and a block of writing paper. The White Book of the Foreign Office for which he has asked could not be placed at his disposal. In view of the voluminous nature of the material entailed by Germany's foreign policy during the last seven or eight years, the defendant von Ribbentrop cannot possibly remember every single detail of events, documents et alia, unless he be afforded some outside help. He will be unable to remember particulars unless his memory be stimulated by discussions with his former colleagues.

Moreover, the defendant von Ribbentrop has been taking a great many soporifics during the last four years, especially bromides, and his memory has suffered in consequence. For a comprehensive realisation of the historical truth in a field which interests not only the Court, but universal public opinion in particular, little would be achieved if, in the course of his examination, he were to declare, over and over again, that he could no longer remember these details.

Defendant von Ribbentrop therefore applies to the Court and begs that his above-mentioned colleagues be brought here, and that he receive permission to discuss with them matters pertaining to the trial, in order that he may prepare for further proceedings.

THE PRESIDENT: The Tribunal has already intimated to defendant's counsel that all applications should, as far as possible, be made in writing and they consider that the applications which have now been made orally should have been made in writing. They will consider the facts with reference to the application in respect of defendant von Ribbentrop's secretary. The other applications, as to witnesses and documents, which have been made in writing, have been considered, or will be considered by the Tribunal.

DR. SAUTER: Mr. President, I would, in addition, like to observe that the applications which I have today submitted have been repeatedly lodged with the Court in writing, but my client is anxious lest he experience difficulties in preparing his own testimony and the examination of the defence witnesses.

THE PRESIDENT: As was announced at the sitting on Friday, counsel for the prosecution were to try and arrange with defendants' counsel some satisfactory arrangement with reference to the production of documents in the German language. In accordance with that announcement, counsel for the prosecution saw counsel for the defence, and representatives of the prosecution and the defence appeared before the Tribunal, and the Tribunal has provisionally made the following arrangement: One, that in future, only such parts of documents as are read in Court by the prosecution, shall in the first instance be part of the record. In that way, those parts of the documents will be conveyed to defendants' counsel through the earphones in German. Two, in order that defendants and their counsel may have an opportunity of inspecting such documents in their entirety in German, a photostatic copy of the original and one copy thereof shall be deposited in the defendants' counsel room at the same time that they are produced in Court. Three, the defendants' counsel may at any time refer to any other part of such documents. Four, prosecuting counsel will furnish defendants' counsel with ten copies of their trial briefs in English and five copies of their books of documents in English, at the time such briefs and books are furnished to the Tribunal. Five, defendants' counsel will be furnished with one copy each of the transcript of the proceedings. That is all.

I call upon the prosecuting counsel for the United States.

MR. ALDERMAN: May it please the Tribunal, may I make, Mr. President, one inquiry with regard to your reference to trial briefs.

On my section of the case I shall not expect to hand up to the Court trial briefs. Whatever I have in the nature of trial briefs will be put over the microphone. I wonder if that is satisfactory.

THE PRESIDENT: I think what I said meets that case.

MR. ALDERMAN: I thought so, yes.

THE PRESIDENT: Because what I said was that the defendants' counsel would be furnished with ten copies of the trial briefs in English at the same time that they are furnished to the Tribunal. Therefore, if you don't furnish the trial briefs to the Tribunal, none will be furnished to the defendants' counsel.

MR. ALDERMAN: Yes.

When the Tribunal rose on Friday last, I had just completed an introductory statement preliminary to the presentation of evidence on the aggressive war aspect of the case. In that introductory statement I had invited attention to the parts of the Charter and to the parts of the Indictment which are pertinent to this aspect of the case. I had also discussed the relationship between recorded history and the evidence to be presented, indicating what sort of additions to recorded history would be made by the evidence contained in the captured documents.

I then indicated to the Court that I would first proceed by presenting singly a handful of captured documents, which, in our opinion, prove the corpus of the crime of Aggressive War, leaving no reasonable doubt concerning the aggressive character of the Nazi war, or concerning the conspiratory premeditation of that war. I indicated to the Tribunal that, after proving the corpus of the crime in this way, I would follow the presentation of this evidence with a more or less chronological presentation of the case on Aggressive War, producing evidence in greater detail of the relevant activities of the conspirators from 1933 to 1941.

As the members of the Tribunal may understand, it is easier to make plans about presentation than to keep them. There have been, by necessity, some changes in our plans. I indicated on Friday that to a certain extent the American case under Count 1 and the British case under Count 2 would interlock. The British Chief Prosecutor, Sir Hartley Shawcross, is by force of circumstances required to be in London this week. He expects to be back next week. The intention now is that he will make his opening statement covering Count 2 of the Indictment, and such interrelated parts of Count 1 of the Indictment as have not by then been presented, when he returns on Monday.

So that what is at the moment planned, if it meets with the Court's views, is that I shall continue as far as I may within two days of this week on the detailed story as to Aggressive War; that thereupon we shall alter the presentation and present some other matters coming under Count 1. Then, following the British Chief Prosecutor's opening on Monday of next week, we shall continue jointly with the Chapters on Poland, Russia, and Japan, as parts of both Count 1 and Count 2. While that may not be strictly logical it seems to us the best method to proceed with under the circumstances.

I turn now to the period of 1933 to 1936, a period characterised by an orderly, planned sequence of preparations for war. This is the period covered by Paragraphs 1 and 2 of IV (F) of the Indictment. This may be found at Page 7 of the printed English text of the Indictment.

The essential character of this period was the formulation and execution of the plan to rearm and to re-occupy and fortify the Rhineland in violation of the Treaty of Versailles and other treaties, in order to acquire military strength and political bargaining power to be used against other nations.

Hitler's own eloquence in a secret speech delivered to all supreme commanders on 23rd November, 1939, at 12.00 hours, is sufficient to characterise this phase of the Nazi conspiracy. This document comes to hand as a captured document found in the OKW files - OKW is Ober Kommando der Wehrmacht, the High Command of the Army, Chief of the High Command of the Armed Forces - and was captured at Flensburg. The document is numbered 789-PS in our numbered series of documents.

I have in my hand, if the Court please, the German original of this document in the condition in which it was captured, and I wish to offer the document in evidence and have it given the proper serial number as the United States Prosecutor's exhibit. The serial number, I understand, is exhibit USA 23. I would ask that the German text of the original be handed to the interpreters, the German interpreters.

If the Court please, understanding the ruling just made by the presiding Justice, although I have offered the entire document, it is a very long speech, and I shall not read it into the record in its entirety. Of course, as the Presiding Judge said, defence counsel may insert any other parts of it as they wish.

I shall begin reading at the beginning, and read a little more than half of the first page in the English text. I am advised that the German original is marked with a blue pencil at the point where I shall stop reading. I will read the English translation:

"November 23rd, 1939, 12.00 hours. Conference with the Fuehrer, to which all supreme Commanders are ordered. The Fuehrer gives the following speech:

The purpose of this conference is to give you an idea of the world of my thoughts, which takes charge of me, in the face of future events, and to tell you my decisions. The building up of our armed forces was only possible in connection with the ideological - the German word is " weltanschaulich" - "education of the German people by the Party."

If I may interpolate just to comment on that interesting German word "weltanschaulich." I take it that ideological is about as close a translation as we can get, but the word means more than that. It means a whole attitude towards the world, the way of looking on the world.

"When I started my political task" - I am quoting again - "in 1919, my strong belief in final success was based on a thorough observation of the events of the day and the study of the reasons for their occurrence. Therefore, I never lost my belief in the midst of setbacks which were not spared me during my period of struggle. Providence has had the last word and brought me success. On top of that, I had a clear recognition of the probable course of historical events, and the firm will to make brutal decisions. The first decision was in 1919 when I, after long internal conflict, became a politician and took up the struggle against my enemies. That was the hardest of all decisions. I had, however, the firm belief that I would arrive at my goal. First of all, I desired a new system of selection. I wanted to educate a minority which would take over the leadership. After 15 years I arrived at my goal, after strenuous struggles and many setbacks. When I came to power in 1933, the period of the most difficult struggle lay behind me. Everything existing before that had collapsed. I had to reorganise everything, beginning with the mass of the people, and extending it to the armed forces. First, reorganisation of the interior, abolishment of appearances of decay and defeatist ideas, education to heroism. While reorganising the interior, I undertook the second task: to release Germany from its international ties. Two particular characteristics are to be pointed out: secession from the League of Nations and denunciation of the Disarmament Conference. It was a hard decision. The number of prophets who predicted that it would lead to the occupation of the Rhineland, was large, the number of believers was very small. I was supported by the nation, which stood firmly behind me, when I carried out my intentions. After that the order for rearmament. Here again there were numerous prophets who predicted misfortunes, and only a few believers. In 1935 the introduction of compulsory armed service. After that the militarisation of the Rhineland, again a process believed to be impossible at that time. The number of people who put trust in me was very small. Then - beginning of the fortification of the whole country, especially in the West.

One year later, Austria came" - I suppose he meant Austria went - "this step also was considered doubtful. It brought about a considerable reinforcement of the Reich. The next step was Bohemia, Moravia and Poland. This step also was not possible to accomplish in one campaign. First of all, the Western fortification had to be finished. It was not possible to reach the goal in one effort. It was clear to me from the first moment that I could not be satisfied with the Sudeten-German territory. That was only a partial solution. The decision to march into Bohemia was made. Then followed the erection of the Protectorate, and with that the basis for the action against Poland was laid, but I wasn't quite clear at that time whether I should start first against the East and then in the West, or vice versa."

There are some curious antitheses of thought in that speech, as in most of Adolf Hitler's speeches. In one sentence he combines guidance by Providence with the making of brutal decisions. He constantly speaks of how very few people were with him, and yet of how the mass of the German people were with him. But he does give a brief summary of the gist of what is contained in the allegations of our Indictment, to which I have invited your attention: the organisation of the mass of the people, then extending to the armed forces, and the various brutal decisions that he did make, about which history knows.

That long document contains other material of great interest. It may be that we shall advert to other portions of it later. At this point, however, I have simply asked the Court to focus attention on the matter I have just read and its hearing on the development of the conspiracy during the period 1933 to 1936.

Another captured document is sufficient to demonstrate the preparations for war in which the Nazi conspirators were engaged during this period. I refer to a top secret letter dated 24th June, 1935, from General von Brauchitsch to the Supreme Commanders of the Army, Navy and Air Forces. Attached to that letter is a copy of a secret Reich Defence law of 21st May, 1935, and a copy of a decision of the Reich Cabinet of 21st May, 1935, on the Council for the defence of the Reich.

These documents were captured in the OKW files at Fechenheim. This group of documents is numbered 2261-PS in our numbered series of documents. It seems to us one of the most significant evidences of secret and direct preparations for aggressive war.

I gave expression to a typographical error. That was General von Blomberg instead of Brauchitsch.

I have the original of these documents. I ask that they be admitted into evidence as exhibit USA 24.

The top page of that document I shall read in full, which is the letter signed "von Blomberg, Berlin, 24th June, 1935, 'Top Secret' " headed "The Reich Minister of War and Supreme Commander of the Armed Forces, No. 1820/35 Top Secret L IIa."

To: The Supreme Commander of the Army

The Supreme Commander of the Navy

The Supreme Commander of the Air Forces

In the appendix I transmit one copy each of the law for the defence of the Reich of the 21st May, 1935, and of a decision of the Reich Cabinet of 21st May, 1935, concerning the Reich Defence Council. The publication of the Reich's Defence Law is temporarily suspended by order of the Fuehrer and Reich Chancellor.

The Fuehrer and Reich Chancellor has nominated the President of the Directorate of the Reichsbank, Dr. Schacht, to be Plenipotentiary-General for war economy.

I request that the copies of the Reich's Defence Law needed within the units of the Armed Forces, be ordered before 1st July, 1935, at Armed Forces Office (L) where it is to be established with the request that the law should only be distributed down to Corps Headquarters outside of the Reich Ministry of War.

I point out the necessity of strictest secrecy once more."

Signed by "von Blomberg." Underneath that is an endorsement "Berlin. 3rd September, 1935; No. 1820/35 L Top Secret II a. To Defence-Economic Group C-3, copy transmitted (signed) Jodl."

There is attached thereto, if the Tribunal please, the statute referred to as the Reich Defence Law of 21st May, 1935, or rather it was enacted by the Reich Cabinet, and it starts with the statement:

"The Reich Cabinet has enacted the following law that is hereby made public." There follows a law in detail covering preparations for state of defence, mobilisation, appointment of this plenipotentiary-general for war economy, with plenipotentiary authority for the economic preparation of the war, and a Part III providing for setting of penalties.

The law is signed "The Fuehrer and Reich Chancellor, Adolf Hitler; the Reich Minister of War, von Blomberg; the Reich Minister of the Interior, Frick," one of the defendants. And at the bottom of it there is this note. That is on Sheet 4 of the original German, I think:

"Note on the law for the Defence of the Reich of 21st May, 1935.

The publication of the Law for the Defence of the Reich on 21st May, 1935, will be suspended. The law became effective 21st May, 1935.

The Fuehrer and Reich Chancellor, Adolf Hitler."

So that although the publication itself stated the law was made public, the publication was suspended by Adolf Hitler; although the law became effective immediately.

There is further attached a copy of the decision of the Reich Cabinet Of 21st May, 1935, on the Council for the Defence of the Realm which deals largely with organisation for economic preparation for the war and which I think was disclosed by my colleague, Mr. Dodd, last week.

There can be no question that this law Of 21st May, 1935, was the corner-stone of war preparations of the Nazi conspirators. The relationship of the defendant Schacht to this preparation is made transparently clear by this captured document.

So much, for the time being, on the preparatory phase of the conspiracy, 1933 to 1936.

As indicated earlier, the next phase of aggression was the formulation and execution of plans to attack Austria and Czechoslovakia, in that order. This is the phase of the aggression covered by paragraphs 3(a), (b), and (c) of Section IV (F) of the Indictment appearing at pages seven to eight of the printed English Text.

One of the most striking and revealing of all the captured documents which have come to hand is a document which we have come to know as the Hoszbach notes of a conference in the Reich Chancellery On 5th November, 1937, from 16.15 to 20-30 hours, in the course of which Hitler outlined to those present the possibilities and necessities of expanding their foreign policy, and requested - I quote, - "That his statements be looked upon in the case of his death as his last will and testament." And so with this document we shall present to the Tribunal and to the public the last will and testament of Adolf Hitler as he contemplated that last will and testament on 5th November, 1937. The document comes to hand through the United States Department of State of the United States. It is numbered document 386-PS in our series of numbered documents. I offer it in evidence as exhibit USA 25.

Before reading it, I note at the start that the recorder of the minutes of this meeting, then Colonel Hoszbach, was the Fuehrer's adjutant. I note also the presence in this conspiratorial meeting of the defendant Erich Raeder. The defendant Constantin von Neurath was present. The defendant Hermann Wilhelm Goering was present. The minutes of this meeting reveal a crystallisation towards the end of 1937 in the policy of the Nazi regime. Austria and Czechoslovakia were to be acquired by force. They would provide Lebensraum (living space) and improve Germany's military position for further operations. While it is true that actual events unfolded themselves in a somewhat different manner than that outlined at this meeting, in essence the purposes stated at the meeting were carried out. The document destroys any possible doubt concerning the Nazis' premeditation of their crimes against peace. This document is of such tremendous importance that I feel obliged to read it in full into the record.

"Berlin, 10th November, 1937. Notes on the conference in the Reichrkanzlei on 5th November, 1937, from 16.15 to 20.30 hours.

Present: The Fuehrer and Reich Chancellor;

The Reich Minister for War, Generalfeldmarschall v. Blomberg;

The C.-in-C. Army, Generaloberst Freiherr von Fritsch;

The C.-in-C. Navy, Generaladmiral Dr. H. C. Raeder;

The C.-in-C. Luftwaffe, Generaloberst Goering;

The Reich Minister for Foreign Affairs Freiherr v. Neurath;

Oberst Hoszbach (the adjutant who took the minutes)."

The Fuehrer stated initially that the subject matter of today's conference was of such high importance that its detailed discussion would certainly in other States take place before the Cabinet in full session. However, he, the Fuehrer, had decided not to discuss this matter in the larger circle of the Reich Cabinet, because of its importance. His subsequent statements were the result of detailed deliberations and of the experiences of his four and a half years in government; he desired to explain to those present his fundamental ideas on the possibilities and necessities of expanding their foreign policy, and in the interests of a far-sighted policy he requested that his statements be looked upon, in the case of his death, as his last will and testament.

The Fuehrer then went on: "The aim of German policy is the security and the preservation of the nation and its propagation. This is consequently a problem of space. The German nation comprises eighty-five million people, which, because of the number of individuals and the compactness of habitation, form a homogeneous European racial body, the like of which cannot be found in any other country. On the other hand it justifies the demand for larger living space more than for any other nation. If there have been no political measures to meet the demands of this racial body for living space, then that is the result of historical development spread over several centuries, and should this political condition continue to exist, it will represent the greatest danger to the preservation of the German nation (the German word used there is not "nation"; it is " Volkstum ") at its present high level. An arrest of the deterioration of the German element in Austria and in Czechoslovakia is just as little possible as the preservation of the present state in Germany itself."

I interpolate that I can but think that this is not a good translation of the German because to me the sentence seems meaningless.

"Instead of growth, sterility will be introduced, and as a consequence tensions of a social nature will appear after a number of years, because political and philosophical ideas are of a permanent nature only as long as they are able to produce the basis for the realisation of the actual claim of the existence of a nation. The German future is therefore dependent exclusively on the solution of the need for living space. Such a solution can be sought naturally only for a limited period, about one to three generations.

Before touching upon the question of solving the need for living space, it must be decided whether a solution of the German position with a good future can be attained, either by way of an autarchy or by way of an increased share in universal commerce and industry.

Autarchy: Execution will be possible only with strict National-Socialist State policy, which is the basis; (that is the basis of autarchy) assuming this can be achieved, the results are as follows:

A. In the sphere of raw materials, only limited, but not total autarchy can be attained:

1. Wherever coal can be used for the extraction of raw materials autarchy is feasible.

2. In the case of ores the position is much more difficult. Requirements in iron and light metals can be covered by ourselves. Copper and tin, however, cannot.

3. Cellular materials can be covered by ourselves as long as sufficient wood supplies exist. A permanent solution is not possible.

4. Edible fats - possible.

B. In the case of foods, the question of an autarchy must be answered with a definite capital NO. The general increase of living standards, compared with thirty to forty years ago, brought about a simultaneous increase of the demand and an increase of personal consumption among the producers, the farmers themselves. The proceeds from the production increases in agriculture have been used for covering the increased demand, therefore they represent no absolute increase in production. A further increase in production by making greater demands on the soil is not possible, because it already shows signs of deterioration due to the use of artificial fertilisers, and it is therefore certain that, even with the greatest possible increase in production, participation in the world market could not be avoided."

I interpolate, that if I understand him he means by that "no autarchy; we must participate in world trade and commerce."

The considerable expenditure Of foreign currency to secure food by import, even in periods when harvests are good, increases catastrophically when the harvest is really poor. The possibility of this catastrophe increases correspondingly to the increase in population, and the annual 560,000 excess in births would bring about an increased consumption in bread, because the child is a greater bread eater than the adult.

Permanently to counter the difficulties of food supplies by lowering the standard of living and by rationalisation is impossible in a continent which has developed an approximately equivalent standard of living. As the solving of the unemployment problem has brought into effect the complete power of consumption, some small corrections in our agricultural home production will be possible, but not a wholesale alteration of the standard of food consumption. Consequently autarchy becomes impossible, specifically in the sphere of food supplies, as well as generally.

Participation in world economy. There are limits to this which we are unable to transgress. The market fluctuation would be an obstacle to a secure foundation of the German position; international commercial agreements do not offer any guarantee for practical execution. It must be considered on principle that since the World War (1914-18), an industrialisation has taken place in countries which formerly exported food. We live in a period of economic empires, in which the tendency to colonies again, approaches the condition which originally motivated colonisation; in Japan and Italy economic motives are the basis of their will to expand, and economic need will also drive Germany to it. Countries outside the great economic empires have special difficulties in expanding economically.

The upward tendency, which has been caused in world economy, due to armament competition, can never form a permanent basis for an economic settlement, and this latter is also hampered by the economic disruption caused by Bolshevism. There is a pronounced military weakness in those States which base their existence on export. As our exports and imports are carried out over those sea lanes which are dominated by Britain, it is rather a question of security of transport than one of foreign currency and this explains the great weakness of our food situation in wartime. The only way out, and one which may appear imaginary, is the securing of greater living space, an endeavour which at all times has been the cause of the formation of States and of movements of nations. It is explicable that this tendency finds no interest in Geneva and in satisfied States. Should the security of our food situation be our foremost thought, then the space required for this can only be sought in Europe, but we will not copy liberal capitalist policies which rely on exploiting colonies. It is not a case of conquering people, but of conquering agriculturally useful space. It would also be more to the purpose to seek raw material- producing territory in Europe directly adjoining the Reich and not overseas, and this solution would have to be brought into effect for one or two generations. What would be required at a later date over and above this must be left to subsequent generations. The development of great world-wide national bodies is naturally a slow process and the German people, with its strong racial root" - I interpolate, there is a German word "Volkstamm", racial root - "has for this purpose the most favourable foundations in the heart of the European Continent. The history of all times - Roman Empire, British Empire - has proved that every space expansion can only be effected by breaking resistance and taking risks. Even setbacks are unavoidable; neither formerly nor today has space been found without an owner; the attacker always comes up against the proprietor."

(A recess was taken.)

MR. ALDERMAN: May it please the Tribunal, after the somewhat jumbled discussion, which I have just read, of geopolitical economic theory and of the need for expansion and "Lebensraum," Adolf Hitler, in these Hoszbach notes, posed the question:

"The question for Germany is where the greatest possible conquest could be made at lowest cost.

German politics must reckon with its two hateful enemies, England and France, to whom a strong German colossus in the centre of Europe would be intolerable. Both these States would oppose a further reinforcement of Germany, both in Europe and overseas, and in this opposition they would have the support of all parties.

Both countries would view the building of German military strong points overseas as a threat to their overseas communications, as a security measure for German commerce, and retrospectively a strengthening of the German position in Europe.

England is not in a position to cede any of her colonial possessions to us owing to the resistance which she experiences in the Dominions. After the loss of prestige which England has suffered owing to the transfer of Abyssinia to Italian ownership, a return of East Africa can no longer be expected. Any resistance on England's part would at best consist in the readiness to satisfy our colonial claims by taking away colonies which at the present moment are not in British hands, for example, Angola. French favours would probably be of the same nature.

A serious discussion regarding the return of colonies to us could be considered only at a time when England is in a state of emergency and the German Reich is strong and well armed. The Fuehrer does not share the opinion that the Empire is unshakeable."

Meaning, I take it, the British Empire.

"Resistance against the Empire is to be found less in conquered territories than amongst its competitors. The British Empire and the Roman Empire cannot be compared with one another in regard to durability; after the Punic Wars the latter did not have a serious political enemy. Only the dissolving effects which originated in Christendom, and the signs of age which, creep into all States, made it possible for the ancient Germans to subjugate ancient Rome.

Alongside the British Empire today a number of States exist which are stronger than it. The British mother country is able to defend its colonial possession only when allied with other States and not by its own power. Now could England alone, for example, defend Canada against attack by America, or its Far Eastern interests against an attack by Japan?

The singling out of the British Crown as the bearer of Empire unity is in itself an admission that the Universal Empire cannot be maintained permanently by power politics. The following are significant pointers in this respect:

(a) Ireland's struggle for independence.

(b) Constitutional disputes in India where England, by her half measures, left the door open for Indians, at a later date, to utilise the non- fulfilment of constitutional promises as a weapon against Britain.

(c) The weakening of the British position in the Far East by Japan.

(d) The opposition in the Mediterranean by Italy which - by virtue of its history, driven by necessity and led by a genius - expands its power position and must consequently infringe British interests to an increasing extent. The outcome of the Abyssinian War is a loss of prestige for Britain which Italy is endeavouring to increase by stirring up discontent in the Mohammedan World.

It must be established in conclusion that the Empire cannot he held permanently by power politics by 45 million Britons, in spite of all the solidity of their ideals. The proportion of the populations in the Empire, compared with that of the motherland, is nine to one, and it should act as a warning to us that if we expand in space, we must not allow the level of our population to become too low."

I take it he meant by that: "Keep the population of occupied territories low in comparison with ours."

"France's position is more favourable than that of England. The French Empire is better placed geographically; the population of its colonial possessions represents a potential military increase. But France is faced with difficulties of internal politics. At the present time only 10 per cent approximately of the nations have parliamentary governments, whereas 90 per cent of them have totalitarian governments. Nevertheless, we have to take the following into our political consideration as power factors:

Britain, France, Russia, and the adjoining smaller States.

The German question can be solved only by way of force, and this is never without risk. The battles of Frederick the Great for Silesia, and Bismarck's wars against Austria and France had been a tremendous risk and the speed of Prussian action in 1870 had prevented Austria from participating in the war. If we place the decision to apply force with risk at the head of the following expositions, then we are left to reply to the questions 'when' and 'how'. In this regard we have to decide upon three different cases."

I interpolate: The Tribunal will recall the specific allegation in the Indictment that at this meeting there emerged three different plans, any of which might be utilised.

"Case 1. Period 1943-45: After this we can only expect a change for the worse. The rearming of the Army, the Navy and the Air Force, as well as the formation of the Officers' Corps, are practically concluded."

I remind the Tribunal that this meeting was on 5th November, 1937, but he is contemplating the period 1943-45.

"Our material equipment and armaments are modern; with further delay the danger of their becoming out-of-date will increase. In particular the secrecy of 'special weapons' cannot always be safeguarded. Enlistment of reserves would be limited to the current recruiting age groups and an addition from older untrained groups would be no longer available.

In comparison with the rearmament, which will have been carried out at that time by other nations, we shall decrease in relative power. Should we not act until 1943-45, then, dependent on the absence of reserves, any year could bring about the food crisis, for the countering of which we do not possess the necessary foreign currency. This must be considered as a 'point of weakness in the regime.'

Over and above that, the world will anticipate our action and will increase counter-measures yearly. Whilst other nations isolate themselves we should be forced on the offensive.

What the actual position would be in the years 1943-45, no one knows today. It is certain, however, that we can wait no longer.

On the one side the large armed forces, with the necessity for securing their upkeep, the ageing of the Nazi movement and of its leaders, and on the other side the prospect of a lowering of the standard of living and a drop in the birth rate, leaves us no other choice but to act. If the Fuehrer is still living, then it will be his irrevocable decision to solve the German space problem no later than 1943-45. The necessity for action before 1943-45 will come under consideration in Cases 2 and 3.

Case 2. Should the social tensions in France lead to an internal political crisis of such dimensions that it absorbs the French Army and thus renders it incapable for employment in war against Germany, then the time for action against Czechoslovakia has come.

Case 3. It would be equally possible to act against Czechoslovakia if France should be so tied up by a war against another State that it cannot "proceed" against Germany.

For the improvement of our military political position it must be our first arm, in every case of entanglement by war, to conquer Czechoslovakia and Austria simultaneously, in order to remove any threat from the flanks in case of a possible advance westwards. In the case of a conflict with France it would hardly be necessary to assume that Czechoslovakia would declare war on the same day as France. However, Czechoslovakia's desire to participate in the war will increase proportionally to the degree to which we are being weakened. Its actual participation could make itself felt by an attack on Silesia, either towards the North or the West.

Once Czechoslovakia is conquered - and a mutual frontier, Germany-Hungary, is obtained - then a neutral attitude by Poland in a German-French conflict could more easily be relied upon. Our agreements with Poland remain valid only as long as Germany's strength remains unshakeable; should Germany have any setbacks then an attack by Poland against East Prussia, perhaps also against Pomerania, and Silesia, must be taken into account.

Assuming a development of the situation, which would lead to a planned attack on our part in the years 1943 to '45, then the behaviour of France, England, Poland and Russia would probably have to be judged in the following manner:

The Fuehrer believes personally, that in all probability England and perhaps also France, have already silently written off Czechoslovakia, and that they have got used to the idea that this question would one day be cleaned up by Germany. The difficulties in the British Empire and the prospects of being entangled in another long-drawn-out European war, would be decisive factors in the non-participation of England in a war against Germany. The British attitude would certainly not remain without influence on France's attitude. An attack by France, without British support, is hardly probable, assuming that its offensive would stagnate along our Western fortifications. Without England's support it would also not be necessary to take into consideration a march by France through Belgium and Holland, and this would also not have to be reckoned with by us in case of a conflict with France, as in every case it would have, as a consequence, the enmity of Great Britain. Naturally, we should in every case have to bar our frontier during the operation of our attacks against Czechoslovakia and Austria. It must be taken into consideration here that Czechoslovakia's defence measures will increase in strength from year to year, and that a consolidation of the inside values of the Austrian Army will also be effected in the course of years. Although the population of Czechoslovakia in the first place is not a thin one, the embodiment of Czechoslovakia and Austria would nevertheless constitute the conquest of food for five to six million people, on the basis that a compulsory emigration of two million from Czechoslovakia, and of one million from Austria could be carried out. The annexation of the two States to Germany, militarily and politically, would constitute a considerable relief, owing to shorter and better frontiers, the freeing of fighting personnel for other purposes, and the possibility of reconstituting new armies up to a strength of about twelve Divisions, representing a new Division per one million population.

No opposition to the removal of Czechoslovakia or Austria is expected on the part of Italy; however, it cannot be judged today what would be her attitude in the Austrian question, since it would depend largely on whether the Duce were alive at the time or not.

The measure and speed of our action would decide Poland's attitude. Poland will have little inclination to enter the war against a victorious Germany, with Russia in the rear.

Military participation by Russia must be countered by the speed of our operations; it is a question whether this needs to be taken into consideration at all in view of Japan's attitude.

Should Case 2 occur - paralysation of France by a Civil War - then the situation should be utilised at any time for operations against Czechoslovakia, as Germany's most dangerous enemy would be eliminated.

The Fuehrer sees Case 3 looming nearer; it could develop from the existing tensions in the Mediterranean, and should it occur, he has firmly decided to make use of it any time, perhaps even as early as 1938.

Following recent experiences in the course of the events of the war in Spain, the Fuehrer does not see an early end to hostilities there. Taking into consideration the time required for past offensives by Franco - the English Text says France: it means Franco - a further three years' duration of war is within the bounds of possibility. On the other hand, from the German point of view, a one hundred per cent victory by Franco is not desirable; we are more interested in a continuation of the war and preservation of the tensions in the Mediterranean. Should Franco be in sole possession of the Spanish Peninsula, it would mean the end of Italian intervention and of the presence of Italy in the Balearic Isles. As our interests are directed towards continuing the war in Spain, it must be the task of our future policy to strengthen Italy in her fight to hold on to the Balearic Isles. However, a solidification of Italian positions in the Balearic Isles cannot be tolerated either by France or by England and could lead to a war by France and England against Italy, in which case Spain, if entirely in his (that is Franco's) hands, could participate on the side of Italy's enemies. A subjugation of Italy in such a war appears very unlikely. Additional raw materials could be brought to Italy via Germany. The Fuehrer believes that Italy's military strategy would be to remain on the defensive against France on the Western frontier and carry out operations against France from Libya, against the North African French colonial possessions.

As a landing of French and British troops on the Italian coast can be discounted, and as a French offensive via the Alps to Upper Italy would be extremely difficult, and would probably stagnate before the strong Italian fortifications, French lines of communication threatened by the Italian fleet will to a great extent be paralysed for the transport of fighting personnel from North Africa to France, so that at its frontiers with Italy and Germany, France will have, at its disposal, solely the metropolitan fighting forces."

There again I think that must be a defective English translation. "French lines of communication by the Italian fleet." must mean "Fresh lines." or something in that connection.

"If Germany profits from this war by disposing of the Czechoslovakian and the Austrian questions, the probability must be assumed that England-being at war with Italy-would not decide to commence operations against Germany. Without British support, a warlike action by France against Germany is not to be anticipated.

The date of our attack on Czechoslovakia and Austria must be made independent of the course of the Italian- French-English war and would not be simultaneous with the commencement of military operations by these three States. The Fuehrer was also not thinking of military agreements with Italy, but in complete independence and by exploiting this unique favourable opportunity, he wishes to begin to carry out operations against Czechoslovakia. The attack on Czechoslovakia would have to take place with the 'speed of lightning'"

- the German words being "blitzartig schnell."

Fieldmarshal von Blomberg and Generaloberst von Fritsch, in giving their estimate on the situation, repeatedly pointed out that England and France must not appear as our enemies, and they stated that the war with Italy would not bind the French Army to such an extent that it would not be in a position to commence operations on our Western frontier with superior forces. Generaloberst von Fritsch estimated the French forces which would presumably be employed on the Alpine frontier against Italy to be in the region of twenty divisions, so that a strong French superiority would still remain on our Western frontier. The French would, according to German reasoning, attempt to advance into the Rhineland. We should consider the lead which France has got in mobilisation, and, quite apart from the very small value of our then existing fortifications - which was pointed out particularly by General Fieldmarshal von Blomberg - the four motorised divisions which had been laid down for the West would be more or less incapable of movement. With regard to our offensive in a South- easterly direction, Fieldmarshal von Blomberg drew special attention to the strength of the Czechoslovakian fortifications, the building of which had assumed the character of a Maginot Line and which would present extreme difficulties to our attack.

Generaloberst von Fritsch mentioned that it was the purpose of a study which he had laid on for this winter to investigate the possibilities of carrying out operations against Czechoslovakia, with special consideration of the conquest of the Czechoslovakian system of fortifications; the Generaloberst also stated that owing to the prevailing conditions, he would have to relinquish his leave abroad, which was to begin on the 10th of November. This intention was countermanded by the Fuehrer, who gave as a reason that the possibility of the conflict was not to be regarded as being so imminent. In reply to statements by General Fieldmarshal von Blomberg and Generaloberst von Fritsch regarding England and France's attitude, the Fuehrer repeated his previous statements and said that he was convinced of Britain's non-participation and that consequently he did not believe in military action by France against Germany. Should the Mediterranean conflict, already mentioned, lead to a general mobilisation in Europe, then we should have to commence operations against Czechoslovakia immediately. If, however, the powers who are not participating in the war should declare their disinterestedness, then Germany would, for the time being, have to side with this attitude.

In view of the information given by the Fuehrer, Generaloberst Goering considered it imperative to think of a reduction or abandonment of our military undertaking in Spain. The Fuehrer agreed to this, insofar as he believed this decision should be postponed for a suitable date.

The second part of the discussion concerned material armament questions."

(Signed) "Hoszbach," and there are other notations.

In this connection I invite the Court's attention to the allegation in paragraph 3(a) of Section IV (F) of the Indictment, on page 7 of the printed English text, relating to a meeting of an influential group of Nazi conspirators on 5th November, 1937. The document just introduced and read in evidence gives the specific evidentiary support for trial allegation.

The record of what happened thereafter is well known to history. The Anschluss with Austria, under military pressure from the Nazis, occurred in March, 1938. We shall give you detailed evidence concerning that in due course. We shall also give evidence as to details of the aggression against Czechoslovakia including the pressure on Czechoslovakia that resulted in the Munich Pact of September, 1938, and the violation of that Pact itself by Germany, on 15th March, 1939. There is much of interest in the secret documents relating to those aggressions.

At this point, however, I desire to bring to the attention of the Tribunal one more captured document, which reveals in all its nakedness the truth concerning the deliberateness of the aggressions against Czechoslovakia. This document consists of a file, a file kept by Colonel Schmundt, Hitler's adjutant. The file was found by one of the units of the 327th Glider Infantry, in a cellar of the Platterhof, Obersalzberg, near Berchtesgaden. The file represents a work- file of originals and duplicates, incidental to the preparations for the annexation of Czechoslovakia. I should like to ask the Tribunal to examine particularly the photostat of the original German of this file. We have copies of those photostats. Something in physical form is lost in transcribing a translation. The picture of the original file, including photographs of the telegrams, gives a sense of the reality of the evidence that is lost in the transcribed translation. The file is numbered document 388- PS, in our numbered series of documents. I have here the original file.

I thought perhaps I might read the German title. It is "Grundlagen zur Studie Gruen," that is the main plan for "Case Green," Green being a code word for the aggression against Czechoslovakia.

I offer the entire file in evidence as exhibit USA 26 and will ask that photostats be passed up to the Court. I offer the file, if the Tribunal please, with, of course, the understanding arid realisation that only such parts of it as I read will immediately go into evidence; but we shall refer to other parts from time to time later, in the presentation of the case. The material in this file will be dealt with in greater detail at a later point in my prosecution. However, at this point, I desire to call attention to Item No. 2 in the file.

Item No. 2 is dated 22nd April, 1938. It is the second sheet of the English translation. It is a summary, prepared by Schmundt, the adjutant, of a discussion on 21st April, 1938, between Hitler and the defendant Wilhelm Keitel.

This item, like the other items in the file, relates to "Case Green." As I said, "Case Green" was a secret code word for the planned operation against Czechoslovakia. This meeting occurred within approximately one month following the successful annexation of Austria. In the carrying out of the conspiracy, it became necessary to revise the "Case Green," to take into account the changed attitude, as a result of the bloodless success against Austria. I shall now read Item 2 of this file.

"Berlin, 22nd April, 1938.

Bases of the Dissertation on 'Gruen.'

Summary of discussion between the Fuehrer and General Keitel of 21st April:-

A. Political Aspect.

(1) Strategic surprise attack out of a clear sky without any cause or possibility of justification has been turned down. The result would be: hostile world opinion which can lead to a critical situation. Such a measure is justified only for the elimination of the last opponent on the mainland.

(2) Action after a time of diplomatic clashes, which gradually come to a crisis and lead to war.

(3) Lightning-swift action as the result of an incident (for example, assassination of German ambassador in connection with an anti-German demonstration).

B. Military Conclusions.

(1) The preparations are to be made for the political possibilities (2 and 3) Case 2 is the undesired one since 'Gruen' will have taken security measures.

(2) The loss of time caused by transporting the bulk of the divisions by rail - which is unavoidable, but should be cut down as far as possible - must not impede a lightning-swift blow at the time of the action.

(3) 'Separate thrusts' are to be carried out immediately with a view to penetrating the enemy fortification lines at numerous points and in a strategically favourable direction. The thrusts are to be worked out to the smallest detail

(knowledge of roads, targets, composition of the columns according to their individual tasks.) Simultaneous attacks by the Army and Air Force.

The Air Force is to support the individual columns (for example dive-bombers sealing of installations at penetration points, hampering the bringing up of reserves, destroying signal communications traffic, thereby isolating the garrisons).

(4) Politically, the first four days of military action are the decisive ones. If there are no effective military successes, a European crisis will certainly arise. Accomplished facts must prove the senselessness of foreign military intervention, draw Allies into the scheme (division of spoils) and demoralise 'Gruen.'

Therefore: bridging the time gap between first penetration and employment of the forces to be brought up, by a determined and ruthless thrust by a motorised army. (For example via Pilsen, Prague.)

(5) if possible, separation of transport movement 'Rot' from 'Gruen.'"

'Rot' was the code name for their then plan against the West.

"A simultaneous strategic concentration 'Rot' can lead 'Rot' to undesired measures. On the other hand, it must be possible to put 'Case Rot' into operation, at any time.

C. Propaganda.

(1) Leaflets on the conduct of Germans in Czechoslovakia (Gruenland).

(2) Leaflets with threats for intimidation of the Czechs (Gruenen)."

(Initialled by Schmundt.)"

In the reading of this document, the Tribunal doubtless noted particularly paragraph 3, under the heading "Political Aspect", which reads as follows: "Lightning-swift action as the result of an incident (example: Assassination of German ambassador as an upshot of an anti-German demonstration)." The document as a whole, establishes that the conspirators were planning the creation of an incident to justify to the world their own aggression against Czechoslovakia. It established, I submit, that consideration was being given to assassinating the German ambassador at Prague to create the requisite incident. This is alleged in paragraph 3(c) of section IV (F) of the Indictment, appearing at page 8 of the printed English text of the Indictment.

As the Indictment was being read, at the opening of the case, when this particular allegation was reached, the defendant Goering shook his head slowly and solemnly in the negative. I can well understand that he would have shaken his head, if he believed the allegation of the Indictment to be untrue. In the course of Mr. Justice Jackson's opening address, when this same matter was referred to, the defendant Goering again solemnly shook his head. On this allegation the prosecution stands on the evidence just submitted, the denials of the defendant Goering notwithstanding.

If the Court please, would this be a convenient time to recess ?

THE PRESIDENT: The Tribunal will adjourn now until 2 o'clock.

(A recess was taken until 14.00 hours.)

THE PRESIDENT: Mr. Alderman.

MR. ALDERMAN: May it please the Tribunal, as I suggested earlier, the next phase of the aggression was the formulation and execution of the plan to attack Poland, and with it the resulting initiation of aggressive war in Poland in September 1939. This is covered by paragraphs 4 a) and (b) of Section IV (in) of the Indictment appearing on page 9 of the printed English text.

Here again the careful and meticulous record-keeping of the Adjutant Schmundt has provided us with a document in his own handwriting, which lets the cat out of the bag. That may be a troublesome colloquialism to translate. I don't know. The document consists of minutes of a conference held on the 23rd May, 1939. The place of the conference was the Fuehrer's study in the New Reich Chancellery. The defendant Goering was present

(The defendant Frick at this point made a statement in German, which was not translated.)

MR. ALDERMAN: I think one of the defendants indicated I had referred to the wrong year. My notes show the 23rd May, 1939. That is shown by the original document.

THE PRESIDENT: Which is the document you are referring to?

MR. ALDERMAN: That is document L-79. As I said, the defendant Goering was present. The defendant Raeder was present. The defendant Keitel was present. The subject of the meeting was, and I quote: "Indoctrination on the political situation and future aims." This document is of historical importance, second not even to the political will and testament of the Fuehrer, recorded by Adjutant Hoszbach.

The original of this document when captured found its way through the complicated channels across the Atlantic to the United States. There it was found by members of the staff of the American prosecution, by them taken to London, and thence to Nuremberg. The "L" on the identifying number indicates that it is one of the documents which were assembled in London and brought here from there. We think the document is of unquestioned validity. Its authenticity and its accuracy as a record of what transpired at the meeting of 23rd May, 1939, stands admitted by the defendant Keitel in one of his interrogations. As I say, the number is document L-79 in our numbered series. I offer it in evidence as exhibit USA 27.

This document also is of such great importance historically and as bearing on the issues now presented to the Tribunal that I feel obliged to read most of it. At the top: Geheime Reichssache "Top Secret."

"To be transmitted by officer only.

Minutes of a Conference on 23rd May, 1939.

Place: The Fuehrer's Study, New Reich Chancellery.

Adjutant on duty: Lt.-Col. (G.S.) Schmundt.

Present: The Fuehrer, Field Marshal Goering, Grand Admiral Raeder, Col.-Gen. Von Brauchitsch, Col.-Gen. Keitel, Col.-Gen. Milch, Gen. (of artillery) Halder, Gen. Bodenschatz, Rear-Adml. Schniewindt, Col. (G.S.) Joschennek, Col. (G.S.) Warlimont, Lt.-Col. (G.S.) Schmundt, Capt. Engel (Army), Lieut.-Commd Albrecht, Capt. V. Below (Army).

Subject: Indoctrination on the political situation and future aims.

The Fuehrer defined as the purpose of the conference

(1) Analysis of the situation.

(2) Definition of the tasks for the Armed Forces arising from that situation.

(3) Exposition of the consequences of those tasks.

(4) Ensuring the secrecy of all decisions and work resulting from those consequences. Secrecy is the first essential for success.

The Fuehrer's observations are given in systematised form below. Our present situation must be considered from two points of view

(1) The actual development of events between 1933 and 1939;

(2) The permanent and unchanging situation in which Germany lies.

In the period 1933-1939, progress was made in all fields. Our military situation improved enormously.

Our situation with regard to the rest of the world has remained the same.

Germany had dropped from the circle of Great Powers. The balance of power had been effected without the participation of Germany.

This equilibrium is disturbed when Germany's demands for the necessities of life make themselves felt, and Germany re-emerges as a Great Power. All demands ire regarded as 'Encroachments'. The English are more afraid of dangers in the economic sphere than of the simple threat of force.

A mass of 80 million people has solved the ideological problems. So, too, must the economic problems be solved. No German can evade the creation of the necessary economic conditions for this. The solution of the problems demands coverage. The principle, by which one evades solving the problem by adapting oneself to circumstances, is inadmissible. Circumstances must rather be adapted to aims. This is impossible without invasion of foreign states or attacks upon foreign property.

Living space, in proportion to the magnitude of the State, is the basis of all power. One may refuse for a time to face the problem, but finally it is solved one way or the other. The choice is between advancement or decline. In fifteen or twenty years' time we shall be compelled to find a solution. No German statesman can evade the question longer than that.

We are at present in a state of patriotic fervour, which is by two other nations: Italy and Japan.

The period which lies behind us has indeed been put to good use. All measures have been taken in the correct sequence and in harmony with our aims.

After six years, the situation is today as follows:

The national-political unity of the Germans has been achieved apart from minor exceptions."

I suppose they were those in the concentration camps. -

"Further successes cannot be obtained without the shedding of blood.

The demarcation of frontiers is of military importance.

The Pole is no 'supplementary enemy.' Poland will always be on the side of our adversaries. In spite of treaties of friendship, Poland has always had the secret intention of exploiting every opportunity to do us harm.

Danzig is not the subject of the dispute at all. It is a question of expanding our living space in the East and of securing our food supplies, of the settlement of the Baltic problem. Food supplies can be expected only from thinly populated areas. Over and above the natural fertility, thoroughgoing German exploitation will enormously increase the surplus.

There is no other possibility for Europe.

Colonies: Beware of gifts of colonial territory. This does not solve the food problem. Remember - blockade.

If fate brings us into conflict with the West, the possession of extensive areas in the East will be advantageous. We shall be able to rely upon record harvests even less in time of war than in peace.

The population of non-German areas will perform no military service, but will be available as a source of labour. The Polish problem is inseparable from conflict with the West.

Poland's internal power of resistance to Bolshevism is doubtful. Thus Poland is of doubtful value as a barrier against Russia.

It is questionable whether military success in the West can be achieved by a quick decision; questionable too is the attitude of Poland.

The Polish government will not resist pressure from Russia. Poland sees danger in a German victory in the West, and will attempt to rob us of that victory.

There is therefore no question of sparing Poland, and we are left with the decision:

To attack Poland at the first suitable opportunity. "

That, if the Court please, is underscored in the original German text.

"We cannot expect a repetition of the Czech affair. There will be war. Our task is to isolate Poland. The success of the isolation will be decisive.

Therefore, the Fuehrer must reserve the right to give the final order to attack.

There must be no simultaneous conflict with the Western Powers (France and England).

If it is not certain that a German-Polish conflict will not lead to war in the West, then the fight must be primarily against England and France.

Fundamentally therefore: Conflict with Poland - beginning with an attack on Poland - will only be successful if the Western Powers keep out of it. If this is impossible, then it will be better to attack in the West and to settle Poland at the same time.

The isolation of Poland is a matter of skilful politics. Japan is a weighty problem. Even if at first, for various reasons, her collaboration with us appears to be somewhat cool and restricted, it is nevertheless in Japan's own interest to take the initiative in attacking Russia in good time.

Economic relations with Russia are possible only if political relations have improved. A cautious trend is apparent in Press comment. It is not impossible that Russia will show herself to be disinterested in the destruction of Poland Should Russia take steps to oppose us, our relations with Japan may become closer.

If there were an alliance of France, England and Russia against Germany, Italy and Japan, 1 would be constrained to attack England and France with a few annihilating blows. The Fuehrer doubts the possibility of a peaceful settlement with England. We must prepare ourselves for the conflict. England sees in our development the foundation of a hegemony which would weaken her. England is therefore our enemy, and the conflict with her will be a life-and-death struggle.

What, will this struggle be like? (Underscored in the German original.)

England cannot deal with Germany and subjugate her with a few powerful blows. It is imperative for England that the war should be brought as near to the Ruhr basin as possible. French blood will not be spared (West Wall). The possession of the Ruhr basin will determine the duration of our resistance.

The Dutch and Belgian air bases must be occupied by armed forces. Declarations of neutrality must be ignored. If England and France intend the war between Germany and Poland to lead to a conflict, they will support Holland and Belgium in their neutrality and make them build fortifications in order finally to force them into co-operation.

Albeit under protest, Belgium and Holland will yield to pressure.

Therefore, if England intends to intervene in the Polish war, we must occupy Holland with lightning speed. We must aim at securing a new defence line on Dutch soil up to the Zuider Zee.

The war with England and France will be a life-and-death struggle.

The idea that we can get off cheaply is dangerous; there is no such possibility. We must burn our boats, and it is no longer a question of justice or injustice, but of life or death for 80 million human beings.

Question: Short or long war?

Every country's armed forces or government must aim at a short war. The government, however, must also be prepared for a war of 10-15 years' duration.

History has always shown that people have believed that wars would be short. In 1914, the opinion still prevailed that it was impossible to finance a long war. Even today this idea still persists in many minds. But on the contrary, every state will hold out as long as possible, unless it immediately suffers some grave weakening (for example Ruhr basin). England has similar weaknesses.

England knows that to lose a war will mean the end of her world power.

"England is the driving force against Germany " (which translated literally means: "England is the motor driving against Germany.")
I suppose that is the French "force motrice."
"Her strength lies in the following:-

(1) The British themselves are proud, courageous, tenacious, firm in resistance and gifted as organisers. They know how to exploit every new development. They have the love of adventure and bravery of the Nordic race. Quality is lowered by dispersal. The German average is higher.

(2) World power in itself. It has been constant for 300 years. Extended by the acquisition of allies, this power is not merely something concrete, but must also

be considered as a psychological force embracing the entire world. Add to this immeasurable wealth, with consequential financial credit.

(3) Geopolitical safety and protection by strong sea power and a courageous air force.

England's weakness.

If in the World War 1 we had had two battleships and two cruisers more, and if the battle of Jutland had been begun in the morning, the British Fleet would have been defeated and England brought to her knees. It would have meant the end of this war" - that war, I take it - " It was formerly not sufficient to defeat the Fleet. Landings had to be made in order to defeat England. England could provide her own food supplies. Today that is no longer possible.

The moment England's food supply routes are cut, she is forced to capitulate in one day. But if the Fleet is destroyed; immediate capitulation will be the result.

There is no doubt that a surprise attack can lead to a quick decision. It would be criminal, however, for the government to rely entirely on the element of surprise.

Experience has shown that surprise may be nullified by:

(1) Disclosure outside the limit of the military circles concerned.

(2) Mere chance, which may cause the collapse of the whole enterprise.

(3) Human failings.

(4) Weather conditions.

The final date for striking must be fixed well in advance. Beyond that time, the tension cannot be endured for long. It must be home in mind that weather conditions can render any surprise intervention by Navy and Air Force impossible.

This must be regarded as a most unfavourable basis of action.

(1) An effort must be made to deal the enemy a significant or the final decisive blow. Consideration of right and wrong or treaties do not enter into the matter. This will only be possible if we are not involved in a war with England on account of Poland.

(2) In addition to the surprise attack, preparations for a long war must be made while opportunities on the on the Continent for England are eliminated.

The army will have to hold positions essential to the Navy and Air Force. If Holland and Belgium are successfully occupied and held, and if France is also defeated, the fundamental conditions for a successful war against England will have been secured.

England can then be blockaded from Western France at close quarters by the Air Force, while the Navy with its submarines can extend the range of the blockade.

Consequences:

England will not be able to fight on the Continent.

Daily attacks by the Air Force and Navy will cut all her life-lines.

Time will not be on England's side.

Germany will not bleed to death on land.

Such strategy has been shown to be necessary by World War I and subsequent military operations. World War I is responsible for the following strategic considerations which are imperative:-

(1)With a more powerful Navy at the outbreak of the War, or a wheeling movement by the Army towards the Channel ports, the end would have been different.

(2) A country cannot be brought to defeat by an air force. It is impossible to attack all objectives simultaneously, and the lapse of time of a few minutes would evoke defence countermeasures.

(3) The unrestricted use of all resources is essential.

(4) Once the Army, in co-operation with the Air Force and Navy, has taken the most important positions, industrial production will cease to flow into the bottomless pit of the Army's battles, and can be diverted to benefit the Air Force and Navy.

The Army must, therefore, be capable of taking these positions. Systematic preparations must be made for the attack.

Study to this end is of the utmost importance. The aim will always be to force England to her knees.

A weapon will only be of decisive importance in winning battles, so long as the enemy does not possess it.

This applies to gas, submarines and Air Force. It would be true of the latter, for instance, as long as the English Fleet had no available countermeasures; it will no longer be the case in 1940 and 1941. Against Poland, for example, tanks will be effective, as the Polish Army possesses no counter-measures.

Where straightforward pressure is no longer considered to be decisive, its place must be taken by the elements of surprise and by masterly handling."

The rest of the document, if the Tribunal please, deals more in detail with military plans and preparations. I think it unnecessary to read further.

The document just read is the evidence which specifically supports the allegations in Paragraph 4(a) of Section IV (F) of the indictment, appearing on page 9 of the printed English text, relating to the meeting of 23rd May, 1939. We think it leaves nothing unproved in those allegations.

THE PRESIDENT: Mr. Alderman, perhaps you ought to read the last page and the last five lines, because they refer in terms to one of the defendants.

MR. ALDERMAN: I didn't read these, Mr. President, simply because I am convinced that they are mistranslated in the English translation. I will be glad to have them read in the original German.

THE PRESIDENT: Very well, if you are of that opinion.

MR. ALDERMAN: We could get it from the original German.

THE PRESIDENT: You mean that the English translation is wrong?

MR. ALDERMAN: Yes.

THE PRESIDENT: You had better inform us then if it is wrong.

MR. ALDERMAN: Did you have a reference to the last Paragraph headed "Working principles"?

THE PRESIDENT: Yes, the one after that.

MR. ALDERMAN: Yes. Might I ask that the German interpreter read that, as it can be translated into the other languages. It is on page 16 of the original.

BY THE INTERPRETER: Page 16.

"Purpose:

(1) Study of the entire problem.

(2) Study of the events.

(3) Study of the means needed.

(4) Study of the necessary training.

Men with great powers of imagination and high technical training must belong to the staff, as well as officers with sober and sceptical powers of understanding.

Working principles:-

(1) No one is to take part in this who does not have to know of it.

(2) No one can find out more than he must know.

(3) When must the person in question know it at the very latest? No one may know anything before it is necessary that he know it.

On Goering's question, the Fuehrer decided that:-

(a) The armed forces determine what shall be built.

(b) In the shipbuilding programme, nothing is to be changed.

(c) The armament programmes are to be modelled on the years 1943 or 1944."

Schmundt certified this text.

MR. ALDERMAN: Mr. President, the translation was closer than I had anticipated.

THE PRESIDENT: Yes.

MR. ALDERMAN: We think, as I have just said, that this document leaves nothing unproved in those allegations in the indictment. It demonstrates that the Nazi conspirators were proceeding in accordance with a plan. It demonstrates the cold-blooded premeditation of the assault on Poland. It demonstrates that the questions concerning Danzig, which the Nazis had agitated with Poland as a political pretext, were not true questions, but were false issues, issues agitated to conceal their motive of aggressive expansion for food and "Lebensraum."

In this presentation of condemning documents, concerning the initiation of war in September 1939, I must bring to the attention of the Tribunal a group of documents concerning an address by Hitler to his chief military commanders, at Obersalzburg, on 22nd August, 1939, just one week prior to the launching of the attack on Poland.

We have three of these documents, related and constituting a single group. The first one, I do not intend to offer as evidence. The other two, I shall offer.

The reason for that decision is this: The first of the three documents came into our possession through the medium of an American newspaperman, and purported to be original minutes of this meeting at Obersalzberg, transmitted to this American newspaperman by some other person; and we had no proof of the actual delivery to the intermediary by the person who took the notes. That document, therefore, merely served to keep our prosecution on the alert, to see if it could find something better. Fortunately, we did get the other two documents, which indicate that Hitler on that day made two speeches, perhaps one in the morning, one in the afternoon, as indicated by the original minutes, which we captured. By comparison of those two documents with the first document, we conclude that the first document was a slightly garbled merger of the two speeches.

On 22nd August, 1939, Hitler had called together at Obersalzberg the three Supreme Commanders of the three branches of the Armed Forces, as well as the commanding generals, bearing the title "Oberbefehlshaber," Commanders- in-Chief.

I have indicated how, upon discovering this first document, the prosecution set out to find better evidence of what happened on this day. In this the prosecution succeeded. In the files of the O.K.W. at Flensburg, the "Oberkommamdo der Wehrmacht," Chief of the High Command of the Armed Forces, there were uncovered two speeches delivered, by Hitler at Obersalzberg, on 22nd August, 1939. These documents are 798 PS and 1014 PS, in our series of documents.

In order to keep serial numbers consecutive, if the Tribunal please, we have had the first document, which I do not intend to offer, marked for identification exhibit USA 28. Accordingly, I offer the second document, 798 PS, in evidence as exhibit USA 29, and the third document 1014 PS as exhibit USA 30.

These are, again, especially the first one, rather lengthy speeches, and I shall not necessarily read the entire speech.

Reading from 798 PS, which is exhibit USA 29, the Fuehrer speaks to the Commanders-in-Chief on 22nd August, 1939. "I have called you together."

THE PRESIDENT: Is there anything to show where the speech took place?

MR. ALDERMAN: Obersalzberg.

THE PRESIDENT: How do you show that

MR. ALDERMAN: You mean on the document?

THE PRESIDENT: Yes.

MR. ALDERMAN: I am afraid the indication "Obersalzberg" came from the first document which I have not offered in evidence. I have no doubt that the defendants will admit that Obersalzberg was the place of this speech.

The place is not very significant; it is the time.

THE PRESIDENT: Very well.

MR. ALDERMAN: *(Reading)*

"I have called you together to give you a picture of the political situation, in order that you may have insight into the individual element on which I base my decision to act, and in order to strengthen your confidence. After this, we will discuss military details.

It was clear to me that a conflict with Poland had to come sooner or later. I had already made this decision in Spring." *(I interpolate, I think he is there referring to the May document, which I have already read, L-79.)* "But I thought I would first turn against the West in a few years, and only afterwards against the East. But the sequence cannot be fixed. One cannot close one's eyes even before a threatening situation. I wanted to establish an acceptable relationship with Poland, in order to fight first against the West, but this plan, [Page 172] which was agreeable to me, could not be executed, since the essential points have changed.

222

It became clear to me that Poland would attack us, in case of a conflict with the West.

Poland wants access to the sea.

The further development became obvious after the occupation of the Memel region, and it became clear to me that under the circumstances a conflict with Poland could arise at an inopportune moment.

I enumerate as reasons for this reflection, first of all, two personal constitutions" -

I suppose he means "personalities." That probably is an inept translation -

"my own personality, and that of Mussolini. Essentially, it depends on me, my existence, because of my political activities."

I interpolate to comment on the tremendous significance of the fact of a war, which engulfed almost the whole world, depending upon one man's personality.

"Furthermore, the fact that probably no one will ever again have the confidence of the whole German people as I do. There will probably never again be a man in the future with more authority. My existence is, therefore, a factor of great value. But I can be eliminated at any time by a criminal or an idiot.

The second personal factor is Il Duce. His existence is also vital. If something happens to him, Italy's loyalty to the alliance will no longer be certain. The basic attitude of the Italian Court is against the Duce. Above all, the Court sees in the expansion of the empire a burden. The Duce is the man with the strongest nerves in Italy.

The third factor, favourable for us, is Franco. We can ask only benevolent neutrality from Spain, but this depends on Franco's personality. He guarantees a certain uniformity and steadiness of the present system in Spain. We must take into account the fact that Spain has not as yet a Fascist Party or our internal unity.

On the other side, a negative picture, as far as decisive personalities are concerned. There is no outstanding personality in England or France."

I interpolate: I think Adolf Hitler must have overlooked one in England, perhaps many.

(MR. ALDERMAN: *continues*)

"For us it is easy to make decisions. We have nothing to lose - we can only gain. Our economic situation is such, because of our restrictions, that we cannot hold out more than a few years. Goering can confirm this. We have no other choice; we must act. Our opponents risk much and can gain only a little. England's stake in a war is unimaginably great. Our enemies have men who are below average. No personalities, no masters, no men of action."

I interpolate again. Perhaps that last sentence explains what he meant by no personalities - no masters having authority that he had over his nation.

"Besides the personal favour, the political situation is favourable for us; the Mediterranean rivalry between Italy, France, and England; in the Orient tension, which leads to the alarming of the Mohammedan world.

The English Empire did not emerge from the last war strengthened. From a maritime point of view, nothing was achieved: there was conflict between

England and Ireland, the South African Union became more independent, concessions had to be made to India England is in great danger, her industries unhealthy. A British statesman can look into the future only with concern.

France's position has also deteriorated, particularly in the Mediterranean.

Further favourable factors for us are these:

Since Albania, there is an equilibrium of power in the Balkans. Yugoslavia carries the germ of collapse because of her internal situation.

Roumania did not grow stronger. She is liable to attack and vulnerable. She is threatened by Hungary and Bulgaria. Since Kemal's death, Turkey has been ruled by small minds, unsteady weak men.

All these fortunate circumstances will no longer prevail in two or three years. No one knows how long I shall live. Therefore conflict is better now.

The creation of Greater Germany was a great achievement politically, but militarily it was questionable, since it was achieved through a bluff of the political leaders. It is necessary to test the military, if at all possible, not by general settlement, but by solving individual tasks.

Relations with Poland have become unbearable. My Polish policy hitherto has been contrary to the ideas of the people. My propositions to Poland, the Danzig corridor, were disturbed by England's intervention. Poland changed her tune towards us. The initiative cannot be allowed to pass to the others. The time is more favourable today than it will be in two to three years. An attempt on my life or Mussolini's would change the situation to our disadvantage. One cannot eternally stand opposite another with rifle cocked. A suggested compromise would have demanded that we change our convictions and make agreeable gestures. They talked to us again in the language of Versailles. There was danger of losing prestige. Now the probability is still great that the West will not interfere. We must accept the risk with reckless resolution. A politician must accept a risk as much as a military leader. We are facing the alternative to strike or to be destroyed with certainty sooner or later."

We skip a paragraph, two paragraphs.

"Now it is also a great risk. Iron nerves, iron resolution." A long discussion follows which I think it is unnecessary to read, and then towards the end, four paragraphs from the bottom, I resume: "We need not be afraid of a blockade. The East will supply us with grain, cattle, coal, lead and zinc. It is a big aim which demands great efforts. I am only afraid that at the last minute some 'Schweinehund' will make a proposal for mediation." And then the last paragraph of one sentence: "Goering answers with thanks to the Fuehrer and the assurance that the Armed Forces will do their duty."

I believe I have already offered exhibit USA 30, which is a shorter note entitled, "Second Speech of the Fuehrer on 22nd August, 1939." Reading, then, from that exhibit headed "Second Speech of the Fuehrer on 22nd August, 1939:

"It may also turn out differently regarding England and France. One cannot predict it with certainty. I figure on a trade barrier, not on blockade, and with severance of relations. Most iron determination on our side. Retreat before nothing. Everybody will have to make a point of it that we were determined from the beginning to fight the Western Powers. A struggle for life or death. Germany has won every war as long as she was united. Iron, unflinching attitude of all superiors, greatest confidence, faith in victory, overcoming of the past by getting used to the heaviest strain. A long period of peace would not do us any good. Therefore it is necessary to expect everything. Manly bearing. It is not machines that fight each other, but men. We have the better quality of men. Mental factors are decisive. The opposite camp has weaker people. In 1918 the nation fell down because the mental pre-requisites were not sufficient. Frederic the Great secured final success only through his mental power.

Destruction of Poland in the foreground. The aim is the elimination of living forces, not the arrival at a certain line. Even if war should break out in the West, the destruction of Poland shall be the primary objective. Quick decision because of the season.

I shall give a propagandistic cause for starting the war, never mind whether it be plausible or not. The victor shall not be asked, later on, whether we told the truth or not. In starting and making a war, not the Right is what matters, but Victory.

Have no pity. Brutal attitude. Eighty million people shall get what is their right. Their existence has to be secured. The strongest has the right. Greatest severity.

Quick decision necessary. Unshakeable faith in the German soldier. A crisis may happen only if the nerves of the leaders give way.

First aim: advance to the Vistula and Narew. Our technical superiority will break the nerves of the Poles. Every newly created Polish force shall again be broken at once. Constant war of attrition.

New German frontier according to healthy principle. Possibly a protectorate as a buffer. Military operations shall not be influenced by these reflections. Complete destruction of Poland is the military aim. To be fast is the main thing. Pursuit until complete elimination.

Conviction that the German Wehrmacht is up to the requirements. The start shall be ordered, probably by Saturday morning."

That ends the quotation. The Tribunal will recall that in fact the start was actually postponed until 1st September.

DR. STAHMER (Counsel for defendant Goering): I should like to make a statement or explanation of the last two documents read. Both these, as well as the third that was not read, but which was taken into consideration, are not recognised by the defence. In order to avoid the appearance that this objection has been raised without due reason, I should like to justify it as follows:

Both the documents that were read contain a number of factual mistakes. They are not signed. Moreover, only one meeting took place, and that is where the documents lack precision. No one it, that meeting was commissioned with taking down stenographically the events in the meeting, and since all signatures are lacking, it cannot be determined who wrote them or who is responsible for their reliability. The third document that was not read is, according to the photostatic copy in the defence's document room, simply written by typewriter. There is no indication of place nor of time.

THE PRESIDENT: Well, we have got nothing to do with the third document, because it has not been read.

DR. STAHMER: Mr. President, this document has nevertheless been published in the Press and was apparently given to the Press by the prosecution. Both the defence and the defendants have consequently a lively interest in giving a short explanation of the facts concerning this document.

THE PRESIDENT: The Tribunal is trying this case in accordance with the evidence and not in accordance with what is in the Press, and the third document is not in evidence before us.

MR. ALDERMAN: May it please the Tribunal, I recognise that counsel wonder how these two documents which I have just read are in our hands. They come to us from an authentic source. They are German documents. They were found in the O.K.W. files. If they are not correct records of what occurred, it surprises us that with the thoroughness with which the Germans kept accurate records, they would have had these records in their O.K.W. files if they did not represent the truth.

THE PRESIDENT: Mr. Alderman, the Tribunal will of course hear what evidence the defendants choose to give with reference to the documents.

MR. ALDERMAN: It has occurred to me in that connection that if any of these defendants have in their possession what is a more correct transcription of the Fuehrer's words on this occasion, the Court should consider that. On the other question referred to by counsel, I feel somewhat guilty. It is quite true that by a mechanical slip, the Press got the first document, which we never at all intended them to have. I feel somewhat responsible. It happened to be included in the document books that were handed up to the Court on Friday, because we had only intended. to refer to it and give it an identification mark and not to offer it. I had thought that no documents would be released to the Press until they were actually offered in evidence. With as large an organisation as we have, it is very difficult to police all those matters.

THE PRESIDENT: Mr. Alderman, the Tribunal would like to know how many of these documents are given to the Press.

MR. ALDERMAN: I can't answer that.

COLONEL STOREY: May it please the Tribunal, it is my understanding that as and when documents are introduced in evidence, then they are made available to the Press.

THE PRESIDENT: In what numbers?

COLONEL STOREY: I think about 250 copies of each one, about 200 or 250 mimeographed copies.

THE PRESIDENT: The Tribunal thinks that the defendants' Counsel should have copies of these documents before any of them are handed to the Press. I mean to say that, in preference to gentlemen of the Press, the defendants' Counsel should have the documents.

COLONEL STOREY: Your Honour, if it pleases the Court, I understand that these gentleman had the ten documents on Saturday morning or Sunday morning. They had them for 24 hours, copies of the originals of these documents that have been read today, down in the Information Centre.

THE PRESIDENT: I stated, in accordance with the provisional arrangement which was made, and which was made upon your representations, that ten copies of the trial briefs and five of the volumes of documents should be given to the defendants' counsel.

COLONEL STOREY: Sir, I had the receipts that they were deposited in the room.

THE PRESIDENT: Yes, but what I am pointing out to you, Colonel Storey, is that if 250 copies of the documents can be given to the Press, then the defendants' counsel should not be limited to five copies.

COLONEL STOREY: If your Honour pleases, the 250 copies are the mimeographed copies in English when they are introduced in evidence. I hold in my hands or in my brief case here a receipt that the document books and the briefs were delivered 24 hours in advance.

THE PRESIDENT: You don't seem to understand what I am putting to you, which is this: that if you can afford to give 250 copies of the documents in English to the Press, you can afford to give more than five copies to the defendants' counsel - one each.

COLONEL STOREY: I see your point, your Honour, and we-

THE PRESIDENT: Well, we needn't discuss it further. In future that will be done.

DR. DIX: May I make the point that of the evidence documents, every defence counsel should receive one copy and not simply one for several members of the defence.

THE PRESIDENT: Go on, Mr. Alderman.

MR. ALDERMAN: The aggressive war having been initiated in September 1939, and Poland having been totally defeated shortly after the initial assaults, the Nazi aggressors converted the war into a general war of aggression extending into Scandinavia, into the Low Countries, and into the Balkans. Under the division of the case between the four Chief Prosecutors, this aspect of the matter is left to presentation by the British Chief Prosecutor.

Another change that we have made in our plan, which I perhaps should mention, is that following the opening statement by the British Chief Prosecutor on Count 2, we expect to resume the detailed handling of the later phases of the aggressive war phase of the case. The British instead of the Americans will deal with the details of aggression against Poland. Then with this expansion of the war in Europe and then as a joint part of the American case under Count 1 and the British case under Count 2, I shall take up the aggression against Russia and the Japanese aggression in detail. So that the remaining two subjects with which I shall ultimately deal in more detail, by presentation of specifically significant documents, are the case of the attack on the Union of Soviet Socialist Republics on the 22nd of June, 1941, and the case on collaboration between Italy and Japan and Germany and the resulting attack on the United States on the 7th of December, 1941.

As to the case on aggression against the Soviet Union, I shall, at this point, present two documents. The first of these two documents establishes the premeditation and deliberation which preceded the attack. Just as, in the case of aggression against Czechoslovakia, the Nazis had a code name for the secret operation "Case Green," so in the case of aggression against the Soviet Union, they had a code name "Case Barbarossa."

THE PRESIDENT: How do you spell that?

MR. ALDERMAN: B-a-r-b-a-r-o-s-s-a -after Barbarossa of Kaiser Friederich. From the files of the O.K.W. at Flensburg we have a secret directive, Number 21, issued from the Fuehrer's headquarters on 18th December, 1940, relating to "Case Barbarossa." This directive is more than six months in advance of the attack. Other evidence will show that the planning occurred even earlier. The document is signed by Hitler and is initialled by the defendant Jodl and the defendant Keitel. This secret order was issued in nine copies. The captured document is the fourth of these nine copies. It is document 446 PS, in our numbered series.

I offer it in evidence as exhibit USA 31.

If the Tribunal please, I think it will be sufficient for me to read the first page of that directive; the first page of the English translation. The paging may differ on the German original.

It is headed "The Fuehrer and Commander-in-Chief of the German Armed Forces" with a number of initials, the meaning of which I don't know, except O.K.W. It seems to be indicated to go to O.K. Chiefs, whom I suppose to be General Kommando Chiefs.

"The Fuehrer's Headquarters, 18th December, 1940. Secret. Only through Officer. Nine Copies. 4th copy. Directive Number 21, case Barbarossa.

The German Armed Forces must be prepared to crush Soviet Russia in a quick campaign before the end of the war against England. (Case Barbarossa).

For this purpose the Army will have to employ all available units with the reservation that the occupied territories will have to be safeguarded against surprise attacks.

For the Eastern campaign the Air Force will have to free such Strong forces for the support of the Army that a quick completion of the ground operations may he expected and that damage of the Eastern German territories will be avoided as much as possible. This concentration of the main effort in the East is limited by the following reservation: That the entire battle and armament area dominated by us must remain sufficiently protected against enemy air attacks and that the attacks on England and especially the supply for them must not be permitted to break down.

Concentration of the main effort of the Navy remains unequivocally against England also during an Eastern campaign.

If occasion arises I will order the concentration of troops for action against Soviet Russia eight weeks before the intended beginning of operations.

Preparations requiring more time to start are - if this has not yet been done - to begin presently and are to be completed by 15th May, 1941.

Great caution has to be exercised that the intention of an attack will not be recognised.

The Preparations of the High Command are to be made on the following basis:

1. General Purpose:

The mass of the Russian Army in Western Russia is to be destroyed in daring operations by driving forward deep wedges within ranks and the retreat of intact battle- ready troops into the wide spaces of Russia is to be prevented.

In quick pursuit a line is to be reached from where the Russian Air Force will no longer be able to attack German Reich territory. The first goal of operations is the protection from Asiatic Russia of the general line Volga- Archangelsk. In case of necessity, the last industrial area in the Urals left to Russia could be eliminated by the Luftwaffe.

In the course of these operations the Russian Baltic Sea Fleet will quickly lose its bases and will no longer be ready to fight.

Effective intervention by the Russian Air Force is to be prevented through powerful blows at the beginning of the operations."

Another secret document, captured from the O.K.W. files--

THE PRESIDENT: Mr. Alderman, perhaps that would be a convenient time to adjourn for ten minutes.

(A recess was taken)

MR. ALDERMAN: If it please the Tribunal, another secret document captured from the O.K.W. files, establishes, we think, the motive for the attack on the Soviet Union. It also establishes the full awareness of the Nazi conspirators of the crimes against humanity which would result from their attack. The document is a memorandum Of 2nd May, 1941, concerning the result of a discussion on that day with the State Secretaries concerning the "Case Barbarossa." The document is initialled by a Major von Giessavet, a member of the staff of General Thomas, set up to handle the economic exploitations of the territory occupied by the Germans during the course of the aggression against Russia. The document is numbered 2718-PS, and our numbered series of documents are offered in evidence as exhibit USA 32.

I shall simply read the first two paragraphs of this document, including the introductory matter:

"Matter for Chief; 2 copies; first copy to files 1a.

Second copy to General Schubert, 2nd May, 1941.

Memorandum about the result of today's discussion with the State Secretaries about Barbarossa.

(1) The War can only be continued if all Armed Forces are fed by Russia in the third year of War.

(2) There is no doubt that as a result many millions of people will be starved to death if we take out of the country the things necessary for us."

That document has already been commented on and quoted from in Mr. Justice Jackson's opening statement. The staggering implications of that document are hard to realise. In the words of the document, the motive for the attack was that the War which the Nazi conspirators had launched in September 1939, could only be continued if all Armed Forces were fed by Russia in the third year of the War. Perhaps there never was a more sinister sentence written than the sentence in this document which reads:-

"There is no doubt that as a result many millions of people will be starved to death if we take out of the country the things necessary for us."

The result is known to all of us.

I turn now to the Nazi collaboration with Italy and Japan and the resulting, attack on the United States on 7th December, 1941. With the unleashing of the German aggressive war against the Soviet Union in June 1941, the Nazi conspirators and, in particular, the defendant Ribbentrop, called upon the Eastern co-architect of the New Order, Japan, to attack in the rear. Our evidence will show that they incited and kept in motion a force reasonably calculated to result in an attack on the United States. For a time, they maintained their preference that the United States should not be involved in the conflict, realising the military implication of an entry of the United States into the War. However, their incitement did result in the attack on Pearl Harbour, and long prior to that attack, they had assured the Japanese that they would declare War on the United States should a United States-Japanese conflict break out. It was in reliance on those assurances that the Japanese struck at Pearl Harbour.

On the present discussion of this phase of the case, I shall offer only one document to prove this point. The document was captured from the files of the German Foreign Office. It consists of notes dated 4th April, 1941, signed by "Schmidt," regarding discussions between the Fuehrer and the Japanese Foreign Minister Matsuoka, in the presence of the defendant Ribbentrop. The document is numbered 1881 PS in our numbered series and I offer it in evidence as exhibit USA 33. In the original, it is in very large, typewritten form in German. I shall read what I deem to be the pertinent parts of this document, beginning with the four paragraphs, first reading the heading, the heading being:

"Notes regarding the discussion between the Fuehrer and the Japanese Foreign Minister, Matsuoka, in the presence of the Reich Foreign Minister and the Reich Minister of State, Reissner, in Berlin, on the 4th April, 1941.

Matsuoka then also expressed the request, that the Fuehrer should instruct the proper authorities in Germany to meet as broad-mindedly as possible the wishes of the Japanese Military Commission. Japan was in need of German help particularly concerning the U- boat warfare, which could be given by making available to them the latest experiences of the war is well as the latest technical improvements and inventions."

For the record, I am reading on what is page six of the German original.

"Japan would do her utmost to avoid a war with the United States. If Japan should decide to attack Singapore, the Japanese Navy, of course, had to be prepared for a fight with the United States, because in that case America probably would side with Great Britain. He (Matsuoka) personally believed that the United States could be restrained by diplomatic exertions from entering the war at the side of

Great Britain. Army and Navy had, however, to count on the worst situation, that is on war against America. They were of the opinion that such a war would extend for five years or longer and would take the form of guerrilla warfare in the Pacific and would be fought out in the South Sea. For this reason the German experiences in her guerrilla warfare were of the greatest value to Japan. It was a question how such a war would best be conducted and how all the technical improvements of submarines, in all details such as periscopes and such like, could best be exploited by Japan.

To sum up, Matsuoka requested that the Fuehrer would see to it that the proper German authorities would place at the disposal of the Japanese those developments and inventions concerning Navy and Army, which were needed by the Japanese.

The Fuehrer promised this and pointed out that Germany too considered a conflict with the United States undesirable, but that it had already made allowances for such a contingency. In Germany one was of the opinion that America's contributions depended upon the possibilities of transportation, and that this again is conditioned by the available tonnage. Germany's war against tonnage, however, means a decisive weakening not merely against England, but also against America. Germany has made her preparations so that no American could land in Europe. She would conduct a most energetic fight against America with her boats and her 'Luftwaffe,' and due to her superior experience, which would still have to be acquired by the United States, she would be vastly superior, and that quite apart from the fact that the German soldiers naturally rank high above the Americans.

In the further course of the discussion, the Fuehrer pointed out that Germany, on her part, would immediately take the consequences if Japan would get involved with the United States. It did not matter with whom the United States would first get involved, whether Germany or Japan. They would always try to eliminate one country at a time, not to come to an understanding with the other country subsequently, but to liquidate this one just the same. Therefore Germany would strike, as already mentioned, without delay in case of a conflict between Japan and America, because the strength of the tripartite powers lies in their joint action; their weakness would be if they would let themselves be beaten individually.

Matsuoka once more repeated his request, that the Fuehrer might give the necessary instructions, in order that the proper German authorities would place at the disposal of the Japanese the latest improvements and inventions, which are of interest to them, because the Japanese Navy had to prepare immediately for a conflict with the United States.

As regards Japanese-American relationship, Matsuoka explained further that he has always declared in his country, that sooner or later a war with the United States would be unavoidable, if Japan continued to drift along as at present. In his opinion this conflict would happen rather sooner than later. His argument went on, why should Japan, therefore, not strike decisively at the right moment and take the risk upon herself of a fight against America? Just thus would she perhaps avoid a war for generations, particularly if she gained predominance in the South Seas. There were, to be sure in his opinion, in Japan, many who would hesitate to follow those trends of thought. Matsuoka was considered in those circles a dangerous man with dangerous thoughts. He, however, stated that, if Japan continued to walk along her present path, one day she would have to fight anyway and that this would then be under less favourable circumstances than at present.

The Fuehrer replied that he could well understand the situation of Matsuoka, because he himself had been in similar situations (the clearing of the Rhineland, declaration of Sovereignty of Armed Forces, etc.). He too was of the opinion that he had to exploit favourable conditions and accept the risk of an anyhow unavoidable fight at a time when be himself was still young and full of vigour. How right he was in his attitude was proven by events. Europe now was free. He would not hesitate a moment to reply instantly to any widening of the war, be it by Russia, be it by America. Providence favoured those who would not let dangers come to them, but who would bravely face them. Matsuoka replied, that the United States or rather their ruling politicians, had recently attempted a last manoeuvre towards Japan, by declaring that America would not fight Japan on account of China or the South Seas, provided that Japan gave free passage to the consignment of rubber and tin to America to their place of destination. However, America would fight against Japan the moment she felt that Japan entered the war with the intention of assisting in the destruction of Great Britain. Such an argument naturally did not miss its effect upon the Japanese, because of the education oriented on English lines which many of them had received.

The Fuehrer commented on this, that this attitude of America did not mean anything but that the United States had the hope, that, as long as the British World Empire existed, one day they could advance against Japan together with Great Britain, whereas, in case of the collapse of the World Empire, they would be totally isolated and could not do anything against Japan.

The Reich Foreign Minister interjected that the Americans definitely under all circumstances wanted to maintain the powerful position of England in East Asia, but that on the other hand it was proved by this attitude, to what extent she fears a joint action of Japan and Germany.

Matsuoka continued that it seemed to him of importance to give to the Fuehrer an absolutely clear picture of the real attitude inside Japan. For this reason he also had to inform him regretfully of the fact that he, Matsuoka, in his capacity as Japanese Minister for Foreign Affairs could not utter in Japan a single word of all that he had expounded before the Fuehrer and the Reich Foreign Minister regarding his plans, as this would cause him serious damage in political and financial circles. Once before, he had committed the mistake, before he became Japanese Minister for Foreign Affairs, of telling a close friend something about his intentions. It seems that the latter had mentioned these things and thus brought about all sorts of rumours, which he as Foreign Minister had to oppose energetically, though as a rule he always tells the truth. Under these circumstances he also could not indicate how soon he could report on the questions discussed, to the Japanese Premier or to the Emperor. He would have to study exactly and carefully in the first place the development in Japan, so as to decide on a favourable moment, for making a clean breast of his proper plans to the Prince Konoye and the Emperor. That decision would have to be made within a few days, otherwise the plans would be spoiled by talk.

Should he, Matsuoka, fail to carry out his intentions, that would be proof that he was lacking in influence, in power of conviction, and in tactical capabilities. However, should he succeed, it would prove that he had great influence in Japan. He himself felt confident that he would succeed.

On his return, being questioned, be would indeed admit to the Emperor, the Premier and the Ministers for the Navy and the Army, that Singapore had been discussed; he would, however, state that it was only on a hypothetical basis.

Besides this Matsuoka made the express decision not to cable in the matter of Singapore, because he had reason to fear that by cabling something might leak out. If necessary, he would send a courier.

The Fuehrer agreed and assured him after all, that he could entirely rely on German reticence.

Matsuoka replied he believed indeed in German reticence, but unfortunately could not say the same for Japan.

The discussion was terminated after the exchange of some personal parting words.

Berlin, the 4th of April, 1941

(Signed) "Schmidt."

This completes the presentation of what I have called the "handful of selected documents," offered not as a detailed treatment of any of these wars of aggression but merely to prove the deliberate planning, the deliberate premeditation with which each of these aggressions was carried out.

I turn to a more detailed and more or less chronological presentation of the various stages of the aggression.

THE PRESIDENT: The Tribunal will now adjourn until ten o'clock tomorrow.

SIXTH DAY:
Tuesday, 27th November, 1945

THE PRESIDENT: I call on the counsel for the United States. Mr. Alderman, before you begin, I think it would be better, for the purpose of the Tribunal, in citing documents if you would refer to them not only by the United States Exhibit number and the PS Exhibit number, but also by the document book identification. Each document book, as I understand it, has either a letter or a number.

MR. ALDERMAN: If the Court please, I am not familiar with the identification numbers of the document book. I suppose the clerk can give them to me.

THE PRESIDENT: They are numbered alphabetically, I think.

MR. ALDERMAN: Yes.

THE PRESIDENT: If that is not done, when we have got a great number of document books before us, it is very difficult to find where the particular exhibit is.

MR. ALDERMAN: I can see that, yes.

May it please the Tribunal, the handful of selected documents which I presented yesterday constitute a cross- section of the aggressive war case as a whole. They do not purport to cover the details of any of the phases of the aggressive war case. In effect they amount to a running account of the entire matter.

Before moving ahead with more detailed evidence, I think it might be helpful to pause at this point to present to the Tribunal a chart. This chart presents visually some of the key points in the development of the Nazi aggression. The Tribunal may find it helpful as a kind of visual summary of some of the evidence received yesterday and also as a background for some of the evidence which remains to be introduced. I am quite certain that, as your minds go back to those days, you remember the maps that appeared from time to time in the public Press as these tremendous movements developed in Europe. I am quite certain that you must have formed the concept as I did, in those days, of the gradually developing head of a wolf.

In that first chart you only have an incipient wolf. He lacks a lower jaw, the part shown in red, but when that wolf moved forward and took over Austria (the Anschluss) - that red portion became solid black. It became the jaw of the wolf, and when that lower jaw was acquired, Czechoslovakia was already, with its head and the main part of its body, in the mouth of the wolf.

Then on chart two, you see the mountainous portions, the fortified portions of Czechoslovakia. In red you see the Sudetenland territories which were first taken over by the Pact of Munich, whereupon Czechoslovakia's head became diminutive in the mouth of the wolf.

And in chart three you see the diminishing head in red with its neck practically broken, and all that was necessary was the taking over of Bohemia and Moravia, and the wolf's head became a solid, black blot on the map of Europe, with arrows indicating incipient further aggressions, which, of course, occurred.

That is the visual picture that I have never been able to wipe out of my mind, because it seems to demonstrate the inevitability of everything that went along after the taking over of Austria.

The detailed, more or less chronological presentation of the aggressive war case will be divided into seven distinct sections. The first section is that concerning preparation for aggression during the period of 1933 to 1936, roughly. The second section deals with aggression against Austria. The third section deals with aggression against Czechoslovakia. The fourth section deals with aggression against Poland and the initiation of actual war. For reasons of convenience, the details of the Polish section will be presented after the British Chief Prosecutor presents his opening statement to the Tribunal. The fifth section deals with the expansion of the war into a general war of aggression by invasions into Scandinavia, the Lowlands and the Balkans. The details on this section of the case will be presented by the British Chief Prosecutor. The sixth section deals with aggression against the Soviet Union, which I shall expect to present. For reasons of convenience again, the details of this section, like the details on aggression against Poland, will be presented after the British Prosecutor has made his opening statement to the Tribunal. The seventh section will deal with collaboration with Italy and Japan and the aggression against the United States.

I turn now to the first of these sections, the part of the case concerning preparation for aggression during the period 1933 to 1936. The particular section of the Indictment to which this discussion addresses itself is Paragraph IV (F) and sub-Paragraph 2 a), (b), (c), (d), (e), f), which I need not read at a glance, as the Tribunal will recall the allegation. It will be necessary, as I proceed, to make reference to certain provisions to the Charter and to certain provisions of the Treaty of Versailles and the Treaty between the United States and Germany restoring friendly relations, 25th August, 1921, which incorporates certain provisions of the Treaty of Versailles and certain provisions of the Rhine Treaty of Locarno of 16th October, 1925.

THE PRESIDENT: Mr. Alderman, is it not intended that this document book should have some identifying letter or number?

MR. ALDERMAN: I suppose it should have, sir, yes. I don't know what the proper letter is.

THE PRESIDENT: Doesn't anybody know?

MR. ALDERMAN: "M,"I am informed.

THE PRESIDENT: "M"?

MR. ALDERMAN: Yes. I do not offer those treaties in evidence at this time, because the British will offer all the pertinent treaties in their aspect of the case.

The Nazi plans for aggressive war started very soon after World War I. Their modest origin aid rather fantastic nature and the fact that they could have been interrupted at numerous points do not detract from the continuity of the planning. The focus of this part of the Indictment, on the theory that it covers events from 1933 to 1945, does not dissociate these events from what occurred in the entire preceding period. Thus, the ascendancy of Hitler and the Nazis to political power in 1933 was already a well advanced milestone on the German road to progress.

By 1933 the Nazi Party, the N.S.D.A.P., had reached very substantial proportions. At that time their plans called for the acquisition of political control of Germany. This was indispensable for the consolidation within the country of all the internal resources and potentialities.

As soon as there was sufficient indication of successful progress along this line of internal consolidation, the next step was to become disengaged from some of the external disadvantages of existing international limitations and obligations. The restrictions of the Versailles Treaty were a bar to the development of strength in all the fields necessary, if one were to make war. Although there had been an increasing amount of circumvention and violation from the very time that Versailles came into effect, such operations under disguise and subterfuge could not attain proportions adequate for the objectives of the Nazis. To get the Treaty of Versailles out of the way was indispensable to the development of the extensive military power which they had to have for their purposes. Similarly, as part of the same plan and for the same reasons, Germany withdrew from the Disarmament Conference and from the League of Nations. It was impossible to carry out their plans on the basis of existing international obligations or of the orthodox kind of future commitments.

The points mentioned in this Paragraph IV (F) 2 of the Indictment are now historical facts of which we expect the Tribunal to take Judicial notice.

It goes without saying that every military and diplomatic operation was preceded by a plan of action and a careful co- ordination of all participating forces. At the same time each point was part of a long prepared plan of aggression. Each represents a necessary step in the direction of the specific aggression which was subsequently committed.

To develop an extensive argument would, perhaps, be an unnecessary labouring of the obvious. What I intend to effect is, largely, the bringing to light of information disclosed in illustrative documents which were hitherto unavailable.

The three things of immediate international significance referred to in this paragraph IV (F) 2 of the Indictment are: first, the withdrawal from the Disarmament Conference and the League of Nations; second, the institution of compulsory military service; and, third, the reoccupation of the demilitarised zone of the Rhineland. Each of these steps was progressively more serious than the matter of international relations. In each of these steps Germany anticipated the possibility of sanctions being applied by other countries, and, in particular, a strong military action from France with the possible assistance of England. However, the conspirators were determined that nothing less than a preventative war would stop them, and they also estimated correctly that no one, or combination of the Great Powers would undertake the responsibility for such a war. The withdrawal from the Disarmament Conference and from the League of Nations was, of course, an action that did not violate any international obligation. The League Covenant provided the procedure for withdrawal. However, in this case and as part of the bigger plan, the significance of these actions cannot be dissociated from the general conspiracy and the plans for aggression. The announcement of the institution of universal military service was a more daring action with a more overt significance. It was a violation of Versailles, but they got away with it. Then came the outright military defiance, the occupation of the demilitarised zone of the Rhineland.

The Indictment, in paragraph IV (F) 2, alleges that the Nazi conspirators determined to remove the restrictions of Versailles, and the fact that their plans in this respect started very early is confirmed by their own statements, indeed they boasted about their long planning and careful execution.

I read to you yesterday at length, from our document 789PS, exhibit USA 23, Hitler's speech to all Supreme Commanders, Of 23rd November, 1939, I need not read it again. He stated there that his primary goal was to wipe out Versailles. After four years of actual war, the defendant Jodl, as Chief of the General Staff of the Armed Forces, delivered an address to the Reich and to tire Gauleiters in which he traced the development of German strength. The seizure of power to him meant the restoration of fighting sovereignty, including conscription, occupation of the Rhineland, and rearmament, with special emphasis on modern armour and air forces.

I have, if the Tribunal please, our document L-172. It is a photostat of a microfilm of a speech by General Jodl, and I offer that photostat as exhibit USA 34. I shall read, if the Tribunal please, only a part of that, but will start at the beginning.

The speech is entitled "The Strategic Position in the Beginning of the 5th Year of War." It is a kind of retrospective summary by the defendant, General Jodl. "A lecture by the Chief of the General Staff of the Armed Forces (West) to the Reich and Gau Leaders, delivered in Munich on the 7th November, 1943."

THE PRESIDENT: Are you reading from the document now?

MR. ALDERMAN: I am reading from the English translation.

THE PRESIDENT: But in my copy Of L-172, as far as I can see, it begins with the word "Introduction".

MR. ALDERMAN: Yes Sir, I was just coming to the Introduction. On my copy -

THE PRESIDENT: There is another heading, too?

MR. ALDERMAN: Yes.

THE PRESIDENT: We haven't got that.

MR. ALDERMAN: You have an index, I think. There is not one on my copy: Page 3.

THE PRESIDENT: Yes, but the index doesn't give that heading; that is all.

MR. ALDERMAN: I see, I am sorry.

THE PRESIDENT: It doesn't matter.

MR. ALDERMAN:

"Introduction: Reichsleiter Bormann has requested me to give you a review today of the strategic position in the beginning of the 5th Year of War.

I must admit that it was not without hesitation that I undertook this none too easy task. It is not possible to do it justice with a few generalities. It is not necessary to say openly what it is. No one, the Fuehrer has ordered, may know more or be told more than he needs for his own immediate task, but I have no doubt at all in my mind, Gentlemen, but that you need a great deal in order to be able to cope with your tasks. It is in your Gaus, after all, and among their inhabitants that all the enemy propaganda, the defeatism, and the malicious rumours concentrate, that try to find a place among our people. Up and down the country the devil of subversion strides. All the cowards are seeking a way out, or - as they call it - a political solution. They say, we must negotiate while there is still something in hand, and all these slogans are made use of to attack the natural sense of the people, who know well that in this war there can only be a fight to the end. Capitulation would mean the end of the Nation, the end of Germany. Against this wave of enemy propaganda and cowardice you need more than force. You need to know the true situation, and for this reason I believe that I am justified in giving you a perfectly open and unvarnished account of the state of affairs. This is no forbidden disclosure of secrets, butt a weapon which may perhaps help you to fortify the morale of the people. For this war will be decided not only by force of arms but by the will to resist of the whole people. Germany was broken in 1918 not at the front but at home. Italy suffered not military defeat but moral defeat. She broke down internally. The result has been not the peace she expected but - through the cowardice of these criminal traitors - a fate a thousand times harder than continuation of the war at our side would have brought her. I can rely on you, Gentlemen, since I give concrete figures and data concerning our own strength, to treat these details as your secret; all the rest is at your disposal, without restriction, for application in your activities as leaders of the people.

Our necessity and objectives were clear to all and everyone at the moment when we entered upon this War of Liberation of Greater Germany and, by attacking, parried the danger which menaced us both from Poland and from the Western Powers. Our further incursions into Scandinavia, in the direction of the Mediterranean and in that of Russia - these also aroused no doubts concerning the general conduct of the war, so long as we were successful. It was not until more serious set-backs were encountered and our general Situation began to become increasingly active, that the German people began to ask itself whether perhaps we had not undertaken more than we could do and had set our aims too high. To provide an answer to this questioning and to furnish you with certain points of view for use in your own explanatory activities, is one of the main points of my present lecture. I shall divide it into three parts:

I. A review of the most important developments up to the present.

II. Consideration of the present situation.

III. The foundation of our morale and our confidence in victory.

In view of my position as Military Adviser to the Fuehrer, I shall confine myself in my remarks to the problems of my own personal sphere of action, fully appreciating at the same time that in view of the Protean nature of this war, I shall in this way be giving expression to only one side of events.

I. The review

1.The fact that the National-Socialist movement and its struggle for internal power were the preparatory stage of the external liberation from the bonds of the Dictate of Versailles is not one on which I need enlarge in this circle. I should like however to mention at this point how clearly all thoughtful regular soldiers realise what an important part has been played by the National- Socialist Movement in re-awakening the will to fight (the "Wehrwillen"); in nurturing fighting strength (the "Wehrkraft") and in rearming the German people. In spite of all the virtue inherent in it, the numerically small "Reichswehr" would never have been able to cope with this task alone, if only because of its own restricted radius of action. Indeed, what the Fuehrer aimed at - and has so happily been successful in bringing about - was the fusion of these two forces.

2. "The seizure of power."

I invite the Tribunal's attention to the frequency with which that expression occurs in all of these documents-"the seizure of power by the Nazi Party in its turn has meant, in the first place, the restoration of fighting sovereignty. "That is the German word "Wehrhoheit" - a kind of euphemism there - the "Highness of Defence." I think it really means "Fighting Sovereignty." "Wehrhoheit" also meant conscription, occupation of the Rhineland and re-armament, with special emphasis being laid on the creation of a modern armoured and air arm.

3. The Austrian "Anschluss"

- "Anschluss" means a locking on to, I think; they "locked on" to Austria - in its turn not only brought with it the fulfilment of an old national aim but has also had the effect both of reinforcing our fighting strength and of materially improving our strategic position. Whereas up till then the territory of Czechoslovakia had projected in a most menacing way right into Germany (a wasp waist in the direction of France and an air base for the Allies, in particular Russia), Czechoslovakia herself is now enclosed by pincers.

I wish the Tribunal would contemplate the chart a moment and see that worm-like form of Czechoslovakia, which General Jodl calls a "wasp waist in the direction of France," and then he very accurately described what happened when Austria was taken by the Anschluss, that the wasp waist was "now enclosed in the pincers."

I resume reading:

"Her own strategic position had now become so unfavourable that she was bound to fall a victim to any attack pressed home with rigour before effective aid from the West could be expected to arrive. This possibility of aid was furthermore made more difficult by the construction of the West-Wall, which, in contra- distinction to the Maginot line, was not a measure based on debility and resignation but one intended to afford rear cover for an active policy in the East.

4. The bloodless solution of the Czech conflict in the autumn Of 1938 and spring of 1939 - that is - the two phases in Czechoslovakia - and the annexation of Slovakia, rounded off the territory of Greater Germany in such a way that it now became possible to consider the Polish problem on the basis of more or less favourable strategic premises."

I think it needs nothing more than a glance at the progressive chart to see what those favourable strategic premises were.

"5. This brings me, said General Jodl, to the actual outbreak of the present War, and the question which next arises is whether the moment for the struggle with Poland, in itself unavoidable, was favourably selected or not. The answer to this question is all the less in doubt since the opponent who was, after all, no inconsiderable one, collapsed unexpectedly quickly, and the Western Powers who were his friends, while they did declare war on us and form a Second Front, yet, for the rest, made no use of the possibilities open to them of snatching the initiative from our hands. Concerning the course of the Polish campaign, nothing further need be said beyond that it proved in a way which made the whole world sit up and take notice, what up till then had not been certain by any means; that is, what a high state of efficiency the young armed forces of Greater Germany had achieved."

If the Court please, there is a long review by General Jodl in this document. I can read on with interest and some enthusiasm, but I believe I have read enough to show that General Jodl by this document identifies himself fully with the Nazi movement. This document shows that he was not a mere soldier. In so far as he is concerned, it identifies the military with the political, and the immediate point on which I had offered the document was to show the deliberation with which the Treaty of Versailles was abrogated by Germany, and the demilitarised zone of the Rhineland was militarised and fortified.

In one of Adolf Hitler's reviews of the six year period between his ascendancy to power and the outbreak of hostilities, he not only admitted but boasted about the orderly and co-ordinated long-range planning. I bring up again, if the Tribunal please, document L-79, which was offered in evidence yesterday, as exhibit USA 27. That is the minutes of the conference of the Fuehrer by Schmundt, his Adjutant. In as large a staff as ours, we inevitably fall into a kind of patoise or lingo, as Americans say. We refer to this as "Little Schmundt." The large file that I offered yesterday, we call "Big Schmundt."

At this point, I merely wish to read two sentences from page 1 of that document which we call "Little Schmundt. "One sentence on page 1. It is found below the middle of the page: "In the period 1933-1939 progress was made in all fields. Our military situation improved enormously." And then, just above the middle of the second page of the English translation: "The period which lies behind us has indeed been put to good use. All measures have been taken in the correct sequence and in harmony with our aims." One of the most significant direct preparations for aggressive war is found in the Secret Reich Defence Law of May 21st, 1935, which I offered in evidence yesterday, as exhibit USA 24 and commented on sufficiently. I need not repeat that comment. The law went into effect upon its passage. It stated at the outset that it was to be made public immediately, but at the end of it Adolf Hitler signed the decree ordering that it be kept secret. I commented on that sufficiently yesterday.

General Thomas, who was in charge of War and Armament Economy, and for some time a high ranking member of the German High Council, refers to this law as "the cornerstone of war preparations." He points out that, although the law was not made public until the outbreak of war, it was put into immediate execution as a programme of preparation.

I ask the Tribunal to take judicial notice of General Thomas' work, "A History of the German War and Armament Economy, 1923 -1944," page 25. We have the volume here, in German, so that anyone may examine it who wishes. I don't care to offer the entire volume in evidence unless the Court thinks I should. We do give it an exhibit number, exhibit USA 35, but I should like to place it in the files merely as a reference work implementing Judicial notice, if that is practicable.

THE PRESIDENT: You want it simply for the purpose of showing that General Thomas said that that law was the cornerstone of war

MR. ALDERMAN: Yes.

THE PRESIDENT: That has already passed into the record.

MR. ALDERMAN: I want to say to counsel for the defendants that it is here if they care to consult it any time.

THE PRESIDENT: Very well.

MR. ALDERMAN: I should have identified it by our number, 2353-PS.

This secret law remained in effect until September 4th, 1938, at which time it was replaced by another secret Defence Law, revising the system of defence organisation and directing more detailed preparations for the approaching status of mobilisation, which 1 think was the euphemism for war.

These laws will be discussed more extensively in connection with other sections of our presentation. They have been discussed by Mr. Dodd in connection with the economic preparations for the war.

The second Secret Defence Law I offer in evidence as our document 2194-PS. It will be exhibit USA 36.

As to that document I only intend to read the two covering letters, "Reich Defence Law, the Ministry for Economy and Labour, Saxony, Dresden ; and 6th December, 1939, Tel." - I suppose - "Telegraph, "52051. Long Distance, Top Secret."

THE PRESIDENT: Does this occur at the beginning Of 2194-PS?

MR. ALDERMAN: It should, yes, sir, unless my English mimeograph is different from yours.

THE PRESIDENT: I don't think I have any letter introducing it.

MR. ALDERMAN: Does it not start after that, "To the Reich Protector in Bohemia and Moravia"?

THE PRESIDENT: Yes, that's right. I beg your pardon.

MR. ALDERMAN:

"Transportation Section, attention of Construction Chief Counsellor Hitch, or representative in the office of the Reich Protector in Bohemia and Moravia, received Prague, 5th September, 1939, No. 274. Enclosed please find a copy of the Reich Defence Law Of 4th September, 1938, and a copy each of the decrees of the Reich Minister of Transportation, dated 7th October, 1938, RL 10.2212/38, Top Secret, and of 17th July, 1939, RL/VL 1.2173/39, Top Secret, for your information and observance, by order, signed Kretschmar. 3 enclosures completed to Dresden, 4th September, 1939, signed Schneider, 3 enclosures. Receipt for the letter of 4th September, 1939, with 3 enclosures, signed 5th September, 1939, and returned to Construction Counsellor Kretschmar."

The whole point being that it was enclosing a second secret Reich Defence Law under Top Secret cover.

I refer next to Indictment, paragraph IV (F) 2A. That paragraph of the Indictment refers to four points: (1) Secret rearmament from 1933 to March, 1935; (2) the training of military personnel (that includes secret or camouflage training); (3) production of munitions of war; (4) the building of an air force.

All four of these are included in the general plan for the breach of the Treaty of Versailles and for the ensuing aggressions. The facts of rearmament and of its secrecy are self-evident from the events that followed. The significant phase of this activity in so far as the Indictment is concerned, lies in the fact that all this was necessary in order to break the barriers of the Versailles Treaty and of the Locarno Pact and to wage the aggressive wars which were to follow. The extent and nature of those activities could only have been for aggressive purposes, and the highest importance which the Government attached to the secrecy of the programme is emphasised by the disguised financing, both before and after the announcement of conscription, and the rebuilding of the army, 16th March, 1935.

I have, if the Court please, an unsigned memorandum by the defendant Schacht dated 3rd May, 1935, entitled "The Financing of the Armament Programme (Finanzierting der Ruestung). "As I say, it is not signed by the defendant Schacht, but he identified it as being his memorandum, in an interrogation on the 16th October, 1945. I would assume that he would still admit that it is his memorandum. That memorandum has been referred to but I believe not introduced or accepted in evidence. I identify it by our No. 1168-PS, and I offer it in evidence as exhibit USA 37.

I think it is quite significant, and with the permission of the Court, I shall read the entire memorandum, reminding you that the German interpreter has the original German before him to read it to the transcript.

"Memorandum from Schacht to Hitler," identified by Schacht as exhibit A, interrogation 16th October, 1945, page 40. 3rd May, 1935 is the date of the memorandum.

Financing of Armament. The following explanations are based upon the thought that the accomplishment of the armament programme with speed and in quantity is the problem of German politics, that everything else therefore should be subordinated to this purpose as long as the main purpose is not imperilled by neglecting all other questions. Even after 16th March, 1935, the difficulty remains that one cannot undertake the open propagandistic treatment of the German people for support of armament without endangering our position internationally (without loss to our foreign trade). The already nearly impossible financing of the armament programme is rendered hereby exceptionally difficult.

Another supposition must also be emphasised. The printing press can only be used for the financing of armament to such a degree, as permitted by maintaining the money value. Every inflation increases the prices of foreign raw materials as well as the domestic prices, and is therefore like a snake biting its own tail. Our armament had to be camouflaged completely till 16th March, 1935, and even after that date the camouflage had to be continued to a larger extent, making it necessary to use the printing press (bank note press) from the very beginning of the whole armament programme, though it would have been natural to start it (i.e., the printing process0 at the final point of finance. In the portefeuille of the Reichsbank are segregated notes for this purpose, that is, armament, of R.M. 3,775 millions and 866 millions, altogether 4,641 millions out of which the armament notes amount to 2,374 million, that is, of issue 30th April, 1935. The Reichsbank has invested the amount of marks under its jurisdiction, but belonging to foreigners, in blank notes of armament. Our armaments are also financed partly with the credits of our political opponents. Furthermore, 500 million Reichsmark were used for financing of armaments which originated out of Reichsanleithe, the Federal Loans placed with the savings banks. In the regular budget the following amounts were provided: for the budget period 1933-34 - R.M. 750 millions; for the budget period 1934-35-R.M. 1,100 millions and for the budget period 1935-36-R.M. 2,500 millions.

The amount of deficits of the budget since 1928 increases after the budget 1935-36 to 5 to 6 millions of Reichsmark. This total deficit is already financed at the present time by short-term credits of the money market. It therefore reduces in advance the possibilities of utilisation of the public market for the armament. The Reichsfinanzminister (Minister of Finance) correctly points out in his defence of the budget: "As a permanent yearly deficit is an impossibility, as we cannot count with security on increased tax revenues to balance such deficit and any other previous debits, and as, on the other hand, a balanced budget is the only secure basis for the impending great task of military policy" - I interpolate that evidently the defendant Schacht knew about the impending great military task to be faced by Germany - "for all these reasons we have to put in motion a fundamental and conscious budget policy which solves the problem of armament financing by organic and planned reduction of other expenditures not only from the point of receipt, but also from the point of expenditure, that is, by saving.

How urgent this question is, can be deduced from the following, that a large amount of cash has been started by the State and Party" - it isn't just the State it is the State and the Party - "and which is now in process, all of which is not covered by the budget, but from contributions and credits, which have to be raised by industry in addition to the regular taxes. The existing of various budgets side by side, which serve more or less public tasks, is the greatest impediment for gaining a clear view about the possibilities of financing the armaments. A whole number of ministries and various branches of the party have their own budget, and for this reason have possibilities of incomes and expenses, though based on the sovereignty of finance of the State, but not subject to the control of the Finanzminister (Minister of Finance) and therefore also not subject to the control of the cabinet. Just as on the sphere of politics the much too far-reaching delegation of legislative powers to individuals brought about various states within the State, exactly in the same way the condition of various branches of State and Party, working side by side and against each other, has a devastating effect on the possibility of finance. If on this territory concentration and unified control is not introduced very soon, the solution of the already impossible task of armament finance is endangered. We have the following tasks:

1) A deputy is entrusted with, I suppose, finding all sources and revenues, which have origin in contributions to the Federal Government, to the State and Party and in profits of public and party enterprises.

(2) Furthermore experts entrusted by the Fuehrer have to examine how these amounts were used and which of these amounts in the future can be withdrawn from their previous purpose.

(3) The same experts have to examine the investments of all public and party organisations, so as to determine to what extent this property can be used for the purpose of armament financing.

(4) The Federal Ministry of Finances is to be entrusted to examine the possibilities of increased revenues by way of new taxes or increasing of existing taxes.

The up-to-date financing of armaments by the Reichsbank, under existing political conditions, was a necessity, and the political success proved the correctness of this action. The other possibilities of armament financing have to be started now under any circumstances. For this purpose all absolutely nonessential expenditure for other purposes must cease and the total financial strength of Germany, limited as it is, must be concentrated for the one purpose of armament financing. Whether the problem of financing, as outlined in this programme, succeeds, remains to be seen, but without such concentration it will fail with absolute certainty."

Being a sort of a hand in finance himself, I can feel some sympathy with the defendant Schacht as he was wrestling with these problems.

May 21st, 1935, was a very important date in the Nazi calendar.

THE PRESIDENT: Would that be a convenient time to adjourn for ten minutes

MR. ALDERMAN: Yes.

(A recess was taken)

MR. ALDERMAN: 21st May, 1935, was a very important date in the Nazi calendar. As I have already indicated, it was on that date that they passed the secret Reich Defence Law, which is our document 2261-PS. The secrecy of their armament operations had already reached the point beyond which they could no longer maintain successful camouflage and since their programme called for still further expansion, they made the unilateral renunciation of the armament provisions of the Versailles Treaty on the same date, 21st May, 1935.

I refer to Hitler's speech to the Reichstag on 21st May, 1935, our document 2288-PS. We have here the original volume of the "Volkische Beobachter " (the "Popular

Observer," I suppose, is the correct translation), Volume 48, 1935, 122- 151, May, and the date 22nd May, 1935, which gave his speech, under the heading (if I may translate, perhaps) "The Fuehrer notifies the world of the way to real peace."

I offer that part of that volume, identified as document 2288-PS, as exhibit USA 38, and from that I shall read, beginning with the fifth paragraph in the English translation:-

"The Treaty of Versailles was not broken." I am starting with the words, "The Treaty of Versailles," in the fifth paragraph.

"The Treaty of Versailles was not broken by Germany unilaterally, but the well-known paragraphs of the Dictat of Versailles were violated, and consequently invalidated, by those powers who could not make up their minds to follow the disarmament requested of Germany with their own disarmament as agreed upon by the Treaty."

I am sorry, I said the fifth paragraph...this is on page 3. It is after he discusses some general conclusions and then there is a paragraph numbered 1, that says:-

"The German Reich Government refuses to adhere to the Geneva Resolution of 17th March...."

The Treaty of Versailles was not broken by Germany unilaterally, but the well-known paragraphs of the Dictat of Versailles were violated and consequently invalidated by those powers.."

I am sorry. May I look at the German original? If the Court please, I did not want to read the whole volume of the "Volkische Beobachter"..

THE PRESIDENT: If it is only a short document you are going to read, only a short extract, perhaps the document could be taken away from the interpreter, and he could follow you.

MR. ALDERMAN: I think I could find it.. I am not very fast in reading German but . . .

THE PRESIDENT: If you read it in English, he will translate it.

MR. ALDERMAN: Yes, but I want the interpreter to have the German.

You will find "1. The German Reich Government refuses to adhere to the Geneva Resolution of 17th March....

"The Treaty of Versailles was not broken by Germany unilaterally, but the well-known paragraphs of the Dictat of Versailles were violated, and consequently invalidated, by those powers who could not make up their minds to follow the disarmament requested of Germany with their own Disarmament as agreed upon by the Treaty. 2. Because the other powers did not live up to their obligations under the disarmament programme, the Government of the German Reich no longer considers itself bound to those articles, which are nothing but a discrimination of the German nation" - (I suppose "against the German nation") - "for an unlimited period of time, since, through them, Germany is being nailed down in a unilateral manner, contrary to the spirit of the agreement."

If the Tribunal please, needless to say, when I cite Adolf Hitler, I don't necessarily vouch for the absolute truth of everything that he presents. This is a public speech he made before the world, and it is for the Tribunal to judge whether he is presenting a pretext or whether he is presenting the truth.

In conjunction with other phases of planning and preparation for aggressive war, there were various programmes for direct and indirect training of a military nature. This included not only the training of military personnel, but also the establishment and training of other military organisations, such as the Police Force, which could be and were absorbed by the Army.

These are shown in other parts of the case presented by the prosecution. However, the extent of this programme for military training is indicated by Hitler's boast of the expenditure of ninety billion Reichsmarks during the period 1933 to 1939, in the building up of the Armed Forces.

I have another volume of the "Volkische Beobachter, " Volume 52, 1939, I think the issue Of 2nd and 3rd September, 1939, which I offer in evidence as exhibit USA 39; and there appears a speech by Adolf Hitler, with his picture, under the heading which, if I may be permitted to try to translate, reads: "The Fuehrer announces the Battle for the justice and Security of the Reich." I hand the original volume ...

This is a speech, if the Court please, by Adolf Hitler, on 1st September, 1939, the date of the attack on Poland, identified by our number 2322-PS ; and I read from that the paragraphs indicated to the interpreter

"For more than six years now .."

I beg your pardon. On the Court's mimeographed copy it is the bottom of page 3, the last paragraph starting on the page.

"For more than six years now, I have been engaged in building up the German Armed Forces. During this period more than ninety billion Reichsmarks were spent in building up the Wehrmacht. To-day, ours are the best- equipped armed forces in the world, and they are superior to those of 1914. My confidence in them can never be shaken."

The secret nature of this training programme and the fact of its early development is illustrated by a reference to the secret training of flying personnel, as far back as 1932, as well as the early plans to build a military air force. A report was sent to the defendant Hess, in a letter from one Schickebaum to the defendant Rosenberg, for delivery to Hess.

I suppose that Schickebaum was very anxious that no one but Hess should get this letter, and therefore sent it to Rosenberg for personal delivery to Hess.

This document points out that the civilian pilots should be so organised as to enable their transfer into the military air force Organisation.

This letter is our document 1143-PS, dated 20th October, 1932, and I now offer it in evidence as exhibit USA 40. It starts: "Lieber Alfred" (referring to Alfred Rosenberg) and is signed "Mit bestem Gruss, Dein Amo." Amo, I think, was the first name of Schickebaum.

"Dear Alfred: I am sending you enclosed a communication from the R.W.M. forwarded to me by our confidential man (Vertrauensmann), which indeed is very interesting. I believe we will have to take some steps so that the matter will not be procured secretly for the Stahlhelm. This report is not known to anybody else. I intentionally did not inform even our long friend"

- I suppose that means "our tall friend." I may interpolate that the defendant Rosenberg, in an interrogation on 5th October, 194S, identified this "long friend" or "tall friend," as being one Von Albensleben.

I am enclosing an additional copy for Hess, and ask you to transmit the letter to Hess by messenger, I do not want to write a letter to Hess for fear that it might be read somewhere. Mit bestem Gruss, Dein Amo."

Then enclosed in that is "Air Force Organisation."

Purpose: Preparation of material and training of personnel to provide for the case of the armament of the airforce.

Entire management as a civilian organisation will be transferred to Col. von Willberg, at present Commander of Breslau, who, retaining his position in the Reichswehr, is going on leave of absence.

(a) Organising the pilots of civilian air-lines in such a way as to enable their transfer to the air force Organisation. (b) Prospects to train crews for military flying.

Training to be done within the organisation for military flying of the Stahlhelm....

I believe that means the "steel helmet."

"... which is being turned over to Col. Hanel, retired.

All existing organisations for sport-flying are to be used for military flying. Directions on kinds and tasks of military flying will be issued by this Stahlhelm directorate. The Stahlhelm Organisation will pay the military Pilots 50 marks per hour flight. These are due to the owner of the plane if he himself carries out the flight. They are to be divided in case of non-owners of the plane, between flight organisation, proprietor and crew in the proportion of 10: 20: 20. Military flying is now paid better than flying for advertisement (40). We therefore have to expect that most proprietors of planes or flying associations will go over to the Stahlhelm organisation. It must be achieved that equal conditions will be granted by the R.W.M., also the N.S.D.A.P. organisation.

The programme of rearmament and the objectives of circumventing and breaching the Versailles Treaty are forcefully shown by a number of Navy documents, showing the participation and co-operation of the German Navy in this rearmament programme, secret at first.

When they deemed it safe to say so, they openly acknowledged that it had always been their objective to break Versailles.

In 1937 the Navy High Command published a secret book entitled "The Fight of the Navy Against Versailles, 1919 to 1935." The preface refers to the fight of the Navy against the unbearable regulations of the peace treaty of Versailles. The table of contents includes a variety of Navy activities, such as saving of coastal guns from destruction as required by Versailles; independent armament measures behind the back of the government and behind the back of the legislative bodies resurrection of the U-boat arm; economic rearmament and camouflage rearmament from 1933 to the freedom from the restrictions in 1935.

This document points out the significant effect of seizure of power by the Nazis in 1933 on increasing the size and determining the nature of the rearmament programme. It also refers to the far-reaching independence in the building and development of the Navy, which was only hampered in so far as concealment of rearmament had to be considered in compliance with the Versailles Treaty.

With the restoration of what was called the military sovereignty of the Reich in 1935 - the reoccupation of the demilitarised zone of the Rhineland - the external camouflage of rearmament was eliminated.

We have, if the Court please, a photostat of the German printed book to which I have referred entitled "Der Kampf der Marine gegen Versailles (The Fight of the Navy against Versailles), 1919 to 1935," written by Sea Captain Schuessler. It has the symbol of the Nazi Party with the Swastika in the spread eagle on the cover sheet, and it is headed "Secret", underscored. It is our document C-156. It is a book of seventy-six pages of text followed by index lists and charts. I offer it in evidence as exhibit USA 41. I may say that the defendant Raeder identified this book in a recent interrogation and explained that the Navy tried to fulfil the letter of the Versailles Treaty and at the same time to make progress in naval development. I should like to read from this book, if the Court please. I certainly shall not read the entire book, but I should like to read the preface and one or two other portions of it.

"The object and aim of this memorandum under the heading 'Preface,' is to draw a technically reliable picture based on documentary records and the evidence of those who took part in the fight of the Navy against the unbearable regulations of the peace Treaty of Versailles. It shows that the Reich Navy, after the liberating activities of the Free Corps and of Scapa Flow, did not rest, but found ways and means to lay with unquenchable enthusiasm, in addition to the building up of the 15,000 man Navy, the basis for a greater development in the future, and so create, by the work of soldiers and technicians, the primary condition for a later rearmament. It must also distinguish more clearly the services of these men, who without being widely known, applied themselves with extraordinary zeal and responsibility to the service of the fight against the peace Treaty. Stimulated by the highest feeling of duty, they risked, particularly in the early days of their fight, themselves and their positions unrestrainedly in the partially self-ordained tasks. This compilation makes it clearer, however, that even such ideal and ambitious plans can be realised only to a small degree if the concentrated and united strength of the whole people is not behind the courageous activity of the soldier. Only when the Fuehrer had created the second and even more important condition for an effective rearmament in the co-ordination of the whole nation and in the fusion of the political, financial and spiritual power, could the work of the soldier find its fulfilment. The framework of this peace Treaty, the most shameful known in world history, collapsed under the driving power of this united will.

Signed, the Compiler."

Now, I wish to invite the Court's attention merely to the summary of contents, because the chapter titles are sufficiently significant for my present purpose.

I. First: "Defensive action against the execution of the Treaty of Versailles (from the end of the war to the occupation of the Ruhr, 1923)."

Second: "Saving of coastal guns from destruction to removal of artillery equipment and ammunition, hand and machine weapons."

Third: "Limitation of destruction in Heligoland."

II. Independent armament measures behind the back of the Reich Government and of the legislative body (from 1923 to the Lohmann case in 1927).

1. Attempt to increase the personnel strength of the Reich Navy.

2. Contribution to the strengthening of patriotism among the people.

3. Activities of Captain Lohmann.

I am ashamed to say, if the Court please, that I am not familiar with the story about Captain Lohmann.

4. Preparation for the resurrection of the German U-boat arm.

5. Building up of the air force.

6. Attempt to strengthen our mine arm (Die Mine).

7. Economic rearmament.

8. Miscellaneous measures

   (a) The M.B. Aerogiadetic, and;

   (b) Secret evidence.

III. Planned armament work countenanced by the Reich Government but behind the back of the legislative body from 1927 to the seizure of power, 1933. IV. Rearmament under the leadership of the Reich Government in camouflage (from 1933 to the freedom from restrictions, 1935)."

The unification of the whole nation which was combined with the taking over of power on 30th January, 1933, was of decisive influence on the size and shape of further rearmament.

While the second chamber, Reichsrat, approached its dissolution and withdrew as a legislative body, the Reichstag assumed a composition which could only take a one- sided attitude toward the rearmament of the armed forces. The government took over the management of the rearmament programme upon this foundation.

Then a heading "Development of the Armed Forces."

This taking over of the management by the Reich Government developed for the Armed Forces in such a manner that the War Minister, General von Blomberg, and through him the three branches of the Armed Forces, received far-reaching powers from the Reich Cabinet for the development of the Armed Forces. The whole organisation of the Reich was included in this way. In view of these powers the collaboration of the former inspecting body in the management of the secret expenditure was from then on dispensed with. There remained only the inspecting duty of the accounting office of the German Reich.

Another heading, "Independence of the Commander-in-Chief of the Navy." The Commander-in-Chief of the Navy, Admiral Raeder, honorary doctor, had been given far-reaching independence in the building and development of the Navy. This was only hampered to the extent that the previous concealment of rearmament had to be continued in consideration of the Versailles Treaty. Besides the public budget there remained the previous special budget, which was greatly increased in view of the considerable credit for the provision of labour which was made available by the Reich. Wide powers in the handling of these credits were given to the Director of the Budget Department of the Navy, up to 1934 Commodore Schuessler, afterwards Commodore Forster. These took into consideration the increased responsibility of the Chief of the Budget.

Another heading, "Declaration of Military Freedom." When the Fuehrer, relying upon the strengthening of the Armed Forces carried out in the meanwhile, announced the restoration of the military sovereignty of the German Reich, the last- mentioned limitation on rearmament works, namely, the external camouflage, was eliminated. "Freed from all the shackles which have hampered our ability to move freely on and under water, on land and in the air for one and a-half decades, and carried by the newly-awakened fighting spirit of the whole nation, the Armed Forces, and part of it, the Navy, can lead with full strength towards its completion the rearmament already under way with the goal of securing for the Reich its rightful position in the world."

If the Tribunal please, at this moment I have a new problem about proof which I believe we have not discussed. I have in my hand an English transcription of an interrogation of the defendant Erich Raeder. Of course, he knows he was interrogated; he knows what be said. I do not believe we have furnished copies of this interrogation to defendant's counsel. I don't know whether under the circumstances I am at liberty to read from it or not. If I do read from it I suggest that the defendant's counsel will all get the complete text of it - I mean of what I read in the transcript.

THE PRESIDENT: Has the counsel for the defendant Raeder any objection to this interrogation being read?

DOCTOR SIEMERS (Counsel for defendant Raeder): As far as I have understood the proceedings to date, I believe that it is a question of procedure in which either proof by way of documents or proof by way of witnesses will be furnished. I am surprised that the prosecution wishes to furnish proof by way of records of interrogations taken at a time when the defence was not present. I should be obliged to the Court if I were told whether, in principle, I, as a defence counsel, may resort to producing evidence in this form, i.e., present documents of the interrogation of witnesses, that is to say, documents in which I myself interrogated witnesses, in the same way as the prosecution has done, without putting witnesses on the stand.

THE PRESIDENT: In future the Tribunal thinks that if interrogations of defendants are to be used, copies of such interrogations should be furnished to defendant's counsel beforehand. The question which the Tribunal wished to ask you was whether on this occasion you objected to this interrogation being used without such a copy having been furnished to you. With regard to your observation as to your own rights with reference to interrogating your defendant, the Tribunal considers that you must call them as witnesses upon the witness stand, and cannot interrogate them and put in the interrogations. The question for you now is whether you object to this interrogation being laid before the Tribunal at this stage.

DR. SIEMERS: I should like first of all to have an opportunity to see this document. Only then shall I be able to decide whether interrogations can be read, the contents of which I as a defence counsellor am not familiar with.

THE PRESIDENT: The Tribunal will adjourn now and it anticipates that the interrogation can be handed to you during the adjournment and then can be used afterwards.

(A recess was taken until 1400 hours.)

MR. JACKSON: May it please the Tribunal. I should like to ask the Tribunal to note the presence and appearance on behalf of the Union of Soviet Socialist Republics of Mr. A. I. Vijshinsky of the Foreign Office, and Mr. K. P. Gorshenin, Chief Prosecutor of the Soviet Republic, who has been able to join us in the prosecution only now.

THE PRESIDENT: The Tribunal notes what Mr. Justice Jackson has said, and observes that Mr. Vijshinsky has taken his seat with the Soviet Delegation of Chief Prosecutors.

DR. SIEMERS: In the meanwhile during the lunch hour I have seen the minutes. I should like to observe that I don't think it is very agreeable that the prosecution should stick to their point that the defence should not see the documents until late during the proceedings, or just before the proceedings, or at times even after the proceedings. I should be most grateful to the prosecution if it should be made possible in the future to let us be informed in good time.

Yesterday a list of the documents which were to be presented to-day was put up in room, No. 54. I find that the documents presented to-day are not [Page 195] included in yesterday's list. You will understand that the task of the defence is thereby rendered comparatively difficult. On principle I cannot, in my statement of to-day, give my agreement to the reading of minutes of interrogations. In order to facilitate matters, I should like to follow the Court's suggestion, and declare my agreement that the minutes presented here should be read. I request, however - and I believe I have already been assured by the prosecution, to that effect - that only that part be read which refers to document C-156, as I had no time to discuss the remaining points with the defendant.

As to the remaining points, five other documents are cited. Moreover, I request that the part which refers to the book by Kapitan zur See Schuessler, should be read in full, and I believe that the prosecutor agrees with this.

THE PRESIDENT: I understood from the counsel for Raeder that you were substantially in agreement as to what parts of this interrogation you should read. Is that right, Mr. Alderman?

MR. ALDERMAN: If I understand the counsel correctly, he asked that I read the entire part of the interrogation which applies to the document C-156, but I understood that he did not agree to my reading other parts that referred to other documents. I handed counsel the original of my copy of the interrogation before the lunch hour, and when he returned it after the lunch hour, I handed him the carbon copy. I do not quite understand his statement about a document being introduced which hadn't been furnished to the defendant. We did file the document book.

THE PRESIDENT: Is this document in the document book?

MR. ALDERMAN: My understandings that the document book contained all of the document which is stated in this interrogation. It didn't contain the interrogation.

THE PRESIDENT: Then he is right to say that.

MR. ALDERMAN: He is right in saying that about this interrogation, yes.

THE PRESIDENT: You are in agreement with him then. You can read what you want to read now, and it is not necessary for you to read that part to which he objects.

MR. ALDERMAN: I think I understand his objection to my reading anything other than the part concerned with C-156, but I anticipate that he may be willing for me to read the other parts tomorrow.

This deals with the book which I offered in evidence this morning, document C-156, exhibit USA 41. The defendant Raeder identified that book, and explained that the Navy had to fulfil the letter of the Versailles Treaty, and at the same time make progress in Naval development. I refer to the interrogation of the defendant Raeder at the part we had under discussion:-

Q. I have here a document, C-156, which is a photostatic copy of a work prepared by the High Command of the Navy, and covers the struggle of the Navy against the Versailles Treaty from 1919 to 1935-. I ask you initially whether you are familiar with the work?

A. I know this book. I read it once when it was published.

Q. Was that an official publication of the German Navy?

A. This Captain Schuessler (indicating the author) was a Commander in the Admiralty. Published by the O.K.M., this book represented an idea of this officer to co- ordinate all those matters.

Q. Do you recall the circumstances under which the authorisation to prepare such a work was given to him?

A. I think he told me that he would write such a book as he says here in the foreword.

Q. And in the preparation of this work he had access to the official Navy files and based his work on the items contained therein?

A. Yes, I think so. He would have spoken with other persons, and he would have had the files which were necessary.

Q. Do you know whether before the work was published, a draft of it was circulated among the officers in the Admiralty for comment?

A. No, I don't think so. Not before it was published. I saw it only when it was published.

Q. Was it circulated freely after its publication?

A. It was a secret subject, I think all Higher Commands in the Navy had knowledge of it.

Q. It was not circulated outside of Navy circles?

A. No.

Q. What then is your opinion concerning the comments contained in the work regarding the circumventing of the provisions of Versailles?

A. I don't remember very exactly what is in here. I can only remember that the Navy had always the object to fulfil the word of the Versailles Treaty, but, in order to obtain some advantages, the flying men were trained one year before they went into the Navy. Quite young men. So that the word of the Treaty of Versailles was fulfilled. They did not belong to the Navy, as long as they were trained in flying, and the submarines were developed, not in Germany, and not in the Navy, but in Holland. There was a Civil Bureau, and in Spain there was an Industrial Bureau; in Finland, too, and they were built only much later, when we began to act with the English Government about the Treaty of thirty-five to one hundred, because we could see that then the Treaty of Versailles would be destroyed by such a Treaty with England, and so in order to keep the word of Versailles, we tried to fulfil the word of Versailles, but we tried to gain advantages.

Q. Would a fair statement be that the Navy High Command was interested in avoiding the limiting provisions of the Treaty of Versailles regarding personnel and the limitation of armaments, but would it attempt to fulfil the letter of the Treaty, although actually avoiding it?

A. That was their endeavour.

MR. ALDERMAN: Now the rest of this is the portion that the counsel for the defendant asked me to read.

Q. Why was such a policy adopted?

A. After the first war we were sorely menaced by the danger that the Poles might attack East Prussia, and we therefore tried to strengthen a little our very, very weak combat forces in this way; consequently all our efforts were directed to the aim of having a little more strength against the Poles should they attack us. It is nonsense to think we could have attacked Poland at this stage-and with the Navy. A second aim was to achieve a certain degree of defence against the possible entry of French forces into the Ostsee (East Sea), since we knew that the French intended coming to the aid of the Poles. Their ships entered the Ostsee and the Navy was therefore a defence against a Polish attack and against a French invasion via the Ostsee. Purely defensive aims.

Q. When did this fear of an attack by Poland arise in Germany's official circles?

A. In the very first years, when Vilna was taken. We felt, at the same time, that they could come to East Prussia. I am not certain about the exact year, since those opinions arose in the German Ministries and were held by the Ministers of the Army and Navy - Groner and Nocke.

Q. And this view, in your opinion, was generally held perhaps as far back as 1919/1920, after the end of the first World War?

A. The whole situation was most uncertain and confirmed and I cannot give you a very precise picture about the beginning of those years, since I was then working for two years in the Navy Archives, writing a book on the War and on how the Cruisers fought in the First World War. So that for two years I was not occupied with such matters."

Likewise the same kind of planning and purposes are reflected in the table of contents of a history of the German Navy, 1919 to 1939, found in captured official files of the German Navy. Although a copy of the book has not been found by us, the project was written by Colonel Scherff, Hitler's special military historian. We have found the table of contents: it refers by numbers to groups of documents and notes on the documents, which evidently were intended as working materials for the basis of chapters to be written in accordance with the table of contents. The titles in this table of contents fairly establish the Navy planning and preparations to get the Versailles Treaty out of the way and to rebuild the Navy strength necessary for aggressive war.

We have here the original captured document which is, as I say, the German typewritten table of contents of this projected work, with a German cover, typewritten, entitled "Geschichte der Deutschen Marine, 1919-1939 (History of the German Navy, 1919-1939)" We identify that as our series C-17 and I offer it in evidence as exhibit USA 42. This table of contents includes such general headings - but perhaps I had better read some of the actual headings:

Part A (1919 - The Year of Transition). Chapter VII. First efforts to circumvent the Versailles Treaty and to limit its effects.

(a) Demilitarisation of the Administration, incorporation of Naval Offices in Civil Ministries, etc. for example: incorporation of greater sections of the German maritime observation station and sea-mark system in Heligoland and Kiel, of the Ems-Jade Canal, etc. into the Reich Transport Ministry up to 1934;

(b) The saving from destruction of coastal fortifications and guns.

1. North Sea (strengthening of fortifications with new batteries and modern guns between the signing and the taking effect of the Versailles Treaty); dealings with the Control Commission - information, drawings, visits of inspection, result of efforts."

Referring to the group of documents numbered 85:

"2. Baltic. Taking over by the Navy of fortresses Pillau and Swinemunde; salvage for the Army of one-hundred and eighty-five movable guns and mortars there.

3. The beginnings of coastal defence.

Part B. (1920-1924. - The Organisational New Order)

Chapter V.

The Navy.

Fulfilment and avoidance of the Versailles Treaty.

Foreign countries.

(a) The inter-allied Control Commissions.

(b) Defence measures against the fulfilment of the Versailles Treaty and independent arming behind the back of the Reich Government and the legislative bodies.

1. Dispersal of artillery gear and munitions, of hand and automatic weapons.

2. Limitation of demolition work in Heligoland.

3. Attempt to strengthen personnel of the Navy, from 1923

4. The activities of Captain Lohmann (founding of numerous associations at home and abroad, participations, formation of 'sports' unions and clubs, interesting the film industry in naval recruitment)

5. Reparation for re-establishing the German U-boat arm since 1920.

(Projects and deliveries for Japan, Holland, Turkey, Argentine and Finland. Torpedo testing.)

6. Participation in the preparation for building of the Luftwaffe (preservation of aerodromes, aircraft construction, teaching of courses, instruction of midshipmen in anti-air raid defence, training of pilots).

7. Attempts to strengthen the mining branch.

Part C- (1925-1932. Replacement of Tonnage).

Chapter IV. The Navy, the Versailles Treaty.

Foreign countries.

(a) The activities of the Inter-allied Control Commission (up to 31.1-27; discontinuance of the activity of the Naval Peace Commission). Independent armament measures behind the back of the Reich Government and legislative bodies up to the Lohmann case.

1. The activities of Captain Lohmann (continuation) their significance as a foundation for the rapid reconstruction work from 1935.

2. Preparation for the re-strengthening of the German U- boat arm from 1925 (continuation), the merit of Lohmann in connection with the preparation for rapid construction in 1925, relationship to Spain, Argentine, Turkey: the first post-war U-boat construction of the German Navy in Spain since 1927; 250 ton specimen in Finland, preparation for rapid assembly; electric torpedo; training of U-boat personnel abroad in Spain and Finland. Formation of U-boat school in 1932 disguised as an anti-U-boat school.

3. Participation in the preparation for the reconstruction of the Luftwaffe (continuation). Preparation for a Naval Air Arm, Finance Aircraft Company Sevra, later Luftdienst CMRH; Naval Flying School Warnemende; Air Station List, training of sea cadet candidates, Military tactical questions 'Air Defence Journeys,' technical development, experimental station planning, trials, flying boat development DOX etc., catapult aircraft, arming, engines, ground organisation, aircraft torpedoes, the Deutschland Flight, 1925 and the Seaplane Race, 1926.

4. Economic re-armament ("The Tebeg' -Technical Advice and Supply Company as a disguised Naval Office abroad for investigating the position of raw materials for industrial capacity and other War economic questions).

5. Various measures. (The NV Aerogeodetic Company - secret investigations.)

(c) Planned Armament Work with the tacit approval of the Reich Government, but behind the backs of the legislative bodies (1928 to the taking over of power).

1. The effect of the Lohmann case on the secret preparations; winding up of works which could not be advocated; resumption and carrying on of other

work.

2. Finance question. ('Black Funds' and the Special Budget.)

3. The Labour Committee and its objectives.

(d) The question of Marine Attaches.

(The continuation under disguise; open reappointment 1932-1933.)

(e) The question of Disarmament of the Fleet abroad and in Germany.

(The Geneva Disarmament Conference 1927; the London Naval Treaty of 1930; the Anglo-French-Italian Agreement 1931. The League of Nations Disarmament Conference 1932.)

Part D (1933-1939)- The German Navy during the Military Freedom Period;" which goes beyond the period with which I am at the moment dealing. A glance at the Chapter headings following that will indicate the scope of this proposed work. Whether the history was ever actually written by Scherff, I do not know.

I would like to call attention just to the first two or three headings, under this

"Part D - The German Navy during the Military Freedom Period;

I. National Socialism and the question of the Fleet and of prestige at sea.

II. Incorporation of the Navy in the National Socialist State."

The main heading III in the middle of the page, "The Re- armament of the Navy under the Direction of the Reich Government in a Disguised Way." The policy development of the Navy is also reflected from the financial side. The planned organisation of the Navy budget for armament measures was based on a co-ordination of military developments and political objectives. Military political development was accelerated after the withdrawal from the League of Nations.

I have here, if the Court please, a captured document, in German, headed "Der Chef der Marineleitung, Berlin, 12th May, 1934," and marked in large blue printing "Geheime Kommandosache" - "Secret Commando Matter" - which is identified as our C-153. It has the facsimile signature of Raeder at the end. I assume it's the facsimile; it may have been written with a stylus on a stencil; I can't tell. I offer it in evidence as exhibit USA 43. It is headed with the title "Armament Plan (A.P.) for the 3rd Armament Phase." This document of 12th May, 1934, speaks of war tasks, war and operational plans, armament targets, etc., and shows that it was distributed to many of the High Command of the Navy. It shows that a primary objective was readiness for a war without any alert period.

I quote from the third numbered paragraphs:

"This organisation of armament measures is necessary for the realisation of this target; this again requires a co- ordinated and planned expenditure in peace time. This organisation of financial measures over a number of years according to the military viewpoint is found in the armament programme and provides

(a) for the military leaders a sound basis for their operational considerations; and

(b) for the political leaders a clear picture of what may be achieved with the military means available at a given time."

One other sentence from paragraph 7 of that document:

"All theoretical and practical A-preparations" (I assume that means Armament Preparations), "are to be drawn up with a primary view to readiness for a war without any alert period."

The conspiratorial nature of these Nazi plans and preparations long before the outbreak of hostilities is illustrated in many other ways. Thus, in 1934 Hitler instructed Raeder to keep secret the U-boat construction programme, also the actual displacement and speed of certain ships. Work on U-boats had been going on, as already indicated, in Holland and Spain.

The Nazi theory was rather clever on that. The Versailles Treaty forbade re-arming by the Germans in Germany, but they said it didn't forbid them to re-arm in Holland, Spain and Finland.

Secrecy was equally important then because of the pending Naval negotiations with England. We have a captured document, which is a manuscript in German script, of a conversation between the defendant Raeder and Adolf Hitler, in June, 1934. It is not signed by the defendant Raeder. I might ask his counsel if he objects to my stating that the defendant Raeder, in an interrogation on 8th November, 1945, admitted that this was a record of this conversation, and that it was in his handwriting, though he did not sign his name at the end.

That document is identified in our series as C-159, and I offer it in evidence as exhibit USA 44.

It is headed, "Conversation with the Fuehrer in June, 1934, on the occasion of the resignation of the Commanding Officer of the' Karlsruhe.'

1. Report by the C-in-C. Navy concerning increased displacement of D. and E.(defensive weapons).

Fuehrer's instructions: No mention must be made of a displacement Of 25-26,000 tons, but only of improved 10,000 ton ships. Also, the speed over 26 nautical miles may be stated.

2. C-in-C. Navy expresses the opinion that later on the Fleet must anyhow be developed to oppose England, that therefore from 1936 onwards, the large ships must be armed with 35 c.m. guns (like the King George Class).

3. The Fuehrer demands to keep the construction of the U- boats completely secret. Plebiscite also in consideration of the Saar."

In order to continue the vital increase of the Navy, as planned, the Navy needed more funds than it had available; so Hitler proposed to put funds of the Labour Front at the disposal of the Navy.

We have another Raeder memorandum of a conversation between Raeder and Hitler, on 2nd November, 1934. Of this, I have a photostatic copy of the German typed memorandum, identified as our C-190. This one, again, is not signed, but it was found in Raeder's personal file and I think he will not deny that it is his memorandum.

I offer it in evidence as exhibit USA 45.

It is headed:

"Conversation with the Fuehrer on 2nd November, 1934 at the time of the announcement by the Commanding Officer of the 'Emden.'

(1) When I mentioned that the total funds to be made available for the armed forces for 1935 would presumably represent only a fraction of the required sum, and

257

that therefore it was possible that the Navy might be hindered in its plans, he replied that he did not think the funds would be greatly decreased. He considered it necessary that the Navy be speedily increased by 1938 with the deadlines mentioned. In case of need he will get Dr. Ley to put 120-150 million from the Labour Front at the disposal of the Navy, as the money would still benefit the workers. Later in a conversation with Minister Goering and myself, he went on to say that he considered it vital that the Navy be increased as planned, as no war could be carried on if the Navy was not able to safeguard the ore imports from Scandinavia.

(2) Then, when I mentioned that it would be desirable to have six U-boats assembled at the time of the critical situation in the first quarter of the following year, 1935, he stated that he would keep this point in mind, and tell me when the situation demanded that the assembling should commence."

Then there is an asterisk and a note at the bottom:-

"The order was not sent out. The first boats were launched in the middle of June, 1935, according to plan."

The development of the armament industry by the use of foreign markets was a programme encouraged by the Navy, so that this industry would be able to supply the requirements of the Navy in case of need.

We have an original German document, again headed "Geheime Kommandosache" - "Secret Commando Matter" - a directive Of 31st January, 1933, by the defendant Raeder, for the German industry to support the armament of the Navy.

It is identified in our series as C-29.

I offer it in evidence as exhibit USA 46.

"TOP SECRET

GENERAL DIRECTIONS FOR SUPPORT GIVEN BY THE GERMAN NAVY TO THE GERMAN ARMAMENT INDUSTRY

The effects of the present economic depression have led here and there to the conclusion that there are no prospects of an active participation of the German Armament Industry abroad, even if the Versailles terms are no longer kept. There is no profit in it and it is therefore not worth promoting. Furthermore, the view has been taken that the increasing 'self-sufficiency' would in any case make such participation superfluous.

However obvious these opinions may seem, formed because of the situation as it is to-day, I am nevertheless forced to make the following contradictory corrective points:-

(a) The economic crisis and its present effects must perforce be overcome sooner or later.

Though equality of rights in war politics is not fully recognised to-day, it will, by the assimilation of weapons, be achieved at some period, at least to a certain extent.

(b) The consequent estimation of the duties of the German Armament Industry lies mainly in the Military-political sphere. It is possible for this industry to

258

satisfy, militarily and economically, the growing demands made of it by limiting the deliveries to our Armed Forces. Its capacity must therefore be increased by the delivery of supplies to foreign countries over and above our own requirements.

(c) Almost every country is working to the same end to- day, even those which unlike Germany, are not tied down by restrictions. Britain, France, North America, Japan, and especially Italy, are making supreme efforts to ensure markets for their armaments industries. The use of their diplomatic representations, of the propaganda voyages of their most modern ships and vessels, of sending missions and also of the guaranteeing of loans and insurance against deficits, are not merely to gain commercially advantageous orders for their armament industries, but first and foremost to expend their output from the point of view of military policy.

(d) It is just when the efforts to do away with the restrictions imposed on us have succeeded, that the German Navy has an ever-increasing and really vital interest in furthering the German Armament Industry and preparing the way for it in every direction in the competitive battle against the rest of the world.

(e) If, however, the German Armament Industry is to be able to compete in foreign countries, it must inspire the confidence of its purchasers. The condition for this is that secrecy for our own ends be not carried too far. The amount of material to be kept secret under all circumstances, in the interest of the defence of our country, is comparatively small. I would like to issue a warning against the assumption that at the present stage of technical development in foreign industrial States, a problem of vital military importance which we perhaps have solved, has not been solved there, too. Solutions arrived at to-day, which may become known, if divulged to a third person by naturally always possible indiscretion, have often been already superseded by new and better solutions on our part, even at that time or at any rate after the copy has been made. It is of greater importance that we should be technically well to the fore in any really fundamental matters, than that less important points should be kept secret unnecessarily and excessively.

(f) To conclude: I attach particular importance to guaranteeing the continuous support of the industry concerned by the Navy, even after the present restrictions have been relaxed. If the purchasers are not made confident that something better is being offered them, the industry will not be able to stand up to the competitive battle and therefore will not be able to supply the requirements of the German Navy in case of need."

This surreptitious rearmament, in violation of treaty obligations, starting even before the Nazis came into power, is illustrated by a 1932 order of the defendant Raeder, Chief of the Naval Command, addressed to the main Naval Command, regarding the concealed construction of torpedo tubes in E-boats. He ordered that torpedo tubes be removed and stored in the Naval Arsenal but be kept ready for immediate refitting. By using only the permitted number - that is, permitted under the Treaty - at a given time and storing them after satisfactory testing, the actual number of operationally effective E-boats was constantly increased.

We have this German order, with the facsimile signature of Raeder, reading "Der Chef der Marine Leitung, Berlin, 10th February, 1932." Our series number is C-141. I offer it in evidence as exhibit USA 47, the order for concealed armament of E-boats. I read C-141 from the first paragraph of the text:-

"In view of our treaty obligations and the Disarmament Conference, steps must be taken to prevent the 1st E-Boat Half-Flotilla, which in a few months will consist of exactly similar newly built E-boats, from appearing openly as a formation of torpedo-carrying boats" - the German word being Torpedotraeger - and it is not intended to count these E-boats against the number of torpedo-carrying boats allowed us.

I therefore order:-

1. S2-S5, will be commissioned in the shipyard Luerssen, Vegesack without armament, and will be fitted with easily removable cover-sheet-metal on the spaces necessary for torpedo-tubes. The same will be arranged by T.M.I." - a translator's note at the bottom says with reference to T.M.I.: "Inspectorate of Torpedoes and Mining" - "in agreement with the Naval Arsenal, for the Boat S-1 which will dismantle its torpedo-tubes on completion of the practice shooting, for fitting on another boat.

2. The torpedo-tubes of all S-boats will be stored in the Naval Arsenal ready for immediate fitting. During the trial runs the torpedo-tubes will be taken on board one after the other for a short time to be fitted and for practice shooting, so that only one boat at a time carries torpedo armament. For public consumption this boat will be in service for the purpose of temporary trials by the T.V.A."

I suppose that is not the Tennessee Valley Authority. The translator's note calls it the Technical Research Establishment.

"It should not anchor together with the other, unarmed boats of the Half- Flotilla because of the obvious similarity of the type. The duration of firing, and consequently the length of time the torpedo-tubes are aboard is to be as short as possible.

3. Fitting the torpedo-tubes on all E-boats is intended as soon as the situation of the political control allows it."

Interestingly enough, that memorandum by the defendant Raeder, written in 1932, was talked about as soon as the situation of the political control allowed it. The seizure of power was the following year.

Along similar lines the Navy was also carrying on the concealed preparation of auxiliary cruisers, under the disguised designation of Transport Ships "O." The preparations under this order were to be completed by 1st April, 1935. At the very time of construction of these ships as commercial ships, plans were made for their conversion.

We have the original German document, again Top Secret, identified by our number C-166, order from the Command Office of the Navy, dated 12th March, 1934, and signed in draft by Groos. It has the seal of the Reichsministerium, Marineleitung, over the draft signature. I offer it in evidence as exhibit USA 48.

I think the defendant Raeder will admit, or at least will not deny, that this is an official document.

"Subject: Preparation of Auxiliary Cruisers.

It is intended to include in the Establishment Organisation 25 (AG-Aufstellungsgliederung) a certain number of auxiliary cruisers which are intended for use in operations on the High Seas.

In order to disguise the intention and all the preparations, the ships will be referred to as 'Transport Ships O.' It is requested that in future this designation only be used.

The preparations are to be arranged so that they can be completed by 1st April, 1935."

Among official Navy files, O.K.M. files, which we have, there are notes kept year by year, from 1927 to 1940, on the reconstruction of the German Navy and in these notes are numerous examples of the Navy's activities and policies of which I should like to point out some illustrations.

One of these documents discloses that the displacement of the battleships "Scharnhorst," "Gneisenau" and "F/G" - whatever that is - was actually greater than the tonnages which had been notified to the British under the treaty. This document, our C-23, I offer in evidence as exhibit USA 49. That is really a set of three separate documents joined together. I read from that document:-

"The true displacement of the battleships "Scharnhorst," "Gneisnau" and "F/G" exceeds by 20 per cent in each case the displacement reported to the British."

And then there is a table, with reference to different ships, and two columns headed "Displacement by Type," one column "Actual Displacement, "and the other column, "Notified Displacement."

On the "Scharnhorst" the actual displacement was 31,300 tons, the notified was 26,000 tons. On the "F" - actual, 41,700, the notified, 35,000. On the "HI," actual, 56,200 tons, notified, 46,850, and so down the list. I need not read them all.

In the second document in that group towards the end, page 2 on the English version, is the statement, "In a clear cut programme for the construction, the Fuehrer and Reich Chancellor has set the Navy the task of carrying out the aims of his foreign policy."

The German Navy constantly planned and committed violations of armament limitation, and with characteristic German thoroughness had prepared superficial explanations of pretexts to explain away these violations.

Following a conference with the chief of "A" section, an elaborate survey list was prepared and compiled, giving a careful list of the quantity and type of German naval armament and munitions on hand under manufacture or construction, and in many instances proposed, together with a statement of the justification or defence that might be used in those instances where the Versailles Treaty was violated or its allotment has been exceeded.

The list contained thirty items under "Material Measures" and fourteen items under "Measures of Organisation." The variety of details covered necessarily involved several sources within the Navy, which must have realised their significance. As I understand it, the "A" section was the military department of the Navy.

We have this very interesting document amongst the captured documents identified by our number C-32. I offer it in evidence as exhibit USA 50. It again is Geheime Kommandosache and it is headed "A survey Report of German Naval Armament with Chief of "A" Section, dated 9th September, 1933, "and captured among official German Navy files.

This is a long document, if the Tribunal please, but I should like to call attention to a few of the more interesting items.

There are three columns, one headed "Measure," one headed "Material Measures, Details," and the most interesting one is headed "Remarks." The remarks contain the pretext or justification for explaining away the violations of the treaty. They are numbered, so I can conveniently refer to the numbers:-

Number 1. Exceeding the permitted number of mines." Then figures are given. "Remarks: Further mines are in part ordered, in part being delivered."

Number 2. Continuous storing of guns from the North Sea area for Baltic artillery batteries." In the remarks column: justification: Necessity for overhauling. Cheaper repairs."

Turning over to Number 6, "Laying gun-platforms in the Kiel area." Remarks, The offence over and above that in Serial Number 3 lies in the fact that all fortifications are forbidden in the Kiel area. This justification make it less severe; pure defence measures."

Number 7. Exceeding the calibre permitted for coastal batteries." The explanation: Possible justification is that, though the calibre is larger, the number of guns are less."

Number 8. Arming of minesweepers. The reply to any remonstrance against this breach: the guns are taken from the Fleet reserve stores, and have been temporarily installed only for training purposes. All nations arm their mine-sweeping forces (equality of rights)."

Here is one that is rather amusing. "Number 13. Exceeding the number of machine guns, etc., permitted." Remarks: "Can be made light of."

Number 18. Construction of U-boat parts." This remark is quite characteristic: "Difficult to detect. If necessary can be denied."

Number 20. Arming of fishing vessels." Remarks: "For warning shots. Make little of it." And so on throughout the list.

I think that must quite obviously have been used as a guide for negotiators who were attending the Disarmament Conference as to the position that they might take.

Now to paragraph IV (F) 2 b) of the Indictment: the allegation that "On 14th October, 1933, they led Germany to leave the International Disarmament Conference and the League of Nations."

That is a historical fact of which I ask the Tribunal to take judicial notice. The Nazis took this opportunity to break away from the International Negotiations and to take up an aggressive position on an issue which would not be serious enough to provoke reprisal from other countries. At the same time Germany attached so much importance to this action, that they considered the possibility of the application of sanctions by other countries. Anticipating the probable nature of such sanctions and the countries which might apply them, plans were made for military preparations for armed resistance on land, at sea and in the air, in a directive from the Reichsminister for Defence, Blomberg, to the Head of the Army High Command, Fritsch, the Head of the Navy High Command, Raeder, and the Reichsminister of Air, Goering.

We have this captured document in our series, C-140, which I offer in evidence as exhibit USA 51. It is a directive dated 25th October, 1933, eleven days after the withdrawal from the Disarmament Conference and the League of Nations.

"Paragraph 1: "The enclosed directive gives the basis for preparations of the armed forces in the case of sanctions being applied against Germany.

Paragraph 2. I request the Chiefs of the Army and Navy High Commands and the Reichsminister for Air to carry out the preparations in accordance with the following points:- a) Strictest secrecy. It is of the utmost importance that no facts become known to the outside world from which preparation for resistance against sanctions can be inferred, or which are incompatible with Germany's existing obligations in the sphere of foreign policy regarding the demilitarised zone. If necessary, the preparations must take second place to this necessity."

I think that makes the point without further reading.

One of the immediate consequences of the action was that following the withdrawal from the League of Nations, Germany's armament programme was still further increased.

I introduced this morning document C-153, as exhibit USA 43, so that is already in. From that, at this point, I wish to read paragraph 5. That, as you recall, was a document dated 12th May, 1934.

Paragraph 5: "Owing to the speed of military political development, since Germany quitted Geneva, and based on the progress of the army, the new A-Plan will only be drawn up for a period of two years. The third "A" phase lasts accordingly from 1st April, 1934, to 31st March, 1936."

Then the next allegation of the Indictment, if the Tribunal please

"On 10th March, 1935, the defendant Goering announced that Germany was building a Military Air Force."

That is an historical fact of which I ask the Court to take judicial notice, and I am quite certain that the defendant Goering would not dispute it.

We have a copy of the German publication known as "Das Archiv" - I suppose that is the way they pronounce it - for March, 1935, and it is page 1890 to which I refer, and I would offer that in evidence, identifying it as our number 2292-PS; I offer it as exhibit USA 52. It is an announcement concerning the German Air Force:-

"The Reich Minister for Aviation, General of the Airmen, Goering, in his talk with the special correspondent of the Daily Mail, Ward Price, expressed himself on the subject of the German Air Force.

General Goering said:-

In the extension of our National Defence (Sicherheit) it was necessary, as we

263

repeatedly told the world, to take care of defence in the air. As far as that is concerned, I restricted myself to those measure which were absolutely necessary. The guiding line of my actions was, not the creation of an aggressive force which would threaten other nations, but merely the completion of a military aviation which would be strong enough to repel, at any time, attacks on Germany."

Then, at the end of that section of the article in "Das Archiv":

"In conclusion, the correspondent asks whether the German Air Force will be capable of repelling attacks on Germany. General Goering replied to that exactly as follows:-

The Germany Air Force is just as passionately permeated with the will to defend the Fatherland to the last as it is convinced, on the other hand, that it will never be employed to threaten the peace of other nations."

As I said, I believe, this morning, when we cite assurances of that kind from Nazi leaders, we take it that we are not prevented from showing that they had different intentions from those announced.

The next allegation of the Indictment is the promulgating of the law for compulsory military service, universal military service.

Having gone as far as they could on rearmament and the secret training of personnel, the next step necessary to the programme for aggressive war was a large-scale increase in military strength. This could no longer be done under disguise and camouflage, and would have to be known to the world. Accordingly, on 16th March, 1935, there was promulgated a law for universal military service, in violation of Article 173 of the Versailles Treaty.

I ask the Court to take judicial notice of that law as it appears in the Reichsgesetzblatt, which is the official compilation of laws, in the Title I of Volume 1, yearly volume 1935, or Jahrgang, at page 369, and I think I need not offer the book or the law in evidence.

The text of the law itself is very brief, and I might read that; it is right at the end of the article. I should refer to that as our document 1654-PS, so as to identify it.

"In this spirit the German Reich Cabinet has to-day passed the following laws Law for the Organisation of the Armed Forces of 16th March, 1935.

The Reich Cabinet has passed the following law which is herewith promulgated:

Section 1.

Service in the Armed Forces is based upon compulsory military duty.

Section 2.

In peace-time, the Germany Army, including the police troops transferred to it, is organised into: 12 Corps and 36 Divisions."

There is a typographical error in the English version of that. It says "16 Divisions," but the original German says 36 Divisions.

"Section 3.

The Reich Minister of War is charged with the duty of submitting immediately to the Reich Ministry detailed laws on compulsory military duty."

Signed, Berlin, 16th March, 1933."

It is signed first by the Fuehrer and Reich Chancellor Adolf Hitler, and then by many other officials, including the following defendants in this case:-

von Neurath; Frick; Schacht; Goering; Hess; and Frank.

Does the Court contemplate a short recess?

THE PRESIDENT: We will adjourn for ten minutes.

(A recess was taken)

COLONEL STOREY: If the Tribunal please, the prosecution expects, to-morrow, to offer in evidence some captured enemy moving pictures and in order to give defence counsel an opportunity to see them before they are offered in evidence - and in response to their request made to the Tribunal some time ago - the showing of these films for defence counsel will be held in this Court Room this evening at 8 o'clock.

THE PRESIDENT: Very well, Colonel Storey.

MR. ALDERMAN: May it please the Tribunal, I have reached now Paragraph IV, F, 2(e) of the Indictment, which alleges: "On 21st May, 1935, they falsely announced to the world, with intent to deceive and allay fears of aggressive intentions, that they would respect the territorial limitations of the Versailles Treaty and comply with the Locarno Pact."

As a part of their programme to weaken resistance in possible Enemy States, the Nazis followed a policy of making false assurances, thereby tending to create confusion and a false sense of security. Thus on the same date on which Germany renounced the armament provisions of the Versailles Treaty, Hitler announced the intention of the German Government to respect the territorial limitations of Versailles and Locarno.

I offered in evidence this morning, as exhibit USA 38, our document 2288-PS, the pertinent volume of the issue of the Volkischer Beobachter containing Hitler's speech in the Reichstag on that date.

In that speech he said:-

"Therefore, the Government of the German Reich shall absolutely respect all other articles pertaining to the co-operation "Euzammenleben" really meaning the living together in harmony of the various nations, including territorial agreements. Revisions which will be unavoidable as time goes by, it will carry out by way of a friendly understanding only.

The Government of the German Reich has the intention not to sign any treaty which it believes itself not to be able to fulfil. However, it will live up to every treaty signed voluntarily even if it was composed before this Government took over. Therefore it will in particular adhere to all the allegations under the Locarno Pact, as long as other partners of the pact also adhere to it."

For convenient reference, the territorial limitations in the Locarno and Versailles Treaties, include the following:-

The Rhine Pact of Locarno, 16th October, 1935, Article 1:-

"The High Contracting Parties, collectively and severally, guarantee, in the manner provided in the following Articles ; the maintenance of the territorial status quo, resulting from the frontiers between Germany and Belgium, and between Germany and France, and the inviolability of the said frontiers, as fixed by, or in pursuance of the Treaty of Peace, signed at Versailles, on 28th June, 1919, and also the observance of the stipulations of Articles 42 and 43 of the said Treaty, concerning the demilitarised zone."

That has reference, of course, to the demilitarised zone of the Rhineland.

Then from the Versailles Treaty, 28th June, 1919, Article 42

"Germany is forbidden to maintain or construct any fortifications, either on the left bank of the Rhine or on the right bank, to the West of the line drawn fifty kilometres to the East of the Rhine.

Article 43: In the area defined above, the maintenance and the assembly of armed forces, either permanently or temporarily and military manoeuvres of any kind, as well as the upkeep of all permanent works for mobilisation, are in the same way forbidden."

The next allegation of the indictment (f):

"On 7th March, 1936, they reoccupied and fortified ,he Rhineland, in violation of the Treaty of Versailles and the Rhine Pact of Locarno of 16th October, 1925, and falsely announced to the world that 'we have no territorial demands to make in Europe.' "

The demilitarised zone of the Rhineland obviously was a sore wound with the Nazis ever since its establishment, after World War I. Not only was this a blow to their increasing pride, but it was a bar to any effective strong position which Germany might want to take on any vital issues. In the event of any sanctions against Germany, in the form of military action, the French and other Powers would get well into Germany, East of the Rhine, before any German resistance could even be put up. Therefore, any German plans to threaten or breach international obligations or for any kind of aggression, required the preliminary reoccupation and refortification of this open Rhineland territory. Plans and preparations for the reoccupation and refortification of the Rhineland started very early.

We have a document, a German captured document, in German script, which we identify as C-139, and which appears to be signed in the handwriting of Blomberg. I offer it in evidence as exhibit USA 53.

The document deals with what is called "Operation Schulung," meaning schooling, or training. It is dated 2nd May, 1935, and even refers to prior Staff discussions on the subject. It is addressed to the Chief of the Army Command, who at that time, I believe, was Fritsch; the Chief of the Navy High Command, Raeder ; and the Reich Minister for Air, Goering.

It does not use the name "Rhineland" and does not, in terms, refer to it. It is our view that it was a military plan for the military reoccupation of the Rhineland, in violation of the Treaty of Versailles and the Rhine Pact of Locarno.

I read from the first part of the document which is headed "Top Secret."

For the operation, suggested in the last Staff Talks of the Armed Forces, I lay down the code name "Schulung" (training).

The supreme direction of operation 'Schulung' rests with the Reich Minister of Defence as this is a joint undertaking of the three services.

Preparations for the operation will begin forthwith according to the following directives:-

I. General.

(1) The operation must, on issue of the code word "Carry out Schulung," be executed by a surprise blow at lightning speed. Strictest secrecy is necessary in the preparations and only the very smallest number of officers should be informed and employed in the drafting of reports, drawings, etc., and these officers only in person.

(2) There is no time for mobilisation of the forces taking part. These will be employed in their peace-time strength and with their peace-time equipment.

(3) The preparation for the operation will be made without regard to the present inadequate state of our armaments. Every improvement of the state of our armaments will make possible a greater measure of preparedness and thus result in better prospects of success."

The rest of the Order deals with military details and I think it is unnecessary to read it.

There are certain points, in the face of this Order, which are inconsistent with any theory that it was merely a training order, or that it might have been defensive in nature. The operation was to be carried out as a surprise blow at lightning speed (Schlagartig als Ueberfall).

The Air Forces were to provide support for the attack. There was to be reinforcement by the East Prussian division. Furthermore, this document is dated 2nd May, 1935, which is about six weeks after the promulgation of the Conscription Law on 16th March, 1935, and so it could hardly have been planned as a defensive measure against any expected sanctions which might have been applied by reason of the passage of the Conscription Law.

Of course the actual reoccupation of the Rhineland did not take place until 7th March, 1936, so that this early plan must necessarily have been totally revised to suit the existing conditions and specific objectives. As I say, although the plan does not mention the Rhineland, it has all of the indications of a Rhineland Operation Plan. That the details of this particular plan were not ultimately the ones that were carried out in reoccupying the Rhineland, does not at all detract from the vital fact that, as early as 2nd May, 193S, the Germans had already planned that operation, not merely as a Staff plan but as a definite operation. It was evidently not on their timetable to carry out the operation so soon if it could be avoided. But they were prepared to do so, if necessary, to resist French sanctions against their Conscription Law.

It is significant to note that the date of this document is the same as the date of the signature of the Franco-Russian Pact, which the Nazis later asserted as their excuse for the Rhineland reoccupation.

The military orders on the basis of which the Rhineland reoccupation was actually carried into execution, on 7th March, 1936, were issued on 2nd March,

1936, by the War Minister and Commander-in-Chief of the Armed Forces, Blomberg, and addressed to the Commander-in-Chief of the Army, Fritsch, the Commander-in-Chief of the Navy, Raeder, and Air Minister and C.-in-C. of the Air Force, Goering. We have that order signed by Blomberg, headed, as usual, "Top Secret," identified by us as document C-159. I offer it in evidence as exhibit USA 54.

The German copy of that document bears the defendant Raeder's initial in green pencil, with a red pencil note "To be submitted to the C-in-C of the Navy."

The first part of the Order reads:-

"Supreme Command of the Navy:

The Fuehrer and Reich Chancellor has made the following decision:

By reason of the Franco-Russian alliance, the obligations accepted by Germany in the Locarno Treaty, as far as they apply to Articles 42 and 43, of the Treaty of Versailles which referred to the demilitarised zone, are to be regarded as obsolete.

2. Sections of the Army and Air Force will therefore be transferred simultaneously in a surprise move to garrisons of the demilitarised zone. In this connection, I issue the following orders:"

There follow the detailed orders for the military operation.

We also have the orders for Naval co-operation. The original German document which we have identified as C-194, was issued on 6th March, 1936, in the form of an order on behalf of the Reich Minister for War, Blomberg, signed by Keitel, and addressed to the Commander-in-Chief of the Navy, Raeder, setting out detailed instructions for the Commander-in-Chief of the Fleet and the Admirals commanding the Baltic and North Sea. I offer the document in evidence as exhibit USA 55.

The short covering letter is as follows:

"To C-in-C Navy:

The Minister has decided the following after the meeting:-

1. The inconspicuous air reconnaissance in the German bay, not over the line Texel-Doggerbank, from midday on Z- Day onward, has been approved. C-in-C Air Force will instruct the air command VI from midday 7th March to hold in readiness single reconnaissance aircraft to be at the disposal of the C-in-C Fleet.

2. The Minister will reserve the decision to set up a U- boat reconnaissance on line, until the evening Of 7th March. The Immediate transfer of U-boats from Kiel to Wilhelmshafen has been approved.

3. The proposed advance measures for the most part exceed Degree of Emergency A, and therefore are out of the question as the first counter-measures to be taken against military preparations of neighbouring States. It is far more essential to examine the advance measures included in Degree of Emergency A, to see whether one or other of the especially conspicuous measures could not be omitted."

That is signed "Keitel."

The rest of the documents are detailed naval orders, operational orders, and I think I need not read further.

For the historical emphasis of this occasion, Hitler made a momentous speech on 7th March, 1936. I have the volume of the "Volkischer Beobachter," Berlin, Sunday, 8th March, 1936, our document 2289-PS, which I offer in evidence as exhibit USA 56.

This is a long speech which the world remembers and of which I shall only read a short portion.

"Men of the German Reichstag! France has replied to the repeated friendly offers and peaceful assurances made by Germany, by infringing the Rhine-Pact through a military alliance with the Soviet Union, exclusively directed against Germany. In this manner, however, the Locarno-Rhine-Pact has lost its inner meaning and ceased in practice to exist. Consequently, Germany regards herself, for her part, as no longer bound by this dissolved Treaty. The German Government are now constrained to face the new situation created by this alliance, a situation which is rendered more acute by the fact that the French-Soviet Treaty has been supplemented by a Treaty of Alliance between Czechoslovakia and the Soviet Union exactly parallel in form. In accordance with the fundamental right of a nation to secure its frontiers and ensure its possibilities of defence, the German Government have to-day restored the full and unrestricted sovereignty of Germany in the demilitarised zone of the Rhineland."

The whole matter of the German re-occupation of the demilitarised zone of the Rhineland caused extensive international repercussions. As a result of the protests lodged with the League of Nations, the Council of the League made an investigation and announced the following finding, of which I ask the Tribunal to take judicial notice, as being carried in the League of Nations Monthly Summary, March, 1936, Volume 6, page 78, and it is also quoted in an article by Quincy Wright, in the American journal of International Law, page 487, 1936.

The finding is this:-

"That the German Government has committed a breach of Article 43 of the Treaty of Versailles, by causing On 7th March, 1936, military forces to enter and establish themselves in the demilitarised zone, referred to in Article 42 and the following articles of that Treaty, and in the Treaty of Locarno. At the same time, on 7th March, 1936, as the Germans reoccupied the Rhineland in flagrant violation of the Versailles and Locarno Treaties, they again tried to allay the fears of other European powers, and lead them into a false sense of security, by announcing to the world 'We have no territorial demands to make in Europe.'"

That appears in this same speech of Hitler's, which I have offered in evidence as exhibit USA 56, which is document 2369-PS. The language will be found on page 6, column 1, "We have no territorial claims to make in Europe. We know above all that all the tensions resulting either from false territorial settlements or from the disproportion of the numbers of inhabitants to their living spaces cannot, in Europe, be solved by war."

Most of the acts set forth in the paragraph of the Indictment, which I have been discussing, do not, I think, need judicial proof, because they are historical facts. We have been able to bring you a number of interesting documents, illuminating that history. The existence of prior plans and preparations is indisputable from the very nature of things. The method and sequence of these plans and their accomplishment are clearly indicative of the progressive and increasingly aggressive character of the Nazi objectives, international obligations and considerations of humanity notwithstanding.

The detailed presentation of the violations of Treaties and International Law will be presented by our British colleagues, in support of Count Two of the Indictment.

In clear relief there is shown the determination of the Nazi conspirators to use whatever means were necessary to abrogate and overthrow the Treaty of Versailles and its restrictions upon the military armament and activity of Germany. In this process, they conspired and engaged in secret rearmament and training, in the secret production of munitions of war, and they built up an air force. They withdrew from the International Disarmament Conference and the League of Nations on 14th October, 1933. They instituted universal military service on 16th March, 1935. On 21st May, 1935, they falsely announced that they would respect the territorial limitations of Versailles and Locarno. On 7th March, 1936, they re-occupied and fortified the Rhineland and at the same time, falsely announced that they had no territorial demands in Europe.

The objectives of the conspirators were vast and mighty, requiring long and extensive preparations. The process involved the evasion, circumvention and violation of international obligations and Treaties: They stopped at nothing.

The accomplishment of all those things, together with getting Versailles out of the way, constituted an opening of the gates toward the specific aggressions which followed.

I pass next, if the Tribunal please, to the presentation of the story of the aggression against Austria. I do not know whether your Honour desires me to start on that or not. I am perfectly willing to do so.

THE PRESIDENT: Are you going to use this volume of documents marked "H" to-morrow?

MR. ALDERMAN: There will be a new one marked "N."

THE PRESIDENT: The Tribunal will adjourn until 10.00 o'clock to-morrow morning.

(The Tribunal adjourned until 28th November, 1945, at 10.00 hours.)

SEVENTH DAY:
Wednesday, 28th November, 1945

THE PRESIDENT: I call upon Counsel for the United States.

MR. ALDERMAN: May it please the Tribunal, at this point we distribute document book lettered "N," which will cover the next phase of the case as it will be presented. Of the five large phases of aggressive warfare, which I undertake to present to the Tribunal, I have now completed the presentation of the documents on the first phase, the phase lasting from 1933 to 1936, consisting of the preparation for aggression.

The second large phase of the programme of the conspirators for aggression lasted from approximately 1936 to March, 1939, when they had completed the absorption of Austria and the occupation of all of Czechoslovakia. I again invite the Court's attention to the chart on the wall, at which you may be interested in glancing from time to time as the presentation progresses.

The relevant portions of the Indictment to the present subject are set forth in Sub-section 3, under Section IV (F), appearing at Pages 7 and 8 of the printed English text. This portion of the Indictment is divided into three parts: First, the 1936 to 1938 phase of the plan, planning for the assault on Austria and Czechoslovakia; second, the execution of the plan to invade Austria, November 1937 to March 1938; third, the execution of the plan to invade Czechoslovakia, April 1938 to March 1939.

As I previously indicated to the Tribunal, the portion of the Indictment headed "(a) Planning for the assault on Austria and Czechoslovakia," is proved for the most part by document 386-PS, which I introduced on Monday as exhibit USA 25. That was one of the handful of documents with which I began my presentation of this part of the case. The minutes taken by Colonel Hoszbach of the meeting in the Reich Chancellery on 5th November, 1937, when Hitler developed his political last will and testament, reviewed the desire of Nazi Germany for more room in Central Europe, and made preparations for the conquest of Austria and Czechoslovakia as a means of strengthening Germany for the general pattern of the Nazi conspiracy for aggression.

I shall present the materials on this second, or Austrian phase of aggression, in two separate parts. I shall first present the materials and documents relating to the aggression against Austria. They have been gathered together in the document book, which has just been distributed. Later I shall present the materials relating to the aggression against Czechoslovakia. They will be gathered in a separate document book.

First, the events leading up to the autumn of 1937, and the strategic position of the National Socialists in Austria. I suggest at this point, if the Tribunal please, that in this phase we see the first full flowering of what has come to be known as "fifth column" infiltration techniques in another country; and first under that, the National

Socialist aim of absorption of Austria.

In order to understand more clearly how the Nazi conspirators proceeded after the meeting of 5th November, 1937, covered by the Hoszbach minutes, it is advisable to review the steps which had already been taken in Austria by the Nazi Socialists of both Germany and Austria. The position which the Nazis had reached by the fall of 1937 made it possible for them to complete their absorption of Austria much sooner, and with much less cost than had been contemplated at the time of the meeting covered by the Hoszbach minutes.

The acquisition of Austria had long been a central aim of the German National Socialists. On the first page of "Mein Kampf," Hitler said, "German Austria must return to the Great German Motherland," and he continued by stating that this purpose of having common blood in a common Reich could not be satisfied by a mere economic union. Moreover, this aim of absorption of Austria was an aim from 1933 on, and was regarded as a serious programme, which the Nazis were determined to carry out.

At this point, I should like to offer in evidence our document 1760-PS, which, if admitted, would be exhibit USA 57. This document is an affidavit executed in Mexico City on 28th August of this year by George S. Messersmith, United States Ambassador, now in Mexico City. Before I quote from a part of Mr. Messersmith's affidavit, I should like to point out briefly that Mr. Messersmith was Consul-General of the United States of America in Berlin from 1930 to the late spring of 1934. He was then made American Minister in Vienna, where he stayed until 1937.

In this affidavit he states that the nature of his work brought him into frequent contact with German Government officials, and he reports it that the Nazi Government officials, with whom he had contact, were on most occasions amazingly frank in their conversation and made no concealment of their aims.

If the Court please, this affidavit, which is quite long, presents a somewhat novel problem of treatment in the presentation of this case. In lieu of reading the entire affidavit into the record, I should like, if it might be done in that way, to offer in evidence, not merely the English original, but also a translation into German, which has been mimeographed.

THE PRESIDENT: Mr. Alderman, some of the Tribunal's documents are not marked with the 'PS " number, which makes it very difficult to find.

MR. ALDERMAN: They are marked in pencil at the foot.

THE PRESIDENT: Well, some of them are not.

MR. ALDERMAN: Oh!

THE PRESIDENT: I wonder if you have a copy of the book, which is numbered.

MR. ALDERMAN: If we could borrow the set that is not numbered, we could number it.

This translation of the affidavit into German has been distributed to counsel for the defendants.

DR. KUBUSCHOK (Counsel for defendant von Papen): An affidavit has just been turned over to the Court, an affidavit of a witness who is obtainable. The contents of the affidavit contains so many subjective opinions of the witness that it seems preferable to hear the witness personally in this matter.

I should like to take this occasion to ask for a decision, as a matter of principle, as to whether that which a witness can present in person may instead be presented in the form of an affidavit; in other words, a witness who can be reached should be brought in instead of an affidavit.

MR. ALDERMAN: If the Tribunal please, I should like to be heard briefly on the matter. May I be heard?

THE PRESIDENT: You have finished what you had to say, I understand.

DR. KUBUSCHOK: Yes.

THE PRESIDENT: Very well, we will hear Mr. Alderman.

MR. ALDERMAN: May it please the Tribunal, I recognise, of course, the inherent weakness of an affidavit as evidence where the witness is not present, not subject to cross- examination. Mr. Messersmith is an elderly gentleman. He is not in good health. It was entirely impracticable to try to bring him here; otherwise we should have done so.

I remind the Court of Article 19 of the Charter:

"The Tribunal shall not be bound by technical rules of evidence. It shall adopt and apply, to the greatest possible extent, expeditious and non-technical procedure, and shall admit any evidence which it deems to have probative value."

Of course, the Court would not treat anything in an affidavit such as this as having probative value unless the Court deemed it to have probative value; and if the defendants have countering evidence, which is strong enough to overcome whatever is probative in this affidavit, the Court will treat the probative value of all the evidence in accordance with this provision of the Charter.

By and large, this affidavit and another affidavit by Mr. Messersmith, which we shall undertake to present, covers background material, which is a matter of historical knowledge, of which the Court could take judicial knowledge. Where he does quote these amazingly frank expressions by Nazi leaders, it is entirely open to any of them, who may be quoted, to challenge what is said, or to tell your Honours what they conceive to be what they said. In any event, it seems to me that the Court can accept an affidavit of this character, made by a well-known American diplomat, and give it whatever probative value it seems to have to the Court.

On the question of reading the whole thing, the whole affidavit, I understand the ruling of the Court, that only those parts of documents which are quoted into the record, will be considered in the record, to have been based upon the necessity of giving the German Counsel knowledge of what was being used. As to these affidavits, we have furnished them with complete German translations, so that it seems to us that a different rule might obtain where that has been done.

THE PRESIDENT: Mr. Alderman, have you finished with what you have to say?

MR. ALDERMAN: Yes.

DR. KUBUSCHOK: The representative of the prosecution takes the point of view that the age and state of health of the witness makes it impossible to summon him as a witness. I do not know the witness personally, and consequently am not in a position to state to what extent he is actually incapacitated. Nevertheless, I have profound doubts regarding the presentation of such evidence of such an old and incapacitated person. I am speaking now not about Mr. Messersmith, but I should like to open the question to what extent the state of health of a witness determines whether or not a person can be heard by this Court.

It is important to know what questions, in toto, were put to the witness, since an affidavit only reiterates the answers to the questions which were put to the person. Very often conclusions can be drawn from questions, which were not in fact put to the witness. It is here a question of evidence on the basis of an affidavit, and for that reason we are not in a position to assume, with absolute certainty, that the evidence of the witness is complete.

I am not of the opinion of the prosecution that in this case there are being introduced two pieces of evidence of different value: namely, on the one hand the evidence of a witness, and on the other hand the evidence as laid down in an affidavit. The situation is rather this: That either the evidence is sufficient, or it is not. I think the Tribunal should confine itself to complete evidence.

MR. ALDERMAN: May it please the Tribunal, I want -

THE PRESIDENT: Yes Mr. Alderman, did you wish to add anything?

MR. ALDERMAN: I wish to make this correction, perhaps, of what I had said.

I did not mean to leave the implication that Mr. Messersmith is in any way incapacitated. He is an elderly man, about 70 years old. He is on active duty in Mexico City, and the main difficulty is that we didn't feel that we could take him away from his duties in that post and make him undergo a long trip at his age.

THE PRESIDENT: That's all, is it?

MR. ALDERMAN: Yes.

THE PRESIDENT: The Tribunal has considered the objection which has been raised and, in view of the powers which the Tribunal has under Article 19 of the Charter, which provides that the Tribunal shall not be bound by technical rules of evidence, but shall adopt and apply to the greatest possible extent expeditious and non-technical procedure, and shall admit any evidence which it deems to have probative value - in view of those provisions - the Tribunal holds that affidavits can be presented, and that in the present case it is a proper course. The question of the probative value of an affidavit as compared with a witness who has been cross-examined would, of course, be considered by the Tribunal and if, at a later stage, the Tribunal thinks the presence of a witness is of extreme importance, the matter can be reconsidered. And the Tribunal would add this: That if the defence wish to put interrogatories to the witness, they will be at liberty to do so.

MR. ALDERMAN: I offer then our document 1760-PS as exhibit USA 57, affidavit by George S. Messersmith; and rather than read the entire affidavit by George S. Messersmith, unless the Court wish me to do so, I had intended to paraphrase the substance of what it covers at various parts of the affidavit.

THE PRESIDENT: The Tribunal thinks it would be better, and that you must adhere to the rule which we have laid down, that only what is read in the Court will form part of the record.

MR. ALDERMAN: I shall read then, if this Tribunal please, on the third page of the English mimeograph; to identify it, it is the fourth paragraph, following a list of names headed by President Miklas of Austria and Chancellor Dollfuss:

"From the very beginnings of the Nazi Government, I was told by both high and secondary Government officials in Germany -"

THE PRESIDENT: Will you tell us again which page you are on?

MR. ALDERMAN: Page 3 of the English version, the fourth paragraph below the list of names. There are two Messersmith affidavits and counsel is confused between the two, I think.

"From the very beginnings of the Nazi Government, I was told by both high and secondary Government officials in Germany that incorporation of Austria into Germany was a political and economic necessity, and that this incorporation was going to be accomplished 'by whatever means were necessary.' Although I cannot assign definite times and places, I am sure that at various times and places, every one of the German officials whom I have listed earlier in this statement told me this, with the exception of Schacht, von Krosigk and Krupp von Bohlen. I can assert that it was fully understood, by everyone in Germany who had any knowledge whatever of what was going on, that Hitler and the Nazi Government were irrevocably committed to this end, and the only doubt which ever existed in conversations or statements to me was how and when."

And in connection with that paragraph, I invite your attention to the list of German officials to whom he refers on page 2 of the affidavit; and they are listed as Hermann Goering, General Milch, Hjalmar Schacht, Hans Frank, Wilhelm Frick, Count Schwerin von Krosigk, Joseph Goebbels, Richard Walter Darre, Robert Ley, Hans Heinrich Lammers, Otto Meissner, Franz von Papen, Walther Funk, General Wilhelm Keitel, Admiral Erich von Raeder, Admiral Karl Donitz, Dr. Bohle, Dr. Stuckert, Dr. Krupp von Bohlen and Dr. Davidson. Now, what the affidavit states is that he was sure that at various times and places, everyone of those listed German officials had made these statements to him, with the exception of Schacht, von Krosigk and Krupp von Bohlen. Continuing with the next paragraph :

"At the beginnings of the Nazi regime in 1933, Germany was, of course, far too weak to permit any open threats of force against any country, such as the threats which the Nazis made in 1938- Instead it was the avowed and declared policy of the Nazi Government to accomplish the same results which they later accomplished, through force, by the methods which had proved so successful for them in Germany: Obtain a foothold in the Cabinet, particularly in the Ministry of the Interior, which controlled the police, and then quickly eliminate the opposition elements. During my stay in Austria, I was told on any number of occasions by Chancellor Dollfuss, Chancellor Schuschnigg, President Miklas, and other high officials of the Austrian Government, that the German Government kept up constant and unceasing pressure upon the Austrian Government to agree to the inclusion of a number of ministers with Nazi orientation. The English and French ministers in Vienna, with whom I was in constant and close contact, confirmed this information through statements which they made to me of conversations which they had with high Austrian officials."

I shall read other portions of the affidavit as the presentation proceeds. On this question of pressure used against Austria, including terror and intimidation, culminating in the unsuccessful "putsch" of 25th July, 1934, to achieve their ends the Nazis used various kinds of pressure. In the first place, they used economic pressure. A law Of 24th March, 1933, German law, imposed a prohibitive 1,000 Reichsmark penalty on trips to Austria, and brought great hardship to that country, which relied very heavily on its tourist trade. For that I cite the Reichsgesetzblatt, 1933, Roman I, page 311, and ask the court to take judicial notice of that German law.

The Nazis used propaganda and they used terroristic acts, primarily bombings. Mr. Messersmith's affidavit, document 176o-PS, from which I have already read, goes into some detail with respect to these outrages. I read again from page 4 of the affidavit, the English version, the second paragraph on the page :

"The outrages were an almost constant occurrence, but there were three distinct periods during which they rose to a peak.

During the first two of these periods, in mid-1933, and in early 1934, I was still in Berlin. However, during that period I was told by high Nazi officials in conversation with them that these waves of terror were being instigated and directed by them. I found no concealment in my conversations with high Nazi officials of the fact that they were responsible for these activities in Austria. These admissions were entirely consistent with the Nazi thesis that terror is necessary, and must be used to impose the will of the Party not only in Germany but in other countries. I recall specifically that General Milch was one of those who said frankly that these outrages in Austria were being directed by the Nazi Party, and expressed his concern with respect thereto and his disagreement with this definite policy of the Party."

And the next paragraph:-

"During the wave of terroristic acts in May and June, 1934, I had already assumed my duties as American Minister in Vienna. The bomb outrages during this period were directed primarily at railways, tourist centres and the Catholic Church, which latter, in the eves of the Nazis, was one of the strongest organisations opposing them. I recall, however, that these outrages diminished markedly for a few days during the meeting of Hitler and Mussolini at Venice in mid-June, 1934. At that time Mussolini was strongly supporting the Austrian Government and was strongly and deeply interested in maintaining Austrian independence and sovereignty, and in keeping down Nazi influence and activity in Austria. At that time also Hitler could not afford an open break with Mussolini, and undoubtedly agreed to the short cessation of these bomb outrages on the insistence of Mussolini because he, Hitler, wished to achieve as favourable an atmosphere for the meeting between him and Mussolini as possible. The cessation of the bomb outrages during the Hitler-Mussolini conversations was considered by me, and by the Austrian authorities, and by all observers at that time as an open admission on the part of Hitler and the German Government that the outrages were systematically and completely instigated and controlled from Germany."

Then turning to page 7 of the English version, following the line which reads, "Official dispatch from Vienna," dated 26th July, 1934, I quote the following paragraph:-

"In addition to these outrages, the Nazis attempted to bring pressure upon Austria by means of the 'Austrian Legion.' This organisation, a para-military force of several thousand men, was stationed near the Austrian border in Germany as a constant and direct threat of violent action against Austria. It was without any question sanctioned by the Nazi Government of Germany, as it could otherwise not have existed, and it was armed by them. It was made up of Austrian Nazis who had fled from Austria after committing various crimes in that country, and by Austrians in Germany who were attracted by the idle life and pay given by the German authorities."

These terroristic activities of the Nazis in Austria continued until 25th July, 1934. It is a well-known historical fact, of which I ask the Court to take judicial notice, that on that day members of the N.S.D.A.P., the Nazi Party, attempted a revolutionary "putsch" in Austria and killed Chancellor Dollfuss. At this point I should like to invite your attention to the fact that the indictment alleges in Count IV, Crimes against Humanity, paragraph B on page 26 of the English printed text, that the Nazis murdered amongst others Chancellor Dollfuss. I have not available an official authenticated account of the details of that "putsch," but I think that it will suffice if I briefly recall to the Court what is after all a well-known matter of history. On 25th July, 1934, about noon, 100 men dressed in the uniform of the Austrian Army invaded the Federal Chancellery. Chancellor Dollfuss was wounded in trying to escape, being shot twice at close quarters. The Radio Building in the centre of the town was overwhelmed, and the announcer was compelled to broadcast the news that Dollfuss had resigned and that Dr. Rintelen had taken his place as Chancellor. Although the "putsch" failed, the insurgents kept control of the Chancellery building, and agreed to give it up only after they had a safe conduct to the German border. The insurgents contacted the German Minister Dr. Rieth by telephone, and subsequently had private negotiations with him in the building. At about 7 P.M. they yielded the building, but Chancellor Dollfuss breathed his last about 6 p.m., not having had the services of a doctor.

It is also a well-known historical fact that the German government denied all complicity in this "putsch" and in this assassination. Hitler removed Dr. Rieth as Minister on the ground that he had offered a safe conduct to the rebels without making inquiry of the German government, and had thus without reason dragged the German Reich into an internal Austrian affair in public sight.

This statement appears in a letter which Hitler sent to defendant Papen on 26th July, 1934. I shall offer that letter a little later.

Although the German government denied any knowledge or complicity in this "putsch," we think there is ample basis for the conclusion that the German Nazis bear responsibility for these events. It is not my purpose, with respect to this somewhat minor consideration, to review the expansive record in the trial of the Austrian Nazi Planetta and others who were convicted for the murder of Dollfuss.

Similarly I have no intention of presenting to the Court the contents of the Austrian "Braunbuch," issued after 25th July, without which the Court will, I think, take judicial notice.

I should like instead to mention a few brief items which seem to us sufficient for the purpose. I quote again from our document 1760-PS, from the Messersmith affidavit, exhibit USA 57, on page 7, the paragraph in the middle of the page:-

"The events of the 'putsch' of 25th July, 1934, are too well known for me to repeat them in this statement. I need say here only that there can be no doubt that the 'putsch' was ordered and organised by the Nazi officials from Germany through their Organisation in Austria, made up of German Nazis and Austrian Nazis. Dr. Rieth, the German Minister in Vienna, was fully familiar with all that was going to happen and that was being planned. The German Legation was located directly across the street from the British Legation, and the Austrian secret police kept close watch on persons who entered the German Legation. The British had their own secret service in Vienna at the time, and they also kept a discreet surveillance over the people entering the German Legation. I was told by both British and Austrian officials that a number of the men who were later found guilty by the Austrian courts of having been implicated in the 'putsch' had frequented the German Legation. In addition, I personally followed very closely the activities of Dr. Rieth, and I never doubted on the basis of all my information that Dr. Rieth was in close touch and constant touch with the Nazi agents in Austria, these agents being both German and Austrian. Dr. Rieth could not have been unfamiliar with the 'putsch' and the details in connection therewith. I recall, too, very definitely, from my conversations with the highest officials of the Austrian Government after the 'putsch' their informing me that Dr. Rieth had been in touch with von Rintelen, who, it had been planned by the Nazis, was to succeed Chancellor Dollfuss, had the 'putsch' been successful.

It may be that Dr. Rieth was himself not personally sympathetic with the plans for the 'putsch,' but there is no question that he was fully familiar with all these plans, and must have given his assent thereto and connived therein.

As this 'putsch' was so important, and was a definite attempt to overthrow the Austrian government, and resulted in the murder of the Chancellor of Austria, I took occasion to verify at the time for myself various other items of evidence indicating that the 'putsch' was not only made with the knowledge of the German government but engineered by it. I found and verified that almost a month before the 'putsch' Goebbels told Signor Corruti, the Italian Ambassador in Berlin, that there would be a Nazi government in Vienna in a month."

I should also like to offer in evidence Ambassador Dodd's diary, 1933-1938, a book published in 1941, our document 2832 PS, and particularly the entry for 26th July, 1934. We have the book with the page to which I refer, two pages. I should like to offer that portion of the book in evidence as exhibit USA 58, further identified as our document 2832 PS.

Mr. Dodd, then Ambassador to Berlin, made the following observations in that entry. First he noted that in February, 1934, Ernst Henfstaengl advised him that he brought what was virtually an order from Mussolini to Hitler to leave Austria alone and to dismiss and silence Theodor Habicht, the German agent in Munich, who had been agitating for annexation of Austria. On 18th June in Venice, Hitler was reported to have promised Mussolini to leave Austria alone. Mr. Dodd further states, and I quote from his entry Of 26th July, 1934:

"On Monday, 23rd July, after repeated bombings in Austria by Nazis, a boat loaded with explosives was seized on Lake Constance by the Swiss police. It was a shipment of German bombs and shells to Austria from some arms plant. That looks ominous to me, but events of the kind have been so common that I did not report it to Washington."

THE PRESIDENT: Mr. Alderman, we don't seem to have this document. Our document 2832-PS begins 28th July, Thursday.

MR. ALDERMAN: That is right. Yes.

THE PRESIDENT: You began something about Monday, didn't you?

MR. ALDERMAN: I think you misunderstood me. I began reading at a sentence which began on Monday, 23rd July.

THE PRESIDENT: I want to know where that is.

MR. ALDERMAN: Yes, sir. It is in the third paragraph.

THE PRESIDENT: Yes, I see, about twelve lines down.

MR. ALDERMAN: Yes, sir.

"To-day evidence came to my desk that last night, as late as 11 o'clock, the government issued formal statements to the newspapers rejoicing at the fall of Dollfuss and proclaiming the greater Germany that must follow. The German Minister in Vienna had actually helped to form the new cabinet. He had, as we now know, exacted a promise that the gang of Austrian and Nazi murderers should be allowed to go into Germany undisturbed, but it was realised about 12 o'clock that, although Dollfuss was dead, the loyal Austrians had surrounded the Government Palace and prevented the organisation of a new Nazi regime. They held the murderers prisoners. The German Propaganda Ministry therefore forbade publication of the news sent out an hour before, and tried to collect all the releases that had been distributed. A copy was brought to me to-day by a friend.

All the German papers this morning lamented the cruel murder, and declared that it was simply an attack of discontented Austrians, not Nazis. News from Bavaria shows that thousands of Austrian Nazis living for a year in Bavaria on German support had been active for ten days before, some getting across the border contrary to law, all drilling, and making ready to return to Austria. The German propagandist Habicht was still making radio speeches about the necessity of annexing the ancient realm of the Hapsburgs to the Third Reich, in spite of all the promises of Hitler to silence him. But now that the drive has failed and the assassins are in prison in Vienna, the German government denounces all who say there was any support from Berlin.

I think it will be clear one day that millions of dollars and many arms have been pouring into Austria since the spring of 1933. Once more, the whole world is considering and condemning the Hitler regime. No people in all modern history have been quite so unpopular as Nazi Germany. This stroke completes the picture. I expect to read a series of bitter denunciations in the American papers when they arrive about ten days from now."

As I stated before, the German government denied any connection with the "putsch" and the murder of Dollfuss. In this connection, I should like to invite attention to the letter of appointment which Hitler wrote to the defendant von Papen on 26th July, 1934. This letter appears in a standard German reference work "Dokumente der Deutschen Politik," Volume2, at page 83. For convenience we have identified it as document 2799-PS, and a copy translated into English is included in the document book. The defendants may examine the German text in the "Dokumente der Deutschen Politik," a copy of which is at present in my hand, page 83 of Volume 2.

I ask the Court if it will take Judicial notice of this original German typing.

THE PRESIDENT: Can you tell us where it occurs in our document book?

MR. ALDERMAN: It is our document 2799-PS, a letter from Adolf Hitler.

THE PRESIDENT: It appears to come opposite 2510-PS, according to the book.

MR. ALDERMAN: I should like to read this letter which Chancellor Hitler sent to Vice-Chancellor von Papen. I think it will provide us with a little historical perspective and perhaps freshen our recollection of the ways in which the Nazi conspirators worked. In considering Hitler's letter to the defendant von Papen on 26th July, we must bear in mind as an interesting sidelight the widespread reports at that time, and I mention this only as a widespread report, that the defendant von Papen narrowly missed being purged on 30th June, 1934, along with the Nazi Ernst Roehm, and others. The letter from Hitler to von Papen is as follows:-

"Dear Herr von Papen,

As a result of the events in Vienna, I am compelled to suggest to the Reichs-President the removal of the German Minister to Vienna, Dr. Rieth, from his post, because he, at the suggestion of Austrian Federal Ministers and the Austrian rebels respectively, consented to an agreement made by both these parties concerning the safe conduct and retreat of the rebels to Germany without making inquiry of the German Reich Government. Thus the Minister has dragged the German Reich into an internal Austrian affair without any reason.

The assassination of the Austrian Federal Chancellor which was strictly condemned and regretted by the German Government has made the situation in Europe, already fluid, more acute, without any fault of ours. Therefore it is my desire to bring about, if possible, an easing of the general situation, and especially to direct the relations with the German Austrian State, which have been so strained for a long time, into normal and friendly channels again.

For this reason, I request you, dear Herr von Papen, to take over this important task, just because you have possessed, and continue to possess, my most complete and unlimited confidence ever since we have worked together in the Cabinet.

Therefore, I have suggested to the Reichs-President that you, upon leaving the Reich-Cabinet and upon release from the office of Commissioner for the Saar, be called on a special mission to the post of the German Minister in Vienna for a limited period of time. In this position you will be directly subordinate to me.

Thanking you once more for all that you have at one time done for the co-ordination of the Government of the National Revolution, and since then together with us for Germany, I remain,

Yours very sincerely,

Adolf Hitler."

Now let us look at the situation four years later, on 25th July, 1938, after the "Anschluss" with Austria. At that time the German officials no longer expressed regrets over the death of Dr. Dollfuss. They were eager and willing to reveal what the world already knew, that they were identified with and sponsors of the murder of the former Chancellor.

I offer in evidence at this point document L-273, which I offer as exhibit USA 59. That document is a dispatch from the American Consul General, Vienna, to the Secretary of State, dated 26th July, 1938. Unfortunately, through a mechanical slip, this document which is in English in the original, was not mimeographed in English and is not in your document book. However, it was translated into German, and is in the document book which counsel for the defendants have. I read from a photostatic copy of the dispatch :-

"The two high points of the celebration" - here was a celebration - "were the memorial assembly on the 24th at Klagenfurt, capital of the Province of Carinthia, where in 1934 the Vienna Nazi revolt found its widest response, and the march on the 25th to the former Federal Chancellery in Vienna by the surviving members of the SS Standarte 89, which made the attack on the Chancellery in 1934"; a reconstruction of the crime, so to speak. "The assembled thousands at Klagenfurt were addressed by the Fuehrer's Deputy, Rudolf Hess, in the presence of the families of the thirteen National Socialists who were hanged for their part in the July "putsch." The Klagenfurt Memorial Celebration was also made the occasion for the solemn swearing in of the seven recently appointed Gauleiters of this Ostmark. From the point of view of the outside world, this picture of Reichsminister Hess was chiefly remarkable for the fact that after devoting the first half of his speech as expected, to praise of the sacrifices of the men, women, and youth of Austria in the struggle for greater Germany, he then launched into a defence of the occupation of Austria and an attack on the lying foreign Press and on those who spread the idea of a new war." The world was fortunate," declared Hess, "that Germany's leader was a man who would not allow himself to be provoked. The Fuehrer does what is necessary for his people in sovereign calm and labours for the peace of Europe, even though mischief makers, completely ignoring the deliberate threat to the peace of certain small States, distinctly claim that he is a menace to the peace of Europe." The march on the former Federal Chancellery, referring back to the "putsch" of four years before, now the "Reichsstatthalterei," followed the exact route and time schedule of the original attack. The marchers were met at the Chancellery by Reichsstatthalter Seyss-Inquart, who addressed them and unveiled a memorial cabinet from the "Reichsstatthalterei," the "Standarte." That is the SS organisation which made the original attack and which marched on this occasion four years later. From the "Reichsstatthalterei" the Standarte marched from the Old Reich Broadcasting Centre, from which false news of the resignation of Dollfuss had been broadcast, and there unveiled a second memorial tablet. Steinhausen, the present police president of Vienna, was a member of the SS Standarte 89."

Now, that original memorial plaque, if the Court please, to- day is rubble, like so much of Nuremberg, but we found a photograph of it in the National Library in Vienna. I should like to offer that photograph in evidence, taken on this occasion four years later, the Nazi wreath encircling the plaque, the memorial tablet, and with a large wreath of flowers with a very distinct Swastika Nazi symbol laid before the wreath. I offer that photograph in evidence, identified as our 2968-PS. I offer it as exhibit USA 60. You will find that in the document book, and I know of no more interesting or shocking document that you could look at. We call that murder by ratification, celebrating a murder four years later.

As that photograph shows, this plaque which was erected to celebrate this sinister occasion reads: "One hundred and fifty-four German men of the 89th SS Standarte stood up here for Germany on 26th July, 1934. Seven found death at the hands of the hangman." The Tribunal may notice that the number 154 at the top of the plaque is concealed in the photograph by the Nazi wreath surrounding the plaque. I must confess that I find myself curiously interested in this tablet and in the photograph which was taken and carefully filed. The words chosen for this marble tablet, and surely we can presume that they were words chosen carefully, tell us clearly that the men involved were not mere malcontent Austrian revolutionaries, but were regarded as German men, were members of a paramilitary organisation, and stood up here for Germany. In 1934, Hitler repudiated Doctor Rieth because he dragged the German Reich into an internal Austrian affair without any reason. In 1938, Nazi Germany proudly identified itself with this murder, took credit for it, and took responsibility for it. Further proof in the conventional sense, it seems to us, is hardly necessary.

Next the programme culminating in the act of 11th July, 1936. In considering the activities of the Nazi conspirators in Austria between 25th July, 1934, and November, 1937, there is a distinct and immediate point, the act of 11th July, 1936. Accordingly, I shall first review developments in the two-year period, July, 1934, to July, 1936.

First, the continued aim of eliminating Austria's independence, with particular relation to the defendant von Papen's conversation and activity. The first point that should be mentioned is this. The Nazi conspirators pretended to respect the independence and sovereignty of Austria, notwithstanding the aim of Anschluss stated in "Mein Kampf." But in truth and in fact they were working from the very beginning to destroy the Austrian State.

A dramatic recital of the position of defendant von Papen in this regard is provided in Mr. Messersmith's affidavit, from which I have already quoted, and I quote now from page nine of the English copy, the second paragraph.

THE PRESIDENT: What is the number?

MR. ALDERMAN: Document 1760-PS, which is exhibit USA 57.

"That the policy of Anschluss remained wholly unchanged was confirmed to me by Franz von Papen when he arrived in Vienna as German Minister. It will be recalled that he accepted this assignment as German Minister even though he knew that he had been marked for execution in the St. Bartholomew's massacre on 30th June, 1934. When, in accordance with protocol, he paid me a visit shortly after his arrival in Vienna, I determined that during this call there would be no reference to anything of importance, and I limited the conversation strictly to platitudes, which I was able to do as he was calling on me in my office. I deemed it expedient to delay my return call for several weeks in order to make it clear to von Papen that I had no sympathy with, and on the other hand was familiar with the objectives of his mission in Austria. When I did call on von Papen in the German Legation, he greeted me with 'Now you are in my Legation and I can control the conversation.'

In the boldest and most cynical manner he then proceeded to tell me that all of South-East Europe, to the borders of Turkey, was Germany's natural hinterland, and that he had been charged with the mission of facilitating German economic and political control over all this region for Germany. He blandly and directly said that getting control of Austria was to be the first Step. He definitely stated that he was in Austria to undermine and weaken the Austrian Government, and from Vienna to work towards the weakening of the Governments in the other states to the South and South-east. He said that he intended to use his reputation as a good Catholic to gain influence with certain Austrians, such as Cardinal Innitzer, towards that end. He said that he was telling me this because the German Government was firmly resolved on this objective of getting this control of South- eastern Europe and there was nothing which could stop it, and that our own policy and that of France and England was not realistic.

The circumstances were such, as I was calling on him in the German Legation, that I had to listen to what he had to say, and, of course, I was prepared to hear what he had to say although I already knew what his instructions were. I was nevertheless shocked to hear him speak so boldly to me, and when he finished I got up and told him how shocked I was to hear the accredited representative of a supposedly friendly State to Austria admit that he was proposing to engage in activities to undermine and destroy that Government to which he was accredited. He merely smiled and said, of course this conversation was between us, and that he would, naturally, not be talking to others so clearly about his objectives. I have gone into this detail with regard to this conversation as it is characteristic of the absolute frankness and directness with which high Nazi officials spoke of their objectives."

And again, reading from the same document on page ten, beginning at the last paragraph at the bottom of the page:-

"On the surface, however, German activities consisted principally of attempts to win the support of prominent and influential men through insidious efforts of all kinds, including the use of the German Diplomatic Mission in Vienna and its facilities and personnel.

Von Papen as German Minister entertained frequently and on a lavish scale.

He approached almost every member of the Austrian Cabinet, telling them, as several of them later informed me, that Germany was bound to prevail in the long run, and that they should join the winning side if they wished to enjoy positions of power and influence under German control. Of course, openly and outwardly he gave solemn assurance that Germany would respect Austrian independence, and that all that she wished to do was to get rid of elements in the Austrian Government like the Chancellor, Schuschnigg and Starhemberg, as head of the Heimwehr, and others, and replace them by a few nationally minded Austrians, which of course meant Nazis. The whole basic effort of von Papen was to bring about Anschluss.

In early 1935, the Austrian Foreign Minister, Berger-Waldenegg, informed me that in the course of a conversation with von Papen, the latter had remarked 'Yes, you have your French and English friends now, and you can have your independence a little longer.' The Foreign Minister, of course, told me this remark in German, but the foregoing is an accurate translation. The Foreign Minister told me that he had replied to von Papen, 'I am glad to have from your own lips your own opinion which agrees with what your chief has just said in the Saar, and which you have taken such pains to deny.' Von Papen appeared to be terribly upset when he realised just what he had said, and tried to cover his statements, but according to Berger-Waldenegg, kept constantly getting into deeper water.

Von Papen undoubtedly achieved some successes, particularly with men like Glaise-Horstenau and others who had long favoured the 'Grossdeutschtum' idea, but who nevertheless had been greatly disturbed by the fate of the Catholic Church. Without conscience or scruple, von Papen exploited his reputation and that of his wife as ardent and devout Catholics to overcome the fears of these Austrians in this respect."

May I inquire if the Court expects to take a short recess?

THE PRESIDENT: Yes. We will adjourn now for ten minutes.

(A recess was taken.)

THE PRESIDENT: The Tribunal wishes to make it clear, if I did not make if clear when I spoke before, that, if defence counsel wishes to put interrogatories to Mr. Messersmith upon his affidavit, they may submit such interrogatories to the Tribunal in writing for them to be sent to Mr. Messersmith to answer.

DR. KRANZBUEHLER (Counsel for defendant Donitz): I do not know whether my question has yet been answered or whether it has been made known to the President of the Court.

In the testimony of Mr. Messersmith, Donitz' name was mentioned. It appears on page four of the German version. I should like to read the whole paragraph:-

"Admiral Karl Donitz was not always in an amicable frame of mind. He was not a National Socialist when the National Socialists came to power" -

THE PRESIDENT: This passage was not read in evidence, was it?

DR. KRANZBUEHLER: No, only the name was mentioned.

THE PRESIDENT: I don't think the name was mentioned, because this part of the affidavit was not read.

DR. KRANZBUEHLER: The name was read, Mr. President.

THE PRESIDENT: Very well; go on.

DR. KRANZBUEHLER:

"Nevertheless, he became one of the first high officers in the Army and Fleet and was in complete agreement with the concepts and aims of National Socialism."

As an introduction to this paragraph, Mr. Messersmith said, on page 2, the last sentence before the Number 1 -

THE PRESIDENT: Which page are you on?

DR. KRANZBUEHLER: I am reading out of document 1760.

THE PRESIDENT: Page what?

DR. KRANZBUEHLER: Page 2, last sentence before the Number 1.

THE PRESIDENT: Yes.

DR. KRANZBUEHLER:

"Among those whom I saw frequently and to whom I have referred in many of my statements were the following."

Then after Number 16 Donitz' name appears. My client has informed me that he has heard the name Messersmith today for the first time; that he does not know the witness Messersmith, has never seen him, nor has ever spoken to him.

I therefore request that the witness Messersmith be brought before the Court to state when and where he spoke to the defendant Donitz.

THE PRESIDENT: The Tribunal has already ruled that the affidavit is admissible in evidence, that its probative value will of course be considered by the Tribunal, and the defendants' counsel have the right, if they wish, to submit interrogatories for the examination of Messersmith; and of course defendants will have the opportunity of giving evidence when their turn comes, when Admiral Donitz, if he thinks it right, will be able to deny the statements of the affidavit.

DR. KRANZBUEHLER: Thank you.

MR. ALDERMAN: I want to call the Court's attention to a slight mistranslation into German of one sentence of the Messersmith affidavit. In the German translation the word "nicht" crept in when the negative was not in the English. The English statement was:

"I deemed it expedient to delay my return call for several weeks, in order to make it clear to von Papen that I had no sympathy with, and on the other hand was familiar with the objectives of his mission in Austria."

The German text contains the negative:

"Und dass ich anderseits nicht mit den Zielen seiner Berufung in Oesterreich vertraut war."

The "nicht" should not be in the German text.

The continued existence of Nazi organisations was a programme of armed preparedness. The wiles of the defendant represented only one part of the total programme of Nazi conspiracy. At the same time Nazi activities in Austria, forced underground during this period, were carried on.

Mr. Messersmith's affidavit at pages 9 and 10, the English text, discloses the following. Reading from the last main paragraph on page 9:

"Nazi activities, forced underground in this period, were by no means neglected.

The Party was greatly weakened for a time as a result of the energetic measures-

THE PRESIDENT: One moment. The French translation isn't coming through.

MR. ALDERMAN: Apparently it is a mechanical difficulty and not the interpretation.

THE PRESIDENT: Will you try again then

MR. ALDERMAN: Nazi activities, forced underground-

THE PRESIDENT: Wait a moment.

MR. ALDERMAN: I am informed that the French line is electrically dead and that it will take some little time to restore it.

THE PRESIDENT: We think it could be translated to the French member of the Tribunal, but we feel there may be some difficulty with the shorthand writers.

MR. ALDERMAN: That would be the main difficulty, yes, unless the shorthand writer could take one of the transcripts in one of the other languages and put it into French.

THE PRESIDENT: Very well, that seems to be possible. Very well.

MR. ALDERMAN: The French prosecutor may object at not being able to hear.

(Pause: Mr. Alderman then began to speak.)

THE PRESIDENT: Speak up, Mr. Alderman, I couldn't hear.

MR. ALDERMAN: The French prosecutor states that not only would he object to not being able to understand the proceedings, but that the French Press is present and he has an interest in the French Press understanding what is going on.

Colonel Dostert thinks a five-minute recess will enable him to fix it.

THE PRESIDENT: Very well, we will adjourn then.

(A recess was taken.)

MR. ALDERMAN: I was just reading from the bottom of page 9 of the Messersmith affidavit:

"Nazi activities, forced underground in this period, were by no means neglected. The Party was greatly weakened for a time as a result of the energetic measures taken against the 'putsch' and, as a result of the public indignation, reorganisation work was soon begun. In October, 1934, the Austrian Foreign Minister, Berger-Waldenegg, furnished me with the following memorandum which he told me had been supplied to the Austrian Government by a person who participated in the meeting under reference."

I quote the first paragraph of the memorandum:

"A meeting of the chiefs of the Austrian National Socialist Party was held on the 29th and 30th of September, 1934, at Bad Aibling in Bavaria."

Then skipping four paragraphs and resuming on the fifth one:

"The Agents of the Party Direction in Germany have received orders in every Austrian district to prepare lists of all those persons who are known to actively support the present Government, and who are prepared closely to co-operate with it.

When the next action against the Government takes place these persons are be proceeded against just as brutally as all those other persons, without distinction of party, who are known to be adversaries of National Socialism.

In a report of the Party leaders for Austria the following Principles have been emphasised:

A. The taking over of the power in Austria remains the principal duty of the Austrian National Socialist Party. Austria has for the German Reich a much greater significance and value than the Saar. The Austrian problem is the problem. All combat methods are consecrated by the end which they are to serve.

B. We must, on every occasion which presents itself, appear to be disposed to negotiate, but arm at the same time for the struggle. The new phase of the struggle will be particularly serious, and there will be this time two centres of the terror, one along the German frontier and the other along the Yugoslav frontier."

That ends the quotation from the memorandum.

I now proceed with the next paragraph of the affidavit:

"The Austrian Legion was kept in readiness in Germany. Although it was taken back some miles further from the Austrian frontier, it remained undissolved in spite of the assurance which had been given to dissolve it. The Austrian Government received positive information to this effect from time to time, which it passed on to me and I had direct information to the same effect from reliable persons coming from Germany to Vienna who actually saw the Legion."

The fact of the reorganisation of the Nazi Party in Austria is corroborated by a report of one of the Austrian Nazis.

I offer in evidence our document 812-PS, as exhibit USA 61. It contains three parts. First, there is a letter dated 22nd August, 1939, from Dr. Rainer, then Gauleiter at Salzburg to the defendant Seyss-Inquart, then Austrian Reich Minister. That letter encloses a letter dated July 6th, 1939, written by Dr. Rainer to Reich Commissar, Gauleiter Josef Burckel.

DR. LATERNSER (Counsel for defendant Seyss-Inquart): I object to the presentation of the letters contained in document 812. Of course, I cannot object to the presentation of this evidence to the extent that this evidence is to prove that these letters were actually written. However, if these letters are to serve as proof for the correctness of their contents, then I must object to the use of these letters, for the following reason. Particularly, the third document is a letter which, as is manifest from its contents, has a particular bias, for this reason, that in this letter it is explained to what extent the Austrian Nazi Party participated in the Anschluss.

It purports, further, to expose the leading role played by the group.

From the bias that is manifest in the contents of this letter, this letter cannot serve as proof for the facts brought forth in it, particularly since the witness Rainer, who wrote this letter, is available as a witness and, as we have discovered, is at present in Nuremburg.

I object to the use of this letter to the extent it is to be used to prove the correctness of its contents, because the witness who can testify to that is, at the present time, in Nuremburg.

THE PRESIDENT: The Tribunal will hear Mr. Alderman in answer to what has been said.

MR. ALDERMAN: I think perhaps it would be better to read the letter before we argue about the significance of its contents.

THE PRESIDENT: Well, are you relying upon the letter as evidence of the facts stated in it?

MR. ALDERMAN: Yes.

THE PRESIDENT: Whom is the letter from, and whom is it to?

MR. ALDERMAN: The first letter is from one Rainer who was, at that time, Gauleiter at Salzburg, to the defendant Seyss- Inquart, then Reich Minister of Austria.

That letter encloses a letter dated 6th July, 1939, written by Rainer to Reich Commissar and Gauleiter Josef Burckel. In that letter, in turn, Rainer enclosed a report on the events in the N.S.D.A.P. of Austria from 1933 to 11th March, 1938, the day before the invasion of Austria.

I had some other matters in connection with this that I did want to bring to the attention of the Tribunal before it passes judgement upon the admissibility.

THE PRESIDENT: I do not think that the defendant's counsel is really challenging the admissibility of the document; it is the contents of the document.

MR. ALDERMAN: Yes. On that, in the first place, we are advised by defendant's counsel that this man Rainer is in Nuremberg. I would assume he is there.

We have also an affidavit by Rainer stating that what is stated in these communications is the truth. However, it seems to us that the communications themselves, as contemporaneous reports by a Party officer at the time, are much more probative evidence than anything that he might testify before you to-day.

DR. LATERNSER: I have already said that this letter has these characteristics, that is it biased, and that it tends to emphasise and decorate the participation of the Austrian Nazi party in the Anschluss. Therefore, I must object to the use of this letter as objective evidence, in that it was not written with the thought in mind that it would be used as evidence before a court. If the writer had known that, the letter undoubtedly would have been formulated differently.

I believe that the witness is in Nuremberg. In that case - a principle which is a basis for all trial procedure - the witness should be presented to the Court personally, particularly since, in this case, the difficulties that apply in the case of Messersmith do not apply here.

THE PRESIDENT: The Tribunal is of the opinion that the letters are admissible. They were written to and received by the defendant Seyss-Inquart. The defendant can challenge the contents of the letters by his evidence.

If it is true that Rainer is in Nuremberg, it is open to the defendant to apply to the Tribunal for leave to call Rainer in due course. He can then challenge the contents of these letters, both by the defendant Seyss-Inquart's evidence and by Rainer's evidence. The letters themselves are admitted.

MR. ALDERMAN: May it please the Tribunal, I agree quite fully with the statement that, if it had been known that these letters were to be offered in evidence in a court of justice, they very probably would have been differently written. That applies to a great part of the evidence that we shall offer in this case. And I would say that if the photographer who took the photograph of the Memorial Plaque had known that his photographs would be introduced in evidence in a conspiracy case, he probably never would have snapped the shutter.

The letter from Rainer to Burckel indicates that he was asked to prepare a short history of the role of the Party. Perhaps I had better read the covering letter, addressed to the defendant Seyss-Inquart:

"Dear Dr. Seyss,

I have received your letter of 19th August, 1939, in which you asked me to inform you what I know of those matters which, among other, are the subject of your correspondence with Burckel.

I do not wish to discuss sundry talks and all that, or what has been brought to my notice in the course of time by different people. I wish to clarify essentially my own attitude.

On the 5th of July, 1939, I was asked by telephone by the Reich Commissar Gauleiter Burckel if I was in possession of the memorandum of Globus regarding the events of March. I told him that I had not this memorandum and that I never possessed a single part of it, and, further, that I did not then participate in the matter, and did not know its contents. Because of official requests by Burckel, I have entrusted him with a report accompanied by a letter written on the 6th of July.

If Burckel now writes to you that certain statements were confirmed by me, I feel obliged to entrust you with a copy of each of those two documents, which were only written in single originals. I shall specially inform Burckel of this. I connect this with the declaration: that I have given - apart from those written explanations - no confirmations, declarations, or criticism whatsoever regarding you and your attitude and that I have authorised nobody to refer to any statements of mine.

Since the beginning of our collaboration, I have always expressed and represented forcefully my ideas regarding yourself and my opinion of your personality.

This conception of mine was the very basis of our collaboration. The events of February and March have not changed this, especially since I considered the political success of the 11th of March merely as a confirmation of the intentions and convictions which have equally induced both of us to collaborate.

As far as Globus is concerned, you are fully aware of his character, which I judged always and in every situation only by its good side. I believe that you have already talked to Globus about the occurrences between the 11th of March, 1938, and to-day; and I am convinced that he will tell you everything that is bothering him, if you will speak to him about this matter, as is your intention.

With best regards and Heil Hitler!

Yours, Friedl Rainer."

And so Rainer writes his report, which is enclosed with this letter, to show that the Party as a whole is entitled to the glory which is exclusively ascribed to one person, Dr. Seyss- Inquart.

I refer to the third paragraph of the first enclosure, the report to Reich Commissar Gauleiter Josef Burckel:-

"We saw in March and April how a false picture about the actual leadership conditions developed from this fact, which could not be corrected in spite of our attempts to that effect. This was an important factor for the varying moods of Globotschnik who hoped particularly that you would emphasise to Hitler, and also to the public, the role of the party during the events preceding 12th March, 1938. I limited myself to address this verbal and written declaration to party member Hess, and furthermore, to secure the documents about the March days. In addition, I spoke at every available opportunity about the fight of the party. I did not take steps to give just credit to other persons for the glory which was exclusively ascribed to one person, Dr. Seyss- Inquart, and I would not do that, primarily because I appear as a beneficiary, and furthermore, because I believe that I would not gladden Hitler by doing so. I am also convinced that Dr. Seyss-Inquart did not act crookedly, and furthermore that Hitler does not want to commit an act of historical injustice by special preference to his person, but that he is attracted to him personally. It really is of no great account to Hitler if this or that person was more or less meritorious in this sector of the great fight of the movement. If, in the last analysis, by far the greatest part is to be ascribed only to him; he alone will be considered by history as the liberator of Austria. I, therefore, considered it best to accept existing conditions and look for new fruitful fields of endeavour in the party.

If I should be asked to describe - without personal interest - the role of the party according to my best conviction, I am ready to do so at any time. For this reason I promised yesterday to submit to you again a short summary, and to make it available for your confidential use. Of this Letter and of this abbreviated description I retain the sole copy.

Heil Hitler! Rainer."

Now, of course, all of these enclosures went to the defendant Seyss-Inquart, and he had knowledge of the contents of all of them.

It is a fact of history, of which the Court will take judicial notice, that Seyss-Inquart was the original Quisling. It so happened that the Norwegian Seyss-Inquart gave his name to posterity as a meaningful name, but all Quislings are alike.

The Tribunal will observe from this that the Rainer report is hardly likely to be tendentious, as counsel says, or to be prejudiced in favour of the defendant Seyss-Inquart's contribution to the Anschluss. It tends, on the contrary, to show that Seyss-Inquart was not quite so important as he might have thought he was. Even so, Rainer gives Seyss- Inquart credit enough.

The Rainer report further tells of the disorganisation of the Nazi Party in Austria and of its reconstruction. I now quote the second and third paragraphs of the report, appearing on pages 3 and 4 of the English text of 812-PS, which is exhibit USA 61; and I believe it is on pages 1 and 2 of the original German of the report or Bericht, which is the third part of the document:-

"Thus began the first stage of battle, which ended with the July rising of 1934. The decision for the Jul rising was right, the execution of it was faulty. The result was a complete destruction of the organisation; the loss of entire groups of fighters through imprisonment or flight into the 'Alt-Reich,'" - the old kingdom - "and with regard to the political relationship of Germany to Austria, a formal acknowledgement of the existence of the Austrian State by the German Government. With the telegram to Papen, instructing him to reinstitute normal relationships between the two States, the Fuehrer had liquidated the first stage of the battle; the Landesleitung Munich was dissolved, and the party in Austria was left to its own resources.

There was no acknowledged leader for the entire party in Austria. New leaderships were forming in the nine Gaus. The process was again and again interrupted by the interference of the police; there was no liaison between the formations, and frequently there were two, three, or more rival leaderships. The first evident, acknowledged speaker of almost all the Gaus in Autumn 1934 was engineer Reinthaler (already appointed Landesbauernfuehrer - leader of the country's farmers - by Hess). He endeavoured to bring about a political appeasement by negotiations with the Government with the purpose of giving the N.S.D.A.P. legal status again, thus permitting its political activities. Simultaneously, Reinthaler started the reconstruction of the illegal political organisations, at the head of which he had placed engineer Neubacher."

Next are the secret contacts between German officials, including the defendant von Papen, and the Austrian Nazis; the use by the Austrian Nazis of personalities. There are two cardinal factors concerning the Nazi Organisation in Austria which should be borne in mind.

First, although the Fuehrer had, on the surface, cast the Austrian Nazis adrift - as indicated in the document I have just read - in fact, as we shall show, German officials, including von Papen, maintained secret contact with the Austrian Nazis in line with Hitler's desires. German officials consulted and gave advice and support to the organisation of the Austrian Nazis. [Page 228] In the second place, the Austrian Nazis remained an illegal organisation in Austria, organising for the eventual use of force in a so-called emergency. But, in the meantime, they deemed it expedient to act behind front personalities, such as the defendant Seyss-Inquart, who had no apparent taint of illegality in his status in Austria.

Mr. Messersmith relates, in his affidavit, that he got hold of a copy of a document outlining this Nazi programme. I quote from page 8 of document 1760-PS, which is exhibit USA 57, the following:-

"For two years following the failure of the 25th July Putsch, the Nazis remained relatively quiet in Austria. Very few terroristic acts occurred during the remainder of 1934 and, as I recall, in 1935, and most of 1936; this inactivity was in accordance with directives from Berlin, as direct evidence to that effect, which came to my knowledge at that time, proved. Early in January, the Austrian Foreign Minister, Berger-Waldenegg, furnished me with a document which I considered accurate in all respects, and which stated" - quoting from that document:-

"The German Minister here, von Papen, on the occasion of his last visit to Berlin, was received three times by Chancellor Hitler for fairly long conversations, and he also took this opportunity to call on Schacht and von Neurath. In these conversations the following instructions were given to him :

During the next two years nothing can be undertaken which will give Germany external political difficulties. On this ground, everything must be avoided which could awaken the appearance of Germany interfering in the internal affairs of Austria. Chancellor Hitler will, therefore, also for this reason, not endeavour to intervene in the present prevailing difficult crisis in the National Socialist Party in Austria, although be is convinced that order could be brought into the Party at once through a word from him. This word, however, he will, for foreign political reasons, give all the less, as he is convinced that the ends desired by him may be reached in another way. Naturally, Chancellor Hitler declared to the German Minister here, this does not indicate any disinterestedness in the idea of Austria's independence. Also, before everything, Germany cannot for the present withdraw Party members in Austria, and must, therefore, in spite of the very real exchange difficulties, make every effort to bring help to the persecuted National Socialist sufferers in Austria.

As a result, Minister of Commerce Schacht finally gave the authorisation that from then on 200,000 Marks a month were to be set aside for this end (support of National Socialists in Austria). The control and the supervision of this monthly sum was to be entrusted to engineer Reinthaler, who, through the fact that he alone had control over the money, would have a definite influence on the Party followers. In this way it would be possible to end most quickly and most easily the prevailing difficulties in the Austrian National Socialist Party.

The hope was also expressed to Herr von Papen that the recently authorised foundation of German 'Ortsgruppen" of the National Socialist Party in Austria (made up of German citizens in Austria) would be so arranged as not to give the appearance that Germany was planning to interfere in Austrian internal affairs."

The report of Gauleiter Rainer to Reich Commissar Burckel in July of 1939 outlines the further history of the Party and the leadership squabbles following the retirement of Reinthaler.

THE PRESIDENT: Do you think this would be a convenient time to break off until 2 o'clock ?

MR. ALDERMAN: Yes, sir.

THE PRESIDENT: Very well, we will adjourn, then.

(A recess was taken until 1400 hours)

MR. ALDERMAN: May it please the Tribunal, I had just referred again to the report of Gauleiter Rainer to Reich Commissar Burckel in July 1939, which outlines the further history of the Party and the leadership-problem, following the retirement of Reinthaler.

In referring to the situation in 1935, he mentioned some of the contacts with the Reich Government, that is, the German Government, in the following terms. I quote from page 4 of the English text of that report, and I believe from page 4 of the German text: "In August some further arrests took place.."

THE PRESIDENT: Which document are you on?

MR. ALDERMAN: The Rainer Report, which is 812-PS.

THE PRESIDENT: 812?

MR. ALDERMAN: Yes, exhibit USA 61.

"In August some further arrests took place, the victims of which were, apart from the Gauleiters (Gau leaders), also Globotschnik and Rainer. Schattenfroh then claimed, because of an instruction received from the imprisoned Leopold, to have been made Deputy Country Leader. A group led by engineer Raffelsberger had at this time also established connection with departments of the Alt- Reich. Ministry of Propaganda, German Racial Agency, etc.) and made an attempt to formulate a political motto in the form of a programme for the fighting movement of Austria."

And, again, the Rainer report sets forth the situation a little later in 1936. I quote from page 6 of the English text, and I think page 5 of the German text:

"The principles of the construction of the organisation were: The organisation is the bearer of the illegal fight and the trustee of the idea to create a secret organisation, in a simple manner and without compromise, according to the principle of organising an elite to be available to the illegal land-party council upon any emergency. Besides this, all political opportunities should be taken, and all legal people and legal chances should be used without revealing any ties with the illegal organisation. Therefore, co-operation. between the illegal party organisation and the legal political aides was anchored at the top of the party leadership. All connections with the party in Germany were kept secret in accordance with the orders of the Fuehrer. These said that the German State should officially be omitted from the creation of an Austrian N.S.D.A.P.; and that auxiliary centres for propaganda, Press, refugees, welfare, etc., should be established in the foreign countries bordering Austria.

Hinterleitner already contacted the lawyer Seyss- Inquart, who had connection with Dr. Wachter which originated from Seyss-Inquart's support of the July uprising. On the other side, Seyss-Inquart had a good position in the legal field and especially well- established relations with Christian-Social politicians. Dr. Seyss-Inquart came from the ranks of the 'Styrian Heimatschutz' (home defence) and became a party member when the entire 'Styrian Heimatschutz' was incorporated into the N.S.D.A.P. Another personality who had a good position in the legal field was Col. Glaise-Horstenau who had contacts with both sides. The agreement of 11th July, 1936. was strongly influenced by the activities of these two persons."

The Rainer report thus discloses the dual tactics of the Austrian Nazis during this period of keeping quiet and awaiting developments. They were maintaining their secret contacts with Reich officials, and using foreign personalities such as Glaise-Horstenau and Seyss-Inquart. The Nazis made good use of such figures, who were more discreet in their activities and could be referred to as nationalists. They presented, supported, and obtained consideration of demands which could not be negotiated by other Nazis like Captain Leopold.

Seyss-Inquart did not hold any public office until January 1937, when he was made Counsellor of State. But Rainer, describing him as a trustworthy member of the Party through the ranks, of this "Styrian Heimatschutz," points him out as one who strongly influenced the agreement of 11th July, 1936. The strategic importance of that agreement will be considered a little later. Rainer's report, as I have said before, was hardly likely to over-emphasise the significance of Seyss-Inquart's contribution'

That the Nazis, but not the Austrian Government, did well to trust Seyss-Inquart is indicated by the next document. I propose to offer in evidence document 2219-PS, which will be exhibit USA 62. This is a letter dated 14th July, 1939, addressed to Field-Marshal Goering. The document is a typed carbon of the letter. It ends with the "Heil Hitler" termination, and it is not signed, but we think it was undoubtedly written by the defendant Seyss-Inquart. It was the carbon copy found among Seyss-Inquart's personal files, and such carbon copies kept by authors of letters usually are not signed. On the first page of the letter there appears a note in English, not indicated in the partial English translation, reading, "Air Mail, 15th July, 1515 hours, Berlin, brought to Goering's office." The main text of the letter consists of a plea for intercession on behalf of one Muhlmann, whose name we shall meet later, and who, unfortunately, got into Buckel's bad graces. I shall quote the extracted part of the document which has been translated into English, and which starts, I believe, on page 7 of the German text: -

"To the General Field Marshal,

At present in Vienna,

14th July, 1939.

Sir,

If I may add something about myself, it is the following: I know that I am not of an active fighting nature, unless final decisions are at stake. At this time of pronounced activity (Aktivismus in the German) this will certainly be regarded as a fault in my personality. Yet I know that I cling with unconquerable tenacity to the goal in which I believe. That is Greater Germany (Gross Deutschland) and the Fuehrer. And if some people are already tired out from the struggle and some have been killed in the fight, I am still around somewhere and ready to go into action. This, after all, was also the development until the year 1938. Until July 1934, I conducted myself as a regular member of the party. And if I had quietly, in whatever form, paid my membership dues (the first one, according to a receipt, I paid in December 1931), I probably would have been an undisputed, comparatively old fighter and party member of Austria, but I would not have done any more for the union. I told myself in July 1934 that we must fight this clerical regime on its own ground in order to give the Fuehrer a chance to use whatever method he desired. I told myself that this Austria was worth a mass. I have stuck to this attitude with an iron determination because I and my friends had to fight against the whole political church, the Freemasonry, the Jewry, in short, against everything in Austria. The slightest weakness which we might have displayed would undoubtedly have led to our political annihilation; it would have deprived the Fuehrer of the means and tools to carry out his ingenious political solution for Austria, as became evident in the days of March 1938. I have been fully conscious of the fact that I am following a path which is not comprehensible to the masses and also not to my party comrades. I followed it calmly, and would without hesitation follow it again, because I am satisfied that at one point I could serve the Fuehrer as a tool in his work, even though my former attitude even now gives occasion to very worthy and honourable party comrades to doubt my trustworthiness. I have never paid attention to such things because I am satisfied with the opinion which the Fuehrer and the men close to him have of me."

Now, that letter was written to one of the men close to him - to Field Marshal Goering. I think that is enough to demonstrate Seyss-Inquart as one whose loyalty to Hitler, a foreign dictator, and to the aims of the Nazi conspiracy, led him to fight for the Anschluss with all the means at his disposal.

It is appropriate at this time to offer in evidence a document from the defendant von Papen, and to see how he thought the doctrines of National Socialism could be used to effect the aim of the Anschluss. I offer document 2248-PS as exhibit USA 63. This document is a letter from von Papen to Hitler, dated 27th July, 1935. It consists of a report entitled "Review and outlook one year after the death of Chancellor Dollfuss." After reviewing the success that the Austrian Government had had in establishing Dollfuss as a martyr, and his principles as the patriotic principles of Austria, von Papen stated, and I quote the last paragraph of the letter, beginning on page 1-146 of the German text :-

"National Socialism must and will overpower the new Austrian ideology. If to-day it is contended in Austria that the N.S.D.A.P. is only a centralised Reich German party, and therefore unable to transfer the spirit of thought of National Socialism to groups of a different political make-up, the answer must rightly be that the national revolution in Germany could not have been brought about in a different way. But when the creation of the people's community in the Reich is completed, National Socialism could, in a much wider sense than this is possible through the present party organisation - at least apparently - certainly become the rallying point for all racially German units beyond the borders. Spiritual progress in regard to Austria cannot be achieved to-day with any centralised tendency. If this recognition would once and for all be stated clearly from within the Reich, then it would easily become possible to effect a break-through into the front of the New Austria. A Nuremberg Party Day designated as 'The German Day' as in old times, and the proclamation of a National Socialist peoples' front, would be a stirring event for all beyond the borders of the Reich. Such attacks would win us also the particularistic Austrian circles, whose spokesman, the legitimistic Count Dubskv, wrote in his pamphlet about the 'Anschluss': The Third Reich will be with Austria or it will not be at all. National Socialism must win it or it will perish, if it is unable to solve this task."

We have other reports from Papen to Hitler, which I shall offer in evidence presently, showing that he maintained covert contact with the National Socialist groups in Austria. It is certainly interesting that from the very start of his mission, defendant von Papen was thinking of ways and means of using the principle of National Socialism for national Germans outside the border of Germany. Papen was working for the Anschluss, although he preferred to use the principles of National Socialism rather than rely on the party organisation as a necessary means of establishing those principles in the German Reich.

Next we have some assurance and reassurance to Austria. The German Government did not do more than keep up a pretence of non-interference with Austrian groups. It employed the psychological inducement of providing assurances that it had no designs on Austrian independence. If Austria could find hope for the execution of those assurances, she could find her way clear to the granting of concessions and obtain relief from the economic and internal pressure.

I offer document 2247-PS in evidence as exhibit USA 64. It is a letter from von Papen while in Berlin to Hitler, dated 17th May, 1935.

Von Papen's letter indicated to Hitler that a forthright, credible statement by Germany, reassuring Austria, would be most useful for German diplomatic purposes and for the improvement of relationships between Austria and German groups in Austria.

He had a scheme for pitting von Schuschnigg and his Social- Christian forces against Starhemberg, the Vice-Chancellor of Austria, who was backed by Mussolini. Von Papen hoped to persuade von Schuschnigg to ally his forces with the N.S.D.A.P. in order to emerge victorious over Starhemberg. Von Papen indicates that he obtained this idea from Captain Leopold, leader of the illegal National Socialists in Austria.

I quote from his letter, starting at the second paragraph of the second page.

This is von Papen writing to "Mein Fuehrer", Hitler:

"I suggest that we take an active part in this game. The fundamental idea should be to pit von Schuschnigg and his Christian Social forces, who are opposed to a home-front dictatorship, against Starhemberg. The possibility of thwarting the measures arranged between Mussolini and Starhemberg should be afforded to him in such a way that he would submit the offer to the government of a definitive German-Austrian compromise of interests. According to the convincing opinion of the Leader of the N.S.D.A.P. in Austria, Captain Leopold, the totalitarian principle of the N.S.D.A.P. in Austria must be replaced in the beginning by a combination of that part of the Christian elements which favours the Greater Germany idea and the N.S.D.A.P. If Germany recognises the national independence of Austria, and guarantees full freedom to the Austrian national opposition, then, as a result of such a compromise, the Austrian Government would be formed in the beginning by a coalition of these forces. A further consequence of this step would be the possibility of the participation of Germany in the Danube Pact, which would take the sting out of its acuteness due to the settlement of relations between Germany and Austria. Such a measure would have a most beneficial influence on the European situation, and especially on our relationship with England. One may object, that von Schuschnigg will hardly be determined to follow such a pattern, that he will rather in all probability immediately communicate our offer to our opponents. Of course, one should first of all explore the possibility of setting von Schuschnigg against Starhemberg through the use of 'go betweens'. The possibility exists. If von Schuschnigg finally says 'no' and makes our offer known in Rome, then the situation would not be any worse, but, on the contrary, the efforts of the Reich government to make peace with Austria would be revealed - without prejudice to other interests. Therefore, even in the case of refusal, this last attempt would be an asset. I consider it completely possible, that in view of the widespread dislike in the Alpine countries of the pro-Italian policy, and in view of the sharp tensions among the Federal Government (that is Bundesregierung), von Schuschnigg will grasp this last straw - always under the supposition that the offer could not be interpreted as a trap by the opponents, but that it bears all the marks of an actually honest compromise with Austria. Assuming the success of this step, we would again establish our active intervention in Central European politics, which, as opposed to the French, Czech and Russian political manoeuvres, would be a tremendous success, both morally and practically. Since there are only two weeks left to accomplish very much work in the way of explorations and conferences, an immediate decision is necessary. The Reich Army Minister (Reichswehrminister) shares the opinion presented above, and the Reich Foreign Minister (Reichsaussenminister) wanted to discuss it with you, my Fuehrer. Signed, Papen."

In other words, Papen wanted a strong assurance and a credible assurance of the preservation of Austria's independence. As he put it, Germany had nothing to lose, with what she could always call a mere effort at peace, and she might be able to persuade von Schuschnigg to establish an Austrian coalition government, with the N.S.D.A.P. If she did this, she would vastly strengthen her position in Europe. Finally, Papen urged haste.

Exactly four days later, in a Reichstag address, Hitler responded to von Papen's suggestion, and asserted Germany neither intends nor wishes to interfere in the internal affairs of Austria, to annex Austria or to conclude an "Anschluss."

The British will present a document covering that speech. I merely wanted to use one sentence at this point. It is a sentence quite well known to history.

It is appropriate to take notice of this assurance at this point, and to note that for a complexity of reasons, Papen suggested, and Hitler announced, a policy completely at variance with their intentions, which had been, and continued to be, to interfere in Austria's internal affairs and to conclude an "Anschluss."

There was then a temporary continuance of a quiet pressure policy.

On 1st May, 1936, Hitler, in a public speech, blandly branded as a lie any statement that "to-morrow or the day after " Germany would fall upon Austria.

I invite the Court's attention to the version of the speech appearing in the "Volkischer Beobachter SD," that is South Germany, 2nd to 3rd May, 1936, page 3, and translated in our document 2367-PS.

Without offering the document, I ask the Court to take Judicial notice of the statement in that well-known speech. If Hitler meant what he said, it was only in the most literal and misleading sense, that is, that he would not actually fall upon Austria "to-morrow or the day after to- morrow." For the conspirators well knew that the successful execution of their purpose required for a little while longer the quiet policy which they had been pursuing in Austria.

I now offer in evidence our document L-150 - memorandum of conversation between Ambassador Bullitt and the defendant von Neurath, on 18th May, 1936 - as exhibit USA 65. This document unfortunately again appears in your document books in German, as, due to an error, it has not been mimeographed in English. German Counsel have the German copies.

I shall read from it, and at the same time, hand to the interpreter reading in German, a marked copy of a German translation.

I might read one sentence from the first paragraph.

"I called on von Neurath, Minister of Foreign Affairs, on 18th May, and had a long talk on the general European situation."

Then skipping a paragraph I will read straight on, if you will pardon me.

"Von Neurath said that it was the policy of the German Government to do nothing active in foreign affairs until the Rhineland had been digested. He explained that he meant that, until the German fortifications had been constructed on the French and Belgium frontiers, the German Government would do everything possible to prevent, rather than encourage, an outbreak by the Nazis in Austria and would pursue a quiet line with regard to Czechoslovakia.

As soon as our fortifications are constructed," he said, "and the countries of Central Europe realise that France cannot enter German territory, all these countries will begin to feel very differently about their foreign policies and a new constellation will develop."

I then skip two paragraphs.

"Von Neurath then stated that no understanding had been reached between Germany and Italy, and admitted that the demonstrations of friendship between Germany and Italy were mere demonstrations without basis in reality. He went on to say that at the present time he could see no way to reconcile the conflicting interests of Germany and Italy in Austria. He said that there were three chief reasons why the German Government was urging the Austrian Nazis to remain quiet at the present time:

The first was that Mussolini had, to-day, the greater part of his army mobilised on the Austrian border, ready to strike, and that he would certainly strike if he should have a good excuse.

The second reason for urging Austrian Nazis to remain quiet for the present was that the Nazi movement was daily growing stronger in Austria. The youth of Austria was turning more and more towards the Nazis, and the dominance of the Nazi Party in Austria was inevitable and only a question of time.

The third reason was that until the German fortifications had been constructed on the French border, an involvement of Germany in war with Italy might lead to a French attack on Germany."

But even if Germany was not yet ready for open conflict in Austria, its diplomatic position was vastly improved over 1934, a fact which influenced Austria's willingness to make concessions to Germany and to come to terms.

I quote again from the Messersmith affidavit, on page 11 of the English text that is document 1760-PS.

"Developments in the fall of 1935 and the spring Of 1936 gave Germany an opportunity to take more positive steps in the direction of the Nazification of Austria. Italy, which had given Austria assurance of support of the most definite character against external German aggression, and on one occasion, by mobilising her forces, had undoubtedly stopped German aggressive action, which had been planned against Austria, embarked on her Abyssinian adventure. This and the reoccupation of the Rhineland in 1936 completely upset the balance in Europe. It is quite obvious that after Italy had launched her Abyssinian adventure, she was no longer in any position to counter German aggressive moves against Austria."

This weakening of Austria helped to leave the way for the Pact of 11th July, 1936. On 11th July, 1936, the Governments of Austria and Germany concluded an accord. That will be offered in evidence also by the British Delegation.

I merely ask a point that the Tribunal take judicial notice of the fact that such an accord was entered into. The formal part of the agreement on 11th July, 1938, will also be proved by our British colleagues. For convenient reference, it will be found in the document which the British will offer, TC-22, and the substance of it is also contained on pages 11 and 12 of Mr. Messersmith's affidavit, document 1760-PS.

Upon the basis of this fight alone, the agreement looked like a great triumph for Austria. It contains a confusing provision to the effect that Austria in her policy, especially with regard to Germany, would regard herself as a German State, but the other two provisions clearly state that Germany recognises the full sovereignty of Austria and that it regards the inner political order of Austria, including the question of Austria and National Socialism, as an internal concern of Austria upon which Germany will exercise neither direct nor indirect influence. But there was much more substance to to-day's events than appears in the text of the accord. I refer to Mr. Messersmith's summary as set forth on page 12 of his affidavit, document 1760-PS, as follows :-

"Even more important than the terms of the agreement published in the official communique, was the contemporaneous informal understanding, the most important provisions of which were that Austria would :

(1) Appoint a number of individuals enjoying the Chancellor's confidence but friendly to Germany, to positions in the Cabinet;

(2) with the devised give the National opposition a role in the political life of

Austri4, within the framework of the Patriotic Front; and

(3) grant an amnesty for all Nazis, save those convicted of the most serious offences."

This amnesty was duly announced by the Austrian Government, and thousands of Nazis were released, and the first penetration of Deutsche-Nationals into the Austrian Government was accomplished by the appointment of justice Guido Schmidt as Secretary of State for Foreign Affairs and Dr. Edmund Glaise-Horstenau as Minister without portfolio.

I now offer in evidence document 2994-PS, which is an affidavit executed by Kurt von Schuschnigg, Foreign Chancellor of Austria, at Nuremberg, Germany on 19th November, 1945. I offer this as exhibit USA 66. The defendants have received German translations of that evidence.

DR. LATERNSER (Counsel for the defendant Seyss-Inquart): In the name of the accused, Seyss-Inquart, I wish to protest against the presentation of written evidence by the witness von Schuschnigg, for the following reasons: To-day, when a resolution was announced, with respect to the use to be made of the written evidence of Mr. Messersmith, the Court was of the opinion that in a case of very great importance it might possibly take a different view of the matter. With respect to the Austrian conflict, this is such a case, since Schuschnigg is the most important witness. He was the witness who at the time had the office of Federal Chancellor which was affected. In the case of such an important witness, the principle of direct evidence must be adhered to in order that the Court be in a position to ascertain the actual truth in this case. The accused and his defence counsel would feel prejudiced in his defence should direct evidence be circumvented. I must, therefore, uphold my viewpoint since it can be assumed that the witness, von Schuschnigg, will be able to confirm certain facts which are in favour of the accused, Seyss-Inquart.

I, therefore, submit an application to the Court that the written evidence of the witness, von Schuschnigg, be not admitted.

THE PRESIDENT: If you have finished the Tribunal will hear Mr. Alderman.

MR. ALDERMAN: May it please the Tribunal, at this point I am simply proposing to offer this affidavit for the purpose of showing the terms of the secret understanding between the German and Austrian Governments in connection with this accord. It is not with any purpose of incriminating the defendant, Seyss-Inquart, that it is being offered at this point.

DR. LATERNSER: May I complete my application by saying that the witness, von Schuschnigg, on the 19th of November, 1945, was questioned in Nuremberg, and that, if an interrogation on the 19th of November was possible, such a short time later it ought to be possible to call him before the Court, especially as the interrogation before this Court is of special importance.

THE PRESIDENT: The Tribunal will recess now to consider this question.

(A recess was taken.)

THE PRESIDENT: The Tribunal has considered the objection to the affidavit of von Schuschnigg and upholds the objection.

If the prosecution desires to call von Schuschnigg as a witness they can apply to do so. Equally the defence, if they wish to call von Schuschnigg as a witness, can apply to do so. In the event of von Schuschnigg not being able to be produced the question of affidavit-evidence by von Schuschnigg being given will be reconsidered.

MR. ALDERMAN: May it please the Tribunal, in view of the strategy and tactics of the Nazis' concessions as indicated in the portion of the Messersmith affidavit that I read, substantial concessions were made by Austria to obtain Germany's diplomatic formal assurance of Austrian independence and non-intervention in Austrian internal affairs.

The release of employed Nazis presented potential police problems, and as Mr. Messersmith pointed out in a 1934 dispatch to the United States State Department quoted on pages 12 to 13 of his affidavit:-

"Any prospect that the National Socialists might come to power would make it more difficult to obtain effective police and judicial action against the Nazis, for fear of reprisals by the future Nazi Government against those taking action against Nazis even in the performance of duty. The preservation of internal peace in Austria was less independent upon Germany's living up to its obligations under the accord."

Next, Germany's continuing programme of weakening the Austrian Government. In the pact of 11th July, 1936, Germany agreed not to influence directly or indirectly the internal affairs of Austria, including the matter of Austrian National Socialism.

On 16th July, 1936, just five days later, Hitler violated that provision. I quote from document 812-PS, which is exhibit USA 61, the reports of Gauleiter Rainer to Commissar Burckel, all of which were forwarded to the defendant Seyss-Inquart, at page 6 of the English and, I believe, also page 6 of the German version:

"At that time the Fuehrer wished to see the leaders of the party in Austria in order to tell them his opinion on what Austrian National Socialists should do. Meanwhile Hinterleitner was arrested, and Doctor Rainer became his successor and the leader of the Austrian party. On 16th July, 1936, Doctor Rainer and Globoznik visited the Fuehrer at the Obersalzberg, where they received a clear explanation of the situation and the wishes of the Fuehrer. On 17th July, 1936, all illegal Gauleiters met in Anif, near Salzburg, where they received a complete report from Ranier on the statement of the Fuehrer and his political instructions for carrying out the fight. At this same conference the Gauleiters received organisational instructions from Globotschnik and Hiedler."

I am skipping a paragraph from this report in the English version.

"Upon the proposal of Globotschnik, the Fuehrer named Lt. Gen. (Gruppenfuehrer) Keppler as chief of the mixed commission which was appointed, in accordance with the state treaty of 11th July, 1936, to supervise the correct execution of the agreement. At the same time Keppler was given full authority by the Fuehrer for the party in Austria. After Keppler was unsuccessful in his efforts to co-operate with Leopold, he worked together with Doctor Rainer,

Globoznik, Reinthaler as leader of the peasants, Kaltenbrunner (that is the defendant Kaltenbrunner in this case) leader of the SS, and Doctor Jury as deputy leader of the Austrian party, as well as von Glaise-Horstenau and Seyss-Inquart." A new strategy was developed for the Austrian Nazis. Mr. Messersmith describes briefly - and I quote from page thirteen of his affidavit, document 1760-PS: "The sequel of the agreement was the only one which could have been expected in view of all the facts and previous recorded happenings." Active Nazi operations in Austria were resumed under the leadership of a certain Captain Leopold who, as was known definitely, was in frequent touch with Hitler. The Nazi programme was now to form an organisation through which the Nazis could carry on their operations openly and with legal sanction in Austria. There were formerly in Austria several organisations which had a legal basis, but which were simply a device by which the Nazis in Austria could organise and later seek inclusion as a unit in the Patriotic Front. The most important of these was the Ostmaerkische Versin, the Union of the East Mark, the sponsor of which was the Minister of the Interior, Glaise-Horstenau. Through the influence of Glaise-Horstenau and pro-Nazi Neustadter Sturmer, this organisation was declared legal by the court.

I make a specific mention of the foregoing because it shows the degree to which the situation in Austria had disintegrated as a result of the underground and open Nazi activities directed from Germany.

At this point I offer in evidence document 2246-PS as exhibit USA 67, a captured German document, which is a report from von Papen to Hitler, dated 1st September, 1936. This document is most interesting because it indicates von Papen's strategy, after 11th July, 1936, for destroying Austria's independence. Von Papen had taken a substantial step forward with the agreement of 11th July. It should be noted, incidentally, that, after that agreement, he was promoted from Minister to Ambassador. Now his tactics were developed in the following terms, I quote the last three paragraphs of his letter of 1st September, 1936, to the Fuehrer and Reich Chancellor. These three paragraphs are all joined as one paragraph in the English text:

"The progress of normalising relations with Germany at the present time is obstructed by the continued persistence of the Ministry of Security, occupied by the old anti-National Socialistic officials. Changes in personnel are therefore of utmost importance. But they are definitely not to be expected prior to the conference on the abolishing of the Control of Finances at Geneva. The Chancellor of the League has informed Minister von Glaise-Horstenau of his intention to offer him the portfolio of the Ministry of the Interior. As a guiding principle 'Marschroute' (a German word meaning the 'Route of March') I recommend on the tactical side continued, patient, psychological treatment with slowly intensified pressure, directed at changing the regime. The proposed conference on economic relations, taking place at the end of October, will be a very useful tool for the realisation of some of our projects. In discussion with Government officials as well as with leaders of the illegal party - Leopold and Schattenfroh - who conform completely with the agreement of 11th July - I am trying to direct the next developments in such a manner as to aim at corporative representation of the movement in the Fatherland front, but nevertheless refraining from putting National Socialists in important positions for the time being. Such positions are to be occupied only by personalities having the support and the confidence of the movement. I have a willing collaborator in this respect in Minister Glaise- Horstenau."

Citing Papen. To recapitulate, this report by von Papen to Hitler discloses the following plan :

  (a) Obtaining a change in personnel in the Austrian Ministry of Security in due course.
  (b) Obtaining corporative representation of the Nazi movement in the Fatherland front.
  (c) Not putting avowed National Socialists in important positions yet, but using Nationalist personalities.
  (d) Using economic pressure and patient psychological treatment with slowly intensified pressure directed at changing the regime.

My next subject is "Germany's Diplomatic Preparations for the Conquest of Austria."

The programme of the Nazi conspiracy with respect to Austria consisted of weakening that country externally and internally by removing its support from without, as well as by penetrating within. This programme was of the utmost significance, especially since, as the Court will remember, the events Of 25th July, 1934, inside Austria, were overshadowed in the news of the day by the fact that Mussolini had brought his troops to the Brenner Pass, and poised there as a strong protector of his Northern neighbour, Austria.

Accordingly, interference in the affairs of Austria, and steady increase in the pressure needed to acquire control over that country, required removal of the possibility that Italy or any other country would come to her aid. But the foreign policy programme of the conspiracy for the weakening and isolation of Austria was integrated with their foreign policy programme in Europe generally.

I should like, therefore, at this juncture, to digress for a moment from the presentation of evidence bearing on Austria alone, and to consider with the Tribunal the general foreign policy programme of the Nazis. It is not my intention to examine this subject in any detail. Historians and scholars exhausting the archives will have many years of exploring all the details and ramifications of European diplomacy during this fateful decade.

It is, instead, my purpose to mention very briefly the highlights of the Nazis' diplomatic preparation for war.

In this connection I should like to offer to the Tribunal document 2385-PS, a second affidavit of George S. Messersmith executed on 30th August, 1945, at Mexico City. This has been made available to the defendants in German, as well as in English.

This is a different affidavit from document I760-PS, which was executed on 28th August. This second affidavit, which I offer as exhibit USA 68, consists of a presentation of the diplomatic portion of the programme of the Nazi party. To a considerable extent it merely states facts of common knowledge, facts that many people who are generally well- informed already know. It also gives us facts which are common knowledge in the circle of diplomats or of students of foreign affairs. It consists of some eleven mimeographed pages, single-spaced. I read from the third paragraph in the affidavit:-

"As early as 1933, while I served in Germany, the German and Nazi contacts, which I had in the highest and secondary categories, openly acknowledged Germany's ambitions to dominate South-eastern Europe from Czechoslovakia down to Turkey. As they freely stated, the objective was territorial expansion in the case of Austria and Czechoslovakia. The professed objectives in the earlier stages of the Nazi regime, in the remainder of South-eastern Europe, were political and economical control, and they did not at that time speak so definitely of actual absorption and destruction of sovereignty. Their ambitions, however, were not limited to South-eastern Europe. From the very beginnings of 1933, and even before the Nazis came into power, important Nazis, speaking of the Ukraine, freely said that 'it must be our granary' and that 'even with South-eastern Europe under our control, Germany needs and must have the greater part of the Ukraine in order to be able to feed the people of greater Germany.' After I left Germany in the middle of 1934 for my post in Austria, I continued to receive information as to the German designs in South-eastern Europe. In a conversation with von Papen shortly after his appointment as German Minister to Austria in 1934, he frankly stated to me that 'South-eastern Europe to Turkey is "Germany's Hinterland" and I have been designated to carry through the task of bringing it within the fold. Austria is the first on the programme.' As I learned through my diplomatic colleagues, von Papen in Vienna and his colleague von Mackensen in Budapest were openly propagating the idea of the dismemberment and final absorption of Czechoslovakia as early as 1935."

Then, skipping a short paragraph, I resume:-

"Immediately after the Nazis came into power, they started a vast rearmament programme. This was one of the primary immediate objectives of the Nazi regime. As a matter of fact, the two immediate objectives of the Nazi regime, when it came into power, had to be, and were, according to their own statements frequently made to me: first, to bring about the complete and absolute establishment of their power over Germany and the German people, so that they would become in every respect willing and capable instruments of the regime to carry through its ends; and second, the establishment of a tremendous armed power within Germany in order that the political and economic programme in South-eastern Europe and in Europe could be carried through by force if necessary, but probably by a threat of force. It was characteristic that, in carrying through this second aim, they emphasised from the very outset the, building of an over-powering Air Force. Goering and Milch often said to me or in my presence that the Nazis had decided to concentrate on air power as the weapon of terror most likely to give Germany a dominant position, and the weapon which could be developed the most rapidly and in the shortest time."

Skipping to the end of that paragraph, and resuming at the next:-

"At the same time that this rearmament was in progress, the Nazi regime took all possible measures to prepare the German people for war in the psychological sense. Throughout Germany, for example, one saw everywhere German youth of all ages engaged in military exercises, drilling, field manoeuvres, practising the throwing of hand grenades, etc.-. In this connection 1 wrote in an official communication in November, 1933, from Berlin as follows. '. Everything that is being done in the country to-day is with the object of making the people believe that Germany is threatened vitally in every aspect of its life by outside influences and by other countries. Everything is being done to use this feeling to stimulate military training and exercises, and innumerable measures are being taken to develop the German people into a hardy, sturdy race which will be able to meet all comers. The military spirit is constantly growing. It cannot be otherwise. The leaders of Germany to-day have no desire for peace, unless it is a peace which the world would make at the expense of complete compliance with German desires and ambitions. Hitler and his associates really and sincerely want peace for the moment, but only to have a chance to get ready to use force if it is found finally essential. They are preparing their way so carefully that there is not, in my mind, any question but that the German people will be with them when they want to use force, and when they feel that they have the necessary means to carry through their objects."

I quote one further sentence:

"Military preparation and psychological preparation were coupled with diplomatic preparation, designed to so disunite and isolate their intended victims amongst the members of the Little Entente as to render them defenceless against German aggression."

In 1933 the difficulties facing Germany in the political and diplomatic field loomed large. France was the dominant military power on the continent. She had a system of mutual assistance in the West and the East.

The Locarno Pact of 1928, supplemented by the Franco-Belgian alliance, guaranteed the territorial status quo in the West. Yugoslavia, Czechoslovakia and Roumania were allied in the Little Entente and each, in turn, was united with France by Mutual Assistance Pacts. Since 1922, France and Poland likewise had been allied against external aggression. Italy had made plain her special interest in Austrian independence.

Nazi Germany launched a vigorous diplomatic campaign to break up the existing alliances and understandings, to create divisions among the members of the Little Entente and the other Eastern European powers.

Specifically, Nazi Germany countered these alliances with promises of economic gain for co-operating with Germany. To some of these countries she offered extravagant promises of territorial and economic rewards. She offered Corinthia and Austria to Yugoslavia. She offered part of Czechoslovakia to Hungary and part to Poland. She offered Yugoslav territory to Hungary, at the same time that she was offering land in Hungary to Yugoslavia.

As Mr. Messersmith states in his affidavit, that's, document 238S-PS, page 5:-
"Austria and Czechoslovakia were the first on the German programme of aggression. As early as 1934, Germany began to woo neighbours of these countries with the promises of a share in the loot. To Yugoslavia in particular they offered Carinthia. Concerning the Yugoslav reaction, I reported at the time:

'The major factor in the internal situation in the last week has been the increase in tension with respect to the Austrian Nazi refugees in Yugoslavia.. There is very little doubt but that Goering, when he made his trip to various capitals in South-eastern Europe about six months ago, told the Yugoslavs that they would get a part of Carinthia, when a National Socialist Government came into power in Austria.. The Nazi seed sown in Yugoslavia had been sufficient to cause trouble, and there are undoubtedly a good many people there who look with a great deal of benevolence on those Nazi refugees who went to Yugoslavia in the days following July 25.'

Germany made like promises of territorial gains to Hungary and to Poland in order to gain their co- operation or at least their acquiescence in the proposed dismemberment of Czechoslovakia. As I learned from my diplomatic colleagues in Vienna, von Papen and von Mackensen in Vienna and in Budapest in 1935 were spreading the idea of division of Czechoslovakia, in which division Germany was to get Bohemia, Hungary to get Slovakia, and Poland the rest. This did not deceive any of these countries, for they knew that the intention of Nazi Germany was to take all.

The Nazi German Government did not hesitate to make inconsistent promises when it suited its immediate objective. I recall the Yugoslav Minister in Vienna saying to me, in 1934 or 1935, that Germany had made promises to Hungary of Yugoslav territory, while at the same time promising to Yugoslav portions of Hungarian territory. The Hungarian Minister in Vienna later gave me the same information.

I should emphasise here in this statement that the men who made these promises were not only the dyed-in-the- wool Nazis, but more conservative Germans who already had begun to lend themselves willingly to the Nazi programme. In an official dispatch to the Department of State from Vienna, dated 10th October, 1935, I wrote as follows:

'Europe will not get away from the myth that Neurath, Papen and Mackensen are not dangerous people and that they are "diplomats of the old school." They are, in fact, servile instruments of the regime, and just because the outside world looks upon them as harmless, they are able to [Page 240] work more effectively. They are able to sow discord just because they propagate the myth that they are not in sympathy with the regime.'"

I find that last paragraph very important and worthy of emphasis. In other words, Nazi Germany was able to promote these divisions and increase its own aggressive strength by using as its agents in making these promises, men who, on outward appearances, were merely conservative diplomats. It is true that Nazis openly scoffed at any notion of international obligations, as I shall show in a moment. It is true that the real trump in Germany's hand was its rearmament and more than that, its willingness to go to war. And yet the attitude of the various countries was not influenced by these considerations alone.

The fact is that with all these countries, and I suppose it is the same with all persons, we are not always completely rational, we tend to believe what we want to believe, so that if an apparently substantial and conservative person, like defendant von Neurath, for example, is saying these things, one might be apt to believe them, or at least, to act upon that hypothesis. And it would be the more convincing if one were also under the impression that the person involved was not a Nazi and would not stoop to go along with the designs of the Nazis.

Germany's approach toward Great Britain and France was in terms of limited expansion as the price of peace. They signed a naval limitations treaty with England and discussed a Locarno Air Pact. In the case of both France and England, they limited their statement of intentions and harped on fears of Communism and war.

In making these various promises, Germany was untroubled by notions of the sanctity of international obligations. High ranking Nazis, including Goering, Frick and Frank, openly stated to Mr. Messersmith that Germany would observe her international undertakings only so long as it suited her interest to do so.

I quote from the affidavit, document 2385-PS, beginning on the tenth line, page 4 of the English version:-

"High ranking Nazis with whom I had to maintain official contact, particularly men such as Goering, Goebbels, Ley, Frick, Frank, Darre and others, repeatedly scoffed at my attitude towards the binding character of treaties, and openly stated to me that Germany would observe her international undertakings only so long as it suited Germany's interest to do so. Although these statements were openly made to me, as they were, I am sure, made to others, these Nazi leaders were not really disclosing any secret, for on many occasions they expressed the same idea publicly."

France and Italy worked actively in South-eastern Europe to counter Germany's moves.

THE PRESIDENT: Would that be a convenient time to break off?

MR. ALDERMAN: Yes, sir.

THE PRESIDENT: Until 10 o'clock to-morrow morning.

(The Tribunal adjourned until 29th November, 1945, at 1000 hours.)

EIGHTH DAY:
Thursday, 29th November, 1945

MR. ALDERMAN: May it please the Tribunal:

Before I resume the consideration of Mr. Messersmith's second affidavit, document 2385-PS, exhibit USA 68, I should like to consider briefly the status of the evidence before this Tribunal, of the matter stated in the first Messersmith affidavit, introduced by the United States, document 1760-PS, exhibit USA 57. You will recall that Mr. Messersmith, in that affidavit, made the following general statement:

First, that although Nazi Germany stated that it would respect the independence of Austria, in fact it intended from the very beginning to conclude an Anschluss, and that Defendant von Papen was working toward that end.

Second, that although Nazi Germany pretended, on the surface, to have nothing to do with the Austrian Nazis, in fact they kept up contact with them and gave them support and instruction.

Third, that while they were getting ready for their eventual use of force in Austria, if necessary, the Nazis were using quiet infiltrating tactics to weaken Austria internally, through the use of Christian-front personalities who were not flagrantly Nazis and could be called, as they were referred to, Nationalist Opposition, and through the device of developing new names for Nazi organisations, so that they could be brought into the Fatherland Front of Austria corporatively, that is, as an entire group.

Now let us see briefly what some of our German documents proved in support of these general statements in the Messersmith affidavit. The excerpts I have already read out of the report from Rainer to Burckel, enclosed in the letter to Seyss-Inquart, document 812-PS, exhibit USA 61, showed first, that the Austrian Nazi groups kept up contacts with the Reich, although they did it secretly, in accordance with instructions from the Fuehrer.

Second, that they continued their organisation on a secret basis so as to be ready in what they referred to as an emergency.

Third, that they used persons like Seyss-Inquart and Glaise- Horstenau, who had what they called good legal positions, but who could be trusted by the Nazis, and that five days after the Pact of 11th July, 1936, between Germany and Austria - a Pact which specifically pledged the German Government not to interfere, either directly or indirectly, in the internal affairs of Austria, including the question of Austrian Socialism - the Austrian Nazis met with Hitler at Obersalzberg and received new instructions, and finally, that Hitler then used Keppler, whose name we shall again meet in a short while, in a significant manner, as his "contact man" with the Austrian Nazis, with full authority to act for the Fuehrer in Austria and to work with the leaders of the Austrian Nazis.

Then we offered document 2248-PS, exhibit USA 63, von Papen's letter of 27th July, 1935, which reviewed the situation one year after Dollfuss' death, and pointed out how National Socialism could be made a link for the Anschluss and could overcome the Austrian ideologies, and in which letter he identified himself completely with the National Socialist goal.

We offered document 2246-PS, exhibit USA 67, von Papen's letter to Hitler of 1st September, 1936, which showed how von Papen advised using both economic and continuing psychological pressure; that he had conferences with leaders of the illegal Austrian Party; that he was trying to direct the next developments in such a way as to get corporative representation of the Nazi movement in the Fatherland Front, and that meanwhile he was not ready to urge that avowed National Socialists be put in prominent positions, but was quite satisfied with collaborators, like Glaise-Horstenau.

I think that practically all of the statements in Mr. Messersmith's affidavits have been fully supported by these documents, German documents which we have introduced. Certain parts of the affidavits cannot be corroborated by documents, in the very nature of things, and I refer specifically to Mr. Messersmith's conversation with the defendant von Papen. in 1934, which I read to the Tribunal yesterday. But I think these matters are manifestly just as true and just as clear as to the defendant's guilt and complicity.

Yesterday, I was reading to the Tribunal selected excerpts from Mr. Messersmith's second affidavit, document 2385-PS, exhibit USA 68, relating to the diplomatic preparations for war. Prior to adjournment, I had read to the Tribunal excerpts which established the following propositions:

First, Nazi Germany undertook a vigorous campaign to break up the diplomatic agreements existing in 1933; first in the West, the Locarno Pact, supplemented by the Franco-Belgian Agreement; second, in the East, the Little Entente, Yugoslavia, Czechoslovakia and Poland, and their respective mutual assistance pacts with France, the French-Polish Pact; third, as regards Austria, the special concern of Italy for her independence, that is, for Austrian independence.

In the second place, Nazi Germany countered these alliances with extravagant and sometimes inconsistent promises of territorial gain to countries in South-Eastern Europe, including Yugoslavia, Hungary and Poland.

In the third place, Mr. Messersmith wrote an official communication to the State Department, pointing out that persons like von Neurath and von Papen were able to work more effectively in making these promises and in doing their other work, just because they, and I quote, "propagated the myth that they were not in sympathy with the regime."

In the fourth place, it is a fact that high ranking Nazis openly stated that Germany would honour her international obligations only so long as it suited her to do so. There are two more excerpts which I wish to read from this affidavit.

France and Italy worked actively in South-Eastern Europe to counter German moves, as I said yesterday. France made attempts to promote an East Locarno Pact and to foster an economic accord between Austria and the other Danubian powers.

Italy's effort was to organise an economic block of Austria, Hungary and Italy. But Germany foiled these efforts by redoubling its policies of loot, by continuing its armament and by another very significant strategy, that is - the Fifth Column strategy; the Nazis stirred up internal dissension within neighbouring countries to disunite and weaken their intended victims.

I read now from page 7 of the English copy of the second Messersmith affidavit, document 2385-PS, exhibit USA 68, the paragraph beginning in the middle of the page.

"At the same time that Germany held out such promises of reward for co-operation in her programme, she stirred up internal dissension within these countries themselves and in Austria and Czechoslovakia in particular, all of which were designed to so weaken all opposition and. strengthen the pro-Nazi and Fascist groups as to ensure peaceful acquiescence in the German programme. Her machinations in Austria I have related in detail, as they came under my direct observation, in a separate affidavit. In Czechoslovakia they followed the same tactics with the Sudeten Germans. I was reliably informed that the Nazi Party spent over 6,000,000 marks in financing the Henlein Party in the elections in the Spring of 1935 alone. In Yugoslavia she played on the old differences between the Croatians and the Serbs and the fear of the restoration of the Hapsburg in Austria. It may be remarked here that this latter was one of the principal instruments, and a most effective one, which Nazi Germany used, as the fear, in Yugoslavia in particular, of a restoration of the Hapsburg was very real. In Hungary she played upon the agrarian difficulties and at the same time openly encouraged the Nazi German elements in Hungary so as to provoke the Government of Hungary to demand the recall of von Mackensen in 1936. In Hungary and in Poland she played on the fear of Communism and Communist Russia. In Roumania she aggravated the existing anti-Semitism, emphasising the important role of the Jews in Roumanian industry and the Jewish ancestry of Lupescu. Germany undoubtedly also financed the Fascist Iron Guard through Codreanou.

Such 'diplomatic' measures reinforced by Germany's vast rearmament programme had a considerable effect, particularly in Yugoslavia, Poland and Hungary, one sufficient at least to deter these countries from joining any combination opposed to German designs, even if not enough to persuade them to ally themselves actively with Nazi Germany. Important political leaders of Yugoslavia began to become convinced that the Nazi regime would remain in power and would gain its ends, and that the course of safety for Yugoslavia was to play along with Germany."

I shall not take the time of the Tribunal to read into evidence the detailed, official dispatches which Mr. Messersmith sent to the American State Department, showing that Yugoslavia, Hungary and Poland were beginning to follow the German line.

As for Italy, Germany's initial objective was to sow discord between Yugoslavia and Italy, by promising Yugoslavia Italian territory, particularly Trieste. This was to prevent France from reaching an agreement with them and to block an East Locarno

Pact. On that I quote again from document 2385-PS, exhibit USA 68, the second Messersmith affidavit, on page 10:

While Italy openly opposed efforts at an Anschluss with Austria in 1934, Italian ambitions in Abyssinia provided Germany with the opportunity to sow discord between Italy and France and England, and to win Italy over to acceptance of Germany's programme in exchange for German support of her plans in Abyssinia."

That, if the Tribunal please, paved the way for the Austro-German Declaration or Pact of 11th July, 1936; and in the fall of 1936, Germany extended the hand of friendship and common purpose to Italy, in an alliance which they called the "Rome-Berlin Axis". This, together with Germany's alliance with Japan, put increasing pressure on England and greatly increased the relative strength of Germany.

And so, by means of careful preparation in the diplomatic field, among others, the Nazi conspirators had woven a position for themselves, so that they could seriously consider plans for war and begin to outline timetables, not binding timetables and not specific ones in terms of months and days, but still general timetables, in terms of years which were the necessary foundation for further aggressive planning, and a spur to more specific planning. That timetable was developed, as the Tribunal has already seen, in the conference of 5th November, 1937, contained in the document 386-PS, exhibit USA 25, the Hoszbach Minutes of that conference, to which I referred in detail on Monday last.

In those minutes we see the crystallisation of the plan to wage aggressive war in Europe, and to seize both Austria and Czechoslovakia, and in that order.

In connection with the exposition of the aggression on Austria, I have shown first the purpose of the Nazi conspiracy, with respect to the absorption of Austria, and then the steps taken by them in Austria up to this period, that is November, 1937.

I have also outlined for the Tribunal the general diplomatic preparations of the Nazi conspirators, with respect to their programme in Europe generally, and with respect to Austria in particular.

It may now be profitable to reconsider the minutes of the meeting of 5th November, 1937, in the light of this more-detailed background. It will be recalled that in that meeting, the- Fuehrer insisted that Germany must have more space in Europe. He concluded that the space required must be taken by force; and three different possible cases were outlined for different eventualities, but all reaching the conclusion that the problem would certainly have to be solved before 1943 to 1945.

Then there was envisaged the nature of a war in the near future, specifically against Austria and Czechoslovakia. Hitler said that for the improvement of Germany's military and political positions, it must be the first aim of the Nazis, in every case of entanglement by war, to conquer Czechoslovakia and Austria simultaneously, in order to remove any threat from the flanks, in case of a possible advance Westward.

Hitler then considered that the embodiment into Germany of Czechoslovakia and Austria, would constitute the conquest of food for from five to six million people, including the assumption that the comprehensive forced emigration of one million people from Austria could be carried out. And he further pointed out that the annexation of the two States to Germany, both militarily and politically, would constitute a considerable relief, since they would provide shorter and better frontiers; would free fighting personnel for other purposes; and would make possible the reconstitution of large new German armies.

Insofar as Austria is concerned, those minutes reveal a crystallisation in the policy of the Nazi conspirators. It had always been their aim to acquire Austria. At the outset a revolutionary putsch was attempted, but that failed. The next period was one of surface recognition of the independence of Austria and the use of devious means to strengthen the position of Nazis internally in Austria.

Now, however, it became clear that the need, or the greed, for Austria, in the light of the larger aggressive purposes of the Nazis, was sufficiently great to warrant the use of force, in order to obtain Austria with the speed that was designed. In fact, as we shall see later, the Nazis were actually able to secure Austria, after having weakened it internally and removed from it the support of other nations, merely by setting the German military machine into motion and making a threat of force.

The German armies were able to cross the border and secure the country without the necessity of firing a shot. Their careful planning for war, and their readiness to use war as an instrument of political action, made it possible, in the end, for them to pluck this plum without having to strike a blow for it.

The German High Command had, of course, previously considered preparation against Austria.

I offer in evidence another German document, C-175, exhibit USA 69. It, again, is "Top Secret," with the added caption in German "Chefsache nur durch Offizier," "Chief Matter only to be delivered through an Officer."

This was a Top Secret directive of 24th June, 1937, of the Reichsminister for War and Commander-in-Chief of the Armed Forces, General von Blomberg. The importance of this Top Secret directive is indicated by the fact that the carbon copy, received by the Commander-in-Chief of the Navy, was one of only four copies, establishing the directive for a unified preparation for war of all the Armed Forces.

This directive from General von Blomberg states, that although the political situation indicates that Germany need not consider an attack from any side, and also states that Germany does not intend to unleash European war, it then states in Part 1, and I quote from page 2 of the English text, which, I believe, is page 4, third paragraph, of the German text:

"The intention to unleash a European War is held just as little by Germany. Nevertheless, the politically fluid world situation, which does not preclude surprising incidents, demands a continuous preparedness for war by the German Armed Forces.

(a) to counter attacks at any time

(b) to enable the military exploitation of politically favourable opportunities, should they occur."

The directive then indicates that there will be certain preparations for war of a general nature. I quote the first two portions of paragraph 2, on page 2 of the English text, and, I think, page 5 of the German text:

"(2) The preparations of a general nature include:

(a) The permanent preparedness for mobilisation of the German Armed Forces, even before the completion of rearmament, and full preparedness for war.

(b) The further working on 'Mobilisation without public announcement' in order to put the Armed Forces in a position to begin a war suddenly and by surprise, both as regards strength and time."

And the directive finally indicates that there might be special preparations for war against Austria. I quote from Part 3 (1) which is on page 4 of the English text, and page 19 of the German text:

"(1) Special Case 'Otto.'

Case 'Otto', as you will repeatedly see, was the standing code name for aggressive war against Austria. I quote:

Armed intervention in Austria in the event of her restoring the Monarchy.

The object of this operation will be to compel Austria by armed force to give up a restoration.

Making use of the domestic political divisions of the Austrian people, the march in will be made in the general direction of Vienna, and will break any resistance."

I should now like to call attention to two conversations, held by United States Ambassador Bullitt with the defendants Schacht and Goering, in November, 1937.

DR. FRANZ EXNER: I am Prof. Exner, defending General Jodl. I should like to state my objection to the manner in which document C-175 has been treated. This document repeats a document of the General Staff, which prepares for all kinds of possibilities of war. The possibility has even been that you have seen in this document that Germany might have had to wage a war with Italy.

This document was only partially read, only the part relating to Austria; and in that way, the impression was created of a plan to march against Austria, whereas it actually says the German Reich had no intention to attack at that time, but was merely preparing for all eventualities.

I should like to request that the reading of this document should be supplemented by the reading at least of the paragraphs of this document which come after it. If these paragraphs of the document are placed before the Court, it will be seen that this was not a plan to march against Austria, but simply a document preparing for all possible eventualities.

THE PRESIDENT: Dr. Exner, your objection does not appear to be to the admissibility of the document, but to the weight of the document. The Tribunal has already informed defendants Keitel and Jodl that they will have the opportunity at the appropriate time, when they come to prepare their defence, to refer to any documents, part of which have been put in by the prosecution, and to read such parts as they think necessary then, and to make what criticism they think necessary then.

Your objection is therefore premature, because it does not go to the admissibility of the document. It simply indicates a wish that more of it should be read. You will have an opportunity later to read any parts of the document which you wish.

MR. ALDERMAN: I suppose, if the Tribunal please, that the fundamental basis of the objection just stated by the distinguished Counsel, must have been his theory that Germany never made any plans to invade Austria, and if so, it would seem to follow that Germany never invaded Austria, and perhaps history is mistaken.

I had referred to two conversations, held by United States Ambassador Bullitt with the defendants Schacht and Goering, in November, 1937.

For this purpose, I offer in evidence our document L-151, offered as exhibit USA 70. It is a dispatch from Mr. Bullitt, American Ambassador in Paris, to the American Secretary of State, on 23rd November, 1937.

Now, again, if the Tribunal please, we are embarrassed because that document is not in the document book before the members of the Tribunal. It has been furnished in German translation to the defence counsel.

THE PRESIDENT: We have got it in German, apparently.

MR. ALDERMAN: I expect you have, yes; you have the German version.

If the Tribunal will permit, I will read from the original exhibit. On top, is a letter from Ambassador Bullitt to the Secretary of State, 23rd November, 1937, stating that he visited Warsaw, stopping in Berlin en route, where he had conversations with Schacht and Goering, among others.

On the conversation with Schacht, I read from page 2 of the report:

"Schacht said that, in his opinion, the best way to begin to deal with Hitler, was not through political discussion, but through economic discussion. Hitler was not in the least interested in economic matters. He regarded money as filth. It was, therefore, possible to enter into negotiations with him in the economic domain without arousing his emotional antipathy; and it might be possible through the conversations thus begun to lead him into arrangements in the political and military field, in which he was intensely interested. Hitler was determined to have Austria eventually attached to Germany, and to obtain at least autonomy for the Germans of Bohemia. At the present moment he was not vitally concerned about the Polish Corridor and again - that is Schacht's opinion - it might be possible to maintain the Corridor, provided Danzig were permitted to join East Prussia, and provided some sort of bridge could be built across the Corridor, uniting Danzig and East Prussia with Germany."

And for the defendant Goering's statement to Ambassador Bullitt, I read from the second memorandum, "Memorandum of conversation between Ambassador Bullitt and General Hermann Goering," on page 2 of that document, the second page, following a part of a sentence which is underlined, just below the middle of the page:

"The sole source of friction between Germany and France was the refusal of France to permit Germany to achieve certain vital and necessary national aims.

If France, instead of accepting collaboration with Germany, should continue to follow a policy of building up alliances in Eastern Europe to prevent Germany from achieving her legitimate aims, it was obvious that there would be conflict between France and Germany.

I asked Goering what aims especially he had in mind. He replied: 'We are determined to join to the German Reich all Germans who are contiguous to the Reich, and are divided from the great body of the German race merely by the artificial barriers imposed by the Treaty of Versailles.'

I asked Goering if he meant that Germany was absolutely determined to annex Austria to the Reich. He replied that this was an absolute determination of the German Government. The German Government, at the present time, was not pressing the matter, because of certain momentary political considerations, especially in their relations with Italy. But Germany would tolerate no solution of the Austrian question other than the consolidation of Austria in the German Reich.

He then added a statement which went further than any I have heard on this subject. He said: 'There are schemes being pushed now for a union of Austria, Hungary and Czechoslovakia, either with or without a Hapsburg at the head of the union. Such a solution is absolutely unacceptable to us, and for us the conclusion of such an agreement would be an immediate casus belli.'"

Goering used the Latin expression "casus belli"; it is not a translation from the German, in which that conversation was carried on.

"I asked Goering if the German Government was as decided in its views with regard to the Germans in Bohemia as it was with regard to Austria. He replied that there could be only one final solution of this question. The Sudeten Germans must enter the German Reich as all other Germans who lived contiguous to the Reich."

These, if the Tribunal please, are official reports made by the accredited representative of the United States in the regular course of business. They carry with them the guarantee of truthfulness of a report made by a responsible official to his own government, recording contemporaneous conversations and events.

My next subject is: Pressure and Threats Resulting in Further Concessions by Austria; a meeting at Berchtesgaden, 12th February, 1938.

As I have stated before, the Austrian Government was labouring under great difficulties imposed by its neighbour. There was economic pressure, including the curtailment of the important tourist trade; and there was what the defendant von Papen called "slowly intensified psychological pressure". There were increasing demonstrations, plots and conspiracies. Demands were being presented by Captain Leopold, and approval of the Nazis was being espoused by the defendant Seyss-Inquart, the new Councillor of State of Austria. In this situation, Chancellor Schuschnigg decided to visit Hitler at Berchtesgaden.

The official communique of this conference is quite calm: I invite the Tribunal to take judicial notice of it. It is document 2461- PS, the official German communique of the meeting of Hitler and von Schuschnigg at Obersalzberg, 12th February, 1938, taken from the official Dokumente der Deutschen Politik, Vol. 6, 1, page 124, number 21-a.

The communique states that the unofficial meeting was caused by mutual desire to clarify, by personal conversation, the questions relating to the relationship between the German Reich and Austria.

The communique lists among those present: Von Schuschnigg and his Foreign Minister Schmidt, Hitler and his Foreign Minister Ribbentrop, and the defendant von Papen.

The communique concludes on a rather bright note, saying, and I quote: "Both statesmen are convinced that the measures taken by them constitute at the same time an effective contribution toward the peaceful development of the European situation."

A similar communique was issued by the Austrian Government.

But, in fact, and as I think history well knows, the conference was a very unusual and a very harsh one. Great concessions were obtained by the German Government from Austria. The principal concessions are contained in the official Austrian communique of the reorganisation of the Cabinet and the general political amnesty, dated 16th February, 1938.

That communique, as taken from the Dokumente der Deutschen Politik, Vol. 6, page 125, number 21-b, is translated in our document 2464-PS, and I invite the Court's judicial notice of it.

That communique announced a reorganisation of the Austrian Cabinet, including most significantly, the appointment of the defendant Seyss-Inquart to the position of Minister of Security and Interior, where he would have control of the police. In addition, announcement was made of a general political amnesty to Nazis convicted of crimes.

Two days later another concession was divulged. I invite the Court's judicial notice to our document 2469-PS, a translation of the official German and Austrian communique concerning the so- called equal rights of Austrian National Socialists in Austria, 18th February, 1938, Dokumente der Deutschen Politik, Vol. 6, 1, page 128, number 21-d.

That communique announced that, pursuant to the Berchtesgaden conference, the Austrian National Socialists would be taken into the Fatherland Front, the single, legal political party of Austria.

THE PRESIDENT: Will you tell us what exhibit numbers those two documents were?

MR. ALDERMAN: I am sorry, Sir; document 2469-PS.

THE PRESIDENT: We haven't had that yet. We have had 2461-PS; which is exhibit what?

MR. ALDERMAN: Well, I hadn't read it in. I was asking the Tribunal to take judicial notice of this as an official communique.

THE PRESIDENT: You are not going to give it an exhibit number?

MR. ALDERMAN: No, sir.

THE PRESIDENT: Nor 2469?

MR. ALDERMAN: No, sir.

In actual fact, great pressure was put on von Schuschnigg at Berchtesgaden. The fact that pressure was exerted, and pressure of a military nature involving the threat of the use of troops, can be sufficiently established from captured German documents.

I have our document 1544-PS, a captured German document, which I offer in evidence as exhibit USA 71. This document consists of the defendant von Papen's own notes on his last meeting with von Schuschnigg, on February 26th, 1938. I quote the last two paragraphs of these notes. This is von Papen speaking:

"I then introduced into the conversation the widespread opinion that he" - that is, von Schuschnigg - "had acted under brutal pressure in Berchtesgaden. I myself had been present and been able to state that he had always and at every point had complete freedom of decision. The Chancellor replied he had actually been under considerable moral pressure, he could not deny that. He had made notes on the talk which bore that out. I reminded him that despite this talk he had not seen his way clear to make any concessions, and I asked, him whether without the pressure he would have been ready to make the concessions he made late in the evening. He answered: 'To be honest, no.'"

And then von Papen says:

"It appears to me of importance to record this statement. In parting I asked the Chancellor never to deceive himself that Austria could ever maintain her status with the help of non- German, European combinations. This question would be decided only according to the interests of the German people. He asserted that he held the same conviction and would act accordingly."

Thus we have, through the words of von Papen, von Schuschnigg's contemporary statement to Papen of the pressure which had been exerted upon him, as recorded by von Papen in an original, contemporaneous entry.

For diplomatic purposes, Papen, who had been at Berchtesgaden, kept up the pretence that there had been no pressure applied.

But the defendant General Jodl, writing the account of current events in his diary, was much more candid. We are fortunate in having General Jodl's hand-written diary, in German script, which I can't read. It is our document 1780-PS, and I offer it in evidence as exhibit USA 72.

I may say that General Jodl, in interrogation, has admitted that this is his genuine diary in his handwriting.

This diary discloses not only the pressure at Berchtesgaden, but also the fact that for some days thereafter defendants Keitel and Admiral Canaris worked out a scheme for shamming military pressure in order, obviously, to coerce President Miklas of Austria into ratifying the agreement. It started from von Schuschnigg at Berchtesgaden. It will be noted that the approval of President Miklas was needed to ratify the Berchtesgaden agreement; that is, with respect to naming Seyss-Inquart as Minister of the Interior and Security.

And so the Nazi conspirators kept up the military pressure with threats of invasion for some days after the Berchtesgaden conference in order to produce the desired effect on President Miklas.

I quote from General Jodl's diary, the entries for 11th February, 13th February, and 14th February, 1938.

The entry of 11th February: "In the evening and on 13th February General K" (Keitel) "with General von Reichenau and Sperrle at the Obersalzberg. Von

Schuschnigg, together with G. Schmidt are again being put under heaviest political and military pressure. At 2300 hours Schuschnigg signs protocol.

13th February: In the afternoon General K" (Keitel) "asks Admiral C" (Canaris) "and myself to come to his apartment. He tells us that the Fuehrer's order is to the effect that military pressure, by shamming military action, should be kept up until the 15th. Proposals for these deceptive manoeuvres are drafted and submitted to the Fuehrer by telephone for approval.

14th February: At 2:40 o'clock the agreement of the Fuehrer arrives. Canaris goes to Munich to the Counter-Intelligence Office VII and initiates the different measures.

The effect is quick and strong. In Austria the impression is created that Germany is undertaking serious military preparations."

The proposal for deceptive manoeuvres reported on by defendant Jodi are set forth in document 1775-PS, a captured German document, which I offer in evidence as exhibit USA 73.

The proposals are signed by the defendant Keitel. Underneath his signature appears a note that the Fuehrer approved the proposal.

In the original document that note is hand-written in pencil.

The rumours which Keitel proposed for the intimidation of Austria make very interesting reading. I quote the first three paragraphs of the suggested order:

"1. To take no real preparatory measures in the Army or Luftwaffe. No troop movements or redeployments.

2. Spread false, but quite credible news, which may lead to the conclusion of military preparations against Austria.

(a) Through V-men (V-Maenner) in Austria.

(b) Through our customs personnel (staff) at the frontier.

(c) Through travelling agents.

3. Such news could be:

(a) Furloughs are supposed to have been barred in the sector of the VII A. K.

(b) Rolling stock is being assembled in Munich, Augsburg and Regensburg.

(c) Major General Muff, the Military Attache in Vienna, has been called for a conference to Berlin. (As a matter of fact, this is the case.)"

That reminds me of a lawyer from my own home town who used to argue a matter at great length, and then he would end up by saying, and, incidentally, it is the truth.

(d) The police stations located at the frontier of Austria have called up reinforcements.

(e) Custom officials report about the imminent manoeuvres of the Mountain Brigade (Gebirgsbrigade) in the region of Freilassing, Reichenhall and Berchtesgaden ".

The total pattern of intimidation and rumour was effective, for in due course, as we have already seen from the communiques referred to, President Miklas verified the Berchtesgaden Agreement, which foreshadowed National Socialist Austria and then the events culminating in the actual German invasion on 12th March, 1938.

Mr. President, would this be a convenient moment for a recess?

THE PRESIDENT: We will adjourn for ten minutes.

(A recess was taken.)

MR. ALDERMAN: May it please the Tribunal, I had reached the subject of the events culminating in the German invasion of Austria on 12th March, 1938, and, first under that, the plebiscite and the preparations for both German and Austrian National Socialists.

The day after his appointment as Minister of the Interior of Austria, Seyss-Inquart flew to Berlin for a conference with Hitler. I invite the Court to take judicial notice of the official German communique covering that visit of Seyss-Inquart to Hitler, as it appeared in the "Dokumente der Deutschen Politik," Volume 6- 1, page 128, number 21-c, a copy of which will be found in our document 464-PS.

On 9th March, 1938, three weeks after Seyss-Inquart had been put in charge of the police of Austria and was in a position to direct their handling of the National Socialists in Austria - three weeks after the Nazis began to exploit their new prestige and position with its quota of further victories - von Schuschnigg made an important announcement.

On 9th March, 1938, Schuschnigg announced that he would hold a plebiscite throughout Austria, the following Sunday, 13th March, 1938. The question to be submitted in the plebiscite was: "Are you for an independent and Social, a Christian, a German and united Austria?" A "Yes" answer to this question was certainly compatible with the agreement made by the German Government on the 11th July, 1936, and carried forward at Berchtesgaden on the 12th February, 1938. Moreover, for a long while the Nazis had been demanding a plebiscite on the question of Anschluss, but the Nazis apparently appreciated the likelihood of a strong "Yes" vote on the question put by von Schuschnigg in the plebiscite, and they could not tolerate the possibility of such a vote of confidence in the Schuschnigg government.

In any case, as events showed, they took this occasion to overturn the Austrian government. Although the plebiscite was not announced until the evening of 9th March, the Nazi Organisation received word about it earlier in that day. It was determined by the Nazis that they had to ask Hitler what to do about the situation (that is, the Austrian Nazis), and that they would prepare a letter of protest against the plebiscite, from Seyss-Inquart to von Schuschnigg; and that, pending Hitler's approval, Seyss-Inquart would pretend to negotiate with von Schuschnigg about details of the plebiscite.

This information is all contained in the report of Gauleiter Rainer to Reich Commissar Burckel, transmitted, as I have already pointed out, to Seyss-Inquart, and which has already been received in evidence -- our document 8122-PS, USA 61.

I quote briefly from page 7 of the English text, the paragraph beginning on page 11 of the German original:-

"The Landesleitung received word about the planned plebiscite, through illegal information services, on 9th March, 1938, at 10 a.m. At the session which was called immediately afterwards, Seyss-Inquart complained that he had known about this for only a few hours, but that he could not talk about it because he had given his word to keep silent on this subject. But during the talks, he made us understand that the illegal information we received was based on truth, and that in view of the new situation, he had been co-operating with the Landesleitung from the very first moment. Klausner, Jury, Rainer, Globotschnik and Seyss-Inquart were present at the first talks, which were held at 10 a.m. There it was decided that first, the Fuehrer had to be informed immediately; secondly, the opportunity for him to intervene must be given to him by way of an official declaration made by Minister Seyss-Inquart to Schuschnigg; and, thirdly, Seyss-Inquart must negotiate with the Government until clear instructions and orders were received from the Fuehrer. Seyss-Inquart and Rainer together composed a letter to von Schuschnigg, and only one copy of it was brought to the Fuehrer by Globotschnik, who flew to him on the afternoon of 9th March, 1938.

Negotiations with the Government were not successful. Therefore they were stopped by Seyss-Inquart in accordance with the instructions he received from the Fuehrer. On the 10th March, all the preparations for future revolutionary actions had already been made, and the necessary orders given to all unit leaders. During the night of the 10th and 11th, Globotschnik returned with the announcement that the Fuehrer gave the party freedom of action, and that he would back it in everything it did."

That means, the Austrian Nazi party.

Next, Germany's actual preparations for the invasion and the use of force. When news of the plebiscite reached Berlin it started a tremendous amount of activity. Hitler, as history knows, was determined not to tolerate the plebiscite. Accordingly, he called his military advisers and ordered the preparation of the march into Austria.

On the diplomatic side, he started a letter to Mussolini indicating why he was going to march into Austria, and in the absence of the defendant Ribbentrop (who was temporarily detained in London), the defendant von Neurath took over the affairs of the Foreign Office again.

The terse and somewhat disconnected notes in General Jodl's diary give a vivid account of the activities in Berlin. I quote from the entry of 10th March.

"By surprise and without consulting his ministers, von Schuschnigg ordered a plebiscite for Sunday, 13th March, which should bring a strong majority for the legitimate party in the absence of plan or preparation.

The Fuehrer is determined not to tolerate it. This same night, March 9th to 10th he calls for Goering. General von Reichenau is ordered back from the Vairo Olympic Committee. General von Schebert is ordered to come as well as Minister Glaise-Horstenau, who is with the District leader (Gauleiter Burckel) in the Palatinia. General Keitel communicates the facts at 1.45. He drives to the Reichskanzlei at ten o'clock. I follow at 10.15, according to the wish of General von Viebahn, to give him the old draft "Prepare Case Otto.'

1300 hours, General K - which I think plainly means Keitel - "informs Chief of Operational Staff and Admiral Canaris; Ribbentrop is being detained in London. Neurath takes over the Foreign Office. Fuehrer wants to transmit ultimatum to the Austrian cabinet. A personal letter is dispatched to Mussolini and the reasons are developed which forced the Fuehrer to take action. 1630 hours, mobilisation order is given to the Commander of the VIII Army, Corps Area 3, 7th and 13th Army Corps, without Reserve Army."

Now, it is to be noted that defendant von Neurath was at this critical hour acting as Foreign Minister. The previous February the defendant Ribbentrop had become Foreign Minister, and von Neurath had become President of the Secret Cabinet Council. But in this critical hour of foreign policy the defendant Ribbentrop was in London handling the diplomatic consequences of the Austrian transaction. As Foreign Minister in this hour of aggression, involving mobilisation and movement of troops, use of force and threats to eliminate the independence of a neighbouring country, the defendant von Neurath reclaimed his former position in the Nazi conspiracy.

I now offer in evidence our document C-102 as exhibit USA 74, captured German document, Top Secret, the directive of the Supreme Command of the Armed Forces, 11th March, 1938. This directive by Hitler, initialled by the defendants Jodl and Keitel, stated, "Hitler mixed political and military intentions." I quote paragraphs one, four, and five of the directive. First, the caption: "The Supreme Command of the Armed Forces," with some initials, referring to Operation Otto." Thirty copies. This is the eleventh copy. Top Secret.

"1. If other measures prove unsuccessful I intend to invade Austria with armed forces to establish constitutional conditions and to prevent further outrages against the pro- German population.

4. The forces of the Army and Air Force detailed for this operation must be ready for invasion and/or ready for action on the 12th of March, 1938, at the latest from 1200 hours. I reserve the right to give permission for crossing and flying over the frontier and to decide the actual moment for invasion.

5. The behaviour of the troops must give the impression that we do not want to wage war against our Austrian brothers; it is in our interest that the whole operation shall be carried out without any violence, but in the form of a peaceful entry welcomed by the population. Therefore any provocation is to be avoided.

If, however, resistance is offered it must be broken ruthlessly by force of arms."

I also offer in evidence captured German document C-103 as exhibit USA 75, special instruction number one, directive, 11th March, 1938. This was an implementing directive, issued by the defendant Jodl, and it provided as follows:

"Top Secret. General. Forty copies, of which this is the sixth. Special instruction number one to the Supreme Commander of the Armed Forces No. 427-38, with some symbols. Directive. Our policy toward Czechoslovakian and Italian troops or militia units on Austrian soil.

1. If Czechoslovakian troops or militia units are encountered in Austria they are to be regarded as hostile.

2. The Italians are everywhere to be treated as friends, especially as Mussolini has declared himself disinterested in the solution of the Austrian question. The Chief of the Supreme Command of the Armed Forces, by order of Jodl."

Next, the actual events of 11th March in Austria. The events of 11th March, 1938, in Austria are available to us in two separate documents. Although these accounts differ in some minor details, such as the precise words used and the precise times when they were used, they afford each other almost complete corroboration. We think it appropriate for this Tribunal to have before it a relatively full account of the way in which the German Government on 11th March, 1938, deprived Austria of its sovereignty. First I shall give the report of the day's events in Austria as given by the Austrian Nazis. I refer to document 812-PS, exhibit USA 61, a report from Gauleiter Rainer to Reich Commissar Burckel, and I shall read from page 8 of the English version. For the purpose of the German interpreter I am starting following a tabulation: First case; second case; third case; and following the sentence: "Dr. Seyss-Inquart took part in these talks with Gauleiters."

"On Friday, 11th March, the Minister Glaise-Horstenau arrived in Vienna after a visit to the Fuehrer. After talks with Seyss- Inquart he went to see the Chancellor. At 11.30 a.m. the 'Landesleitung' had a meeting at which Klausner, Rainer, Jury, Seyss-Inquart, Glaise-Horstenau, Fishbock, and Muhlmann participated. Dr. Seyss-Inquart reported on his talks with von Schuschnigg, which had ended in a rejection of the proposal of the two ministers.

In regard to Rainer's proposal, von Klausner ordered that the Government be presented with an ultimatum, expiring at 1400 hours, signed by legal political 'front' men, including both ministers and also State Councillors Fishbock and Jury, for the establishment of a voting date in three weeks and a free and secret ballot in accordance with the constitution.

On the basis of written evidence which Glaise-Horstenau had brought with him, a leaflet, to be printed in millions of copies, and a telegram to the Fuehrer calling for help were prepared.

Klausner placed the leadership of the final political actions in the hands of Rainer and Globotschnik. Von Schuschnigg called a session of all ministers for 2 p.m. Rainer agreed with Seyss-Inquart that he should send the telegram to the Fuehrer and the statement to the population at 3 p.m., and at the same time he would start all necessary actions to take over power unless he received news from the session of the ministers' council before that time. During this time all measures had been prepared. At two-thirty Seyss-Inquart phoned Rainer and informed him that von Schuschnigg had been unable to stand the pressure, and had recalled the plebiscite, but that he had refused to call a new plebiscite and had ordered the strongest police measures for maintaining order. Rainer asked whether the two ministers had resigned, and Seyss-Inquart answered 'No.' Rainer informed the 'Reichskanzlei' through the German Embassy, and received an answer from Goering through the same channels, that the Fuehrer will not consent to partial solutions and that von Schuschnigg must resign. Seyss-Inquart was informed of this by Globotschnik and Muhlmann. Talks were had between Seyss-Inquart and von Schuschnigg. Von Schuschnigg resigned. Seyss-Inquart asked Rainer what measures the Party wished taken. Rainer's answer: 'Re-establishment of the government by Seyss-Inquart, legalisation of the Party, and calling up of the S.S. and S.A. as auxiliaries to the police force. Seyss-Inquart promised to have these measures carried out, but very soon the announcement followed that everything might be threatened by the resistance of Miklas, the President. Meanwhile word arrived from the German Embassy that the Fuehrer expected the establishment of a government under Seyss-Inquart with a national majority, the legalisation of the Party, and permission for the Legion (that is the Austrian Legion in Germany) to return, all within the specified time of 7.30 p.m.; otherwise German troops would cross the border at 8 p.m. At 5 p.m. Rainer and Globotschnik, accompanied by Muhlmann, went to the Chancellor's office to carry out this errand.

Situation: Miklas negotiated with Ender for the creation of a government which included Blacks, Reds, and National Socialists, and proposed the post of Vice-Chancellor to Seyss- Inquart. The latter rejected it, and told Rainer that he was not able to negotiate by himself because he was personally involved, and therefore a weak and unpleasant political situation might result. Rainer negotiated with Zernatto. Director of the cabinet Huber, Guido Schmidt, Glaise- Horstenau, Legation Councillor Stein, Military Attache General Muff, and the 'Gruppenfuehrer' Keppler (whose name I told you would reappear significantly), who had arrived in the meantime, were already negotiating. At 7 p.m. Seyss-Inquart entered the negotiations again. Situation at 7-30 P-m.: stubborn refusal of Miklas to appoint Seyss-Inquart as Chancellor; appeal to the world in case of a German invasion.

Gruppenfuehrer Keppler explained that the Fuehrer did not yet have an urgent reason for the invasion. This reason must first be created. The situation in Vienna and in the country is most dangerous. It is feared that street fights will break out any moment, because Rainer ordered the entire Party to demonstrate at three o'clock. Rainer proposed storming and seizing the government palace in order to force the reconstruction of the government. The proposal was rejected by Keppler, but as carried out by Rainer after he discussed it with Globotschnik. After 8 p.m. the S.A. and S.S. marched in and occupied the government buildings and all important positions in the city of Vienna. At 8.30 p.m. Rainer, with the approval of Klausner, ordered all Gauleiters of Austria to take over power in all eight 'gaus' of Austria, with the help of the S.S. and S.A., and with instructions that all government representatives who try to resist should be told that this action was taken on the order of Chancellor Seyss-Inquart.

With this the revolution broke out, and this resulted in the complete occupation of Austria within three hours and the taking over of all important posts by the Party.

The seizure of power was the work of the party supported by the Fuehrer's threat of invasion, and the legal standing of Seyss-Inquart in the government. The national result in the form of the taking over of the government by Seyss-Inquart was due to the actual seizure of power by the Party on one hand, and the political efficiency of Dr. Seyss-Inquart in his territory on the other; but both factors may be considered only in relation to the Fuehrer's decision on 9th March,

1938, to solve the Austrian problem under any circumstances, and the orders consequently issued by the Fuehrer."

We have at hand another document which permits us virtually to live again through the events of 11th March, 1938, and to live through them in most lively and interesting fashion. Thanks to the efficiency of the defendant Goering and his Luftwaffe Organisation, we have a highly interesting document, obviously an official document from the Luftwaffe Headquarters headed as usual "Geheime Reichssache," Top Secret. The letter head is stamped "Reichsluftfahrtministerium Forschungsamt." If I can get the significance of the German, "Forschungsamt" means the "Research Department" of Goering's Air Ministry. The document is in a characteristic German folder, and on the back it says " Gespracche Fall Oesterreich." " Conversation about the Case on Austria," and the paper cover on the inside has German script writing. In time I will ask the interpreter to read it, but it looks to me as if it is "Privat, Geheime Archive," which is "Secret Archive," Berlin, Gespraeche Fall Oesterreich (Case About Austria). I offer that set of documents in the original file as they were found in the Air Ministry, identified as our 2949-PS. I offer them as exhibit USA 76,and, in offering them, I am reminded of Job's outcry: "Oh, that mine enemy would write a book."

The covering letter in that file, signed by some member of this research organisation within the Air Ministry, and addressed to the defendant Goering, states in substance - well, I will read the English translation. It starts: "To the General Fieldmarshal. Fieldmarshal. Enclosed I submit, as ordered, the copies of your telephone conversations." Evidently the defendant wanted to keep a record of important telephone conversations which he had with important persons regarding "Case Austria," and had the transcriptions provided by his research department. Most of the conversations, transcribed and recorded in the volume I have offered, were conducted by the defendant Goering, although at least one interesting one was conducted by Hitler. For purposes of convenience our staff has marked these telephone calls in pencil with identifying letters running from "A" through "Z" and then to "AA." Eleven of these conversations have been determined, by a screening process, to be relevant to the evidence of this particular time. All the conversations which have been translated have been mimeographed and are included in the document books handed to the defendants. The original binder contains, of course, the complete set of conversations. A very extensive and interesting account of events with which we are much concerned can be developed from quotations from these translated conversations. The first group in part "A" of the binder took place between Field Marshal Goering, who was identified by the letter "F" for Field Marshal, and Seyss-Inquart, who was identified as "S." The transcript prepared by the Research Institute of the Air Ministry is in part in the language of these two persons, and is in part a summary of the actual conversations. I quote from part "A" of this binder, and because of the corroborated nature of this transcript and its obvious authenticity I propose to quote this conversation in full.

"F - (hereafter I shall use Goering and Seyss-Inquart)-F. How do you do, doctor? My brother-in-law; is he with you?

Seyss-Inquart: No."

Thereupon the conversation took approximately the following turn:-

"Goering: How are things with you? Have you resigned, or have you any news? Seyss-Inquart: The Chancellor has cancelled the elections for Sunday, and therefore he has put "S" (Seyss-Inquart) and the other gentlemen in a difficult situation. Besides having called off the elections, extensive precautionary measures are being ordered, among others curfew at eight p.m.

Goering replied that in his opinion the measures taken by Chancellor Schuschnigg were not satisfactory in any respect. At this moment he could not commit himself officially. Goering will take a clear stand very shortly. In calling off the election he could see a postponement only, not a change of the present situation which had been brought about by the behaviour of the Chancellor Schuschnigg in breaking the Berchtesgaden agreement.

Thereafter a conversation took place between Goering and the Fuehrer. Afterwards Goering phoned Seyss-Inquart again. This conversation was held at 1505 hours.

"Goering told Seyss-Inquart that Berlin did not agree at all with the decision made by Chancellor Schuschnigg, since he did not enjoy any longer the confidence of our Government, because he had broken the Berchtesgaden agreement, and therefore further confidence in his future actions did not exist. Consequently the National Ministers, Seyss-Inquart, and the others are being requested to immediately hand in their resignation to the Chancellor, and also to ask the Chancellor to resign. Goering added that if, after a period of one hour, no report had come through, the assumption would be made that Seyss-Inquart would no more be in a position to phone. That would mean that the gentlemen had handed in their resignations. Seyss-Inquart was then told to send the telegram to the Fuehrer as agreed upon. As a matter of course, an immediate commission by the Federal President for Seyss- Inquart to form a new cabinet would follow Schuschnigg's resignation."

Thus you see that at 2.45 p.m. Goering told Seyss-Inquart over the phone that it was not enough for von Schuschnigg to cancel the elections; and twenty minutes later he telephoned Seyss-Inquart to state that von Schuschnigg must resign. That is your second ultimatum. When informed about an hour later that von Schuschnigg had resigned, he pointed out that in addition it was necessary to have Seyss-Inquart at the head of the cabinet. Shall I go into another one?

THE PRESIDENT: I think we had better adjourn until 2 o'clock.

(A recess was taken.)

MR. ALDERMAN: May it please the Tribunal, an hour later, following the conversation between Goering and Seyss-Inquart, with which I dealt this morning, the defendant Goering telephoned to Dombrowski in the German Embassy in Vienna. I refer to the telephone conversation marked TT on page 2, Part C, of document 2949-PS. In that conversation, in the first place, the defendant Goering showed concern that the Nazi Party and all of its organisations should be definitely legalised promptly. I quote from page 2 of the transcript:-

"Goering: Now to go on, the Party has definitely been legalised?

Dombrowski: But that is ... it isn't necessary to even discuss that.

Goering: With all of its organisations.

Dombrowski: With all of its organisations within this country.

Goering: In uniform?

Dombrowski: In uniform.

Goering: Good."

Dombrowski calls attention to the fact that the SA and SS have already been on duty for half ail hour, which means everything is all right.

In addition Goering stated that the Cabinet, the Austrian Cabinet, must be formed by 7.30 p.m., and he transmitted instructions to be delivered to Seyss-Inquart as to who should be appointed to the Cabinet. I quote from page 3 of the English text of the transcript of the conversation:-

"Goering: Yes, and by 7.30 he also must talk with the Fuehrer, and as to the Cabinet, Keppler will bring you the names. One thing I have forgotten. Fishbock must have the Department of Economy and Commerce.

Dombrowski: That is understood.

Goering: Kaltenbrunner is to have the Department of Security, and Bahr is to have the Armed Forces. The Austrian Army is to be taken by Seyss-Inquart, and you know all about the Justice Department.

Dombrowski: Yes, yes.

Goering: Give me the name.

Dombrowski: Well, your brother-in-law, isn't that right?"

(That is, Subert, the brother-in-law of the defendant Goering.)

"Goering: Yes.

Dombrowski: Yes.

Goering: That's right, and then also Fishbock."

And about twenty minutes later, at 5.26 p.m., Goering was given the news that Miklas, the President, was refusing to appoint Seyss- Inquart as Chancellor, and he issued instructions as to the ultimatum that was to be delivered to Miklas. I quote from the telephone conversation between Goering and Seyss-Inquart, in Part E of the folder, the part marked with capital R, pages 1 and 2 of Part E. I'm sorry, I thought the interpreters had the letter marked. They have not, I understand.

"Goering: Now remember the following: You go immediately together with Lt.-General Muff and tell the Federal President that if the conditions which are known to you are not accepted immediately, the troops who are already stationed at and advancing to the frontier will march in to-night along the whole line, and Austria will cease to exist. Lt.-General Muff should go with you and demand to be admitted for conference immediately. Please do inform us immediately about Miklas' position. Tell him there is no time now for any joke. Just through the false report we received before, action was delayed, but now the situation is that to-night the invasion will begin from all the corners of Austria. The invasion will be stopped, and the troops will be field at the border, only if we are informed by 7.30 that Miklas has entrusted you with the Federal Chancellorship." There follows in the transcript a sentence which is broken up. "M," - I suppose that means Lt. General Muff - "does not matter whatever it might be, the immediate restoration of the Party with all its organisations." There is again an interruption in the transcript. "And then call out all the National Socialists all over the country. They should now be in the streets; so remember report must be given by 7.30. Lt.-General Muff is supposed to come along with you. I shall inform him immediately. If Miklas could not understand it in four hours, we shall make him understand it now in four minutes."

An hour later, at 6.20 p.m., Goering had an extensively interrupted telephone conversation with Keppler and Muff and Seyss- Inquart. When he told Keppler that Miklas had refused to appoint Seyss-Inquart, Goering said - I read from Part H - it is about a third of the way down on the page.

"Goering: Well, then Seyss-Inquart has to dismiss him. Just go upstairs again and just tell him plainly that Seyss-Inquart (S.I.) shall call on the National-Socialists guard, and in five minutes the troops will march in by my order."

After an interruption, Seyss-Inquart came to the telephone and informed the defendant Goering that Miklas was still sticking to his old view, although a new person had gone in to talk to him, and there might be definite word in about ten minutes. The conversation proceeded as follows: I quote from page 2 of Part H, beginning about the middle of the page:-

"Goering: Listen, I shall wait a few more minutes, till he comes back; then you inform me via Blitz conversation in the Reich Chancellery as usually, but it has to be done fast. I hardly can justify it as a matter of fact. I am not entitled to do so; if it can not be done, then you have to take over the power, all right?
Seyss-Inquart: But if he threatens?
Goering: Yes.
Seyss-Inquart: Well, I see; then we shall be ready.
Goering: Call me via Blitz."

In other words, Goering and Seyss-Inquart had agreed on a plan for Seyss-Inquart to take over power if Miklas remained obdurate. The plan which was already discussed involved the use of both the National Socialist forces in Austria and the German troops who bad been crossing the borders. Later that night Goering and Seyss- Inquart had another conversation at about 11 o'clock. This was after the ultimatum had expired. Seyss-Inquart informed Goering that Miklas was still refusing to name Seyss-Inquart as Chancellor. The conversation then proceeded as follows, and I quote from Part 1 of this folder:-

"Goering: O.K." What's the German word for O.K.? Schon. "I shall give the order to march in and then you make sure you get the power. Notify the leading people about the following which I shall tell you now: Everyone who offers resistance or organises resistance will immediately be subjected to our court-martial, the court- martial of our invading troops. Is that clear?
Seyss-Inquart: Yes.

Goering: Including leading personalities; it does not make any difference.

Seyss-Inquart: Yes, they have given the order not to offer any resistance.

Goering: Yes, it does not matter; the Federal President did not authorise you and that also can be considered as resistance.

Seyss-Inquart Yes.

Goering: Well, now you are officially authorised.

Seyss-Inquart Yes.

Goering: Well, good luck, Heil Hitler."

I'm sorry; that conversation took place at 8 o'clock not 11. I meant to say 8 o'clock. It is quite interesting to me that when the defendant Goering was planning to invade a peaceful neighbouring State, he planned to try those whom he referred to as major war criminals, the leading personalities, before a German court-martial. So much for the conversation with respect to the plan of action for taking over power. Then something very significant was sent on that subject over the telephone, at least so far as those transcripts indicate. But there was another historical event which was discussed over the telephone. I refer to the famous telegram which Seyss-Inquart sent to the German Government, requesting the German Government to send troops into Austria to help Seyss- Inquart put down disorder. A conversation held at 8.48 that night between Goering and Keppler proceeded as follows: I read from page 1 of Part L:-

"Goering: Well, I do not know yet. Listen, the main thing is that if Inquart takes over all powers of government he keeps the radio stations occupied.

Keppler: Well, we represent the Government now.

Goering: Yes, that's it. You are the Government. Listen carefully. The following telegram should be sent here by Seyss- Inquart. Take the notes: "The provisional Austrian Government which, after the dismissal of the Schuschnigg Government, considered it its task to establish police and order in Austria, send to the German Government the urgent request to support it in its task to help it to prevent bloodshed. For this purpose, it asks the German Government to send German troops as soon as possible."

Keppler: Well, SA and SS are marching through the streets, but everything is quiet."

THE PRESIDENT: Did you say "quiet"?

MR. ALDERMAN: Quiet.

THE PRESIDENT: In my copy, it is "quick."

MR. ALDERMAN: That is a typographical error. It is "Quiet."

THE PRESIDENT: Yes.

MR. ALDERMAN:

"Everything has collapsed with the professional groups. Now let us talk about sending German troops to put down disorder."

The SA and the SS were marching in the streets, but everything was quiet. And a few minutes later, the conversation continued thus, reading from page 2 of Part L:-

Goering: Then our troops will cross the border to-day.

Keppler: Yes.

Goering: Good, he should send the telegram as soon as possible.

Keppler: Well, send the telegram to Seyss-Inquart in the office of the Federal Chancellor.

Goering: Please show him the text of the telegram and do tell him that we are asking him - well, he doesn't even need to send the telegram. All he needs to do is to say, 'Agreed.'

Keppler: Yes.

Goering: He doesn't know me at the Fuehrer's or at my place. Well, good luck. Heil Hitler." Of course, he didn't need to send the telegram because Goering wrote the telegram. He already had it. It must be recalled that in the first conversation, Part A, held at 3.5 p.m., Goering had requested Seyss-Inquart to send the telegram agreed upon, but now the matter was so urgent that he discussed the direct wording of the telegram over the telephone. And an hour later, at 9.54 p.m. a conversation between Dr. Dietrich in Berlin and Keppler in Vienna went on as follows, reading from Part M:-

"Dietrich: I need the telegram urgently.

Keppler: Tell the General Field Marshal that Seyss-Inquart agrees.

Dietrich: This is marvellous. Thank you.

Keppler: Listen to the radio. News will be given.

Dietrich: Where?

Keppler: From Vienna.

Dietrich: So Seyss-Inquart agrees?

Keppler: Jawohl."

Next the actual order to invade Austria. Communications in Austria were now suspended but the German military machine had been set in motion. To demonstrate that, I now offer in evidence captured document C-182, offered as exhibit USA 77, a directive of 11th March, 1938, at 2045 hours, from Supreme Commander of the Armed Forces. This directive, initialled by General Jodl and signed by Hitler, orders the invasion of Austria in view of its failure to comply with the German ultimatum. The directive reads.-

"Top secret. Berlin, 11th March, 1938, 2045 hours. Supreme Commander of the Armed Forces, OKW," with symbols. 35 copies, 6th copy. C-in-C. Navy (pencil note) has been informed. Re: Operation Otto. Directive No. 2."

(1) The demands of the German ultimatum to the Austrian Government have not been fulfilled.

(2) The Austrian Armed Forces have been ordered to withdraw in front of the entry of German troops and to avoid fighting.

The Austrian Government has ceased to function of its own accord.

(3) To avoid further bloodshed in Austrian towns, the entry of the German Armed Forces into Austria will commence, according to directive No. 1, at day-break on 12.3.

I expect the set objectives to be reached by exerting all forces to the full as quickly as possible. Signed Adolf Hitler. Initialled by Jodl and by a name that looks like Warlimont."

And then some interesting communications with Rome, to avoid possibility of disaster from that quarter. At the very time that Hitler and Goering had embarked on this military undertaking they still had a question mark in. their minds, and that was Italy. Italy had massed on the Italian border in 1934 on the occasion of 25th July, 1934, the putsch, Italy had traditionally been the political protector of Austria.

With what a sigh of relief did Hitler hear at 10.25 p.m. that night from Prince Phillipp von Hessen, his Ambassador at Rome, that he had just come back from the Palazzo Venezia, where Mussolini had accepted the whole thing in a very friendly manner. The situation can really be grasped by the reading of the conversation. The record of the conversation shows the excitement under which Hitler was operating when he spoke over the phone. It is a short conversation, and I shall read the first half of it from Part "N" of the transcript of document 2949-PS. I'm afraid Part "N" may be blurred on the mimeographed copy. "H" is Hessen and "F" is the Fuehrer.

"Hessen: I have just come back from Palazzo Venezia. The Duce accepted the whole thing in a very friendly manner. He sends you his regards. He had been informed from Austria, von Schuschnigg gave him the news. He had then said it would be a complete impossibility; it would be a bluff; such a thing could not be done. So he was told that it was unfortunately arranged thus, and it could not be changed any more. Then Mussolini said that Austria would be immaterial to him."

Hitler: Then please tell Mussolini I will never forget him for this.

Hessen: Yes.

Hitler: Never, never, never, whatever happens. I am still ready to make a quite different agreement with him.

Hessen: Yes, I told him that, too.

Hitler: As soon as the Austrian affair has been settled, I shall be ready to go with him through thick and thin; nothing matters.

Hessen: Yes, my Fuehrer.

Hitler: Listen, I shall make any agreement - I am no longer in fear of the terrible position which would have existed militarily in case we had become involved in a conflict. You may tell him that I do thank him ever so much, never, never shall I forget that.

Hessen: Yes, my Fuehrer.

Hitler: I will never forget it, whatever will happen. If he should ever need any help or be in any danger, he can be convinced that I shall stick to him whatever might happen, even if the whole world were against him.

Hessen: Yes, my Fuehrer.

The Tribunal will recall the reference in Jodl's diary to the letter which Hitler had sent to Mussolini. It is dated 11th March. It may be found in the official publication "Dokumente der Deutschen Politik," Volume 6, 1, page 135, number 24A. I ask the Court to take judicial notice of it and you will find a translation of it appearing in our document 2510-PS. In this letter, after stating that Austria had been declining into anarchy, Hitler wrote - and I quote:-

"I have decided to re-establish order in my fatherland - order and tranquillity -

and to give to the popular will the possibility of settling its own faith in unmistakable fashion openly and by its own decision."

He stated that this was an act of self-defence; that he had no hostile intentions towards Italy. And after the invasion, when Hitler was at Linz, Austria, he communicated his gratitude to Mussolini once more, in the famous telegram which the world so well remembers. I again cite Dokumente der Deutschen Politik, Volume 6, page 145, number 29, the translation of the telegram being in our document 2467-PS, and the document reads:-

"Mussolini, I shall never forget you for this."

We now shift our scene from Vienna to Berlin. We have shifted our scene I mean, from Vienna to Berlin. It may now be appropriate to come back to Vienna just long enough to recall that late in the evening of 11th March, President Miklas did appoint defendant Seyss-Inquart as Chancellor. The radio announcement of Seyss-Inquart's appointment was made at 11.15 p.m. This is noted in Dokumente der Deutschen Politik, Volume 6, 1, page 137, number 25- A, and a translation of the announcement is in our document 2465- PS. Then something had to be done in London to smooth things over there and accordingly, one more act, played on the international scene, is set down in Air Ministry telephone transcript. On Sunday, 13th March, 1938, the day after the invasion, defendant Goering, who had been left in Berlin in charge of the Reich by Hitler, who had gone to his fatherland, phoned defendant Ribbentrop in London. I find this conversation very illuminating as to the way in which these defendants operated, using, if I may employ American vernacular, a kind of international "double talk" to soothe and mislead other nations. I quote from Part 1 of item "W" of document 2949-PS.

"Goering: As you know - speaking to Ribbentrop in London - "As you know, the Fuehrer has entrusted me with the administration of the current government procedures (Fuhrung der Regierungsgeschaefte), and therefore I wanted to inform you. There is overwhelming joy in Austria, that you can hear over the radio.
Ribbentrop: Yes, it is fantastic, isn't it?
Goering: Yes, the last march into the Rhineland is completely overshadowed. The Fuehrer was deeply moved, when he talked to me last night. You must remember it was the first time that he saw his homeland again. Now, I mainly want to talk about political things. Well, this story that we had given an ultimatum is just foolish gossip. From the very beginning the National Socialist ministers and the representatives of the people (Volksreferenten) have presented the ultimatum. Later on, more and more prominent people of the Movement Party participated, and as a natural result, the Austrian National Socialist ministers asked us to back them up, so that they would not be completely beaten up again and subjected to terror and civil war. Then we told them we would not allow von Schuschnigg to provoke a civil war, under any circumstances. Whether by von Schuschnigg's direct order or with his consent, the Communists and the Reds had been armed, and were already making demonstrations, which were photographed with "Heil Moskau " and so on. Naturally, all these facts caused some danger for Wiener-Neustadt. Then you have to consider that von

Schuschnigg made his speeches, telling them the Fatherland Front (Vaterlaendische Front) would fight to the last man. One could not know that they would capitulate like that, and therefore Seyss-Inquart, who already had taken over the Government, asked us to march in immediately, before we had already marched up to the frontier, since we could not know whether there would be a civil war or not. These are the actual facts which can be proved by documents."

There the defendant Goering was giving to the defendant Ribbentrop the proper line that he should take in London, as to how to explain what had happened in Austria. Of course, when the defendant Goering said that his story about this matter could be proved by documents, I don't think he had in mind that his own telephone calls might constitute documents.

Another rather interesting item begins on page 3 of the English text of this Part "W" - still Goering talking to Ribbentrop in London. This is at the bottom of the page.

"Goering: No, no, I think so, too. Only, I did not know if you had spoken already to these people. I want you once more - but no - not at all once more, but generally speaking - to tell the following to Halifax and Chamberlain: It is not correct that Germany has given an ultimatum. This is a lie by von Schuschnigg, because the ultimatum was presented to him by Seyss-Inquart, Glaise-Horstenau and Jury. Furthermore, it is not true that we have presented an ultimatum to the Federal President, but that also was given by the others, and as far as I know, just a military attache came along, asked by Seyss- Inquart, because of a technical question" - you will recall that he was a Lieutenant-General directed by Goering to go along - "he was supposed to ask whether, in case Seyss-Inquart asked for the support of German troops, Germany would grant this request. Furthermore, I want to state that Seyss-Inquart asked us expressly, by 'phone and by telegram, to send troops because he did not know about the situation in Wiener- Neustadt, Vienna, and so on; because arms had been distributed there. And then he could not know how the Fatherland Front might react, since they always had had such a big mouth."

Ribbentrop: Tell me, how is the situation in Vienna; is everything settled yet?
Goering: Yes. Yesterday I landed hundreds of airplanes with some companies, in order to secure the airfields, and they were received with joy. To-day the advance unit of the 17th division marches in, together with the Austrian troops. Also, I want to point out that the Austrian troops did not withdraw, but that they got together and fraternised immediately with the German troops, wherever they were stationed."

These are quite interesting explanations that the ultimatum was by Seyss-Inquart alone and not by Goering; that Lieutenant General Muff, the Military Attache, was along just to answer a technical question; and that Seyss-Inquart asked expressly by telephone and telegram for troops. But, perhaps to understand this conversation, we must try to create again the actual physical scene of the time and place as Goering talked over the phone. I quote nine lines from page 11 of the English text, about in the middle, Part "W."

"Goering: Well, do come! I shall be delighted to see you.

Ribbentrop: I shall see you this afternoon.

Goering: The weather is wonderful here. Blue sky. I am sitting here on my balcony - all covered with blankets-in the fresh air, drinking my coffee. Later on I have to drive in; I have to make the speech, and the birds are twittering, and here and there I can hear over the radio the enthusiasm, which must be wonderful over there" - that is Vienna.

Ribbentrop: That is marvellous."

May it please the Tribunal, I have nearly come to the end of the material relating to the aggression against Austria. In a moment I shall take up quite briefly the effect of the Anschluss, some of the developments which took place after the German troops marched across the border. What is to come after that is an epilogue, but before developing the epilogue, it may be appropriate to pause briefly for just a moment. I think that the facts which I have related to the Tribunal to-day show plainly certain things about the defendants involved in the conspiracy, and among the conspirators who particularly took action in the Austrian matter were von Papen, Seyss-Inquart, Ribbentrop, von Neurath, and Goering.

First I think it is plain that these men were dangerous men. They used their power without a bridle. They used their power to override the independence and freedom of others. And they were more than bullies. They compounded their force with fraud. They coupled threats with legal technicalities and devious manoeuvres, wearing a sanctimonious mask to cover that duplicity. I think they were dangerous men.

In accordance with the directive of 11th March, our document C- 1S2, exhibit USA 77, the German Army crossed the Austrian border at daybreak, 12th March, 1938. Hitler issued a proclamation to the German people announcing the invasion, and purporting to justify it. I refer again to Dokumente der Deutschen Politik, Volume 6, page 140, number 27, "Proclamation of Hitler." The British Government and the French Government filed protests. The German Government and the Austrian National Socialists swiftly secured their grip on Austria. Seyss-Inquart welcomed Hitler at Linz, and they both expressed their joy over the events of the day. Seyss-Inquart in his speech declared Article 88 of the Treaty of St. Germain inoperative. I refer to the speech of Seyss-Inquart at Linz on 12th March, 1938, as contained in the Dokumente der Deutschen Politik, Volume 6, 1, page 144, number 28-A, of which I ask the Tribunal to take judicial notice, and which you will find translated in our document 2485-PS.

For a view of what was happening in Vienna, I offer in evidence our document L-292, telegram 70, American Legation, Vienna, to the American Secretary of State, 12th March,1938 - that is L-292,and I offer it as exhibit USA 78. I quote it in full.

"Secretary of State, Wien.

March 12th, noon.

"Numerous German bombers flying over Vienna dropping leaflets 'National Socialist Germany greets its possession, National Socialist Austria and its new Government in true indivisible Union.'

Continual rumours small German troops movements into Austria and impending arrival Austrian Legion. S.S. and S.A. in undisputed control in Vienna. Police wear Swastika arm bands, von Schuschnigg and Schmidt rumoured arrested. Himmler and Hess here."

Signed "Wiley."

The law-making machine was put to work immediately on the task of consolidation. For all of this material I shall merely refer the Tribunal to the German sources and to the document number of the English translation, but I think I need not offer these legislative acts in evidence but shall merely invite the court to take judicial notice of them.

First, Miklas was forced to resign as President. I refer to Dokumente der Deutschen Politik, Volume 6, 1, page 147, number 30- B. Our translation is in our document 2466-PS.

In this connection the Court will no doubt recall Goering's telephone conversation as shown in document 2949-PS, that in view of Miklas' delay in appointing Seyss-Inquart, Miklas would be dismissed. Seyss-Inquart became both Chancellor and President.

He then signed a Federal Constitutional Law of March 12th, 1938, for the reunion of Austria with the German Reich, which in turn was incorporated into the Reich Statute of Reunion, passed the same day, German law. I cite for that the Reichsgesetzblatt 1938, Volume 11 page 237, number 21, a translation of which will be found in our document 2307-PS.

This Federal Constitutional Law declared Austria to be a province of the German Reich. By annexing Austria into the German Reich, Germany violated Article 80 of the Treaty of Versailles, which provided - by the way, on the constitutional law to which I just referred there appear as signatories the following names: Adolf Hitler, Fuehrer and Reich Chancellor; Goering, General Field Marshal, Reich Minister of Aviation; Frick Reich Minister of the Interior; von Ribbentrop, Reich Minister of Foreign Affairs; R. Hess, Deputy Fuehrer.

By annexing Austria into the German Reich, Germany violated Article 80 of the Treaty of Versailles, which provides, and I quote:-

"Germany acknowledges and will respect the independence of Austria within the Frontier, which may be fixed in a treaty between that State and the principal Allied and Associated Powers. She agrees that this independence shall be inalienable."

Similarly, the Austrian action violated Article 88 of the Treaty of St. Germain, which provides: "The independence of Austria is inalienable otherwise than with the consent of the Council of the League of Nations. Consequently, Austria undertakes, in the absence of the consent of the said Council, to abstain from any act which might directly or indirectly or by any means whatever compromise her independence, particularly until her admission to membership of the League of Nations, by participation in the affairs of another power."

This basic constitutional Law provided for a plebiscite to be held on 10th April, 1938, on the question of reunion, but this was a mere formality. The plebiscite could only confirm the union declared in the law. It could not undo Germany's union with and control over Austria.

To illustrate the way in which legal consolidation was swiftly assured under conditions of occupation of Austria by troops, it is not necessary to do more than review some of the acts passed within the month.

Hitler placed the Austrian Federal Army under his own command and required all members of the Army to take an oath of allegiance to Hitler as their Supreme Commander. A translation of the pertinent document will be found in our 2936-PS, and I refer to the instruction of the Fuehrer and Reich Chancellor, concerning the Austrian Federal Army, 13th March, 1938, Dokumente der Deutschen Politik, Volume 6, 1, page 150.

Public officials of the province of Austria were required to take an oath of office swearing allegiance to Hitler, Fuehrer of the German Reich and people. Jewish officials as defined were not permitted to take the oath.

I refer to "Decree of the Fuehrer and Reich Chancellor concerning the administration of oath to the officials of the Province of Austria, 15th March, 1938, Reichsgesetzblatt, 1938, Volume 1, page 245, number 24, the translation being in our document 2311-PS.

Hitler and Frick signed a decree applying to Austria various Reich laws, including the law of 1933 against the formation of new political parties, and the 1933 law for the Preservation of Unity of Party and State.

I refer to "First Decree of the Fuehrer and Reich Chancellor concerning the introduction of German Reich Law in Austria, 15th March, 1938," Reichsgesetzblatt, Volume 1, page 247, number 25, the translation being in our document 2310-PS.

Hitler, Frick and Goering ordered that the Reich Minister of the Interior be the central authority for carrying out the reunion of Austria with the German Reich, 16th March, 1932, Reichsgesetzblatt, 1938 - that must be 1938 - Volume 1, page 249, number 25, translated in our document 1060-PS.

In connection with Germany's extensive propaganda campaign to insure acceptability of the German regime, it may be noted that Goebbels established a Reich Propaganda Office in Vienna.

I cite "Order concerning the Establishment of a Reich Propaganda Office in Vienna, 31st March, 1938," Reichsgesetzblatt 1938, Volume 1, page 350, number 46, translated in our document 2935-PS.

The ballot addressed to soldiers of the former Austrian Army as "German soldiers" asked the voters whether they agreed with the accomplishment and ratification on 13th March, 1938, of the reuniting of Austria with Germany.

I cite "Second Order concerning Plebiscite and Election for the Greater German Reichstag of 24th March, 1938, " Reichsgesetzblatt, 1938, Volume 1, page 303, translated in our document 1659-PS.

The ground work was fully laid before the holding of the plebiscite "for German men and women of Austria" promised in the Basic Law of 13th March."

Then, the importance of Austria in further plans of aggression. Could we run that screen up, or is the chart still behind it? Well, the Court will remember the chart.

The seizure of Austria had now formed that lower jaw to the head of the wolf around the head of Czechoslovakia. Germany's desire to consummate the Anschluss with Austria, and its determination to execute that aim in the way and at the time that it did - that is, with threat of military force, quickly, and despite political risk - was due to the importance of Austria in its further plans of aggression.

The conference held on 5th November, 1937, planning for aggressive war in Europe outlined as objectives in Austria the conquest through expulsion of a million people and the effective increase in fighting strength, in part through the improvement in the Frontier.

I cite again document 386-PS, exhibit USA 25. Austria was to yield to Germany material resources, and moreover she provided ready cash, taken from the Jews and from the Austrian Government.

One of the first orders passed after the Anschluss was an order signed by Hitler, Frick, Schwerin von Krosigk and Schacht for the transfer to the Reich of the assets of the Austrian National Bank. I refer to the "Order for the Transfer of the Austrian National Bank to the Reichsbank, 17th March, 1938," Reichsgesetzblatt, 1938, Volume 1, page 254, number 27, translated in our document 2313-PS.

Austria also yielded human resources. Three months after the Anschluss there was enacted a decree requiring the 21-year-old men, Austrian men, to report for active military service. I refer to the decree regarding registration for active military service in Austria during 1938, Reichsgesetzblatt, 1938, Volume 11, page 631, translated in our document 1660-PS.

The acquisition of Austria improved the military strategic position of the German Army. I invite the Court's attention to a document which I introduced in the case on preparation for aggression, document L-I72, exhibit USA 34, which was a lecture delivered by General Jodl, Chief of the German Staff of the Armed Forces, on 7th November, at Munich, to the Gauleiters. Only one page of that lecture appears in this particular document book, and I quote from one paragraph on page 1 of the English text, which is page 7 of Jodl's lecture, which reviewed the situation in 1938:-

"The Austrian 'Anschluss,' in its turn, brought with it not only the fulfilment of an old national aim but also had the effect both of reinforcing our fighting strength and of materially improving our strategic position. Whereas up till then the territory of Czechoslovakia had projected in a most menacing way right into Germany (a wasp waist in the direction of France and an air base for the Allies, in particular Russia), Czechoslovakia herself was now enclosed by pincers. Her own strategic position had now become so unfavourable that she was bound to fall a victim to any attack pressed home with rigour before effective aid from the West could be expected to arrive."

The Nazi conspirators were now ready to carry out the second part of this second phase of their aggression, and to take over Czechoslovakia.

Logically, if the Tribunal please, we should proceed at this point with the story about Czechoslovakia. For reasons that I explained earlier in the week we have had to change our plans somewhat from a strictly logical order, and the plan at present is that on Monday I shall go forward with the Czechoslovakian part of the aggressive war case.

At this point it is planned by our staff to show a motion picture, and it will take some few minutes to make physical arrangements in the courtroom, so that if the Court should feel like recessing those arrangements could be made.

THE PRESIDENT: Could you tell me how long the showing of the picture will take?

MR. ALDERMAN: My understanding is about an hour.

THE PRESIDENT: We will adjourn for ten minutes then, shall we now, or until the picture is ready?

(A recess was taken.)

COLONEL STOREY: Mr. President, if the Tribunal please, Sir, supplementing what Mr. Alderman has said, we have had to adjust our presentation to some extent. To-morrow morning, the witness will be offered for interrogation. Then Mr. Alderman on Monday, and Sir Hartley Shawcross will make the opening statement for the British Empire on Tuesday morning.

The film this afternoon, at the request of the defendants' counsel, made in writing to the Court, was exhibited to defendants' counsel the day before yesterday evening in this courtroom. I personally requested Dr. Dix to convey the invitation to defence counsel to witness the film. Eight of them came. Dr. Dix advised me kindly that he would not come unless he were forced to come.

I now present Mr. Dodd, who will have charge of the presentation.

MR. DODD: If it please the Tribunal, the prosecution for the United States will at this time present to the Tribunal, with its permission, a documentary film on concentration camps. This is by no means the entire proof which the prosecution will offer with respect to the subject of concentration camps, but this film which we offer represents in a brief and unforgettable form an explanation of what the words "concentration camp" imply.

This subject arises appropriately in the narrative of events leading up to the actual outbreak of aggressive war, which, as Mr. Alderman's presentation shows, was planned and prepared by the Nazi conspirators. We propose to show that concentration camps were not an end in themselves but, rather, they were an integral part of the Nazi system of government. As we shall show, the black- shirted guards of the S.S. and the Gestapo stood ranged behind the official pages of the Reichsgesetzblatt.

We intend to prove that each and every one of these defendants knew of the existence of these concentration camps; that fear and terror and nameless horror of the concentration camps were instruments by which the defendants retained power and suppressed the opposition to any of their policies, including, of course, their plans for aggressive war. By this means they enforced the controls imposed upon the German people, as required to execute these plans, and obliterated freedom in Germany and in the countries invaded and occupied by the armies of the Third Reich.

Finally, we ask the Tribunal in viewing this film to bear in mind the fact that the proof to be offered at a later stage of this trial will show that on some of the organisations charged in this indictment lies the responsibility for the origin, the control and the maintenance of the whole concentration camp system. On the S.S., the S.D. - a part of the S.S. which tracked down the victims - upon the Gestapo, which committed the victims to the camps, and upon other branches of the S.S. which were in charge of the atrocities committed therein.

Commander James Donovan will introduce the film with a statement explaining its source and its authenticity. Commander James Donovan.

COMMANDER DONOVAN: May it please the Tribunal, I refer to document 2430-PS, concerning the motion picture entitled "Nazi Concentration Camps " and to the affidavits of Commander James B. Donovan, Lt.-Colonel George C. Stevens, Lieutenant E. R. Kellogg and Colonel Erik Tiebold contained therein. The affidavits of Colonel Stevens and of Lieutenant Kellogg are also contained in the motion picture, and thus will be in the record of the Tribunal. With the permission of the Tribunal, I shall now, however, read into the record those affidavits not appearing in the film.

THE PRESIDENT: In the absence of any objection by the defence counsel, we don't think it is necessary to read these formal affidavits.

COMMANDER DONOVAN: Yes, sir. The United States now offers in evidence an official film, a documentary motion picture report on Nazi Concentration Camps. This report has been compiled from motion pictures taken by Allied military photographers as the Allied armies in the West liberated the areas in which these camps were located. The accompanying narration is taken directly from the reports of the military photographers who filmed the camps.

While these motion pictures speak for themselves in evidencing life and death in Nazi concentration camps, proper authentication of the films is contained in the affidavits of the United States Army and Navy officers, to which I have referred.

As has been stated, this motion picture has been made available to all defence counsel, and they possess copies in their information room of the supporting affidavits duly translated.

If the Tribunal please, we shall proceed with the projection of the film, document 2430-PS, which is exhibit USA 79.

(Photographs of the two affidavits were then projected on the screen and the voices of the respective deponents were reproduced reading them.)

"I, George C. Stevens, Lieutenant-Colonel, Army of the United States, hereby certify:-

1. From 1st March, 1945, to 8th May, 1945, I was on active duty with the United States Army Signal Corps attached to the Supreme Headquarters, Allied Expeditionary Forces, and among my official duties was direction of the photographing of the Nazi concentration camps and prison camps as liberated by Allied forces.

2. The motion pictures which will be shown following this affidavit were taken by official Allied photographic teams in the course of their official duties, each team being composed of military personnel under the direction of a

commissioned officer.

3. To the best of my knowledge and belief, these motion pictures constitute a true representation of the individuals and scenes photographed. They have not been altered in any respect since the exposures were made. The accompanying narration is a true statement of the facts and circumstances under which these pictures were made.

Signed) George C. Stevens, Lieutenant Colonel, U.S.A."

Sworn to before me this 2nd day of October, 1945.

(Signed) James B. Donovan, Commander, United States Naval Reserve.

I, E. R. Kellogg, Lieutenant, United States Navy, hereby certify that:-

1. From 1929 to 1941 I was employed at the Twentieth Century Fox Studios in Hollywood, California, as a director of film effects, and am familiar with all photographic techniques. From 6th September, 1941, to the present date 27th August, 1945, 1 have been on active duty with the United States Navy.

2. I have carefully examined the motion picture film to be shown following this affidavit, and I certify that the images of these excerpts from the original negative have not been retouched, distorted or otherwise altered in any respect, and are true copies of the originals held in the vaults of the United States Army Signal Corps. These excerpts comprise 6,000 feet of film selected from 80,000 feet, all of which I have reviewed and all of which is similar in character to these excerpts.

(Signed) E. R. Kellogg, Lieutenant, United States Navy.

Sworn to before me this 27th day of August, 1945. (Signed) John Ford, Captain, United States Navy."

NINTH DAY:
Friday, 30th November, 1945

THE PRESIDENT: I call on the prosecutor for the United States.

MR. JUSTICE JACKSON: Colonel Amen will represent the United States this morning.

COLONEL JOHN H. AMEN: May it please the Tribunal, I propose to call as the first witness for the prosecution, Major- General Erwin Lahousen.

THE PRESIDENT: The Tribunal wish me to state that the evidence of the witness, whom you propose to call, must be strictly confined to the Count with which the United States are dealing, Count One.

COLONEL AMEN: May I have a moment to discuss that with the Chief Counsel of the United States?

THE PRESIDENT: Yes, certainly.

DR. OTTO NELTE: Mr. President, so far as I know the prosecution -

THE PRESIDENT: Could you state for whom you appear? Do you appear for the defendant, Keitel?

DR. NELTE: Yes.

As far as I know, an agreement was reached between the prosecution and the defence, to the effect that whenever possible, questions to be discussed on the following day should be communicated beforehand. The obvious purpose of this understanding, which seems reasonable to me, was to give the defence counsel the possibility to discuss forthcoming questions with their clients, and thus expedite the rapid and smooth progress of the trial.

I did not hear that the witness, Lahousen, was to be summoned by the prosecution today, nor did I hear on what questions he was to be heard.

This was particularly important, because today, I believe, we were not to deal with questions, nor was the witness, Lahousen, to be heard on questions connected with the address delivered by the prosecution during the preceding days.

THE PRESIDENT: That is the contrary of what I said. What I said was that the witness was to be confined to evidence relating to Count One, which is the count that has been solely discussed up to the present date.

DR. NELTE: Does the President wish to say that in order to make it possible for the defence to subject the witness to cross-examination, they will be given the possibility, after interrogation by the prosecution, to speak with the defendant during a recess, so that they will know what questions to ask? The witness, Lahousen, as far as I recall, has not been mentioned in the address of the prosecution.

THE PRESIDENT: Is that all you have to say?

DR. NELTE: Yes.

THE PRESIDENT: I think the Tribunal would like to hear counsel for the United States upon the agreement which counsel for the defendant, Keitel, alleges, namely, an agreement to the effect that what was to be discussed on the following day should be communicated to the defendants' counsel beforehand.

MR. JUSTICE JACKSON: I know of no agreement to inform defendants' counsel of any witness, nor of his testimony; nor would I want to make such. There are security reasons involved in disclosing to defence counsel the names of witnesses, which I don't need to enlarge.

I am quite sure we did advise them that they would be given information as to the documentary matters, and I think that has been adhered to.

As to witnesses, however, a matter of policy arises. These witnesses are not always prisoners. They have to be treated in somewhat different fashion to prisoners; and the protection of their security is a very important consideration, when we are trying this case in the very hotbed of the Nazi Organisation with which some of defence counsel were identified.

THE PRESIDENT: I think, Mr. Justice Jackson, that that is sufficient. If you tell the Tribunal that there was no such agreement, the Tribunal will, of course, accept that.

MR. JUSTICE JACKSON: I know of nothing of that character, relating to witnesses, that does apply.

We find it very difficult to know just the meaning of the ruling which the Court has just announced. Count One of the Indictment is a conspiracy count, covering the entire substantive part of the Indictment. There are problems, of course, of overlapping, which I had supposed to have been worked out between the prosecutors until this morning. It is impossible, in trying a conspiracy case, to keep from mentioning the fact that the act, which was the object of the conspiracy, was performed. In fact, that is a part of the evidence of the conspiracy.

I know I do not need to enlarge upon the wide scope of evidence in a conspiracy case. I think, perhaps, the best thing to do is to swear the witness, and that the other prosecutors, if they feel their field is being trespassed upon, or the judges, if they feel that we are overlapping, raise the objection specifically; because I don't know how we can separate, particularly on a moment's notice, Count One from the other counts.

We have tried our best to work out an arrangement that would be fair, as between ourselves and the other prosecutors, but we find it impossible always to please everybody.

With the greatest deference to the ruling of the Court, I would like to suggest that we proceed. I don't know just what the bounds of the ruling might be, but I think the only way we can find out is to proceed, and have specific objections to the specific things, which anyone feels have been transgressed; and in doing that, I want to say that we do it with the greatest respect to the ruling, but that we may find ourselves in conflict with it, because of the difficulty of any boundary on the subject.

THE PRESIDENT: Doctor Stahmer?

DR. STAHMER (counsel for defendant Goering): Mr. President, I must return to the matter, raised by Doctor Nelte, namely, his assertion that before the beginning of the trial the defence and the prosecution reached an agreement to the effect that the next day's programme should always be made known to the defence on the day before. Such an agreement has actually been reached, and I cannot understand that the prosecution should not have been informed of it. In a conference we considered this possibility, and were given assurances by Doctor Kempner, our liaison man, that it would be reached. I should further like to point out the following:

The prosecution has stated that, for security reasons, the defence could not be furnished with the names of witnesses to be summoned during next day's proceedings. The Press, however, received, as early as yesterday, information concerning the witnesses to be heard today. We were informed of this, this morning, by representatives of the Press and, as far as I know, a statement to this effect appeared in to- day's papers. I cannot understand why such information should be withheld from us because, for security reasons, such statements are not to be made. It seems to me that this amounts to an unjustified distrust of the discretion of the defence. It is, furthermore, incorrect that we are now being furnished with documents in good time. Documents still reach us belatedly. This morning, for instance, a document to be dealt with to-day was put on our desks and, moreover, the language it was written in could not be understood by most of the defence counsel since they do not know English.

As I have already submitted this objection in writing, I should be glad if the Tribunal will decide this matter as soon as it may.

THE PRESIDENT: Have you finished?

DR. STAHMER: Yes.

MR. JUSTICE JACKSON: It is quite correct that the name of the witness who is to be used to-day was given to the Press. The question of our policy as to giving witnesses' names was submitted to me last night after the Court recessed, because we had not been using witnesses heretofore; and I then stated to Colonel Storey that witnesses' names must not be given to the defence counsel for security reasons. He communicated that, I believe, to Doctor Dix. I found that later it had been given to the Press. They, of course, have had adequate information therefore as to this witness. However, I am speaking about the policy. We cannot be under an obligation to inform those counsel of the names of witnesses who will be called. who are here in Nuremberg, but not in prison; the situation does not permit of that. Neither can we furnish transcripts of testimony or that sort of thing of witnesses in advance.

Now we want to give the defence counsel everything that in the fair conduct of the trial they ought to have. They are now receiving much more than any citizen of the United States gets on trial in the courts of the United States, in some respects, as to advance information and copies and help and service, and I do think that to ask us to disclose to them in advance either the names or substance of testimony- oftentimes the substance would disclose the witness-would not be proper. It was stated yesterday that we would take up a witness to-day.

THE PRESIDENT: We have already heard two counsel on behalf of the defence.

Have you anything to add which is different to what they have said?

DR. DIX (Counsel for defendant Schacht): Yes. I believe that I can elucidate a misunderstanding and contribute to the simplification of the whole problem. May I address the Court?

I believe that there is a misunderstanding here. I do not know what was discussed before I attended the Court, but the situation so far has been the following:-

No agreement was reached between the prosecution and the defence counsel. There is, as your Lordship knows, only an agreement regarding documents, which is known to the Court and which I therefore need not repeat. As far as witnesses are concerned, I believe that I may presuppose that we are all of one mind in finding justified the wish of the defence to know beforehand what witnesses will appear.

The high Tribunal must decide to what extent this wish, which is in itself justified, cannot be granted for security reasons. That is a matter which lies outside the determination of the defence. But I believe that I understood Mr. Justice Jackson correctly in thinking that if the Press is being informed what witnesses will appear the next day, it is a matter of course that the same communication should be made to defence counsel, but that it was only an unhappy concatenation of circumstances, an incident that can always happen, and which can and will be obviated in future by mutual understanding and good will.

As I said, I do not know what was agreed upon before I was present here. I cannot therefore contradict my colleague, Dr. Stahmer, in this matter. I think it possible, however, that the misunderstanding arose because the readiness of the Court to have documents submitted and notice given to us forty-eight hours ahead of time, and even the film shown to us beforehand, led my colleagues to the conclusion, which I consider justified, that all evidence was to be submitted to them. We do not, of course, expect to be informed of the contents of the witness' account, because the contents evolve during the session and cannot be determined prior to it.

After this elucidation I should like to express the wish that we be informed in future what witness is to be called, and to add a further wish, that security considerations be guided by the certainty that the counsellors of the defence are reliable, determined and capable of assisting the Court in passing judgement by maintaining the discipline of proceedings. In consequence, the cases in which the security officer believes that he should not communicate the name of the witness beforehand, should be reduced to an absolute minimum.

THE PRESIDENT: The Tribunal will consider the submissions which have been made to them on behalf of defence counsel with reference to what shall or what shall not be communicated to them. With reference to the witness whom the United States desire to call, they will now be permitted to call him. With reference to what I said about confining his evidence to Count One, the Tribunal thinks that the best course would be for the other prosecutors to have the opportunity now to ask any questions which they think right, and that they may have the opportunity, if they wish, of calling the witness later upon their own counts.

As to cross-examination by the defendants' counsel, that will be allowed to them in the most convenient way possible, so that if they wish to have an opportunity of communicating with their clients before they cross-examine, they may have the opportunity of doing so. Now we will continue.

COLONEL AMEN: May we have General Lahousen brought before the Tribunal?

THE PRESIDENT: Will you stand in front of the microphone there so that you can be heard?

Q. What is your name

A. Erwin Lahousen.

Q. Will you please spell it?

A. L-a-h-o-u-s-e-n.

Q. Will you say this oath after me? I swear by God the Almighty and Omniscient, that I will speak the pure truth and will withhold and add nothing.

(The witness repeated the oath after the President.)

THE PRESIDENT: Don't you think the witness had better sit down?

COLONEL AMEN: I think he should be allowed to sit down, particularly since he has a heart condition which may be aggravated.

THE PRESIDENT: Very well; you can sit down.

BY **COLONEL AMEN:**

Q. Where were you born?

A. I was born in Vienna.

Q. On what date?

A. On 25th of October, 1897.

Q. What has been your occupation?

A. I was a professional soldier.

Q. Where were you trained?

A. I was trained in Austria, in the Military Academy in Wiener Neustadt.

Q. Were you immediately commissioned as an officer?

A. In 1915 I was commissioned a lieutenant in the infantry.

Q. Did you serve in the first World War?

A. Yes, as first and second lieutenant in the infantry.

Q. Were you promoted from time to time thereafter?

A. Yes, I was promoted according to the normal regulations valid in Austria at the time.

Q. By 1930 what rank had you attained?

A. In 1930 I was captain.

Q. And commencing in 1930 did you take any additional training?

A. In 1930 I entered the Austrian War School, which corresponds to the Military Academy in the German Army. I received the education of an officer of the General Staff.

Q. How long did this training last?

A. This training lasted three years.

Q. In 1933 to what regular army unit were you assigned?

A. In 1933 I was serving in the Second Austrian Division, the so-called Vienna Division.

Q. What type of work did you do there?

A. I was an Intelligence officer; that branch of the service for which I was destined already during my training with the General Staff.

Q. Did you then receive a further promotion?

A. I was promoted in accordance with the regulations valid in Austria, and roughly at the end of 1933 I became a Major. About 1935 or the beginning of 1936 I was transferred into the General. Staff - and, in June or at any rate, in the summer of 1936, I became lieutenant Colonel of the Austrian General Staff.

Q. And were you assigned to the intelligence division at or about that time?

A. I entered the Austrian Intelligence Service; that corresponds technically to what is called in the German Army "Abwehr." I must add that a "Nachrichten Abteilung" was only added to the Austrian Army about this time, i.e., 1936; before that there was no such department. Because the plan was to re-establish, within the framework of the Austrian Federal Army, the military intelligence service, which had ceased to exist after the collapse of the Austrian- Hungarian Empire, I was trained for it in order to organise the "Nachrichtenabteilung" which had by then come into existence.

Q. After being assigned to the Intelligence Division, how were your activities principally directed?

A. My responsible chief, or rather the responsible chief at that time, was Colonel of the General Staff, Boehme; the section chief to whom I was subordinate, was the chief of the Intelligence Service, that is to say, the man responsible to me or rather the one to whom I was responsible, from whom I received my orders and instructions; later on it was the Chief of the Austrian General Staff.

THE PRESIDENT: Can't you shorten this, Colonel Amen? We really needn't have all this detail.

COLONEL AMEN: Very good, Sir. It is, however, I think important for the Tribunal to understand more of this information than they ordinarily would by virtue of the fact that he was transferred subsequently to a corresponding position in the German Army, a point which I did want the Tribunal to appreciate.

BY COLONEL AMEN:

Q. Now, will you state to the Tribunal what your principal activities were after being assigned to the Intelligence Division? What information were you interested in and seeking to obtain?

A. If I understand your question correctly, I was a member of the Austrian Intelligence Service, that is to say, in the Austrian Intelligence Service and not in the German so- called "Abwehr."

Q. After the Anschluss, what position did you assume?

A. After the Anschluss I was automatically taken into the High Command of the German Armed Forces, and did the same job there. My chief there was Admiral Canaris.

Q. And what was the position of Admiral Canaris?

A. Canaris was, at that time, Chief of the Bureau of the "Ausland-Abwehr," that is to say, of the Intelligence.

Q. And will you explain briefly the responsibility of the principal departments of the Abwehr under Admiral Canaris?

A. When, in 1938, I entered the Ausland-Abwehr, after the "Anschluss," there were three Abwehr Divisions, and the division then called Ausland-Abwehr at least, I was acquainted with this Organisation. How it was before, I cannot say exactly.

Q. And what were your duties?

A. First of all, I was automatically placed in "Abwehr" Division 1. That is the section which was concerned with collecting information on secret communications, as it was also called. At the time I worked under the Chief of Section, Colonel-General Pieckenbrock, as well as Canaris, whom I knew from my Austrian past.

Q. Admiral Canaris was your immediate superior?

A. Admiral Canaris was my immediate superior.

Q. From time to time did you act as his personal representative?

A. Yes, in all cases and on all occasions when his immediate representative - that is, Colonel Pieckenbrock-was not present, or when Canaris, for one reason or another, considered it necessary or advisable for me to appear as his representative.

Q. And in this capacity did you have any contact with Field -Marshal Keitel?

A. Yes.

Q. Did you also have contact with Jodl

A. To a much lesser degree, but occasionally ...

Q. And did you occasionally attend conferences at which Herr Hitler was also present?

A. Yes, I attended a few of the sessions or meetings at which Hitler was present and which he conducted.

Q. Will you tell the Tribunal whether the leaders of the Abwehr were in sympathy with Hitler's war-programme?

A. I have to make it clear in this connection that we chiefs, at that time, in the Intelligence Department were deeply influenced and captivated by the personality of Canaris, his inner orientation, which was perfectly clear and unequivocal to a small group of us.

Q. And was there a particular group or groups in the Abwehr who worked against the Nazis?

A. Within the Ausland-Abwehr Office there were two groups which, as far as their intentions and actions were concerned, were closely connected, but which, nevertheless, must be strictly kept apart.

Q. And what were those two groups?

A. Before I answer this question, I must briefly discuss the personality of Canaris, who was the centre and focus of this group.

Q. Please make it as brief as you can.

A. Canaris was a personality of pure intellect. We relied on his inner, very unique and complicated nature, for this reason. He hated violence and hated and abominated therefore Hitler, his system, and particularly his methods. Canaris was, in whatever way you may look upon him, a human being.

Q. Now, will you refer back to the two groups of which you spoke and tell me about each of those two groups and their respective memberships?

A. One might characterise one of the groups as Canaris' circle. It included, in the "Ausland-Abwehr," and particularly amongst its leaders, Canaris himself as its spiritual leader; General Oster, Chief of the Central Division (the Fuehrer of the Abwehr) and my predecessor, Lieutenant-Colonel Grosskurt, who had joined the circle along with Canaris in Vienna as early as 1938. Further, the Chief of Abwehr Section 1, Colonel Pieckenbrock, who was a close friend of Canaris; and Pieckenbrock's successor, Colonel Hansen, who was executed on 28th June; then there was my successor, Colonel Freytag-Lorrindhofen, who was executed, or rather, who committed suicide on 26th July, 1944, before his arrest; also, somewhat differentiated, the Chief of Abwehr Section III, Colonel Bentivigny. There were, too, various people in all these sections; most of them were executed or imprisoned in connection with the events of 20th July, 1944.

In this connection I have to mention a person who did not belong to the said groups, but who knew about certain actions designed to prevent orders or foil the execution of orders for murder and other atrocities: namely, Admiral Burckner who was chief of the Auslandsabteilung at that time. These were essentially the leaders of the group called the Canaris-circle.

The second and smaller group was attached to General Oster, who was the spiritual leader of the persons in the office of the Ausland-Abwehr who, as early as 1938 - I could recognise this clearly by 1939-1940 and later on - were actively concerned with schemes and plans designed to do away by force with Hitler, the instigator of this catastrophe.

Q. What was the purpose of the group to which you belonged; that is, Canaris' inner circle?

A. As regards the political motives or aims, I was not informed. I can only reiterate the train of thought best known to me, having been one of Canaris' most intimate confidants, which determined his basic attitude. This, his inner attitude, which determined the actions not only of myself but of the other people whom I mentioned, was as follows:-

We did not succeed in preventing this war of aggression. The war signified the annihilation of Germany and of ourselves and, as such, would be a misfortune and a catastrophe of the greatest extent. However, a misfortune even greater than this catastrophe would be a triumph of this system. To prevent this was the ultimate aim and purpose of our struggle.

What I have just said was often expressed by Canaris in the group of which I am speaking.

Q. Now, did this group of which you and Canaris were members meet frequently?

A. I must explain that this group or circle was not to be regarded as an organisation in the technical sense, or as a sort of conspirators' club. That would have been completely contradictory to Canaris' nature. It was more of a spiritual organisation of people of the same convictions, who were perspicacious and well informed. Their official functions provided them with the necessary knowledge. These people understood each other and acted jointly, while maintaining their complete individuality.

This is the reason for the differentiation of which I spoke in the beginning. Different demands were made on each individual. Canaris approached at any one time the person whose character he knew from his personal knowledge to be the fittest to carry out a certain task.

Q. Did you have conversations at those official meetings, at which Canaris expressed his views with respect to the use of force in Poland, for example?

A. These and similar methods were repeatedly, I may say, discussed in our circle. They were repudiated as a matter of course.

Q. Do you recall what Canaris said about the Polish war at the time of its commencement?

A. I very well recall the hour at which Canaris entered, completely broken, and informed us of the fact that the situation had become serious after all, although it had appeared before as if the matter might still be postponed. He told us then: "This is the end."

Q. Did you have conversations with Canaris and the other members of your group with respect to eliminating Nazis from your staff?

A. While I was still in Vienna, before entering service in the O.K.W., I received instructions from Canaris not to admit to his office in Berlin any National Socialists. I was also instructed, whenever possible, not to admit any Party members or officers sympathising with the Party to high positions in my section. Thus the actual organisation -

Q. Did Canaris keep a diary?

A. Yes, Canaris kept a diary - he had done so even before the beginning of the war - a diary to which I personally contributed many portions.

Q. Was it a part of your duties to make entries in that diary?

A. No, it was not a part of my immediate duties, but it just turned out as a matter of course that, as regards those conferences which I attended as Canaris' representative, or at which I was present, I recorded such conferences in his diary.

Q. And did you keep copies of the entries which you made in Canaris' diary?

A. Yes, I kept copies, with Canaris' knowledge and approbation.

Q. I have you the original of some of those copies with you here to-day?

A .I have not got them on my person, but they are available.

Q. And you have refreshed your recollection in reference to those entries

A. Yes.

Q. What was the purpose of Canaris in keeping such a diary

A. If I answer this question I must, in the interests of truth, repeat the words that Canaris addressed to me on this subject. Others know also what I am saying now.

The purpose of his diary - and it is Canaris' voice speaking now through me - the purpose of his diary was to show the German people and the world, once and for all, how those who were guiding the fate of the people at this time acted.

Q. Now, do you recall attending conferences with Canaris at the Fuehrer's headquarters just prior to the fall of Warsaw?

A. I and Canaris took part in a conference which did not take place in the Fuehrer's headquarters, but in the so- called Fuehrer's train, shortly before the fall of Warsaw.

Q. And having refreshed your recollection from reference to the entries in Canaris' diary, can you tell the Tribunal the date of those conferences?

A. According to the notes and documents at my disposal, it was on 12th September, 1939.

Q. Did each of these conferences take place on the same day?

A. The conferences in the Fuehrer's train took place on 12th September, 1939.

Q. And was there more than one conference on that day? Were they split into several conferences?

A. I cannot call them sessions; they were discussions, conversations, of shorter or longer duration, but not actually conferences.

Q. And who was present on this occasion?

A. Present, independent of time and location, were the following: Foreign Minister von Ribbentrop; Keitel, the Chief of the O.K.W.; the president of the "Wehrmacht-Fuehrungstab" at that time, Jodl; Canaris; and myself.

Q. Do you see Ribbentrop in this court room?

A. Yes.

Q. Will you indicate for the record where he is sitting?

A. Over there - (indicating) - in the first row, third from the left.

Q. Do you also see Keitel in the court room

A. Yes; he is next to Ribbentrop.

Q. Do you also see Jodl in the court room?

A. Yes; he is in the second row, next to Herr von Papen.

Q. Now, to the best of your knowledge and recollection, will you please explain, in as much detail as possible, to the Tribunal, exactly what was said and what took place at this conference in the Fuehrer's train?

A. First of all, Canaris had a short talk with Ribbentrop, in which von Ribbentrop explained political aims in general, with regard to the Polish regions, and in particular with regard to the Ukrainian question. Later the Chief of the O.K.W. took up the Ukrainian question in subsequent discussions which took place in his private working carriage. These are recorded in the notes which I took down immediately, on Canaris' commission. While we were still in the train of the Chief of the O.K.W., Canaris expressed serious scruples regarding the bombardment of Warsaw, stressing the devastating repercussions on foreign policy of such a bombardment. The Chief of the O.K.W. at that time, Keitel, answered that these measures had been laid down directly by the Fuehrer and Goering, and that he, Keitel, had had no influence on these decisions. He spoke these words - I can repeat them only after having read my notes - the Fuehrer and Goering telephoned frequently back and forth; sometimes I heard something of what was said, but not always.

Secondly, Canaris gave an earnest warning against the measures which he knew about, i.e., the projected shooting and extermination which were to be directed particularly against the Polish intelligentsia, the nobility, the clergy, as well as all elements that could be regarded as embodying the national resistance movement. Canaris said at that time - I am quoting more or less verbatim - "the world will at some time make the armed forces under whose eyes these events occurred also responsible for these events."

The then Chief of the O.K.W. replied - and what I am now going to say is based on my notes, which I looked through a few days ago - that these things had been determined by the Fuehrer, and that the Fuehrer, the Commander in Chief of the Army, had made it known that, should the armed forces refuse to have any part in these things or should they not agree with them, they would have to accept the fact that the S.S., the S.I.P.O. and such organisations would be simultaneously employed to carry out these very measures. Thus, at the side of each military commander, a corresponding civilian official would be appointed. This, in outline, was the subject of the discussion dealing with extermination measures and the policy of shooting.

Q. Was anything said about a so-called political house- cleaning?

A. Yes, the then Chief of the O.K.W. used an expression in this connection which was certainly derived from Hitler, and which characterised these measures "political housecleaning." This expression remains very clearly in my recollection without the aid of my notes.

Q. In order that the record may be perfectly clear, exactly what measures did Keitel say had already been agreed upon?

A. According to the then Chief of the O.K.W., the bombardment of Warsaw and the shooting of those categories of people whom I characterised before, had been agreed upon already.

Q. And what were they?

A. Foremost of all, the Polish intelligentsia, the nobility, the clergy, and, of course, the Jews.

Q. What, if anything, was said about possible co-operation with a Ukrainian group?

A. Canaris was ordered by the then Chief of the O.K.W., who stated that he was transmitting a directive which he had apparently received from Ribbentrop in connection with the political plans of the Foreign Minister, to instigate a resistance movement in the Galician part of the Ukraine, which should have as its goal the extermination of Jews and Poles.

Q. At what point did Hitler and Jodl enter this meeting?

A. Hitler and Jodl entered either after what I have just described took place, or towards the conclusion of this discussion, and Canaris had already begun his report on the situation in the West: that is to say, on the news that had come in in the meantime, regarding the attitude of the French army at the West Wall.

Q. And what further discussions took place then?

A. After this discussion in the private working carriage of the Chief of the O.K.W., Canaris left the coach and had a short talk with Ribbentrop, who, returning to the theme of the Ukraine, told him once more that the uprising or the resistance movement should be so arranged that all farms and dwellings of the Poles should go up in flames, and all Jews be killed.

Q. Who said that?

A. The Foreign Minister at that time, Ribbentrop, said this to Canaris. I was standing next to him.

Q. Is there any slightest doubt in your mind about that?

A. No. I have not the slightest doubt about that. I remember with particular clarity the somewhat new formulation that "all farms and dwellings should go up in flames" because previously only terms like "liquidation" and "killing" had been used.

Q. Was there any note in Canaris' diary which helped to refresh your recollection on that point also?

A. No.

Q. What, if anything, was said on the subject of France?

A. On the subject of France a discussion took place in the carriage of the Chief of the O.K.W. Canaris explained the situation in the West according to reports he had received from the "Abwehr" intelligence service. Canaris described the situation by saying that in his opinion a great attack was being prepared by the French in the sector of Saarbrucken. Hitler, who had entered the room in the meantime, intervened, took charge of the discussion and rejected in a lively manner the opinion which Canaris had just expressed, putting forward arguments which, looking back now, I must recognise as factually correct.

Q. Do you recall whether, in the course of this conference, Ribbentrop said anything about the Jews?

A. During the conversation, which was taking place in the private conference coach of the Chief of the O.K.W., Ribbentrop was not present.

Q. Do you recall whether at any time in the course of the conferences Ribbentrop said anything about the Jews?

A. In this discussion, I repeat - the one that took place in the coach - no.

Q. For purposes of keeping the record straight, whenever you have referred to the Chief of the O.K.W., you were referring to Keitel?

A. Yes.

Q. Was the Wehrmacht ever asked to furnish any resistance for the Polish campaign?

A. Yes.

Q. Did that undertaking have any special name?

A. As it is recorded in the diary of my section, the name of this undertaking that took place just before the Polish campaign, was given the name "Himmler."

Q. Will you explain to the Tribunal the nature of the assistance required?

A. The matter in which I am now giving testimony is one of the most mysterious actions which took place in the atmosphere of the Abwehr office. Sometime, I believe it was the middle of August - the precise date can be found in the corresponding entry of the diary - Abwehr Section I, as well as my section, Abwehr Section II, were charged with the job of providing or keeping in readiness Polish uniforms and equipment, as well as identification cards, and so on, for the undertaking "Himmler". This request, according to an entry in my diary made by my aide-de-camp, was received by Canaris from the Wehrmacht Fuehrungstab or from the "Landesverteidigung" - National Defence.

Q. Do you know whence this request originated?

A. Whence the request originated I cannot say. I can only repeat how it reached us in the form of an order. It was, to be sure, an order on which we, the chiefs of sections concerned, already had some misgivings without knowing what, in the last analysis, it was about. The name Himmler, however, was eloquent enough. In the pertinent entries of the diary, expression is given to the fact that I asked the question why Mr. Himmler was to receive uniforms from us.

Q. To whom was the Polish material to be furnished by the Abwehr?

A. These articles of equipment had to be kept in readiness, and one day some man from the S.S. or the S.D. - the name is given in the official war-diary of the department - fetched them.

Q. At what time was the Abwehr informed as to how this Polish material was to be used?

A. The real purpose, which we do not know in its details even to-day, was concealed from us, we did not learn it, though at the time we had a very understandable suspicion that something crooked was afoot, particularly because of the name of the undertaking.

Q. Did you subsequently find out from Canaris what in fact had happened?

A. The actual course of events was the following: When the first war-bulletin appeared, which spoke of the attack of Polish units on German territory, Pieckenbrock, who had the report in his hand, and read it, observed that now we knew what our uniforms had been needed for. the same day or a few days later, I cannot say exactly, Canaris informed us that people from concentration camps disguised in these uniforms had been ordered to make a military attack on the radio station at Gleiwitz. I cannot recall whether any other locality was mentioned. Although we were greatly interested, particularly General Oster, to learn details of this action, that is, where it had occurred and what had happened in detail - as a matter of fact we could well imagine it - we did not know for certain, and I cannot even to-day say exactly what happened.

Q. Did you ever find out what happened to the men from the concentration camps that wore the Polish uniforms and created the incident?

A. It is strange, this matter held my interest ever since, so much so that even after the capitulation, I spoke about these matters with an S.S. Hauptsturmfuehrer who was confined in the same hospital as I was, and I asked him for details on what had taken place. The man - his name was Burckel - told me, "It is peculiar, but even we in our circles only found out about these matters much, much later, and then what we did find out was only by implication. So far as I know," he said, "all members of the S.D. who took part in that action were presumably put out of the way; that is to say, were killed." That is the last I heard of this matter.

Q. Do you recall attending a meeting in 1940 at which the name of Weygand was under discussion?

A. Yes.

Q. Do you happen to recall the particular month in which this discussion took place?

A. The discussion took place in the winter of 1940, either November or December, if my memory does not deceive me. I have retained the precise date in my personal notes; in accordance with the wish and desire of Canaris.

Q. To the best of your knowledge and recollection, who was present?

A. At that time, we usually met at the conference, i.e., the three chiefs of sections and the Chief of the Ausland Section, the former Admiral Burckner.

Q. What were you told at this meeting by Canaris?

A. In this conversation Canaris told us that for a considerable time Keitel had put pressure on him to execute an action leading to the elimination of the French Marshal Weygand; and that I - that is to say, my section - would be charged with the execution of this task, as a matter of course.

Q. When you say "elimination", what do you mean?

A. Killing.

Q. What was Weygand doing at this time?

A. Weygand was, so far as I recall, at that time in North Africa.

Q. What was the reason given for attempting to kill Weygand?

A. The reason given was the fear that the unbeaten part of the French Army in North Africa might find in Weygand a point of crystallisation for resistance. That, of course, is only the main outline of what I still remember to-day. It may be that there were other contributing factors.

Q. After you were so informed by Canaris, what else was said at this meeting?

A. This request, which was put to the military Abwehr openly and without restraint by a representative of the Armed Forces, was repudiated strongly and indignantly by all those present. I, myself, as the person most involved, since MY department was charged with the action, stated before all present that I had no intention of executing this order. My section and my officers are fighters but they are not a murderers' organisation or murderers.

Q. What then did Canaris say?

A. Canaris said: "Calm down. We'll talk it over later on."

Q. Did you then talk it over later with Canaris?

A. After the other gentlemen had left the room, I spoke alone with Canaris. Canaris told me immediately, "It is obvious that this order will not only not be carried out, but it will not even be communicated any further;" and so it happened.

Q: Were you subsequently questioned as to whether you had carried out this order?

A. At an audience that Canaris had with Keitel, at which I was present, I was addressed by the then Chief of the O.K.W., Keitel, on this subject. He asked me what had happened or what had been undertaken so far with regard to this matter. The date of this event is recorded in my notes, with Canaris' knowledge and with his approval.

Q. What reply did you make to Keitel?

A. Naturally I cannot recall the precise words I spoke, but one thing is certain; I certainly did not answer that I had no intention of carrying out this order. I could not do this, and did not do it; otherwise, I would not be sitting here to-day. Probably, as in many similar cases, I gave the answer that it was very difficult but whatever was possible would be done, or something of that sort. Naturally, I cannot recall my precise words.

Q. Incidentally, are you the only one of this intimate Canaris group who is still alive to-day?

A. I believe that I am at least one of the very few. Possibly Pieckenbrock is still alive; perhaps, Bentivigny, who, however, did not belong to the inner circle. Most of the others fell as a result of the events of July 20th.

COLONEL AMEN: I have another subject to take up now. I don't know if you want me to start in before recess.

THE PRESIDENT: We will continue until 12.45.

(Further examination of the witness by Colonel Amen.)

Q. In 1941 did you attend a conference at which General Reinecke was present?

A. Yes.

Q. Who was General Reinecke?

A. General Reinecke was at that time Chief of the General Army Office; that is to say, i.e., a member-office of the O.K.W.

Q. Do you recall the approximate date of that meeting?

A. It was roughly in the summer of 1941, shortly after the beginning of the Russian campaign; possibly in July.

Q. To the best of your knowledge and recollection, will you state exactly who was present at that conference?

A. At this conference, which is also recorded in the notes taken for Canaris, in which I participated as his representative, the following were present: General Reinecke as the presiding officer, ObergruppenFuehrer Muller, of the R.S.H.A., General Breuer representing the office in charge of prisoners of war, and I, as a representative of Canaris, i.e., "Ausland-Abwehr".

Q. Will you explain who Muller was and why he was at this meeting?

A. Muller was a Division Chief in the main office of Reichsecurity (R.S.H.A.) and took part in the session because he was responsible for the measures regarding the treatment of the Russian prisoners; i.e., the executions.

Q. Will you explain who Colonel Breuer was and why he was there?

A. Colonel Breuer was in charge of matters relating to prisoners of war. I do not know in which precise front Organisation detachment he worked at the time. He took care of questions regarding prisoners of war within the O.K.W.

Q. What was the purpose of this conference?

A. The purpose of this conference was to examine the orders received so far, regarding the treatment of prisoners of war, and also to comment on, explain and give reasonable grounds for these commands.

Q. Did you learn from the conversation at this conference what the substance of these orders under discussion was?

A. Its content concerned itself essentially with two groups of measures that were to be taken. First of all was the killing of Russian commissars. Second was the killing of all those elements among the Russian prisoners of war who, according to a special segregation by the S.D., could be identified as Bolshevists or as active representatives of the Bolshevistic attitude toward life.

Q. Did you also learn from the conversation what the basis for these orders were?

A. The basis for these orders was explained by General Reinecke in its essential features as this: That the war between Germany and Russia was not a war between two States or two armies but between two attitudes toward the world, namely, the National Socialist and the Bolshevistic. The Red Army soldier was not to be looked upon as a soldier in the ordinary sense of the word, such as our Western opponents, but as an ideological enemy. That is, as an enemy-to-the- death of National Socialism, and he was to be treated accordingly.

Q. Did Canaris tell you why he had selected you to go to this conference?

A. Canaris gave me two or perhaps three reasons for ordering me to this session, although he was himself present in Berlin. First, he wanted to avoid a personal contact with Reinecke, whom he regarded as the prototype of the always willing National Socialist Generals and whom he personally considered very antipathetic. Secondly, he told me my guiding principle was to be to attempt through factual argument - that is to say, through appeals to reason - to oppose this brutal and senseless order, or at least to mitigate its evil effects as far as that might be possible. He selected me for tactical reasons also since, as department chief, he could by no means be as outspoken as I, who, thanks to my subordinate position, could use much stronger language.

Thirdly, he was well acquainted with my personal attitude, an attitude that I manifested, wherever practical, in my many trips to the front where I saw mistreatment of prisoners of war. This fact is also clearly recorded in my notes.

Q. Did Canaris and the other members of your group have a particular name for Reinecke?

A. Not only in our group but in other places, he was called the "small" or the "other Keitel".

Q. Prior to your going to this conference, did Canaris make any other comment on those orders?

A. Even at the time when these orders were given, Canaris said to our circle - and when I say our circle I mean the section chiefs - that he had put himself in a position of sharp opposition to this command and protested through Burckner. I cannot say now whether that was done in writing or orally, whether that was communicated to Keitel in writing or orally, I don't know, but, at any rate, Burckner communicated it to Keitel; probably by both media.

Q. When you say "protested through Burckner", what do you mean?

A. When I say Burckner, I mean the group or perhaps even a representative in his office.

Q. Will you repeat that?

A. This protest or this counter-argument, and the question regarding the treatment of the Russian prisoners of war, was communicated by Canaris via the Foreign Office, Ausland-Amt, and, through Burckner, communicated further. The Ausland office had a section that dealt with questions of International Law. The expert in that section was Count Moltke who, like some other men, belonged to Oster's inner circle. After 20th July he was executed.

THE PRESIDENT: Would that be a convenient time to break off?

COLONEL AMEN: Yes, sir.

THE PRESIDENT: Until 2.00 o'clock.

(A recess was taken until 1400 hours.)

THE PRESIDENT: Yes, Colonel Amen.

(Erwin Lahousen resumed the stand and testified further as follows:)

BY COLONEL AMEN:

Q. Prior to the luncheon recess you were testifying about a conference in 1941 with Reinecke and others. Prior to that conference did Canaris tell you what kind of appeal to make to those present at the meeting?

A. Before the discussion Canaris said, as I have already stated, that I should use arguments in order to ruin the case or to weaken its effects, but that otherwise I should not take it into my head to use arguments of a humanitarian nature, lest I should so make a fool of myself.

Q. And now will you explain to the Tribunal, to the best of your recollection, exactly what happened and what was said in the course of that conference?

A. The discussion was opened by General Reinecke, and he explained these orders in the manner in which I described them before the recess. He said that these measures were necessary, and that it was particularly necessary that this idea should also be made clear to the Wehrmacht, and above all to the officers corps, as they apparently still had ideas which belonged to the Ice Age and not to the present age of National Socialism.

Q. What views did you present at this conference?

A. According to my instructions from the Amt Ausland-Abwehr and as representative of Canaris, in the main I pointed out, first of all, the most unfavourable effect of such measures on the troops, namely, on the Front troops; that they would never understand such orders, particularly not the simple soldier. Besides, I said, we had reports that the executions were sometimes carried out before their eyes.

Secondly, I brought forward the objections of my office in regard to activities which referred to the office itself, the effect on the enemy of these measures which were, practically speaking, the hindering of deserters, to prevent Russians from deserting, who were surrendering without any opposition; and then the great difficulties which the Abwehr Division had in fighting agents, that is, people who for any reasons had voluntarily kept themselves prepared to help the Germans.

Q. In order that this may be clear on the record, because I think there was quite a bit of confusion in the translation, I want to point out one or two of those arguments again. What did you say at this conference about the effect of the execution of these orders on Russian soldiers?

A. I pointed out, first of all, that through these orders some elements among the Russian soldiers who were inclined to surrender were prevented from doing so. Secondly, that people who for any reason had offered their services to the Abwehr would also be prevented by these measures. And that, taking it all together, above all, the effect attained would be the opposite to that which they had desired, and that the resistance of the Russians would be increased to the utmost.

Q. And in order that we may be perfectly clear, what did you say about the effect of the execution of these orders on the German troops?

A. I said that, from several reports which we had from the Front, the effect on the morale and on the discipline of the troops was terrible, devastating.

Q. Was there any discussion about International Law at this conference?

A. No. In this connection there was no discussion of International Law. The manner of selection of the prisoners of war was particularly stressed. It was completely arbitrary, apart from the order in itself, the general order itself.

Q. We will get to that in a moment. Were your views accepted at this conference?

A. My views, which were the views of the Amt Abwehr which I was representing, were opposed in the sharpest possible manner by Muller, who, with the usual cliches, rejected the arguments that I had produced, and who made the sole concession that the executions, in order to consider the feelings of the troops, should not take place in the face of the troops but at a secret place. He also made a few concessions in the question of the selection, which was completely arbitrary, and was just left to the Kommando leaders or their viewpoints.

Q. And subsequent to this conference did you learn whether an order was issued with respect to having these killings take place out of the sight of the German troops?

A. Except for Muller's promise, which I have just mentioned, I heard no more about it at the time. I found a confirmation of the results of this conference; and the promises then made to me, in an order which was submitted to me only now.

Q. Was there a conversation at this conference about the manner in which these orders for the killings were being executed?

A. Yes; in the course of discussions the entire problem was under discussion as well as the manner in which these orders were carried out by the riot-squads (Einsatzkommandos) of the S.D. - according to my recollection. These S.D. squads were in charge both of singling out of persons in camps, and in assembly centres for prisoners of war, and of carrying out the executions.

Reinecke also discussed measures regarding the treatment of Russian prisoners of war in the camps. Reinecke emphatically accepted the arguments put forth by Muller and not by myself, and voiced his conviction in very sharp words.

Q. Now, will you explain to the Tribunal, from what you learned at this conference, the exact manner in which the sorting of these prisoners was made and in what way it was determined which of the prisoners should be killed?

A. The prisoners were sorted out by commandos of the S.D. and according to peculiar and utterly arbitrary points of view. The leaders of these "Einsatzkommandos" were guided by racial characteristics; particularly if someone was a Jew or Jewish type or could otherwise be classified as racially inferior, he was picked for execution. Other leaders of the S.D. selected people according to their intelligence. Some had views all their own and usually most peculiar, so that I felt compelled to ask Muller, "Tell me, according to what principles does this selection take place? Do you determine it by the height of a person or the size of his shoes?"

Muller was very emphatic in rejecting these and any other objections, and Reinecke adopted rigidly the same point of view, instead of accepting my opinions, i.e., those of the Amt Ausland-Abwehr, which were offered him as a "golden bridge" for his acceptance. That was essentially the contents of the discussion in which I participated.

Q. Did you receive knowledge about the manner in which these orders were executed through official reports?

A. We were currently informed of all happenings by the organs either at the front or active in the camps. Officers of the Abwehr Division were active in these camps, and in this way, and through the normal service channels, we were informed by reports and oral presentation of all these measures and of their effects.

Q. Was the information which you received secret and confidential information not open to others?

A. The information was confidential since almost all which took place in our offices was treated confidentially. De facto, however, it was known to large groups of the Wehrmacht that these things happened in the camps, respectively in due execution.

Q. Now, at this conference did you learn anything from Reinecke with respect to the treatment of Russian prisoners in prison camps?

A. In this discussion the treatment of Russian prisoners in the camps was discussed by Reinecke, and Reinecke was of the opinion that in the camps their treatment must not be the same as the treatment of other Allied prisoners of war, but that here too, according to the principles laid down, discriminating measures must be used. The camp guards should be furnished with whips, and, in case of an attempted escape or other undesirable act, the guards should have the right to resort to arms.

Q. Besides the whips, what other equipment were the Stalag guards given?

A. Those are details which I do not remember for the moment. I can only say what was mentioned in this discussion.

Q. What, if anything, did Reinecke say about the whips?

A. Reinecke said that the guards, i.e., the guard details, should make use of their whips or sticks or whatever other primitive instruments they had.

Q. Now, through official channels did you learn of an order for the branding of Russian prisoners of war?

THE PRESIDENT: Colonel Amen, I think you should refer to them as "Soviet", not "Russian" prisoners.

COLONEL AMEN: Yes, Your Honour.

BY COLONEL AMEN:

Q. Did you learn of such an order?

A. Yes, in one of the discussions at which most of the previously mentioned divisional chiefs were usually present. At least one of them must have been present.

Q. Do you know whether any protests were made with respect to that order?

A. When the intention was made known of branding these prisoners, a very sharp protest was voiced at once by Canaris, probably through Burckner himself.

Q. What, if anything, did Canaris tell you with regard to this order?

A. Canaris told us that the question had already been expounded in a medical opinion by some sort of physician; that there actually were people low enough to consent to giving a medical opinion on such madness. That was the main topic of this discussion.

Q. What information, if any, did you receive through official channels regarding plans to bring Soviet prisoners back to German territory?

A. Under similar circumstances, that is, during discussions between Canaris and the chiefs of his divisions, as well as in the General Staff talks, I heard that it had been planned to bring some Soviet prisoners into Germany, but that those projects were suddenly abandoned, and I remember that this was by direct order of Hitler. The reason for it was the conditions found in camps in the theatre of operations, where prisoners were crowded together and could not be adequately fed, housed or clothed, resulting in epidemics and cannibalism in these camps.

Q. I am not sure but what we missed some of your previous answer. Will you start again to tell us about the change which was made in these orders?

A. Will you please repeat the question once more?

Q. You referred to a change in the plans to take the Soviet prisoners back to German territory. Is that correct?

A. Yes, they were not brought back into Germany.

Q. And what was the result of this action, namely, of their not being brought back, at the direct order of Hitler?

A. The result was as described just now.

Q. But I want you to repeat it because we lost some of the answer in the interpreting process. Please just repeat it again.

A. The greater number of prisoners of war remained in the theatre of operation, without proper care - care in the sense of PW conventions, with regard to housing, food, medical care; and many of them died on the bare floor. Epidemics broke out and cannibalism - human beings devouring each other - driven by hunger - manifested itself.

Q. Were you personally at the front to observe these conditions?

A. I made several trips with Canaris and I saw some of these things which I have just described with my own eyes. I made notes of my impressions at the time, which were found amongst my papers.

Q. Did you also obtain information as to these matters through official channels of the Abwehr?

A. Yes, I received this information through our own legal department and through the Ausland-Abwehr.

Q. From your official information, to what extent was the Wehrmacht involved in the mistreatment of these prisoners?

A. According to my information, the Wehrmacht was involved in all matters which referred to prisoners of war, except the executions, which were the concern of the "Kommandos" of the S.D. and the Reichssicherheitshauptamt.

Q. But is it not a fact that the prisoner-of-war camps were entirely under the jurisdiction of the Wehrmacht?

A. Yes, prisoners of war were under the jurisdiction of the Supreme Command of the Wehrmacht.

Q. But before they were placed in these camps, the Special Purpose Kommandos of the S.S. were responsible primarily for the executions and the selection of the people to be executed, is that correct?

A. Yes.

Q. Did you receive through official channels information regarding the existence of an order for the killing of British Commandos?

A. Yes.

Q. What action, if any, did Canaris or yourself take with respect to this order?

A. The order, as far as I remember, and even the intention that such an order was to be issued, was discussed in our circle, that is, between Canaris and his section chiefs. We all, of course, absolutely agreed on its rejection. The reasons, apart from the aspects of International Law, being that the Amt Ausland had under its jurisdiction a formation, which was attached to our section, named "Regiment Brandenburg", which had a task similar to that of the Kommandos. I immediately and most emphatically protested against this order, as the head of the section to which this regiment was attached, and for which I considered myself responsible, and also in view of the retaliation measures which were to be expected as a result.

Q. Did you personally assist in the drafting of these protests?

A. I know that twice a protest was lodged against this order by Canaris, and by Amt Ausland, through Burckner. The first time as soon as the order was issued orally or in writing, and the second time after the first executions had been carried out. I drafted one of these written protests - I do not know whether the first or the second; this very contribution was made in the interest of my section, and the Regiment Brandenburg, whose functions were similar, very similar, to those of the Kommandos.

Q. To whom in the ordinary course did these protests go?

A. The protests were addressed to Canaris' superior officer, that is to say, to the Chief of the O.K.W.

Q. Who was that?

A. It was Keitel, at that time.

Q. Did these protests in the ordinary course go also to Jodl?

A. That I cannot say, but it is possible.

Q. Now, will you tell the Tribunal what the grounds of the protests which you made were.

A. The basis was, above all, that it was contrary to the interpretation of International Law that soldiers, that is to say, not agents or spies, but soldiers clearly recognisable as such, should be killed after they had been taken prisoner. That was the main point and one also of concern to my section, since it also comprised soldiers who had to carry out such or similar tasks in their capacity as soldiers.

Q. Were there any other grounds urged in protest against these orders?

A. Certainly. Other reasons were also mentioned in accordance with the interests of the different sections affected by these orders. For the Amt Ausland, it was the point of view of International Law. The Abwehr Division III was particularly interested to interrogate soldiers captured in commando raids, rather than see them killed.

Q. Were there any other chiefs of the Amt Abwehr who assisted in the preparation of these protests?

A. As far as I remember to-day, no.

Q. You mentioned Admiral Burckner, did you not?

A. Yes, Burckner belonged to the Amt-Ausland Abwehr, but he wasn't the chief, but only Section Chief of Amt Ausland.

Q. Now, have you ever heard of an operation known as "Gustav"?

A. The name "Gustav" was applied not to an operation but to an undertaking very like or similar to the one which was demanded for the elimination of Marshal Weygand.

Q. Will you tell the Tribunal what was the meaning of "Gustav"?

A. "Gustav" was the expression used by the Chief of the O.K.W. as a cover name to be used in conversations on the question of General Giraud.

Q. When you say the Chief of the O.K.W., are you referring to Keitel?

A. Yes.

Q. And are you referring to General Giraud of the French Army?

A. Yes, General Giraud of the French Army who, according to my recollection, fled from Koenigstein in 1942.

Q. Do you know of any order issued with respect to General Giraud?

A. Yes.

Q. Who issued such an order?

A. The Chief of the O.K.W., Keitel, gave an order of this kind to Canaris, not in writing but an oral order.

Q. How did you come to know about this order?

A. I knew of this order in the same way as certain other chiefs of the sections, e.g., Chief of Abwehr Section 1, Bentivigny, and a few other officers. We all heard it at a discussion with Canaris.

Q. What was the substance of the order?

A. The essential part of this order was to eliminate Giraud in the same way as Weygand.

Q. When you say "eliminate" what do you mean?

A. I mean the same as in the case of Marshal Weygand, that is, he was to be killed.

Q. Do you recall the approximate date when this order was given by Keitel to Canaris?

A. This order was given to Canaris repeatedly. I cannot say for certain when it was given for the first time as I was not present. It was probably after the flight of Giraud from Koenigstein and it was probably given for the first time prior to the attempt on the life of Heydrich, in Prague. According to my notes, this subject was discussed with me by Keitel in July of the same year. Canaris also being present.

Q. Well now, what did Keitel first say to you personally about this affair?

A. I cannot give the exact text, but the meaning was that he proclaimed the intention of having Giraud killed, similarly as in the case of Weygand, and asked me how the matter was progressing.

Q. And what did you say to him on that occasion?

A. I cannot remember the exact words. I probably gave some evasive answer, or one that would permit time to be gained.

Q. Now, was this question later discussed by you at any time?

A. According to my recollection, this question was once more discussed in August. The exact date can be found in my notes. Canaris telephoned me in my private apartment one evening and said impatiently that Keitel was urging him again about Giraud, and the Section Chiefs were to meet the next day on this question.

The next day that meeting was held and Canaris repeated in this larger circle what he had said to me over the phone the night before, that he was being continually pressed by Keitel that something must at last be done in this matter. Our attitude was the same as in the matter of Weygand. All those present rejected flatly this new demand to carry out a murder. We mentioned our decision to Canaris, who also was of the same opinion, and Canaris thereupon went down to Keitel in order to induce him to leave the Military Abwehr out of all such matters and to request that, as agreed prior to this, such matters should be left to the S.D.

In the meantime, while we were all there, I remember Pieckenbrock spoke, and I remember every word he said. He said it was about time that Keitel was told clearly that he should tell his Herr Hitler, that we, the Military Abwehr, were no murder organisation like the S.D. or the S.S. After a short time, Canaris came back and said it was now quite clear that he had convinced Keitel that we the Military Abwehr, were to be left out of such matters, and further measures were to be left to the S.D.

I must observe here and recall that Canaris had said to me that once this order had been given, the execution must be prevented at any cost. He would take care of that and I was to support him.

Q. I don't think you have yet told us just who were present at this conference?

A. The three Abwehr Chiefs were present, Colonel Pieckenbrock, whom I have already mentioned, Colonel-General Bentivigny, and I. Probably, also, General Oster, and possibly Burckner, but I cannot remember clearly. In my notes only those three chiefs are mentioned who all strictly rejected the proposal

Q. What was the next occasion when this matter was brought to your attention again?

A. A little later, it must have been September - the exact date has been recorded - Keitel rang me up in my private apartment. He asked me what was happening with "Gustav". "You know what I mean by 'Gustav'? " I said, "Yes, I know." "How is the matter progressing, I must know, it is very urgent." I answered, "I have no information on the subject. Canaris has reserved this matter to himself, and Canaris is not here, he is in Paris." Then came the order from Keitel, or rather, before he gave the order, he put one more question. "You know that the others are to carry out the order." By the others, he means the S.S. and S.D. respectively. I answered,

"Yes, I know." Then came an order from Keitel to ask Muller immediately how the whole matter was progressing. "I must know it immediately," he said. I said, "Yes." I went at once to the office of the Ausland- Abwehr, General Oster, and informed him of what had happened, and asked for his advice as to what was to be done by Canaris and me in this extremely critical and difficult matter. I told him what, as Oster knew nothing yet of what it was expected to do, Canaris so far had told the S.D. concerning the murder of Giraud. General Oster advised me to fly to Paris immediately and to inform Canaris and to warn him. I flew the next day to Paris, and met Canaris at an hotel at dinner in a small circle, which included Admiral Burckner, and told Canaris what had happened. Canaris was horrified and amazed, and for a moment he saw no way out.

During the dinner Canaris asked me in the presence of Burckner and two other officers, i.e., Colonel Rudolph, and another officer whose name I have forgotten, as to the date when Giraud had fled from Koenigstein, and when Abwehr III had been in Prague, and at what time the assassination of Heydrich had taken place. I knew these dates, and told them to him. When he had the three dates, he was instantly relieved, and his face which had been very clouded, relaxed. He was certainly relieved in every way. I must say that in particular - at the three days' conference of the Abwehr, Heydrich was present. It was a meeting between Amt Abwehr III and the co-ordinating functionaries at the meeting of Prague.

Canaris then based his whole plan on these three dates. His plan was to attempt to show that Heydrich, during the conference, had passed on the order to carry out the action. That is to say, his plan was to use the death of Heydrich to wreck the whole proposition. The next day we flew to Berlin, and Canaris reported to Keitel that the matter was taking its course, and that Canaris had given Heydrich the necessary instructions at the three days' conference in Prague, and Heydrich had prepared everything, that is, a special purpose action had been started in order to have Giraud murdered, and that the matter was completed and all mapped out.

COLONEL AMEN: There was a mistake I think in the translation a little way back. If you don't mind will you please go back to where you first referred to Heydrich with Canaris, and repeat the story, because I think that the translation was incorrect. In other words, go back to the point where Canaris suddenly seemed relieved, and started to tell you what the apparent solution might be.

THE WITNESS: All those present saw that Canaris was much relieved, when he heard from me the three dates. His whole plan or his manoeuvring was a purely mental combination, possibly on the basis of his three dates, of which the essential part was the date of the escape of Giraud, and the three-day conference, and typical of his mentality. Had this combination been made prior to Giraud's escape, it would probably not have stood the test.

THE PRESIDENT: Colonel Amen, what is the reason for the repetition?

COLONEL AMEN: There was a mistake in the record. If it is the wish of the Tribunal, I shall not get him to repeat it any further.

THE PRESIDENT: It seems clear to the Tribunal what was said.

COLONEL AMEN: Very well.

Q. What, if anything, happened next in so far as the affair Giraud was concerned?

A. Nothing more happened. Giraud fled to North Africa, and I only heard that Hitler was very indignant about this escape, and said that the S.D. had failed miserably, that it would be written down in the records of the Hauptquartier. The man who told me this is in the American zone.

Q. Were you acquainted with Colonel Rowehls?

A. Yes.

Q. Who was he?

A. He was an officer. He was a colonel of the Luftwaffe.

Q. What was the work of the special squadron to which he was attached?

A. He had a special squadron for altitude flying, which operated together with the Ausland-Abwehr reconnaissance, in respect to certain States.

Q. Were you ever present when he reported to Canaris?

A. I was present occasionally.

Q. Do you recall what Rowehls told Canaris on those occasions?

A. He reported on the result of the reconnaissance flight and submitted his findings to Abwehr 1 - that is, Amt Abwehr 1. I was responsible for this, and noted the results.

Q. Did you know over what territories these reconnaissance flights had been made?

A. They were taken over Poland and England and in the South- east sphere. I cannot say in any greater detail what territory, and what State in the South-east, but I know that this squadron was stationed in Budapest for such reconnaissance.

Q. Did you personally see some of these photographs?

A. Yes.

Q. Now will you tell the Tribunal the dates when you know that these reconnaissance flights over London and Leningrad were being made?

A. I cannot give the exact dates. I only remember being present at the Abwehr with Canaris, or with Bentivigny who was there sometimes, and Pieckenbrock; that these reconnaissance flights did take place, and that photographic material was furnished, and that the squadron operated from Hungarian airfields. I flew back to Berlin with them at one time. I knew some of the pilots from their activities.

Q. What I am going to ask you about now is the year, or years we will say, when these reconnaissance flights were being made?

A. In a certain part of 1939 before the beginning of the Polish campaign.

Q. Were these flights kept secret?

A. Yes, of course, they were secret.

Q. And why were these flights being made from Hungary, do you know?

A. A Luftwaffe expert would have to give this information.

Q. Have you in your possession a report of the treatment of the Jews in certain territories?

A. Yes, I have a report which probably came to us through Department III, and I made several copies for Canaris and one for myself, regarding incidents in Borisov.

Q. Is that an official report?

A. Yes, and it was a report. The files would show from what office it came to us. In this connection Borisov to me recalls the particular name of an Abwehr officer in connection with this shooting of Jews, an officer whom I knew quite well.

COLONEL AMEN: Now, may it please the Tribunal, I should like to offer in evidence a photostatic copy or copies of the entries made by the witness in every detail, together with a photostatic copy of the report. The originals are here in court, but cannot be lifted out of the box in which they are contained. They are so much damaged by a bomb explosion that if they were to be lifted out of the box, they would be destroyed beyond use, but we have had them photostated, and the photostatic copies are now available. That letter would be exhibit USA 80 - document 3047-PS.

THE PRESIDENT: Do I understand, Colonel Amen, that only such portions of these documents as are read in court will be in evidence?

COLONEL AMEN: Well, these have been used by the witness to refresh his recollection.

THE PRESIDENT: Yes, I know they have.

COLONEL AMEN: And none of them have been read in full in Court, but they may be so read at any time, Sir.

THE PRESIDENT: If you want them to go into evidence as documents, you must read them, of course. Colonel Amen, do you want to use the documents any more than you already used them for the purpose of refreshing the witness's memory?

COLONEL AMEN: I do not, Sir, except that having used them in this fashion, I now think it is only fair to offer them in evidence for the information and scrutiny of the Tribunal; for my own purpose they have served their ends.

THE PRESIDENT: If the defence wants to see them for the purpose of cross-examination, of course, they may do so.

COLONEL AMEN: Oh, yes, Sir. I have offered it already, Sir, to be exhibit USA 80 - document 3047-PS.

THE PRESIDENT: But otherwise they may not be put in evidence?

COLONEL AMEN: Correct.

THE PRESIDENT: From this damaged paper, it seems to contain a report on the execution of the Jews in Borisov.

COLONEL AMEN: Yes.

THE PRESIDENT: That again will not be in evidence unless you read it.

COLONEL AMEN: Correct, Sir. We will include that in the offer which I just made to you, that, unless what we are offering is desired by the Court, I will not offer it in evidence or read it.

THE PRESIDENT: Very well, the Court does not desire it.

COLONEL AMEN: Very well.

COLONEL AMEN: to witness: As a member of the Abwehr, were you generally well informed on the plan of the German Reich for waging of war?

WITNESS: In so far as the office of the Abwehr was concerned in the preparation for these matters.

Q. Did any intelligence information ever come to your attention which was not available to an ordinary person, or to an ordinary officer in the army?

A. Yes, certainly. It is a function of my office.

Q. And, on the basis of the knowledge which you so obtained, did you in your group come to any decisions as to whether or not the attack on Poland, for example, was an unprovoked act of aggression?

THE PRESIDENT: Well -

WITNESS: Would you be kind enough to repeat the question?

THE PRESIDENT: That is one principal question which this Court has to decide. You cannot produce evidence upon a question which is within the province of the Court to decide.

COLONEL AMEN: Very well, sir. The witness is now available for cross-examination.

THE PRESIDENT: Is it the Soviet prosecutor's wish to ask any questions of this witness? General Rudenko

DIRECT EXAMINATION BY GENERAL RUDENKO: You have made definite replies to questions and I should like to have certain details. Am I to understand you rightly that the insurgent units of the Ukrainian nationalists were organised under the direction of the German High Command?

A. They were Ukrainian immigrants from Galicia.

Q. And from these immigrants were formed insurgent units (Commandos).

A. Yes, "Commando" perhaps is not quite the right expression. They were people who were brought together in tents and were given a military or a semi-military training.

Q. What was the function of these Commandos?

A. They were organisations of immigrants from the Ukraine Galicia, as I already previously stated, who worked together with the Amt Abwehr.

Q. What were these troops supposed to accomplish?

A. Tasks were assigned to them from time to time at the beginning of the operation by the office in charge of the command. That is, in the case of orders originating from the office to which I belonged, they were determined by the OKW.

Q. What functions did these groups have?

A. These Commandos were to carry out sabotage behind the enemy's front line.

Q. That is to say, in what territory?

A. In those territories with which Germany had entered into war or, speaking of a concrete case, such as the trial is concerned with, in Poland.

Q. Of course, in Poland. Well, sabotage and what else.

A. Sabotage, wrecking of bridges and other objectives of military importance. The Wehrmacht operational staff determined what was of military importance; details of that activity I have just described, namely, destruction of militarily important objectives or objectives important for a particular operation.

Q. But what about terroristic activities? I am asking you about the terroristic activities of these units.

A. Political tasks were not assigned to them by us, i.e., the Amt Ausland-Abwehr. Political assignments were made by the respective Reich office where it should be said, often as a result of erroneous ...

Q. You have misunderstood me. You are speaking about sabotage and I was asking you concerning terroristic acts of these organisations. Do you understand me? Was terror one of their tasks? Let me repeat again; as well as the sabotage acts, were there any terror acts assigned to them?

A. On our part never.

Q. You have told me that from your side there was no question of terrorism. From whose side was there? Who worked on this aspect?

A. Well, that was the whole point at the time. Each one of these military Abwehr units was being asked again and again to use their purely military organisation, which was established to take care of the tasks of the Armed Forces operation, for political or terroristic methods, as is clearly shown by the memorandum on our files concerning the campaign against Poland.

Q. Answering the question of Colonel Amen as to whether the Red Army men were looked upon as an ideological enemy and was subjected to corresponding measures, what do you mean by corresponding measures? I repeat the question. You have said that the Red Army man was looked upon by you, I mean by the German High Command, as an ideological enemy, and was to be subjected to the corresponding measures. What does it mean? What do you mean by "corresponding measures"?

A. By special measures I mean quite clearly all those brutal methods which were actually used and which I have already mentioned, and of which I am convinced there were many more, more than I could possibly have seen in my restricted field and more than were known to me.

Q. You have already told the Tribunal that there were special commandos for the screening of prisoners of war. I understand that they were screened in the following way: into those who were to be killed and the others who were to be interned in camps, is that right?

A. Yes, but these special commandos of the S.D. alone were concerned with the execution of those selected amongst the prisoners of war.

Q. That, of course, makes the chief of the commandos responsible and decisive for the question as to who was to die and who was not to die.

A. Yes, it was this very subject that was under discussion with Reinecke. The fact was mentioned that he was to be the head of one such commando which was to decide who, in view of the order, was to be looked upon as Bolshevistically tainted and who was not.

Q. And the chief of the commando decided upon his own authority, what to do with them.

A. Yes, at least up to the date of the discussion in which I participated upon an order from Canaris, this point, amongst others, was one of the most important ones of this discussion.

Q. You have told us about your protest and the protest of Canaris against these atrocities, killings and so forth. What were the results of these protests?

A. As I have already stated, there were some very modest results, so modest that you can hardly call them results at all. The fact that executions were to take place out of sight of the troops or at least at a 500-metres distance, I can in no way call a result.

Q. What conversation did you have with Muller on this subject, concerning his concessions? You told us when you were asked by General Alexandrov (please who is Alexandrov?) you were questioned by Colonel Rosenblith, a representative of the Soviet Delegation. I am sorry I made a mistake. Perhaps you will remember your communication to Colonel Rosenblith regarding the conversation and the concession that Muller made. I shall ask you to tell us that part again.

A. Yes, correct. Yes, if the name is Alexandrov, though I do not know what Alexandrov meant in this connection.

Q. Alexandrov was a mistake on my part, forget it. I am interested in the question of Muller, concerning the shootings, torturings, and so forth.

A. I had a long conversation with Muller, especially with regard to the selections. I cited, to be concrete, the case of the Crimean Tartars, i.e., the case of Soviet Russian soldiers who, according to their nationality, originated from the Crimea; and cases where, for certain reasons, Mohammedan people were declared Jews, and were then executed. Apart from the brutality of these and all other similar measures, these cases proved the entirely irrational point of view, or points of view, incomprehensible to any normal person, which characterised the handling of the entire matter. To that, among other things, I made reference.

Q. You told us where these measures were carried out.

THE PRESIDENT: He doesn't hear you, carry on but do a little bit more slowly.

GENERAL RUDENKO: Have you finished your conversation with Muller?

WITNESS: No, I didn't quite finish, I had many discussions with Muller and all this was a consensus of these discussions. All the subjects about which I have given evidence were discussed first with Muller as the man in authority in at least one sector. As for Reinecke, he then merely decided according to his own ideas, and his own point of view, and contrary to my views or those held by the Amt. I would be grateful if you would tell me what particular points you would like me to explain and I will gladly repeat them.

Q. Your usual topic of discussion was murders, shootings, and so forth, especially shootings. I am interested in all that. What did Muller say about it? How were shootings to take place, especially in relation to your protests?

A. He told me in a rather cynical form that in this case the shootings would take place somewhere else if the troops were too disturbed by them and if, as I described it, "their morale suffers," etc ., and that was the main meaning of what he said.

Q. That was the result of your protest?

A. Yes, that was the very poor result of our protest, and then still a certain concession...

Q. And one last question. The conditions of the concentration camps where Soviet prisoners were taken and where mass destruction of prisoners was committed; were all these orders the result of directives of the German High Command?

A. In some sort of co-operation with the competent authorities, the Reichs-Sicherheitshauptamt. Corroborating all I have stated, I must point out that at the time, I myself did not read the orders, and that I learned of the work alone on parallel lines, or the collaboration, or the co-ordination in this question only from conversations and primarily from the conversations with Reinecke, and wherever I encountered a representative of the O.K.W. in the persons of Reinecke and of the afore-mentioned Muller.

Q. Excuse me, did you get to know that information in private or unofficial sessions or conversations?

A. It was a strictly official meeting called by General Reinecke. I was not there as "Lahousen", but as a representative of the Ausland-Abwehr.

Q. The orders which are passed on in these sessions, did they come to you directly from the German High Command?

A. They came from the German High Command and from one of the highest officers of the R.S.H.A., according to what Reinecke said during one of these discussions. I have never seen them with my own eyes, therefore this is all I can state.

Q. But you have heard during these meetings where and when they were discussed?

A. Yes, during the discussions, the course of which I have already described, or at least in its essential aspects, of course.

Q. And during these sessions which you mentioned were the questions raised about murders, and burning of cities?

A. There was no talk at these discussions about setting on fire, but mention was made of the orders which had been issued with respect to the prisoners.

Q. About the murders only.

A. About the executions.

GENERAL RUDENKO: That is all.

THE PRESIDENT: Does the French prosecutor wish to ask any questions?

BY M. DUBOST: One single question.

Q. Who gave the orders for the liquidation of the army leaders?

A. I did not understand that - the destruction of the "Kommandos"? What was it exactly that you meant? Presumably the killing of members of the Kommando troops?

Q. Who gave the orders for the execution?

A. I did not read the order myself, but according to what was said in our circles about this subject, the idea came from Hitler himself, who was instrumental in reorganising the S.D., but who also has helped in the reforming of the S.D. I do not know.

Q. The defendants Keitel, Jodl, what orders did they handle; what orders did they give?

A. I cannot say that because I do not know.

Q. What were the reasons for these orders, as far as you know?

A. Not merely was it my opinion, but it was common knowledge, that the reasons for these orders were, to have an intimidating effect and thus to crush and paralyse the activity of the commandos.

Q. Who gave the order to have Generals Giraud and Weygand executed or murdered?

A. I did not hear the first part of the question. Who gave the order to kill Weygand

and Giraud? The order to liquidate, that is, to be explicit, to murder Weygand and Giraud, as Canaris told me, came from Keitel. This order and this intention regarding the case Weygand, were furthermore directly transmitted to me in a personal remark on the part of Keitel. Keitel asked me after Canaris had read to him a report in my presence, On 23rd December, 1940, according to my notes, about the progress in the case Weygand.

As regards the second case, that is the case Giraud, it is a fact that the order came from Keitel to Canaris - this I heard first from Canaris himself - and so did the other chiefs who were present. I further heard of it a second time during a report from Canaris to Keitel, in my presence, in July, 1942, when this order was communicated to me in a manner similar to that of case Weygand, and, finally, in a direct manner, that is, a telephone conversation which I described here, received from Keitel and transmitted as urgent intelligence.

(The British Chief Prosecutor indicated that he had no questions to ask.)

THE PRESIDENT: Do you want to ask any questions, Dr. Nelte?

DR. NELTE (Counsel for defendant Keitel): The witness, Lahousen, has given very important evidence, particularly -

THE PRESIDENT: Are you going to make a speech now?

DR. NELTE: My client, the defendant Keitel, would like to put numerous questions to the witness after he has had a discussion with me. I therefore ask the Tribunal to allow either that there may be a considerable adjournment now, or that at the next session this question may be discussed in cross-examination.

THE PRESIDENT: Very well. You shall have an opportunity to cross-examine at 10 o'clock to-morrow. Does any member of the Tribunal wish to ask any questions of the witness now?

BY THE TRIBUNAL (Mr. Biddle):

Q. I should like to ask the witness whether the orders for the killing of the Russians and in connection with the treatment of the prisoners were in writing?

A. As far as I know, yes, but I did not see or read these orders myself.

Q. Were they official orders?

A. Yes, they were official orders, of course, though the facts were brought out in a roundabout way. It was these orders which Reinecke and the others discussed and this is how I learned about their essential points; I did not read them myself at any time. Still, that they were not oral agreements I knew, because they were commented upon; consequently I knew that something existed in writing. Only, I cannot say whether there were one or more orders, or who signed them. This I did not claim to know. I submitted my knowledge which is based solely on discussions and reports from which I quite clearly could deduct the existence of orders.

Q. Do you know to whom or to what organisations such orders were usually addressed?

A. Orders of this kind, involving the question of principle, went to the O.K.W., because things relating to prisoners of war were the concern of the O.K.W., and in particular of Reinecke, which also explains the discussions with Reinecke.

Q. So usually the members or some of the members of the General Staff would have known of such orders, would they not?

A. Certainly, in accordance with its essential contents, many members of the Wehrmacht knew of this order, and the reaction of the Wehrmacht against it was tremendous. Apart from the service view, which is what I have reported here, and elsewhere, these orders were discussed a great deal, in casino clubs, because all these matters became manifest in the most undesirable form and had a most undesirable effect on the troops. As a matter of fact, officers and high- ranking officers at the front, either did not transmit these orders or sought to evade them in some way, and this was discussed a great deal. I have named some of these officers; some are listed in the notes, diary, etc. It was not an everyday occurrence, and it was then the topic of the day.

Q. And were the orders known to the leaders of the S.A. and S.D.?

A. They must have been known to them, for the ordinary soldiers who watched all these proceedings knew and spoke about them, and partly they were also known to the civilian populace; civilians and men from the front, as well as wounded soldiers, told far more details about these matters than I could tell here.

THE PRESIDENT: General Nikitchenko wants to ask a question.

BY THE TRIBUNAL (Gen. Nikitchenko):

Q. You have told us that you received instructions about the murder of prisoners of war and brutal treatment. You received these orders from Reinecke?

A. Well, I must correct something that I said. We didn't get the order in the Ausland-Abwehr because it had nothing to do with us, but I knew about it, and went into this conference as a representative of the Ausland- Abwehr. But we ourselves had nothing to do with the treatment of prisoners of war, and certainly not in this negative sense.

Q. Apart from these meetings, the meetings of the High Command, were such instructions ever given? Were there any meetings of the High Command headquarters about killings and ill-treatment of prisoners of war?

A. There certainly had been a number of discussions about this subject, but I was present at only one of them, which I described, so I cannot say anything more about it.

Q. At headquarters?

A. In the O.K.W. - at headquarters.

Q. At the headquarters of the German Army?

A. Certainly, in the O.K.W., where Amt Abwehr had been requested to send a delegate in my person, particularly because of its protests. As a matter of fact our Amt had nothing to do with prisoners of war in this sense. But we were, because of technical and natural reasons, interested in proper treatment of the prisoners.

Q. But the meetings were not about treating prisoners, about killing and murdering them? At these meetings, Ribbentrop was also present?

A. No; these discussions, I mean the one conference about which I have given testimony, took place after the accomplished fact. Everything had already happened; executions had already taken place, and the results had already been shown. Protests of all kinds had already been made, they had come from the front and from other places. For example, from our own office, Abwehr; this conference was intended to show the necessity for the orders which had already been given, and to justify measures already taken. These discussions took place after the beginning of operations, after the orders which had been given had already been carried out. All that I have touched upon or stated had already happened and its effect had already been felt in the worst sense. Facts that had already happened were being discussed with the idea of making one more attempt, a last attempt on our part, to get a grip of the situation.

Q. All these reports brought about results?

A. That is what I talked about, and that was the subject of the discussions with Reinecke. I did not take part in the other discussions and therefore have nothing to say.

Q. At which other meetings had orders been given about killings and burning of towns and villages?

A. I must make something clear, relative to what the General has in mind. Am I being asked about the conference in the Fuehrer's train prior to the fall of Warsaw? According to the entries in Canaris' diary, it took place on the 12th September, 1939. The meaning of this order which Ribbentrop gave, and which Keitel gave them in a brief discussion, was again referred to by Ribbentrop, and was in reference to the organisations of National Ukrainians with which Amt Abwehr co-operated along military lines, that is, in the matter of military operations to bring about an uprising in Poland, with the Ukrainians--an uprising which aimed to exterminate the Poles and the Jews, that is to say, above all such elements as were always being discussed in these conferences. When Poles are mentioned, the intelligentsia especially is meant, and any persons who would be prototypes of the national will of resistance. This was the order given Canaris in the connection I have already described and as it has already been noted in the memorandum. The idea was not to kill Ukrainians but, on the contrary, for us to carry out this task of a purely political and terroristic nature together with the Ukrainians. The co-operation and what actually occurred in the connection between Ausland-Abwehr and these people who were only about five hundred or a thousand - all this can be clearly seen from the diary. This was simply a preparation for military sabotage.

Q. These instructions were received from Ribbentrop and Keitel?

A. They came from Ribbentrop. Such orders which concerned the political contents couldn't possibly come from Amt- Ausland-Abwehr because any -

Q. I am not asking you whether they could or could not. I am asking where they came from.

A. They came from Ribbentrop, as is seen from the memorandum that I made for Canaris.

THE PRESIDENT: yes, Doctor

DR. DIX (Counsel for defendant Schacht): I have three short questions, May I put them?

THE PRESIDENT: It is now past four, and we have to hear the requests of the defendant Hess, and the Court has to be cleared for them. So I think you had better postpone then, until tomorrow.

(A short recess was taken, and all the defendants except Hess were removed from the courtroom.)

THE PRESIDENT: I call upon counsel for the defendant Hess.

DR. VON R0HRSCHEIDT (counsel for the defendant Hess): May it please the Tribunal, I am speaking here as counsel for the defendant Rudolf Hess.

In the proceedings which have already been opened against Hess, the Court should solely decide on the question whether the defendant is fit or unfit to be heard, and further, whether he might be considered entirely irresponsible.

The Court itself has expressed this judicial conception by asking the experts to state their opinion with regard to his fitness to plead; firstly, is the defendant in a state in which he can plead on the charge; secondly, as to his mental stability; the question here was formulated as to whether the defendant is mentally sound or not

In respect to question 1, is the defendant in a state fit to plead, the Tribunal on the basis of its determination of the issue "is the defendant fit to plead his case?" asked the experts specifically whether the defendant is sufficiently in possession of his mental faculties to understand the proceedings, and whether he is qualified for an adequate defence - that is, to repudiate a witness to whom he objects and to understand details given in evidence.

During several sessions the experts to whom this task was entrusted, acting as commissions, have examined Hess on several days and have given their expert opinion concerning these questions to the Tribunal, and I, as the defendant's counsel, after having studied this experts' opinions (which I couldn't do very thoroughly because time was so short) and in view of the experience and knowledge I gained in almost daily discussions with the defendant, consider it my duty to state that, in my opinion, the defendant Hess is not capable of pleading.

As his defence counsel I am therefore in duty bound to file the following motions on behalf of the defendant Hess:

Firstly, I ask for a Court decision that the proceedings against Hess be temporarily suspended. Secondly, in case his inability to plead should be admitted by the Tribunal, I should request the Tribunal not to proceed against the defendant in absentia. Thirdly, in case the Tribunal should consider Hess fit to plead, I should ask for a consensus of opinion of further competent psychiatrists.

Here, however, before I come to the reasons for my applications, I should like to say, on behalf of the defendant, that Hess himself thinks he is fit to plead and would like to tell the Court so.

I would now like to give the reasons for my application:

As regards (1): If my defendant - my client, rather - is not fit to plead, I should like the proceedings against Hess to be temporarily suspended.

In connection therewith and to explain the reasons for my application it is permissible for me, I believe, to refer to the opinions already submitted to the Tribunal.

Pursuant to the questions placed before them by the Tribunal, the experts come to the following conclusion which I infer from the consensus of opinions as - I must term it - having been rendered by a mixed delegation, which as far as I could determine consisted of English, Soviet, and American experts, the opinion bearing the date of 14th November, 1945, and I should like to cite textually from it. In this opinion it is stated, "that the capability of the defendant Hess is impaired"; that is to say, the capacity to defend himself and to face a witness and to understand the details of evidence. I have cited this formulation of the opinion because it is closest to the questions put to the experts by the Tribunal.

Going further, another opinion says that even if Hess' amnesia does not prevent the defendant from understanding what happens around him-and to follow the proceedings in Court -

THE PRESIDENT (interposing): Would you speak a little more slowly? The interpreters are not able to interpret so fast.

Would you also refer us especially to those parts of the medical reports to which you wish to draw our attention?

Do you understand what I said?

DR. VON ROHRSCHEIDT: Yes.

I should like to mention that I cannot refer to quotations according to the pages of the original text, or English text, as I only have the German translation, so I can only state that the first quotation -

The first quotation -

THE PRESIDENT (interposing): You can read the words in German, and they will be translated into English.

Which report are you referring to?

DR. VON ROHRSCHEIDT: For the quotation that I gave I was referring to the expert report, as far as I can see from my German translation which was given on the 14th November, 1945, which was drawn up by the delegation of English, Soviet and American experts and which accompanied the report of the 17th of November, 1945. What I quoted was the following - may I repeat it?

The passage runs: "The capability of the defendant Hess in respect to his being able to defend himself, to face a witness, and to understand details of the evidence given, is impaired". I should like the Tribunal to tell me -

THE PRESIDENT: Can you say which of the doctors you are quoting?

DR. VON ROHRSCHEIDT: It is the report which, in my copy, is dated the 14th of November, 1945, and, as I said, was presumably signed by Soviet, American and English doctors.

Unfortunately, when returning the material after completion of translation into German yesterday evening, I did not succeed in my attempt to obtain the original text, because of lack of time.

THE PRESIDENT: Have the English prosecutors got a copy, and can you tell us which it is?

SIR DAVID MAXWELL FYFE: I think I am in the same difficulties as your Lordship. On the order that I have, I have copies of four medical reports. Your Lordship will see at the end of the document headed "Order", it says, "Copies of four medical reports are attached."

The first one of these is signed by three English doctors on the 19th of November. Then there is a report signed by three Soviet doctors, dated the 17th of November. Another one is signed by three Soviet doctors and the French doctor dated the 16th of November.

These are the ones which I have with the Court's order. The fourth, dated 20th November, is signed by Drs. Delay, Lewis and Cameron, and Colonel Paul Schroder.

THE PRESIDENT: Yes.

I don't know what this report is that you are referring to.

SIR DAVID MAXWELL FYFE: Dr. von Rohrscheidt seems to have an unsigned report of the 14th.

THE PRESIDENT: Dr. von Rohrscheidt, have you got the four reports which are really before us? I will read them out to you:

The first one I have got in my hand is the 19th of November, 1945, by Lord Moran, Dr. Reece, and Dr. Riddoch. Have you got that? That is the English report.

DR. VON ROHRSCHEIDT: I only have this report in the German translation and not in the original.

THE PRESIDENT: But if you have got it in the German translation, that is quite good enough.

Then the next one is dated the 20th of November, 1945, by Dr. Delay, Dr. Nolan Lewis, Dr. Cameron and Colonel Paul Schroeder.

Have you got that?

DR. VON ROHRSCHEIDT: Yes, I have that one.

THE PRESIDENT: That is two.

Then, the next one is dated the 16th of November, and is signed by three Soviet doctors and one French doctor, Dr. Jean Delay, dated the 16th of November. Have you got that?

Then there is another report of the 17th November, signed by the three Soviet doctors alone, without the French doctor.

Now, will you refer to the passages in those reports upon which you rely?

There is another report by the two English doctors which is practically the same. That is the one I have already referred to, that does not contain the name of Lord Moran on it, dated the 19th of November.

DR. VON ROHRSCHEIDT: If the Tribunal please, I think I can shorten this speech to the Tribunal. My view is that all the experts' opinions can be summed up as stating that the capability of the accused Hess to defend himself, to face a witness, and to understand details of the evidence given - I did not keep exactly to these words in my statement -

If we assume that all the medical opinions agree as to the fact that defendant Hess' capacity to defend himself is impaired, I, as his defence counsel, would draw the conclusion that defendant Hess' capacity to plead must be considered as being nil. The reduced capacity of the defendant to defend himself, which is recognised as amnesia by all experts, who describe it as a mental condition of a mixed character rather than a mental abnormality, must be accepted as meaning that he is unfit to plead.

I am of the opinion that the conclusion drawn by the medical experts implies, that in whatever way the question be formulated its answer will be, "Hess cannot be suitably defended on account of his mental defect." The medical report is based on the assumption "that the defendant is not insane". That is not the important point at the moment because according to the medical report it is, in my opinion, convincingly stated, that because of reduced mental ability the defendant is not in a condition to understand the proceedings.

Speaking for myself - and I think that my opinion is in agreement with the medical opinion - I believe that the defendant is quite incapable of making himself understood in the manner that is to be expected from a mentally normal person.

In view of my own experience I consider that the defendant is incapable of grasping the charges which the Tribunal will bring against him, to the extent that is required for his defence, because his memory is very unreliable. Because of his loss of memory he remembers neither events of the past nor the persons who were associated with him in the past. I am, therefore, of the opinion that defendant's own claim that he is fit to plead is irrelevant. The reduction of the defendant's capacity will not improve within a given time, according to the medical report and therefore I think that the proceedings against him should be suspended.

It is not certain that the treatment of narcotic analysis suggested by the medical experts would bring about the desired effect, nor that a determined period of time can be given, during which this treatment would result in the complete recovery of the defendant's health. The reproach has been raised in the medical report against the defendant of deliberately refusing to undergo such medical treatment. The defendant tells me that, on the contrary, he would readily undergo treatment, but that he refuses the suggested cure because he thinks first of all, that he is already fit to plead and therefore considers this cure as unnecessary, and secondly, because he disapproves on principle of such violent methods, and finally because he is of the opinion that such an operation, at precisely this time, might render him unfit to plead or to take part in the proceedings, which is the very thing he wishes to avoid.

If, however, defendant is incapable of pleading and of defending himself, as stated in the medical report, and if the aforesaid condition is likely to last for a long time, this would, in my opinion, provide the basis for a temporary suspension of the proceedings against him.

My second motion is the following: In case this Tribunal should accept my former motion and declare the defendant Hess unfit to plead, then, according to Article 12 of the Charter, it would be possible to proceed against the defendant in absentia. Article 12 provides that the Tribunal has the right to proceed against a defendant in absentia if he cannot be found, or if this procedure is, for other reasons, in the interests of justice.

Is it then in the interests of justice to proceed against the defendant in absentia? In my opinion it is incompatible with objective justice if actual proofs are available, as in the present case, that the defendant's capacity is reduced owing to illness, i.e., amnesia which has been recognised in all medical reports, and that he is, therefore, unable to personally safeguard his rights and to attend Court- sessions.

In a trial where charges are being brought against the defendant, so grave that they might entail the death penalty, it seems incompatible with objective justice that the defendant should be deprived of the rights granted to him under Article 16 of the Charter, although medical opinion confirms the existence of reasons of health.

Article 16 of the Charter makes, however, provisions for the defendant's defence, for the possibility of furnishing evidence to this end, for cross-examining every witness called before the Court, all of which is of so great an importance for the defence that failure to make use of any of these privileges would, in my opinion, constitute a grave injustice to the defendant. Therefore a trial in absentia cannot be accepted as a fair trial.

If, as I have stated, the defendant's capacity to defend himself is reduced owing to the reasons already mentioned, it is equally established that the defendant is not in a position to give his counsel the necessary information and to enable his counsel to defend him in his absence.

Since the Charter has precisely laid down the rights of the defendants, it seems unjust to me as defence counsel that the defendant should be deprived of these rights in a case where, by reason of illness, he is handicapped in safeguarding his interest in his defence and in Court proceedings.

The regulation laid down in Article 12 of the Charter, on proceedings in absentia against a defendant, must surely be looked upon as an exceptional measure, which in my opinion should only be applied against a defendant if he endeavours to evade the proceedings in any way except through force of circumstances. But defendant Hess has told me, and he will probably emphasise this before the Tribunal, that he wishes to attend the proceedings, and he will certainly feel that it is particularly unfair if the proceedings were carried on in absentia, and regardless of his own readiness to plead.

I therefore request the Tribunal, if it should declare the defendant not competent to plead, that it will not proceed in his absence.

And now I wish to submit an additional motion:-

Should the Tribunal consider defendant Hess fit to plead - which, in my opinion, would be contrary to the opinion expressed in the medical reports - I request that a further medical test be made in order to investigate the question once more, for, as I have seen from the reports, each of the doctors examined and talked to the defendant for only a few hours during one day (during two days in one case). In a case as outstanding as this one, it seems to me, that, in order to obtain a complete picture of the defendant's case, it would be advisable to place him in a suitable hospital, for an examination over an extended period of time, in order to obtain a reliable picture based on several weeks of observation. The experts themselves are, obviously, not quite sure whether defendant Hess is mentally ill, apart or beyond the admitted unfitness to plead, This clearly emerges from the fact that all the medical statements emphasise that should the accused, when called upon by the Court, not be considered fit to plead, he should again be subjected to a psychiatric examination. I think this course should be followed in accordance with the suggestion made by the psychiatrists who have already examined him. I should therefore request - in case the Tribunal considers the defendant fit to plead - that the suggestion of the psychiatrists who have already examined him be followed, and that another medical opinion be obtained.

THE PRESIDENT: I want to ask you one question: Is it not consistent with all the medical opinions that the defendant is capable of understanding the course of the proceedings, and that the only defect from which he is suffering is forgetfulness about what happened before he flew to England?

DR. VON ROHRSCHEIDT: Mr. President, it is true that the experts find defendant Hess capable of following the proceedings. But when answering the questions put to them they emphasise on the other hand, that the defendant is incapable of defending himself. The Tribunal asked the experts to give their opinion on the following questions, and I beg to read them again: "Is the defendant mentally healthy or not?" The question was answered in the affirmative by all experts, i.e., that he is not mentally ill, which does not, however, exclude the fact that the defendant might, at this moment, be incapable of pleading. This is borne out again by the answer of the experts to the next question: "Is the defendant mentally capable of following the proceedings so as to adequately defend himself, to understand a witness he wishes to repudiate, and to comprehend evidence submitted?" This is the wording of the translation in my possession. It seems to me that this question is answered by the experts, to the effect that the defendant is incapable of suitably defending himself, of rejecting a witness he wishes to repudiate and of comprehending evidence submitted. That I consider is contained in all the experts' reports with the exception of the report given by the Russians. Looking at the report given by the Franco-American delegation, if I may submit that to the Court, dated 20th November, it is stated under G, "as a result of our examination and investigations, we find that Hess is suffering from hysteria which partly manifests itself in a loss of memory." Now I come to the passage to which I should like to draw the Court's attention, "The loss of memory is of a kind that will not impair his understanding of the proceedings, but will do so with regard to his reactions to questions about his past, which would reduce the weight of his defence."

This report thus establishes that Hess's defence will be impaired. And I believe that the experts' admission "that his memory is affected" means that his fitness to plead is greatly reduced. The report of the Soviet-French delegation, signed by the Russian professors and Professor Delay, goes even further in stating that, although the defendant is able to comprehend all that happens around him, amnesia affects his capacity to defend himself and to understand details of the proceedings, and that this amnesia must be considered an impediment. If one is to interpret this report in the spirit of the doctors who wrote it, it clearly means that the defendant is not insane, that he can follow the proceedings - to all appearances - but that he cannot defend himself, as he is suffering from a credible form of amnesia based on hysteria.

THE TRIBUNAL (Mr Biddle): Do you accept the opinion of the experts?

DR. VON ROHRSCHEIDT: Yes.

THE TRIBUNAL (GENERAL NIKITCHENKO): I should like to draw the attention of the defence counsel to the fact that he has referred inaccurately to the decision reached by the Soviet and French experts. He has rendered this decision in a free translation which does not correspond to the original content.

DR. VON ROHRSCHEIDT: May I ask whether the report of 16th November is meant? May I once more read what my translation says? I can only refer to the translation of the English text that was given to me. This translation was made in the Translation Division of the Secretariat and handed over to me in this shape.

May I repeat that the translation in my possession refers to the report of 16th November, 1945, which was signed by members of the Soviet delegation and by Professor Delay of Paris?

Under Point 3 of this report the following is stated:

"The defendant is not insane in the strict sense of the word at present. His amnesia does not prevent him from following everything that is going on around him. But it affects his capacity to defend himself and to understand all details of the defence which might be presented as actual facts."

That is the text which I have here before me in the authentic German version.

THE PRESIDENT: That is all we wish to ask you. Does the Chief Prosecutor for the United States wish to address the Tribunal?

MR. JUSTICE JACKSON: I think General Rudenko would like to open discussion, if that is agreeable.

THE PRESIDENT: Yes. Are you going on?

GENERAL RUDENKO: In connection with the statement made by the defence counsel acting for Hess, concerning the results of the evidence regarding Hess' certified psychological condition, I consider it essential to make the following declaration: his psychological condition was certified by experts appointed by the Tribunal. These experts appointed by the Tribunal came to the unanimous conclusion that he is sane and responsible for his actions. The chief prosecutors after discussing the results of the decision and acting in accordance with the order of the Tribunal, replied as follows to the inquiry of the Tribunal: First of all, we have no questions to ask, no doubts to cast on the Commission. We consider that the defendant, Rudolf Hess, is perfectly able to stand his trial. This is the unanimous statement made by the chief prosecutors.

THE PRESIDENT (interposing): Will you speak more slowly, please?

GENERAL RUDENKO: I consider that the findings of the experts are quite sufficient to declare Hess sane and able to stand his trial. We therefore request the Tribunal to make the requisite decision this very day.

The defence counsellor, in his statement, when submitting to the Tribunal his reasons either for the postponement of the proceedings or for the settlement of the defendant's case, refers to the decision of the experts. I must, however, declare that this decision (and I do not know on what principle it was reached) has been quoted absolutely inaccurately. In the summary submitted by the defence counsel it is pointed out that the mental condition of the defendant Hess did not permit him to defend himself, to reply to the witnesses or to understand all the details of the evidence. This is contrary to the decision submitted by the experts, in their statement. The final conclusion of the experts definitely states that a similar loss of memory would not entirely prevent him from understanding the trial, but would preclude the possibility of defending himself and of remembering particulars of the past. I consider that these particulars, which Hess is unable to remember, would not interest the Tribunal unduly. The most important point is that which was emphasised by the experts in their decision, a point which they never doubted themselves and which, incidentally, was never doubted by Hess' defence counsel, namely, the fact that Hess was sane, in which case he, Hess, comes under the jurisdiction of the International Tribunal. On the strength of the above- mentioned data, I consider that the petition of the defence should be declined as being devoid of foundation.

SIR DAVID MAXWELL FYFE: May it please the Tribunal:

It has been suggested that I might say just a word, and as shortly as the Tribunal desires, as to the legal conceptions which govern the position in which the Tribunal and this defendant are placed at the present time.

The question before the Tribunal is whether this defendant is able to plead to the Indictment, and should be tried at the present time.

If I might very briefly refer the Tribunal to the short passages in the report, which I submit are relevant, it might be useful at the present time. According to the attachments to the order, which I have, the first report is that signed by the British doctors on the 19th November, 1945. And in that report, I beg the Tribunal to refer to paragraph 3, in which the signatories say: "At the moment he is not insane in the strict sense. His loss of memory will not entirely interfere with his comprehension of the proceedings, but it will interfere with his ability to make his defence and to understand details of the past, which arise in evidence."

The next report is that signed by the American and French doctors, and in paragraph I, the Tribunal will see: "We find, as a result of our examinations and investigations, that Rudolf Hess is suffering from hysteria, characterised in part by loss of memory. The nature of this loss of memory is such that it will not interfere with his comprehension of the proceedings, but it will interfere with his response to questions relating to his past, and will interfere with his undertaking his defence."

If the Tribunal will proceed to the third report, signed by the Soviet doctors, at the foot of page 1, of the copy that I have, there is a paragraph beginning "Psychologically - ", which I submit is of importance - "Psychologically, Hess is in a state of clear consciousness. He knows that he is imprisoned at Nuremberg, under Indictment as a War Criminal; has read and, according to his own words, is acquainted with the charges against him. He answers questions rapidly and to the point. His speech is coherent. His thoughts are formed with precision and correctness and they are accompanied by sufficient emotionally expressive movements. Also, there is no kind of evidence of paralogism. It should also be noted here, that the present psychological examination, which was conducted by Lieut. Gilbert, Doctor of Medicine, bears out the testimony, that the intelligence of Hess is normal and in some instances, above average. His movements are natural and not forced."

Now, if I may come to the next report, I am sorry - the report which is signed by the three Soviet doctors, and Professor Delay of Paris, dated the 16th, which is the last in my bundle; that says in paragraph 3:

"At present he is not insane in the strict sense of the word. His amnesia does not prevent him completely from understanding what is going on around him, but it will interfere with his ability to conduct his defence and to understand details of the past, which would appear as factual data."

I refer, without quoting, because I do not consider that they are of such importance at this point, to the explanation of the kind and reason of the amnesia which appeared in the Soviet report, dated the 17th November, under the numbers one, two and three, at the end of the report. But I remind the Tribunal that all these reports unite in saying that there is no form of insanity.

In these circumstances, the question in English Law, and I respectfully submit that to the consideration of the Tribunal as being representative of natural justice in this regard, is, in deciding whether the defendant is fit to plead, the issue is whether the defendant be insane or not, and the time which is relevant for the deciding of that issue is at the date of the arraignment and not at any prior time.

Different views have been expressed as to the party on whom the onus of proof lies in that issue, but the later, and logically the better view, is that the onus is on the defence, because it is always presumed that a person is sane until the contrary is proved.

Now, if I might refer the Court to one case which I suspect, if I may so use my mind, has not been absent from the Court's mind, because of the wording of the notice which we are discussing to-day, it is the case of Pritchard in 7 Carrington and Pike, which is referred to in Archibold, Criminal Pleading on the 1943 edition, at page 147:

In Pritchard's case, where a prisoner arraigned on an indictment for felony appeared to be deaf, dumb, and also not of sane mind, Baron Alderson put three distinct issues to the jury, directing the jury to be sworn separately on each: (1) whether the prisoner was mute of malice, or by the visitation of God, (2) whether he was able to plead, (3) whether he was sane or not. And on the last issue they were directed to inquire whether the prisoner was of sufficient intellect to comprehend the course of the proceedings of the trial so as to make a proper defence, to challenge a juror, that is, a member of the jury, to whom he might wish to object, and to understand the details of the evidence; and he directed the jury that if there was no certain mode of communicating to the prisoner the details of the evidence, so that he could clearly understand them, and be able properly to make his defence to the charge against him, the jury ought to find that he was not of sane mind.

I submit to the Tribunal that the words there quoted, "to comprehend the course of the proceedings of the trial so as to make a proper defence", emphasise that the material time, the only time which should be considered, is whether at the moment of plea and of trial the defendant understands what is charged against him, and the evidence by which it is supported.

THE PRESIDENT: And does not relate to his memory at that time.

SIR DAVID MAXWELL FYFE: That is, I respectfully agree with your Lordship, it does not relate to his memory. It has never, in English jurisprudence, to my knowledge, been held to be a bar either to trial or punishment, that a person who comprehends the charge and the evidence, has not got a memory as to what happened at the time. That, of course, is entirely a different question which does not arise either on these reports or on this application, as to what was the defendant's state of mind when the act was committed. No one here suggests that the defendant's state of mind when the action charged was committed was abnormal, and it does not come into this case. ,

THE PRESIDENT: He will, it seems to me, be able to put forward his amnesia as part of his defence.

SIR DAVID MAXWELL FYFE: Certainly, my Lord.

THE PRESIDENT: And to say, "I should have been able to make a better defence if I had been able to remember what took place at the time."

SIR DAVID MAXWELL FYFE: Yes, Sir. If I might compare a very simple case within my experience, and I am sure within the experience of members of the Court where this has arisen scores of times in English courts, after a motor accident when a man is charged with manslaughter or doing grievous bodily harm, he is often in the position of saying, "because of the accident, my memory is not good, or fails as to the exact charge". That should not, and no one has ever suggested that it could be a matter of relief from criminal responsibility. I hope that the Tribunal will not think that I have occupied too much of their time, but I thought it was useful just to present the matter on the basis of the English law as I understand it.

THE TRIBUNAL (Mr. Biddle): As I understand you, one of the tests under the Pritchard case is whether or not the defendant can make a proper defence?

SIR DAVID MAXWELL FYFE: With the greatest respect, will the learned judge read the preceding words which limit it? They say, "Whether a prisoner was of sufficient intellect to comprehend the course of the proceedings of the trial so as to make a proper defence."

THE TRIBUNAL (Mr. Biddle): And would you interpret that to mean that this defendant could make a proper defence under the procedure of the trial, if you also find as a fact, which you, I think, do not dispute, and which you quoted in fact, that although not insane - now I quote: "He did not understand, or rather his amnesia does not prevent him completely from understanding, what is going on around him but it will interfere with his ability to conduct his defence, and understand details of the past." You don't think that is inconsistent with that finding?

SIR DAVID MAXWELL FYFE: No, I am submitting it is not. It is part of his defence, and it may well be "I don't remember anything about that at all." And he could actually add to that: "From my general behaviour or from other acts which I undoubtedly have done, it is extremely unlikely that I should do it." That is the defence which is left to him. And he must take that defence, and that is my submission.

THE TRIBUNAL (Mr. Biddle): So even if we assume for the purpose of argument that his amnesia is complete, and that he remembers nothing that occurred before the indictment, though now understanding the proceedings, you think he should be tried?

SIR DAVID MAXWELL FYFE: I submit he should be tried. That is my submission as to the legal position. I especially did not discuss of course - the Tribunal will appreciate that - I did not discuss the quantum of amnesia here, because I am not putting that to the Tribunal, I wanted to put before the Tribunal the legal basis on which this application is opposed. Therefore I accept readily the extreme case which the learned American judge put to me.

THE TRIBUNAL (M. de Vabres): I ask in what period the real amnesia of Hess applies. He pretends to have forgotten facts which occurred more than fifteen days ago. It may be simulation or, as they say in the report, it may be real simulation. I would like to know if according to the reports Hess has really lost his memory of facts, which are referred to in the Indictment, facts which pertain to the part covered by the Indictment.

SIR DAVID MAXWELL FYFE: The facts which are included in the Indictment, the explanations that the doctors give as to his amnesia, are most clearly set out in these paragraphs of the Soviet report, that is the third report dated the 17th of November, 1945, page two, and the numbered paragraphs one to three. They say first:

"In the psychological personality of Hess there are no changes typical of the progressive schizophrenic disease. That is, there are no changes typical of a progressive double personality developing, from which he suffered periodically while in England. I am sorry, therefore, the delusions from which he suffered periodically while in England cannot be considered as manifestations of a schizophrenic paranoia, and must be recognised as the expression of a psychogenic paranoia reaction, that is, the psychologically comprehensible reaction."

Now I ask the learned French judge to note the next sentence. "Of an unstable personality to the situation, the failure of his mission, arrest and incarceration. Such is the interpretation of the delirious statements of Hess in England, as bespoken by the disappearance, appearance, and repeated disappearance, depending on external circumstances which affected the mental state of Hess."

Paragraph two: "The loss of memory by Hess is not the result of some kind of mental disease, but represents hysterical amnesia, the basis of which is a subconscious inclination towards self-defence." Now I ask the learned French judge to note again the next words: As well as a deliberate and conscious tendency towards it." Such behaviour often terminates when the hysterical person is faced with an unavoidable necessity of conducting himself correctly. Therefore the amnesia of Hess may end upon his being brought to trial."

Three: "Rudolf Hess, prior to his flight to England, did not suffer from any kind of insanity, nor is he now suffering from it. At the present time he exhibits hysterical behaviour with signs of - and again I ask the learned French judge to note this point - with signs of a conscious intentional simulated character, which does not exonerate him from responsibility under the Indictment.

The last sentence is a matter for the Tribunal. But in these circumstances it would be impossible to say that the amnesia may continue to- be complete or is entirely unconscious. That is deliberately avoided by the learned doctors. Therefore the prosecution do not say that that is the case, but they do say that even if it were complete, the legal basis which I have suggested to the Court is a correct one for action in this matter.

THE PRESIDENT: Thank you, Sir David. Would Doctor Rohrscheidt like to add anything by way of reply? One moment: Mr Justice Jackson, I gathered from what Sir David said that he was speaking on behalf of you and of the French prosecution. Is that correct?

MR. JUSTICE JACKSON: I intend to adopt all that he said. I would only add a few more words, if I may.

THE PRESIDENT: Doctor Rohrscheidt, Mr. Justice Jackson has something to say first of all.

MR. JUSTICE JACKSON: I adopt all that has been said, and will not repeat. We have three applications before the Tribunal. One is for another examination. I will spend very little time on that. I think that we have made, up to this point in the examination, medical history in having seven psychiatrists from five nations who are completely in agreement. An achievement of that kind is not likely to be risked.

The only reason suggested here is that a relatively short time has been devoted to the examination, but I suggest to your Honour that that is not the situation, because there have been available the examinations and observations and medical history during the incarceration of Hess in England, extending from 1941, and the reports of the psychiatrists of the American Forces since he was brought to Nuremberg, and they all agree. So that there is a more complete medical history in this case than in most cases.

The next application was as to trial in absentia. I shall spend no time on that, for there seems to be no occasion for trying Hess in absentia if he should not be tried in his presence. If he is unable to be tried, why, he simply should not be tried at all. That is all I can see to it.

I would like to call your attention to the one thing in all this, the one statement on which any case can be made here for postponement. That is the statement with which we all agree: That Hess' condition will interfere with his response to questions relating to his past, and will interfere with his undertaking his defence. Now, I think it will interfere with his defence if he persists in it, and I am sure that Counsel has a very difficult task. But Hess has refused the treatment, and I have filed with the Court the report of Major Kelly, the American psychiatrist, in whose care he was placed immediately after he was brought here.

He has refused every simple treatment that has been suggested. He has refused to submit to the ordinary things that we submit to every day, blood tests, examinations, and says he will submit to nothing until after the trial. The treatment which was suggested to bring him out of this hysterical condition every psychiatrist agrees that this is simply a hysterical condition if it is genuine at all-was the use of intravenous drugs of the barbital series, either sodium amytal or sodium phenotal, the ordinary sedative that you perhaps take on a sleepless night. We did not dare administer that, to be perfectly candid, against his objection, because we felt that however harmless - and in over a thousand cases observed by Major Kelly there had been no ill-effects, although some cases are reported where there has - we felt that should be he struck by lightening a month afterward it would still be charged that something we had done had caused his death; and we did not desire to impose any such treatment upon him.

But I respectfully suggest that a man cannot stand at the bar of the Court and assert this his amnesia is a defence to his being tried, and at the same time refuse the simple medical expedients which all agree might be useful.

He is in the volunteer class with his amnesia. When he was in England, he is reported to have made the statement that his earlier amnesia was simulated. He came out of this state during a period in England, and went back into it. It is now highly selective. That is to say, you cannot be sure what Hess will remember and what he will not remember. His amnesia is not of the type which is a complete, blotting out of the personality, of the type that would be fatal to his defence.

So we feel that so long as Hess refused the ordinary, simple expedients, even if his amnesia is genuine, he is not in a position to continue to assert that he must not be brought to trial. We think he should be tried, not in absentia, but that this trial should proceed.

THE TRIBUNAL (Mr. Biddle): Is not Hess asserting that he wants to be tried?

MR. JUSTICE JACKSON: Well, I don't know about that. He had been interrogated and interrogated by us, interrogated by his co-defendants, and I would not attempt to say what he would now say he wants. I have not observed that it is causing him any great distress. Frankly, I doubt very much if he would like to be absent, but I would not attempt to speak for him.

THE PRESIDENT: Does M. Dubost wish to add anything?

(M. Dubost indicated that he did not.)

DR. VON ROHRSCHEIDT: May I just say a few words to the Tribunal to make my point of view clear once more?

As Hess' defence counsel this is my point of view. First of all, it is a fact that Hess, according to the reports of the doctors which, all agree, is not mentally ill. It is therefore, not a question of his mental faculties being impaired.

Secondly, the defendant Hess is suffering from amnesia, which, as all medical experts admit, exists. They all agree, however, that this amnesia is caused by a pathological condition of his mind. The result is that the defendant is not insane, but has a mental defect. In a legal sense, I think, from this it can be deducted that the defendant cannot disdain responsibility for his actions, because at the time when the acts he is charged with were committed, he was certainly not mentally insane, consequently he can be held responsible. But there is a difference, according to German law at any rate, when the question is whether the defendant is at this moment in a position to follow the trial, that is, whether he is capable of participating in the proceedings. This question should, in my opinion, as I have already said, on the basis of the medical reports, be answered in the negative. He is not capable of pleading his case.

I admit that doubts are possible, and that the Court may not be completely satisfied that the answers of the experts, in the definition given, are sufficient to establish that the defendant's ability to plead is actually impaired, in the light of the language, perhaps deliberately used by the Court, which speaks of ability to plead "adequately." I believe that, perhaps, this is the point to be stressed.

It is my considered opinion that the amnesia, confirmed by all experts, would impair the ability to present an adequate defence.

The possibility exists that at times he might be able to plead or raise objections, and then at such times he may appear to follow the proceedings. But even then his defence could not be termed "adequate" and would not be comparable to that of a person in full possession of his mental faculties.

May I perhaps add one word. I have already explained that the defendant has expressed the wish to me that he would like to attend the sessions, as he does not feel himself unfit to plead, but that, in the opinion of the defence, is completely irrelevant. It is up to the Court to settle this question. The personal preference of the defendant is of no account. With respect to the conclusion which the American prosecutor might draw about the defendant's refusal to be treated by narcotic means, that is not a question of truculence. He refused it because he was afraid that the intravenous injections at this particular moment might, in his weakened state, make him incapable of following the proceedings, which is exactly what he did not want to happen, and, as I have already mentioned, he himself thinks he is healthy and therefore says, "I do not need any intravenous treatment, I shall recover in the course of time." The defendant also tells me that he has an abhorrence of such treatments, and that in the unhappy times of the National Socialist regime, he was always for the homeopathy. He even founded the Rudolf Hess Hospital in Dresden, which is conducted on a natural, rather than medical, therapeutical plane.

MR. JUSTICE JACKSON: May I make one observation, Your Honour?

THE PRESIDENT: Yes.

MR. JUSTICE JACKSON: The argument illustrates the selectivity of the memory of which I spoke to you. Hess apparently can inform his counsel about his attitude toward this particular matter during the National Socialist regime. His counsel is able to tell us how he felt about medical things during the National Socialist regime, but when we ask him about anything in which he participated that might have a criminal aspect, the memory becomes bad. I hope that the Court has not overlooked the statement of the matters that he does well recollect.

DR. VON ROHRSCHEIDT: May I make a correction?

THE PRESIDENT: It is unusual to hear counsel in a second reply, but as Mr. Justice Jackson has spoken again we will hear what you have to say.

DR. VON ROHRSCHEIDT: I would merely like to observe that I was misunderstood. It was not the defendant who told me that he was an adherent of natural medicine, thus proving that his memory works, but it was I who, from my own experience, ascertained this, and I know that he was an adherent. I gave that as my opinion and my experience in order to show that he has an instinctive aversion to medical treatments, but this remark was not based on memory of the defendant Hess but on a fact based on knowledge of my own.

THE PRESIDENT: Dr. Rohrscheidt, the Tribunal would like, if you consider it proper, that the defendant Hess should state what his views on this question are.

DR. VON ROHRSCHEIDT: As his defence counsel, I have certainly nothing to say against it, and I think it would be the defendant's own wish, and the Tribunal would then be in a position to judge the mental state of the defendant, thus giving the Court an opportunity to observe Hess' mental state.

THE DEFENDANT HESS: Mr. President, I would like to say this: At the beginning of the trial of this afternoon's session, I gave my defence counsel a note that I am of the opinion that these proceedings could be shortened if I could be allowed to speak for myself. I wish to say the following:

In order to forestall the possibility of my being pronounced incapable of pleading in spite of my willingness to take part in further proceedings, and in order to receive sentence alongside my comrades, I would like to make the following declaration before the Tribunal, although, originally, I intended to make this declaration during a later part of the proceedings:

Henceforth my memory will again respond to the outside world. The reasons why I simulated loss of memory were tactical. The fact is that it is only my ability to concentrate that is somewhat reduced. However, my capacity to follow the trial, to defend myself, to put questions to witnesses or even to answer the questions, is not being affected hereby.

I emphasise that I bear the full responsibility for everything that I have done or signed as signatory or co- signatory. My attitude, in principle, that the Tribunal is not competent, is not affected by the statement I have just made. So far in conversations with my official defence counsel I have also simulated loss of memory. He has, therefore, represented me in good faith.

THE PRESIDENT: The trial is adjourned.

(The Tribunal adjourned until 10.00 hours on 1st December, 1945)

TENTH DAY:
Saturday, 1st December, 1945

THE PRESIDENT: I will begin the session by reading the judgement of the Tribunal upon the application made by counsel for the defendant Hess.

The Tribunal has given careful consideration to the motion of counsel for the defence of the defendant Hess, and it has had the advantage of hearing full argument upon it both from the defence and the prosecution. The Tribunal has also considered the very full medical reports, which have been made on the condition of the defendant Hess, and has come to the conclusion that no grounds whatever exist for a further examination to be ordered.

After hearing the statement of the defendant Hess in Court yesterday, and in view of all the evidence, the Tribunal is of the opinion that the defendant Hess is capable of standing his trial at the present time, and the motion of the counsel for the defence is, therefore denied, and the trial will proceed.

Now the witness under examination should come back to the witness box.

(ERWIN LAHOUSEN resumed the stand.)

MR. ROBERTS: May it please the Tribunal, Sir David Maxwell Fyfe yesterday said he had no questions to ask this witness. He has now requested me very shortly to cross-examine this witness on one incident mentioned in the Indictment, namely, the murder of fifty R.A.F. officers who escaped from Stalag Luft 3 in March of 1944.

THE PRESIDENT: You said "to cross-examine."

MR. ROBERTS: I realise that this is a matter which falls in the part of the Indictment which is being dealt with the prosecutors for the U.S.S.R. My Lord, I have mentioned that matter to General Rudenko, who with his usual courtesy and kindness has said that he has no objection to my asking some questions on that matter.

THE PRESIDENT: Very well.

Q. By MR. ROBERTS: Might I ask you this? Do you know anything of the circumstances of the death of fifty R.A.F. officers in March 1944, who had escaped from Stalag Luft 3 at Zagreb and were recaptured?

A. WITNESS: No, I have nothing to say because at that time I was at the East front, as commander of my regiment, and had no contact any longer with my former duties.

Q. Did you hear of the matter from any of your fellow officers?

A. No, I heard nothing about it whatsoever.

Q. You cannot assist the Court at all with the matter?

A. No; in no way.

CROSS-EXAMINATION.

By DR. EGON KUBUSCHOK (counsel for defendant von Papen):

Q. Witness, you stated yesterday that you were the intimate friend and collaborator of Admiral Canaris. Since I no longer can address my question directly to Admiral Canaris, I ask you to answer the following questions for me: Did Admiral Canaris know of defendant von Papen's attitude toward Hitler's war policies, and how did Admiral Canaris express himself to you on this point?

A. First, I should like to make a slight correction on the question addressed to me. I never asserted that I was the intimate friend of Canaris. Pieckenbrock was a friend of Canaris, while I was merely one of his confidants. From this relationship, however, I recall that von Papen's and Canaris' attitude towards the question, which counsel has just brought up, was negative.

Q. Was this negative attitude only towards the war policy, or was it also towards all the violent methods used in the execution of such a policy?

A. According to my recollection I have to answer this question in the affirmative in accordance with a conversation between Admiral Canaris and von Papen, during the latter's visit in Berlin and at which I was present.

Q. Did you know that von Papen told Canaris that from political quarters no resistance against Hitler's aggressive policies was possible, but that such resistance would have to be sought among the ranks of the military?

A. In this connection, that is to say, in the direct connection as it is now being presented, I personally do not know anything. In other words I personally was not witness at any such conversation between Canaris and von Papen touching this question; and I cannot recall today whether Canaris ever told me anything regarding such conversations with von Papen. It is quite possible, but I cannot recall it, and consequently my oath as witness does not permit me to make any statement other than I have made.

Q. Witness, do you conclude that Canaris believed von Papen to intentionally retain an exposed political office in order to exercise a mitigating influence?

A. I believe so, though I have no tangible proof through any of his statements, but that is my impression, from what I still recollect to-day.

By DR. OTTO NELTE (counsel for defendant Keitel):

Q. My client requested me to ask you the following questions: Since when have you known Canaris and Pieckenbrock?

A. I have known Canaris and Pieckenbrock since 1937 through my previous activity in the Austrian Intelligence.

Q. Did at that time any relationship of a military nature exist between the Abwehr, then headed by Admiral Canaris, and yourself?

A. Not only did such connections exist with the Austrian Intelligence, but the Austrian Federal Army and the German Wehrmacht maintained at that time an absolute legal and purely military exchange of information. Legal in the sense that this exchange and collaboration of military intelligence was carried on with the knowledge of the Austrian authorities. To state it clearly, this was purely military collaboration concerning intelligence exchange about Austria's neighbouring countries.

Q. May I ask if this contact between you and Canaris was also of a personal nature, i.e., to determine how the Austrian Army felt about the question of the Anschluss?

A. This and similar questions, that is to say, all questions of a political nature, particularly the question of the Anschluss, or the then very intense illegal Nazi activities, were and had to continue to be completely ignored in this connection. This agreement was essentially kept by Count Margona, the official liaison man - (he was also executed after the 2oth of July) - and by Canaris and Generaloberst Beck.

Q. Do I understand you to wish to say that the personal contact did not mean that the Austrian officers of the General Staff gave information on everything regarding their attitude to the idea of the Anschluss, or that they were willing or able to give this information?

A. This personal contact took place for the first time on the day, when I saw Canaris - (it was the first time) - while he was still an Austrian officer. It was in the Office for Defence of the Federal Government, where Canaris was with the then Chief of the Austrian General Staff.

THE PRESIDENT: Can you not hear what was said?

DR. NELTE: No.

THE PRESIDENT: Would you please repeat the question?

BY DR. NELTE:

Q. I asked the witness to what extent a personal contact existed between the officers of the German General Staff and the Abwehr, and between the officers of the Intelligence Section and the German General Staff, for the purpose of determining the trend towards the Anschluss.

A. First of all, there was no such personal contact in the sense that the word is used here. The contact which actually did take place - (and there are witnesses in this room who can confirm this statement - von Papen must be thoroughly informed of this) - took place on a single day, during which I never spoke with Canaris alone, but always in the presence of my superior. officers. In any case, no questions relating to the Anschluss and no political questions which touched on internal Austrian problems were discussed there, naturally not by myself, and naturally not consciously and willingly by Canaris.

Q. What was your job in the Abwehr Office II?

A. In the Abwehr Section II, which I took over at the beginning of 19391 described it yesterday, and I am willing to repeat it if you wish-this particular job did not have its own designation; it embraced various functions and actions, which I can define very precisely: acts of destruction, acts of sabotage, or prevention of sabotage, or in general those activities that are carried out by commandos. It was the function of this division to co- ordinate these activities and to bring them into relationship with the military necessities, or the plans of the General Staff.

Q. Who, in general, gave you your orders as regards co- ordinating these activities with the military activities?

A. My orders were usually received from my Chief, Canaris.

Q. I was referring to the office, whether they came from the OKH or the OKW?

A. They did not come from the OKW as a rule. Usually they came through channels from the OKW represented by the then Chief of the OKW, Keitel, or the chief of the "Fuehrungsstab" of the Wehrmacht; and when the General Staff or the Air Force "Fuehrungsstab" were interested in any undertaking, the orders, as far as I can remember, were also transmitted by way of the Armed Forces Fuehrungsstab, and the representatives of the three Armed Forces, i.e., the Army, Air Force and Navy appointed to it. All these orders came through the same channels to the Ausland-Abwehr, and Canaris transmitted them to me, as my allotted task.

Q. Are you now describing the official channels through which you received the orders, or are you defining where the orders came from, whether they came from the OKW, the Army, the OKH, or the Fuehrungsstab; or whether they were simply transmitted by way of or via the OKW?

A. Speaking strictly for myself I can say that I was in touch with my immediate superior, Canaris, with regard to that question; also with Keitel and with the officers of the Army Fuehrungsstab. Sometimes I had to deal with officers of the General Staff of the Army in connection with questions concerning my section. I could mention specific cases from memory. But in general the procedure was such as I described it.

Q. Is it true that Keitel, as the Chief of the OKW, at first every year, and then from 1936 onwards, in shorter periods, spoke to the officials and section chiefs of the OKW; and on such occasions pointed out to them, specifically, that everyone who believed that something was being asked of him that his conscience would not allow him to carry out, should be so kind as to tell him, namely, Keitel?

A. It is true that the then Chief of the OKW spoke before the aforementioned circle several times, but I cannot, of course, remember his precise words, or that he made a statement which could be so interpreted. Whatever the wording of Keitel's statement, I definitely did not obtain the impression that one could have spoken to him as clearly and openly as I and others, who are still alive, were able to speak to Canaris at any time.

Q. Do I understand you correctly to mean that you do not wish to challenge, in principle, the fact that Keitel actually said these words?

A. I can neither challenge it, nor can I add anything to it, because I do not precisely recall it. I do recall that these addresses or conferences took place, and it is altogether possible that the then Chief of the OKW might have used those words. I can only add what I have already said.

Q. Is it true that on several occasions, you, in the company of Admiral Canaris, as well as alone, were in the presence of the Chief of the OKW, in order to discuss plans or undertakings with Keitel, which were in the purview of your official duties?

A. Of course, I said a great deal about that yesterday; and I do not feel I have the right to talk about such things unless I personally was there.

Q. I had the impression, that in many respects you were being used as a mouthpiece for Admiral Canaris, among other things, through your quotations in his diary.

A. The impression is completely fallacious. I was not a mouthpiece, and am now as I was then, inwardly completely independent in what I state. I have never allowed myself, nor shall I ever allow myself, to become the mouthpiece of any conception, or to make any statements that are contrary to my inner convictions and to my conscience.

Q. You misunderstood me if you believe that I used the word "mouthpiece" derogatorily. I simply wanted to bring attention to the remarks that have their source in Canaris' diary.

A. Yes, I did assist Canaris, in matters which were of personal concern to him and which, being dead, he could not take up. Since I knew a great deal of it, and in great detail, I took it upon myself to say what I knew.

Q. Did the defendant Keitel ever ask the question, or communicate with Abwehr Section, as regards whether or not there were Nazis in that section?

A. He gave unequivocal answers to such questions at the aforementioned conferences, namely that there can be no doubt that in such an office as the OKW, no officers or trends of thought could be tolerated that did not have an unshakeable belief in a final victory, or give proof of complete obedience to the Fuehrer, etc.

Q. Could not these statements be interpreted as requirements of a military nature, obedience in a military set, or must they be understood politically?

A. Of course, they were military, but there could be no doubt that they were clearly also political, since no discrimination was recognised in this matter. The Wehrmacht was supposed to be a unit, the National Socialistic Wehrmacht. That touches the basic problem.

Q. Do you then believe that the basic attitude was still essentially military?

A. The basic attitude was or should have been a National Socialistic one, in the first place; and only in second place a military attitude, or anything else.

Q. You said "should have been".

A. Yes, because such was not actually the case.

Q. You said that in the first place it was military and not National Socialistic.

A. It should have been a purely military one, according to our interpretation, but according to the point of view represented by the then Chief of the O.K.W - whether he received an order in this matter or not, I am not in a position to say, as I wasn't there - the basic attitude should have been one of absolute obedience in a National Socialistic sense.

Q. Do you know anything about the attitude of the generals towards this problem?

A. Of course, I do, because immediately after such conferences, as has been mentioned here, a lively exchange of opinions took place on this subject and a large number of those who were present - I could name them and some of them are present here - took a negative attitude to the fact that the orientation should be so exclusively political in accordance with "regulations from higher quarters," as they were called then, and scarcely ever of a technical or military nature.

Q. Yesterday, on the occasion of the discussion of the meeting that took place in the Fuehrer's train, in September of 1939, as regards the communication of the Chief of the O.K.W. to you, you said that the defendant Keitel had expressed himself to you, or rather had expressed himself to the gentlemen present, as follows, viz.: "That these measures had been determined between the Fuehrer and Goering, and that he, Keitel, had no influence on them. You added that the Fuehrer and Goering telephoned frequently back and forth. Sometimes he knew something about it; sometimes you did, too."

A. That is correct. I have made a verbal transcript of everything which was said in my presence; and I repeated it here because it is true.

Q. May I ask whether your remark: "Sometimes I find out about it, sometimes I don't", relates to a concrete, specific case, or was that a general rule?

A. That was to be understood as a general statement, to the best of my present recollection.

Q. At this conference in the Fuehrer's train, on the 12th of September, 1939, you spoke further of the transmission of the political goals which, according to you, had their source in Ribbentrop.

A. That is correct.

Q. And you said that the defendant Keitel transmitted these political goals to those who were present; and the same way with respect to the order regarding Warsaw, namely, the bombardment of Warsaw.

A. According to my recollection this was true as far as the air bombardment of Warsaw was concerned; and in accordance with my notes. I can also state in this respect that as far as the matter of the shootings in Poland is concerned, Canaris took the initiative in these matters by provoking discussions during which he pointed out the terrible political international repercussions that such behaviour might have. The details are no longer quite clear in my mind.

Q. I should now like to ask you whether, on the occasion when the order to bombard Warsaw was made known, Keitel did not specifically point out that that action was planned only to take place if Warsaw did not surrender, after it had been approached through parliamentary channels; and that first of all, Warsaw should be given an opportunity to capitulate without being bombarded.

A. I cannot recall the precise words he used, but judging by my knowledge of that general situation, it is quite possible, indeed probable, that the Chief of the O.K.W., Keitel, did make this remark.

Q. Do you know that before the Polish War began, the Commander in Chief of the Army at that time, von Brauchitsch, and the Chief of the O.K.W., Keitel, specifically objected to the use of Commandos and Gestapo, and rejected their use; and in so doing, had the agreement of Hitler?

A. No, that is not known to me, and could not have been known to me, because of my subordinate position at that time. Please do not over-rate the importance of my official position at the time.

Q. There is also here a question of knowledge of a document, which was transmitted to all departments and sections of the O.K.W., as you probably remember from yesterday. They were the so-called directives; and in these directives, there appears, contrary to what happened later -

THE PRESIDENT: I think you were going a little bit too fast.

Q. (continuing) I said that in connection with such military actions, the orders and directives were mimeographed and generally made known, no doubt.

A. Yes, but these orders did not concern my specific department, I stress the word "specific", and I did not even see them.

Q. Since later you were brought into a discussion of these questions, and since you emphasise that the orders were not literally known to you -

A. Of course, a great deal was known to me, because I heard of it.

Q. For that reason, I want to ask you whether you recall that the Gestapo and S.D. were used, contrary to the specific intentions and wishes of the O.K.W., in the matter of the Polish War?

A. I cannot remember. I can only refer to what I remember, and what is registered in the files, in which there is mention made of a remark of Hitler's, which was transmitted by Keitel at that time; stating that, if the Armed Forces objected to these measures, the latter as well as the O.K.W. would have to realise that the Gestapo and the S.D. would go ahead anyhow. That is probably what you are referring to. I know that because I was present at these discussions.

Q. During this conversation, were you not told that an objection to the behaviour of the S.S. was brought up, on the part of General Blaskowitz?

A. Whether or not this question was brought up in this conference, I cannot recall. I can hardly assume that it was so, since otherwise the question would have been registered in the minutes of that conference, particularly in the case of General Blaskowitz, whose attitude in such matters was quite clear cut. But apart from this conversation in the Fuehrer's train, I remember in its essence something about the subject - which was just brought up - namely, Blaskowitz' objections. I cannot say what form those objections took at the time, whether they were in writing or verbal, but I do remember the general theme, though I cannot recall whether it happened at one of the conferences which I attended.

Q. What appears to me to be important in this matter, is the fact that actually the Armed Forces, the troops, protested, or at least had a negative attitude toward the behaviour of the S.S.

A. That the Armed Forces did object, is, of course, quite evident.

Q. That is what I wanted to know.

A. One moment, please. When I say "the Armed Forces", I mean the masses of common soldiers, the ordinary human beings. Of course, there were in these Armed Forces - other men whom I wish to exclude. I do not wish to be misunderstood. The concept "Armed Forces" does not include everybody, but does include the greater majority of common soldiers and thinking human beings.

Q. You use the term "Wehrmacht" to differentiate between the common soldiers and the High Command.

A. As far as the then prevailing methods and conditions were concerned, which became apparent for the first time in this shape to the broad masses of the Wehrmacht, I think I have summed them up fairly accurately within the small section I have described.

Q. Who gave the order regarding the collaboration with the Ukrainian Group? You spoke yesterday of that group.

A. I have to go further back, and state first of all, that this group was composed of citizens from various countries; Hungarians, Czechs and Poles, who, because of their oppositionist attitude, had emigrated or gone to Germany. I cannot say who ordered this collaboration, because these matters came up quite a long time back, and because at that time, I was not even a member of the Abwehr Section, and was not in touch with the department, which I took over only in 1939. However, I remember the period after 1938 quite clearly. I should like to add to this connection, because it has been already mentioned yesterday, that these Ukrainians, as a whole, had no ties whatsoever with Germany. To be specific, a great many of these people with whom the Abwehr Division had any dealings were in German concentration camps, and some of them were fighting for their country in Soviet-partisan groups. Those are the facts.

Q. Did not Admiral Canaris say to you that the chief of the O.K.W.- when the demand was made on him for Polish uniforms and equipment, demands made by the S.S. - that Keitel specifically ordered that, the Abwehr Division should more or less let the matter drop?

A. I mentioned this matter also yesterday, saying that it was treated altogether in a mysterious way. Until it actually happened, neither I nor others knew what game was being played. This can be clearly seen from the war diary of the section, which relates how one day so many uniforms were requested for an operation called "Himmler", by order of Canaris. My amazement and my question, how Himmler came to request new Polish uniforms, is registered in the diary by the officer who had the job of keeping it, and the question was answered to the effect that these uniforms would simply be picked up on such and such a day by somebody, without any further explanations, and that was the end of the matter as far as I was concerned.

Of course, this matter not only became immediately mysterious but also very suspicious, because of its connection with the name "Himmler". All of us, from the highest level to the non-com. who had to deliver the equipment to the S.S. Hauptsturmfuehrer, whose name has been recorded in the War-Diary, felt that way about it. Everybody had his own opinion on this matter; that could not be forbidden.

Q. You also made statements yesterday regarding the treatment of war prisoners. In what regard was Abwehr Section II concerned with this problem?

A. The functions of Abwehr II were such that it was of the greatest possible interest to see to it that these war prisoners were being treated decently; the same applies to any Intelligence Services in the whole world.

Q. Do I understand you to mean that the Division Abwehr II as such was not admittedly concerned with problems concerning war prisoners?

A. Not at all with prisoners of war.

Q. You spoke of this problem of the treatment of war prisoners in connection with the talk that took place the end of July, 1941.

A. Yes, and during this conversation I did not merely represent my section, but the whole department, "Ausland- Abwehr", namely, the section that has to concern itself mainly with general questions of International Law, military politics, and general questions on foreign territories common to all Abwehr groups. Abwehr Section III, rather than my own section, were, of course, interested in these matters because some of their officers served in P.W. camps, and from the point of view of counter-intelligence it was important to know about these things. For me the entire problem rather than the partial details were of importance, namely, that people in camps, for many reasons, should be treated decently, rather than mistreated or killed.

Q. You said yesterday that the war prisoner camps in the Eastern field were under the jurisdiction of the O.K.W.

A. Yes, what I said about the war prisoner camps, as I specifically said yesterday I learned from my talk with Reinecke and not from any direct knowledge of the orders themselves, which I did not see or read. This conversation with Reinecke, who as Chief of the P.W. Division and on behalf of the O.K.W. expounded the matter, elucidated the problem of war prisoners for me.

Q. My question dealt with the limits of the jurisdiction. Did you not know who in the Operation Section of the Army held responsibility for war prisoners, and that the O.K.W. took over this responsibility at the moment in which the war prisoners reached Germany?

A. Yes, as far as I recall, the General Staff of the Army had prepared everything to bring these people back; and an order originating with Hitler authorised the O.K.W. to overrule and cancel this, and the General Staff then made the O.K.W. responsible for all the consequences. What happened after that I do not know and have no right to judge; I can only repeat what I saw and heard.

Q. I thought that yesterday you expressed the conjecture that by Hitler's order the movement of P.W's. was stopped?

A. I did not express any conjecture; I simply repeated what I had heard at the time and what I knew - I could, of course, be wrong.

Q. From whom had you heard this?

A. I learned it through the people with whom I was in daily contact, such as Canaris, the section chiefs, and others who were present at daily situation reports and conversations and that sort of thing where these matters were discussed. It was under such circumstances that I heard these things, which were frequently discussed, and as I have emphasised repeatedly in the past since my first interrogation, I told Reinecke to his face that what he himself at that time said regarding these matters.

Q. That does not apply to my questions.

A. I quite understand your question, but I wish to define it as clearly as possible so as to make plain to you what I said yesterday in order to describe the specific organisational limits.

Q. But you know that as a matter of principle the O.K.W. had charge of war prisoners only in Germany?

A. That is evident.

Q. Could it happen that the Abwehr office that had to do with commando activities took an attitude such as you defined it yesterday, insofar as you had to do with these things from the German side, but you were not officially concerned with these things?

A. No, not immediately. The Ausland Office had something to do with these things because somehow it received intelligence of any order that was under consideration, even before it was put into shape, and certainly as soon as it was drawn up. The Order in question had, of course, a bearing on an essential question of International Law, and the Ausland Section of the Abwehr Division or the "Sachbearbeiter" as it was called - was naturally concerned with it. My division was, as a matter of fact, directly concerned with these things, for reasons explained before, regarding the possible consequences arising thereof to persons for whom I was responsible.

Q. As regards the division for International Law in the Ausland-Abwehr, did it take an official position toward this?

A. I wrote, as I pointed out yesterday, a contribution on that subject from the point of view of my section, which was transmitted to Canaris and was to be part of the long document. I only learned from what Burckner said at the time what use was made of it. Whether he, i.e. his department, lodged these objections and counter objections, cognisance was taken of the danger these measures represented. This was done a second time and again I cannot say whether in writing or orally, after executions had already taken place and I had protested anew. This was the logical development.

THE PRESIDENT: It would help the interpreter if, when giving a very long answer like that that you pause between the intermediate parts of the answer.

THE WITNESS: Shall I repeat?

THE PRESIDENT: No, no; go on.

BY DOCTOR NELTE:

Q. You also spoke yesterday of some sort of branding used on Russian prisoners. Are you not aware that a scheme on this question, presented by the then chief of the O.K.W., who had gone to the Fuehrer's Headquarters, was cancelled by an order transmitted by telephone, and that owing to a terrible misunderstanding this order was issued in but a very few copies?

A. No, I do not know about this, because, in general, I heard merely of occurrences that took place within Canaris' Section in the Abwehr division. I knew of these occurrences either because I had promoted or directed them. What happened in higher quarters I only learned if I was appointed to collaborate with them.

Q. You yourself did not see the order?

A. Which order are you referring to?

Q. The one concerning the branding of Russian prisoners.

A. No. As in the matter of the commando orders, I only attended the very lively discussion of this question with regard to the branding of Russian prisoners. I remember Canaris mentioning that a doctor had furnished a medical report as to how this could be done most efficiently.

Q. You stated yesterday that Admiral Canaris had said that the defendant Keitel had issued the order to do away with General Weygand. The defendant Keitel denies that. Now, he would like to ask whether there is in your possession any document or any written evidence that could serve as proof of the source of such a remark regarding General Weygand?

A. This order was not transmitted in writing, but was given directly to me. It was given to me because I was to carry it out through my department. To a certain circle round Canaris, a certain limited public, it was known, and I was initiated into this matter by a lecture which Canaris delivered at Keitel's O.K.W. after which I was spoken to by Keitel on this matter. I have noted this in my diary. It had not been an everyday occurrence. This took place on December 23rd 1940.

Q. Do you not remember the actual wording of the question that defendant Keitel asked you?

A. Of course I cannot remember the precise wording; the incident happened too long ago. I remember the meaning very well. The meaning was: "What has been done in this matter? How do things stand?"

Q. You said yesterday that you answered evasively.

A. I cannot remember the precise wording of my answer, but I certainly didn't say what I had said to Canaris, namely: "I wouldn't consider the execution of such a murderous order; my section and my officers are not an organisation of murderers." What I probably said to Keitel was something about how difficult the matter was; I gave any evasive answer that I may have thought of.

Q. If the Chief of the O.K.W. had ordered such an action on his own initiative or on higher orders, it would, because of the high rank of General Weygand, have amounted to an act of State. You didn't tell us whether after December 23rd, 1940, anything transpired in this matter, that is to say, whether the chief of the O.K.W. took up this question again.

A. No, I didn't say that yesterday, but I frequently mentioned during the cross examination, that after this nothing further happened on the part of the Chief of the O.K.W. Canaris' attitude made it obvious that nothing further had been heard of it, for in the hierarchy of commands, he would have had to transmit orders to me. On the other hand, the information which I received in the matter of Giraud was authoritative.

Q. We shall come to that presently. It is extraordinary that if an act of State such as the murder of General Weygand, should have been ordered, nothing more should have been heard of it. Can you give me an explanation for that?

A. I can give only the explanation which corresponded to our interpretation of the matter then. The situation at that time was full of agitation; events followed each other very quickly and something was happening all the time; and we assumed - I shall come back to why we assumed it - that this matter and the interest attached to it had been superseded by some more important military or political event, and that therefore this interest had been thrust into the background.

Q. Do you wish to say anything else?

A. Yes. I want to state that what I am saying now bears a certain relationship to the inner development of the affair Giraud, in which Canaris and the others, who knew about this when the matter began, had hoped that it would follow the same course as the affair Weygand; namely, that, wherever the order might have originated, whether from Hitler, Keitel or Himmler, down to Canaris and then to me, it would have been relatively simple to stop it once it had reached our circle. That was our hope when the case Giraud cropped up, a hope based on the practical experience of the case Weygand. Whether this was right or wrong, I do not know. This is the explanation.

Q. For a less important matter your assumption might hold water, but in such an important matter as the case of Weygand it doesn't seem to me to do so. But even if it had been so, had the intention to do away with Weygand existed in any quarters and for any reason, how do you explain the fact that Weygand, who later was taken to Germany and housed in a villa, lived undisturbed and honoured and met with no harm? It would have been understandable that, if the order to eliminate him had been seriously expressed in any quarters, it would have been carried out on this occasion.

A. I can only answer to this that the attitude towards personalities in public life whether at home or abroad was very varied. There were high personalities who were at one moment in great favour and thought of very highly, and at the next moment were to be found in a concentration camp.

Q. Now, as to the case of Giraud, you said that Admiral Canaris said in your and other people's presence that General Giraud was to be done away with on orders from higher quarters.

A. Yes; that can be assumed from the remark that Pieckenbrock made, that Keitel should tell these things to Hitler once and for all.

Q. So according to the communication made to you by Admiral Canaris, it was not an order of Keitel's but an order of Hitler's.

A. As far as we knew in the Abwehr Office about it, it was Keitel who gave the order to Canaris. I can only assume this in view of a remark Hitler made to this effect. I do not know who actually gave this order, because I had no insight into the hierarchy of command beyond Canaris. It was, as far as I was concerned, an order from Canaris, an order which I could discuss immediately with him in the same way as I can discuss it here.

Q. You yourself didn't personally hear this order?

A. No, I did not personally hear it; I never stated that.

Q. But you mentioned that at a later time you were spoken to by Keitel about this matter?

A. The development was the same as in the case of Weygand.

Q. Do you remember that a precise, or positive expression such as "killing," "elimination" or something of the sort was used on this occasion?

A. The word generally used was "elimination" ("Umlegen").

Q. What I mean is whether in this connection such a word was used in your presence by the defendant Keitel?

A. Yes, of course - after my lecture, the notes of which I have together with the date, just as in the Weygand case. For reasons unknown to me the Giraud affair was apparently carried further than the Weygand affair, for Canaris and I could determine different stages in its development.

Q. You didn't answer my question. What did the defendant Keitel say to you on this occasion, on the occasion when you and Canaris were present and the question of Giraud was brought up? What did he say?

A. The same thing: how does the situation stand, and by "situation" he clearly meant Giraud's elimination, and that was the very subject we discussed under similar conditions in the Weygand affair.

Q. That is your opinion, but that is not the fact. I wish to find out from you what Keitel actually said to you. In your presence, he did not use this expression "dispose of", did he?

A. I cannot remember the precise expression that he used, but it was perfectly clear what the general subject was. Whatever it was, it was not a question of sparing Giraud's life or imprisoning him. There was the opportunity to do away with him because he was in occupied territory.

Q. That is what I want to speak about now. You are familiar with the fact that after Giraud's flight and his return to unoccupied France, a conference took place in Occupied France.

A. Yes, I heard of that.

Q. Ambassador Abetz had a talk with General Giraud, which dealt with the question of his voluntary return to confinement. You know that?

A. Yes, I heard of that.

Q. Then you probably also know that at the time the local military commander immediately called up the Fuehrer's H.Q. by way of Paris to say that he believed that an important communication was to be made; namely that Giraud was in Occupied France and could be taken prisoner?

A. I know about this in its broad outlines.

Q. Then you also know that thereupon the O.K.W. - that is to say in this case, Keitel - decided that it should not take place.

A. No, that I did not know.

Q. But you do know that General Giraud returned to Unoccupied France without having been harmed?

A. Yes, I do know that.

Q. Well, in that case, the answer to my previous question is self-apparent.

THE PRESIDENT: Don't go so fast.

Q. Did you know that General Giraud's family lived in Occupied France?

A. No, I did not know that.

Q. I thought the Abwehr Division was charged with the surveillance of this region?

A. No, by no means - certainly not my department. I don't know whether another department was in charge.

Q. The question was asked simply to prove that the family did not suffer from the fact that General Giraud escaped and that he later refused to return to captivity. I have one more question which you may be able to answer.

A. I beg your pardon. May I return, please, to the question of General Giraud?

Q. This question also has to do with General Giraud.

A. Very well.

Q. Did you know that one day your chief, Canaris, received by special courier a letter from Giraud in which Giraud asked whether he might be allowed to return to France? Do you know that?

A. No. No, I do not know about it. Perhaps I was not in Berlin at the time. I was not always in Berlin.

Q. I am aware of that. I thought it might be mentioned in the diary.

A. No, I didn't keep Canaris' diary. I simply made additions to it so far as my particular department was concerned, but I was not familiar with the diary in its entirety.

Q. Thank you.

THE PRESIDENT: The Tribunal will adjourn now for ten minutes.

(A recess was taken.)

DR. OTTO KRANZBUEHLER (counsel for the defendant Donitz):

I would like to propose a motion in connection with the technical side of the proceedings. In the course of these proceedings many German witnesses will be heard. It is important that the statement of the witnesses be brought correctly to the attention of the Court. In the course of the hearing of this witness I have tried to compare the real statements of the witness with the English translation. I think I can state that in many essential points the translation did not entirely correspond to the statements of the witness.

I would, therefore, like to suggest that German stenographers take down directly the statements of the witness in German, so that defence counsel will have an opportunity to compare the real statements of the witness with the English translation and, if necessary, to make a motion for the correction of the translation. That is all.

THE PRESIDENT: Yes, Mr. Justice Jackson.

MR. JUSTICE JACKSON: I just want to inform the Court and counsel, in connection with the observation that has just been made, that that has been anticipated; and that every statement of the witness is recorded in German so that if any question arises, if counsel addresses a motion to it, the testimony can be verified.

THE PRESIDENT: Is that German record available to defendants' counsel.

MR. JUSTICE JACKSON: I don't think it is. It is not, so far as I know. It would not be available unless there were some occasion for it.

THE PRESIDENT: It is transcribed, I suppose?

MR. JUSTICE JACKSON: I don't know how far that process is carried. I will consult the technicians and advise about it, but I know that it is preserved. The extent of my knowledge is that it is preserved in such a form that, if the question does arise, it can be accurately determined by the Tribunal, so that if they call attention to some particular thing, either the witness can correct it or we can have the record produced. It would not be practicable to make the recording available without making reproducing machines available. While I am not a technician in that field, I should not think it would be practicable to place that at their disposal.

THE PRESIDENT: Would it not be practicable to have a transcription made of the shorthand notes in German and, within the course of one or two days after the evidence has been given, place that transcription in the defendants' counsel room?

MR. JUSTICE JACKSON: I think that is being done. I think perhaps Colonel Dostert can explain just what is being done better than I can, because he is the technician in this field. I am sure that no difficulty need arise over the matter of correct translations.

COLONEL DOSTERT: Your Honour, the reports of the proceedings are taken down in all four languages, and every word spoken in German is taken down in German by German Court stenographers. The notes are then transcribed and can be made available to defence counsel. Moreover, there is a mechanical recording device which registers every single word spoken in any language in the court room, and in case of doubt about the authenticity of the reporters' notes, we have the further verification of the mechanical recording, so that defence counsel should have every opportunity to check the authenticity of the translation.

MR. JUSTICE JACKSON: I am advised further by Colonel Dostert that twenty-five copies of the German transcript are being delivered to the defendants each day.

B Mr. President, I was not informed that the German testimony is being taken down in shorthand in German. I understood that the records handed over to us were translations from the English. If German shorthand notes are being taken in the Court, I withdraw my motion.

THE PRESIDENT: I think we should get on faster if the defendants' counsel, before making motions, inquire into the matters about which they are making them.

DR. FRITZ SAUTER: I would like to ask a few questions of the witness.

CROSS-EXAMINATION BY DR. SAUTER (counsel for the defendant Ribbentrop)

Q. Witness, you have previously stated that at some time an order was given, according to which, Russian prisoners of war were marked in a certain manner, and that this order had been withdrawn by the defendant Keitel. You did say that, didn't you?

A. Yes, I have said that I have knowledge of it.

Q. This is interesting from the point of view of defendant Ribbentrop, and I would like to hear from you whether you know about the following. Ribbentrop maintains that when he heard about the order to brand Russian prisoners of war, he, in his capacity as Reich Foreign Minister, went immediately to the Fuehrer's Headquarters to inform General Field Marshal Keitel of this order, and pointed out to him that he, Ribbentrop, in his capacity as Foreign Minister, as well as in his capacity as the guarantor of matters of International Law, objected to such treatment of Russian prisoners of war.

I would be interested to know, witness, whether in your circle something was said as to who drew Keitel's attention to this order and asked him to retract it.

A. I was not informed of that and I only knew, as I said yesterday, that this intention had existed and was not carried out.

Q. Then I have another question.

Witness, you spoke of remarks of the defendant Ribbentrop yesterday, especially of one statement to the effect that an uprising should be staged in Poland - not in Russia - and that all Polish farmhouses should go up in flames and all Jews should be killed. That is just about the contents of your yesterday's statement.

A. Yes.

Q. Now, later on, I believe in answering a question of one of the Russian prosecutors, you amplified your statement by mentioning an order of the defendant Ribbentrop. I would now like to know whether you really meant to say that it was an order from Ribbentrop to a military department.

A. No.

Q. Just a minute please, so that you can answer both questions together.

I would also like to remind you that yesterday, during the first session to deal with this matter, you spoke of a directive which, I believe, your superior officer had, as you said, received from Ribbentrop.

A. No, the then Chief of the O.K.W. received it, not my superior officer. This was Canaris. I would like to repeat it in order to clarify this matter. It was a matter that was taken up on the 12th of September, 1939, in the Fuehrer's train. These meetings took place in the following sequence with respect to time and locality:

At first, a short meeting took place between Reich Foreign Minister Ribbentrop and Canaris in his train, where general political questions in regard to Poland and the Ukraine were raised. I was present. I do not know any more about the first meeting.

Later another meeting took place in the coach of Keitel, the then Chief of the O.K.W., and Keitel summarised and amplified the general political directives, issued by Ribbentrop, in regard to the treatment of the Polish problem. From a foreign-political point of view he mentioned several possibilities: this or that could happen. In this connection he said: "You, Canaris, have to promote an uprising with those Ukrainian organisations co-operating with you, and this should have as its aims Poles and Jews."

Thirdly, not a special meeting but just a short conversation between Ribbentrop and Canaris took place. A remark was made casually in this connection, which showed even more explicitly how this uprising should be carried out and what was to happen. I remember this very clearly because he demanded: "The farms must go up in flames."

Canaris spoke with me at great length in this connection in regard to this remark. And this is what happened. Directives or orders received by Keitel were passed on to Canaris. It was later repeated to him in the form of a casual remark, which I recall because of the unusual referring to farms going up in flames.

THE PRESIDENT: It would assist the Tribunal if one question at a time were asked and if the witnesses would answer "yes" or "no" to the question asked, and explain, if they must, afterwards. But questions and answers should be put as shortly as possible, and only one question should be asked at a time.

Q. (continuing) Now, witness, something else has come to my attention.

THE PRESIDENT: You heard what I said, did you? Do you understand it?

Q. (continuing) This has come to my attention. Yesterday you said that these remarks of Ribbentrop are not in the diary, if I understood you correctly.

A. No - this is not from the diary but a contribution to Canaris' diary. This is a remark which was -

Q. You also said yesterday that this remark especially aroused your attention.

A. Yes.

Q. And to-day, you said that the then General Blaskowitz also made a striking remark. You also mentioned, however, that these remarks of Blaskowitz were not entered into the diary.

A. No.

Q. Now, I would like to know, and I would like you to answer this question: why, if this remark of the defendant Ribbentrop aroused your special attention, was it not entered in the diary?

A. As to Blaskowitz I have to say or, better, repeat the following:

I have said: I did not hear the subject Blaskowitz mentioned in this way during the meeting, and I cannot assume that this subject had fallen into this category, otherwise it would have been entered in the diary. It can also be, of course, that the matter Blaskowitz discussed was at a time when I was not actually there. I have only put down what I heard or what Canaris told me to enter into the record.

Q. But did you personally hear that from Ribbentrop?

A. Yes, but the essence was not altered. In the final analysis whether it was extermination, elimination or the burning of farms, all of them were terroristic measures.

Q. Did von Ribbentrop really talk of killing Jews? Do you definitely remember that?

A. Yes, I definitely remember this particular remark he made to Canaris, because Canaris talked not only to me but also to others in Vienna about this matter, and called time and again upon me as a witness.

Q. You heard that too.

A. The matter was not settled thereby, but these words of Ribbentrop's were frequently discussed.

Q. Witness, something else. You have told us about murderous designs with which you or your department, or other offices, were charged. Did you make the prescribed report at any police station? I would like to point out that failure to make a report of intended crimes according to German Law is punishable with imprisonment or in some serious cases with death.

A. Well, when you talk about German Law, I cannot follow you. I am not a lawyer, but just a simple man.

Q. As far as I know, this is also punishable according to Austrian Law.

A. At that time the Austrian Law as far as I know was not valid any more.

THE PRESIDENT: It is too fast.

Q. (continuing). In other words, you never made a report of the intended crime either as a private person or as an official?

A. I should have had to make a great many reports of about 100,000 intended murders of which I knew and could not help but know. You can read about them in the records - and about shootings and the like - of which I necessarily had knowledge, whether I wanted to or not, because, unfortunately, I was in the midst of it.

Q. This is not a matter of shootings which had taken place and could no longer be prevented, but rather a matter of intended murders at a time when it could have, perhaps, been prevented.

A. I can only answer: why did the person who received this order first hand not do the same thing? Why didn't he report to Hitler for instance?

Q. You, as a General of the German Wehrmacht, should have asked Hitler...

A. I am sorry, you overestimate my rank; I had only been a General in the German Wehrmacht since the first of January, 1945, i.e., only for four months. At that time I was Lt.-Colonel, of the High Command and later Colonel of the General Staff, not in the General Staff.

Q. But, in 1938, right after Hitler's attack on Austria, you had immediately made a request to be taken into the German Wehrmacht by Hitler.

A. I did not make a request, I didn't have to do this. Wherever I was in the service, 1 was known for my efficiency. I was not a stranger. With the knowledge of the Austrian Government and also, in a restricted sense, with the knowledge of the German authorities (i.e., of certain persons) I was working for the Austrian Government in a matter which exclusively concerned things outside the scope of Austrian internal policy. I co-operated with the Wehrmacht and the Italian and I Hungarian Governments at the wish of the Austrian Government and the competent authorities. There were matters of politics which were not my domain.

Q. But, I believe, witness, your memory deceives you, because immediately after Hitler's attack on Austria, you called on the General Staff in Berlin and there - what you deny - tried to get a commission in the German Wehrmacht. You had also made out a questionnaire in which you declared your complete allegiance to the Greater German Reich, to Adolf Hitler; and shortly afterwards you took the oath of allegiance to Adolf Hitler.

A. Yes, of course I did it, just as everybody else who was in the position of being transferred from one office and capacity to another.

Q. Previously you said you did not try to get this appointment but I have been informed to the contrary; that you, in the company of two or three other officers, were the first to go to Berlin with the sole purpose of asking the Chief of the German General Staff - Beck - to take you into the German Army.

A. I am very glad that you are talking about this, especially so that I may fully clarify my position. It was necessary for me to make an application for my new position in the German Wehrmacht. I was known because of my military activities, just as any military attachí is known in the country where he is serving.

Moreover, I can easily explain why I rose in office so fast. I have said that in my activities and in this co-operation, which was not determined by me, but by my superior Austrian Officer in the Austrian Intelligence Service with other States, was at that time directed against the neighbouring country of Czechoslovakia - Czechoslovakia was the country that was next after Austria. Therefore, it was natural that my later Chief, Canaris, who knew me from my former position, should be very much interested in my coming up into his department. He put in a request for me and, beyond that, so did Beck, whom I was visiting. Other people also know this: and I have now told everything that General Beck told me at that time.

Q. Then it is true, you did go to Berlin and try to be transferred into the German Wehrmacht, which you at first denied?

A. No, that is not true, I did not try to do this. Others made the request. I can even say that I did not go there - I flew there. Canaris, who knew me, not only in my military capacity, but also in regard to my personal attitude (just as Maroga had known me and just as General Col. Beck, who was informed about me by Canaris), requested me. I did not request a position, but others requested me for reasons which only later became clear to me, because they knew my personal attitude, just as my Austrian comrades - they were necessarily few-knew about this and about me. That's the way it was.

DR. SAUTER: I have no other questions to ask this witness.

THE PRESIDENT: Before the cross-examination I wish to announce that there will be no public session of the Tribunal this afternoon.

DR. STAHMER: I am counsel for the defendant Goering, and I would like to address a few questions to the witness.

CROSS-EXAMINATION BY DR. STAHMER (counsel for the defendant Goering)

Q. Witness, if I understood you correctly, you said yesterday that, according to the inner basic conviction of General Canaris, the war on Poland, which was not successful, was the end of Germany and our misfortune. This misfortune, however, would become greater by a triumph of the system which it was the purpose of General Canaris to prevent. Did I understand you correctly?

A. With one exception, you did not understand me. He did not fail to succeed in preventing it; the attack was not preventable, but Canaris had no way of knowing this.

Q. Is it known to you that Admiral Canaris, within the first years of the war, had very active sabotage organisations behind the front, and that he personally was very busy with these organisations?

A. This is naturally known to me, and I have fully informed the American departments who have been interested in this, on this subject.

Q. But how is that possible? This would not be in conformity with his inner political beliefs.

A. This is explained by the fact that in the circle in which he was active he could never say what he really thought, and thousands of others could not do so either. The essential thing is not what he said, or what he had to say; but what he did and how he did it. This I know and others know too.

Q. This is not a question of what he said, but of what he has actually done. He has not only proposed such measures, but has also applied himself to their execution; is this true?

A. Ostensibly he had, of course, to remain within the limits of his office, in order to keep his position. That was the important thing, that he had to remain in this position, to avoid in 1939 the thing that actually happened in 1944. He then tried to get things in hand, and I wish to compare Canaris with Himmler; there is no need to mention what the goal was, if he took part .

Q. You mentioned the name of Himmler; in this connection I would like to ask the following questions.

Is it known to you that Admiral Canaris, during the first years of the war, kept up close connections with the S.S. and that the necessity of close co-operation with the SS. was emphasised by him repeatedly, so that the defendant Goering had to advise him to be more independent in his military functions?

THE PRESIDENT: You are going too quickly and I do not think you are observing what I said just now, that it will help the Tribunal if you will ask one question at a time.

DR. STAHMER: I would like to summarise my question this way; did the witness know that Admiral Canaris, during the first years of the war, had good connections with the SS. and recognised the necessity of close co-operation with the formation, a fact which he always emphasised?

THE WITNESS: Yes, this is known to me. I also know why.

Q. *(continuing)*: And why?

A. Because in this position he was able to see and to get information of everything that happened to these people, and so could intervene if and whenever feasible.

Q. Was it the duty of your organisation and of the department of Canaris respectively, to pass on enemy intelligence in good time to Higher Headquarters?

A. I do not understand what the office of Canaris has to do with this.

Q. Your section, of the office of Canaris?

A. Why, of course, the Department I -

Q. Now, according to my information your office did not pass on the information of the Anglo-American landing in North Africa. Is that true?

A. I do not know, I do not wish to be held responsible for the Department. This is a question which could easily be answered by Oberst Pieckenbrock, but not by myself.

Q. As to the case Rowehls, you said yesterday that a colonel of the Air Force, Rowehls, was leading a special troop which had the job of making reconnaissance flights over Poland, England and the South East, prior to the Polish campaign, and you also said that Colonel Rowehls went to see Admiral Canaris and to report on the result of these flights, and presented his photographic maps. Is that true?

A. Yes. How should I have known about it otherwise? I did not invent it.

Q. I didn't say that.

How did Colonel Rowehls come to tell Admiral Canaris about this?

A. I believe I mentioned yesterday, that this was a function of the department Ausland-Abwehr, Obere Abteilung.

Q. Have you yourself seen the pictures that were made over England?

A. Yes, I have seen them.

Q. When and where have these pictures been shown to you?

A. In the office of Canaris, but they were none of my business. I happened to be present at the time. I was interested to see what was going on.

Q. What did these pictures show?

A. I do not remember the details now. They were pictures taken from airplanes.

Q. The pictures were not shown to you?

A. No, the pictures were not shown to me, I was merely an interested bystander on this occasion, just as I previously told you.

Q. Did Rowehls give any written reports about these test flights to the Amt?

A. I do not know.

Q. You do not know?

You also said that Rowehls' squadron made flights from Budapest later?

A. Yes.

Q. Do you know that of your own experience or information?

A. I know it through personal investigation; the time is fixed through the diary of the section, and because at that time I was in Budapest, and because at that time I was asked to attend a Citation Ceremony at the Palace.

Q. And why were these flights executed from Budapest?

A. I do not know; I said that yesterday. A gentleman of the Air Force would have to answer that.

DR. DIX (counsel for defendant Schacht): You probably do not know me. I am Dr. Dix, the attorney for the defendant Schacht.

CROSS-EXAMINATION BY DR. DIX

Q. Witness, do you know Captain Struenck from the Abwehr?

A. I would like you to tell me something about the name. The name alone does not mean anything to me. Give me a few points that will refresh my memory.

Q. He is a lawyer who was a reserve officer with the Abwehr, I do not know in which department, but I should say it was in the department of Pieckenbrock. However, if you do not know him I will not question you any further.

A. If he was with Pieckenbrock I do not know him. I knew a few. Is Struenck still alive?

DR. DIX: No, he is no longer living.

THE WITNESS LAHOUSEN: Was he executed?

DR. DIX: He suffered the same death as Canaris and Oster. For the information of the Court, I should like to add that I asked this question because I named Struenck as a witness, and the Court has admitted him as such. I wish to take this opportunity ... but if you do not know him I will not continue questioning you.

LAHOUSEN: As to the question whether he is still alive, I seem to recall that this man, in connection with others whom I knew, very well might have been killed, but I cannot be more definite on this point.

DR. FRITZ (counsel for the defendant Fritzsche): I would like to ask the witness a few questions.

CROSS-EXAMINATION BY DR. FRITZ:

Q. Witness, do you know that the defendant Fritzsche, after May, 1942, was transferred to the Sixth Army as a soldier, and that there he heard for the first time of the existence of an order for execution and that he recommended to the Supreme Commander of the Sixth Army, Paulus, to have this order suspended within the jurisdiction of his army and to have this decision made known by leaflets to be dropped over the Russian front.

THE PRESIDENT: Be careful only to ask one question at a time. You have just asked three or four questions at once.

Q. (continuing.) Yes, Sir. Is it known to you that Fritzsche gave Paulus the advice to rescind the order for his army area?

A. That order had already been given to his army. Will you kindly give me the approximate date?

Q. That was during the Russian campaign, as I mentioned yesterday. Most of these things occurred in May, 1942.

A. No. In connection with the person of Fritzsche, this is not known to me. In connection with the name Reichenau, which was mentioned before, I do remember a conversation between Reichenau and Canaris. That for me was very impressive, and Reichenau's concept and judgement of things in this conversation, in this circle, where there were several other gentlemen present, showed him to be entirely different from what I expected him to be, and the way I thought of him. I don't know anything about this particular question.

Q. Also nothing concerning the fact that Paulus had then already rescinded the order within the boundaries of his Army?

A. No, not in connection with the name Paulus, but in general I believe, as I also mentioned yesterday, that several army commanders, whose names are no longer in my memory to-day, all those names have been recorded, and I have already informed you about them.

CROSS-EXAMINATION BY DR. KAUFFMANN (counsel for defendant Kaltenbrunner):

Q. Do you know Kaltenbrunner?

A. Kaltenbrunner? I met Kaltenbrunner once in my life, on a date that will always be in my memory. It was also the first meeting between Canaris and Kaltenbrunner. It took place in Munich in the Regina Hotel, and it was on that day when two young people, a student and his sister, were arrested and executed. They had distributed leaflets from the auditorium of the University of Munich. I read the contents of the leaflets, and I remember, amongst other things, that they contained an appeal to the Wehrmacht.

I can easily reconstruct that day. It was the first and last time that I saw Kaltenbrunner, with whose name I was familiar. Of course, Kaltenbrunner mentioned this subject to Canaris, in the presence of witnesses, and everybody got a terrible impression of what had happened, and Kaltenbrunner spoke about it to Canaris in a manner of which cynicism would be a very mild description. This is all that I can say to this question.

Q. Kaltenbrunner claims that Himmler retained full executive powers for himself, while he was only in charge of information. Is this in accord with the conversation that you just mentioned?

A. I would like you to know what connection this has with the matter Kaltenbrunner and Himmler-the power politics which took place, in the S.S.I have merely given this very plain description of this event - I can give you the names and the people present, who were very much impressed.

CROSS-EXAMINATION BY DR. BOEHM (counsel for S.A.)

Q. You were asked yesterday, whether the orders as to the treatment of Soviet prisoners of war were known to the leaders of the S.A. and other organisations, and your answer was, that these orders must have been known to them, and I would now like to ask you who these leaders were at the time and what were their names.

A. Who they were and what their names were, I do not know. I have also stated explicitly yesterday why I said so. These orders should have been known both to them and to a large circle, through the execution thereof and, of course, through the return of the wounded. The German people would have learned of it.

Q. In other words, it was only an opinion of yours but in no way a fact based on information?

A. No, it was not based on information. I have never spoken to any S.A. leader about it. I never had anything to do with them, and I do not think any one of them knew me well.

Q. Could you make a statement on this, that is, that the orders which were named yesterday were given to the formations of the S.A., emphasising S.A.?

A. Would you kindly formulate that question again?

Q. Could you make another statement, whether it was known to you whether the contents of these orders, which were talked about yesterday, were sent to formations of the S.A. through channels?

A. No, not through channels, no, but in the way I have previously indicated in other words, members of the S.A. who were also in the Wehrmacht would see outside actually what happened, and when they came back or came in contact with them they talked about the Jews as anyone else would. It was only in this connection

Q. Is it known to you whether members of the S.A. had anything to do, at all, with the management of the prisoners of war?

A. Within the frame of the employment of S.A. in the Wehrmacht, yes.

Q. Have you any personal information on that?

A. No, I never said that. I said I had already talked about the S.A.

Q. I have asked you what leaders of the S.A. formations have known about it, and you yourself answered that they should have known it.

A. I said the leaders of these organisations, in this way, have known about it.

Q. And to-day I ask you whether the specific formations of the S.A. had received these orders.

A. I can only repeat what I said yesterday, and I think I was very clear on the subject, in other words, how these orders, that I did not read myself, but I know the effects anyway -

Q. I can imagine myself how this happened, but I have asked you whether you know anything about having these orders actually given to the S.A.?

A. No.

Q. You do not know? Is anything known to you to show that members of the S.A. were employed for the supervision of prisoners of war, according to your personal information?

A. Yes, because I, myself, on a trip to the Army Group North, once got hold of an S.A. man, who kicked a Russian prisoner of war, and I told him off, accordingly. Surely somewhere I have this in my records, and also an episode about an Arbeitsdienst Mann.

Q. Did you report any of these incidents to any superior officers?

A. I did report them to my superior officers, and also made reports about these trips, either orally or in written shape, and on many of these occasions discussions took place.

Q. Have you got anything in your records?

A. Yes.

Q. Will you kindly present these?

(Discussion between counsel and witness in German, not translated.)

A. I am looking it up. This is about the Arbeitsdienst Mann, this document.

Q. It is not about the S.A.?

A. I have not got it here. I would have to look it up.

Q. Is there any possibility that you might find some records?

A. I would have to obtain the entire material which the American authorities have, and I would have to look through it thoroughly for this one possibility.

DR. GEORG BOEHM (counsel for S.A.): I will ask the Court to have it made possible at some time.

Q. (continuing): I would also like to ask you if you have any other information that S.A. members, who you previously said were employed in supervisory capacities, were made to execute these orders, according to statements about Russian prisoners of war.

A. No, not personally.

Q. Thank you.

DR. STAHMER (counsel for Goering): I would like to ask the Court for a fundamental ruling, whether the defendant also has the right to personally ask the witness questions. According to the German Charter, Paragraph 16, I believe this is permissible without a doubt.

THE PRESIDENT: The Tribunal will consider the point you have raised and will let you know later.

MR. JUSTICE JACKSON: The United States prosecution would desire to be heard, I am sure, if there were any probability of that view being taken by the Tribunal.

THE PRESIDENT: Perhaps we had better hear you now then, Mr. Justice Jackson.

MR. JUSTICE JACKSON: Well, I think it is very clear that these provisions are mutually exclusive. Each has the right to conduct his own defence or to have the assistance of counsel. Certainly this would become a performance rather than a trial if, we go into that sort of thing. In framing this Charter, we anticipated the possibility that some of these defendants, being lawyers themselves, might conduct their own defence. If they do so, of course, they have all the privileges of counsel. If they avail themselves of the privileges of counsel, they are not, we submit, entitled to be heard in person.

DR. STAHMER: I would like to point out once more that paragraph 16 (e), according to my opinion, speaks very clearly in support of my point of view, and says that the defendant has the right, either personally or through his attorney, to present evidence, and according to the German text it is clear that the defendant has the right to cross- examine each witness called by the prosecution.

THE PRESIDENT: Does any other German counsel, defendant's counsel, wish to cross-examine the witness?

DR. SERVATIUS (counsel for defendant Sauckel): I would only like to point out that in the written forms that have been given to us by the Court, the defendant as well as his lawyer can propose a motion. There is room for two signatures on the questionnaire. I request, therefore, that the defendant himself have the right to speak on the floor.

THE PRESIDENT: What I asked was whether any other defendant's counsel wished to cross-examine the witness.

(Dr. Boehm approached the lectern.)

THE PRESIDENT: What is it? Would you put the earphones on, please, unless you understand English?

What is it you want to ask now? You have already cross-examined the witness.

DR. BOEHM: Yes, I have cross-examined him, but I have heard from him that he has written statements, that he has made a report, according to something he has witnessed. I cannot dismiss the witness as yet.

I would like to make a motion that it be made possible for the witness for the prosecution to look through all the reports and all the records, and for us to go through all the materials.

THE PRESIDENT: I think you must conclude your cross- examination now.

DR. BOEHM: Surely.

THE PRESIDENT: The Court thinks it would be better, if you want to make any further application with reference to this witness, that you should make it in writing later.

DR. BOEHM: Yes.

THE PRESIDENT: Then, as no other defendant's counsel wishes to cross-examine the witness, the Tribunal will now retire for the purpose of considering the question raised by **DR. STAHMER:** whether a defendant has the right to cross-examine as well as his own counsel.

(A recess was taken.)

THE PRESIDENT: The Tribunal has carefully considered the question raised by

Dr. Stahmer, and it holds that defendants who are represented by counsel have not the right to cross- examine witnesses. They have the right to be called as witnesses themselves and to make a statement at the end of the trial.

Do the prosecutors wish to ask any questions of this witness in re-examination?

COLONEL AMEN: just one question, your Lordship.

THE PRESIDENT: Let the witness come back here.

THE MARSHAL OF THE COURT: He was taken away.

THE PRESIDENT: Taken away?

THE MARSHAL: That's right. He was taken away by some Captain who brought him here for the trial. They have sent after him now.

THE PRESIDENT: Do you know how far he has been taken away?

THE MARSHAL: No, Sir, I do not. I will find out immediately.

THE PRESIDENT: Colonel Amen, are the questions that you wish to ask of sufficient importance for the Tribunal to wait for this witness, or can he be recalled on Monday?

COLONEL AMEN: I do not think they are so important, your Lordship.

THE PRESIDENT: Very well then. The Tribunal will adjourn, and it will be understood that in future no witness will be removed, whilst he is under examination, from the precincts of this Court, except on the orders of the Tribunal.

COLONEL AMEN: I do not know how that happened, your Lordship, I understood he was still here.

(The Tribunal adjourned until 10.00 hours on 3rd December, 1945)

About Coda Books

Most Coda books are edited and endorsed by Emmy Award winning film maker and military historian Bob Carruthers, producer of Discovery Channel's Line of Fire and Weapons of War and BBC's Both Sides of the Line. Long experience and strong editorial control gives the military history enthusiast the ability to buy with confidence.

The series advisor is David McWhinnie, producer of the acclaimed Battlefield series for Discovery Channel. David and Bob have co-produced books and films with a wide variety of the UK's leading historians including Professor John Erickson and Dr David Chandler.

Where possible the books draw on rare primary sources to give the military enthusiast new insights into a fascinating subject.

The English Civil Wars

The Zulu Wars

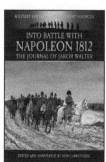

Into Battle with Napoleon 1812

Waterloo 1815

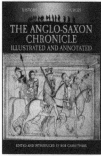

The Anglo-Saxon Chronicle

The Battle of the Bulge

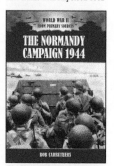

The Normandy Campaign 1944

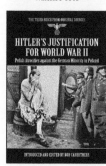

Hitler's Justification for WWII

Hitler's Mein Kampf -
The Roots of Evil

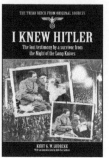

I Knew Hitler

Mein Kampf - The 1939
Illustrated Edition

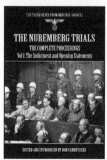

The Nuremberg Trials Volume 1

For more information, visit codahistory.com

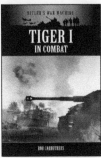

Tiger I in Combat

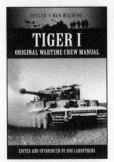

Tiger I Crew Manual

Panzers at War 1939-1942

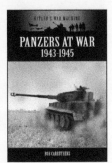

Panzers at War 1943-1945

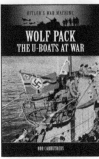

Wolf Pack - the U boats

Poland 1939

Luftwaffe Combat Reports

Eastern Front Night Combat

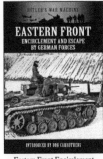

Eastern Front Encirclement

Panzer Combat Reports

The Panther V in Combat

The Red Army in Combat

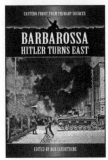

Barbarossa - Hitler Turns East

The Russian Front

The Wehrmacht in Russia

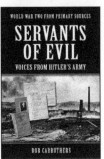

Servants of Evil